THE ACCOUNTABILITY OF ARMED GROUPS UNDER HUMAN RIGHTS LAW

The Accountability of Armed Groups under Human Rights Law

KATHARINE FORTIN

OXFORD
UNIVERSITY PRESS

OXFORD
UNIVERSITY PRESS

Great Clarendon Street, Oxford, OX2 6DP,
United Kingdom

Oxford University Press is a department of the University of Oxford.
It furthers the University's objective of excellence in research, scholarship,
and education by publishing worldwide. Oxford is a registered trade mark of
Oxford University Press in the UK and in certain other countries

First Edition published in 2017

Published in the United States of America by Oxford University Press
198 Madison Avenue, New York, NY 10016, United States of America

British Library Cataloguing in Publication Data
Data available

Library of Congress Control Number: 2017943901

ISBN 978–0–19–880838–1

Foreword

This book asks some hard questions about whether armed groups have human rights obligations and, having concluded that there is considerable practice that points in this direction, it asks how and when can these groups be bound by human rights law in a more 'technical sense'. The questions are of more than theoretical interest; in 2015 it was estimated that the so-called 'Islamic State' had control over around 10 million people in Iraq. Thousands of other groups around the world are in control of vulnerable men, women, and children. One of the key merits of Dr Fortin's research is that she takes us beyond the often polarized debate and into the overlooked area of 'rebel governance', and the continuance of 'everyday life'. She shows us, by using social science materials, how armed groups are compelled to impose a form of law and order involving not only basic policing and administration, but also control over all sorts of issues including, for example, public broadcasting and assembly. The implications for the people living under such control are obvious. The fact that international humanitarian law is silent on most of these matters makes the case for the application of the human rights framework to such situations.

An equally important contribution comes in the form of Dr Fortin's careful examination of the ways in which international law has attached obligations to armed groups in the context of belligerency, insurgency, and international humanitarian law. Her conclusion based on an examination of historical incidents is that one may need to see legal personality as something which operates on a sliding scale giving rise to various obligations which could vary, not only according to whether one derives them from treaty, custom, or some bilateral arrangement, but also according to the capability of the group. Dr Fortin's analysis does not end with the easy cases but rather pushes on to find the limits of her own logic. She asks some very hard questions about groups that are not in situations of armed conflict and have no control of territory. Here she admits that the legal foundations of her thesis are more fragile. Personality and practice seem to be wanting, and yet she explains how international law has come to accommodate the idea of international crimes in such a situation. We are then exposed to the parameters of prosecuting crimes against humanity and genocide. At this point she suggests that other *jus cogens* norms and an obligation to respect the right to life may come into play.

What stands out from this analysis is that, while previous academic focus has been exclusively on the sources of obligations for armed groups, Dr Fortin has highlighted how important it is additionally to develop routes for accountability. We are reminded that accountability can include procedural obligations which go way beyond issues of responsibility. Nevertheless, as Dr Fortin is at pains to stress, accountability can be neither free-floating nor entirely dependent on the will of the armed group or any single government. Dr Fortin wants us to see effective accountability as flowing from a greater confidence in the foundations of obligations. Her theories which ground the obligations of armed groups in established international doctrines represent a significant contribution to the knowledge in this field and have taken us considerably forward in our understanding of how to achieve greater accountability for human rights violations committed by armed groups.

Andrew Clapham
Professor of International Law,
Graduate Institute of International
and Development Studies, Geneva

Acknowledgements

The seeds of this book were sown in 2002 when I was working in Sierra Leone on a child rights programme. I spent long trips visiting parts of the country which had only recently been under rebel control, and was struck by the arbitrariness of armed conflict. I was particularly troubled by how a decision to run in a particular direction in the middle of the night when a village is attacked can affect whether an individual ends up in territory controlled by an armed group or in government controlled territory. In many ways, this book is a legal exploration of this observation.

In these acknowledgements, I wish to thank those individuals without whose support this book would not have been written. While I am unable to name everyone who has assisted me on my journey, there are a number of individuals and organisations I would very much like to mention.

First, I want to thank the Netherlands Organisation for Scientific Reseach (NWO) for funding the research which led to this book. I also want to extend my thanks to my three PhD supervisors, Professor Kees Flinterman (Utrecht University), Professor Terry Gill (University of Amsterdam and the Netherlands Defence Academy), and Professor Harmen van der Wilt (University of Amsterdam), who provided me with invaluable support and inspiration during the project. Together they challenged my developing thoughts and urged me to look at the subject from new and different angles. Special thanks are due to the members of my reading committee, Professor Cedric Ryngaert, Professor Fred Soons, Professor Andrew Clapham, Professor Elies van Sliedregt, and Professor Jann Kleffner for the time they took to assess my manuscript and provide comments on its content. My gratitude is due to Sir Nigel Rodley and Professor Sandesh Sivakumaran who formed the *cum laude* committee for my manuscript and who provided valuable critical commentary on the book's text. My thanks also goes to the anonymous reviewers at Oxford University Press who improved the manuscript with their insights and comments. I am also grateful for the individuals who have read parts of this book and provided valued comments on their contents. In particular, I am grateful to Marthe Lot Vermeulen, Brianne McGonigle, Jonathan Somer, Jessica Dorsey, Rogier Bartels, and Professor Mark Bovens. I would also like to thank Amy Shepherd and Hendrik Vandekerckove who, at different moments, have provided me much valued assistance with referencing.

My gratitude is also due to my colleagues at the Netherlands Institute of Human Rights (SIM), past and present, for their inspiration and friendship. Outside academia, there are many people that I should thank but I will mention only a few. Indeed, my special thanks goes to Nuala Mole, Catherina Harby, Frances Nicholson, Rosina Conteh, Deirdre Walker, Pat Watson, Jim Goldston, Hans Bevers, Norman Farrell, Serge Brammertz, Gavin Ruxton, and Frederick Swinnen. Your commitment, passion, and work ethic continue to be an inspiration to me as I go forward through my professional life.

I also thank my parents, Jane and Richard, and sisters Abigail and Elizabeth for their unwavering support and love. I owe my biggest thanks to Timme, my husband, for his unwavering belief in me and his sense of humour, and Una and Eloïse, our two daughters, whose mischief, joy, and laughter kept me sane during the writing process.

Utrecht, January 2017

Contents—Summary

Contents—Detailed

Table of Cases

INTERNATIONAL COURTS

Permanent Court of International Justice

International Court of Justice

INTERNATIONAL CRIMINAL COURTS AND TRIBUNALS

International Criminal Court

International Criminal Tribunal for the former Yugoslavia

International Military Tribunal at Nuremberg

Permanent Military Tribunal at Metz

United States Military Tribunal, Nuremburg

Franco-Italian Conciliation Commission

REGIONAL HUMAN RIGHTS COURTS

European Court of Human Rights

Inter-American Court of Human Rights

MISCELLANEOUS COMMISSIONS AND COUNCILS

General Claims Commission of 1923 between the United States and Mexico

International Council for Commercial Arbitration

NATIONAL COURTS

Colombia

United Kingdom

United States

EUROPEAN UNION

General Chamber

Table of Instruments

TABLE OF INTERNATIONAL INSTRUMENTS

Table of Other Materials

Human Rights Committee

Office of the High Commissioner of Human Rights (OHCHR)

Security Council Documents

Security Council Resolutions

United Nations Field office reports

NON-GOVERNMENTAL REPORTS

List of Abbreviations

CAT	Convention against Torture and other Cruel, Inhuman or Degrading Treatment or Punishment
CEDAW	Committee on the Elimination of Discrimination against Women
CERD	International Convention on the Elimination of all forms of Racial Discrimination
CPN-M	Communist Party of Nepal - Maoist
CRC	Convention on the Rights of the Child
CRPD	Convention on the Rights of Persons with Disabilities
DRC	Democratic Republic of the Congo
ELN	National Liberation Army (Columbia)
FARC	Revolutionary Armed Forces of Columbia
FDLR	Democratic Forces for the Liberation of Rwanda
FMLN	Farabundo Marti National Liberation Front
FPLC	Forces Patriotiques pour la Libération du Congo
FSA	Free Syrian Army
ICC	International Criminal Court
ICCPR	International Covenant on Civil and Political Rights
ICESCR	Internatinal Covenant on Economic, Social and Cultural Rights
ICJ	International Court of Justice
ICRC	Interational Committee of the Red Cross
ICTR	International Criminal Tribunal for Rwanda
ICTY	International Criminal Tribunal for the former Yugloslavia
IDP	internally displaced person
IHL	International Humanitarian Law
IHRL	International Human Rights Law
IMT	International Military Tribunal
KLA	Kosovan Liberation Army
LRA	Lord's Resistance Army
LTTE	Liberation Tigers of Tamil Eelam
MILF	Moro Islamic Liberation Front
MONUC	United Nations Organization Mission in the Democratic Republic of the Congo
NGO	non-governmental organization
NLA	Albanian National Liberation Army
OHCHR	United Nations Office of the High Commissioner of Human Rights
PLO	Palestinian Liberation Organization
RUF	Revolutionary United Front
SWAPO	Southwest African People's Organization
TRNC	Turkish Republic of Northern Cyprus
UDHR	Universal Declaration of Human Rights
UNAMA	United Nations Assistance Mission in Afghanistan
UNHRC	United Nations Human Rights Council

UNITA	National Union for the Total Independence of Angola
UNMISS	United Nations Mission to the Republic of South Sudan
UNOCI	United Nations Operation in Côte d'Ivoire
UPC	Union des Patriotes Congolais

PART I

INTRODUCTION

1

Introduction

1. Introduction

The purpose of this book is to inject clarity into the much contested question of when armed groups can be held to account under human rights law. In doing so, the book aims to bring answers to an academic debate which has existed for more than two decades about when and how armed groups can be bound by human rights law. During this time, some authors have argued that armed groups do not have obligations under human rights law.[1] Others have argued that they only have obligations under human rights law when they control territory.[2] A third category of authors have argued that armed groups have obligations under human rights law outside of armed conflict situations.[3] Yet, despite the existence of considerably divergent academic views on the question, there has been surprisingly little in-depth analysis of the various positions on the debate and their legal basis remains 'under-theorized'.[4] Moreover, strangely, despite the debate's shaky theoretical underpinnings, the practice of holding armed groups accountable under human rights law has been gaining pace over recent years. While it used to be somewhat exceptional for armed groups to be held bound by human rights law, nowadays statements from commissions of inquiry and United Nations Special Rapporteurs holding armed groups to account under human rights law are quite commonplace.[5] Indeed, the United Nations Office of the High Commissioner of Human

[1] L. Moir, *The Law of Internal Armed Conflict* (CUP, Cambridge 2002) 45 (hereafter Moir, *Internal Armed Conflict*).

[2] N. S. Rodley, 'Can Armed Opposition Groups Violate Human Rights?' in K. E. Mahoney and P. Mahoney (eds), *Human Rights in the Twenty-First Century* (Kluwer, Dordrecht 1993) 297–313 (hereafter Rodley, 'Armed Opposition Groups'); L. Zegveld, *The Accountability of Armed Opposition Groups in International Law* (OUP, Oxford 2002) 52 (hereafter Zegveld, *Accountability of Armed Opposition Groups*).

[3] T. Rodenhäuser, 'Human Rights Obligations of Non-State Armed Groups in Other Situations of Violence: The Syria Example' (2012) 3 International Humanitarian Legal Studies 263 (hereafter Rodenhäuser, 'The Syria Example').

[4] A. Clapham, 'Focusing on Armed Non-State Actors' in A. Clapham and P. Gaeta (eds), *The Oxford Handbook of International Law in Armed Conflict* (OUP, Oxford 2014) 788. A recent addition to the literature adding considerable analysis is found in D. Murray, *Human Rights Obligations of Non-State Armed Groups* (Bloomsbury, West Sussex 2016) (hereafter Murray, *Human Rights Obligations*).

[5] See e.g. 'Report of the Secretary General's Panel of Experts on Accountability in Sri Lanka' (31 March 2011) (hereafter Report of Sri Lanka Panel of Experts); United Nations Human Rights Council

Rights (OHCHR) has recognized that the application of human rights standards to armed groups is particularly relevant in circumstances where they exercise 'some degree of control over a given territory and population'.[6] Yet, it has provided little worked-out legal justification for its position.[7]

Uncertainties about when it is possible for armed groups to have obligations under human rights law clearly cause problems. Despite the growing trend to hold armed groups accountable under human rights law, many of the reports from UN accountability mechanisms approach the question of armed groups and human rights law in different ways. The inconsistencies in these reports demonstrate that the lack of clarity on the topic is an operational problem for these kinds of monitoring mechanisms. On more than one occasion, reports have explicitly referred to the fact that the extent to which international human rights law binds armed groups is contested.[8] On some occasions, the existence of uncertainty surrounding the question of human rights and armed groups has been explicitly cited as a reason for mechanisms to adopt a minimalist approach to the normative human rights framework.[9] Moreover, it is the starting premise of this book that 'accountability' is a process which is dependent upon the legitimacy of the norms upon which it is based. As a result, the lack of clarity on the question of armed groups and human rights law inflicts damage on the accountability framework. For as long as grave doubts remain about whether and when armed groups are bound by human rights law, the legitimacy of any claims that they have violated

(UNHRC), 'Report of the United Nations Fact-Finding Mission on the Gaza Conflict' (23 September 2009) UN Doc A/HRC/12/48 (hereafter Gaza Fact-Finding Mission Report); United Nations Human Rights Council (UNHRC), 'Report of the Independent International Commission of Inquiry on the Syrian Arab Republic' (5 February 2013) UN Doc A/HRC/22/59; OHCHR, 'Report of the United Nations High Commissioner of Human Rights, Situation of Human Rights in the Central African Republic' (12 September 2013) UN Doc A/HRC/24/59 (hereafter OHCHR CAR Report 2013); UNAMA, 'Afghanistan Mid-Year Report on the Protection of Civilians in Armed Conflict' (July 2013) (hereafter UNAMA Afghanistan Report July 2013); UN Security Council, 'Midterm Report of the Group of Experts on the Democratic Republic of Congo' (19 July 2013) UN Doc S/2013/433; 'Report of the United Nations Joint Human Rights Office on Human Rights Violations committed by the M23 in North Kivu Province, April 2012–November 2013' (October 2014) (hereafter M23 Report); UNMISS, 'Conflict in South Sudan, A Human Rights Report' (8 May 2014) (hereafter UNMISS South Sudan Report 2014); UN Security Council, 'Preliminary Report of the International Commission of Inquiry on the Central African Republic' (26 June 2014) UN Doc S/2014/373.

6 OHCHR, *International Protection of Human Rights in Armed Conflict* (UN New York/Geneva 2011) 25 (hereafter OHCHR, *Human Rights in Armed Conflict*).

7 The report cites evolving practice from the Security Council and reports from several Special Rapporteurs as evidence of the fact that it is increasingly considered that non-State actors can be held bound by human rights law.

8 UN Human Rights Council (UNHRC), 'Report of the International Commission of Inquiry to investigate all alleged violations of international human rights law in the Libyan Arab Jamahiriya' (1 June 2011) UN Doc A/HRC/17/44, [72] (hereafter Libya ICI Report June 2011); Report of Sri Lanka Panel of Experts (n 5) see e.g. [188].

9 Report of Sri Lanka Panel of Experts (n 5) [188], where the panel states that in the light of the differing views on the subject of whether armed groups can be bound by human rights law it proceeds on the basis that the LTTE were bound to respect the 'most basic human rights of persons within its power'. See also [243] where the Panel of Experts states that the panel did not address LTTE abuses outside the conflict zone 'because of the uncertainty surrounding whether non-state actors have human rights obligations beyond the territories they control'.

it will be greeted with caution. Moreover, so long as the theoretical underpinnings of this practice remain unclear, the legal framework as applied to armed groups will not develop. It is primarily with these problems in mind that the book seeks to address the question of when and how armed groups are bound by human right law.

2. Definition of Accountability

Indeed, it is explained below why a lack of clarity about when and how armed groups are bound by human rights law compromises the effectiveness of efforts to hold armed groups accountable under this body of law. Menno Kamminga, the author of a notable study into accountability, found the concept 'accountability' to be wider than 'responsibility'. He argued that the term 'responsibility' denoted a 'limited subcategory of the wider concept of *accountability* (italics in the original)'.[10] In part, he based this assertion on the basis of one of the observations made by the International Court of Justice in the *Corfu Channel* case. Here the ICJ found that 'a State on whose territory an act contrary to international law has occurred may be called upon to given an explanation'.[11] The ICJ found that a State's duty to give an explanation existed independently from a finding that the State had prima facie responsibility for such an act. To Kamminga, the Court's finding illustrated that there is a difference between an actor being *accountable* under international law and an actor being *responsible* under international law. An actor which is found responsible for a wrongful act has a duty to provide reparation to the entity that has suffered loss as a result. An actor which is found accountable for a wrongful act may not ultimately be found responsible as a result of that process. However, during that process, the actor has a duty or opportunity to provide an explanation for the allegations it faces. In other words, Kamminga asserted that the notion of accountability has an added procedural element which distinguishes it from the notion of responsibility. It is noteworthy that the procedural nature of the term is also captured in the etymological roots of the term.[12]

The idea that the notion of 'accountability' has distinct procedural characteristics has been the subject of a great deal of writing in the field of public administration. Much of this writing was generated out of concerns that the term

[10] M. T. Kamminga, *Inter-State Accountability for Violations of Human Rights* (University of Pennsylvania Press, Pennsylvania 1992) 5.

[11] *Corfu Channel (United Kingdom of Great Britain and Northern Ireland v Albania) (Judgment)* [1949] ICJ Reports 4, [18] (hereafter *Corfu Channel).*

[12] These can be traced to the reign of William I's England when all landowners were forced to render 'a count' of their possessions for the Domesday Books. See M. Bovens, 'Analysing and Assessing Accountability: A Conceptual Framework' (2007) 13 European Law Journal 447, 448 (hereafter Bovens, 'Analysing and Assessing Accountability'), referring to M. J. Dubnick, 'Seeking Salvation for Accountability' (Paper presented at the 2002 Annual Meeting of the American Political Science Association, Boston).

accountability in that field was becoming an 'ever-expanding concept' that was no longer able to be empirically evaluated.[13] In an attempt to reclaim the word, a succession of authors tried to identify the concept's key features and distinguish the core sense of the term from related peripheral concepts.[14] A review of the literature in this area reveals a consensus that the core of the term 'accountability' is associated with the *process* of being 'called "to account" to some authority for one's actions'.[15] It has been commented that this 'original' or core sense of 'accountability' has 'the longest pedigree in the relevant literature and in the understanding of practitioners'.[16] Mulgan identifies accountability as a 'process' that has several core features. Perhaps most importantly, he argues that the process needs to be external, in that the explanation of an actor's conduct is given to a third party. He comments that a process of accountability usually involves 'social interaction'; one side gives an account and the other side receives the account. He comments that through this process, one side is seeking answers and rectification while the other side is responding and agreeing to sanctions. Mulgan states that the process of accountability 'implies rights of authority, in that those calling for an account are asserting rights of superior authority over those who are accountable'.[17]

In exploring the issue, Mulgan identifies four key features of 'accountability' as a procedural mechanism: (i) the accountability forum must be a third party; (ii) the person or entity being held accountable must have the opportunity to explain his conduct; (iii) the accountability forum has 'rights of authority' over the entity under scrutiny; and (iv) the accountability forum must have the possibility of imposing sanctions.[18] These same key features also appear in Bovens's description of accountability, which he defines as:

> a relationship between an actor and a forum, in which the actor has an obligation to explain and to justify his or her conduct, the forum can pose questions and pass judgement, and the actor must face consequences.[19]

It is noteworthy that Bovens prefers the term 'consequences' to Mulgan's term 'sanction'. He clarifies that 'consequences' may be positive or negative; formal or even implicit.[20]

[13] R. Mulgan, '"Accountability": An Ever-Expanding Concept' (2000) 78 Public Administration 555, 555 (hereafter Mulgan, 'Ever-Expanding Concept'). Bovens stated that the term 'accountability', 'is one of those golden concepts that no one can be against… However, its evocative powers make it also a very elusive concept because it can mean many different things to different people.' See Bovens, 'Analysing and Assessing Accountability' (n 12) 448.

[14] Applied more expansively, the term has also been employed to refer to the inward sense of moral obligation that is required from public servants, any mechanism that controls government power, transparency, responsiveness, and democratic dialogue.

[15] Mulgan, 'Ever-Expanding Concept' (n 13) 555. [16] Ibid. [17] Ibid.

[18] Ibid.

[19] M. Bovens, 'Two Concepts of Accountability: Accountability as a Virtue and as a Mechanism' (2010) 5 West European Politics 946, 951 (hereafter Bovens, 'Two Concepts of Accountability').

[20] Bovens clarifies that the possibility of sanctions makes the difference between the non-committal provision of information and being held to account. Ibid, 952.

There is less legal literature on the notion of accountability, but Curtin and Nollkaemper's article on the topic is an important addition to the field. Curtin and Nollkaemper provide the following definition of accountability:

> [Accountability] refers to a process in which an actor explains conduct and gives information to others, in which a judgment or assessment of that conduct is rendered on the basis of prior established rules or principles and in which it may be possible for some form of sanction (formal or informal) to be imposed on the actor.[21]

Significantly Curtin and Nollkaemper's definition is similar to those studied above, but adds the extra requirement that the behaviour of the actor being held to account must be scrutinized against 'prior established rules or principles'. In many ways, this extra requirement is similar to Mulgan's requirement that the accountability forum has 'rights of authority' over the entity under scrutiny. In the legal context, the requirement that a forum has a 'right of authority' most obviously refers to the question of mandate and jurisdiction. It also refers to the idea that the legitimacy or effectiveness of the accountability process is reliant upon the legitimacy of the norm at its centre. If there is any uncertainty about the validity of the norm on which the process of accountability is based, the process of accountability itself will inevitably be compromised.

It has been remarked that accountability in international law has traditionally been achieved by courts and tribunals scrutinizing State conduct against primary rules.[22] However in recent years, accountability processes have extended significantly beyond the State responsibility paradigm and a wide variety of new accountability mechanisms have been established.[23] Some of these new mechanisms routinely assess the conduct of non-State actors, such as armed groups, against international norms. Assessing the features of these various accountability mechanisms (e.g. Commissions of Inquiry, Special Rapporteurs mandates, etc) against the definitions of accountability above is informative and insightful. In particular, it prompts a questioning of whether these mechanisms, as they are currently set up, are capable of achieving 'accountability' for armed groups. While the mechanisms are external, the armed groups themselves are often given little opportunity to give an 'account' of the allegations against them. Likewise, while the mechanisms conduct an assessment of the armed group's behaviour against rules and principles, there is considerable uncertainty about the legitimacy of some of these norms to armed groups. Perhaps most significantly, it remains uncertain whether and when it is legally justifiable to apply human rights norms to armed groups. When examining the definitions of accountability above, it can be seen that these types of issues prevent effective accountability being attained. So long as these legal uncertainties remain, there will remain significant doubt about the legal

[21] D. Curtin and A. Nollkaemper, 'Conceptualizing Accountability in International and European Law' (2005) 36 Netherlands Yearbook of International Law 3, 8.

[22] Ibid, 5.

[23] J. Brunnée, 'International Legal Accountability through the Lens of State Responsibility' (2005) 36 Netherlands Yearbook of International Law 21, 39.

legitimacy of these mechanisms' findings. The overriding purpose of this study is to bring greater clarity and understanding to the accountability of armed groups under human rights law, by clarifying the circumstances in which it may be justifiable for UN accountability mechanisms to hold armed groups to account under human rights law.

3. Scope of the Book

The book focuses on armed groups which are engaged in an ongoing non-international armed conflict against a government. As a result, the book does not include paramilitary organizations that may be fighting on the same side as the government. The book looks only at armed groups which are operating within the context of non-international armed conflicts which have reached, or exceeded, the threshold of common Article 3 of the 1949 Geneva Conventions. It does not examine armed groups which operate in situations of internal disturbances and tensions, such as riots, isolated and sporadic acts of violence.[24] This book is written against the context of the hugely divergent ways in which the responsibility of armed groups is referred to by accountability mechanisms operating within the context of the United Nations. The study adopts a wide definition of 'accountability mechanisms' to include Security Council Resolutions, General Assembly Resolutions, Commissions of Inquiry set up under the auspices of the United Nations, reports by field offices documenting violations by armed groups, and reports by Special Rapporteurs working under the auspices of the Human Rights Council's special procedures. All these mechanisms seek to hold actors to account for their behaviour against a well-established and elaborate legal framework of international rules, which includes the human rights framework.

4. Background to Legal Debate

The question of whether armed groups can be bound by human rights law emerged over twenty years ago, in the early 1990s. In 1990, Peru and Colombia were keen to put the 'activities of armed groups and drug dealers' on the agenda of the UN Commission of Human Rights in Geneva, asking for special rapporteurs and working groups to be created on 'acts of violence committed by armed groups and drug dealers that infringe human rights'.[25] The two countries also proposed the creation of a separate Commission agenda item for the subject.[26] Several

[24] See Article 1 of Additional Protocol II, which is instrumental for clarifying that common Article 3 of the Geneva Conventions 1949 does not apply to such internal tensions.

[25] See Rodley, 'Armed Opposition Groups' (n 2) 311; D. Matas, 'Armed Opposition Groups' (1997) 3 Manatoba Law Journal 621, 622–3 (hereafter Matas, 'Armed Opposition Groups'); R. Brody et al., 'Major Developments in 1990 at the UN Commission on Human Rights' (1990) 4 Human Rights Quarterly 560, 585 (hereafter Brody, 'Major Developments') for an account of this debate.

[26] Brody, 'Major Developments' (n 25) 585.

non-governmental human rights organizations and several country delegations expressed opposition to the proposition that the Commission of Human Rights should turn its attention to armed groups. They articulated a fear that a focus on armed groups might allow governments to deflect criticism of their own human rights violations.[27] In response to this criticism, Peru presented a revised resolution calling on existing special rapporteurs to 'pay particular attention to the activities of irregular armed groups and drug traffickers' and requesting the secretary-general to collect information on these issues.[28] In presenting the revised text, Peru made clear that the resolution was 'not aimed at national liberation movements but at irregular bands seeking to overthrow democratically elected governments and that it did not intend to diminish state responsibility for protecting human rights'.[29] The Commission adopted the resolution with abstentions from Sweden and Cuba. Subsequent resolutions were then passed again in 1991, 1992, and 1993 entitled 'Consequences on the enjoyment of human rights of acts of violence committed by armed groups that spread terror among the population and by drug traffickers'.[30]

In the years immediately after the passing of these resolutions, both Nigel Rodley and David Matas published articles on the question of whether armed groups could be held accountable under human rights law. Interestingly, their early approaches to the subject reflect the same differences of opinions that are often still seen to characterize the debate on the question of armed groups and human rights law today. As a result, each view will be set out in some detail. Writing in 1993, Rodley divided his examination of the question into three perspectives: the 'conceptual perspective', the 'international law perspective', and the 'political perspective'.[31] Only the conceptual and legal perspectives will be reviewed here, as they are most relevant to the legal debate. From a conceptual perspective, Rodley found that the notion that armed groups can violate human rights law 'misconceives the significance of "human rights", both as a historical construct and as a notion distinguishable from other notions such as "crime" or, simply, "rights" '.[32] Rodley saw human rights law as a pragmatic response to the rise of the modern nation state. As a body of law, human rights law was developed to provide a 'buffer' between the middle classes and the sovereign and safeguard against excesses of power and

[27] Ibid.

[28] UN Commission on Human Rights, 'Consequences of acts of violence committed by irregular armed groups and drug traffickers for the enjoyment of human rights' (7 March 1990) UN Doc E/CN.4/RES/1990/75.

[29] UN Commission on Human Rights, 'Consequences on the enjoyment of human rights of acts of violence committed by armed groups that spread terror among the population and by drug traffickers' (5 March 1991) UN Doc E/CN.4/RES/1991/29; also further resolutions with the same title: (28 February 1992) UN Doc E/CN.4/RES/1992/42 and (9 March 1993) UN Doc E/CN.4/RES/1993/48. See also Brody, 'Major Developments' (n 25) 585.

[30] Sweden was of the opinion that special rapporteurs' functions should be restricted to the monitoring of government's compliance with their human rights obligations. It felt that any attempt to focus on armed groups would merely cause a diversion from their proper function. Cuba abstained on the basis that it believed that the resolution should have only covered armed groups related to drug trafficking and not irregular armed groups *and* drug traffickers. Matas, 'Armed Opposition Groups' (n 25) 622.

[31] Rodley, 'Armed Opposition Groups' (n 2) 297.

[32] Ibid, 298.

arbitrary rule.[33] From these historical origins, Rodley saw human rights as the 'concept of rules applicable to the relations between governments and governed'.[34] Basing his understanding of the concept of human rights law on 'governance', Rodley conceded that the operation of human rights law might also be triggered in circumstances where entities are exercising effective power analogous to governments over a significant segment of the population.[35] Accordingly, Rodley made a distinction between armed groups exercising '"effective power" over a significant segment of population and conduct[ing] sustained organized armed hostilities' and 'armed opposition group[s] not exercising effective power'.[36] For him, for both conceptual and legal reasons, the former kind of group could be considered as capable of violating human rights but the latter kind of group could not.[37]

The second reason why Rodley found it misconceived to use the notion of human rights to examine harms inflicted by private actors was that he was fearful that the practice confused the conception of a human rights violation with the notion of a crime. Rodley feared that the special meaning contained in the term 'human rights violation' would be lost if it were also applied to wrongs by non-State actors. In particular, people would no longer be able to tell from the terminology employed whether it had been a State or a non-State actor that had been the wrong-doer in a particular case. He argued that this dilution of the human rights terminology would be harmful to the human rights discourse. He also argued that it was unnecessary, as 'wrongs' by non-State actors could be better described by using domestic law terminology, such as as 'crimes' or 'torts'.[38] Addressing the legal perspective of the question, Rodley argued that finding private actors responsible for human rights violations overreached the natural parameters of international law. By tradition, international law was addressed to the behaviour of States, as personified by their governments, rather than individuals. In the few instances where it concerned itself with the behaviour of individuals or groups (e.g. the crimes of piracy, aircraft hijacking, sabotage, hostage-taking, and offences against diplomats) it still mainly addressed itself to States, authorizing or requiring States to prevent or repress the crimes.[39] Even in the field of international criminal law, Rodley found that the law only targeted individuals who were responsible for the behaviour of the State.[40] According to

[33] Ibid, 299.

[34] Ibid, 299–300. Rodley also acknowledges that this definition must be amended in order to take into account the fact that human rights law has developed from imposing limitations on the authority of governments over their subjects to imposing positive obligations on governments too. In response to this development, he amends his definition of human rights to become 'rules that mediate the relationship between governments and their subjects'.

[35] Ibid, 300.

[36] Ibid, 300, 313. Rodley borrows this term from the UN Declaration against Torture.

[37] Ibid, 298. See also N. Rodley, 'Non-State Actors and Human Rights' in S. Sheeran and N. Rodley (eds), *Routledge Handbook of International Human Rights Law* (Routledge, Abingdon 2013) 532.

[38] Rodley, 'Armed Opposition Groups', (n 2) 301–2.

[39] Ibid, 303.

[40] Writing before the establishment of the International Criminal Tribunal for the former Yugloslavia (ICTY) and the International Criminal Tribunal for Rwanda (ICTR), Rodley found prosecutions had only occurred where the accused were either state officials or private individuals acting in 'collusion with the state, in the context of a fundamental event involving interstate relations'. Ibid, 303.

Rodley, a review of the major human rights instruments confirmed this theoretical perspective. Apart from the Genocide Convention, he found no instances of duties being imposed on individuals or groups. Any mention of individuals having duties was in language of 'fact or faith', rather than in the language of legal obligation.[41]

Writing a few years later than Rodley, Matas took a starkly different approach. Conducting a review of the Universal Declaration of Human Rights (UDHR) and the International Covenant on Civil and Political Rights (ICCPR), Matas found their principal purpose to be to declare the rights of individuals, rather than to assert the obligations of States.[42] However, he argued that under the ICCPR, the State should be construed as being constituted by all of its citizens, governmental officials, and non-governmental civilians as well.[43] To support his argument, he drew attention to the industrialists who were prosecuted after the Second World War, in the cases of Flick, I. G. Farben, Krupp, and Zykon B. Matas points out that in the case of Flick the US Military Tribunal stated:

> Acts adjudged criminal when done by an officer of the government are criminal also when done by a private individual. The guilt differs in magnitude, not in quality. The offender in either case is charged with personal wrong and punishment falls on the offender in propria persona. There is no justification for a limitation of responsibility to public officials.[44]

In conclusion, Matas found that it may not be possible to say to an armed opposition group 'you have violated your international commitments to respect human rights. But it is possible to say something very similar'.[45] He stated that 'to use the difference in formulation to generate a substantially different approach belies the international legal reality. It creates an imbalance that is not required by international law'.[46]

Since the early 1990s when Rodley and Matas wrote, the subject of armed opposition groups and human rights law has received repeated academic attention, as violence by armed groups in various conflicts around the world has spiralled. Yet to a large extent, academic responses to the question have remained divided.[47] Writing in 2002 Lindsay Moir categorically rejected the idea that armed groups are bound by human rights law, stating: 'human rights obligations are imposed upon States ...

[41] Ibid, 306.

[42] Matas, 'Armed Opposition Groups' (n 25) 631. This was a view also expressed by C. Tomuschat, 'The Applicability of Human Rights Law to Insurgent Movements' in H. Fischer et al. (eds), *Krisensicherung Und Humanitarer Schutz—Crisis Management and Humanitarian Protection: Festschrif Fur Dieter Fleck* (BWV Berliner-Wissenschaft, Berlin 2004) 588 (hereafter Tomuschat, 'Insurgent Movements').

[43] Matas, 'Armed Opposition Groups' (n 25) 632. [44] Ibid, 633. [45] Ibid.

[46] Ibid, 634.

[47] See for example D. Fleck, 'Humanitarian Protection Against Non State Actors' in J. A. Frowein et al. (eds), *Verhandeln Fur Den Frieden—Negotiating for Peace: Liber Amicorum Tono Eitel* (Springer, Berlin 2003) 79, who states: 'If non-state actors have human rights, it appears logical that they must also have responsibilities, no different from the obligations insurgents have under international humanitarian law.'

and have no binding force for the insurgents'.[48] However, he acknowledged that international law seems likely to move towards the imposition of human rights obligations upon individuals as human rights law in general assumes greater horizontal effect.[49] Liesbeth Zegveld, also writing in 2002, conducted a review of instances in which international bodies have asserted the applicability of human rights law to armed opposition groups and concluded that 'practice [was] insufficient both in quantity and quality to challenge the principle that human rights law binds only the state in its relation with individuals living under its jurisdiction and not armed opposition groups involved in internal conflict'.[50] Looking at the question from a conceptual angle, she also added that she did not see a *need* for human rights law to extend to armed groups, finding international humanitarian law sufficient to protect individuals during internal conflict. Agreeing with Rodley, she found that the application of human rights norms to armed groups would cause the concept of human rights to lose its specific meaning. Moreover, she argued that such application would render human rights norms identical to norms of international humanitarian law.[51] She also found the suggestion that armed groups could be bound by human rights law problematic because human rights law 'purports to govern the relations between the government representing the state and the governed'.[52] Accordingly, she agreed with Rodley that human rights law might only be applied to armed opposition groups in instances where they exercise *de facto* governmental functions and have a 'stable presence in part of the state territory'.[53] However, reviewing international practice in this respect, she found it ambiguous as to whether such a contention could be supported.[54]

Tomuschat, writing in 2004, noted that in 1999 the *Institut de Droit International* had adopted a resolution explicitly recognizing armed groups to be bound by the 'principles and rules of international law guaranteeing fundamental human rights'.[55] Reviewing the practice of the UN Security Council and General Assembly, he found multiple examples of instances where parties to non-international armed conflicts were either urged to 'adhere' to human rights law or chastized for 'violating' human rights law. For him, this was a manifestation of the view that a movement struggling to become a 'legitimate government' of a nation is treated by the international community as 'an actor who, already at an embryonic stage, is subject to the essential obligations and responsibilities every State must shoulder in the interest of a civilized state of affairs between nations'.[56] He also stated his view that it was irrelevant that armed groups had not consented to the norms in question because the rule that a party may only be bound by international law in circumstances where it has consented 'has long been abandoned'.[57] Ryngaert, who addressed the debate in 2008, came to the opposite conclusion finding, at the end of a detailed review of the subject, that armed groups will only incur liability under international human rights

[48] Moir, *Internal Armed Conflict* (n 1) 44–5.
[49] Ibid, 45, fn 50. [50] Zegveld, *Accountability of Armed Opposition Groups* (n 2) 52.
[51] Ibid, 53. [52] Ibid. [53] Ibid, 54, 149. [54] Ibid, 151.
[55] Tomuschat, 'Insurgent Movements' (n 42) 577. [56] Ibid, 577–85.
[57] Ibid, 587.

law in instances where they 'consent to be bound by human rights law'.[58] In other cases, Ryngaert found that armed groups will remain subject only to the 'demand of the international community' which can take them to task if they fail to comply with human rights norms.[59] In 2010, Constantinides conducted a review of the practice of the United Nations Security Council with regards to armed groups and human rights law and found a 'clear and unrelenting trend' of the Security Council to address armed opposition groups directly in human rights terms.[60] At the same time, he noted that the Security Council used the terms 'abuses' and 'violations' somewhat interchangeably in a 'confusing and inconclusive way'.[61] Reviewing the Security Council's practice in relation to: (i) country situations; (ii) armed opposition groups in control of territory; and (iii) thematic resolutions, he found that it would not be an overstatement to assert that a customary rule has emerged extending human rights obligations to armed groups in control of territory.[62]

A key voice in the literature on non-State actors more generally and on the question of armed groups more specifically is that of Andrew Clapham who more than any other author has grappled with the questions relating to holding non-State actors accountable under human rights law. In his book *Human Rights Obligations of Non-State Actors* in 2006, Clapham challenges the notion that the structure of international law prevents non-State actors being the addressees of duties. Like Matas, he points to the prosecutions of non-State actors for violations of international criminal law as evidence of international law placing duties on individuals.[63] Analysing the language of the UDHR he finds that its wording supports a view that human rights are to be respected by all persons.[64] He also mentions numerous examples of international organizations addressing non-State actors in respect to their human rights obligations.[65] At the heart of Clapham's analysis lies a re-conceptualization of the traditional approach to international law under which only States are 'subjects'.[66] Following in the footsteps of Rosalyn Higgins, Clapham proposes that determination of whether a particular entity is a 'subject' of international law should be reconceived.[67] His suggestion is that it should be simplified to an examination of its capacity to enjoy those rights and bear those obligations. He states:

> We have an international legal order that admits that states are not the only subjects of international law. It is obvious that non-state entities do not enjoy all the competences,

[58] C. Ryngaert, 'Human Rights Obligations of Armed Groups' (2008) 2 Revue Belge de Droit International 355, 380.

[59] Ibid.

[60] Constantinides, 'Human Rights Obligations and Accountability of Armed Opposition Groups: The Practice of the UN Security Council' (2010) 4 Human Rights and International Legal Discourse 89, 98 (hereafter Constantinides, 'Armed Opposition Groups and the UN Security Council').

[61] Ibid, 96. [62] Ibid, 102–3.

[63] A. Clapham, *Human Rights Obligations of Non-State Actors* (OUP, Oxford 2009) 29–30 (hereafter Clapham, *Non-State Actors*).

[64] Ibid, 33–5. [65] Ibid, 35–41.

[66] L. Oppenheim, *International Law: A Treatise* (3rd edn, Longmans, Harlow 1920) 25, cited by Clapham, *Non-State Actors* (n 63) 61.

[67] R. Higgins, *Problems and Process, International Law and How We Use It* (Clarendon Press, Oxford 1994) 49 (hereafter Higgins, *Problems and Process*).

privileges and rights that states enjoy under international law, just as it is also clear that states do not have to have all the rights that individuals have under international law … We need to admit that international human rights and duties depend on the capacity of the entity to enjoy those rights and bear those obligations; such rights and obligations do not depend on the mysteries of subjectivity.[68]

From this premise, Clapham proceeds to conduct a review of the 'capacity' of non-State actors to enjoy rights and bear obligations with reference to statements by international organizations and judicial bodies.

With regard to how armed groups specifically might be bound to international human rights law, Clapham considers the various theories of how armed groups are bound by international humanitarian law by analogy, which in his view remain 'misty'.[69] Writing more recently on the subject in 2010, Clapham comments that 'lawyers have done hardly any work in developing a theory as to why such groups might have human rights obligations at all'.[70] Writing in 2012, Rodenhäuser finds, in line with Rodley's view above, that it is generally accepted that where armed groups exercise *de facto* control over territory, they must respect the fundamental human rights norms of the people that live there.[71] Taking this position as his starting point, but not explaining it from a theoretical perspective, he explores whether armed groups might also be bound by human rights norms in situations where they do not exercise control over territory. In doing so, he argues that rights should not primarily be considered as obligations of States but as entitlements of the individual. He also identifies a number of human rights treaties which are sometimes argued to be deliberately designed to bind armed groups (i.e. the Optional Protocol to the Convention on the Rights of the Child on the Involvement of Children in Armed Conflicts and the African Union Convention for the Protection and Assistance of Internally Displaced Persons in Africa). He sees these to be evidence of a 'trend in international law' considering armed groups to be bound by human rights law in 'certain circumstances'.[72] He continues by examining how arguments might be made that armed groups are bound by peremptory norms of international law. During the course of his argument, he rejects the idea that armed groups need to consent to norms before they can be bound by them.[73] The most recent voice on the debate is that of Murray who investigates the possibility of subjecting armed groups to international human rights law obligations and tests the application of human rights law to armed groups in practice.[74] As Murray's book was completed contemporaneously to this study, his book is not always cited in instances where the same case law or theories are reviewed.

[68] Clapham, *Non-State Actors* (n 63) 68. [69] Ibid, 281.

[70] Rodenhäuser, 'The Syria Example' (n 3) . In particular, see 276–7.

[71] Ibid, in particular see 267 where Rodenhäuser cites Rodley, 'Armed Opposition Groups' (n 2) and Tomuschat, 'Insurgent Movements' (n 42) for wide acceptance of this fact.

[72] Ibid. In particular, see 276–7. [73] Ibid.

[74] D. Murray, *Human Rights Obligations of Non-State Armed Groups* (n 4).

It is seen from the above review, that although many articles and recent studies have addressed the topic of armed groups and human rights law, certain key questions remain. Firstly, there is disagreement on whether and when armed groups may be bound by international human rights law. Secondly, there is disagreement on whether armed groups need to consent to international norms, before they can be bound by them. While there may be an emerging acceptance that armed groups are bound by international human rights law while they control territory, there is a lack of understanding about how this may be justified from a legal perspective. Additionally, there is a lack of agreement about whether armed groups may be bound by human rights norms without control of territory. And yet, somewhat paradoxically, when one considers this backdrop of academic uncertainty, the practice of holding armed groups accountable under human rights law is only increasing. It has already been commented that while it used to be somewhat exceptional for armed groups to be held bound by human rights law, nowadays it is common practice for commissions of inquiry and UN special rapporteurs to hold armed groups accountable under human rights law. Indeed, as was observed in the first paragraph of this introduction, it is noteworthy that the UN OHCHR, has now publicly stated that it is its policy to hold armed groups accountable in circumstances where they exercise 'some degree of control over a given territory and population'.[75] Likewise, in 2013 the Committee on the Elimination of Discrimination against Women (CEDAW) was the first human rights treaty body to recognize that armed groups with an identifiable political structure exercising significant control over territory or population are obliged to respect international human rights law.[76]

5. Damage to the Accountability Framework

It was argued above that the legal uncertainty about how and when armed groups are bound by human rights law risks inflicting damage to the accountability framework. A review of practice in this regard confirms that this is the case. Indeed, while it is becoming more commonplace to hold armed groups accountable under human rights law, practice remains distressingly inconsistent across UN accountability mechanisms. Moreover, the inconsistencies between and within these various mechanisms exist at a number of levels. The first inconsistency is whether human rights law is applied to armed groups at all, in documents setting out the legal framework in times of armed conflict.[77] Another inconsistency, which is more

[75] See OHCHR, *Human Rights in Armed Conflict* (n 6), 25.

[76] See CEDAW, 'General Recommendation No. 30 on Women in Conflict Prevention, Conflict and Post-Conflict Situations' (18 October 2013) UN Doc CEDAW/C/GC/30, [16] (hereafter CEDAW General Recommendation No. 30) [16].

[77] Compare, for example, OHCHR, 'Twelfth periodic report of the United Nations High Commissioner on Human Rights on the situation of human rights in the Sudan, Attacks on civilians in Western and Central Equatoria States, Southern Sudan, between 15 December 2008 and 10 March 2009 by the Lords Resistance Army (LRA)' (December 2009) UN Doc A/HRC/18/2,

common, is how human rights law is referenced. Sometimes breaches of human rights law by armed groups are called 'violations' and sometimes they are called 'abuses'. While some UN accountability mechanisms seem to have no qualms about using the term 'human rights violation' when referring to armed groups, others like the Security Council, have in more recent years developed a more or less consistent practice of referring to acts of armed groups as 'human rights abuses' and the acts of States as 'human rights violations'.[78] The distinction may seem slight, but it is generally interpreted to reflect a more fundamental disagreement about whether armed groups are bound by human rights obligations, or not. The word 'violation' is broadly understood to refer to the breach of a hard legal obligation whereas the word 'abuse' refers to the breach of a soft, non-binding norm.[79] Interestingly, it is noted that many of these same resolutions call upon 'all parties to the conflict' to comply with their obligations under international law or rules and principles of human rights law.[80] It is argued that these varying approaches to terminology reflect the fundamental uncertainty at the heart of the legal framework

with OHCHR, 'Special Report: Summary of fact finding missions on alleged human rights violations committed by the Lords Resistance Army (LRA) in the districts of Haut-Uélé and Bas-Uélé in Orientale province of the Democratic Republic of Congo, United Nations Joint Human Rights Office in the DRC (United Nations Organization Mission in the Democratic Republic of the Congo and Office of the High Commissioner for Human Rights)' (December 2009) (hereafter LRA Report, December 2009). In the first report, the violations by the LRA are analysed under international criminal law and national criminal law. The obligations of the Government of Sudan are analysed under the ICCPR and the Constitution of the Government of Sudan. The second report explicitly analyses the operations of the Lords Resistance Army under international human rights law grouping the violations into: (i) violations of the rights to life; (ii) rape, sexual slavery, and other violations of physical integrity; (iii) abductions of civilians; and (iv) forced displacement. There is no reference to the applicable human rights instruments. The report concludes in the language of international criminal law: 'LRA members and its leader, Joseph Kony, are clearly guilty of war crimes and crimes against humanity, they must be held accountable under international law... These human rights violations against the civilian population as well as violations of international humanitarian law, which continue despite the successive past and present military operations, sharply raise the issue of protection of civilians.'

78 A review of the Security Council Resolutions from 2014 to 2016 reveal a more consistent use of the term 'violations' for State and 'abuses' for armed groups than prior to 2014. It may be assumed but it is not always explicitly clear that the term 'abuses' is used to refer to acts by armed groups. See for example UN Security Council Resolutions: 'Reports of the Secretary-General on the Sudan and South Sudan' (12 August 2016) UN Doc S/RES/2304 (2016); 'The Situation in the Central African Republic' (26 July 2016) UN Doc S/RES/2301 (2016); 'The situation concerning Iraq' (25 July 2016) UN Doc S/RES/2299 (2016); 'Situation in Mali' (29 June 2016) UN Doc S/RES/2295 (2016); 'The situation concerning the Democratic Republic of Congo' (29 June 2016) UN Doc S/RES/2293 (2016); 'The situation in Afghanistan' (15 March 2016) UN Doc S/RES/2274; 'Reports of the Secretary-General on the Sudan and South Sudan (15 December 2015) UN Doc S/RES/2252; 'Iraq' (29 July 2015) UN Doc S/RES/2233; 'Children and armed conflict' (18 June 2015) UN Doc S/RES/2225.

79 See for examples the inconsistencies highlighted in Constantinides, 'Armed Opposition Groups and the UN Security Council' (n 60) 96.

80 See for example UNSC Resolutions: 'The situation concerning Iraq' (25 July 2016) UN Doc S/RES/2299 (2016); 'Situation in Mali' (29 June 2016) UN Doc S/RES/2295 (2016); 'The situation in Afghanistan' (15 March 2016) UN Doc S/RES/2274, 'Iraq' (29 July 2015) UN Doc S/RES/2233; 'Children and armed conflict' (18 June 2015) UN Doc S/RES/2225.

about whether and when it is legitimate to hold armed groups responsible under human rights law.

A further inconsistency relates to the question of when human rights law is said to apply to armed groups. Inconsistencies on this issue are not often brought to the fore because the majority of UN accountability mechanisms are working against a backdrop of armed conflict. As a result, most accountability mechanisms are operating in a legal framework in which the threshold of international humanitarian law has already been met. That being said, there are several instances in which UN commissions have found armed groups to be bound by human rights law outside of the international humanitarian law framework, either *before* the threshold of international humanitarian has been reached or *after* international humanitarian law has ceased to apply.[81] These varying practices expose an uncertainty in the legal doctrine about 'when' armed groups are bound by human rights law. For those accountability mechanisms working within the framework of armed conflict, there is yet another inconsistent practice which again reflects an uncertainty on the law. While some accountability mechanisms state that armed groups are only bound by human rights law in instances where they control territory, others have found that armed groups are bound by human rights when they do not hold any territory at all.[82] This reflects the existence of a lack of clarity about the role territory plays in the acquisition of obligations under human rights law.

The last and arguably most important inconsistency which is demonstrated by the practice of the various monitoring mechanisms is the way in which the various

[81] See for example the Syria Commission of Inquiry, 'Report of the Independent International Commission of Inquiry on the Syrian Arab Republic' (22 February 2012) UN Doc A/HRC/19/69, [106] (hereafter Syria Commission of Inquiry Report, February 2012), which found that the FSA groups were bound by, 'at a minimum human rights obligations constituting peremptory international law (jus cogens)' at a time when the threshold of international humanitarian law had not yet been met. The decision of the International Commission of Inquiry to include human rights obligations for the FSA groups at this juncture is the subject of Rodenhäuser, 'The Syria Example' (n 3). For international human rights law continuing to apply at the end of an armed conflict, see International Commission of Inquiry on Libya, 'Report of the International Commission of Inquiry on Libya' (2 March 2012) UN Doc A/HRC/19/68, [26], which confirms that after the close of hostilities in Libya on 24 October 2011, human rights law became the predominant applicable framework again, save for 'residual humanitarian law matters'. See also UNMISS South Sudan Report 2014 (n 5) which states at [18]: 'The most basic human rights obligations, in particular those emanating from peremptory international law (jus cogens) bind both the State and armed opposition groups in times of peace and during armed conflict.'

[82] In the Report of Sri Lanka Panel of Experts (n 5) the experts expressed uncertainty about whether non-state actors, in this case the LTTE, might have human rights obligations beyond the territories they control, [243]. The majority of reports limit their observations to instances in which the armed group in question has effective control. See for example, Gaza Fact-Finding Mission Report (n 5) [304]; Libya ICI Report June 2011 (n 8) [72]. For examples of reports where territorial control is not required see Syria Commission of Inquiry Report, February 2012 (n 81); UNMISS South Sudan Report 2014 (n 5). See also UN Human Rights Council, 'Report of the Special Rapporteur on freedom of religion or belief, Heiner Bielefeldt' (29 December 2014) UN Doc A/HRC/28/66 (hereafter 2014 Report on Special Rapporteur on freedom of religion), [54], where he states: 'an evolving approach recognizes the importance and impact of certain non-State actors, arguing that some human rights obligations also apply to them, including non-State armed groups with (or arguably even without) effective control over territory'.

mechanisms justify the application of human rights to armed groups in legal terms, if any justification is given at all. Firstly, legal justifications for statements holding armed groups to account under human rights law are all too often very light on law.[83] It is astonishing to see how often reports or documents holding armed groups accountable under human rights law fail to give any *legal* justification for their practice at all.[84] It is also remarkable how often reports which do provide a footnote to their statement that armed groups are bound by human rights law simply cite other reports of commissions of inquiry or special rapporteurs as their justification rather than sources of law.[85] In doing so, these reports serve to create and perpetuate the already identified disconnect between practice and theory on this topic. They perpetuate the notion that armed groups are bound by international human rights law while offering almost no legal explanation for this being the case. As a result, they leave the hard questions, such as, 'how', 'why', and 'when' unanswered. The reports which do provide a legal explanation for their claim that armed groups are bound by human rights law usually rely on one of four explanations for this position. These explanations include reliance on the UDHR, reference to the armed group's control of territory, reference to the fact that the human rights norms which are being relied upon are *jus cogens*, and reference to crimes against humanity. A short description of these four explanations is given below.

6. Theories Relied upon by Accountability Mechanisms

6.1 Universal Declaration of Human Rights

In some cases where UN mechanisms have the notion indicated that armed groups have obligations under human rights law, they have referred to the UDHR. It is noteworthy that reports holding armed groups accountable under human rights law have also cited, either directly or indirectly, the important report which was written on Sri

[83] There are many instances in which the application of human rights law to armed groups is not explained with either a footnote or any reference to a legal source. See for example, Gaza Fact-Finding Mission Report (n 5) [188]; UNMISS South Sudan Report 2014 (n 5) [18]; OHCHR, 'Report for the United Nations High Commissioner for Human Rights on the situation of human rights in Mali' (7 January 2012) UN Doc A/HRC/22/33 (hereafter OHCHR Mali Report January 2012). See also M23 Report (n 5) [11].

[84] See for example CEDAW General Recommendation No. 30 (n 76) above [16].

[85] In the OHCHR CAR Report 2013 (n 5), the statement that it is 'increasingly accepted that non-State armed groups must respect and ensure respect for human rights in the territory it controls' was supported in fn 10 by a statement by the President of the Security Council in the context of the conflict in the DRC that all parties must abide by human rights in the sectors they control: UN Security Council, 'Presidential Statement on DRC' (18 October 2002) UN Doc S/PRST/2002/27. See also OHCHR Mali Report January 2012 (n 83). This report contains no statement of law justifying its application of human rights law to the armed groups in the north of the country. The UNAMA Report July 2013 (n 5) refers to the Report of Sri Lanka Panel of Experts (n 5) [188] and the Libya ICI Report June 2011 (n 8). It is noted that the statement in [188] of the Sri Lanka Panel of Experts has no reference to legal authority at all. The referenced paragraph to the Libya report also refers to [188] of the Sri Lanka Panel of Experts as a reference.

Lanka by Philip Alston, the Special Rapporteur on extrajudicial, summary or arbitrary executions in 2006 as their authority.[86] Here Philip Alston stated:

The Government has assumed the binding legal obligation to respect and ensure the rights recognized in the International Covenant on Civil and Political Rights (ICCPR). As a non-State actor, the LTTE does not have legal obligations under the ICCPR, but it remains subject to the demand of the international community, first expressed in the Universal Declaration of Human Rights, that every organ of society respect and promote human rights.[87]

In doing so, Alston stated a view, albeit implicitly, that the source of human rights obligations for armed groups is customary international law. Yet Alston was silent about the details and consequences of this claim. Did Alston mean to express a view that armed groups are bound to secure all the rights contained in the UDHR? Or did he mean that armed groups are only bound by the human rights norms that have gained the status of customary international law? It is notable that Special Rapporteur Alston did not elaborate on when an armed group would constitute an 'organ of society' and nor did he cite any further legal sources to support his position.

6.2 Control of territory

Special Rapporteur Alston went on to comment that it is 'especially appropriate and feasible to call for an armed group to respect human rights norms when it "exercises significant control over territory and population and has an identifiable political structure"'.[88] Indeed today, this is the legal justification given most often by accountability mechanisms holding armed groups accountable under human rights law.[89] In his early article on the subject, Matas wrote that '[w]hen a government undertakes an obligation on behalf of the state, the obligation is taken on behalf of the whole state, governmental and non-governmental people alike, and not just on behalf of the government'.[90] Likewise, Tomuschat, writing in 2004, wrote that '[t]o the extent that elements of governmental authority have fallen into the hands of a rebel movement, that movement cannot escape its responsibilities under the CCPR—and other human rights instruments, including the elementary rules that have crystallized as customary law'.[91] Yet, beyond this, the idea that

[86] OHCHR, 'Report of the Special Rapporteur on Extrajudicial, Summary or Arbitrary Exectutions, Philip Alston; the Special Rapporteur on the Right to Health, Paul Hunt; the Special Rapporteur on the human rights of internally displaced persons; and the Special Rapporteur on Adequate Housing' to Lebanon and Israel (2 October 2006) UN Doc A/HRC/2/7, footnote 19.

[87] OHCHR, 'Report on the Special Rapporteur on Extrajudicial, Summary or Arbitrary Executions, Mission to Sri Lanka' (27 March 2006) UN Doc E/CN.4/2006/53/Add.5, [24–33]. See likewise Gaza Fact-Finding Mission Report (n 5 above), footnote 186.

[88] Ibid, [26].

[89] See (n 82). See also S. Sivakumaran, *The Law of Non-International Armed Conflict* (OUP, Oxford 2014) 96 (hereafter Sivakumaran *Non-International Armed Conflict*), who states that this is the 'predominant view to date'.

[90] Matas, 'Armed Opposition Groups' (n 25) 632.

[91] Tomuschat, 'Insurgent Movements' (n 42) 588.

territorial control holds the key to understanding how and when armed groups are bound by human rights law has only been moderately explored.

6.3 *Jus cogens*

Bodies holding armed groups to account under human rights law have sometimes employed the argument that armed groups are bound because *jus cogens* norms are binding upon every subject of international law. This argument was articulated by the Commission of Inquiry on Syria which found that 'at a minimum, human rights obligations constituting peremptory international law (*jus cogens*) bind States, individuals and non-State collective entities, including armed groups'.[92] It was also asserted by the United Nations Mission to the Republic of South Sudan (UNMISS) which has stated:

> the most basic human rights obligations, in particular those emanating from peremptory international law (jus cogens) bind both the State and armed opposition groups in times of peace and during armed conflict. In particular, international human rights law requires States, armed groups and others to respect the prohibitions of extrajudicial killing, maiming, torture, cruel inhuman or degrading treatment of punishment, enforced disappearance, rape, other conflict related sexual violence, sexual and other forms of slavery, the recruitment and use of children in hostilities, arbitrary detention as well as of any violations that amount to war crimes, crimes against humanity, or genocide.[93]

The truth of such an assertion needs closer examination, as it raises several important questions. In particular, it is questionable whether the fact that a norm has *jus cogens* status means that it is binding upon every subject of international law. The explanation based on *jus cogens* also leads to another common explanation that is given for why armed groups may be bound by human rights law: the overlap between the *jus cogens* norms which are often said to be binding upon armed groups and crimes against humanity.

6.4 Crimes against humanity

In some instances, reports from UN accountability mechanisms refer to crimes against humanity as legal justification for holding armed groups bound by human rights law.[94] Yet an accompanying explanation is lacking, and there is no attempt at the legal and conceptual analysis that needs to be done before such a proposition can be accepted. This evaluation would require first addressing whether crimes against humanity really equate with human rights violations, in a technical rather than just semantic sense. Second, it would require addressing the question whether

[92] See United Nations Human Rights Council (UNHRC), 'Report of the Independent International Commission of Inquiry on the Syrian Arab Republic' (15 August 2012) UN Doc A/HRC/21/50, [106]. For a discussion of this argument see Rodenhäuser, 'The Syria Example' (n 3) 267, 279–83. See also 2014 Report on Special Rapporteur on freedom of religion (n 82).

[93] UNMISS South Sudan Report 2014 (n 5) [18].

[94] See (n 77).

the fact that *members* of armed groups can commit crimes against humanity can be cited as evidence of *armed groups* committing crimes against humanity. It is only if both questions are answered in the affirmative that it can be said that the law on crimes against humanity supports the contention that armed groups are bound by human rights law. Yet even in these circumstances, a number of important questions remain. For example, what would such a conclusion say about the normative scope of the responsibility of armed groups under human rights law? And what kind of armed groups can commit crimes against humanity? The preliminary questions required by this legal argument are profound, yet are overlooked in footnotes or reports that simply cite 'Rome Statute, Article 7' or passages which, like that in the South Sudan report referred to above, clearly seem to be referring to the law on crimes against humanity, but only do so implicitly.[95]

7. Design of the Book

In the light of the above discussion, it can be seen that there are several key areas of uncertainty relating to the question of the accountability of armed groups under human rights law. The first uncertainty relates to why the accountability of armed groups under human rights law matters in the first place. Does the practice of applying human rights norms to armed groups bring normative 'added-value' to the legal framework or is humanitarian law sufficient on its own? If human rights law does not bring any added normative value, then the practice of holding armed groups accountable under human rights law is of little worth. A second important area of uncertainty relates to the international legal personality of armed groups. In particular, there is a lack of clarity on several fundamental theoretical questions that relate specifically to human rights law. For example, is it justified to say that armed groups can have legal personality under international human rights law? If so, how and when is that international legal personality acquired? These theoretical questions relating to the international legal personality of armed groups pertain to the heart of the legal framework and have been given only minimal attention in legal scholarship. A review of the reports published by the International Law Commission on important topics of international law contain repeated and tantalizing references to the importance of establishing the conditions required for a given insurrectional movement to gain international legal personality. Yet each time the reports conclude that such questions fall outside the scope of the particular study which is focused on States.[96] Yet it is argued that questions relating

[95] See LRA Report December 2009 (n 77) 4.

[96] See, for example, ILC, Yearbook of the International Law Commission 1975 (5 May–25 July 1975) Vol II, UN Doc A/CN.4/SER.A/1975/Add.1, where it is stated: 'It is not, of course, the purpose of this draft to codify the rules governing the international responsibility, if any, of the insurrectional movements but—once again—to proceed from the premise that, as soon as they begin their separate existence on the international scene, such movements may be capable within certain limits of committing internationally wrongful acts of their own. But taking these problems into consideration certainly does not make it necessary, in the course of the present codification project, to spell out the

to international legal personality are the primary and crucial building blocks in any quest to better understand how and when human rights law can be applied to armed groups.

A third uncertainty relates to the question of when and how armed groups are bound by human rights law, if at all. This is an equally fundamental issue. What is the source of human rights obligations for armed groups and when will they apply? It has been illustrated above that there are several competing theories on how the application of human rights norms to armed groups can be justified, from a normative perspective. It is argued that more evaluative research is needed to find out which explanation is most convincing, in which circumstances. Another fourth key area of uncertainty relates to the normative scope of the legal personality of armed groups. It is observed that statements calling armed groups to account under human rights law rarely comment on the normative scope of those obligations. This omission means that there is little clarity on issues such as whether armed groups are bound by the full range of human rights or only those which match their functional capacity. A final level of uncertainty relates to the manner in which existing human rights mechanisms or institutions can secure the accountability of armed groups under human rights law and ensure their compliance with the obligations identified above. This requires a consideration of when and how human rights monitoring mechanisms can and should engage with armed groups in their reports. The purpose of the present book is to address only the first four areas of uncertainty above, by addressing four major questions.

Firstly, the book seeks to evaluate whether there is any added value in the practice of holding armed groups to account under human rights law, from a normative perspective. Secondly, the book seeks to gain insight into the manner in which the legal community is, and has been, willing to understand the legal personality of armed groups per se today and in the past. Thirdly, the book considers what these conclusions can tell us about *when* and *how* armed groups can gain international legal personality under human rights law. Fourthly, the book considers what these conclusions can tell us about when and how armed groups can be held bound by human rights law, in a more technical sense. In adopting this narrow focus, the study leaves much of the normative inquiry to future projects. This study also does not address the practical implications of engaging with armed groups in an accountability process. The book also does not analyse the legal bindingness of

requirements imposed by international law for a given movement to be classified as an "insurrectional movement", or to specify under what conditions, at what time and in relation to whom such a movement can be regarded as endowed with international personality and what is then the scope-which will in any event vary from one case to another and, in any one case, with the passage of time—of its international legal capacity.' See similar examples of statements recognizing the importance of this topic but passing over it see ILC, Yearbook of the International Law Commission 1958 (28 April–4 July 1958) Vol II, UN Doc A/CN.4/SER.A/1958/Add.1, 24, 32; 'Draft Articles on the Law of Treaties with Commentaries' in ILC, Yearbook of the International Law Commission 1966 (3–28 January 1966) Vol II, UN Doc A/CN.4/SER.A/1966/Add.1 186-9; ILC, Yearbook of the International Law Commission 1967 (8 May–14 July 1967) UN Doc A/CN.4/SER.A/1967, 15 [29], 19–21 (Special Missions).

unilateral declarations or deeds of commitment by armed groups under international law. While the book recognizes these to be important vehicles of accountability in their own right, the book's aim is to bring greater insight to how *all* armed groups are bound by human rights law and not just armed groups which have signed such a commitment. It also takes note that important research on this topic has already been conducted by Sivakumaran in his far-reaching study on non-international armed conflict.[97] The decision to draw the parameters of this study in this manner is justified by a view that a single study could not do sufficient justice to all the remaining areas of uncertainty.

With this stated focus in mind, Chapter 2 of the book considers whether holding armed groups accountable under human rights law brings any added value to the legal framework that applies in non-international armed conflicts. By comparing international humanitarian law with international human rights law, the chapter seeks to identify the value of human rights law vis-à-vis international humanitarian law. In order to identify the 'value' of human rights law, the study takes into account the factual paradigm of non-international armed conflict, the role of armed groups and the experiences of individuals on the ground. To do this, the comparative legal research is complemented by further desk-based research into political sciences literature and anthropology literature. The purpose of Chapter 2 is to establish whether the question of whether armed groups are bound by human rights law is more than just a question of legal theory and whether it actually matters to people on the ground whether armed groups are bound by human rights law.

Chapters 3, 4, 5, and 6 are designed to shed light on when and how armed groups acquire legal personality under international human rights law, in the form of obligations. The book seeks answers to these questions by analysing other frameworks of international law which are less controversially binding upon armed groups: the law of belligerency, the law of insurgency and international humanitarian law. The virtue of these bodies of law is that there is a general acceptance that armed groups are bound by them. As a result, these legal frameworks present a valuable opportunity to dissect the mechanics of 'how armed groups can be bound by international law' without the distraction of parallel discussions about the desirability of them being bound in the first place. However, the book's handling of this analysis includes an acknowledgement that the concept of international legal personality under international law is inescapably subjective in character. Indeed, it can be observed that the debates about the legal personality of armed groups under human rights law reflect the same fault lines which underlie and divide discussions about international legal personality more generally. It is argued that this observation poses a problem for any author writing on the topic of armed groups and legal personality, because it risks the author evaluating the legal personality of armed groups in a way that either consciously or sub-consciously, reflects his or her own personal approach to legal personality. The book employs two major methods to combat this subjectivity.

[97] Sivakumaran, 'Non-International Armed Conflict' (n 89).

First, the book introduces the study of legal personality by utilizing an evaluative framework through which the legal frameworks above can be analysed. This short evaluative framework is set out in Chapter 3 and consists of the five dominant conceptions of international legal personality identified by Portmann on his monograph on legal personality in international law: the 'State-only', 'recognition', 'formal', individualistic' and 'actor' conception of international legal personality. The adoption of this evaluative framework allows the three legal frameworks examined in Chapters 4, 5, and 6 to be evaluated against an identifiable benchmark of analysis. The inclusion of this evaluative framework has the effect of forcing a more painstaking examination of how the legal personality of armed groups is acquired, under each legal framework. It also helps the author escape somewhat from, or at least be more aware of, her own inevitable scholarly biases.[98] Perhaps most importantly, the adoption of such a framework means that the conclusions of the study on legal personality are immediately transparent and able to be challenged. This has the effect of facilitating a continuing debate on the topic and gives the study's conclusions more legitimacy. Secondly, whenever citing a jurist as an authority on the law for a particular point, the study deliberately notes whether that author is either openly or arguably allied to a particular conception of international legal personality. The study argues that it is only by adding this level of meta-analysis that it is possible to combat the subjectivity inherent in the debate and draw transparent conclusions about what the various legal frameworks demonstrate regarding the legal personality of armed groups.[99]

As a result of its approach, Chapters 3–6 do not seek to determine how and when an armed group may gain international legal personality per se as if there is an objective truth on the topic.[100] Instead, these chapters shed light on the dominant manner in which the legal personality of armed groups is conceived under international law. The question 'when' consists of an enquiry into the temporal and material circumstances that are necessary for an armed group to acquire legal personality under international law. The question 'how' includes an enquiry into the theoretical dimension of when an armed group acquires legal personality under international law. It is with respect to the 'how' question that the conclusions of the theoretical evaluation above will be mainly relevant. Here, the chapters will utilize the evaluative framework to enquire into the legal mechanics of an armed group acquiring legal personality under international law. In doing so, the chapters evaluate *inter alia* the role of functionality and State consent in an armed group's acquisition of legal personality.

The final five chapters of the book consider *when and how is it justifiable to find armed groups responsible under international human rights law.* While these chapters

[98] Higgins, *Problems and Process* (n 67) 5. [99] Ibid.

[100] T. Schultz, *Transnational Legality: Stateless Law and International Arbitration* (OUP, Oxford 2014) 16–17, where he states: 'Let me repeat, and I offer not apology for the repetition because the argument is important: nothing is intrinsically of a legal nature or not of that nature. As Paul Bohannan put it, law is a noetic unity: it is a concept not represented by anything except our ideas about it.'

also address 'when' and 'how' questions, they approach the questions from a different angle. Rather than considering how armed groups acquire legal personality generally under international law, they give attention to the theories of how armed groups are bound by human rights law. As a first step, Chapter 7 examines the main theories which exist as to how armed groups are bound by international humanitarian law and considers the relative merits of each. The rationale behind this chapter is similar to the methodology employed in Part II of the book. Its inclusion constitutes a recognition that other bodies of law can be instructive when seeking to understand armed groups' obligations under human rights law. The purpose of Chapter 7 is to extract theories which can provide assistance when examining the main explanations for how armed groups might be bound by human rights law.

The next four chapters of the book are devoted to examining the major theories which have been put forward for 'how' armed groups are bound by international human rights law. Chapter 8 examines whether armed groups might be bound by human rights treaty law. It first examines the two main human rights Covenants which are together often referred to as the Bill of Rights: the International Covenant on Civil and Political Rights and the International Covenant on Economic, Social and Cultural Rights. It then looks at the Convention against Torture which is an example of a human rights treaty whose text holds potential to apply to armed groups in certain circumstances. It then focuses on the two human rights treaties which explicitly address armed groups: the Optional Protocol on the Convention on the Rights of the Child and the African Union Convention for the Protection and Assistance of Internally Displaced Persons in Africa 2009. Chapter 9 explores the extent to which territorial control provides answers as to when and how it may be justifiable to find armed groups responsible under international human rights law.

Chapter 10 examines the extent to which the law on crimes against humanity may provide answers to how armed groups are bound by human rights law. In approaching this question, it broadly addresses the steps of the argument which are identified as necessary above. First, it examines the relationship between international human rights law and crimes against humanity from a historical and contemporary perspective. Secondly, it considers whether armed groups themselves may be argued to commit crimes against humanity, as opposed to their individual members. Finally, Chapter 11 of the book considers whether customary international law provides an explanation for how armed groups may be bound by human rights law. In doing so, it examines documents from UN mechanisms that have addressed the issue of accountability of armed groups under human rights law. These include reports from the Human Rights Council's special procedures, reports written by independent commissions of inquiry, fact-finding missions and field offices. It also reviews Security Council Resolutions, Human Rights Council Resolutions, and statements from the Office of the High Commissioner of Human Rights. In analysing these reports and statements, the chapter examines how they employ customary law in order to explain how and when armed groups might be bound by customary international human rights law. It then evaluates these statements against conclusions extracted from Chapters 6, 7, 9, and 10 of the study to evaluate whether the arguments that have been employed by the accountability mechanisms, have been articulated in a manner that justify holding armed groups responsible under human rights law. The overall conclusions of the book are found in Chapter 12 which brings together the various complementary strands of research throughout the book and orders them thematically in order to provide comprehensive answers to the study's question about when and how human rights law can be binding upon armed groups.

2

Added Value of Application of International Human Rights Law to Armed Groups

1. Introduction

Although the overriding purpose of this book is to consider *how* and *when* armed groups may be bound by human rights law, the first substantive chapter begins by considering whether there is any normative added value in holding armed groups to account under human rights law. Notably, some influential authors have concluded that the contribution of human rights standards to the legal framework which applies in non-international armed conflicts is 'not significant'.[1] For example, in Zegveld's view, common Article 3 and Additional Protocol II provide the 'most essential protections' which are needed in times of armed conflict and are almost identical to non-derogable human rights norms. If this is true, it can be questioned whether the practice of holding armed groups to account under human rights law has any normative value at all. It can also be questioned whether lawyers only articulate abuses by armed groups in the language of human rights law in order to take advantage of human rights' procedural mechanisms. In addition, it also allows doubt to creep in as to whether the multiple statements holding armed groups accountable under human rights law are simply numerous examples of bad lawyering; statements written by persons who do not properly know the difference between human rights law and international humanitarian law.[2] A failure to address this issue at the beginning of the book would cast doubt on the normative validity of this study whose purpose is to seek to understand better from a legal perspective when and how armed groups can be bound by human rights law. In

[1] L. Zegveld, *The Accountability of Armed Opposition Groups in International Law*, (CUP, Cambridge 2002) 52 (hereafter Zegveld, *Armed Opposition Groups*). Indeed, it has often been commented that the added value of invoking human rights law remains unclear. See for example J. Peijic, 'Conflict Classification and the Law Applicable to Detention and the Use of Force' in E. Wilmshurt (ed), *International Law and the Classification of Conflicts* (OUP, Oxford 2002) 53.

[2] This possibility with respect to General Assembly and Security Council Resolutions has specifically been rejected by C. Tomuschat, 'The Applicability of Human Rights Law to Insurgent Movements' in H. Fischer et al. (eds), *Krisensicherung Und Humanitarer Schutz—Crisis Management and Humanitarian Protection: Festschrif Fur Dieter Fleck* (BWV Berliner-Wissenschaft, Berlin 2004) 585: 'Both the General Assembly and the Security Council are firmly in the hands of lawyers who know perfectly well what words mean... when a clause is inserted into a resolution indicating what legal rules a State is bound to respect, nobody is unaware of the thrust of such a specification.'

the light of this opening observation, the purpose of this chapter is to identify the value of applying human rights law to armed groups, from a normative perspective, vis-à-vis international humanitarian law.[3]

2. Relationship between IHRL and IHL

2.1 IHL applying to non-international armed conflicts

When seeking to understand the potential value that human rights law brings to the legal framework of non-international armed conflict, it is first important to clarify what norms we are referring to within that framework and in the context of this study. From an international humanitarian law perspective, the relevant norms are those found in common Article 3 of the Geneva Conventions, Additional Protocol II and the customary international humanitarian law which applies to non-international armed conflicts. Common Article 3 provides basic protections for individuals not taking an active part in hostilities such as civilians, fighters who have been captured or have surrendered, and those placed *hors de combat* as a result of being wounded or falling ill. The norms in common Article 3 apply at the lowest level of non-international armed conflicts.[4] The norms in Additional Protocol II apply at a higher threshold of non-international armed conflict, when an armed group has attained control over a portion of the territory and gained sufficient capacity to adhere to its norms.[5] Additional Protocol II contains a number of fundamental guarantees which apply to all persons who do not take part in the hostilities.[6] It contains special provisions intended to provide protection to those who are detained or prosecuted for reasons related to the armed conflict.[7] It also contains provisions intended to protect the wounded, sick, and shipwrecked and provisions relating to the protection of the civilian population.[8] It is increasingly accepted

[3] The notion that human rights law brings added normative value has also been identified by C. Ryngaert, 'Human Rights Obligations of Armed Groups' (2008) 2 Revue Belge de Droit International 355, 378; A. Constantinides, 'Human Rights Obligations and Accountability of Armed Opposition Groups: The Practice of the UN Security Council' (2010) 4 Human Rights and International Legal Discourse 89, 94.

[4] The threshold for the application of common Article 3 is laid out in *Prosecutor v Tadić (Decision on the Defence Motion for Interlocutory Appeal on Jurisdiction)* IT-94-1-AR72 (2 October 1995) [70] (hereafter (*Tadić* Jurisdiction Decision), and has been elaborated comprehensively in *Prosecutor v Boškoski and Tarčulovski (Trial Judgment)* IT-04-82-T (10 July 2008) [172–92] (hereafter *Boškoski*). This case law is discussed in more detail in Chapter 5.

[5] See Article 1 of Additional Protocol II to the Geneva Conventions of 1949 (8 June 1977) which states that it will apply to non-international armed conflicts between a State's armed forces and 'dissident armed forces or other organized armed groups which, under responsible command, exercise such control over a part of its territory as to enable them to carry out sustained and concerted military operations and to implement this Protocol'.

[6] See Article 4 (Fundamental Guarantees) of Additional Protocol II.

[7] See Additional Protocol II, Articles 5 (Persons whose liberty has been restricted) and 6 (Penal prosecutions).

[8] See Additional Protocol II, Articles 7 (Protection and Care), 8 (Search), 9 (Protection of medical and religious personnel), 10 (General protection of medical duties), 11 (Protection of medical units and transports), 12 (The distinctive emblem), 13 (Protection of the civilian population), 14

that some of the norms found in the Geneva Conventions and Additional Protocol I are also widely accepted to apply in situations of non-international armed conflicts, as a matter of customary international law. This is particularly the case for the key international humanitarian law provisions relating to the conduct of hostilities found in Additional Protocol I and the fundamental guarantees contained in Article 75 of Additional Protocol I.[9]

2.2 IHRL applying to non-international armed conflicts

From a human rights perspective, the most core norms under examination are those found in the International Covenant on Civil and Political Rights (ICCPR) and the International Covenant on Economic, Social and Cultural Rights (ICESCR). Further human rights norms are also contained in the Convention on the Elimination of all forms of Discrimination against Women (CEDAW), the Convention on the Rights of the Child (CRC), the Convention against Torture and other Cruel, Inhuman or Degrading Treatment or Punishment (CAT), the International Convention on the Elimination of all forms of Racial Discrimination (CERD), and the Convention on the Rights of Persons with Disabilities (CRPD). For the purpose of identifying the added value of human rights law vis-à-vis international humanitarian law, this chapter focuses primarily on the two Covenants which, together with the Universal Declaration of Human Rights (UDHR), have been referred to as the International Bill of Rights. When examining those Covenants, one could take the view, like Zegveld, that one should only look at the non-derogable rights contained therein, i.e. the rights which cannot be derogated from in times of armed conflict.[10] Such an approach would arguably include the majority of the rights contained in the ICESCR which has no derogation clause but only about a third of the total articles in the ICCPR.[11] Alternatively, one could

(Protection of objects indispensable to the survival of the civilian population), 15 (Protection of works and installations containing dangerous forces), 16 (Protection of cultural objects and of places of worship), 17 (Prohibition of forced movement of civilians) and 18 (Relief societies and relief actions).

[9] See e.g. Additional Protocol I to the Geneva Conventions of 1949 (8 June 1977), Articles 48 (principle of distinction), 52(2) (definition of military objectives), 52(1) (definition of civilian objects), and 51(4) (prohibition of indiscriminate attacks). See also J. Henckaerts and L. Doswald-Beck, *Customary International Humanitarian Law, Volume I: Rules* (CUP, Cambridge 2005) 3–76 (hereafter Henckaerts and Doswald-Beck, *Rules*).

[10] Zegveld, *Armed Opposition Groups* (n 1) 52.

[11] According to Article 4 of the ICCPR, adopted and opened for signature, ratification, and accession by General Assembly, 'Resolution 2200 A (XXI)' (16 December 1966), no derogation may be made from Articles 6 (the right to life), 7 (the right not to be subjected to torture or cruel, inhuman or degrading treatment or punishment), 8 (the right not to be held in slavery or servitude), 11 (the right not to be deprived of liberty on the ground of an inability to fulfil a contractual obligation), 15 (*nullum crimen sine lege* and *nulla poena sine lege*), 16 (the right to recognition before the law), and 18 (the right to freedom of thought, conscience and religion). See A. Műller, 'Limitations to and Derogations from Economic, Social and Cultural Rights' (2009) 4 Human Rights Law Review 557 (hereafter Műller, 'Limitations to and Derogations from') for a discussion of whether derogations may still be possible from the International Covenant on Economic, Social and Cultural Rights (ICESCR), despite the absence of a derogation clause.

take the view that all the rights listed in both Covenants are relevant in times of non-international armed conflict, in some form.

It is submitted that the latter approach is more appropriate. A first reason not to exclude the derogable norms in the ICCPR from the evaluation is that more of the rights contained in the ICCPR are non-derogable in character than those which are listed as being non-derogable in Article 4. In its General Comment 29, the Human Rights Committee found that many other rights in the ICCPR are non-derogable, by virtue of their peremptory nature (*jus cogens*).[12] Another important reason to include derogable norms when evaluating the added value of human rights law vis-à-vis international humanitarian law is that the Human Rights Committee has found that even in instances where a State derogates from a particular enumerated 'right', it is only allowed to derogate to the extent required by the exigencies of the particular situation. As a result, even in situations where a State has derogated from a particular right, the core of that right will nevertheless remain applicable. It has stated: '[i]n practice this will ensure that no provision of the Covenant, however validly derogated from, will be entirely inapplicable to the behaviour of a State party'.[13] This is a strong reason to argue that it cannot be sufficient only to compare the non-derogable norms of the ICCPR and ICESCR with common Article 3 and Additional Protocol II when seeking to understand the relative normative scope of international human rights law vis-à-vis international humanitarian law. Instead, it is suggested that one must compare all the norms of the ICCPR and the ICESCR with the international humanitarian law which applies in non-international armed conflicts.

2.3 Different purposes of IHL and IHRL

As a legal regime, international humanitarian law is designed to regulate the acts of two opposing entities confronting each other in a competition for control over territory or persons. International humanitarian law takes the existence of armed conflict as a given, and within that reality, has the purpose limiting harm to civilian life and civilian infrastructure. As a result, it is infused with a sense of pragmatism which arises from its acceptance of the realities of the existence of armed conflict. International humanitarian law conceives armed conflict to be a temporary and exceptional situation.[14] Within that factual paradigm, it allows the parties to the armed conflict to achieve their military goals to the extent possible within the principle of humanity. Unlike human rights law, international humanitarian law does not offer protection to individuals which is solely premised on the 'inherent

[12] UN Human Rights Committee, 'General Comment 29 (States of Emergency: Article 4)' (31 August 2001) UN Doc CCPR/C/21/Rev.1/Add.11, [11–13], [12] (hereafter HRC General Comment 29, Emergency) suggests that the definition of crimes against humanity in Article 7 of the Rome Statute may be used as evidence that a norm is 'non-derogable'.

[13] Ibid, [4].

[14] This is implicit in the notion that international humanitarian law has a 'threshold of application'. It is also implicit in the notion that international humanitarian law will largely cease to apply at the 'end of the armed conflict'. See e.g. Article 2 of Additional Protocol II.

dignity' of the human person.[15] Instead, international humanitarian law offers a status based protection, which is conditioned upon individuals belonging to, or not belonging to, a number of categories, e.g. civilians, medical personnel, combatants, fighters, persons *hors de combat*. Although it seeks to secure civilians' protection, international humanitarian law does not make the protection of vulnerable individuals its single goal. Instead, it constantly balances the principle of humanity with the principle of military necessity in order to create a realistic framework of legal protection that also takes into account the goals of the fighting parties.[16] It also offers protection to several categories of inanimate objects such as civilian objects, cultural and religious property, medical units, and protected emblems, such as the red cross and the symbol of the United Nations.[17] While it can be argued that the ultimate purpose of these provisions is the protection of human life in the widest sense, it is a reflection of international humanitarian law's pragmatism that this goal is not explicitly stated in these provisions.[18]

Compared to international humanitarian law, human rights law places the individual more squarely at the centre of the legal framework. The preamble of the Vienna Declaration and Programme of Action, adopted on 25 June 1993, articulates this focus clearly:

> Recognizing and affirming that all human rights derive from the dignity and self-worth inherent in the human person, and that the human person is the central subject of human rights and fundamental freedoms, and consequently should be the principal beneficiary and should participate actively in the realization of these rights and freedoms.[19]

Unlike international humanitarian law which is inherently provisional and concerned with limiting the damage that occurs within an adverse situation, human rights is aspirational in character.[20] It not only identifies the rights we all have as human beings but also sets out institutional benchmarks with which those rights can be realized. In some instances, particularly with regard to economic, social, and cultural rights, the human rights framework explicitly acknowledges that the

[15] See Preamble to the Universal Declaration of Human Rights, adopted and proclaimed by General Assembly, 'Resolution 217A (III)' (10 December 1948).

[16] This is seen most clearly in the definition of proportionality in international humanitarian law which applies to international and non-international armed conflicts and is articulated in Article 57(2)(b) of Additional Protocol I. This article recognizes that loss of civilian life and injury to civilians will be permitted by international humanitarian law, as long as it is incidental to an attack on a military objective and is not excessive in relation to the concrete and direct military advantage anticipated.

[17] See e.g. articles in Additional Protocol I: Articles 52 (civilian objects), 53 (cultural objects and places of worship), 12 (medical units), and 38 (recognized emblems), and the equivalent provisions in Additional Protocol II: Articles 11 (medical units and transports), 12 (the distinctive emblem), and16 (cultural objects and places or worship).

[18] Compare the drafting of Article 1 of Protocol I, European Convention of Human Rights 1950 ('Every natural or legal person is entitled to the peaceful enjoyment of his possessions') with Article 52 of Additional Protocol I ('Civilian objects shall not be the object of attack or of reprisals').

[19] See Preamble to the Vienna Declaration and Programme of Action (World Conference on Human Rights, Vienna 25 June 1993).

[20] Despite this, it is noted that both the ICCPR and the ICESCR contain obligations of immediate effect. See also (n 21) and (n 22).

full realization of the rights in question may only be realized progressively over a period of time.[21] Unlike international humanitarian law which has a minimum of two duty-bearers (i.e. the two parties to an armed conflict), human rights law is generally understood as presenting a vertical paradigm whereby a single duty-bearer owes duties to the individual. Human rights law is concerned with governance structures and the vertical relationship between the government and the governed. Importantly, it relies upon traditional methods of law enforcement to achieve its implementation. This is seen through the fact that human rights law repeatedly refers to law enforcement institutions in its provisions. For example, the articles protecting individuals from arbitrary detention and securing fair trial make clear that a court system and an established legal code are required, in order for these rights to be effectively protected.[22] Having provided a brief outline of the respective purposes of the two bodies of law, the chapter's next task is to identify the value that international human rights law brings to the legal framework.

2.4 Historical background to the relationship between IHL and IHRL

When examining the history of the two bodies of law, the present author has shown elsewhere that when the UDHR and Geneva Conventions were respectively drafted in 1948 and 1949, their drafters already understood the two bodies of law to have potential to be complementary in nature.[23] Yet the idea that human rights law and international humanitarian law are 'complementary' was first explicitly enunciated in the ICJ's *Advisory Opinion on the Legal Consequences of the Construction of a Wall in the Occupied Palestinian Territory*.[24] Here the ICJ confirmed that some rights in times of armed conflict will be 'exclusively matters of international humanitarian law; others may be exclusively matters of human rights law; yet others may be matters of both these branches of law'.[25] In its Advisory

[21] See Article 2 ICCPR. For a discussion as to the concept of progressive realization, see UN Committee on Economic, Social and Cultural Rights, 'General Comment 3 (The Nature of States Parties' Obligations)' (14 December 1990) UN Doc E/1991/23, [9] (hereafter CESCR General Comment 3, State Party Obligations).

[22] See for example the text of Article 9(1) which confirms that no one shall be deprived of their liberty except on grounds 'established by law' and subject to a procedure 'established by law'. Article 9(3) confirms that people who have been arrested must be brought promptly before a 'judge or other officer authorized by law to exercise judicial power and shall be entitled to trial'. The quoted words evidence the requirement for a court system and an established legal code.

[23] K. Fortin, 'Complementarity between the ICRC and United Nations and International Humanitarian Law and International Human Rights Law, 1948–1968' (2012) 888 International Review of the Red Cross 1433.

[24] *Advisory Opinion on Legal Consequences of the Construction of a Wall in the Occupied Palestinian Territory* [2004] ICJ Reports 136 (9 July 2004) 106 (hereafter *Wall Advisory Opinion*). See also UN Human Rights Committee, 'General Comment 31 (Nature of the General Legal Obligation Imposed on States Parties to the Covenant)' (26 May 2004) UN Doc CCPR/C/21/Rev.1/Add.13, [11], (hereafter HRC General Comment 31, Legal Obligation): 'While, in respect of certain Covenant rights, more specific rules of international humanitarian law may be specially relevant for the purposes of the interpretation of Covenant rights, both spheres of law are complementary, not mutually exclusive.'

[25] See *Wall Advisory Opinion* (n 24) 106.

Opinion, the ICJ also confirmed its earlier statement in the *Nuclear Weapons* that the principle of *lex specialis* will be a relevant tool of interpretation when deciding which body of law should govern a particular right.[26] With its origins in Roman law, the principle of *lex specialis* was described by Grotius in his *De jure belli ac pacis* as the principle that '[a]mong agreements that are equal in respect to the qualities mentioned that [rule] should given preference which is most specific and approaches most nearly to the subject at hand'.[27] The principle of *lex specialis* is also referred to in texts by Vattel and Pufendorf where it is broadly defined as the principle that where two different norms cover the same question, preference should be given to the rule which is the least general, and comes closest to the matter in question.[28]

By referring to the *lex specialis* principle, the ICJ inadvertently raised more questions than it answered on the relationship between human rights law and international humanitarian law. An explosion of literature followed its pronouncement, opining differently on its meaning. Academic views varied on *inter alia* whether the *lex specialis* principle should be applied at the level of a legal regime or at the level of a norm.[29] Academic views also differed as to the scope of the principle of *lex specialis*. Some scholars argued that it should only be applied in instances where norms are in conflict, whereas others argued that the principle had an interpretative function too.[30] In 2004, the scope of the *lex specialis* principle was studied in depth by the work of the Study Group on the Fragmentation of International Law. Its conclusions are helpful when seeking clarification on these two areas of dispute above. The Study Group found that the *lex specialis* principle works at two different levels.[31] First, it applies in situations where two

[26] *Advisory Opinion on the Legality of the Threat of Use of Nuclear Weapons* [1996] ICJ Reports 226 (8 July 1996) [25] (hereafter *Nuclear Weapons Advisory Opinion*).

[27] Grotius (Bk. II, Cap. xvi. sec. xxix(I)), cited by C. W. Jenks, 'The Conflict of Law-Making Treaties' [1953] British Year Book of International Law 401, 446.

[28] E. de Vattel, *Le Droit des Gens ou Principes de la Loi Naturelle* (London 1758) Vol. I, Bk. II, Ch. xvii, 316, cited by C. Droege, 'Elective Affinities? Human Rights and Humanitarian Law' (2008) 871 International Review of the Red Cross 501, 522 (hereafter Droege, 'Elective Affinities?'); Pufendorf, *Le droit de la nature et des gens ou système general des principes les plus important de la morale, de la jurisprudence, et de la politique* (Amsterdam 1732) Bk. V, Ch. XII, 138–40, cited by A. Lindroos, 'Addressing Norm Conflicts in a Fragmented Legal System: The Doctrine of *Lex Specialis*' [2005] Nordic Journal of International Law 27, 35–6 (hereafter Lindroos, 'Norm Conflicts').

[29] For example, even during the International Law Commission's work at times it seemed to apply the *lex specialis* principle at the level of a 'regime', stating: 'A general type of lex specialis, constituting an exception to legal normality are the laws of war. It seems clear that, at least in the absence of evidence to the contrary, the laws of war must be regarded as leges speciales in relation to—and thus override—rules laying out peace-time norms relating to the same subjects.' M. Koskenniemi, 'Study on the Function and Scope of the Lex Specialis Rule and the Question of Self-Contained Regimes' (4 May 2004) UN Doc ILC(LVI)/SG/FIL/CRD.1 Add.1, [2.5.2].

[30] W.A. Schabas, 'Lex Specialis? Belt and Suspenders? The Parallel Operation of Human Rights Law and the Law of Armed Conflict, and the Conundrum of *Jus Ad Bellum*' [2007] Israel Law Review 592.

[31] 'Conclusions of the Work of the Study Group on the Fragmentation of International Law: Difficulties Arising from the Diversification and Expansion of International Law', ILC, Yearbook of the International Law Commission 2006 (1 May–9 June 2006; 3 July–11 August 2006) Vol II, Part II, UN Doc A/CN.4/SER.A/2006, [2], [5] (hereafter ILC Study Group on the Fragmentation of International Law).

or more norms assist in each other's interpretation. In these instances, the norms in question will not be in conflict with one another.[32] Secondly, it can apply in situations where two norms are in conflict.[33] In these instances, the principle can assist in efforts to decide which norm should have precedence in a particular situation.[34] It is relevant to note that it is increasingly acknowledged that there may be instances in an armed conflict when a human rights law norm may be the 'special norm' vis-à-vis a norm of international humanitarian law.[35] At a conceptual level, this reflects an increased recognition that many modern armed conflicts contain elements of both peace (defined by a lack of fighting, daily life, personal agendas) and war (defined largely by fighting) and that there is often a symbiosis between these two situations.[36]

[32] Some scholars have expressed the view that the notion that international human rights law norms and international humanitarian law norms can assist each other on issues of interpretation would be more effectively captured by recourse to Article 31(3)(c) of the Vienna Convention on the Law of Treaties 1969. See Droege, 'Elective Affinities?' (n 28) 524; N. Prud'homme, '*Lex Specialis:* Oversimplifying a More Complex and Multifaceted Relationship?' [2007] Israel Law Review 356, 392 (hereafter Prud'homme, 'Oversimplifying'). See also *Hassan v UK,* Application No. 29750/09 (ECHR, 16 September 2014) (Grand Chamber Judgment) [100–7].

[33] ILC Study Group on the Fragmentation of International Law (n 31) [2]. See also Lindroos, 'Norm Conflicts' (n 28) 46.

[34] Some scholars argue that international humanitarian law will always be the *lex specialis.* However, a counterweight of scholarship argues that the question of which norm should prevail should be determined at the normative level. See M. Milanovic, 'A Norm Conflict Perspective on the Relationship between International Humanitarian Law and Human Rights Law' (2010) 3 Journal of Conflict and Security Law 459, 463–4; H. Krieger, 'A Conflict of Norms: The Relationship between Humanitarian Law and Human Rights Law in the ICRC Customary Law Study' (2006) 2 Journal of Conflict and Security Law 265, 269; S. Sivakumaran, 'International Humanitarian Law' in D. Moeckli, S. Sangeeta, and S. Sivakumaran (eds), *International Human Rights Law* (OUP, Oxford 2014) 479 (hereafter Sivakumaran, 'International Humanitarian Law'). On the notion that the 'lex specialis' principle is almost always applied at the level of a 'norm', see Lindroos 'Norm Conflicts' (n 28) 42, 44.

[35] See Sivakumaran, 'International Humanitarian Law' (n 34) 479; J. Kleffner, 'Human Rights and International Humanitarian Law' in T. Gill and D. Fleck (eds), *The Handbook of International Law of Military Operations* (OUP, Oxford 2010) 51–77 (hereafter Gill and Fleck, *Military Operations*). See also M. Sassòli and L. M. Olson, 'The Relationship between International Humanitarian and Human Rights Law Where it Matters: Admissible Killing and Internment of Fights in Non-International Armed Conflicts' (2008) 871 International Review of the Red Cross 599, 621–4 (hereafter Sassòli and Olson, 'Admissible Killing and Internment of Fights'); N. Melzer, *Targeted Killing in International Law* (OUP, Oxford 2009) (hereafter Melzer, *Targeted Killing*). It is interesting to note that Melzer at 81 agrees that international human rights law may be referred to in instances where IHL does not provide a rule or where international humanitarian law contains insufficient guidance on a particular issue, but he continues to identify international human rights law as the '*lex generalis*' and international humanitarian law as the '*lex specialis*' in these instances.

[36] See V. Gowlland-Debbas, 'The Relevance of Paragraph 25 of the ICJ's Advisory Opinion on Nuclear Weapons' [2004] American Society of International Law Proceedings 358, 361: 'A view of the law of armed conflict as *leges specilis* totally preempting the *leges generalis* of the rest of international law, including human rights law, could only be tenable when conditions of peace and conditions of war could be strictly compartmentalized. In the situations of neither peace nor war which are prevalent today, it would be untenable to consider that neither the one nor the other applied and in this way to create a vacuum of protection.'

2.5 Relationship between IHL and IHRL in the context of a non-international armed conflict

It has often been pointed out that the potential for complementarity between international human rights law and international humanitarian law is greatest in non-international armed conflicts.[37] Kooijmans states that non-international armed conflict is the 'true shadowland' between international humanitarian law and international human rights law.[38] Likewise, Kalshoven has written:

> Precisely in regard to the non-international armed conflict the two spheres are in closest contact, though; both the citizen-government relations and those between adversaries are here indissolubly linked.[39]

The close relationship between the two bodies of law in non-international armed conflicts is largely due to the fact that the members of the armed groups are simultaneously fighters under international humanitarian law and criminals under domestic law.[40] Moreover, in many instances, non-international armed conflicts escalate out of situations of violent confrontation between the State and the civilian population. In that sense, non-international armed conflicts are often armed extensions of the traditional confrontation between the State and the population, which is the classical domain of human rights law. It will be seen that the tension and overlap between the respective conceptual parameters of international humanitarian law and international human rights law is a key and returning theme of this chapter.

3. Assessment of the Added Value of IHRL in Non-International Armed Conflicts

When seeking to identify the value of human rights law in the non-international armed conflict framework, the chapter takes the words of the ICJ as its starting point: some rights in times of armed conflict will be 'exclusively matters of international humanitarian law; others may be exclusively matters of human rights law; yet others may be matters of both these branches of law'.[41] With these words in mind, the chapter's task is to determine: (i) which issues in non-international

[37] Droege, 'Elective Affinities?' (n 28) 521, defines 'complementarity' as follows: 'Complementarity means that human rights law and humanitarian law do not contradict each other but, being based on the same principles and values, can influence and reinforce each other mutually.'

[38] P. H. Kooijmans, 'In the Shadowland between Civil War and Civil Strife: Some Reflections on the Standard-Setting Process' in A. Delissen and G. Tanja (eds), *Humanitarian Law of Armed Conflict Challenges Ahead* (T.M.C. Asser Institute, The Hague 1991) 226.

[39] F. Kalshoven, 'Applicability of Customary International Law in Non-International Armed Conflicts' in A. Cassese (ed), *Current Problems of International Law* (University of Milan 1975) 267, 284.

[40] G. Gaggioli, 'The Use of Force in Armed Conflicts: Interplay between the Conduct of Hostilities and Law Enforcement Paradigms' (ICRC Report, November 2013) 1.

[41] See *Wall Advisory Opinion* (n 24) 106.

armed conflict are exclusively matters of human rights law; and (ii) how human rights law contributes to matters which are governed by both human rights law and international humanitarian law. The chapter's primary focus on human rights law reflects its overriding purpose to determine human rights law's value in the particular context of a non-international armed conflict. In the light of this purpose, the chapter does not take pains to identify matters which are 'exclusively matters of international humanitarian law', unless they are relevant to the analysis of human rights law. Importantly, the chapter's focus on human rights law should not be interpreted as an indication that international humanitarian law is insignificant or that international human rights law is more important. On the contrary, this book's foundational premise is that international humanitarian law constitutes one of the most important aspects of the legal framework which applies in times of non-international armed conflict, because unlike human rights law, it was designed with the exclusive purpose to address the particular problems that arise in armed conflict.

3.1 Conduct of hostilities

When seeking to identify the value of human rights law in non-international armed conflict, the starting point of analysis is the law enforcement paradigm, rather than the conduct of hostilities paradigm. This observation stems from the idea that there are two dominant factual and legal paradigms which are relevant in armed conflicts. The first is the 'conduct of hostilities paradigm' and the second is the 'law enforcement paradigm'. The conduct of hostilities paradigm has been said to comprise 'all activities that are specifically designed to support one party to an armed conflict against another, either by inflicting death, injury, or destruction, or by adversely affecting its military operations or military capacity'.[42] In substantive terms, the conduct of hostilities paradigm is governed almost exclusively by international humanitarian law. There are occasions when situations occurring in the conduct of hostilities paradigm have been addressed through a human rights lens, but in many of these instances the human rights principles have often been interpreted differently to take into account international humanitarian law principles.[43] The most well-known example of this is when the ICJ said that the term 'arbitrary' in Article 6 of the ICCPR (stating that 'no one shall be arbitrarily deprived of his life') should be interpreted through international humanitarian law rules on the conduct of hostilities.[44] The words of the ICJ confirm that the conduct of hostilities paradigm is one of the key matters which, in operational terms, is

[42] N. Melzer, 'Law Enforcement and the Conduct of Hostilities' in T. Gill and D. Fleck (eds), *The Handbook of International Law of Military Operations* (OUP, Oxford 2010) (hereafter Melzer, 'Law Enforcement and Conduct of Hostilities').

[43] Melzer conducts a review of the role of human rights law in the paradigm of hostilities in Melzer, *Targeted Killing* (n 35) 382–93. In doing so, he shows that in many cases where the conduct of hostilities has been analysed in human rights terms, the substantive content has been drawn from the *lex specialis* of international humanitarian law.

[44] *Nuclear Weapons Advisory Opinion* (n 26) [25].

almost exclusively governed by international humanitarian law. Human rights law generally only adds value in terms of its procedural obligations to investigate and prosecute operations on the battlefield.

The reason that international humanitarian law has a position of such precedence in the conduct of hostilities paradigm is that it contains specific provisions which are designed to limit the effects of armed conflict by protecting persons who are not participating in hostilities and restricting the means and methods of warfare. The different, and sometimes overlapping, categories of protected *persons* under international humanitarian law include civilians, medical and religious personnel and those placed *hors de combat* by sickness, wounds, detention, or any other cause.[45] The categories of protected *objects* include civilian objects, religious and cultural buildings, and medical units.[46] International humanitarian law also elaborates important principles such as the principle of distinction, precautions in attack, and proportionality *in bello* which inform how targeting decisions should be made.[47] Furthermore, it contains provisions which place restrictions on the weapons that the parties use and important protections for the environment.[48] As a result, when two parties to a non-international armed conflict are engaged in hostilities, and neither has control over persons or territory, their actions are governed almost exclusively by international humanitarian law.[49] In that sense, it is no coincidence that conduct of hostilities has a clear and irrefutable nexus to the armed conflict. The fact that the conduct of hostilities paradigm is governed almost exclusively by international humanitarian law enables us to conclude that we principally need to look at the law enforcement paradigm when seeking to identify the value of human rights law.

3.2 Law enforcement paradigm

While the concept of 'law enforcement' is also relevant in peacetime and international armed conflicts, this chapter focuses only on the parameters of law enforcement in non-international armed conflicts. The law enforcement paradigm has been described in a variety of ways by different authors but the definition which is adopted in the chapter is as follows: 'all activities connected to the exercise of authority over persons or territory; the maintenance of public order; and the suppression of criminal or subversive activity outside the conduct of hostilities'.[50]

[45] See *inter alia* common Article 3; Articles 10, 21–31 of Additional Protocol I; Articles 7, 11 of Additional Protocol II.

[46] See Articles 11, 14, 16 of Additional Protocol II.

[47] See Articles 48, 51(4), 57 of Additional Protocol I.

[48] See Article 35(1)–(3) of Additional Protocol I.

[49] See T. Gill, 'Some Thoughts on the Relationship between International Humanitarian Law and International Human Rights Law: A Plea for Mutual Respect and a Common Sense Approach' in Y. Haeck et al. (eds), *The Realisation of Human Rights when Theory Meets Practice* (Intersentia, Cambridge 2013) 345 (hereafter Gill, 'Mutual Respect and a Common Sense Approach') for elaboration of this notion.

[50] Ibid, 346.

It is noteworthy that this definition is broader than activities which relate to the literal enforcement of a body of law.[51] Accordingly, it will not be surprising to note that the concept of law enforcement as it applies in times of armed conflict is generally thought to be governed not only by international humanitarian law but also by international human rights law, international criminal law, and general international law.[52] It can be concluded from the wording of common Article 3 and Additional Protocol II that the international humanitarian law provisions relating to law enforcement presuppose that the party to the armed conflict has control over persons or territory.[53] When considering the scope of this paradigm, it is immediately clear that many key human rights norms will be important to the law enforcement paradigm, alongside international humanitarian law. Indeed, the provision of a legal 'buffer' between governments and the governed is often seen to be the *raison d'être* of human rights law.[54]

It will be clear from the definition of 'law enforcement' given above that detention is one of the key issues that falls within the law enforcement paradigm. During a non-international armed conflict some individuals may be detained because they have committed a common crime. In this case, it will be shown below that they will fall squarely within the parameters of international human rights law. For persons detained for reasons *related to the conflict*, the situation is more complex. In international armed conflict, there are clear regulations determining when people may be detained for reasons related to the conflict.[55] The legal framework also provides rules about how and when any detention or internship is authorized and when it should be reviewed.[56] However, the rules on detention in non-international armed conflict are much less detailed, particularly when it comes to procedural guarantees. As a result, it is often said that this is one of the areas in which recourse to human rights law may be appropriate.[57] International human rights law adds

[51] Instead, in many ways, the law enforcement paradigm is often presented as referring to all parts of the legal framework that falls outside of the conduct of hostilities paradigm. This interpretation is supported by Melzer's subheading 'Applicability "by default" of the Law Enforcement paradigm'. Melzer, 'Law Enforcement and Conduct of Hostilities' (n 42) 42.

[52] Gill, 'Mutual Respect and a Common Sense Approach' (n 49) 346.

[53] Common Article 3 of the Geneva Conventions seems to envisage that the individuals to whom the article applies will either be in the physical custody of the relevant party to the armed conflict or positioned in territory under its control. Likewise, Article 1 of Additional Protocol II requires that an armed group has 'such control over a part of its territory as to enable them to carry out sustained and concerted military operations and to implement this Protocol'.

[54] See N. S. Rodley, 'Can Armed Opposition Groups Violate Human Rights?' in K. E. Mahoney and P. Mahoney (eds), *Human Rights in the Twenty-First Century* (Kluwer Academic Publishers, The Netherlands 1993) 297–313, 299.

[55] See Geneva Convention III relative to the Treatment of Prisoners of War of 12 August 1949 (Geneva Convention III) and Geneva Convention IV relative to the Protection of Civilians in Time of War of 12 August 1949 (Geneva Convention IV).

[56] See in particular Articles 4, 5, 21, 118 of Geneva Convention III and Articles 41, 42, 43, 68, 78 of Geneva Convention IV.

[57] Henckaerts and Doswald-Beck, *Rules* (n 9) 347–52. See also D. Casalin, 'Taking Prisoners: Reviewing the International Humanitarian Law Grounds for Deprivation of Liberty by Armed Opposition Groups' (2011) 883 International Review of the Red Cross 743, 746. It has been argued by some academics and the ICRC that human rights law norms on detention are inherently ill-suited

considerably in terms of procedural guarantees on detention matters requiring *inter alia* that States confirm whether the detention is 'lawful'.[58] Within the discussion about how the two bodies of law interact on issues relating to detention, there is an ongoing conversation about whether the international humanitarian law of non-international armed conflict provides a 'legal basis' to detain.[59] While there is no doubt that the international humanitarian law applying in non-international armed conflicts provides an implicit authorization to detain, it does not provide an explicit authorization of the kind sufficient for a human rights body to determine that a State's detention is lawful.[60] To satisfy that standard, a State will generally have to be able to justify its detention on the basis of national law as well or a Security Council resolution.[61]

3.2.1 Relevance of law enforcement paradigm for armed groups

3.2.1.1 Definition of 'governance' versus 'law enforcement'

Before looking more specifically at areas in which human rights law adds value, the chapter first considers the factual relevance of the law enforcement paradigm in territory controlled by armed groups. In doing so, the chapter presents findings from social science disciplines that show that armed groups exert control over persons or territory more often than has hitherto been appreciated.[62] This research, which originates from researchers in political sciences and

to the factual dynamics of a non-international armed conflict. See for example, Sassòli and Olson, 'Admissible Killing and Internment of Fights' (n 35) 622. Certainly, it is easy to see how it will be unrealistic for a State to adhere to the procedural safeguards of human rights law, if it wishes to detain surrendering members of an armed group in the heat of the battle near the frontlines or while it is moving through territory or operating far away from urban centres. However, in UN Human Rights Committee, 'General Comment 35 (Liberty and Security of Person: Article 9)' (28 October 2014) UN Doc CCPR/C/GC/35, [15], [64] (hereafter HRC General Comment 35, Liberty and Security), the Human Rights Committee suggested that States might be given a wider margin of appreciation to implement 'security detention' in instances where individuals presented a 'direct and imperative threat'.

[58] Article 9 ICCPR prohibits 'unlawful detention'. See HRC General Comment 35, Liberty and Security (n 57) [10], [11].

[59] The ICRC argues that Additional Protocol II contains an 'inherent power to intern' which may be seen to be the legal basis for internment under international humanitarian law in non-international armed conflicts: ICRC, 'Internment in Armed Conflict: Basic Rules and Challenges' (ICRC Opinion Paper, November 2014) 7 (hereafter ICRC, Internment). See also 'Report from Expert Meeting at Chatham House on Procedural Safeguards for Security Detention in Non-International Armed Conflicts' (Chatham House and ICRC, London, 22–23 September 2008) 3–4, where there was 'prevailing agreement' among the experts that any party to a non-international armed conflict has an inherent power or 'qualified right' to intern persons captured; N. van Amstel, 'In Search of Legal Grounds to Detain for Armed Groups' (2012) 3 International Humanitarian Legal Studies 160.

[60] The fact that the international humanitarian law in non-international armed conflicts authorizes or confers legality on detention was refuted by the UK House of Lords in *Serdar Mohammed & Others v Secretary of State for Defence* [2017] UKSC 2.

[61] Ibid. See also ICRC, Internment (n 59) 8.

[62] J. Weinstein, *Inside Rebellion: The Politics of Insurgent Violence* (CUP, Cambridge 2007) 163 (hereafter Weinstein, *Inside Rebellion*).

anthropology, has been rarely taken note of in legal literature. Yet, it injects an important nuance into our perception of conflict zones and the structures of power that exist within them. In social science literature the phenomenon of a party to an armed conflict exercising authority over a civilian population is often analysed from a 'governance' perspective. On the basis that the term 'governance' is not one used in legal literature, it is first necessary to show how the term relates to the law enforcement paradigm. When applied to armed groups, the term 'governance' has been defined as the manner in which an insurgent group regulates life within a defined territory and provides public services.[63] To perform governance functions, it has been noted that an armed group will usually establish institutions which are either contained within, or separate to, the armed group's military wing. Generally, the purpose of these institutions is to enable the armed group to manage its relations with the civilian population.[64] Importantly, it has been pointed out that the concept of governance is a 'more encompassing phenomenon than government'.[65] In other words, from a political science perspective 'it is possible to conceive of governance without government'.[66]

In his study on insurgent governments and civilian life, Mampilly observes that governance activities performed by armed groups may range from providing the civilian population with security from private actors and the State, ensuring the provision of health care or education, establishing or preserving systems of food production and distribution, taking a role in land management, providing housing, shelter or other public resources to civilian populations and internally displaced persons, resolving civil disputes, tackling social problems such as prostitution, theft and drug use, and regulating market transactions.[67] Contemplating this definition, it is seen that there is a significant overlap between the notion of 'governance' and the law enforcement paradigm described above. The different aims of the different academic disciplines (i.e. law versus social sciences) are reflected in the different perspective each discipline takes. While the law enforcement paradigm described by lawyers is defined largely with reference to what the parties to the armed conflict are doing and the contextual circumstances in which they are doing it, the micro-level political science research on governance focuses mainly on the relationship between the entity and the population and the dynamics behind that relationship. It is on the basis of this overlapping definition, that the chapter finds the political science literature on this topic instructive for lawyers working with the legal framework.

[63] Z. C. Mampilly, *Rebel Rulers: Insurgent Governance and Civilian Life during War War* (Cornell University Press, Ithaca and London 2011) 4 (hereafter Mampilly, *Rebel Rulers*).

[64] Weinstein, *Inside Rebellion* (n 62) 164.

[65] Mampilly, *Rebel Rulers* (n 63) 3, citing J. Rosenau, 'Governance, Order and Change in World Politics' in J. Rosenau and E. Czempiel (eds), *Governance without Government: Order and Change in World Politics* (CUP, Cambridge 1992) 12.

[66] Ibid. [67] Ibid, 4.

3.2.1.2 Degree of order in rebel-held areas

Perhaps the most interesting point to note from political science literature is that there is often a surprising degree of order in situations of armed conflict, even in the areas outside of State control.[68] Making this point, Verhoeven points out that at the moment when Somalia, the archetypal example of total State collapse, resembled a 'terrifying war zone' to outsiders, it was in reality a 'complex mosaic of traditional and imaginative informal mechanisms and pacts [which] provided a reasonable degree of stability'.[69] Moreover, researchers who have spent significant periods in conflict zones report that 'everyday life is much more structured than imagined'.[70] This belies the oft-made assumption that where the State is absent, areas are wracked with Hobbesian chaos.[71] The literature from the political sciences shows 'armed actors are often willing to eliminate common crime'[72] and often feel 'forced' to develop and maintain structures for maintaining civilian life, in instances where they control territory more than fleetingly.[73] This leads to the related observation that armed groups may perform law enforcement activities without having full control over an extended swathe of territory. For example, there may be situations in which an armed group takes control of a town only for a brief period, and, overnight, finds itself in control of the town's population, including its prison population. In such circumstances, an armed group will often take immediate steps to control the local population by instigating a curfew, patrolling the streets, and preventing public rallies.[74] Conversely it may convene public rallies to elicit the local population's support.[75] It may set up checkpoints and promulgate its own laws. It may also take control of the news media, by disconnecting radio

[68] See T. Kolomba Beck, *The Normality of Civil War: Armed Groups and Everyday Life in Angola* (Campus, Frankfurt 2012) 123–4 (hereafter Kolomba Beck, *Normality of Civil War*): 'Only rarely, the interviewees described their experience of war as an exposure to violent chaos. Instead, the focus of their narratives is on their re-organisation of everyday life in view of the presence of armed groups and the latent or actual threat of violence.' See also D. Ellsberg, *Secrets: A Memoir of Vietnam and the Pentagon Papers* (Penguin, New York 2003) 114, who, recalling his time in the Vietnamese countryside, concluded: 'The widespread perception of chaos appears to be the result of superficial observation', as cited by S. Kalyvas, *The Logic of Violence in Civil War* (CUP, Cambridge 2009) 71 (hereafter Kalyvas, *Logic of Violence*).

[69] H. Verhoeven, 'The Self-Fulfilling Prophecy of Failed States: Somalia, State Collapse and the Global War on Terror' (2009) 3 Journal of Eastern African Studies 405, 411, 412, 414.

[70] Kalyvas, *Logic of Violence* (n 68) 71.

[71] This is an idea which is particularly explored by Mampilly, *Rebel Rulers* (n 63) 7, 28, 35, 40. See also Kalyvas, *Logic of Violence* (n 68) 384: 'Counter to Hobbes, civil war cannot be reduced to a mere mechanism that opens up the floodgates to random and anarchical private violence.'

[72] Kalyvas, *Logic of Violence* (n 68) 70.

[73] Mampilly, *Rebel Rulers* (n 63) 31.

[74] 'M23 curfew 'unacceptable', says UN' (*Mail & Guardian*, 5 September 2013) <https://mg.co.za/article/2013-09-05-m23-curfew-unacceptable-says-un> accessed 6 July 2017; 'Goma falls to Congo's 'M23' rebels without expected bloodbath' (*Telegraph*, 20 November 2012) <http://www.telegraph.co.uk/news/worldnews/africaandindianocean/democraticrepublicofcongo/9691489/Goma-falls-to-Congos-M23-rebels-without-expected-bloodbath.html> accessed 20 January 2017.

[75] See also the public rally convened by M23 after it took Goma. 'Congo rebel army vows to take control of all DR Congo' (*Telegraph*, 21 November 2012) <http://www.telegraph.co.uk/news/worldnews/africaandindianocean/democraticrepublicofcongo/9693043/Congos-rebel-army-vows-to-take-control-of-all-DR-Congo.html> accessed 20 January 2017.

signals and television stations, or controlling the content of public broadcasts.[76] Furthermore, it may round up and punish people for alleged collaboration with the enemy.[77] In a similar vein, political science literature shows that even when an armed group does not hold sustained control over civilian populations in the traditional sense, it may still engage in governance activities as regards its own fighters and their family members. This is particularly likely if the armed group is nomadic, exiled, or positioned in training camps away from the general population. For example, in her study of UNITA in Angola, Kalomba Beck tells of how UNITA fighters' lives were micro-managed by the armed group in bush encampments.[78] She relates how leadership insisted on making the combatants and their families work in the fields and attend school. In many cases, women were forced to marry several times and forced to have multiple children.[79] She also tells how the 'alternative' version of everyday life that UNITA created in their camps was accompanied by a draconian punishment system for domestic violence, adultery, rape, robbery, drinking, and other 'incivilities'.[80]

3.2.1.3 Varied approach to governance activities

The literature from political sciences also demonstrates that not every armed group will perform the full range of governance activities, even if its control of territory is very consolidated. For example, when the Forces Nouvelles controlled the North of Côte D'Ivoire, it administered the education system, had a police force, collected taxes and customs, and ran the prison services, but it did not have a functioning judiciary for the majority of the conflict.[81] This was due to an almost complete lack of judges in the north of the country. Conversely, when the LTTE controlled the north of Sri Lanka, it had a court system consisting of six district courts, two high courts, an appeals court and a special bench, and a network of police stations.[82] It also had a taxation system and currency but it did not run the healthcare or the education systems, which continued to be administered by the incumbent government.[83] The literature from political sciences on insurgent governance and non-international armed conflict, particularly the studies by Weinstein, Mampilly, and Kalyvas, demonstrates

[76] 'TV Stations Silenced by M23 Resume Retransmitting in Goma' (*Reporters without Borders*, 4 December 2012) <http://en.rsf.org/drc-concern-about-m23-s-news-control-21-11-2012,43706.html> accessed 20 January 2017.

[77] 'M23 rebels Rape, Kill Civilians' (*Human Rights Watch*, 22 July 2013) <http://www.hrw.org/news/2013/07/22/dr-congo-m23-rebels-kill-rape-civilians> accessed 20 January 2017.

[78] Kolomba Beck, *Normality of Civil War* (n 68) 113–17.

[79] Ibid, 114–15.

[80] Ibid, 116.

[81] D. Balint-Kurti, 'Cote D'Ivoire's Forces Nouvelles, Chatham House' (Africa Programme Armed Non-State Actors Series, September 2007) 26 (hereafter Balint-Kurti, 'Cote D'Ivoire's Forces Nouvelles'). See also UN Secretary-General, 'Eighteenth Progress Report on the UN Operation in Côte d'Ivoire' (13 October 2008) UN Doc S/2008/645, Section E; UN Secretary-General, 'Twenty-fourth report on the UN Operation in Côte d'Ivoire' (20 May 2010) UN Doc S/2010/245, on the restoration of the judiciary and parallel system of administration maintained by the Forces Nouvelles.

[82] S. Sivakumaran, 'Courts of Armed Opposition Groups, Fair Trials or Summary Justice?' (2009) 7 Journal of International Criminal Justice 489, 494 (hereafter Sivakumaran, 'Fair Trials or Summary Justice?').

[83] Mampilly, *Rebel Rulers* (n 63) 110–11.

that an armed group's decision about which services it will provide, if any, will be motivated by a number of context-specific factors, including its ideology, funding structures, relationship with the incumbent government, and the manner in which public services were provided in the country, before the conflict broke out.[84] A few of the most major motivations are examined below.

3.2.1.4 Motivations for performing law enforcement/governance activities

(a) Control of territory and populations

It was mentioned above that research from political sciences suggests that often an armed group will feel compelled to provide governance activities, as a result of its control over territory or people. Indeed, in his research on the Democratic Republic of the Congo (DRC), Mampilly tells how the vice president of the RCD-Goma, Arthur Zahidi Ngoma, stated that he considered the armed group to be under an 'obligation' to set up what was 'more or less a government', as a result of its control over territory.[85] A similar sentiment was expressed by the LTTE's chief negotiator in 2002 when he was asked about the group's court system and network of police stations. Mr. Anton Balasingham denied that the institutions constituted a means by which the LTTE was consolidating its position militarily. According to Mr Balasingham, the establishment of this law enforcement infrastructure was simply a 'necessity' for a group responsible for such a large area. He stated:

> We explained that these courts and Police stations have been functional for the last 12 years and that the ground reality is that as a consequence of this war the LTTE has established control over 70 percent of the area in the northeast. There are huge populations here and we have to administer them and for the purpose of maintaining law and order, or rather social order and cohesion we need to have certain institutions....these Police stations are necessary instruments to maintain law and order because we cannot allow anarchy and social disorder in areas controlled by us.[86]

The explanation that an armed group felt 'compelled' to provide governance activities was also repeatedly given in respect to the courts established by the rebel administrations in the early years of the Syrian conflict.

Indeed, many of the courts which have been established in rebel-held Syria are reported to be dealing with minor civil matters such as divorces, land disputes, unfair price fixing for foodstuffs, and fuel and food quality. Their responsibilities

[84] See Weinstein, *Inside Rebellion* (n 62), who argues that an armed group with an income stream from abroad or natural resources will be less reliant upon the civilian population for survival, and therefore will be less likely to create a form of governance that encourages support from the civilian population. See also Mampilly, who argues that the nature of the pre-conflict relationship between the State and society will shape the rebel command's preferences for civilian governance strategy. Mampilly, *Rebel Rulers* (n 63) 234; Kalyvas, *Logic of Violence* (n 68).

[85] Mampilly, *Rebel Rulers* (n 63) 190.

[86] 'LTTE Police Stations "not a new phenomenon"—Balasingham' (*TamilNet*, 3 December 2002) <http://www.tamilnet.com/art.html?catid=13&artid=7932> accessed 20 January 2017. A similar sentiment was stated by the vice president of RCD Goma in 1998 when it took power in the Kivus. He said: 'We hadn't realized that we would have to set up what is more or less a government so fast, but it's an obligation now', BBC Monitoring 1998, cited by Mampilly, *Rebel Rulers* (n 63) 190.

have ranged from fining shopkeepers to more serious cases like rape and murder allegations.[87] In Aleppo, the United Courts Council was reported to issue birth and death certificates, sign divorce papers, and listen to lawyers pleading their cases in family property disputes. Marwan Gayad, a former appeals court judge who defected from the Syrian government and was serving as the general prosecutor for the United Courts Council at the time of his interview in 2012, said of this court:

> We created this temporary judicial council as an emergency solution, like when a doctor removes a bullet from a patient without using anaesthetic.[88]

The United Courts Council, which was established in the hope that it would provide an alternative to the more hard-line Islamic courts which had been established by rebel-factions, was, the council members admitted, 'a desperate strategy … aimed at preventing Syria descending into further chaos'.[89] In the early years of the armed conflict in Syria, similar stories came out of towns throughout rebel-held Syria. In Maaret Misreen, a market town of 40,000 people, local communities were left to organize their own security and work together to obtain enough food and fuel. Local residents explained that as a result of the Syrian government focusing all of its energy on the military struggle, the State became almost entirely absent in Maaret Misreen. Mamaar, a local shopkeeper who played a role in coordinating local efforts to keep civilian life ticking over in the town reported in June 2012 that he now spent his time dispensing advice, mediating in local disputes, and issuing orders alongside his day-job of selling light-bulbs, power cords, and circuit breakers. He said: 'There is no police station, there is no state, so who else can they go to? … We have to solve peoples' problems.'[90] This points to another observation that often public administration in areas outside the control of the government, is provided equally by armed groups and the civilian population. The legal relevance this observation falls outside this study, but certainly deserves further attention elsewhere.

(b) Battle for legitimacy

Another explanation for armed groups providing governance roles within the law enforcement paradigm is the observation that many non-international armed conflicts are just as much a battle for legitimacy, as they are a battle for territory.

[87] 'Fighting Shortages, Syrian Civilians Take Reins in Rebel Areas' (*Associated Press*, 28 February 2013) <http://www.nytimes.com/2013/03/01/world/middleeast/syrian-civilians-take-reins-in-test-of-self-government.html?ref=world&_r=0> accessed 20 January 2017.

'In Rebel-held Syria, Revolutionary Courts decide matters of life, death' (*Miami Herald*, 18 June 2012) <http://www.miamiherald.com/2012/06/18/2855841/in-rebel-held-syria-revolutionary.html> accessed 20 January 2017.

[88] 'Rebel Court Fills Void Amid Syrian Civil War' (*CNN*, 26 January 2012) <http://edition.cnn.com/2013/01/25/world/meast/syria-rebel-court/> accessed 20 January 2017.

[89] Ibid.

[90] 'Rebel-held Syrian town struggles to keep the peace' (*Associated Press*, 25 June 2012) <https://www.yahoo.com/news/rebel-held-syrian-town-struggles-keep-peace-170918224.html> accessed 20 January 2017.

Kilcullen, a counterinsurgency theorist and an adherent to this view, identifies a pattern that is seen repeatedly in counterinsurgency operations:

> Local nonstate actors gain influence through the local exercise of law and order, especially dispute resolution and mediation, and then translat[e] that influence into formal political authority through processes of state formation from the bottom up.[91]

In the words of Bernard Fall, a French counterinsurgency theorist of the 1950s and 60s: 'a government that is losing to an insurgency isn't being out-fought, it's being out-governed'.[92] The truth of Fall's statement is illustrated by the words of Colonel Major Bamba Sinima, a representative of the Forces Nouvelles during the non-international armed conflict in Côte d'Ivoire. When, at a certain point in the conflict, children under the Forces Nouvelles' control achieved better examination marks than those under the incumbent government's control in the South, Colonel Major Sinima, the Head of the Forces Nouvelles, Education Committee at the time, expressed his pride in the better result in the North, saying: 'it *is* a competition'.[93] Moreover, in a non-international armed conflict where fighting is not only between the State and an armed group, but also between armed groups, the battle for legitimacy may also exist *between* those armed groups. This was seen in the early months of the armed conflict in Syria. As government officials fled and crime proliferated, competing rebel leaders responded to local residents' demands for security by opening 'dozens of courts'.[94] Commenting on this phenomenon, Mazen Jumaa of the lawyers association which monitored the new courts said: 'It's almost the fashion to have your own courthouse now.'[95]

The identification of a link between governance and legitimacy feeds into another important observation from political science literature, that the support of a civilian population in a non-international armed conflict is often driven by security concerns, rather than ideology.[96] The significance of these findings is profound

[91] D. Kilcullen, *Counterinsurgency* (Hurst & Co Publishers Ltd, London July 2010) 147–9 (hereafter Kilcullen, *Counterinsurgency*).

[92] Kilcullen, *Counterinsurgency* (n 91) 149, referring to B. Bernard and B. Fall, 'The Theory and Practice of Insurgency and Counterinsurgency' (U.S. Naval War College Review, Newport Rhode Island April 1965).

[93] In 2006, over 4,000 children in the rebel-held area in Côte d'Ivoire sat the 2006 baccalauréat, with a pass rate of just over 30% compared with just over 40% in the north. The pass rate for the Brevet d'Etudes de Premier Cycle, taken by children aged 13 and above, was higher in the north (42.4%) than in the south (35.75%). See Balint-Kurti, 'Cote D'Ivoire's Forces Nouvelles' (n 81) 26.

[94] See 'A Battle for Syria One Court at a Time' (*New York Times*, 13 March 2013) <http://www.nytimes.com/2013/03/14/world/middleeast/a-battle-for-syria-one-court-at-a-time.html?ref=world&_r=2&> accessed 20 January 2017.

[95] Ibid.

[96] Research shows that the relationship between the population and armed groups is often converse to how it was traditionally perceived. The old saying in guerrilla warfare that 'the people are the water to the fish who inhabit it' was intended to suggest that the people are the lifeblood of the rebels in a civil conflict. It indicates that the power and authority of the rebels will follow from, or will be dependent on, the support of the people. This is true in instances where the struggle is ideological and the people have a political idealism that is equal to those of the fighting rebels. In his seminal work on guerrilla warfare, Mao refers to a 'unity of spirit' between the people and the troops. M. Tse-tung, 'Guerilla Warfare' in *Guerilla Warfare by Mao Tse-Tung and by Che Guevara with a Forward by Captain B. H. Liddell Hart* (Cassell, London 1969) 67. But such a 'unity of spirit' between people and armed

when trying to understand the provision of law enforcement activities by armed groups. For when civilian support is uncoupled from ideology, it is revealed to be a commodity to be won by the party to the conflict which is either strongest or makes the civilian population feel safest.[97] In many instances a feeling of safety may be achieved by the party that institutes the best or most efficient structures to address local disputes, tackle crime, promulgate local laws, rein in its own fighters, and protect the civilians from the attacks of the other party to the conflict. This explains why in Afghanistan, according to Kilkullen, the Taliban deliberately focused on rule of law issues as a strategy to win the war.[98] With their mobile court system, the Taliban was able to establish themselves in some parts of the country as the entity that is best able to deal with people's disputes.[99] The establishment of a police force and judiciary by an armed group will often be an effective way for it to demonstrate its power over the civilian population, while at the same time establishing itself as a contender to the State in the eyes of the local population.[100]

Indeed, the notion that the provision of public services is an important component of the battle for hearts and minds explains why armed groups sometimes provide governance activities in parallel with the government. In these instances, an armed group is able to enter into a direct competition with the government by providing shadow institutions. This was seen in the non-international armed conflicts in Afghanistan and Nepal. In Nepal, the Maoists exercised parallel law enforcement activities including prosecutions and policing activities.[101] In Afghanistan, the Taliban likewise deliberately set up alternative dispute resolution mechanisms for local people which they held out as being more efficient and less susceptible to corruption than those offered by the government. In doing so, it set itself up as a direct competitor to the government even in areas when the government was nominally in control.[102] A similar phenomenon was seen in Sri Lanka where the

groups is seldom seen in modern non-international armed conflict. On the contrary, civilians and civilian infrastructure increasingly bear the brunt of violence in non-international armed conflicts and rebel groups are increasingly fighting for material gain rather than the pursuit of political ideologies. See B. A. Valentino, 'Why we kill: the Political Science of Political Violence against Civilians' (2014) 17 Annual Review of Political Science 89. With these two observations, it is easy to see how the delicate balance of Mao's correlation may be upset. Indeed, research now indicates that the opposite is more often true: rather than the supremacy of the fighting parties following the support of the people, the support of the people *follows* the power of the fighting parties. See Kalyvas, *Logic of Violence* (n 68) 91–104. See also M. P. Glaser, 'Humanitarian Engagement with Non-State Actors, the Parameters of Negotiated Access' (Network Paper, Humanitarian Practice Network 2005) 50, who indicates that conflicts involving national liberation movements may be an example of a 'type' of armed conflict where a symbiosis between an armed group and the civilian population may still exist.

[97] See Kalyvas, *Logic of Violence* (n 68) 91–145, on the connections between civilian support for an armed group and a variety of factors including coercion, fear, success, and control.

[98] Kilcullen, *Counterinsurgency* (n 91) 60–1.

[99] E. Lee Walker, *Culturally-Attuned Governance and Justice in Helmand Province, Afghanistan* (ISAF/International Media Ventures April 2010) 86, on file with the author (hereafter Walker, *Culturally Attuned Governance*).

[100] Mampilly, *Rebel Rulers* (n 63) 63.

[101] See Sivakumaran, 'Fair Trials Or Summary Justice?' (n 82) 492–3, for details of the parallel legal system run by the CPN-M in Nepal.

[102] See Walker, *Culturally Attuned Governance* (n 99) 48–51.

LTTE marketed its legal system as being incorruptible, more effective, and cheaper than that in government held areas.[103] Indeed, Mampilly tells how Tamils in government-controlled areas sometimes chose to file complaints in the LTTE legal system, because they perceived it to be more efficient.[104] The LTTE court would then issue a summons to the respondent in government-held territory requesting the individual's attendance in the insurgent court. To sum up, the political science literature reviewed above has shown that armed groups may perform law enforcement activities more often than legal literature tends to acknowledge. This points to the possibility that human rights law may add more value to the legal framework than has sometimes been appreciated.

3.2.2 Conceptual scope of IHL within the law enforcement paradigm

3.2.2.1 Nexus requirement for common Article 3

When trying to understand how international humanitarian law and international humanitarian law work together within the law enforcement paradigm, the most important observation is the fact that generally everyday life which has no nexus to the armed conflict will fall outside the scope of international humanitarian law and be governed by human rights law and/ or national law. The fact that the protections contained in common Article 3 require a nexus to the armed conflict is not clear from the wording of the article itself but has been articulated explicitly in the case law from the ICTY and ICTR focusing on jurisdiction. It can be seen to stem from the fact that the purpose of international humanitarian law is limited to the regulation of 'armed conflict'. The fact that there needs to be a 'relationship between the conflict and the deprivation of liberty' for a person's detention to be governed by international humanitarian law was first recognized by the Appeals Chamber in the *Tadic* Jurisdiction Decision.[105] The judgment asserted that although international humanitarian law applies to the whole country in a non-international armed conflict, it does not govern every act of violence or detention.[106] More recently, the *Boskoski* Trial Chamber stated:

> The nexus requirement serves to distinguish war crimes from purely domestic crimes and also prevents purely random or isolated criminal occurrences from being characterised as war crimes.[107]

In a similar vein the *Kunarac* Appeals Chamber said that although war crimes could occur in circumstances temporally and geographically remote from the actual fighting (i.e. in the law enforcement paradigm), they needed to be 'closely

[103] Mampilly, *Rebel Rulers* (n 63) 118. [104] Ibid, 119.

[105] See also *Prosecutor v Delalić, Mucić, Delić and Landžo (Trial Judgment)* IT-96-21-T (16 November 1998), [193]: 'It is axiomatic that not every serious crime committed during the armed conflict in Bosnia and Herzegovina can be regarded as a violation of international humanitarian law. There must be an obvious link between the crime and the armed conflict.'

[106] *Tadić* Jurisdiction Decision (n 4) [69].

[107] *Boškoski* (n 4) [293].

related to hostilities occurring in other parts of the territories to be governed by international humanitarian law.'[108] The need for a nexus requirement was also confirmed by ICTR in the *Akayesu* Appeals Chamber which stated 'common Article 3 requires a close nexus between violations and the armed conflict'.[109]

The appreciation that there needs to be a nexus with the armed conflict prompts reflection on what this means in practice.[110] The *Kunarac* Appeals Judgment provides further guidance on this point stating that:

> The existence of an armed conflict must, at a minimum, have played a substantial part in the perpetrator's ability to commit [the crime], his decision to commit [the crime], the manner in which it was committed or the purpose for which it was committed.[111]

In other words, the nexus requirement would be satisfied if it could be proved that an individual acted under 'the guise of the armed conflict'.[112] The Appeals Chamber continued by identifying a number of factors which may indicate that a particular crime constitutes a war crime or a domestic crime. These include:

> The fact that the perpetrator is a combatant; the fact that the victim is a non-combatant; the fact that victim is a member of the opposing party; the fact that the act may be said to serve the ultimate goal of a military campaign; and the fact that the crime is committed as part of or in the context of the perpetrator's official duties.[113]

These concrete factors suggest that in reality a more stringent relationship between the armed conflict is required, than the fact that the perpetrators took advantage of the enabling environment of an armed conflict. The nexus test focuses on the roles that the perpetrator and victim have within the armed conflict and their statuses under international humanitarian law.

3.2.2.2 Nexus requirement for Additional Protocol II and Article 75 of Additional Protocol I

The fact that the international humanitarian law norms that form part of the law enforcement paradigm require a nexus to the armed conflict is also seen in Additional Protocol II. In particular, it is noted that Additional Protocol II states at Article 2, paragraph 1 that:

> [T]his Protocol shall be applied [...] to all persons *affected* by an armed conflict as defined in Article 1. (emphasis added)[114]

Likewise, paragraph 2 of the same article states:

> [A]t the end of the armed conflict, all the persons who have been deprived of their liberty or whose liberty has been restricted for reasons related to such conflict, as well as those

[108] *Prosecutor v Kunarac* et al. *(Appeals Judgment)* IT-96-23-A, 23/1-A (12 June 2002) [57] (hereafter *Kunarac* Appeals Judgment).

[109] *Prosecutor v Akayesu (Trial Judgment)* ICTR-96-4-T (2 September 1998) [444].

[110] See H. van der Wilt, 'War Crimes and the Requirement of a Nexus with an Armed Conflict' [2012] Journal of International Criminal Justice 1, for a thorough review of the case law from international criminal tribunals and Dutch courts on the 'nexus requirement'.

[111] *Kunarac* Appeals Judgment (n 108) [58].

[112] Ibid.

[113] Ibid, [59].

[114] See also *Tadić* Jurisdiction Decision (n 4) [69].

deprived of their liberty or whose liberty has been restricted *for reasons related to such conflict*, as well as those deprived of their liberty or whose liberty is restricted after the conflict for the same reasons, shall enjoy the protection of Articles 5 and 6 until the end of such deprivation or restriction of liberty. (emphasis added)

In a similar vein, Articles 5 and 6 of Additional Protocol II state that they apply to 'persons deprived of their liberty for reasons related to the armed conflict' and 'the prosecution of criminal offences *related to the armed conflict*' (emphasis added).

Research into the history of these provisions reveals that the drafters of both Additional Protocols felt strongly that the Additional Protocols should only regulate issues connected to the armed conflict. The *travaux préparatoires* demonstrate that the drafters' wish to limit their scope arose out of their apprehension that in situations of armed conflict, even non-international armed conflicts reaching the threshold of Additional Protocol II, the armed conflict might only affect a small part of the territory and a small proportion of its population. This prompted a 'long discussion' on whether the scope of the Additional Protocol II should be limited by geography, i.e. the zone of the fighting. But eventually, the drafters rejected this approach and decided that it would be more effective to limit the scope of the Protocol by 'criteria related to persons, and not to places'.[115] In essence, the inclusion of the phrase 'affected by an armed conflict' in Articles 2, 5, and 6 of the Additional Protocol II was driven by a similar rationale to that expressed by the *Tadic* Appeals Decision.[116] Importantly, the words 'affected by an armed conflict' in Article 2 also have the effect of limiting the scope of Article 4 of Additional Protocol II (fundamental guarantees) to persons affected by the armed conflict.[117] They also mirror the scope of 5 and 6 of Additional Protocol II to people detained or interned 'for reasons connected to the armed conflict' or persons prosecuted for 'crimes connected with the armed conflict'.[118]

[115] See ICRC, *Commentary on the Additional Protocols of 8 June 1977 to the Geneva Conventions of 12 December 1949,* (Martinus Nijhoff, Geneva 1987) 1360 [4490] (hereafter ICRC, *Commentary on the Additional Protocols*). See also ICRC, *Official Records of the Diplomatic Conference on the Reaffirmation and Development of International Humanitarian Law Applicable in Armed Conflicts* (Geneva 1974–1977) Vol VII, CDDH/SR.5.1/annex, 211 [43], where Mrs Bujard of the ICRC is recorded explaining that there had been a long discussion of whether the application of the Additional Protocol should be geographically limited at the Conference of Government Experts, but the experts had pointed out that in a large, federal State, for example, it might be better that the Protocol should apply to the persons affected by an armed conflict rather than to the territory where the armed conflict took place. To meet that wish, the ICRC did not include an article concerning the territorial scope of the Protocol in its draft.

[116] A similar discussion can be seen in the *Tadić* Jurisdiction Decision (n 4) [66–70]. Here, the notion that the scope of international humanitarian law should be limited by geography was also discussed and rejected.

[117] Although not explicitly stated in the article itself, this can be discerned from Article 2, Additional Protocol II, which limits the scope of the protocol *in toto* to persons 'affected by the armed conflict'. It can also be discerned from the fact that Article 75, Additional Protocol I, the equivalent to provision to Article 4, Additional Protocol II, is explicitly limited to persons 'affected by the armed conflict'.

[118] See text of Articles 5 and 6, Additional Protocol II for these limitations.

While the notion that fundamental guarantees in Article 4 might be limited *ratione personae* might seem surprising, it is significant that a similarly restrictive scope is found in Article 75 of Additional Protocol I. Although drafted to apply to international armed conflicts, Article 75 contains the fundamental guarantees that are generally thought to apply as a matter of customary international law in non-international armed conflicts too.[119] The chapeau to Article 75 states that persons will benefit from the protections of the article 'in so far as they are affected by a situation referred to in Article 1'.[120] The commentary to Article 75 of Additional Protocol I provided a similar rationale for its scope, saying:

> In general those who contravene the normal laws of the State (ordinary criminals) and who are punished on these grounds, are not "affected" within the meaning of this article. On the other hand, if security measures are taken against certain individuals because of their attitude, whether true or alleged, with regard to the conflict, Article 75 certainly applies to them.[121]

In other words, the commentary advocates a narrow definition of the term 'affected by the armed conflict' which excludes persons who are in the power of a party to the conflict because they have broken the ordinary criminal law from Article 75's scope.

When one pieces this interpretative guidance together, it becomes apparent that international humanitarian law will generally only apply to the aspects of the law enforcement paradigm which are connected to the armed conflict. For example, rather than applying to all instances in which persons are detained and prosecuted by a party to a non-international armed conflict, Articles 5 and 6 of Additional Protocol II only provide protection for individuals who have been arrested, detained, interned, or prosecuted as a result of their attitude to the armed conflict. These might include individuals being prosecuted for taking part in the insurrection or assisting the insurrection or persons interned as a result of the imperative security threat that they are deemed to pose in relation to the armed conflict.[122]

[119] Henckaerts and Doswald-Beck, *Rules* (n 9) 299.

[120] The commentary to Article 75 clarifies that the term 'affected by' means 'touched by or concerned.' Recognizing that to a certain extent 'all those who find themselves in the territory of . . . countries at war' are affected 'in some way or another', it also states that such an expansive definition of the term was probably not what was meant by the provision. Instead, it advocates that a narrow approach should be taken to the phrase. It justifies its view on this by pointing to the phrase 'in so far', and saying that it suggests that there will be some people in the country who will not be affected by the armed conflict in the sense of the article. ICRC, *Commentary on the Additional Protocols* (n 116) [3011].

[121] Ibid.

[122] Further support for this conclusion is found in Article 5's sub-paragraph one refers to people having been deprived of their liberty as a result of being 'interned or detained'. Reference to the term 'internment', which is repeated several times later in the Article too, implies that the drafters of Article 5 envisaged that it would to apply to people being 'interned' on grounds similar those which justify internment in Articles 42 and 78, Geneva Convention IV, i.e. if the security of the detaining power makes it absolutely necessary or for imperative reasons of security. A further indication that Article 5 was intended to apply to *inter alia* persons interned for security reasons, rather than common crime, is found in the fact that Article 5(2)(a) acknowledges the possibility of 'men and women of a family' being 'accommodated together'. The commentary to the Additional Protocol notes that this provision was based on Article 82, Geneva Convention IV in relation to civilian internment. The notion that the Article anticipates that an entire family could be detained together is a further

Indeed, commenting on the scope of Article 75 of Additional Protocol I, Meron observed that it reflected the fact that the purpose of the drafters was not to 'revise the entire range of human rights that would otherwise apply between a government and its people'.[123] In a similar vein, Bothe, in his authoritative commentary to the Additional Protocols, confirmed that 'the purpose of the Conference was not to draft a Convention on Human Rights'.[124] The fact that both authors distinguished international humanitarian law from international human rights law, confirms a view that international humanitarian law is generally the *lex specialis* on issues related specifically to the armed conflict. In a similar vein, human rights law will apply to issues which do not have a clear nexus to the armed conflict.

3.2.3 Conceptual scope of IHRL within the law enforcement paradigm

Employing the *Kunarac* Appeals Judgment for guidance, it can be seen that issues which do not have a clear nexus to the armed conflict will be those which do not arise out of an individual's status as a fighter or civilian, are not related to a person's official duties or a person's membership to a particular group, and are not connected to the military strategy of either party. Instead, they will generally relate to issues which exist equally in peacetime and in armed conflict, e.g. the ability to travel to work, move around freely, access healthcare, express an opinion freely, gather in public places, and be protected from common crime. In the light of the analysis above, and in consideration of the narrow purpose of international humanitarian law, it will be no surprise that these are some of the key issues in the law enforcement paradigm which are regulated *only* by international human rights law. Unlike international humanitarian law, human rights law contains a right to freedom of movement, a right to freedom of expression, and a right to freedom of assembly.[125] Likewise, only human rights law contains provisions articulating the right to work, the right to just and favourable conditions of work, the right to an adequate standard of living, including adequate food, clothing and housing.[126] Only human rights law contains a provision on the right to health, in the sense of a positive right which extends to healthy people as well as those who are already sick.[127] This is particularly important for people seeking vaccinations or medical services related to nutrition, hygiene, or contraception. Likewise, only human rights law contains provisions relating to people's right to marry freely and

indication that the Article's drafters intended the Article to provide protection to individuals, who had been detained or interned, for reasons connected to the armed conflict. It also provides further confirmation that the Article was not intended to cover persons detained on suspicion of committing, or as a result of committing, common crimes.

[123] T. Meron, 'On the Inadequate Reach of Humanitarian and Human Rights Law and the Need for a New Instrument' (1983) 3 American Journal of International Law 589, 596.

[124] M. Bothe et al., *New Rules for Victims of Armed Conflicts: Commentary on the Two 1977 Protocols Additional to the Geneva Conventions of 1949* (Brill 1982) 460, citing a statement by the Canadian delegation as cited by ibid, 597.

[125] See Articles 12, 19, 22 ICCPR.

[126] See Articles 6, 7, 11 ICESCR.

[127] See Article 12 ICESCR.

children's rights to be registered after birth. Human rights law also contains detailed provisions on the rights of women, including their right not to be discriminated against in society.[128] These are all key rights which are necessary to protect people's everyday life from unnecessary interference and they are all issues addressed predominantly by human rights law, rather than by international humanitarian law.

3.2.3.1 Enforcement of laws relating to common crime

Moreover, human rights law has a key role in providing protection for persons subject to the criminal justice system, such as the right to life, the right to freedom from arbitrary detention, and the right to fair trial. Combating common crime is a notable means for a party to an armed conflict to maintain public order and suppress criminal behaviour. Human rights norms are relevant at every stage of the criminal justice system: they govern the actions of police as they patrol the streets, they govern the employment of lethal force in a law enforcement paradigm, the manner in which police officers arrest people, the manner in which people are detained, and the manner in which individuals are prosecuted on criminal charges.[129] Likewise, human rights law contains a unique system of positive obligations that require a duty-bearer to protect individuals from harms by others.[130] In the area of combating sexual violence against women for example, a State is generally considered to be under a duty to legislate to ensure that sexual violence crimes are effectively criminalized.[131] In specific situations where a woman has been the victim of abuse, a State is obliged to exercise due diligence by preventing, punishing, investigating, or providing redress for the harm committed by a

[128] See Articles 3, 10 ICESCR; Article 23 ICCPR.

[129] The employment of lethal force in a law enforcement paradigm was considered by the UN Human Rights Committee in *Pedro Pablo Camargo v Colombia,* Communication No. 45/1979 (31 March 1982) UN Doc CCPR/C/OP/1, [13.2]; *John Khemraadi Baboeram* et al. *v Suriname,* Communication Nos. 146/1983 and 148–54/1983 (4 April 1985) UN Doc A/40/40, [14.3]. Together these cases indicate that person may only be killed if they pose an imminent danger to the law enforcement official or a third party. Even then lethal force may only employed after a warning has been given and if the application of lethal force is deemed 'necessary' in the circumstances. Article 9 ICCPR contains important protections for persons on arrest. Article 14 sets out the minimal guarantees of fair trial for persons facing criminal charges.

[130] HRC General Comment 31, Legal Obligation (n 24) [8]: 'However the positive obligations on States Parties to ensure Covenant rights will only be fully discharged if individuals are protected by the State, not just against violations of Covenant rights by its agents, but also against acts committed by private persons or entities that would impair the enjoyment of Covenant rights in so far as they are amenable to application between private persons or entities. There may be circumstances in which a failure to ensure Covenant rights as required by article 2 would give rise to violations by States Parties of those rights, as a result of States Parties' permitting or failing to take appropriate measures or to exercise due diligence to prevent, punish, investigate or redress the harm caused by such acts by private persons or entities. States are reminded of the interrelationship between the positive obligations imposed under article 2 and the need to provide effective remedies in the event of breach under article 2, paragraph 3.'

[131] See e.g UN Human Rights Committee, 'Concluding Observations on the Second Periodic Report of Burundi' (21 November 2014) UN Doc CCPR/C/BDI/CO/2, [12]; UN Human Rights Committee, 'Concluding Observations on the Initial Report of Haiti' (21 November 2014) UN Doc CPPR/C/HTI/CO/1, [13]; UN Human Rights Committee, 'Concluding Observations on the Initial Report of Malta' (21 November 2014) UN Doc CPPR/C/MNE/CO/1, [11].

private individual.[132] The existence of these positive obligations in human rights law shows that human rights law can have an important role to play in establishing and maintaining public order, because human right law's positive obligations require a duty-bearer to ensure that the law protecting the rights of others are enforced against private citizens. While similar positive obligations exist in international humanitarian law too, it is not clear to what extent they extend to armed groups.[133] Importantly, human rights law also includes a right to a remedy which provides individuals with an important manner of vindicating any rights violations that they suffer. This right entails an obligation on the duty-bearer to establish administrative or judicial mechanisms which can address claims that a person's rights have been violated.[134]

3.2.3.2 Protection of everyday life

Having shown that human rights law has much to add in relation to the enforcement of laws relating to common crime, the discussion below will demonstrate that the need to protect everyday life is particularly pressing in times of armed conflict. In the climate of fear and suspicion which often accompanies a non-international armed conflict, there will be a more pressing imperative than ever to protect some of the rights mentioned above. For example, there will be a need to protect the family unit and people's privacy, home, and correspondence from intrusive searches or surveillance. Far-reaching curfews or regular checkpoints may lead to a violation not just of the right to freedom of movement, but also the right to work, the right to education, and even the right to food. People may be prevented from getting to their work, getting to market, and working their land. Children may be prevented from attending school. Radio and television stations may be prevented from broadcasting freely, in a manner that constitutes an undue interference with people's freedom of expression. Likewise, people may be prevented from attending or convening public rallies, in a manner that interferes with their right to freedom of association. People may become more susceptible to abuse from private persons or corporations who seek to exploit their vulnerability by imposing harsher conditions of work or employment. Common and violent crime may increase, as a result of people living in poverty, suffering trauma from the conflict, or taking advantage of reduced policing. Similarly, the authorities

[132] See the concluding observations referred to above for articulations of States' obligations to investigate and prosecute cases of domestic violence.

[133] Indeed, Article 1 of the Geneva Conventions contains the same 'respect and ensure respect' wording, from which the legal basis of some of the earliest articulations of 'due diligence' obligations in human rights law have emerged. See *Velasquez Rodriguez* Inter-Am.Ct.H.R. (Ser. C) No. 4 (1988) (Judgment) (29 July 1988) [165–72]. Adopting the same reasoning as the Inter-American Court in the international humanitarian law framework, the words 'ensure respect' in Article 1 of the Geneva Conventions can be argued to place an obligation on High Contracting Parties to prevent private individuals violating common Article 3 and Additional Protocol II. However, on the basis that Article 1 only refers to High Contracting Parties, the ICRC has taken the position that common Article 1 is not binding upon armed groups. See ICRC, 'Updated Commentary on the First Geneva Convention' (Published Online 22 March 2016) [131].

[134] See Article 2(3)(a) and (c) of the ICCPR.

may institute an over-zealous response to common crime that results in arbitrary detentions, corporal punishment, violations of the right to a fair trial, or violations of the right to life. This observation supports a view that in order for everyday life to be maintained during an armed conflict, the human rights framework becomes more important than ever.

(a) Definition of the so-called 'life goes on driver'

It is easy to see how it might be assumed that the regulation of everyday life is not a relevant dynamic to take into account when appraising the legal framework, except in State-controlled territory far away from the hostilities. However, the emerging body of social science literature referred to above contradicts this. It shows that everyday life is an important aspect of the human experience in armed conflict that has been routinely overlooked in empirical research. It also shows that daily life continues much more than it is often thought, both in the midst of armed conflict and in territory under rebel control. For the purposes of this chapter and in the rest of the book, the notion that daily life continues in the midst of armed conflict is called the 'life goes on driver'. The use of the term 'driver' is intended to capture the observation that life going on is a force which, although to some extent is defined by the armed conflict, also exists outside of the armed conflict and has a momentum and durability that is hard to suppress. In many ways, the 'life goes on driver' can be seen to be the other side of the governance coin. For, just as governance structures are required in order for life to go on effectively; very often, the fact that life goes on in rebel-held areas compels the armed group to respond by providing some kind of governance structures or service provisions. In that sense, the 'life goes on driver' and the provision of basic services by armed groups can be seen as two interdependent and mutually reinforcing phenomena impacting on the legal landscape.

Indeed, it is increasingly becoming noticed in research emerging from political science and anthropology that the experience of everyday life in times of armed conflict has all-too-often been excluded from empirical research.[135] Instead, there has been a general tendency to analyse civil wars exclusively in a top-down manner, focusing mainly on the identity of the parties and their motivations.[136] As a result, the dominant narrative of armed conflict has often revolved almost exclusively around the manner in which civilians 'cop[e] with violence' as 'victims'.[137] Literature on armed conflict has also tended to portray countries or areas affected by armed conflict as being completely disordered; a state of chaos.[138] In an effort

[135] Kalyvas, *Logic of Violence* (n 68) 39; Mampilly, *Rebel Rulers* (n 63) 27.

[136] Kalyvas, *Logic of Violence* (n 68) 39.

[137] S. C. Lubkemann, *Culture in Chaos: A Social Anthropology of the Social Condition of War* (University of Chicago Press, Chicago 2010) 11, 12, 21 (hereafter Lubkemann, *Culture in Chaos*); Mampilly, *Rebel Rulers* (n 63) 6.

[138] Lubkemann, *Culture in Chaos* (n 137) 12, states that places affected by armed conflict are often 'cast as sites of pervasive and uncontrollable violence, warscapes are viewed as "socially unstable places" in which historically constituted social relations and cultural meanings have been thoroughly "undone" by that violence'.

to redress this imbalance, a growing body of researchers from the social and political sciences have taken a micropolitical approach to experiences of armed conflict, focusing on the social dynamics of daily life.[139] A micropolitical approach is one which looks at how individuals and groups use formal and informal power to achieve their goals within organizations. The research that has emerged from this bottom-up approach has significantly challenged these dominant narratives of non-international armed conflict in a manner that is particularly relevant when seeking to identify the value of human rights law in the legal framework. On the basis it has not been highlighted before in legal literature, it is set out in some detail below.

(b) Not every aspect of human experience in times of armed conflict relates to 'armed conflict'

One of the key observations that has emerged out of this micropolitical approach is that people's personal lives continue within the context of armed conflict. Indeed, while it has long been observed that population centres far away from the fighting may remain largely unaffected by the fighting, recent empirical research now also highlights the reality that even in areas closer to the fighting everyday life will to a large extent continue.[140] For the civilians who live in these areas, lives will inevitably become harder, more insecure, and changed by the dynamics of armed conflict in the territory around them. They may suffer from or greatly fear terrorist attacks. They may lose loved ones in the fighting. They may be affected by the promulgation of emergency laws or the erosion of human rights that are often the consequences of long years of a state of emergency. Life may become harder as a result of restrictions on the availability of goods, difficulties moving about the country, or the influx of internally displaced persons.[141] But in spite of these difficulties, in many situations, people will carry on as best as they can to maintain their livelihoods and lives. The literature demonstrates that the human drive to survive is strong and includes more than simply physical security.[142] Commenting on this reality, it has been observed that the war is not an 'event' that suspends 'normal' social processes'[143] but the 'normal—in the sense of 'expected'—context for

[139] Kolomba Beck, *Normality of Civil War* (n 68) 16, 23, where she defines 'micropolitical studies' as those which aim to 'understand and theoretically construct social processes in wars based on an inquiry into micro-level dynamics'.

[140] In some instances, life in the capital city of countries suffering non-international armed conflicts remain completely free from hostilities for the majority—if not all—of the armed conflicts. See also Kalyvas, *Logic of Violence* (n 68) 133.

[141] See, for example, Kolomba Beck, *Normality of Civil War* (n 68) 126, where interviews cited restrictions on the circulation of persons and goods as being one of the major problems during the armed conflict.

[142] Kolomba Beck, *Normality of Civil War* (n 68) 133, suggests that holding on to normality may be an important form of 'defiance' for local communities against their circumstances and a form of 'self-preservation'. She comments in this regard that the villagers' stubborn return to their fields even under the most dangerous of circumstances served a function to affirm their independence and capability.

[143] Lubkemann, *Culture in Chaos* (n 137) 1.

the unfolding of social life'.[144] Likewise, political scientists have made the related observation that civilians retain a little remarked upon degree of agency in times of armed conflict. In social sciences literature, the term 'agency' refers to an individual's ability to act independently and make free choices. Agency is demonstrated through an individual's pursuit of daily life projects in a changed environment.[145]

This observation challenges the perception that in times of armed conflict, violence is the civilians' only concern. It also challenges the dominant narrative under which individuals, rather than retaining their status as 'brothers, workers, neighbours and elders', are distilled down to reductionist categories such as ' "refugees", whose only recognizable role is to flee violence, or as "combatants" whose only analyzed role is to perpetrate violence, or as "victims", whose only role of relevance is to suffer violence'.[146] Indeed, authors taking a micropolitical approach have repeatedly pointed out that civilians are rarely only victims.[147] Instead, they point out that civilians continue to prioritize personal agendas that are not connected per se to the fighting or survival in the physical sense.[148] They continue to pursue and be preoccupied by 'social struggles, interpersonal relations, and life projects'.[149] They point out that retaining agency is partly a survival mechanism in that it allows people to build a personal narrative which, although defined by the armed conflict, remains also independent from the armed conflict.[150] In other words, empirical research challenges what has been called 'state of emergency thinking' on violent conflict. Instead, it presents a counter-image of everyday life persisting in the midst of armed conflict.[151] It is important to note that by identifying the durability of everyday life in the context of non-international armed conflicts, researchers do not have the intention of downplaying civilians' experiences of war, but the intention of highlighting 'the dignity preserved by people who live through war situations'.[152]

(c) Importance of 'life goes on driver' in protracted armed conflicts

The notion that 'life goes on' in situations of non-international armed conflict has been shown to be particularly relevant in protracted or inconclusive armed conflicts, where territory may be frozen under the control of one of the actors.[153] This may be the reason why the phenomenon of normality amidst armed conflict is receiving increasing attention in political science literature today. As the ICRC stated in their 2009 Annual Report:

> The first noticeable characteristic of today's conflicts is their average duration. In most cases, the ICRC has now been present for two, three or even four decades.[154]

144 Ibid, 1. 145 Kalyvas, *Logic of Violence* (n 68) 71; Mampilly, *Rebel Rulers* (n 63) 67.
146 Kalyvas, *Logic of Violence* (n 68) 13.
147 Mampilly, *Rebel Rulers* (n 63) 67; Lubkemann, *Culture in Chaos* (n 137) 12.
148 Kalyvas, *Logic of Violence* (n 68) 390. 149 Ibid, 13.
150 Kolomba Beck, *Normality of Civil War* (n 68) 132–3. 151 Ibid, 16.
152 Ibid, 147. 153 Kalyvas, *Logic of Violence* (n 68) 138.
154 ICRC, *Annual Report of the International Committee of the Red Cross 2009* (Geneva 21 June 2010).

Since 2009, the trend towards protractedness in modern armed conflict has only increased.[155] The protractedness of modern non-international armed conflict has had an inevitable effect on nature of armed groups. Hottinger has stated:

> NSAs have doubled their life expectancy within the last twenty years. An average rebel force in Africa could either achieve its objectives, or decide to negotiate, within a life span of roughly six years. This was in the sixties and seventies. Today, most NSAs on the African continent have either existed or fought for either 12 to 16 years. They have spread geographically and their combatants have become more diverse.[156]

The continuing truth of Hottinger's observation today is illustrated by the ongoing existence of groups like the FARC and the ELN in Colombia, the LRA in East Africa, the FDLR in Rwanda, and the Taliban in Afghanistan, all of which demonstrate the considerable survival-power of many armed groups in the modern world. In many cases, the longevity of a group will be accompanied by a period of consolidated control of territory and some form of governance.[157] However, it is important to note that an armed group's control of territory and level of organization will often be in a state of flux during a protracted armed conflict and may vary tremendously during the lifetime of the armed group.[158]

In protracted armed conflict conflicts especially, the semblance of ordinary life will often continue, levels of common crime will persist and possibly even increase, children will be born and people will die.[159] Wherever possible, children will go to school, people will go to work and take their goods to the market. They will borrow money, have disputes with their neighbours, marry, divorce, and travel around the country to the extent that it is possible.[160] The literature referred to above makes explicitly clear that the 'life goes on driver' is just as much a force to be reckoned with in areas controlled by armed groups, as it is in

155 ICRC, Protracted Conflict and Humanitarian Action: Some Recent ICRC Experiences 2016 (Geneva).

156 J. T. Hottinger, 'The Engagement to Respect Humanitarian Law and Human Rights: A Prerequisite for Peace Negotiations, or a "Future" Component within Peace Negotiations, Exploring Criteria and Conditions for Engaging Armed Non-State Actors to Respect Humanitarian Law and Human Rights Law' (UNIDIR Conference Report 4–5 June 2007) 29.

157 The LRA is a notable exception.

158 Mampilly, *Rebel Rulers* (n 63) 3, citing J. Rosenau, 'Governance, Order and Change in World Politics' in J. Rosenau and E. Czempiel (eds), *Governance without Government: Order and Change in World Politics* (CUP, Cambridge 1992) 1–29, 59.

159 'Bombardments can't stop the Disco beat in Aleppo' (*Malay Mail Online*, 23 November 2014) <http://m.themalaymailonline.com/features/article/bombardments-cant-stop-the-disco-beat-in-aleppo> accessed 20 January 2017.

160 Commenting on how in the 'throes of war' Mozambicans 'still lived everyday lives, remained social beings, and pursued key life projects, such as marrying and bearing children', Lubkemann, *Culture in Chaos* (n 137) 217, recalls the words of an artist in Mozambique: '[A]lthough the bloodshed was all around then, you could still find some lovers. They would say all is gone, but let's at least love one another to create the future … I was joking around one day with a friend as I often do. I saw she was pregnant and said "You're pregnant, but we are in the middle of a war!" And my friend responded, "Yes, it is war, but even here on the street we still make love".'

areas controlled by State actors.[161] Empirical research makes clear that even under rather temporary rebel control, there will be many aspects of people's lives which are not directly connected to the armed conflict. Indeed, it has been commented that in times of non-international armed conflicts 'most people most of the time are interacting in non-violent ways'.[162] As a result, in areas controlled by rebel groups, it remains true that human existence remains more complex than simply victimhood and violence. As a result, disputes on matters such as land, marriage, grazing, water, and many other civil matters will continue. Indeed, in Syria at the beginning of the conflict, reporters repeatedly reported how local residents clamoured for security and public services after the Assad regime retreated in some areas.[163] It was repeatedly reiterated that despite the fact that there was no functioning government in some parts of Syria, the need for public administration was strong because problems relating to everyday life, such as legal cases, had not ceased.

(d) Relevance of 'life goes on driver' to legal framework

The notion that life goes on more than it has often been appreciated for individuals experiencing armed conflict is relevant to the legal framework. Indeed, it highlights the importance of the law enforcement paradigm in non-international armed conflicts for persons falling under State control and under the control of armed groups. The identification of the 'life goes on driver' is also key to understanding the value of human rights law within that paradigm. For when one thinks of armed conflict situations, it might be tempting to consider rights such as the right to freedom of movement, the right to marry, or common crime as considerations that will have been displaced by more pressing considerations of physical safety and survival. But when one examines the empirical research from social sciences, one realizes that this is often not the case. Moreover when the two legal frameworks of international humanitarian law and international human rights law are compared side-by-side, one sees that international human rights law has a particularly valuable role to play in regulating everyday life. For while the international humanitarian law framework brings crucial protections in times of armed conflict, it also reproduces a reductionist narrative of non-international armed conflict where individuals are reduced to being either fighters or civilians. In the humanitarian law framework individuals who are not fighters are generally portrayed as powerless and defined entirely by their vulnerability; they feature in common Article 3 and Additional Protocol II as either being in danger of violence or attack, in the hands of the

[161] 'Daily Life in Aleppo: The Struggle for Normality amid the Ruins of War' (*Spiegel Online*, 26 February 2013) <http://www.spiegel.de/international/world/the-struggle-to-maintain-order-in-rebel-controlled-aleppo-in-syria-a-885396.html> accessed 20 January 2017.

[162] Mampilly, *Rebel Rulers* (n 63) 7, citing C. Tilly, *The Politics of Collective Violence* (CUP, Cambridge 2003) 12.

[163] 'A Battle for Syria One Court at a Time' (*New York Times*, 13 March 2013) <http://www.nytimes.com/2013/03/14/world/middleeast/a-battle-for-syria-one-court-at-a-time.html?ref=world&_r=2&> accessed 20 January 2017.

enemy, or sick and wounded.[164] The empirical research referred to above demonstrates that the civilian experience of armed conflict is more than this.

The observation that international humanitarian law may not capture the whole civilian experience of armed conflict does not diminish its fundamentally important role in times of armed conflict or suggest that it should be otherwise. International humanitarian law is, in its very conception, a reflection of state of emergency thinking and rightly so; its purpose is to protect people who are not or are no longer participating in the hostilities and restrict means and methods of warfare.[165] In doing so, it naturally takes a top-down approach which starts with an identification of the parties to the armed conflict. This is crucial for the legal framework, as it is essentially the identification of its obligation-bearers. International humanitarian law has no reason to pay attention to people's roles as brothers, fathers, elders, or neighbours because the only real status that is important for its goal is whether an individual is an civilian or fighter.[166] Human rights law, on the other hand, is a body of law which is much more capable of responding to multidimensional experiences of non-international armed conflicts that has been portrayed above. It avoids categorizing individuals as anything but individuals and in doing so, allows for the recognition that individuals can play multifaceted roles in the complicated context of armed conflict. Most particularly, it conceives the individual as a participant in the social fabric of life with a full measure of agency.[167] In this sense, it is seen that human rights law has a unique and important role to play in the law enforcement paradigm non-international armed conflicts, alongside international humanitarian law. The question of how these rights may be respected, protected, and fulfilled by armed groups is considered in more detail in the final part of this chapter.

3.3 Humanitarian assistance

3.3.1 Obligation to provide essential services in times of need

Another area in which the two bodies of law work alongside each other is in the field of humanitarian assistance. The term humanitarian assistance has been

[164] It is noted that this is less true in international armed conflicts. Both Geneva Convention III and IV reflect a strong appreciation of life 'going on' in prisoner of war camps and situations of occupation.

[165] ICRC Advisory Service on International Humanitarian Law, 'What is International Humanitarian Law?' (July 2004).

[166] It is noted in this respect that international humanitarian law that applies in non-international armed conflicts does pay passing attention to individual's roles as mothers and the family unit. See for example, Article 4 of APII which states that the death penalty shall not be carried out on 'pregnant women or mothers of young children'. See also the notion that children should be educated 'in keeping with the wishes of their parents', Article 4(3)(a). The status of medical personnel and the 'sick and wounded' is also important.

[167] See again the text of the Preamble to the Vienna Declaration and Programme of Action (n 19): 'Recognizing and affirming that all human rights derive from the dignity and self-worth inherent in the human person, and that the human person is the central subject of human rights and fundamental freedoms, and consequently should be the principal beneficiary and should participate actively in the realization of these rights and freedom.'

defined as the provision of goods and services which are essential for the survival of those directly affected by armed conflicts or natural disasters.[168] For example, it has been noted by commentators that the positive obligations under human rights law are more far-reaching that the obligations which can be found in international humanitarian law which apply in non-international armed conflicts.[169] The right to life which is found in the ICCPR is recognized to encompass not only a prohibition from taking action which infringes an individual's right to life but an obligation upon States' parties to take positive measures to ensure that an individual's right to life is protected. The right to life is also interconnected with the core subsistence rights in the ICESCR which are necessary for human survival.[170] The ICESCR recognizes 'the right of everyone to an adequate standard of living ... including adequate food, clothing and housing' and the right to freedom from hunger.[171] It also includes the right to enjoy the highest attainable standard of physical and mental health and the right to water.[172] While the ICESCR provides for the progressive realization of rights to the maximum of a State's available resources, it also obliges States to take immediate steps to adhere to a set of core obligations which are designed to 'ensure the satisfaction of, at the very least, minimum essential levels of each of the rights'.[173] The Committee on Economic, Social and Cultural Rights has said that the consequence of this is that any State in which 'any significant number of individuals is deprived of essential foodstuffs, of essential primary health care, of basic shelter and housing, or of the most basic forms of education is, prima facie, failing to discharge its obligations under the Covenant'.[174]

These positive primary obligations to provide food, water, and basic healthcare contained in human rights law are important components of the web of protection offered by international humanitarian law and international human rights law on humanitarian assistance. Moreover, the specific value of human rights law on this issue stems from the fact that there are not many provisions in international

[168] For definition of 'humanitarian assistance' see H. Spieker, 'The Right to Give and Receive Humanitarian Assistance' in H. Heintze and A. Zwitter (eds), *Humanitarian Assistance: A Cross-Cut through Legal Issues Pertaining to Humanitarianism* (Springer, Heidelberg 2011) 7.

[169] See R. A. Stoffels, 'Legal Regulation of Humanitarian Assistance in Armed Conflict: Achievements and Gaps' (2004) 855 International Review of the Red Cross 515, 516; R. Barber, 'Facilitating Humanitarian Assistance in International Humanitarian Law and Human Rights Law' (2009) 874 International Review of the Red Cross 371, 395 (hereafter Barber, 'Facilitating Humanitarian Assistance'); F. Schwendimann, 'The Legal Framework of Humanitarian Access in Armed Conflict' (2011) 844 International Review of the Red Cross 993, 1004 (hereafter Schwendimann, 'Legal Framework'). See also Barber, 'Facilitating Humanitarian Assistance' 391–6; Schwendimann, 'Legal Framework' 1003–4, for a detailed discussion of the human rights provisions which apply in a non-international armed conflict.

[170] Műller, 'Limitations to and Derogations from' (n 11) 601.

[171] Article 11 of the ICESCR.

[172] See Article 12 of the ICESCR for the right to the enjoyment of the highest attainable standard of physical and mental health. The right to water is not explicitly mentioned in the ICESCR but has been found in Articles 11 and 12 of the Covenant. See UN Committee on Economic Social and Cultural Rights, 'General Comment 15 (The Right to Water: Articles 11 and 12)' (20 January 2003) UN Doc E/C.12/2002/11 (hereafter CESCR General Comment 15, Water).

[173] CESCR General Comment 3, State Party Obligations (n 21) [10].

[174] Ibid.

humanitarian law which require parties to the armed conflict to provide essential goods and services to the civilian population. While the ICRC has stated that 'the object and purpose' of international humanitarian law allows an inference that each party to a non-international armed conflict is under an obligation to 'meet the needs' of the population under its control, the details of these obligations are only minimally articulated.[175] In a conflict reaching the threshold of common Article 3 of the Geneva Conventions, the positive obligations are especially minimal. Common Article 3 requires the parties to a non-international armed conflict to treat the civilian population 'humanely' but it does not oblige them to provide essential services, at least not explicitly.[176] Common Article 3 also prohibits the parties to a non-international armed conflict from committing violence to life and person, taking hostages, committing outrages upon personal dignity, and passing sentences and carrying out executions without the provision of due process guarantees. If a State were to take acts to deny civilian populations access to essential services or impede or prevent humanitarian agencies providing relief to civilian populations in a humanitarian emergency, this might arguably fall within the prohibition of violence to life.

The obligations in Additional Protocol II regarding basic services are more far-reaching than common Article 3, but not as far-reaching as the positive obligations in human rights law. Article 5 of Additional Protocol II states that parties to a non-international armed conflict must provide persons deprived of liberty with food and drinking water 'to the same extent as to the local civilian population'. From the wording of Article 5, an inference could be drawn that a concurrent obligation to provide food and drinking water to the civilian population exists but Additional Protocol II does not provide further details of what this obligation might entail. Article 14 of Additional Protocol II prohibits parties from employing starvation as a method of combat. It also prohibits parties from attacking, destroying, removing, or rendering useless objects indispensable to the survival of the civilian population such as food-stuffs, agricultural areas for the production of food-stuffs, crops, livestock, drinking water installations, and supplies. The scope of this provision has been interpreted widely to prohibit not only starvation as a means of killing but also a general deprivation or denial of an essential commodity needed for survival. While it is arguable that this provision includes an obligation to provide essential goods required to stave off starvation, the fact that this positive obligation is not explicitly articulated detracts from its strength. In the light of this, human rights law contains important complementary obligations relating to the provision of food, water, and housing. It also brings value on the question of whether the parties to a non-international armed conflict are obliged to consent to the provision of services by humanitarian organizations in circumstances where their primary obligations to supply basic services are not being met.

[175] ICRC, 'Q&A and Lexicon on Humanitarian Access' (June 2014) (hereafter ICRC, Q&A and Lexicon).

[176] Barber, 'Facilitating Humanitarian Assistance' (n 169) 385.

3.3.2 *Obligation to consent to humanitarian assistance*

Article 18 of Additional Protocol II makes clear that humanitarian organizations can only provide humanitarian assistance if they obtain the consent of the State and this is generally accepted to be the position for common Article 3 conflicts too.[177] Despite Article 18's focus on State consent, in practice, humanitarian organizations will also have to obtain the consent of the armed group if the persons in need of assistance are in territory under an armed group's control.[178] Although Article 18 does not explicitly *require* a State to provide its consent, the ICRC has found that under customary international humanitarian law a State cannot withhold its consent: (i) on arbitrary grounds; or (ii) if it will result in the starvation of the population.[179] The ICRC notes in this respect that the 26th International Conference of the Red Cross and Red Crescent in 1995 emphasized that all parties to armed conflicts were under an 'obligation to accept, under the conditions prescribed by international humanitarian law, impartial humanitarian relief operations for the civilian population when it lacks supplies essential to its survival'.[180] However, in the light of the fact that neither common Article 3 nor Article 18 of Additional Protocol contains an explicit obligation to consent, this is another issue on which recourse is often additionally had to human rights law.[181]

[177] It is noteworthy that the original draft of Additional Protocol II contained a much more far-reaching provision on relief operations than the final wording which is found in Article 18. Draft Article 33(1) of the Additional Protocol required the parties to the non-international armed conflict to 'agree to facilitate, to the fullest extent possible' relief actions which were exclusively humanitarian in circumstances where the 'the civilian population is inadequately supplied, in particular, with foodstuffs, clothing, medical and hospital stores and means of shelter'. See 'Official Records of the Diplomatic Conference on the Reaffirmation and Development on International Humanitarian Law Applicable in Armed Conflicts' (Geneva 1974–1977) Vol I, Part III, Draft Additional Protocol II, 43. For the latter point, see Article 14 of Additional Protocol II.

[178] In practice, the ICRC usually seeks consent from both parties. See ICRC, Q&A and Lexicon (n 175) 10. See also OCHA, Oxford Institute for Ethics, Law and Armed Conflict and University of Oxford, Oxford Guidance on the Law Relating to Humanitarian Relief Operations in Situations of Armed Conflict (October 2016) (hereafter 'Oxford Guidance') [31]

[179] For the latter point see Article 14 of Additional Protocol II. For the fact that parties to a non-international armed conflict cannot refuse consent to humanitarian relief on arbitrary grounds, see Henckaerts and Doswald-Beck, *Rules* (n 9) 197. The ICRC states that the only valid grounds on which a party can refuse humanitarian relief actions is if the organization is (a) not humanitarian and impartial or (b) if the population is not in need. The ICRC takes the view that 'military necessity' may not be invoked to deny humanitarian access but may be invoked in exceptional circumstances in order to regulate humanitarian access. See ICRC, Q&A and Lexicon (n 175) 5, 10. See also Oxford Guidance (n 178) [49].

[180] ICRC 26th International Conference, 'Resolution II: Protection of the Civilian Population in Period of Armed Conflict' (7 December 1995) [E(b)].

[181] See Institute of International Law 16th Commission, 'Resolution on Humanitarian Assistance' (2 September 2003) [VIII(I)], which states that States must not refuse consent 'if such refusal is likely to endanger the fundamental human rights of the victims or would amount to a violation of the ban on starvation of civilians as a method of warfare'. See also Institute of International Humanitarian Law, 'Guiding Principles on the Right to Humanitarian Assistance' (1993) 33 International Review of the Red Cross 519, Principle 1: 'Every human being has the right to humanitarian assistance in order to ensure respect for the human rights to life, health, protection against cruel and degrading treatment and other human rights which are essential to survival, well-being and protection in public emergencies.' See further Advisory Committee on Issues of Public International Law, 'Advisory Report No. 25 on Humanitarian Assistance' (The Hague, August 2014), for discussion of these sources.

Human rights law is generally thought to support the view that a State must not refuse humanitarian assistance, in instances where its population is in need. Relevant rights in this respect include the right to life, the right to freedom from torture, cruel and inhuman treatment, the right to an adequate standard of living, including adequate food, clothing, and housing, and the right to the enjoyment of the highest attainable standard of health. In particular, the ICSCR has consistently drawn attention to the obligation of States to cooperate with international partners when taking steps to realize the rights recognized in the Covenant.[182] Indeed, the 'obligation to cooperate' is expressly articulated in the wording of Article 11 of the ICESCR which contains the right to an adequate standard of living, including adequate food, clothing, and housing, Article 2(1) which articulates the nature of the State parties' obligations in general and Article 23 which gives some examples of the sort of cooperation which might be appropriate. These articles combined present a strong argument that a State would be in breach of these provisions if it refused to allow a humanitarian organization permission to operate in an area where it was clear that the civilian population was suffering as a result of its failure or inability to provide adequate access to food, water, medical supplies, and shelter.[183] An obligation for States to consent to the provision of emergency assistance by third parties can also be seen to be inherent in State parties' obligations to *respect* and *fulfil* the rights to food, water, and health contained within the Covenant.[184]

3.4 Complementarity in the drafting details

It has been seen above that the issue of humanitarian assistance is another major issue on which human rights law brings important value, alongside international humanitarian law. It provides a further example of the observation that it is *because* the two bodies of law have slightly different scopes of application or slightly different normative content that they can provide a holistic protection for individuals. For example, while international humanitarian law provides important protections for people who are sick and wounded, international human rights law provides protection for people who are healthy but nevertheless need medical assistance. In

[182] See CESCR General Comment 3, State Party Obligations (n 21) [13], [14]. See also UN Committee on Economic Social and Cultural Rights, 'General Comment 12 (The Right to Adequate Food)' (12 May 1999) UN Doc E/C.12/1999/5, [36] (hereafter CESCR General Comment 12, Food); UN Committee on Economic Social and Cultural Rights, 'General Comment 14 (The Right to the Highest Attainable Standard of Health)' (11 August 2000) UN Doc E/C.12/2000/4, [38] (hereafter CESCR General Comment 14, Health); CESCR General Comment 15, Water (n 172) [30].

[183] The conceptualization of international cooperation on the provision of food aid as an element of the human right to adequate food is supported by the Special Rapporteur on the Right to Food, 'The role of development cooperation and food aid in realizing the right to adequate food: moving from charity to obligation' (11 February 2009) UN Doc A/HRC/10/5, 5 [15].

[184] See CESCR General Comment 12, Food (n 182) [15]; CESCR General Comment 14, Health (n 182) [33]; CESCR General Comment 15, Water (n 172) [20–9]. The obligation to respect the rights in the Covenant includes an obligation upon States to refrain from interfering directly or indirectly with the enjoyment of the right to health. The obligation to *fulfil* requires States to adopt appropriate legislative, administrative, budgetary, judicial, promotional and other measures towards the full realization of the right in question.

this sense, the right to life may be particularly important for the provision of family planning services, hygiene, and nutrition information which are needed irrespective of whether people are sick and wounded. Likewise, while humanitarian law prohibits people from being moved against their will, international human rights law protects people from being confined to a single location against their will in an arbitrary manner. Both bodies of law provide a different perspective on the same issue. Both are equally relevant and necessary to address the myriad problems that civilians may face in times of non-international armed conflict. The two bodies of law work together in a complementary fashion to produce a net-normative gain. Moreover, even when the substance of two norms in international humanitarian law and international human rights law are substantively very similar, the small differences between them are often helpful, and in a practical sense complementary.

For example, international humanitarian provisions are generally articulated as 'prohibitions' binding upon the parties to an armed conflict, human rights law is generally articulated in terms of 'rights' owned by the population. For example, while international humanitarian law 'requires' that children shall 'receive an education', international human rights law 'recognises the right of everyone to education'. In a similar manner, while international humanitarian law 'prohibits' slavery and the slave trade in all its forms, human rights law states that 'no one shall be held in slavery'. Although small, the difference in the way these provisions are worded or conceptualized can be helpful to humanitarian actors on the ground. For example, it is often seen that humanitarian organizations taking a 'rights-based' approach may prefer to use human rights treaties as their primary advocacy tool, in combination with international humanitarian law. More than international humanitarian law treaties, human rights treaties facilitate a bottom-up approach under which the possession of the right by the individual is the starting place for advocacy and action. As one humanitarian agency has stated, the first three questions its staff have to examine when an emergency arises is: (i) what rights do people have?; (ii) what rights are people being denied?; and (iii) what opportunities exist to change people's access to their rights?[185] These questions are easier to answer when looking at human rights law, than under international humanitarian law which is framed largely in terms of prohibitions. This is another aspect of international human rights which may be helpful for those working on the ground in situations of non-international armed conflict. Likewise, it is seen that in instances where international humanitarian law and international human rights law cover the same issues, human rights law can sometimes provide interpretative guidance on its counterpart provisions in international humanitarian law.[186] For example, the meaning of the term 'regularly constituted court' in common Article 3 has been interpreted with reference to human rights norms on fair trial guarantees.[187]

[185] 'The Rights-Based Approach to Emergencies' (ActionAid, undated) <http://www.actionaid.org.uk/doc_lib/110_1_rights_based_approach_guide.pdf> final page, accessed 20 January 2017.

[186] See Sivakumaran, 'International Humanitarian Law' (n 34) 490–1.

[187] Sivakumaran, 'Fair Trials Or Summary Justice?' (n 82) 498–9.

4. Relationship between Territory and Added Value

It can be seen from the above analysis that there is a clear correlation between the amount of territory that an armed group controls and the added value that can be brought by human rights to the legal framework. Indeed, in situations where an armed group is controlling territory, the chapter has demonstrated that there is a high likelihood that everyday life will continue for the people under the armed group's control. It has also been shown that there is a high likelihood that the armed group will be exercising governance activities such as policing functions, taking measures to tackle common crime, holding people in detention, administering courts, instituting road blocks, imposing restrictions on people's freedom of movement, freedom of association, and the many other rights relating to everyday. It has been shown in this chapter that it is primarily in relation to the performance of these activities, that the added value of human rights law is found. In addition, it has been demonstrated that in situations of protracted armed conflict, there will be the largest scope to argue that certain activities do *not* have a nexus to the armed conflict with the result that the protective scope of international humanitarian law vis-à-vis international human rights law will be less far-reaching. However, the chapter has shown that human rights law will also add important normative value in instances where an armed group only controls a small pocket of territory (e.g. a town) for short period of time. In these circumstances, an armed group may quickly institute a system of basic security on the streets where people live and exercise policing activities. It may also interfere with people's ability to exercise their freedom of association, freedom of expression, and freedom of movement, by forbidding public meetings, radio broadcasts or public dissent, or setting up far-ranging road blocks or curfews. These activities bring the value of the extra norms and perspectives that are brought by human rights norms to the fore.

In contrast, in situations where an armed group does not exercise control over an area, the factual situation on the ground will often be more akin to the conduct of hostilities paradigm than the law enforcement paradigm. Moreover, in instances where an armed group does exercise authority over persons in these situations, those people will be more 'affected' by the armed conflict, than in situations where an armed group exercises control over territory. Consequently, the armed group's law enforcement actions will be more likely to have a nexus with the armed conflict, thereby falling under international humanitarian law. Indeed, research indicates that in instances where an armed group does not control territory, it will almost inevitably not be focusing on the provision of public services.[188] Instead, its priority will tend to be on building its military operations and securing its survival as a military organization. Accordingly, from a capacity perspective, the armed group will not be in a position to provide education, healthcare, security, justice, and other public services. Moreover, it will not be seen as a provider of public

[188] Mampilly, *Rebel Rulers* (n 63) 235.

services in the eyes of the civilian population, so the civilian population will likely continue appealing to the State for the provision of governance and public services. However, it is noteworthy that an armed group which does not control territory may still be in a position to interfere considerably with peoples' freedom of movement, physical security, property, and liberty by instituting curfews, arrests, and administering physical punishment. It will be able to prevent people enjoying rights like the right to health and the right to education, by destroying schools or making medical clinics the subject of attack. It may also be able to prevent people enjoying their rights to health and food by refusing humanitarian organizations access to the territory. However, an armed group will rarely be able to do more than simply 'respect' these rights, i.e. refrain from interfering with these rights. It will rarely be able to 'protect' and 'fulfil' them, as this needs a more consolidated control of territory, more sophisticated governance structures and a law enforcement system.[189]

The observation that armed groups will not be able to bear extensive obligations under human rights law in situations where they do not control territory is examined in more detail in Chapter 6. Here, it is argued that an armed group's obligations under human rights law should be modified to match its organizational capacity and the rights 'in play' in a given situation. Indeed, it is demonstrated in Chapter 6 that an approach that tailors the obligations of armed groups to their capacity has precedent in the international humanitarian law framework and the historical law on belligerency. Such an approach also correlates with the fact that when a State has lost control over a portion of its territory, its obligations with respect to that territory are also adjusted and reduced.[190] It also has similarities with the position taken by the Grand Chamber in the *Al-Skeini* et al *v UK* case when the court recognized that rights can be divided and tailored when a State does not have full control of territory.[191] In this case, the Court recognized that in instances where a State has the power to violate only some of an individual's rights, it can be held responsible for only those violations.[192] As a result, in instances where control of territory is fluid between the parties, it is suggested that it would be most appropriate for an armed group to be held responsible to

[189] D. Murray, *Human Rights Obligations of Non-State Armed Groups* (Bloomsbury, West Sussex 2016), 181–97 for an excellent overview of the 'respect', 'protect', 'fulfil' obligations with respect to armed groups.

[190] See *Ilaşcu and Others v Moldova and Russia,* Application No. 48787/99, Judgment, 8 July 2004, para 340–5. Here, the Court clearly considered that it was unrealistic to expect Moldova to have managed to re-establish its control over the Transdniestrian territory. As a result, the European Court of Human Rights seemed to take the view that Moldova's obligations to re-establish its control could have been fulfilled largely by its diplomatic efforts to assert sovereignty over the territory and its efforts to secure the release of the individuals from custody in its bilateral negotiations with the Russian Federation.

[191] *Al-Skeini and Others v UK,* Application No. 55721/07 (ECHR, 7 July 2011)(Grand Chamber Judgment) [137].

[192] But this does not equate to a recognition that the individual in question only 'has' those rights, and not the others. The restriction is effected by issues of jurisdiction and responsibility.

respect the human rights that are relevant to the civilians in the territory in question, while the State is held responsible to respect, protect, and fulfil those rights. The State's positive obligations may include an obligation to protect civilians in the course of its military operations against the armed group.[193] In that sense, the human rights obligations in the International Bill of Rights would be divided and tailored between two duty-bearers according to their capabilities and immediate relevance.

It is argued, therefore, that where the threshold of international humanitarian law has already been reached but an armed group does not control any territory, international human rights law will still bring some added value but it will be less, than when an armed group controls territory. Its value lies mainly in the fact that human rights law contains some important norms that do not exist in international humanitarian law, such as the right to work, the right to freedom of expression, and the right to freedom of movement. With respect to issues covered by both bodies of law (e.g. the right to health) the value of human rights law will often be small vis-à-vis international humanitarian law. For when human rights norms are stripped down to the obligation to 'respect', they contain largely similar protections to the norms found in the international humanitarian law framework, although sometimes reach a wider group of beneficies.[194] As a result, within an armed conflict situation, it can be seen that human rights law adds the most value in situations where an armed group exercises control over population or territory, even for short periods. Outside these circumstances, the main situation in which such human rights law can bring significant normative value is if the threshold of international humanitarian law has not yet been met, or has recently passed. In these situations, it may be particularly valuable to rely on the right to health, for example, to condemn attacks on healthcare facilities by armed groups. The chapter shows that human rights law will also bring value in instances when an armed group *without* control over a civilian population per se, nevertheless exercises significant control over its own fighters and their family members. This chapter has demonstrated that this is an important but little-noted area in which the human rights law framework can bring significant added value in instances where an armed group does not have control of civilian populations, as the concept is most often understood.

5. Conclusions

This chapter has shown that the myriad instances in which accountability mechanisms have referred to human rights law, alongside international humanitarian law, are not instances of bad-lawyering on the part of their drafters but in many cases have real normative value. Indeed, the chapter has demonstrated that human rights law has most to add in the area of the law enforcement paradigm. Often

[193] See Chapter 6 for a fuller elaboration of this argument.

[194] See comment above in paragraph 3.4 about the right to health providing a right to health services for people who are healthy, as well as those who are sick and wounded.

considered solely as a paradigm relevant to State controlled territory, the chapter has drawn on political science literature to show that it is also deserves attention in territory held by armed groups. In particular, the chapter demonstrates that everyday life is an important dynamic in non-international armed conflicts and too often overlooked. It also shows that governance activities are performed by armed groups more often than has often been thought. Finding a strong overlap between the notion of governance and law enforcement, the chapter finds that these connected observations give validation to the idea that human rights law brings value on issues that do not have any nexus to the armed conflict, such as the regulation of everyday life and the enforcement of common crime. Indeed, the chapter finds that human rights law provides an important complement to international humanitarian law which requires a nexus to the armed conflict. In particular, it contains norms relating to the right to freedom of expression, the right to freedom of movement, the right to freedom of association, the right to health, and the right to work. Likewise, in many instances in which it covers the same issues as international humanitarian law, the chapter has shown that human rights law contains *different* norms or provides a *different* perspective on the same norm. In its final section, the chapter demonstrates that there is clear normative merit to the notion that armed groups have obligations under human rights law, especially in situations where they control territory or towns. In situations where armed groups do not have control over territory, the chapter finds the normative added value of human rights law to be less significant, but still notable especially in situations outside of the international humanitarian law framework or in situations where the armed group exercises control over its fighters and their families.

PART II

LEGAL PERSONALITY OF ARMED GROUPS UNDER HUMAN RIGHTS LAW

3

Evaluative Framework: Legal Personality under International Law

1. Introduction

The purpose of Part II of the book is to examine what can be learnt about the international legal personality of armed groups under human rights law from other fields of international law. The rationale behind Part II's focus on legal personality is the observation that international legal personality is one of the key foundation blocks from which our understanding of rights and obligations flows.[1] Legal personality can be defined as 'the capacity to be the bearer of rights and duties under international law'.[2] In the light of this definition, it can be seen that our understanding of legal personality is also key to an understanding of the circumstances in which rights and obligations are acquired in international law. This connection between international legal personality and 'rights and duties' explains why a focus on the legal personality of armed groups is crucial when seeking to achieve a better understanding of *how* and *when* armed groups may have obligations under international human rights law. Yet such an undertaking is not for the faint-hearted. Discussions of international legal personality inevitably raise complex questions of international law to which there are often no clear answers. Moreover, it is a highly subjective notion that is linked to, and formed by, individual scholars' conceptions of the whole system of international law.[3] This makes it especially difficult to find a consensus on questions of international legal personality, especially when the enquiry pertains to non-State actors in general and armed groups in particular.[4]

[1] R. Portmann, *Legal Personality in International Law* (CUP, Cambridge 2010) 19 (hereafter Portmann, *Legal Personality*).

[2] J. Crawford, *The Creation of States in International Law* (2nd edn, Clarendon Press, Oxford 2006) 28 (hereafter Crawford, *Creation of States*).

[3] See J. d'Aspremont, 'Inclusive Law Making and Law-Enforcement Processes for an Exclusive International System' in J. d'Aspremont (ed), *Participants in the International Legal System: Multiple Perspectives on Non-State Actors in International Law* (Routledge, Abingdon 2011) 433 (hereafter d'Aspremont, 'Inclusive Law Making'); J. Nijman, 'Non-State Actors and the International Rule of Law: Revisiting the 'Realist Theory' of International Legal Personality' in M. Noortmann and C. Ryngaert (eds), *Non-State Actor Dynamics in International Law: from Law-Takers to Law-Makers* (Ashgate, Farnham 2010) 102 (hereafter Nijman, 'Revisiting the 'Realist Theory'').

[4] See d'Aspremont, 'Inclusive Law Making' (n 3) 433.

The idea that armed groups possess legal personality presents a particularly blatant challenge to the idea that personality needs to be conferred by States. Unlike some other non-State actors, such as international organizations, armed groups clearly do not factually exist, as a result of the consent of States. Instead, they usually exist *contrary* to the will of most States. As a result, States are often reluctant to acknowledge that armed groups have international legal personality at all. Even when a State recognizes an armed group's personality at international level, it may persist in denying that it exists at national level. Chapter 2 has shown that the tension between international and national law is a recurring and difficult feature of the legal framework relating to non-international armed conflict. Also, the distinctive character and composition of armed groups raise a number of uniquely thorny legal issues relating to international legal personality. A particular difficulty arises from the fact that armed groups come into being organically. This means that there is generally no clearly identifiable moment at which an armed group starts to exist, in either factual or legal terms. As a result, any attempt to identify such a moment for legal purposes will inevitably involve an element of conjecture and a degree of artificiality. This sets armed groups apart from other non-State actors whose moment of formal incorporation or creation is often evidenced by the signing of constitutional documents.[5] It also makes it doubly challenging as a matter of law to identify how and when armed groups acquire legal personality under human rights law.

In the light of the reflections above, the purpose of the second part of the book is to clarify how and when armed groups attain international legal personality under human rights law. The book seeks clarification on these issues primarily through a study of the law of belligerency and the contemporary law of non-international armed conflict. During the course of analysing the framework of belligerency, significant attention is also given to the framework of insurgency; the body of law which applies to situations which fall short of a formal belligerency. The decision to seek insights into the legal personality of armed groups in areas of law outside human rights law is motivated by a view that the legal landscape relating to armed groups' accountability under human rights law is too embryonic to form a solid or consistent enough legal paradigm against which the questions can be properly analysed.[6] Moreover, it is the central premise of the study that the academic controversy and uncertainty surrounding the questions of how and when armed groups are bound by international human rights law casts doubt on aspects of its validity. As a result, the author chooses to seek clarification on the international legal personality of armed groups under human rights law in alternative firmer

[5] See e.g. *Advisory Opinion on Reparations for Injuries Suffered in the Service of the United Nations* [1949] ICJ Reports 174 (11 April 1949) [178–9] (hereafter *Advisory Opinion on Reparations*), where the Court relied heavily on the Charter of the United Nations which 'establishes' the United Nations and sets out its anticipated functions.

[6] See the introduction of the book for an overview of some of the uncertainties within this framework.

legal frameworks which are less controversially binding upon armed groups. It is demonstrated that these legal frameworks contain valuable information about the way in which the international legal personality of armed groups has been conceived from a historical and contemporary perspective.

In examining how armed groups may acquire legal personality under international law, the second part of the book seeks to shed light on the factual conditions that are required for armed groups to acquire international personality. It also considers how the international legal personality of armed groups manifests itself, e.g. does it exist along a spectrum? Or is it fixed? Attention is also given to how the legal personality of armed groups is achieved or acquired. As part of this enquiry, consideration is given to the role that State consent plays in the acquisition of legal personality by armed groups. General answers to these questions are sought by analysing first the frameworks of belligerency and insurgency and second by analysing the framework of international humanitarian law. Synthesizing this analysis, Chapter 6 evaluates whether these general conclusions shed any light on the identical questions in human rights law. The evaluation of these questions not only has an important intrinsic value in furthering the debate on whether and when armed groups are bound by human rights law, it also plays an important methodological role for the chapters that follow by allowing the author to take a more objective position later in the book on two key questions which have been the subject of debate in academic literature. The first is the question of whether the consent of armed groups is necessary before they can be bound by international law. The second is whether the practice of armed groups should be taken into account when determining the legal framework of customary international law which is binding upon them.

2. Rationale behind Evaluative Framework on Legal Personality

It was commented above that writings on international legal personality are intrinsically and inexorably subjective.[7] It is no coincidence that two of the major works on international legal personality are organized into chapters representing individual legal theorists, rather than themes.[8] Theories on international legal personality are generally influenced by their authors' understanding of the whole system of international law.[9] As a consequence, legal

[7] See e.g. D. P. O'Connell, *International Law* (Stevens & Sons Limited, London 1965) 89–105 (hereafter O'Connell, *International Law*) for an example of a text book in which the author's personal views on international legal personality are very clear. Here, O'Connell makes it clear that he is not a proponent of the recognition theory of international legal personality.

[8] Portmann, *Legal Personality* (n 1) 19; J. Nijman, *The Concept of International Legal Personality: an Inquiry into the History and Theory of International Law* (T.M.C. Asser Press, The Hague 2004) (hereafter Nijman, *International Legal Personality*).

[9] See d'Aspremont, 'Inclusive Law Making' (n 3) 433.

cases and text books on the topic of legal personality are particularly susceptible to what has been called 'auto-theorizing'.[10] This is the notion that the rule of law always includes a 'theory of its own legitimacy' within its very fabric.[11] This chapter argues that the only appropriate response to this problem is to seek a heightened level of transparency when analysing issues pertaining to international legal personality. As a result, the second part of the book analyses the legal frameworks of belligerency, insurgency, and international humanitarian law against five pre-defined conceptions of international legal personality which are identified by Portmann in his monograph on the topic and set out in this chapter.[12] Also, whenever citing a jurist as an authority on the law for a particular point, the chapter deliberately notes whether that author is either openly or arguably allied to a particular conception of international legal personality.

It is argued that this level of meta-analysis assists in efforts both to combat the subjectivity inherent in the debate about armed groups and to draw transparent conclusions about what the various legal frameworks demonstrate regarding the state of the law. The adoption of this evaluative framework allows the legal frameworks to be investigated against an identifiable benchmark of analysis. The employment of an evaluative framework also has the effect of forcing a more painstaking examination and helps the author of this study escape somewhat from, or at least be more aware of, her own inevitable scholarly biases.[13] Perhaps most importantly, the adoption of such a framework means that the conclusions of the study on legal personality are immediately transparent and able to be challenged. This has the effect of facilitating a continuing debate on the topic and gives the study's conclusions more legitimacy. As a result, Part II does not seek to determine how and when an armed group may gain international legal personality per se as if there is an objective truth on the topic.[14] Instead, it seeks to determine what the various legal frameworks tell us about the dominant manner in which the legal personality of armed groups is conceived.

[10] P. W. Kahn, *The Cultural Study of Law* (University of Chicago Press, Chicago 1999) 87.

[11] Ibid, 86–7. See in particular Kahn's comment: 'Law is not simply command, but command that holds itself out as legitimate … The rule of law, accordingly, always includes a theory of its own legitimacy. Such reflections about law do not attach to an already-complete practice. Reflection is not separate and after the fact; it is a part of the practice. This self-reflective moment makes possible normative critique of any particular aspect of the existing practice. The grounds of law's legitimacy provide a ground for interpretation and thus a critique of what the law is or should be. This is why Dworkin can describe law as an interpretative practice'.

[12] See Portmann, *Legal Personality*, (n 1).

[13] R. Higgins, *Problems and Process, International Law and How We Use It* (Clarendon Press, Oxford 1994) 5 (hereafter Higgins, *Problems and Process*).

[14] T. Schultz, *Transnational Legality: Stateless Law and International Arbitration* (OUP, Oxford 2014) 16–17, where he states: 'Let me repeat, and I offer no apology for the repetition because the argument is important: nothing is intrinsically of a legal nature or not of that nature. As Paul Bohannan put it, "law is a noetic unity: it is a concept not represented by anything except our ideas about it" '.

3. Introduction to Evaluative Framework on Legal Personality

The five main conceptions of international legal personality utilized in this study are those put forward by Portmann in his monograph on legal personality in international law.[15] They include the 'States-only', 'recognition', 'individualistic', 'formal', and 'actor' conceptions of international legal personality. While Portmann's groupings are not exhaustive or conclusive, it is argued that they provide a valuable conceptual framework through which the vast legal scholarship on international legal personality can be viewed. In describing these five conceptions of international legal personality, this chapter takes pains to highlight the features which are most relevant to the analysis of the international legal personality of armed groups. These features include the role of State consent in the acquisition of legal personality, the relevance of the participation of the actor concerned, whether international legal personality is viewed as a graduated or absolute concept, how this conception sees international rights and duties in relation to national legal systems, and the extent to which it relies on sources of law beyond the strict volition of States, e,g. natural law or general principles of law. The chapter also pays attention to the manner in which each theory views the role of the individual and other non-State actors in the international legal system. It makes efforts to point out that there are commonalities between these conceptions of international legal personality. It also emphasizes that these conceptions of international legal personality are in essence merely theories about the way in which the system of law is understood. In this respect, the chapter espouses the view that the conceptions of international legal personality should be seen mainly as analytical tools. Rather than being determinative, they are intellectual constructions or analytical groupings which reflect several common ways of thinking about international legal personality.

At times during the evaluative chapters on belligerency and international humanitarian law, reference is made to the 'constitutive' and 'declaratory' approaches to international legal personality. These terms refer to the two most widely known conceptions of international legal personality which are more widely delineated than Portmann's five conceptions. A constitutive approach to legal personality is largely the same as that which Portmann terms the 'recognition' conception of international legal personality. It holds that the international legal personality of a non-State actor can be conferred or withheld at will by States. Under this conception of international legal personality, recognition is a political act from which a normative framework flows.[16] A declaratory approach to international legal personality finds that personality is acquired through an entity's intercourse in legal relations. It is not therefore a status explicitly conferred by States. In other words,

[15] Portmann, *Legal Personality* (n 1).

[16] See I. Brownlie, *Principles of Public International Law* (7th edn, OUP, Oxford 2008) 87: 'According to the [constitutive view], the political act of recognition is a precondition of the existence of legal rights: in its extreme form this is to say that the very personality of a state depends on the political decision of States.'

an act of recognition is an acknowledgement of an already existing state of 'law and fact'.[17] It will be shown below that the declaratory approach has much in common with the 'individualistic', 'formal', and 'actor' conception of international legal personality identified by Portmann. While discussions of the constitutive versus declaratory approaches to recognition most often take place in relation to the recognition of States, the basic features of the two approaches are also applicable to a discussion of the international legal personality of armed groups. It will be shown in Chapter 4 that this is particularly the case in the context of the law of belligerency. Here, just as in the creation of new States, an explicit recognition of belligerency by States plays a major, although contested, role in an armed group's acquisition of international legal personality.[18]

It has been asserted in literature relating to State recognition that it would oversimplify the legal situation to suggest that the declarative and constitutive theories of legal personality are exclusive of each other, or polar opposites. In that sense, it has been pointed out that is not a matter of simply choosing which theory matches the legal and factual landscape the best. Rather, the analysis of both theories allows the identification of the complex interplay of normative, legal, and political forces at play before a new State is recognized. This observation leads to an important related comment relating to the purpose of the evaluative framework in this book. It is not the chapter's principal purpose to form a conclusion about which single conception of international legal personality triumphs over the others, when analysing the frameworks of belligerency, insurgency, and international humanitarian law. While such a conclusion is of course instructive, the chapter principally uses the five conceptions of legal personality as an analytical tool to inject an objective element into the analysis, so that its conclusions are transparent and less open to be impugned as representing a bias on the part of their author. It also provides an evaluative framework which justifies a more rigorous analysis of certain key issues. The following section describes the five conceptions of international legal personality identified by Portmann. In doing so, it seeks to identify the main components which are relevant to this study on armed groups.

4. States-Only Conception of International Legal Personality

The 'States-only' conception of international legal personality is a true positivist approach to the idea of legal personality which is rarely seen in modern scholarship.[19] Portmann finds this conception of international legal personality to be articulated in writings by scholars such as Henrich Triepel, Lassa Oppenheim, and

[17] Ibid, 86–7: 'According to the declaratory view, the legal effects of recognition are limited, since recognition is a mere declaration or acknowledgment of an existing state of law and fact, legal personality having been conferred previously by operation of law.'

[18] See L. Oppenheim, *International Law, A Treatise* (Longmans 1948) 249 (hereafter Oppenheim, *International Law*), who states that the principles governing recognition of belligerency are exactly the same as those governing the recognition of States and governments.

[19] Under the classic positivist perspective, 'law is regarded as a unified system of rules that, according to most variants, emanate from state will': S. R. Ratner and A. Slaughter, 'Symposium in Method

Dionisio Anzilotti.[20] This approach to international legal personality emanates from a view of international law that understands States to be the highest entity in international law.[21] It finds that only States can be subjects of international law and believes that international law is only binding on States.[22] As a result, those who adhere to what has been called the 'States-only' conception of international legal personality do not consider that international legal personality can exist along a spectrum and nor do they think that non-State actors, such as armed groups, can be subjects of international law. The States-only approach to international legal personality sees international law to emanate exclusively from the will of States and makes a stark differentiation between national law and international law.[23] The fact that the States-only approach distinguishes so acutely between international law and national law impacts on the way that this conception of international personality conceives the role of individuals within the international legal system. More particularly, it means that it sees individuals to be subjects of the domestic legal order, rather than the international system.[24] As a result, the States-only conception of international legal personality holds that international law is never directly binding upon individuals or other non-State actors. Another important feature of the States-only conception of international law is that it rejects natural law elements entirely.[25] Its rejection of natural law can be seen as a direct result of its foundational premise that international law is strictly founded in State volition.

5. Recognition Conception of International Legal Personality

The second conception of international legal personality that Portmann identifies is the 'recognition' conception of international legal personality. This conception of international legal personality is mainly manifested in the writings of Karl Strupp, Arrigo Cavaglieri, and Georg Schwarzenberger.[26] While agreeing with the States-only conception that States are the primary subjects of international law, the 'recognition conception' of international legal personality finds that States are able to bestow international legal personality upon other non-State entities by recognizing them as legal subjects.[27] According to the recognition conception of international law, States are the kingmakers of the international legal order because

in International Law: Appraising the Methods of International Law: A Prospectus for Readers' (1999) 93 American Journal of International Law 291, 304 (hereafter Ratner and Slaughter, 'Symposium in Method').

[20] Portmann, *Legal Personality* (n 1) 41. [21] Ibid, 41, 43.

[22] See Oppenheim, *International Law* (n 18) 99 [63]: 'The conception of International Persons is derived from the conception of the Law of Nations. As this law is the body of rules which the civilised State consider legally binding in their intercourse, every State which belongs to the civilised States, and is, therefore, a member of the Family of Nations, is an International Person. Sovereign States exclusively are International Persons— i.e. subjects of International Law'.

[23] Portmann, *Legal Personality* (n 1) 43 refers to Triepel, who described the international and the national legal order as 'two circles touching each other but never overlapping'.

[24] Ibid, 46. [25] Ibid, 44. [26] Ibid, 79. [27] Ibid.

they can confer or withhold international legal personality at will.[28] The recognition conception of international legal personality is largely encapsulated by a 'constitutive' approach to recognition which holds that entities, particularly States, can be conferred with legal personality through the act of 'recognition' by the international community.[29] Unlike the States-only conception of international legal personality, the recognition conception accepts that international legal personality may exist along a spectrum.

The recognition conception recognizes that non-State actors can be subjects of international law, albeit with a more limited personality than States. But like the States-only conception of international legal personality, it finds that international law emanates exclusively from the will of States and holds that the 'creation and scope' of international law is limited to norms to which States have consented.[30] As a result, the recognition conception of international law also rejects the notion of there being natural law principles which exist outside of treaty law or custom.[31] It also shares the dualist approach of the States-only conception which finds that individuals are largely outside the scope of international law, as their rights and obligations exist at national level and only are represented at international level by the State.[32] Having outlined the main features of the 'recognition' conception of international legal personality, the chapter now turns to the individualistic, formal, and actor conceptions of international legal personality. Because these three conceptions of international legal personality emerged out of similar impulses, a few general words are given on their background before they are examined individually.

6. Background to Individualistic, Formal, and Actor Conceptions of International Legal Personality

The final three conceptions of international legal personality together represent a clear shift away from a positivist approach to international legal personality. This shift in legal thinking was caused largely by changing power dynamics within the global order. It has also been driven by writings on legal theory which have challenged some of the key features of the States-only and recognition conceptions of international legal personality. The forces behind this theoretical challenge include a revised understanding of the role of the individual in the international legal order and a growing appreciation that the traditional doctrine of subjectivity, which saw States as the only subjects of the international legal order, was essentially a human creation. This brought the accompanying consciousness that the legal framework

[28] See H. Lauterpacht, *International Law and Human Rights* (Stevens & Sons, London 1950) 69 (hereafter Lauterpacht, *International Law and Human Rights*), where he refers to the widely accepted view of recognition being the 'gift' of 'existing States'.

[29] M. Dixon, *Textbook on International Law* (OUP, Oxford 2007) 128 (hereafter Dixon, *Textbook on International Law*).

[30] Portmann, *Legal Personality* (n 1) 83. [31] Ibid, 83, 93. [32] Ibid, 92.

of international legal personality, like any other artificial construct, can be changed. Perhaps one of the most famous articulations of this idea is found in the words of Rosalyn Higgins when she stated:

> First of all, international law is not only 'rules'; moreover, its norms are not fixed indefinitely and are thus wholly responsive to the needs of the system. Further, the positivist definition assumes that some specific rule is required 'permitting' the individual to be a 'subject' of international law. Finally, the whole notion of 'subjects' and 'objects' has no credible reality, and, in my view, no functional purpose. We have erected an intellectual prison of our own choosing and then declared it to be an unalterable construct.[33]

Out of a consciousness that the 'rules' on international legal personality are not set in stone came an increased move away from a constitutive approach to a declaratory approach, according to which personality is thought to be acquired through an entity's intercourse in legal relations or the international sphere. These theoretical developments have particularly influenced the development of theories on how non-State actors may acquire international legal personality under international law.

In tracing these developments through the twentieth century, Portmann identifies three distinct theoretical conceptions of international legal personality which have emerged. Portmann labels these three conceptions of international legal personality: (i) the individualistic conception; (ii) the formal conception; and (iii) the actor conception.[34] It is clear from Portmann's analysis that these three conceptions of international legal personality have much in common. This stems from the fact that they were all in part developed in reaction to the States-only and recognition conception of international personality described above. All three approaches give more precedence to the role of the individual in the international legal system, give less weight to the hierarchical superiority of the State, and find that new subjects of international law can emerge without the explicit consent of States. But despite these similarities, Portmann shows that they have a number of major differences. For although all three conceptions of international legal personality give a heightened precedence to the individual, they each understand the role of the individual in the international legal system differently. Moreover, while the formal conception of international legal personality rejects natural law, the individualistic conception relies upon natural law, albeit a particular kind of natural law. Furthermore, all three conceptions take a different view on the role of State consent in the international system and the creation of international law. To illustrate these differences more fully, a brief sketch of the three distinct conceptions of legal personality is presented below.

[33] Higgins, *Problems and Process* (n 13) 49.
[34] See Portmann, *Legal Personality* (n 1) 126–42.

7. Individualistic Conception of International Legal Personality

It will be of little surprise to those familiar with his writings to learn that Portmann identifies Hersch Lauterpacht as being the main proponent of what he calls the individualistic conception of international legal personality.[35] Lauterpacht's views on the notion of international legal personality are particularly articulated in his writings after the Second World War.[36] Portmann explains that the key idea behind the individualistic approach to international legal personality is the idea that the individual has an international legal personality which exists independently from the will of States. Portmann shows how the individualistic conception of international law was formulated as a response to the 'positivist doctrine' of international personality.[37] In particular, it was intended to challenge the classical understanding of the place of individuals in the international legal order and its rejection of natural law principles.[38] In Lauterpacht's conception of the international legal system, the State is a legal vehicle composed of individuals and international law is a tool to protect individuals' interests and well-being.[39] Lauterpacht famously understood the individual as being the ultimate unit of international law.[40] As a result, the individualistic conception of international personality rejects the idea that international law and national law are irreconcilably separate. It not only finds that individuals can participate on the international legal sphere but also finds that individuals and non-State actors can be directly addressed by international law.[41] The individualistic conception's understanding of the individual within the greater system of international law is famously articulated in the Nuremberg judgment which found that not only States, but also individuals should be held responsible for their actions under international law.[42]

Unlike the other approaches to international legal personality, the individualistic conception claims to rely upon natural law principles, albeit defined quite specifically. According to Lauterpacht, natural law principles were principles

[35] Ibid, 126. Portmann also finds support for the individualistic conception of international legal personality in writings by George Scelle, Hugo Krabbe, James Leslie Brierly, Nicolas Politis, Maurice Bourquin, and Alejandro Alvarez.

[36] Ibid, 126. [37] Ibid, 128. [38] Ibid, 131.

[39] See Lauterpacht, *International Law and Human Rights* (n 28) 19, 70: 'The recognition of the individual, by dint of the acknowledgment of his fundamental rights and freedoms, as the ultimate subject of international law, is a challenge to the doctrine which in reserving that quality exclusively to the State tends to a personification of the State as a being distinct from the individuals who compose it, with all that such personification implies … It denies, by cogent implication, that the corporate entity of the State is of a higher order than its component parts'. See also Portmann, *Legal Personality* (n 1) 129–32.

[40] Lauterpacht, *International Law and Human Rights* (n 28) 69. [41] Ibid, 28.

[42] *International Military Tribunal (Judgement and Sentence)* (1947) 41 American Journal of International Law 172, 221: 'Crimes against international law are committed by men, not by abstract entities, and only by punishing individuals who commit such crimes can the provisions of international law be enforced'.

not founded in philosophy or religion but in the principles of law recognized by civilized nations or a 'generalization of the legal experience of mankind'.[43] Portmann explains how it is the individualistic conception's reliance on natural law principles that provides it with a means to break out of the States-only paradigm. Locating a source of law beyond the explicit consent of States enables an understanding that international law is more than State-made law.[44] Moreover, to some extent, the individualistic conception of international legal personality breaks out of the traditional positivist framework by turning the international legal system on its head. By finding power at the bottom of the system rather than at the top, the individualistic conception of international legal personality facilitates a bottom-up approach whereby the international legal personality of individuals, traditionally at the bottom of the system, can be an equal driver of international legal personality. As a force, individuals exist independently from the will of States. This reconfiguration of the international legal system enables a view that non-State actors can acquire international legal personality without the explicit or implied agreement of States. Perhaps most important of all, the individualistic conception of international personality relies on general principles of law to find that individuals are the direct holders of a set of fundamental rights under international law.[45] It also finds that the procedural capacity to assert a right against a given subject of international law is not an essential component of international legal personality.[46]

Another feature of the individualistic conception of international legal personality is its openness to the notion that an entity can acquire legal personality through its intercourse in legal relations with third States. Writing in 1950 immediately after the *Reparations Opinion* was handed down by the International Court of Justice, Lauterpacht stated his view that:

An international public body—such as the United Nations—may possess or acquire international personality *by virtue of facts* other than formal attribution of such capacity. Such a result may be brought about by the fact of that body being entrusted with *or exercising functions compatible with or implying international personality.* (emphasis added)[47]

[43] Portmann, *Legal Personality* (n 1) 131–2. In explaining his understanding that the rights of man exist outside the 'uncontrolled will of the sovereign State', Lauterpacht, *International Law and Human Rights* (n 28) 93, has recourse first to natural law and secondly to 'a body of rules which are voluntarily accepted or imposed by the existence of international society and which govern the conduct of States and are subject to enforcement by external sanction'. He seemed to have in mind in this respect a principle similar to that articulated in Article 53 of the Vienna Convention on the Law of Treaties that certain norms are 'accepted and recognized by the international community of States as a whole as … norm[s] from which no derogation is permitted', i.e. *jus cogens*.

[44] Portmann, *Legal Personality* (n 1) 132.

[45] Ibid, 132. See also (n 43).

[46] Lauterpacht, *International Law and Human Rights* (n 28) 27. See also Higgins, *Problems and Process* (n 13) 52, for her discussion of this issue and in particular her reference to the statement of the Permanent Court of Justice in 1933: 'It is scarcely necessary to point out that the capacity to possess civil rights does not necessarily imply the capacity to exercise those rights oneself'. *Appeal from a Judgment of the Hungaro/Czecoslovak Mixed Arbitral Tribunal (The Peter Pázmány University)* Ser. A/B, No. 61 (15 December 1933) [231].

[47] Lauterpacht, *International Law and Human Rights* (n 28) 20.

Lauterpacht's position demonstrates that a focus on the 'actual' is a central feature of the individualistic conception of international legal personality.[48] As Lauterpacht states elsewhere:

In each particular case the question whether a person or a body is a subject of international law must be answered in a pragmatic manner by reference to actual experience and the reason of the law as distinguished from a preconceived notion as to who can be subject of international law.[49]

This focus on the actual participation of an entity will also be seen to be a feature of the 'actor' conception of international legal personality which is examined later in this chapter. However, unlike the actor conception of international legal personality, the individualistic conception is mainly interested in an entity's '*legal* participation' with third States which involves the application of international law.[50] According to Lauterpacht, examples of such intercourse might include an entity entering into legal relations with third States, asserting jurisdictional or legislative powers, or exercising sovereignty over a territory.[51]

8. Formal Conception of International Legal Personality

Portmann shows that the 'formal' conception of international legal personality has some elements in common with the individualistic conception but also several important differences. He locates the origin of the formal conception of

[48] It is noteworthy that a close reading of the *Advisory Opinion on Reparations* (n 5) demonstrates that it is more properly seen to be a manifestation of the formal or recognition conception of international legal personality. For although it is clear that the ICJ saw the United Nation's rights and functions as an important sign of its international legal personality, it did not find its participation on the international sphere to be a *source* of its international legal personality. It is noteworthy that the ICJ took pains to link the United Nation's actual rights and functions with the purposes and functions specified or implied in its constituent documents. See for example 179–81. Ultimately, the Court's view that the United Nations had legal personality seemed to originate from the fact that the powers exercised by the United Nations were 'implied' into its constitution. In other words, where States bestow a particular entity with international legal personality to fulfil a particular purpose, States concurrently bestow that entity with all the powers and capacities required to fulfil that purpose. This is similar to the view which was articulated in the ICJ's *Advisory Opinion on the Legality of the Use by a State of Nuclear Weapons in Armed Conflict* [1996] ICJ Reports 66 (8 July 1996) [79], where the court stated: 'The powers conferred on international organizations are normally the subject of an express statement in their constituent instruments. Nevertheless, the necessities of international life may point to the need for organizations, in order to achieve their objectives, to possess subsidiary powers which are not expressly provided for in the basis instruments which govern their activities. It is generally accepted that international organizations can exercise such powers, known as "implied powers"'. See also Dixon, *Textbook on International Law* (n 29) 112, for a discussion of this case 'clearly [explaining] the concept of derived personality'. The implied powers doctrine has been recognized to combine aspects of the formal conception of international legal personality and the recognition conception of international legal personality.

[49] Lauterpacht, *International Law and Human Rights* (n 28) 12.

[50] Ibid, 20–1, where Lauterpacht analyses the functions that the United Nations is exercising which are 'compatible with or imply' international legal personality.

[51] Ibid, 12.

international legal personality mainly in the writings of Hans Kelsen in his pure theory of law.[52] This was a major work of legal theory published in Germany in 1934 which separated the science of law from sociology, politics, and metaphysics. According to Kelsen's theoretical framework, the international legal system is 'completely open' and any entity can be a subject of international law.[53] Kelsen states that international legal personality arises whenever international legal norms, whether rights, duties, or capacities, are addressed to particular entities. As a result, international legal personality is an '*a posteriori* concept'.[54] By that it is meant that international legal personality is not the 'precondition for holding international obligations or authorizations, but is the consequence of possessing them'.[55] In a sense, like the individualistic conception of international legal personality, the formal conception turns the States-only conception of international legal personality on its head, but in a different way.[56] Rather than starting with the subject of international law and then evaluating the norm, the formal conception of international legal personality starts with the norm. Consequently, it contains no presumption that certain entities, i.e. States, should be the primary subjects of international law.[57] Like Lauterpacht, Kelsen was a strong believer that individuals are a fundamentally important actor in the international legal system. Recognizing that all rights and obligations in the international legal system have the behaviour of human beings as their content, he believed that individuals were the primary addressee of all norms.[58] But Kelsen based his theoretical framework less on the quality of being 'human' per se than Lauterpacht and made less reference to the principle of humanity. To Kelsen, the fact that individuals were the subject of rights and obligations was a simple reflection of the fact that 'human behaviour is the content of legal obligations and legal rights'.[59] In other words, human beings were only relevant to the legal system because of the sum of normative rights and obligations which they represented. In *The Pure Theory of Law,* Kelsen states: '[t]he physical or juristic person who "has" obligations and rights as their holder, *is* these obligations and rights—a complex of legal obligations and rights whose totality is expressed figuratively in the concept of "person"'.[60]

As a result, under the 'formal conception' of international legal personality expounded by Kelsen, it is natural that international law can be directly binding upon individuals and other non-State actors. Indeed, according to Kelsen, States and other corporations are only bound by international law when the rights and obligations which are imposed upon human beings are attributed to the juristic person of the State or corporation.[61] Moreover, because the 'formal conception'

[52] Portmann, *Legal Personality* (n 1) 172. [53] Ibid, 173. [54] Ibid, 173.

[55] Ibid, 173.

[56] J. Griffiths. 'What is Legal Pluralism?' (1986) 24 Journal of Legal Pluralism 1, 3 (hereafter Griffiths, 'What is Legal Pluralism'). Here Griffiths points out that while Austinian positivism can be seen to be a pyramid with the sovereign at the top, the Kelsenian view of international law can be seen to be like an inverted pyramid with the grundnorm at the bottom.

[57] Portmann, *Legal Personality* (n 1) 172.

[58] H. Kelsen, *Pure Theory of Law* (University of California Press 1967) 179, 188.

[59] Ibid, 173. [60] Ibid. [61] Ibid, 176; Portmann, *Legal Personality* (n 1) 175.

of international legal personality takes the norm as the starting point of legal personality, it attributes no further normative consequences to international legal personality.[62] For example, unlike Lauterpacht, the formal conception of international law finds no fundamental rights and obligations to flow from the acquisition of legal personality.[63] This amounts to a very strict reading of the notion that legal personality is attained *a posteriori*. According to the 'formal conception' of international legal personality, international legal personality is simply a confirmation of an already existing factual situation. From this perspective, it makes sense that international legal personality is not perceived to be a quality which can be conferred or recognized by States. Moreover, the fact that an entity has international legal personality does not give it the immediate right to take part in norm creation.[64] According to Kelsen, an entity will only be able to take part in the creation of international law if there is a 'hierarchically higher norm' giving it the authority to do so, e.g. a customary international law rule confirming States' ability to enter into binding treaty obligations.[65] Importantly, Kelsen did not see the consent of States to be necessary for the making of customary international law because he conceived custom to be a law which arose from 'general use among competent organs and as such generally pertinent in international relations'.[66] As a result, the 'formal conception' of international legal personality finds that customary international law applies irrespective of whether its subjects took part in its creation. Another feature of note is that unlike the individualistic conception of international legal personality, the formal conception of international legal personality also rejects the notion that natural law can play any part in the international legal system.[67]

9. Actor Conception of International Legal Personality

The fifth and final conception of international legal personality is the 'actor conception'. It is the view of international legal personality associated with the New Haven School of International Law and the policy-orientated jurisprudence established by Harold Lasswell and Myres McDougal in the mid-1940s.[68] This school of legal thinking famously saw the international legal system as a 'decision making process'.[69] It eschewed the notion of 'subjects of international law', and focused on the notion of participants instead.[70] It did this for the reasons so famously articulated by Higgins above, although it took the notion of 'participant' much

62 Portmann, *Legal Personality* (n 1) 174, 176. 63 Ibid, 176. 64 Ibid, 176.
65 Ibid. 66 Ibid, 177. 67 Ibid, 192. 68 Ibid, 208.
69 See M. S. McDougal, H. D. Lasswell, and W. M. Reisman, 'The World Constitutive Process of Authoritative Decision' in R. A. Falk and C. E. Black (eds), *The Future of the International Legal Order, Volume I, Trends and Patterns* (Princeton University Press, Princeton 1969) 77 (hereafter McDougal, Lasswell, and Reisman, 'World Constitutive Process').
70 Ibid, 81: 'By a participant in constitutive process, as distinguished from the more general effective power process, we mean an individual or an entity which has at least minimum access to the process of authority in the sense that it can make claims or be subjected to claims'.

further than Higgins.[71] Proponents of the actor school felt that the distinction between subjects and objects, that since Roman times had been the lens through which international legal personality had been analysed, failed to do justice to the special position of individuals. According to many scholars, individuals were not only the base units from which States are made up but also the entities at the heart of the international legal order.[72] Recognizing the importance of individuals, it was felt to be somewhat incongruous to group them together with a miscellany of other mainly inanimate entities such as ships, boundaries, rivers, and territories.[73] Finding the subject–object dichotomy to be 'fallacious', O'Connell (a writer sometimes also associated with the 'formal conception of international legal personality') elaborated:

> There is something offensive to reason in the doctrine that international law addresses itself only to States, leaving the human beings who compose them, and who in reality make the decisions that create and implement and violate the law, to fulfil no more significant role in the legal process than stocks and shares and ships.[74]

Proponents of the New Haven School of International Law also found that the distinction between subjects and objects reinforced the positivist distinction between rules and human actions.

Under the actor school put forward by McDougal and Lasswell, there were only 'participants' within the international legal system. This re-classification rendered the traditional subject–object dichotomy to be no longer relevant as participants could be individuals, States, international organizations, multinational corporations, or private non-governmental groups.[75] The actor conception of international legal personality rejected the positivist focus on rules, and chose to focus its attention instead on what participants in the legal system said and did.[76] International law was understood to be an 'ongoing process of authoritative and controlling decision'.[77] As a result, in contrast to the 'formal' conception of international legal personality which saw law to be exclusively normative, the 'actor' conception of international legal personality was based more on what was happening in the real

[71] Higgins, *Problems and Process* (n 13) 50: 'I believe that there is room for another view: that it is not particularly helpful, either intellectually or operationally, to rely on the subject–object dichotomy which runs through so much of the writings. It is more helpful, and closer to a perceived reality, to return to the view of international law as a particular decision-making process … Now in this model, there are no "subjects" and "objects", but only *participants*. Individuals *are* participants, along with states, international organizations (such as the United Nations, or the International Monetary Fund (IMF) or the ILO), multinational corporations, and indeed private non-governmental groups.' While Higgins clearly found the notion of 'participant' at the heart of the actor school persuasive, it is argued that her writings actually reflect a stronger leaning towards the ideas expressed by Lauterpacht who took a more legal definition of the concept of 'intercourse'.

[72] O'Connell, *International Law* (n 7) 92. See also Lauterpacht, *International Law and Human Rights* (n 28) 69: 'In relation to both rights and duties, the individual is the final subject of all law'.

[73] O'Connell, *International Law* (n 7) 92.

[74] Ibid, 92.

[75] The major but explicitly non-exhaustive classes of participants enumerated by McDougal, Lasswell, and Reisman, 'World Constitutive Process' (n 69) 83–7, consist of territorial units, international governmental organs, political parties, pressure groups, and private associations.

[76] Ratner and Slaughter, 'Symposium in Method' (n 19) 320.

[77] Ibid, 319.

world. By that it is meant that authors of the New Haven School of International Law set out to engage in an 'empirical investigation' to find out which actors were involved in decision-making processes.[78] They enquired into the actors' involvement in international affairs and the effectiveness of their functions. An appraisal of an actor's participation at the international level was a matter of objective fact rather than dependent on the view or judgment of States. Authors associated with the New Haven School recognized that there was often no dependable relationship between power structures *de jure* and power structures *de facto*. As a result, they adopted a 'functional' analysis of the decision process and its participants.[79] Accordingly, the actor conception of international legal personality advocated a rapprochement between the actual and the normative.[80] Fundamentally, it was a descriptive approach to international law. It has been commented above that to a degree, a similar rapprochement between the normative and the actual can be seen in the individualistic conception of international legal personality, which has been seen to have a similar focus on 'participation'. But it is clear that the New Haven School of International Law takes a much wider definition of 'participation' than the individualistic conception of international legal personality, which retains its normative focus, by concentrating primarily on *legal* intercourse.[81]

An important extension to the New Haven School of International Law is the form of legal pluralism which has been referred by Berman as the 'new' New Haven School of International Law.[82] A legal pluralist approach to international legal personality is not referred to by Portmann but is particularly relevant to any study of non-State actors. Berman shows the New Haven School's shift from a State-based viewpoint to an empirical ground-level analysis which takes into account the decision making of multiple non-State actors 'open[ed] the door for a pluralist approach' to international law.[83] He explains how legal pluralists drew on the works of McDougal and Lasswell, but also others such as Cover, to argue that law is made up of 'all collective behaviour entailing systematic understandings of

[78] See Nijman, *International Legal Personality* (n 8) 326–7.

[79] McDougal, Lasswell, and Reisman, 'World Constitutive Process' (n 69) 79.

[80] See Higgins, *Problems and Process* (n 13) 10: 'The further one moves away from positivism and rules, the less important becomes the distinction between *lex lata* and *lex ferenda*—the law as it is and the law as it might be. If law as rules requires the application of outdated and inappropriate norms, then law as process encourages interpretation and choice that is more compatible with values we seek to promote and objectives we seek to achieve. But it is only to a rule-based lawyer that this is to be classified as 'law as it ought to be', standing in false dichotomy, a cleavage which we can ourselves can banish from existence'.

[81] This is clear from Lauterpacht's analysis of the functions that the United Nations is exercising which are 'compatible with or imply' international legal personality. Here, he provides examples of intercourse which might include an entity having legal personality which include an entity entering into legal relations with third States, asserting jurisdictional or legislative powers or exercising sovereignty over a territory. These are all inherently legal forms of 'participation'. See Lauterpacht, *International Law and Human Rights* (n 28) 18, 20–1, and compare with the wider conception of participation in McDougal, Lasswell, and Reisman, 'World Constitutive Process' (n 69) 74–7.

[82] P. S. Berman. 'A Pluralist Approach to International Law' (2007) 32 Yale Journal of International Law 301, 309 (hereafter Berman, 'A Pluralist Approach').

[83] Ibid, 306.

our commitments to future worlds'.[84] In deconstructing law and finding it to be present at every level of social interaction, legal pluralists reconceived international law as being constituted by plural voices, which do not exclusively emanate from the State.[85] Like the policy orientation jurisprudence of Lasswell and McDougal, legal pluralism advocates a descriptive rather than prescriptive theory of law. In doing so, it takes as its starting point the fact that social action takes place in 'multiple, overlapping, semi-autonomous social fields'.[86] It aims to see what effect this will have on the legal framework and finds normative heterogeneity to be the result.[87] As a result of this approach, international lawyers of the pluralist school find that it is less important to consider what is 'law' or 'not law'. The reason for this is that the consequence of a norm being law is less significant than the force of the norm.[88] A determination of the force of a norm requires an empirical inquiry into 'which statements of authority tend to be *treated* as binding in actual practice and by whom'.[89] From this perspective, it is seen there is much less need to consider whether a particular non-State entity is a subject of international law or whether it has international legal personality at all. More relevant is whether a particular entity is considered to be bound by a particular norm, irrespective of whether it is binding or non-binding in a formal sense.

10. Commonalities and Differences between the Conceptions of International Legal Personality

It will be clear from the above descriptions that a number of features are common to the various conceptions of international personality described above. Yet, there are also some important differences. For, while the proponents of different conceptions of international legal personality may all agree on the *relevance* of a certain feature of the factual situation, their understanding of the *legal significance* of the event of recognition may be different. For example, the descriptions above demonstrate that proponents of the four latter conceptions of international legal personality would all be likely to agree that an armed group 'recognized' by States as a belligerent has international legal personality. But, they would differ on *when* that armed group's international legal personality is thought to crystallize. Under

[84] R. M. Cover, 'The Folktales of Justice: Tales of Jurisdiction' (1985) 14 Capital University Law Review 179, 181 (hereafter Cover, 'Folktales of Justice'), cited by Berman, 'A Pluralist Approach' (n 82) 307.

[85] Cover, 'Folktales of Justice' (n 84) 181–2: 'The upshot of such a claim, of course, is to deny to the nation state any special status for the collective behavior of its officials or for their systematic understandings of some special set of "governing" norms. The status of such "official" behavior and "official" norms is not denied the dignity of "law." But it must share the dignity with thousands of other social understandings. In each case the question of what is law and for whom is a question of fact about what certain communities believe and with what commitments to those beliefs'.

[86] Griffiths, 'What is Legal Pluralism?' (n 56) 3, 38. See also Berman, 'A Pluralist Approach' (n 82) 327.

[87] Griffiths, 'What is Legal Pluralism?' (n 56).

[88] Berman, 'A Pluralist Approach' (n 82) 323.

[89] Ibid.

the 'recognition' conception of international legal personality, the armed group's international legal personality is understood to flow from the act of recognition and is therefore subsequent to the act of recognition by States. Under the 'formal conception' of international personality, the triggering factor for an entity to acquire international legal personality is the application of a normative framework to the entity. As a result, in practical terms the moment at which an entity becomes the subject of international norms may coincide with an act of recognition. Under the individualistic conception of international legal personality, an act of recognition by States is understood to confirm an already existing legal state. Under the 'actor' conception of international law, an entity which is 'recognized' by States will inevitably already have all the qualifying features of a subject of international law. It will be a participant in the international legal order with functional effectiveness and actual power.

Likewise, four out of the five conceptions of international legal personality agree that participation is a relevant factor in considering an entity's legal personality. But each school of thought understands the relevance and consequences of that participation differently. For example, the recognition conception of international legal personality sees armed groups' intercourse with third States to be a factor that might convince a parent State or a third State to recognize an armed group as a subject of international law, i.e. a belligerent. In other words, it acknowledges that international legal personality may be a consequence of an entity's participation on the international stage, but does not find its participation to be legally determinative in that respect. The opposite is true of the individualistic and actor conceptions of international legal personality. Both these conceptions of international legal personality find an entity's participation on the international stage to be a sign that it has already achieved a degree of international legal personality. However, in observing that commonality, it is important to note that their approach to what constitutes of 'participation' is different. Within the actor conception of international legal personality, there is no requirement that an entity's participation be specifically legal. Instead, it is simply required that an entity is involved in 'authoritative' decisions which contribute to the 'world public order'.[90] In contrast, under the individualistic conception of international law, there seems to be a requirement that the entity participates in a legal manner with third States. This might include the assumption or exercise of legal rights and duties governed by international law or the exercise of jurisdiction.[91] Finally, it has been seen that participation is relevant under the formal conception of international legal personality, but only to the extent that it is evidence of the application of legal norms which in turn are the source of international legal personality.

Another common feature of the recognition, formal, individualistic, and actor conceptions of international legal personality is that they all recognize that international legal personality operates along a sliding scale. The fact that international

[90] Ibid, 306; McDougal, Lasswell, and Reisman, 'World Constitutive Process' (n 69) 81.
[91] Lauterpacht, *International Law and Human Rights* (n 28) 18, 20–1.

legal personality is understood to be a graduated concept was already recognized by the ICJ in its *Reparations Opinion* as early as 1949.[92] In finding the United Nations to possess international personality with regard to its members, the Court famously stated:

> The subjects of law in any legal system are not necessarily identical in their nature or in the extent of their rights, and their nature depends upon the needs of their community.[93]

In a later passage, the Court continued:

> Accordingly, the Court has come to the conclusion that the Organization is an international person. That is not the same thing as saying that it is a State, which it certainly is not, or that its legal personality and rights and duties are the same as those of a State.[94]

With this statement, the Court recognized that entities other than States can be subjects of international law, without necessarily having the same objective characteristics of States and without having the same legal capacities. It also recognizes that some entities may have a more extensive legal personality than others, as a result of being bound by more legal norms or more far-reaching legal norms.

[92] d'Aspremont, 'Inclusive Law Making' (n 3) 433, argues that he is unconvinced by the notion that international legal personality can be graduated, elaborating: 'However, whilst legal personality cannot be subjected to a scale, there surely is room for variations in the *capacities that accompany such a personality*' (emphasis added).

[93] *Advisory Opinion on Reparations* (n 5) 178.

[94] Ibid, 179.

4

The Law on Belligerency and Insurgency, and International Legal Personality

1. Introduction

Because there are no recent examples of the law of belligerency having been applied since the drafting of the Geneva Conventions in 1949, it is often assumed to be irrelevant to the modern framework of international law.[1] Yet this chapter shows that the law on belligerency, and its counterpart the law of insurgency, holds vital information that allows us to better understand how armed groups may acquire legal personality under human rights law. By comparing the legal frameworks of belligerency and insurgency, the chapter demonstrates that in the late nineteenth century and early twentieth century, there was already a view that armed groups could acquire international legal personality in a variety of ways that did not involve formal State consent, including through control of territory or persons. The chapter also shows that the parameters of the legal framework of belligerency were much wider than are often portrayed. The legal obligations that an armed group incurred in belligerency situations related not only to its warlike operations but also related to the protection of people and assets in the territory under its control.

The general methodology behind this chapter, which is common to Chapters 4 and 5, is set out in more detail in Chapter 3. The chapter begins by providing a definition of the term 'belligerency'. It then proceeds by describing the different circumstances in which a belligerency could arise. It describes what belligerencies would consist of in terms of legal obligations for the armed group. The chapter then proceeds by analysing what the legal framework can tell us about the legal personality of armed groups. It does this by comparing the legal frameworks of belligerency to the evaluative framework of legal personality set out in Chapter 3. The second half of the chapter also considers how the framework of belligerency

[1] Y. M. Lootsteen, 'The Concept of Belligerency in International Law' (2000) 166 Military Law Review 109, 111 (hereafter Lootsteen, 'Concept of Belligerency'); A. Clapham, *Human Rights Obligations of Non-State Actors* (OUP, Oxford 2006) 492 (hereafter Clapham, *Non-State Actors*). However, note S. Sivakumaran, *The Law of Non-International Armed Conflict* (OUP, Oxford 2014) 20 (hereafter Sivakumaran, *Non-International Armed Conflict)*, who finds there to be nothing to prevent a State from recognizing a situation as one of belligerency in the future.

compares with the framework of insurgency. It demonstrates that this comparison is helpful in pinpointing more clearly the circumstances in which armed groups could acquire obligations under international law.

2. Law on Belligerency

2.1 Definition of belligerency

The term belligerency is a legal term used describe a civil war of a high degree of intensity, in which the armed group fighting the incumbent State has been recognized as a 'belligerent'. The conditions of fact which were deemed to justify a recognition of belligerency were generally thought to include: (i) the existence of a civil war accompanied by a state of general hostilities; (ii) the occupation and a measure of orderly administration of a substantial part of national territory by the insurgents;[2] (iii) the observance of the rules of warfare by insurgent forces acting under responsible authority; and (iv) the practical necessity for third States to define their attitude to the civil war.[3] The requirement that third States' interests be engaged explains why belligerencies arose most commonly in maritime wars. In circumstances where hostilities between an armed group and a parent State took place at sea, it was almost inevitable that the shipping and trade of third States would be adversely affected.[4] Other circumstances which were considered relevant to whether or not a belligerency existed included the length of the contest between the parties, the number, order and discipline of the rebel forces, their subordination to a *de facto* existing government, the group's ability to maintain international relations with foreign States, and the acts of the parent State towards the rebels and foreign States.[5] Historical writings and case law shows that a belligerency could come about in two different ways. It could either come about as a result of an explicit recognition of belligerency by the parent State or it could

[2] For details of what this 'orderly administration' might look like, it is helpful to see G. Grafton Wilson, 'Insurgency and International Maritime Law' (1907) 1 American Journal of International Law 46, 48 (hereafter Wilson, 'Insurgency and International Maritime Law') 57–8, citing US President Grant's Message of 7 December 1875 which explains the reasons that the US did not recognize the belligerent status of the Cuban people fighting Spain. The President refers to: 'The existence of such a substantial political organization, real, palpable, and manifest to the world, having the forms and capable of the ordinary functions of government towards its own people and to other states, with courts for the administration of justice, with local habitation, possessing such organization of force, such material, such occupation of territory, as to take the contest out of the category of a mere rebellious insurrection or occasional skirmishes and place it on the terrible footing of war, to which a recognition of belligerency would aim to elevate it to.'

[3] For the definition in full, see L. Oppenheim, *International Law, A Treatise* (Longmans, Harlow 1948) 249 (hereafter Oppenheim, *International Law*).

[4] Sivakumaran, *Non-International Armed Conflict* (n 1) 13.

[5] A. D. McNair, *International Law Opinions* (CUP, Cambridge 1956) 144–5 (hereafter McNair, *International Law Opinions*), citing a Report by British Law Officers Karslake, Selwyn, and Phillimore dated 14 August 1867.

come about by recognition by a third State.[6] Sometimes the recognition of the parent State or third State could be inferred from the circumstances.[7] It will be shown below that the normative scope of the legal framework was dependent in part on how the belligerency came about. When a parent State recognized a belligerency a wider set of rights and obligations were conferred on the armed group than when a third State recognized a belligerency. Because the legal framework of 'belligerency' has been so long out of use and to a large part replaced by international humanitarian law, it will generally be referred to in this chapter in the past tense.

2.2 Normative scope of belligerencies recognized by parent State

When a parent State recognized an armed group as having belligerent status, it was thought to usher in a 'new legal situation' which resulted at a minimum in the full scope of the law of armed conflict becoming applicable between the two parties to the non-international armed conflict.[8] This meant that the entire *jus in bello* traditionally associated with international armed conflict would apply to both the State and the rebels.[9] As a result, the rebels would be eligible to prisoner of war status and belligerent immunity if they were captured.[10] It would also mean that the other rights and obligations which are traditionally associated with the law of neutrality and *jus ad bellum* would apply to the conflict. It entitled the armed group to search and visit ships which it suspected of carrying contraband to the enemy. It also allowed an armed group to issue letters of marque to privateers, enforce a blockade of enemy ports, and administer prize courts.[11] It is seen therefore that recognition of a belligerency on the part of the parent State not only affected the armed group's relations with the parent State, but also affected both parties' relations with third States. In effect, the recognition of belligerency by a parent State

[6] See also L. Moir, *The Law of Internal Armed Conflict* (CUP, Cambridge 2002) 7–10 (hereafter Moir, *Internal Armed Conflict).*

[7] The imposition of a blockade by a parent State was likely to be conceived by a third State as necessitating the recognition of belligerency. As such, in effect, it was considered by third States to amount to an implicit declaration of belligerency by the parent State. Likewise, a declaration of neutrality by a third State was thought to amount to an implicit recognition of belligerency. See Oppenheim, *International Law* (n 3) 250. See also the Report dated 14 August 1867 from Law Officers Karslake, Selwyn, and Phillimore, in which they advise the British government that a declaration of neutrality might operate as 'a public recognition of the insurgents as belligerents', cited by McNair in McNair, *International Law Opinions* (n 5) 145. However, it is noteworthy that the imposition of a blockade by a group of insurgents would not force a third State or parent State to recognize a belligerency: see Oppenheim, *International Law* (n 3) 249; J. W. Garner, 'Questions of International Law in the Spanish Civil War' (1937) 31 American Journal of International Law 66, 73 (hereafter Garner, 'International Law in the Spanish Civil War').

[8] ICRC, *Commentary on the Additional Protocols of 8 June 1977 to the Geneva Conventions of 12 December 1949* (Commentary to Additional Protocols) (Martinus Nijhoff, Geneva 1987) 1321 [4345] (hereafter ICRC, *Commentary to Additional Protocols*).

[9] Moir, *Internal Armed Conflict* (n 6) 10.

[10] Lootsteen, 'Concept of Belligerency' (n 1) 110.

[11] McNair, *International Law Opinions* (n 5) 139.

put the armed group's warlike operations on the same level as a belligerent in an international armed conflict between two States.[12]

It was because the recognition of belligerency by a parent state conferred such wide-ranging legal rights on an armed group that parent States were generally reluctant to recognize an armed group as a belligerent. Their act of recognition would also have far-reaching non-legal consequences. For a start, it would confer the armed group with a certain level of quasi-political recognition. This would make it easier for the armed group to obtain loans abroad and make it easier for it to have its flag acknowledged by third States.[13] Such developments might allow an armed group to raise finance more easily with the consequent risk that its military capabilities might increase more quickly afterwards. Yet, in some circumstances, it might be beneficial for a parent State to recognize an armed group as a belligerent. This was particularly the case in circumstances where a parent State desired to impose a blockade on the armed group's ports or wished to exercise powers of stop, search, and capture against foreign merchant vessels.[14] After a recognition of belligerency, these measures would be possible for both parties to the conflict. A parent State might also be attracted to the fact that after the recognition of belligerency, it would cease to be responsible to third States for what happened in areas of the country under the armed group's control. Henceforth, the armed group would be responsible for its own wrongful acts. For example, it would be directly responsible to a third State for any failure to protect its nationals and assets.[15]

2.3 Normative scope of belligerencies recognized by third States

The effect of recognition of a belligerency by a third State was more limited than the recognition by a parent State.[16] Unlike the effect of recognition by a parent State which affected the insurgent group's relations with all States, recognition by a third State mainly affected its bilateral relations with that armed group. Yet the recognition of belligerency by a third State would undoubtedly affect the parent State to a certain extent. For a start, it triggered the application of the law of neutrality which, by its nature, affects all parties to the conflict, including the parent State.[17]

12 ICRC, *Commentary to Additional Protocols* (n 8) 1321 [4343]. See also Oppenheim, *International Law* (n 3) 248: 'International Law recognizes the status of war and its effects as regards rights and duties between the belligerents on the one hand, and between the belligerents and neutral States on the other'.

13 H. Wheaton, *Elements of International Law* (Stevens & Sons, London 1904) 42 (hereafter Wheaton, *Elements of International Law*). See also F. Snow, *Cases and Opinions on International Law with Notes and a Syllabus* (Boston Book Company, Boston 1893), citing Opinion of Dana, 25–6 (hereafter Snow, *Cases and Opinions*).

14 McNair, *International Law Opinions* (n 5) 138.

15 W. E. Hall, *International Law* (Clarendon Press, Oxford 1880) 26 (hereafter Hall, *International Law*); Wheaton, *Elements of International Law* (n 13) 42–3.

16 See ILC, Yearbook of the International Law Commission 1967 (8 May–14 July 1967) UN Doc A/CN.4/SER.A/1967, 20 [25]; ICRC, *Commentary to Additional Protocols* (n 8) 1321 [4346].

17 Oppenheim, *International Law* (n 3) 653 defines neutrality as: 'The attitude of impartiality adopted by third States towards belligerents and recognised by belligerents, such attitude creating rights and duties between the impartial States and the belligerents.' For the significance of this see

Accordingly, the parent State would be forced to treat the third State as a neutral, unless the good faith of the third State could be impugned.[18] The parent State would not be permitted to commit war-like acts against the third State's territory. It would also be duty-bound not to interfere with the third State's intercourse with the belligerent armed group, which would be legitimate under international law.[19] Recognition of belligerency by a third State also had the formal effect of releasing the parent State from any responsibility it may have previously had to that third State for acts done by the armed group in territory under its control.[20] It also released the parent State from any responsibility for a failure to prevent those acts by the armed group. While it will be shown later in this chapter that third States sometimes held armed groups responsible in this way even before a belligerency was declared (i.e. in the insurgency framework) this formal consequence might have been an important incentive for a third State to recognize a belligerency. In some situations it made more sense for a third State to enter into correspondence with an armed group, in its efforts to secure meaningful security for its citizens in locations where the *de jure* government was no longer in *de facto* control.[21]

In general, a parent State was able domestically to disregard a recognition of belligerency by third States and continue to treat the insurgent fighters as criminals.[22] A recognition of a belligerency by a third State did not force the parent State to confer rebel fighters with prisoner of war status. Likewise, if a third State recognized the flag of the rebels and ceased to treat its ships as piratical, the parent State was generally not obliged to do the same. The only situation when it was sometimes argued that a parent State was compelled to confer recognition

Y. Dinstein, 'The Laws of Neutrality' (1984) 14 Israel Yearbook on Human Rights 80: 'The laws of neutrality are based on two fundamental rationales which are closely interlinked: (a) the desire to guarantee to the neutral State that it will sustain minimal injury as a result of the war; (b) the desire to guarantee to the belligerents that the neutral State will be neutral not only in name but also in fact – that is to say, that it will not aid and abet one of the belligerents against its adversary.'

[18] Hall, *International Law* (n 15) 26. Likewise, in instances where a third State accorded belligerent rights to the parent State, it was also obliged to recognize the insurgent group as belligerents. See McNair, *International Law Opinions* (n 5) 142. It was important that the third State could justify its decision to recognize a belligerency with reference to a need to protect its citizens or assets and the objective size and scale of the conflict. Hall, *International Law* (n 15) 28.

[19] Neutrality involves a duty to abstain from assisting either belligerent either actively or passively, but does not involve a duty to break off all intercourse with belligerents. See Oppenheim, *International Law* (n 3) 659.

[20] Hall, *International Law* (n 15) 26.

[21] In this respect see the note of 26 November 1861 from the British Secretary of State for Foreign Affairs, Earl Russell, to United States Ambassador Adams, referring to complaints by the United States concerning the relations Great Britain maintained with the Confederate insurgents against the Federal government. Earl Russell justified the need for these relations, pointing out *inter alia* that: 'Her Majesty's Government hold it to be an undoubted principle of international law, that when the persons or the property of the subjects or citizens of a state are injured by a de facto government, the state so aggrieved has a right to claim from the de facto government redress and reparation.' It is noteworthy that at the time of the note, the British government had not recognized the Confederate government as a *de facto* government. In this respect the Confederate government was an 'unrecognized *de facto* government' only. See McNair, *International Law Opinions* (n 5) 147. This will also be illustrated in the section below relating to insurgency. See for example n 57.

[22] Oppenheim, *International Law* (n 3) 251.

on the rebels was where the intensity of the uprising against the government had reached such a scale that independent statehood was anticipated and the application of the parent State's own criminal law could no longer be considered the only 'legally relevant element' in the situation.[23] Likewise, scholars have argued that in circumstances where a considerable proportion of the population had taken up arms against the government, it would be 'inhuman' for the parent State to continue to treat these subjects under its criminal law.[24] In such circumstances, it has also been suggested that the parent State might have been in danger of facing 'justifiable retaliation' from third States if it persisted in treating the insurgents as ordinary criminals.[25] Similarly a minority of scholars have argued that a parent State was obliged to recognize a belligerency, in instances where the conditions of a belligerency were met.[26]

2.4 Summary of obligations imposed on an armed group in a belligerency recognized by third State or parent State

It is clear from the descriptions above that the main legal obligations which were imposed on an armed group in a belligerency related to its military operations against its parent State. Certainly, these are the kind of obligations which are most often referred to when talking about belligerencies. They related to blockades, stop and search at sea, the administration of prize courts, and the conduct of hostilities. But the paragraphs above also show that a belligerent armed group could also be held bound to obligations that did not immediately relate to its role as a party to the conflict. For example, after a declaration of belligerency by a parent State or third State, the parent State was discharged of its obligations with regard to the protection of foreign nationals or assets in areas under its control.[27] This reflects the important fact that after being recognized as a belligerent, the armed group became responsible for keeping foreign nationals and assets unharmed in the territory under its control. Evidence of this view in practice is seen in an opinion written in 1863 by the Law Officers of the Government of the United Kingdom during the American Civil War. Here, the British Law Officers expressed their concern about a British citizen who had been abducted from the Bahamas and enslaved in the Southern States by a private citizen. The Law Officers stated their

[23] See ibid, 253. See also E. Vattel, *The Law of Nations* (6th edn, T. & J. W. Johnson 1844) Book III Of War, 421–4 (hereafter Vattel, *Law of Nations*).

[24] Hall, *International Law* (n 15) 27–8; Wheaton, *Elements of International Law* (n 13) 42.

[25] See Oppenheim, *International Law* (n 3) 252–3, and Hall, *International Law* (n 15) 28, who takes a similar view to Oppenheim but contests whether or not this reflects a principle of international law or flows from 'the moral duty of human conduct'.

[26] See Oppenheim, *International Law* (n 3) 250; (n 22); (n 3). Oppenheim acknowledges that this is a minority view.

[27] See Hall, *International Law* (n 15) 26. See e.g. also Article 6 of the Draft Convention on the Responsibility of States for injuries caused in their territory to the person or property of aliens, prepared by the German International Law Association in 1930, cited in ILC, Yearbook of the International Law Commission 1969 (2 June–8 August 1969) Vol II, UN Doc A/CN.4/SER. A/1969/Add.1, 150, 153.

view that the Confederate government was 'bound' to exercise its criminal jurisdiction over the kidnapper, if he was found in the area of the Southern government's *de facto* authority.[28] The opinion provides evidence of the fact that the British government considered the Confederacy to be bound by the due diligence obligations which under normal circumstances would have been owed to foreign nationals and assets, as a matter of customary international law.[29]

There is also evidence that third States considered belligerent armed groups to be bound by the treaty obligations binding on the parent State before the conflict began.[30] A report by British Law Officers dated 1864 shows law officers advising the British government that it could consider the San Domingo belligerents bound to the terms of a treaty which had been signed by the parent State, Spain, before the armed conflict began.[31] In the case in hand, the treaty obligations in question related to warlike activities but there is no suggestion that the principle is restricted to these kinds of activities. There is also evidence that belligerent armed groups would sometimes be held bound by obligations contained in bilateral agreements brokered with third States on practical issues that arose out of their control of territory. For example, when giving examples of 'treaties made by the insurgent community', McNair highlights the fact that during the American Civil War there was much intercourse between the British government and the Confederate government which resulted in agreements being brokered between them. The main example McNair gives of such intercourse was the presence of British consuls in the Confederate States and the presence of Confederate consuls in Britain. But he also draws attention to the fact that third States often felt the need to enter into legal intercourse with belligerents on practical matters that arose out of their control of territory, rather than their belligerent activities as such. To illustrate his point, he refers to the fact that on 25 June 1861, one month after Britain's proclamation of neutrality, the British Law Officers advised the British government to open postal relations with the Confederate government.[32]

In summary, a review of the formal legal framework of belligerency above has identified three distinct sorts of responsibility that could arise for an armed group in a time of belligerency. The first relates to the legal rights and duties relating to the parties warlike operations. These are the obligations which are traditionally associated with the law of belligerency and are directly linked with the 'recognition' of belligerency. They include the main rules relating to maritime warfare (e.g. blockade, prize courts, flags, etc) and also rules relating to what we refer to today

[28] 'Report of Law Officers dated 12 September 1863', cited by McNair, *International Law Opinions* (n 5) 146–7.

[29] For a summary of the kind of obligations a State was usually deemed to owe to foreign nations and assets, see ILC, Yearbook of the International Law Commission 1978 (8 May–28 July 1978) Vol II, Part I, UN Doc A/CN.4/SER.A/1978/Add.1 (Part 2), 106–23.

[30] A. D. McNair, *The Law of Treaties* (Clarendon Press, Oxford, 1961) 676 (hereafter McNair, *Law of Treaties*).

[31] This meant that the San Domingo insurgents were considered to be prohibited from using privateers against neutral States because Spain had signed the Declaration of Paris before the conflict broke out. Ibid, 680.

[32] See ibid, 680.

as the 'conduct of hostilities' and 'protected persons'. The second kind of responsibility that has been seen is that arising out of the armed group's control of the control of territory in default of the government. This relates to obligations of the armed group to protect foreign assets and persons within its territory. This type of obligation is less often identified in writings describing the law on belligerency but is arguably the most relevant to this study of armed groups and human rights law because it is related to the armed group's control over persons or territory in default of the government. It was seen to be a product partly of the capacities of the group, but also partly of the incapacities of the State.[33] The third kind of responsibilities which an armed group might bear in a situation of belligerency were those arising out of explicit agreements brokered with third States. Typically, these obligations would also not relate specifically to the parties' warlike operations. Instead, they would relate to practical matters which arose out of the specific context of the armed conflict, such as consular relations and commerce. Having described the legal framework of belligerency, the following section will consider what the legal framework tells us about the international legal personality of armed groups and how it was acquired.

3. Legal Personality of Belligerent Armed Groups

3.1 Non-State actors having legal personality

The first point to note is that the above description of the law of belligerency evidences an approach to international legal personality that goes beyond the States-only conception of international legal personality set out above. It is clear that the law on belligerency shows that already in the nineteenth century there was an acknowledgement that international legal personality could be held by non-State actors, in this case, belligerent armed groups. Indeed, even though the recognition of belligerency by a parent State was thought to place the parties to the armed conflict on an equal footing in terms of their military operations, the international legal personality that was accrued by an armed group in such circumstances was considered to be of a different character to that of a State.[34] The legal framework

[33] Hall, *International Law* (n 15) 26: 'So soon as recognition takes place, the parent State ceases to be responsible to such states as have accorded recognition, and when it has itself granted recognition to all states, for the acts of the insurgents, and for losses or inconveniences suffered by a foreign power or its subjects *in consequence of the inability of the state to perform its international obligations in such parts of its dominions as are not under its actual control*' (emphasis added).

[34] Some writers have suggested that an insurgent government to which belligerency has been accorded 'is considered to have all the normal rights and liabilities of a state'. See H. Smith, *Great Britain and the Law of Nations* (P. S. King Publishing, New York, London 1932) Vol 1, 325; Vattel, *Law of Nations* (n 23) [293]: 'A civil war breaks the bands of society and government, or at least suspends their force and effect; it produces in the nation two independent parties, who consider each other as enemies, and acknowledged no common judge. Those two parties, therefore, must necessarily be considered as constituting, at least for a time, two separate bodies, two distinct societies. Having no common superior to judge between them, they stand in precisely the same predicament as two nations

makes clear that armed groups which had been recognized as belligerents were not considered to have achieved Statehood per se.[35] This is evidenced by the fact that a declaration of belligerency was rarely followed by a recognition of government. Unlike the international legal personality that accompanies Statehood, the international legal personality that attached to belligerency was clearly of a temporary character and would only last for the duration of the armed conflict.[36] Belligerent armed groups were treated as subjects of international law *sui generis* which emerged out of the specific factual circumstances of a prolonged armed conflict between two evenly matched parties.

3.2 Legal personality existing along a spectrum

It can also be concluded from the above description of the law of belligerency that the legal framework supports the notion that legal personality under international law can exist along a spectrum. For according to the legal framework, belligerents did not have as extensive international legal personality as States. The legal framework also suggests an acceptance of the fact that there could be differences between the legal personality of different belligerent armed groups. For example, the legal framework makes clear that the international legal personality that was accrued by armed groups which had been recognized as belligerents by their parent State was more far-reaching than the international legal personality realized by groups recognized by third States. When an armed group was recognized as a belligerent by its parent State, it gained a status vis-à-vis the international community as a whole. In contrast, when a third State recognized an armed group as a belligerent, it only affected the armed group's status vis-à-vis the third State and the other warring parties.

This highlights a distinction between what has been called ' "general" or "objective" and "special" or "particular" legal personality'. General legal personality 'arises against the world (*erga omnes*)' and particular legal personality binds only 'consenting States'.[37] In circumstances where an armed group was recognized by a third State, the extent of its legal personality would be less extensive than when an armed group had been recognized by its parent State. Such a group would have less normative responsibility and the obligations it accrued would be binding against fewer parties. There is also a suggestion that within these two situations, some armed groups might have more extensive legal personality than others, depending on their functions and capacities. For example, it was demonstrated that an

who engage in a contest and have recourse to arms.' But see McNair, *International Law Opinions* (n 5) 146, who, citing Smith, finds 'scanty' evidence to support this proposition.

[35] Indeed this is specifically stated in 'Report of Law Officers dated 25 June 1861', cited by McNair, *International Law Opinions* (n 5) 147, which makes clear that a government which has been recognized as a 'belligerent' falls short of a government which has been recognized as a 'de facto' government.

[36] McNair, *International Law Opinions* (n 5) 148.

[37] J. Crawford, *The Creation of States in International Law* (2nd edn, Clarendon Press, Oxford 2006) 30 (hereafter Crawford, *Creation of States*).

armed group with extensive control over a population or territory containing foreign assets or individuals would be held responsible for obligations relating to that control. It was also seen that an armed group which made bilateral agreements with third States, would be held responsible for the obligations contained in those agreements. This shows that already in the nineteenth century, there was implicit cognizance of the legal principle confirmed by the ICJ in its *Reparations Opinion* in 1949, i.e. that subjects of international law are not necessarily identical in their nature or in the extent of their rights. [38]

3.3 Manner in which legal personality of belligerent armed groups was acquired

3.3.1 Legal personality often seen to be result of 'declaration' of belligerency by States

Having made these preliminary observations on the nature of the international legal personality of armed groups under the law of belligerency, the next question is what the framework demonstrates about the way in which armed groups acquired their legal personality. Considering the relatively formal manner in which belligerency was often explicitly 'declared', it may seem tempting to see the legal framework of belligerency as wholly supporting the 'recognition' conception of international legal personality set out above. At first glance at least, the legal framework on belligerency presents a picture in which the normative framework imposed upon armed groups flowed from the bestowal of international legal personality by third States or the parent State. This view is supported by writings on belligerency which often suggest that the 'recognition' of an armed group as a belligerent had an immediately transformative effect on the legal framework that governed the parties' relations. The act of recognition has been said to 'create' a 'new legal situation'.[39] Likewise, a declaration of belligerency has been described as triggering the application of the law on neutrality and belligerency and causing the *jus in bello* to apply to both the State and the rebels.[40] However, on closer inspection, the situation may not be so black and white as it first appears. More

[38] See the statement by the ICJ in *Advisory Opinion on Reparations for Injuries Suffered in the Service of the United Nations* [1949] ICJ Reports 174 (11 April 1949) [178] (hereafter *Advisory Opinion on Reparations*): 'The subjects of law in any legal system are not necessarily identical in their nature or in the extent of their rights, and their nature depends upon the needs of their community.' This was discussed in the introduction to Part II of the book.

[39] See e.g. ICRC, *Commentary to Additional Protocols* (n 8) 1320 [4341]: 'Such an act [recognition of belligerency by the parent State] creates a new legal situation. The relationship between the established government and the insurgents follows from the state of war which makes the law of armed conflict as a whole applicable between them. Recognition is a manifestation of the competence of a State to wage war, which keeps its national sovereignty. It grants insurgents merely a sort of legal personality as subjects of rights and duties within the confines of the laws of war.'

[40] See also H. W. Briggs, *The Law of Nations, Documents and Notes* (2nd edn, Appleton-Century-Crofts, New York 1952) 992 (hereafter Briggs, *Law of Nations*): 'Recognition of the belligerency of the insurgents ... changes the legal situation under international law.'

particularly, it will be demonstrated in the rest of this chapter that there is room for a view that the law on belligerency supports a conception of international legal personality whereby the recognition of an armed group as a belligerent was partly a confirmation of an already existing situation of fact and law. For example, it will be shown that a declaration of belligerency by either the parent State or a third State was not as substantively transformative as it is often presented to have been. It seems also questionable whether the international legal personality achieved by the armed group in times of belligerency can realistically be wholly attributed to the recognition of that armed group's belligerent status.

3.3.2 Indications that States did not entirely control point at which belligerent armed group acquired international legal personality

Initial indications that the legal framework on belligerency does not entirely adhere to the recognition conception of international legal personality can be seen in the view held by some scholars that States did not entirely control the point at which a state of belligerency was reached. This is implicit in the view held by some legal scholars that a population in a 'belligerent' territory was legally 'entitled' to be treated as a belligerent in circumstances where the factual situation of the armed conflict met all the conditions of a belligerency.[41] It is also supported by the view, albeit rather vaguely stated by Oppenheim, that a State which persists in treating the soldiers of the opposing side as common criminals in the face of recognition of the belligerency by third States will expose itself to 'justifiable retaliation'.[42] Furthermore, it is contained in the suggestion that a third State was bound to ensure that its attitude towards insurgent groups not only accorded with its obligations towards a friendly state, but also with the 'laws of humanity'.[43] Implicit in these observations is a view that the threshold of when a belligerency had been met was not in fact exclusively in the hands of individual States, but was rather determined by an objective benchmark of fact. This poses a challenge to the view that the parent State was the ultimate arbiter of the conferral of international legal personality *erga omnes* and constitutes an indication of the fact that the legal framework relating to belligerency does not fully reflect the 'recognition conception' of international legal personality.

A further challenge to the notion that the belligerency framework reflects a pure recognition conception of international legal personality is found in the fact

[41] H. Lauterpacht, *International Law and Human Rights* (Stevens & Sons, London 1950) 12 (hereafter Lauterpacht, *Human Rights*), found that 'substantial practice supports what is probably the accurate view on the subject, namely, that insurgents are entitled as a matter of law to recognition of belligerency provided that the requisite conditions of fact are met'.

[42] See Oppenheim, *International Law* (n 3) 252–3, although it is not clear whether the use of the term 'justifiable' by Oppenheim in this instance refers to legal justification or justification in the moral or political realm.

[43] Wilson, 'Insurgency and International Maritime Law' (n 2) 55. See also Briggs, *Law of Nations* (n 40) 991, who recognized that '[r]easons of humanity' sometimes motivated a parent State to recognize the belligerency of the insurgents.

that a situation of belligerency did not always need to be explicitly declared, but could be inferred from a parent State's behaviour. In the American Civil War, the British government maintained that by enforcing a blockade on Southern ports, the United States had effectively recognized a belligerency. It was also generally thought that a third State's declaration of neutrality could be interpreted as a recognition of belligerency by that State. The notion that a belligerency could be recognized implicitly by either the parent State or third States is somewhat contrary to the recognition conception of international legal personality's general requirement that non-State actors may only acquire legal personality through a the explicit recognition of States. It is an indication of an acceptance that in assessing whether a belligerency exists, equal store was given to States' actions, especially in the absence of explicit declarations. The acceptance that a belligerency could be recognized implicitly reflects an approach more akin to the ideas contained in the individualistic and actor conceptions of international legal personality, which put greater store on issues such as an entity's participation in the legal framework than States' formal declarations of international legal personality.

3.3.3 Armed groups were held bound by similar legal obligations in situations falling short of belligerency, i.e. insurgencies

3.3.3.1 Definition of insurgency

Interestingly, the notion that an armed group could incur legal personality through means other than a declaration of belligerency is supported most forcefully by a comparison of the law of belligerency with the law of insurgency. Such a comparison demonstrates that the distinction between a state of 'insurgency' and a state of 'belligerency' was sometimes small, both as a matter of fact and of law. Before illustrating this more thoroughly, a description of the term 'insurgency' is given below. The term insurgency is employed in this chapter to refer to an 'intermediate state' between peace and belligerency, occurring before the Geneva Conventions were drafted in 1949.[44] It was a label for a situation of non-international armed conflict which had proceeded beyond an internal rebellion but had not been recognized as a belligerency.[45] Some have argued that the term 'insurgency' is not a 'legal' term at all because it does not comprise of a fixed set of rights and obligations. Instead, it refers mainly to the patchwork of ad hoc obligations which sometimes arose between the parties to a non-international armed conflict *inter se* and between the parties to a non-international armed conflict and third parties.[46]As a result, it has

[44] Since the drafting of the Geneva Conventions in 1949, the term 'insurgency' is generally used exclusively as a non-legal term to refer to an armed uprising.

[45] H. Lauterpacht, 'Recognition of Insurgents as a De Facto Government' (1939) 3 Modern Law Review 1, 2 (hereafter Lauterpacht, 'Recognition of Insurgents as a De Facto Government'). See also Wilson, 'Insurgency and International Maritime Law' (n 2) 49: 'It is evident that a status between peace and belligerency is recognised by the various departments of the government of the United States. This is not the status of non-hostile redress which has long been mentioned in books on international law, but a status which while not war may have certain consequences and characteristics of war.'

[46] Lauterpacht, 'Recognition of Insurgents as a De Facto Government' (n 45) 4.

been said that to 'search for a definition of insurgency' would be to 'misconstrue its nature'.[47] That being said, it is possible to describe the circumstances in which an insurgency could come about.

The term 'insurgency' is employed in this chapter to refer to situations of armed conflict in which international legal obligations were incurred by armed groups, outside of the belligerency framework. As a result, when describing an 'insurgency', it will not be surprising to note that the first requirement for an insurgency is a lack of recognition of belligerency. In addition, an insurgency has been said to have four distinct requirements.[48] The first requirement is that the situation of armed uprising has exceeded the control of the State's civilian authority. The second is that the insurgent group is pursuing 'public ends' by force, e.g. is trying to change the government or reform the political system. The third is that the situation within the State is so serious as 'to materially affect outside States'. The fourth is that because of the absence of control by the State, third States are forced to have some kind of relation with the insurgents. A review of this definition instantly shows that the differences between situations of insurgency and belligerency were inevitably small, as a matter of reality. The main difference between the two definitions is that the definition of insurgency does not require that the armed group occupy and have orderly administration over a substantial portion of the national territory. It also does not require that the armed group observe the rules of warfare.

3.3.3.2 Potential for considerable similarities between legal frameworks of belligerency and insurgency

In practical terms, the reason that there was often a considerable similarity between situations of insurgency and situations of belligerency was that the conferral of recognition to an armed group was essentially a political decision by States.[49] As a result, it was perfectly possible for a non-international armed conflict to meet and surpass the objective requirements of a belligerency while still not being recognized as a belligerency in legal terms. In such situations, the legal framework governing the armed conflict would often have many of the same features of a belligerency. One such similarity would be the application of at least *some* of the rules of warfare to the conflict.[50] For example, the parties to an insurgency would draw up special agreements declaring that they would declare the laws of war between them.[51]

[47] Wilson, 'Insurgency and International Maritime Law' (n 2). See also Sivakumaran, *Non-International Armed Conflict* (n 1) 10.

[48] Wilson, 'Insurgency and International Maritime Law' (n 2) 51.

[49] See also Snow, *Cases and Opinions* (n 13) 26, citing Opinion of Dana, where he emphasizes that a decision as to whether to recognize a situation as a belligerency must be taken by the political department of a State, not by law officers.

[50] It is noted in this regard that an observance of the rules of warfare by insurgent forces was one of the conditions for a declaration of belligerency to be made. Oppenheim, *International Law* (n 3) 249.

[51] For details of how this came about in the Spanish Civil War, see F. Siordet, 'Les Conventions de Genève et La Guerre Civile, Revue Internationale de la Croix Rouge' (1950) 81 Bulletin International des Sociétés de la Croix Rouge (hereafter Siordet, 'Revue Internationale de la Croix Rouge'). See also (n 65).

Indeed, there is evidence that there was often an expectation by third States and international organizations that the basic laws on conduct of hostilities and protection of civilians would also be applied in situations falling short of a belligerency, irrespective of whether such agreements had been brokered.[52] It is also observed that in many instances where a third State's interests were affected by an armed conflict abroad, it might also draw up a set of rules to govern its own conduct and determine its treatment of the parties to the conflict.[53] A third State might also pass neutrality laws forbidding its citizens from accepting commissions, enlisting in the foreign struggle, or fitting out vessels on behalf of either party to the conflict.[54] It might also, as is demonstrated in more detail later below, choose to seek redress for wrongs done to its citizens or assets from the insurgent body, rather than the parent State.

Just as in a belligerency, a third State sometimes chose to make bilateral agreements with an armed group to protect its assets and citizens in the areas under its control. Such a move generally stemmed from a sense of pragmatism on the part of third States and a desire to put their relations with the armed group on 'a regular, although clearly provisional basis'.[55] The truth of this statement is illustrated in an article in the American Journal of International Law at the beginning of the twentieth century. Writing in 1907, Grafton Wilson highlighted that often when a domestic struggle was not recognized as a belligerency, foreign States were nonetheless affected and needed to 'have some rules to govern their conduct and to determine their treatment of the party to the struggle which is not yet recognized as a state or as a belligerent'.[56] A similar truth is illustrated by Lord Eden's lengthy statement to the House of Commons in November 1937 during the Spanish Civil War, which shows that it was mainly commercial considerations which led the British to broker special agreements with Franco's insurgent government during the Spanish Civil War.[57] The fact that the Franco insurgents controlled two-thirds of continental Spain in which many million British sterling pounds were invested, gave the British government little choice but to

[52] See Vattel, *Law of Nations* (n 23) [294]. See also United Kingdom House of Commons Debate (Hansard 21 June 1938) Vol 337, 919–1045, 938, where the British Prime Minister makes it clear that Britain considered Franco's insurgents to be bound by the international law prohibiting deliberate attacks on civilian populations. See also Garner, 'International Law in the Spanish Civil War' (n 7) 66: 'In general the rules of international law governing the conduct of war in the technical sense apply equally in case of an insurrection.' See also the statement by the ICRC on 11 November 1936 to the parties of the Spanish Civil War reminding the parties that the general principles relating to civilians who have fallen into the power of the enemy and the prohibition on the taking of hostages apply just as much to a civil war, as they do to an international armed conflict, cited in C. Rousseau, 'La Non-Intervention en Espagne—Section II' (1938) 3 Revue de Droit International et de Législation Comparée 473, 475–6 (hereafter Rousseau, 'La Non-Intervention en Espagne—Section II').

[53] Wilson, 'Insurgency and International Maritime Law' (n 2) 50.

[54] Ibid, 59.

[55] Lauterpacht, *Recognition in International Law* (CUP, Cambridge 1947) 270–1, cited by Moir, *Internal Armed Conflict* (n 6) 4.

[56] Wilson, 'Insurgency and International Maritime Law' (n 2) 50.

[57] United Kingdom House of Commons Debate (Hansard 8 November 1937) Vol 328, 1381–9 (hereafter Hansard, 8 November 1937).

set up some channels of direct communication between Britain and Franco's administration.

4. Insurgency and the Legal Personality of Armed Groups

4.1 Spanish Civil War: general legal framework

Indeed, the Spanish Civil War provides a vivid example of the similarities between 'war in a material sense' and 'war in a legal sense'.[58] Somewhat astonishingly, the Spanish Civil War was never recognized as a belligerency despite the fact that it would easily have qualified as one in legal terms. Even a few weeks after the fighting began in July 1936, the insurrection was reported to have acquired a 'magnitude and an organisation' which would have justified any third government from recognizing a belligerency.[59] By November 1937, General Franco, who had instigated a coup against the Republican government, held at least two-thirds of continental Spain and all its overseas territories.[60] His Nationalist forces had a well-established government in Burgos and significant army and air force.[61] The reason that third States and the Spanish government refused to recognize Franco's government as insurgents were political. Records show that there was a fear by third States and Spain that a declaration of belligerency would appear to give support to the rebels. There was also a feeling that a declaration of belligerency would have the effect of further deflating the morale of the struggling Republican government. Statements from governments of third States indicate that third States saw a declaration of belligerency to be an inappropriate 'reward' for a group that had taken up arms against its government.[62] Yet when the patchwork web of ad hoc relations which arose during the Spanish Civil War are compared next to the belligerency framework, it is seen that, in practical terms, there was not very much difference between the two legal frameworks despite the fact that the situation was never recognized as a belligerency.

[58] The phrases 'war in the material sense' and 'war in the legal sense' were used by the US Supreme Court in the case of *The Three Friends* to refer to the difference between insurgency and belligerency: *The Three Friends* 166 US 1 (US Supreme Court, 1897). See Wilson, 'Insurgency and International Maritime Law' (n 2) 49.

[59] See Garner, 'International Law in the Spanish Civil War' (n 7) 70.

[60] Hansard, 8 November 1937 (n 57).

[61] See C. Rousseau, 'La Non-Intervention en Espagne' (1938) 3 Revue de Droit International et de Législation Comparée 217, 256–9 (hereafter Rousseau, 'La Non-Intervention en Espagne'), for an account of the government function and territorial control of the Nationalist forces. See also Rousseau, 'La Non-Intervention en Espagne—Section II' (n 52) 512, 517, where Rousseau confirms that by the second year of the war, the Nationalist forces occupied 41 of the 50 provinces in Spain, representing approximately two thirds of the total country (323,000 km^2 out of 504,000 km^2) and total population (14.5 million inhabitants out of 23 million).

[62] See Rousseau, 'La Non-Intervention en Espagne—Section II' (n 52) 510–49 for a full discussion of the precise considerations at play in the decision not to recognize Franco's forces as belligerents.

4.2 General similarities between the legal framework that applied in the Spanish Civil War and a belligerency

The Republican government's loss of control over territory had serious implications for foreign States' ability to protect their commercial assets and citizens, with the result that they were forced to initiate and consolidate dialogue and legal relations with the insurgents.[63] Just as Britain had exchanged agents with the belligerent Confederate government during the American Civil War, so Britain exchanged agents with Franco's government even though it had not been recognized as a belligerent.[64] After the International Committee of the Red Cross (ICRC) visited the government of Madrid and the Franco authorities in August 1936, both parties to the conflict agreed to apply the two 1929 Geneva Conventions for the rest of the conflict.[65] In November 1936, Franco's insurgent authorities informed the British government that it intended to prevent the importation of munitions or implements of war via the port of Barcelona and proceeded to pursue an aggressive aerial campaign of bombardment against British vessels.[66] On a number of occasions during the armed conflict, both parties informed third States of their intention to blockade certain ports.[67] In the early years of the war, twenty-seven governments made declarations of non-intervention confirming that they were going to refrain from interference in the war and essentially maintain a neutral position.[68]

4.3 Requests for reparations directed by third States to Franco rebels

The complex web of legal obligations which arose during the Spanish Civil War between the Republican government and the Franco rebels on the one hand, and the Franco rebels and third States on the other, provides evidence of how the legal framework governing an insurgency could be startlingly similar to that of a belligerency. Moreover, there are records of several countries, including Norway, Britain, and Portugal, directing claims for reparations for financial compensation to Franco's government, rather than to the Spanish Republican government.[69] As early as 1937, the British government sought reparations from the Franco authorities for the bombing of the British steamer 'Jean Weems'. In response to this request, the Nationalist authorities expressed their official regret for the incident, provided an assurance that orders would be given to Nationalist forces to avoid the incident's

[63] Rousseau, 'La Non-Intervention en Espagne' (n 61) 259–75, gives an account of relations between the Nationalist forces and third States and international entities. See also (n 57).

[64] Ibid, 265–9; see also (n 57).

[65] Siordet, 'Revue Internationale de la Croix Rouge' (n 51) 112–14.

[66] See United Kingdom House of Commons Debate (Hansard 21 June 1938) Vol 337, 926.

[67] See Rousseau, 'La Non-Intervention en Espagne—Section II' (n 52) 528–38.

[68] N. J. Padelford, 'The International Non-Intervention Agreement and the Spanish Civil War' (1937) 4 American Journal of International Law 578, 580 (hereafter Padelford, 'Non-Intervention Agreement').

[69] See Rousseau, 'La Non-Intervention en Espagne—Section II' (n 52) 508.

repetition, and agreed to submit the case, if necessary, to arbitration so that compensation and liability could be agreed between the parties.[70] In 1938, the British government addressed a formal request for reparation to the Nationalist authorities for the destruction of a destroyer, a steamer, and a British cargo ship by Nationalist mines and air attacks.[71] However, records indicate that the British government did not always seek reparations from the Nationalist insurgents and the Franco authorities were not always so receptive, as in the Jean Weems incident.[72] But the fact that the British pursued the Franco authorities for these claims constitutes evidence that as a matter of policy, the British considered the Franco insurgents responsible for the incidents as a matter of law despite there being no specific agreement to that effect. Similarly, there is evidence that the Norwegian government claimed monetary compensation from the Franco insurgents for the attack on its cargo ship, the *Gulnes* in December 1936 near Seville.[73]

4.4 Franco insurgents held responsible for international obligations as a result of their control of territory

In a similar manner, records show that in August 1936, the Spanish government instructed the Portuguese government to pursue a claim for reparation against the Franco insurgents rather than against Spain, for harm caused by a 'group of armed Spaniards' during an incursion onto Portuguese territory in August 1936.[74] According to the Spanish government, the insurgents' were responsible under 'international conventions' for their actions.[75] Following the Spanish government's advice, the Portuguese government presented their original claims to the Nationalist insurgents (still drafted against the Spanish government) with the observation that the Junta had in effect been exercising sovereignty over the Spanish territory on the border with Portugal at the time of the incursion. The Junta in Burgos replied that it accepted the claim and provided an assurance that no such incident would happen again. It stated that it was willing to respond to the claim because the Spanish government had lost the ability to protect its borders and the assets and lives of foreign citizens. It stated that it was responding to the Portuguese claim in its capacity as the 'representative exercising sovereignty over all its territory'.[76] The assumption of responsibility by the Nationalist rebels and the denial of responsibility by the Spanish government for those acts will be discussed

[70] Hansard, 8 November 1937 (n 57).

[71] See Report of the Commission to the General Assembly on the Law of Treaties', ILC, Yearbook of the International Law Commission 1975 (5 May–25 July 1975) Vol II, UN Doc A/CN.4/SER.A/1975/Add.1, 99 [28], citing Rousseau, 'La Non-Intervention en Espagne' (n 61) 278 fn 105–7.

[72] See United Kingdom House of Commons Debate (Hansard, 21 June 1938) Vol 337, 919–1045, which shows that already by June 1938 the attacks against British shipping had escalated significantly. It also suggests that the British did not make a habit of pursuing the Franco authorities for damage, unless the facts suggested that it had been a deliberate attack.

[73] Rousseau, 'La Non-Intervention en Espagne—Section II' (n 52) 508.

[74] Rousseau, 'La Non-Intervention en Espagne' (n 61) 279. [75] Ibid, 279.

[76] Ibid, 279–80.

in greater detail later in this study.[77] For now, it is remarked that these incidents support the observation that in situations falling short of formal belligerencies, insurgent groups were sometimes also held bound by the international legal obligations usually incumbent on the State, in instances where they were in control of territory or people.

4.5 Concluding remarks on the Spanish Civil War

This analysis of the Spanish Civil War demonstrates that a 'recognition' of a belligerency by a parent State or third State was often not as transformative as it is sometimes suggested. Indeed, the description of the legal obligations which arose during the Spanish Civil War indicates that an armed group could incur the same three kinds of obligations in an insurgency, as it would usually incur during a belligerency. An armed group could be held bound by the rules relating to what we refer to today as the 'conduct of hostilities' and 'protected persons'. It could also be held bound to obligations arising out of its control of the control of territory in default of the government. Furthermore, it could be held bound by explicit agreements brokered with third States. Ultimately, the fact that these obligations were sometimes also held to bind armed groups outside the belligerency framework indicates an acceptance by States that armed groups could gain legal personality not only through explicit State consent, but also through their participation on the international legal sphere. In other words, both the legal frameworks of belligerency and insurgency have been shown to have an affinity to the individualistic, formal, and actor approaches to international legal personality which will be examined more closely below.

5. General Intercourse between Armed Groups and States as a Source of Legal Obligations

In the light of this observation, it will not be surprising to note that Hersch Lauterpacht was one of the early champions of the idea that armed groups could acquire legal personality outside of the belligerency framework. Writing in the aftermath of the Spanish Civil War, Lauterpacht challenged the frequent assumption that 'unrecognized insurgents are not and cannot be subjects of international rights and duties'.[78] He elaborated his view as follows:

> There is no sufficient warrant for any such assumption. Moreover, it is clear that unrecognised insurgents, without having acquired a specific status of belligerency, may be admitted to various forms of intercourse with outside States. Such intercourse, which involves the application of international law by and in relation to the insurgents, may include the

[77] See in particular Chapter 9 which examines the relevance of 'control of territory' to an armed group acquiring obligations under international law.

[78] Lauterpacht, *Human Rights* (n 41) 12–13.

conclusion of agreements, diplomatic and consular relations, and recognition of the insurgent authority as a government ... It would therefore appear that not only insurgents recognised as belligerents, but also insurgents not recognised as such, may be subjects of international rights and duties.[79]

From this statement, and Lauterpacht's other analytical writings on the legal personality of non-State actors, it is clear that in his view, the determinative factor which made armed groups 'subjects of international rights and duties' was their 'intercourse' or participation with third States, which, according to him, 'involves the application of international law'.[80] The various elements of this argument, which on its face has strong elements of the actor and individualistic conception of international legal personality, will be examined further in the paragraphs below.

5.1 Bilateral agreements between armed groups and States

Before examining whether armed groups can acquire legal personality through 'general intercourse' with third States, the paragraphs below explore Lauterpacht's observation that armed groups can acquire international legal personality through the conclusion of bilateral agreements with States. The need to look more closely at this question arises out of the observation, already made in this chapter, that armed groups and States often brokered such bilateral agreements in both belligerencies and insurgencies. The following paragraphs will consider whether such agreements can be considered the source of international legal personality for armed groups today. Indeed, it is noteworthy that decisions by the Appeal Chamber of the Special Court for Sierra Leone and the Constitutional Court of Colombia adopt a States-only view of legal personality which is hard to justify in modern times.[81] In the Sierra Leone case, the Court was asked *inter alia* whether the Lomé agreement between the Revolutionary United Front (RUF) and government of Sierra Leone was an agreement which created legal rights and obligations under international law. Having considered arguments on both sides, the Appeals Chamber found that the Lomé agreement was not a 'treaty nor an agreement in the nature of a treaty' and could not be characterized as an 'international agreement'.[82] Based on that conclusion, the Appeals Chamber found that the Lomé Agreement did not 'create an obligation in international law' on the Sierra Leone government to provide an amnesty to the rebels.[83]

In coming to this conclusion, the Appeals Chamber rejected the argument that the RUF had international personality under international law, as a result of being bound by common Article 3 of the Geneva Conventions.[84] Its conclusion on this

[79] Ibid.

[80] Ibid, 19–23. See for example, Lauterpacht's discussion of the international legal personality of the United Nations, where this is made clear.

[81] *Prosector v Morris Kallon* (SCSL-2004-15-AR72(E)); *Brima Bazzy Kamara* (SCSL-2004-16-AR72(E)) (*Decision on Challenge to Jurisdiction: Lomé Agreement Amnesty*) (*Appeals Chamber Decision*) [2004] SCSL 6 (13 March 2004).

[82] *Brima Bazzy Kamara* (n 81), [48–9].

[83] Ibid, [49].

[84] Ibid, [45].

point seems logically untenable in the light of the fact that it earlier accepts that the RUF was bound by common Article 3 but later in the judgment it becomes clear that the Appeals Chamber understood the concept of international legal personality as being reserved for States only.[85] Finally, the Appeals Chamber rejected the notion that the RUF had 'treaty-making capacity' and found this to be strong evidence for its conclusion that the Lomé Agreement had not been 'a treaty or an agreement in the nature of a treaty'.[86] Although there may be merit to the Appeals Chamber's final conclusion that the Lomé Agreement did not contain international obligations, it is argued that its process of reasoning reflects a conception of international legal personality which errs too far towards the States-only approach to legal personality to be sustained in modern legal doctrine.[87] A similar States-only approach was taken by the Constitutional Court of Colombia in a judgment in 1995 where the Court argued that armed groups are subjects of international humanitarian law, but not subjects of public international law. In denying the armed group legal personality under public international law, the Colombian court went on to conclude that any special agreements between the parties to a non-international armed conflict could not be 'treaties' and would not have legally binding effect.[88]

In reaching these conclusions, both courts seemed to disregard the fact that international legal personality can exist along a spectrum and be held by entities other than States.[89] Furthermore, neither court made reference to Article 3 of the Vienna Convention on the Law of Treaties 1969 which explicitly recognizes that there may be other forms of 'international agreements' between States and other subjects of international law.[90] There was also no attention given to analogous areas of law where bilateral agreements between States and non-State actors have been found to contain 'international obligations', for example case law relating to corporate concessionary contracts. In this area, it has been found that such agreements can be governed by international law if it can be demonstrated that this was

[85] This can be gleaned by the Court's reference to 'international legal personality of such a nature as to make it possible for them to be a party to the Geneva Conventions', ibid, [47].

[86] Ibid, [49].

[87] See Cassese who calls the decision 'convoluted' and 'legally flawed'. He notes that the decision takes a particularly circuitous route to a finding that the amnesty granted by the Government of Sierra Leone in the Lomé Agreement could not cover crimes under international law that are the subject of universal jurisdiction. A. Cassese, 'The Special Court and International Law: The Decision concerning the Lomé Agreement Amnesty' (2004) 2 Journal of International Criminal Justice 1130, 1130–1 (hereafter Cassese, 'Lomé Agreement Amnesty').

[88] Constitutional Court of Colombia, Sentencia No. C-225/95 (1995) [14].

[89] Support for this is found in, e.g., *Advisory Opinion on Reparations* (n 38).

[90] For further critique of the Special Court of Sierra Leone decision on this point, see P. Okowa, 'Interpreting Constitutive Instruments of International Criminal Tribunals: Reflections on the Special Court for Sierra Leone' in M. Fitzmaurice, I. A. Olufemi, and Panos Merkouris (eds), *Treaty Interpretation and the Vienna Convention on the Law of Treaties: 30 Years On* (Brill, Leiden 2010) 341–2, which refers to the 'outdated character of the pure form of legal positivism advanced by the prosecution ... and adopted by the Court.' See also 345 for Okowa's discussion of Article 3 of the Vienna Convention. See also C. Bell, 'Peace Agreements: Their Nature and Legal Status' (2006) 100 American Journal of International Law 373, 387, who says that the 'tautologies of the decision ... point to the difficulties of the positivist law project in this area, but not its irrelevance'.

the intention of the parties.[91] There was also no mention made of the Convention on the Settlement of Investment Disputes of 1964 which establishes a permanent dispute resolution machinery where participating States and individuals or corporations can settle investment agreements which are governed *inter alia* by international law. Article 42 Convention explicitly recognizes the possibility that disputes between States and non-State actors may be governed by international law. These sources show that agreements between States and armed groups can be governed by international law in instances where it can be shown that this was the intention of the parties.[92]

One can see that it will be especially impractical for an agreement between an armed group and a State to be governed by national law when the State in question is a third State, as was mainly the case in the belligerency framework. In instances where a third State makes an agreement with an armed group, it will be unlikely that either the third State or the armed group will agree to the agreement being governed by domestic law, e.g. the national law of the third State or the national law of the parent State of the armed group.[93] From the armed group's perspective, the national law of the parent State will be a symbol of the State against which it considers itself to be fighting and the national law of the third State will be unknown and untrustworthy. From the third State's perspective, the legitimacy of the national law of the parent State will also be severely compromised by the parent State's lack of control over territory and the breakdown of its law enforcement capabilities. More fundamentally, the questions which were addressed by bilateral agreements which were brokered between armed groups and States during the course of an ongoing armed conflict often pertained to issues governed by international law, and not domestic law (e.g. diplomatic protections, protests about incursions into territory, treatment of prisoners of war, exercise of belligerent activity at sea).

An acceptance that armed groups may gain a measure of international legal personality through the brokering of bilateral agreements with third States is not incompatible with the recognition conception of international legal personality. Legal obligations brokered between an armed group and a State are expressions of

[91] See *Texaco v Libya* [1977] 53 ILR 389 (Arbitral Tribunal) (19 January 1977). See R. Portmann, *Legal Personality in International Law* (CUP, Cambridge 2010) 119–24, for a discussion of this case and topic.

[92] It is likely that a debate will remain between scholars as to how these intentions may be evidenced. For example, some lawyers will argue like Cassese that intentions may be evidenced from the spirit of the document while others will argue that they need to be stated explicitly. See Cassese, 'Lomé Agreement Amnesty' (n 87) 1135. Differing views on this matter will again reflect different views on how and when international legal personality can be acquired in international law.

[93] This is a reflection of the fact that in many internal armed conflicts, the legitimacy of the national law of the parent State will be severely diminished for both the armed group and third States. An illustration of this can be seen in the interview conducted by Shaun Walker with Igor Bezler, rebel chief in Ukraine. Led to the bathroom, he noted that the Ukrainian legal code was being used as toilet paper, with half its pages ripped out. 'An audience with Ukraine rebel chief Igor Bezler, the Demon of Donetsk' (*Guardian Newspaper*, 29 July 2014) <http://www.theguardian.com/world/2014/jul/29/-sp-ukraine-rebel-igor-bezler-interview-demon> accessed 20 January 2017.

State consent. However, the notion that armed groups can make international law agreements with third States is also compatible with the formal, individualistic, and actor conception of international law. It recognizes that an armed group has a degree of agency in the international sphere that may result in it acquiring legal obligations. Under the formal conception of international legal personality, such an agreement may be considered to be the source of international legal personality for the armed group. Under the individualistic and actor conception of international legal personality, the brokering of such an agreement may be deemed to be evidence of the group's already existing international legal personality, rather than its source. Yet no matter which conception of international legal personality is adopted, it is important to note that the legal personality that an armed group will accrue through such an agreement is limited. Rather than leading to international legal personality *erga omnes,* an agreement between a State and an armed group leads to, or demonstrates, an international legal personality *inter se* that is restricted to the terms and parties of the agreement.

6. General Functionality on International Sphere as a Source of Legal Personality

As a final point in this section, it is important to consider Lauterpacht's statement that insurgent groups can gain a measure of personality not only through explicit agreements but also through their more general 'intercourse' with third States.[94] This view accords with an argument Lauterpacht makes elsewhere in his writings on non-State actors where he indicates that non-State entities can gain legal personality under international law by 'exercising functions compatible with or implying international legal personality'.[95] With these words, Lauterpacht seems to argue that a non-State actor can gain international legal personality from a variety of sources, one of which is its participation on the international plane. The notion that an armed group may gain international legal personality through 'participation' is a view which Chapter 3 showed to be central to the actor conception of international legal personality. Yet it was also argued in Chapter 3 that when Lauterpacht refers to the term 'intercourse', he referred to something more specifically legal than the kind of participation which is referred to by the actor conception of international legal personality by McDougal and Lasswell.[96]

[94] Lauterpacht, *Human Rights* (n 41) 12–13.

[95] This is clear from Lauterpacht's analysis of the functions that the United Nations is exercising which are 'compatible with or imply' international legal personality. Here, he provides examples of intercourse which might include an entity having legal personality which include an entity entering into legal relations with third States, asserting jurisdictional or legislative powers or exercising sovereignty over a territory. These are all inherently legal forms of 'participation'. See ibid, 20–1. See also the final paragraph of section 7 in Chapter 3 of this book.

[96] M. S. McDougal, H. D. Lasswell, and W. M. Reisman, 'The World Constitutive Process of Authoritative Decision' in R. A. Falk and C. E. Black (eds), *The Future of the International Legal Order, Volume I, Trends and Patterns* (Princeton University Press, Princeton 1969) 81–94.

Instead, Lauterpacht refers to an armed group's actual exercise of international rights or observance of international duties in accordance with international law.[97] It is argued that this has similarities with the view which has been articulated by Andrew Clapham where he suggested that an entity's international legal personality might be measured according to its 'capacity to fulfil obligations'.[98] Like the individualistic conception of international legal personality, Clapham's view has features of the actor conception of international legal personality, in that it focuses on 'function', but also has features of the formal conceptions of international legal personality, in that it focuses on 'norms'.[99]

The argument that armed groups can acquire legal personality under international law due to their capacity or functioning on the international sphere finds support in the legal framework of belligerency which has been set out above. In particular, the comparison of the legal frameworks of belligerency and insurgency demonstrates that armed groups were often held bound to the laws of war by parent States and third States before a declaration of belligerency had been declared. It also shows that an insurgent group could be held responsible for the unlawful acts it had committed in instances where it had control over territory or people, in default of the State. Indeed, the correspondence between Portugal and Spain on the subject of who should bear responsibility for insurgents' incursion into Portuguese territory, suggests that the Spanish government considered that the Franco insurgents had acquired legal obligations under international law, by virtue of having supplanted the functions of the government in the territory in question. The Spanish government's reference to the insurgents being responsible under 'international conventions' seems to indicate that it saw the Franco insurgents as having supplanted the Spanish government as the duty-bearer under those conventions.

Similar evidence that armed groups were sometimes held to accrue obligations under international law on the basis of their functionality was seen in the instances where the British and Norwegian governments pursued the Franco authorities for damage to their commercial shipping. These incidents demonstrate a view by the British and Norwegian authorities that the Franco insurgents had gained sufficient international legal personality to answer the claim, even though no declaration of belligerency had been made. Moreover, their

[97] Lauterpacht, *Human Rights* (n 41) 18.

[98] Clapham, *Non-State Actors* (n 1). Clapham bases his suggestion on a close reading of the words of the ICJ in its *Advisory Opinion on Reparations* (n 38) [179]: 'In the opinion of the Court, the Organization was intended to exercise and enjoy, and is in fact exercising and enjoying, functions and rights which can only be explained on the basis of the possession of a large measure of international personality *and the capacity to operate on an international plane …* ' (emphasis added).

[99] The fact that Clapham was influenced by Lauterpacht is seen in his citation of Lauterpacht's writings on the subjects of international law which he states he finds 'convincing and far-reaching'. See ibid, 72. Clapham's interest in theories about legal personality with commonalities with the actor conception of international legal personality is evidenced by his citation of Higgins. The latter influence is seen in Clapham's suggestion ibid, 83: 'I suggest we concentrate on the rights and obligations of entities rather than their personality.'

view that the Franco insurgency had this measure of international legal personality seems to have been based equally on two factors: first, on the insurgency's functions and second on the incumbent government's lack of capacity in the territory in question.[100] Notably, it was not based on any explicit conferral of legal personality by third States.[101] Interestingly, it would seem that the international legal personality which is evidenced by the claims made by Portugal, Norway, and Britain was a 'general' legal personality, effective against the world, rather than 'particular' against one or two consenting States. The invocation by third States of legal obligations which relate to the armed group's control of territory, in default of the State, support Clapham's theory above that an armed group may acquire international legal personality through its capacity to fulfil international legal obligations. It is argued that it is this aspect of the chapter's conclusions will be most interesting for its study of the modern framework of human rights law, because it shows armed groups taking over the parent State's legal obligations, in situations where it has control of a territory in default of the States. However, it is recalled below that participation by an armed group in the international legal order can only be achieved with the acquiescence or consent of third States.

7. Conclusions

The example of the Spanish Civil War demonstrates the extent to which a declaration of belligerency was a political act which could be withheld for political reasons.[102] More than anything, the comparison of the legal frameworks of belligerency and insurgency above illustrates how arbitrary a declaration of recognition, or lack therefore, could be in legal terms. However, ultimately, it provides strong support for the idea that the act of recognition was largely a *post posteriori* measure. Indeed, when a group of government experts convened in 1971 to discuss the law of non-international armed conflicts, they expressed broadly the same opinion, stating:

> Now-a-days the application of the law of armed conflicts as a whole no longer depends on the recognition of the insurgents by the legal government – recognition which is longer ever met with in practice. Indeed, if such recognition of belligerency were to occur, it should no

[100] Significantly these are the same two factors which led an armed group to gain obligations relating to territory under the belligerency framework. See (n 33).

[101] This is less true of the legal obligations which arise as a result of ad hoc agreements between armed groups and State because even though these agreements do not flow from a declaration of belligerency, they still accord with the recognition conception of international legal personality. This is particularly the case when they contain a clause nominating international law as the governing law clause.

[102] See (n 62); Oppenheim, *International Law* (n 3) 251, who speaks approvingly of the refusal by third States to recognize the Spanish Civil War as a belligerency, on the basis that the illegal intervention of foreign States had caused the conflict to lose the character of a civil war.

longer be considered as a unilateral juridical act creating a state of law, *but as the acknowledgment of a pre-existing state of law.* (emphasis added)[103]

The truth of this observation is also seen in the definition of belligerency provided at the beginning of a chapter. For in order for a recognition of belligerency by a third State to be justified, it was required that the armed group in question exercised a state of occupation and measure of orderly administration of a substantial part of a territory by the insurgents, observed the rules of warfare, and caused third States to define their attitude to the civil war.[104] In situations where these conditions of fact existed, it has been demonstrated that the armed group in question may have often achieved a level of international legal personality through its control of territory, brokering of agreements on the laws of war, and assumption of bilateral agreements with third States.

To conclude, it is seen that the overlap between the two legal frameworks of belligerency and insurgency adds credence to a conclusion that the belligerency framework does not sit easily with a pure recognition conception of international law. This is particularly true of the legal obligations which relate to the armed group's control of territory, in default of the State, because unlike bilateral agreements, these types of obligation cannot be explained solely on the basis of State consent.[105] Instead, they support Clapham's theory that an armed group may acquire international legal personality through its functioning on the international level. The comparison of the legal frameworks of belligerency and insurgency also provides support for the idea that an armed group may acquire international legal personality through a multiplicity of sources: agreements with third States or other international organizations, declarations by third States (e.g. of belligerency), and its capacities on the ground. Each element of its personality will be characterized by the character of the norm on which it is based and how it has been acquired. For example, some aspects of an armed group's legal personality may be general in character and exist *erga omnes.* Other aspects of an armed group's legal personality may be specific in the sense that they only extend to certain States.

A further conclusion that emerges from this chapter's analysis is the comment that despite the similarities between the legal frameworks that applied to the Spanish Civil War and a belligerency, some differences between the frameworks in the formal sense remained. The first of these differences stems from the observation that although many States passed domestic neutrality laws and issued declarations of neutrality in the Spanish Civil War, they did not have a *duty* of neutrality under international law. As a result, under international law, third States could have

[103] 'Protection of Victims of Non-International Armed Conflict' (ICRC Report, January 1971), submitted to the Conference of Government Experts on the Reaffirmation and Development of International Humanitarian Law applicable in Armed Conflicts (Geneva, 24 May–12 June 1971) 15.

[104] Oppenheim, *International Law* (n 3) 249.

[105] It is less true of the legal obligations which arise as a result of ad hoc agreements between armed groups and State because even though it shows that these agreements do not necessarily flow from a declaration of belligerency, they may still accord with the recognition conception of international legal personality. This is particularly the case when the agreement contains a clause nominating international law as the governing law clause.

assisted the Spanish government if they wished, without violating international law.[106] Moreover, without a recognition of belligerency, third States also remained under a duty not to recognize the blockade imposed by Franco forces upon government ports. They were also legitimately able to continue to resist the insurgents' attempts to interfere with their shipping.[107] In reality, these small differences had far-reaching effects. For there is no doubt that the refusal of third States to recognize the situation as a belligerency posed an obstacle to Franco's forces' ability to exercise a more extensive legal personality. A declaration of belligerency would have allowed Franco's naval forces legitimacy to blockade government ports, board foreign vessels, and prevent armaments being delivered to the Republican government. While Franco's forces were already doing all these things, there was a strong feeling among third States that they would do them more often and more effectively, if they could do them legitimately.[108]

This leads to an important further observation that despite the conclusion that a declaration of belligerency was largely a recognition of an already existing legal situation, a lack of recognition of belligerency by States remained an effective blocking force for the international legal personality of armed groups. When reflecting on this reality, it is helpful to recall the definition of 'recognition' under international law put forward by O'Connell. O'Connell, an author whose writings have features of both the 'formal' and 'actor' approaches to legal personality, defines 'recognition' as a political action by a State which demonstrates two elements: (i) a willingness to acknowledge the actual situation; *and* (ii) a willingness to bring about certain legal consequences of that acknowledgement.[109] It is clear from this definition, that even though O'Connell sees recognition to be a *a posteriori* confirmation of an already existing legal framework, he recognizes that it is also an act capable of bringing about legal consequences. In this sense, O'Connell observes that States retain a formidable ability to prevent non-State actors exercising rights and duties under international law. The ability of States to block a non-State actor's exercise of legal personality goes some way to explain why in many respects the recognition of belligerency by third States or a parent State could appear to be so practically *transformative*. Because even if a view is taken that the participation or intercourse

[106] See Wilson, 'Insurgency and International Maritime Law' (n 2) 51, for details of the US and the UK passing neutrality laws in the face of an insurrection. In the particular context of the Spanish Civil War, see Padelford, 'Non-Intervention Agreement' (n 68) 580, 582. Padelford points out that as a result of the 'Non-Intervention Agreement' reached between twenty-seven governments in the Spanish Civil War, twenty-seven governments prohibited the direct or indirect exportation of arms, munitions, and materials of war to the Spanish colonies. He also pointed out that at the time of the Spanish Civil War, ten countries already had laws on their statute books prohibiting the export of arms and munitions in times of insurgencies.

[107] Wheaton, *Elements of International Law* (n 13) 42. It is noted by Rousseau that there was several attempts by the Spanish government to impose blockades upon ports but they were repeatedly not respected by third States on the basis that the government had not recognized the insurgents as belligerents and that the blockades were not effective. See Rousseau, 'La Non-Intervention en Espagne—Section II' (n 52) 523.

[108] Ibid, 514–18, 523.

[109] D. P. O'Connell, *International Law* (Stevens & Sons Limited, London 1965) 137–8.

of an entity on the international plane is the key to its subjectivity, it should not be forgotten that States ultimately remain in control of that participation and are able to veto an entity's further interaction on the international sphere and acquisition of a more extensive legal personality. This is a reflection of Crawford's observation that States remain to a large extent the 'gatekeepers' of the international system.[110]

The Spanish Civil War illustrates that even if an armed group had the capacity to exercise belligerent rights, it was still possible for third States to block their ability to exercise certain rights and participate fully on the international plane.[111] In a similar vein, the example of the Spanish Civil War shows that even though armed groups could acquire aspects of their legal personality through bilateral agreements and the control of territory, it was only with the 'consent' and 'acquiescence' of States that these obligations were actually enforced against them as a matter of law.[112] The observation that States have a strong gate-keeping function when it comes to the acquisition of legal personality by non-State actors, highlights that the acquisition of international legal personality by a non-State actor will often need to be accompanied by a degree of acquiescence by State parties. In McCorquodale and Dixon's words:

> The precise ambit of this personality [the personality of entities which are not States or international organisations] will usually depend on the acquiescence of, or recognition by, States.[113]

This observation identifies the fact that the notion of 'participation' or 'intercourse' which is central to the individualistic and actor conception of international legal personality is inevitably a two-way street, and can rarely achieved by a non-State actor alone. An armed group may only participate or have intercourse with third States, if third States allow that participation and intercourse.

In conclusion, this chapter has demonstrated that to say that the law of belligerency wholly reflects the recognition conception of international legal personality would ignore the fact that some of the belligerent armed group's rights and duties seem to be more linked to their control over territory and persons than to their functioning as a belligerent. It would also ignore the fact that many of the rights and duties which are usually associated with a belligerency were also capable of existing outside the belligerency framework. Indeed, the chapter has shown that the legal framework of belligerency and insurgency seems to reflect many of the features of the individualistic conceptions of international legal personality, which has a dual emphasis on functionality and norms. It also recognizes that non-State actors have a degree of agency in the manner under which they can acquire legal personality under international law. However, despite this conclusion, the chapter

[110] Crawford, *Creation of States* (n 37) 29.

[111] Rousseau, 'La Non-Intervention en Espagne—Section II' (n 52) 530–8.

[112] For example, it was only through the Portuguese government's agreement to pursue the Franco insurgent government for its wrongful acts that its obligations were recognized.

[113] R. McCorquodale and M. Dixon, *Cases and Materials on International Law* (4th edn, OUP, Oxford 2003) 152.

has demonstrated that there is a strong element of the recognition conception reflected in the legal framework. It has been argued that are two main reasons for this. The first stems from the observation that participation by an armed group in the international legal order is a 'two-way street' and cannot be achieved without the acquiescence of third States. The second is O'Connell's observation that even if the act of recognition is seen to be *post posteriori* confirmation of an existing legal framework, it will also likely be the *source* of further rights and duties for the armed group. In other words, the belligerency framework shows that even if an act of recognition is ultimately just a confirmation of pre-existing legal personality, it will also have a further constitutive element to it, as it will have the effect of deepening and expanding the legal capacities of the entity in question. An analysis of what these conclusions tell us about when and how armed groups may gain international legal personality under international human rights law is conducted in Chapter 6.

5

International Humanitarian Law and International Legal Personality

1. Introduction

The next task of the book is to consider what modern international humanitarian law can tell us about the way in which the international personality of armed groups is generally perceived. The chapter begins by examining the threshold test for the application of international humanitarian law to see what it can tell us about the moment at which armed groups are said to acquire international legal personality under international humanitarian law. At the moment at which it can be said for sure that international humanitarian law applies to a particular situation, it can also be said for sure that there is an acceptance that the armed group in question has acquired international legal personality. This makes the 'threshold' test for the application of international humanitarian law a rich source of information when seeking to determine how, and when, the international legal personality of armed groups is acquired under international humanitarian law. Using the evaluative framework set out in Chapter 3, the chapter sheds light on how armed groups acquire international legal personality in this framework. It will be seen that the lower threshold of common Article 3 is most interesting in this regard because it identifies most clearly what is needed for an entity to transition from being an entity with 'no' international legal personality to 'some' international legal personality. In contrast, the threshold of Additional Protocol II, identifies what is required for an entity to change from having 'some' international legal personality into having 'more' extensive international legal personality.

2. Threshold of IHL: Procedural Perspective

The current section starts by analysing the threshold of international humanitarian law from a procedural perspective. In other words, it does not ask, '*when is the threshold of international humanitarian law met?*' but '*who decides when it is met?*'. This step of analysis provides a helpful procedural context against which the substance of the test can later be understood. It also provides important information about *how* armed groups acquire international legal personality under international humanitarian law. Specifically, it provides insights into the role that State consent plays in the acquisition of legal personality by armed groups. Crucially, the first point to be noted is that the Geneva Conventions and their Protocols provide little guidance as to where the threshold of armed conflict lies and appoint no independent mechanism to decide when it has been reached. In particular, common Article 3 of the Geneva Conventions is lacking in a definition of the 'armed conflict[s] not of an international character'. However, section 3 of this chapter shows that the non-international armed conflict must reach a certain level of intensity and the armed group must reach a certain level of organization before international humanitarian law will apply. Apparently the drafters of common Article 3 deliberately chose not to include a formal definition of a non-international armed conflict as they thought that the provision of a strict set of criteria might limit the article's application.[1]

2.1 Omission of a definition was deliberate

There is no doubt that the absence of a definition of non-international armed conflict has enabled different actors to advocate that international humanitarian law applies at different levels, higher or lower, according to their agenda. For example, the International Committee of the Red Cross (ICRC) and many other writers with a humanitarian agenda have argued over the years that the threshold should be lowered as far as possible.[2] The commentary to Article 3 states: 'We think ... that the Article should be applied as widely as possible'.[3] Justifying this view, the commentary continues:

> There can be no reason against this. For, contrary to what may have been thought, the Article in its reduced form does not in any way limit the right of a State to put down rebellion. Nor does it increase in the slightest the authority of the rebel party. It merely demands respect for certain rules, which were already recognized as essential in all civilized countries, and enacted in the municipal law of the States in question, long before the Convention was signed.[4]

This push to lower the threshold of common Article 3 was particularly strong in the early 1980s when there was concern that there was an area of legal uncertainty or perhaps even a lacuna in instances of internal strife where States denied the applicability of humanitarian law and yet derogated from their human rights

[1] Flexibility in this regard was very much the effect that the drafters had hoped for in omitting a definition. They realized that a lack of definition was likely to be infinitely better than a definition that might have the effect of making the article prohibitively narrow. Instead, the rather stringent criteria which had been proposed as for possible inclusion in the article itself, were relegated to the commentary where they could constitute 'convenient criteria' while remaining 'in no way obligatory'. See J. Pictet, *Commentary to the Geneva Convention for the Amelioration of the Condition of the Wounded and Sick in Armed Forces in the Field of August 12, 1949* (ICRC, Geneva 1952) 50 (hereafter Pictet, *Commentary to Geneva Convention I*).

[2] G. Abi-Saab, *Non-International Armed Conflicts* (Henry Dunant Institute, Geneva 1988) 217–39, 224 (hereafter Abi-Saab, *Non-International Armed Conflicts*).

[3] Pictet, *Commentary to Geneva Convention I* (n 1) 50.

[4] Ibid.

obligations.[5] In addition, international humanitarian law was deemed to have considerable advantages over human rights law in that it was non-derogable and applied uncontroversially to non-State actors.

Indeed, the application of Article 3 to all situations of unrest whatever the level of violence was considered a 'humanitarian' initiative.[6] It was considered to be a means of achieving the legal framework's aim to give humanitarian protection to victims of armed conflict. Abi-Saab comments:

> In the face of such difficulties [difficulties of definition], the consistent strategy of the ICRC was to strive to extend its activities to all situations of internal conflict, disturbances or tension; in other words, to use the ambiguities of the text in order to push the threshold as far down as possible, and to establish its locus standi to act even in situations falling below it. In particular, the ICRC strove to have access in all such situations to prisoners and detainees with a view to ensuring their humane treatment.[7]

In line with the humanitarian push for the threshold of international humanitarian law to be low, the prevailing trend has generally been for States to deny its application by arguing for a higher threshold. Meron stated in 1984 that the 'rule' was for States to routinely reject the application of common Article 3.[8] The fact that it might be advantageous for States to deny the application of international humanitarian law was expressed succinctly by Baxter in the 1970s, when he said '[t]he first line of defense against international humanitarian law is to deny that it applies at all'.[9] In many situations his words remain true today.

Indeed States have many reasons to deny the application of international humanitarian law to a particular situation. They may be reluctant to admit that a situation of domestic turmoil has become an armed conflict because they fear that such an admission will be tantamount to a concession that they have lost control over their territory. The application of international humanitarian law is a strong indication that a situation of international or internal disturbance has reached a level of seriousness of international proportions. The threshold marks the moment at which domestic law and ordinary law enforcement strategies are

[5] T. Meron, *Human Rights in Internal Strife, Their International Protection* (CUP, Cambridge 1987) 136.

[6] See for example, F. Hampson, 'Human Rights and Humanitarian Law Internal Conflicts' in M. Meyer (ed), *Armed Conflict and the New Law* (British Institute for Comparative and International Law, 1990) 55–80, 67.

[7] Abi-Saab, *Non-International Armed Conflicts* (n 2) 224.

[8] T. Meron. 'On the Inadequate Reach of Humanitarian and Human Rights Law and the Need for a New Instrument' (1983) 77 American Journal of International Law 589–606, 598 (hereafter Meron. 'On the Inadequate Reach of Humanitarian and Human Rights Law'). See also Y. Dinstein. 'The International Law of Civil Wars and Human Rights' (1976) 6 *Israel Yearbook on Human Rights* 62–80, 78: 'As a rule, it is possible to state that the legitimate Government is inclined to lag behind the facts by one step'.

[9] Meron, 'On the Inadequate Reach of Humanitarian and Human Rights Law (n 8), 598, citing R. Baxter, *Some Existing Problems of Humanitarian Law in the Concept of International Armed Conflict: Further Outlook 1* (Proceedings of the International Symposium on Humanitarian Law, Brussels 1974) 2.

no longer sufficient to contain the violence. As a result, domestic politicians will often be reluctant to admit that there is a 'non-international armed conflict' as such a concession will almost inevitably be interpreted as a failure. They worry that such a concession will pigeon-hole the country as being in armed conflict, which will harm its reputation, downgrade its currency, and scare off international trading partners or investors. They may also be reluctant to accept the fact that the application of international humanitarian law will mean that there is, nominally at least, international criminal jurisdiction over some of their soldiers' actions. Any transgressions or excess violence by the military may henceforth be 'war crimes' and subject to international prosecution. Political leaders may also be reluctant to submit themselves to the international scrutiny that inevitably accompanies a situation of armed conflict, feeling that it will frustrate their freedom to combat the unrest in their own way.

Yet in recent years, the trend for States to deny the application of international humanitarian law and humanitarian organizations and encourage the application of international humanitarian law has, in some circumstances, been turned on its head. In recent years, certain States have shown themselves to be keen to declare that international humanitarian law applies.[10] With this shift, has come a growing appreciation and fear that the application of international humanitarian law might in fact bring disadvantages to civilians.[11] Suddenly, the commentary's assertion that '[t]here can be no reason against' the application of common Article 3 may seem somewhat naïve.[12] In the words of the UN Special Rapporteur on Extrajudicial, Summary, or Arbitrary Executions:

> The appeal is obvious: the IHL applicable in armed conflict arguably has more permissive rules for killing than does human rights law or a State's domestic law, and generally provides immunity to State armed forces. Because the law of armed conflict has fewer due process safeguards, States also see a benefit to avoiding compliance with the more onerous requirements for capture, arrest, detention or extradition of an alleged terrorist in another States.[13]

[10] See Final Report on the Meaning of Armed Conflict in International Law, International Law Association, The Hague Conference 2010, 4 and see also D. Kretzmer, 'Rethinking the Application of IHL in Non-International Armed Conflicts' (2009) 42 Israel Law Review 8–45, 22 for a discussion of this. See also M. Sassòli. 'The Status of Persons Held in Guantánamo under International Humanitarian Law' (2004) 2 Journal of International Criminal Justice 96–106.

[11] It is interesting to note that the International Law Association's Report on threshold states: 'The challenge seems to have become greater in recent years with the clash today between advocates of a broad, flexible understanding of armed conflict that affords states belligerent rights and advocates of a narrow definition that better protects individuals.' See 'Final Report on the Meaning of Armed Conflict in International Law', International Law Association, The Hague Conference, 2010, 4. This conclusion illustrates the shift of opinion that has taken place on whether the application of international humanitarian law is to be desired, from a humanitarian perspective.

[12] ICRC, *Commentary on the Additional Protocols of 8 June 1977 to the Geneva Conventions of 12 December 1949* (Martinus Nijhoff, Geneva 1987) (Commentary to Additional Protocols), 50 (hereafter ICRC, *Commentary to the Additional Protocols of 8 June 1977*).

[13] United Nations Human Rights Council, Report by Special Rapporteur on extrajudicial, summary or arbitrary executions, Philip Alston, 'Study on targeted killings' (28 May 2010) UN Doc A/HRC/14/24/Add.6, [47].

In essence, the shift of position by States has drawn attention to the more dangerous side of the international humanitarian law framework which allows more permissive rules for killing and detention than human rights law.[14] The above discussion exposes that, just as with the law of belligerency, the application, or non-application, of international humanitarian law is capable of serving political ends. It also demonstrates that the legal framework is vulnerable to advocacy campaigns by entities with differing agendas.

Yet despite the fact that no definition of 'non-international armed conflict' was provided by the Geneva Convention's drafters, international humanitarian law is much less at risk to political manipulation than the law on belligerency. The main reason for this is that unlike the belligerency framework which was reviewed in Chapter 4, the question of whether international humanitarian applies to a particular non-international armed conflict is a matter of objective assessment beyond the consent of any particular State.[15] The view of a parent State or third State on the matter may be taken into account, but will certainly not be determinative.[16] A parent State and an armed group will be considered bound by international humanitarian law provisions irrespective of whether they agree that it applies.[17] While this may go some way to preventing the legal framework from manipulation, a problem remains that there is no designated authority to determine whether and when international humanitarian law applies. It is notable that the question of whether such a body should be established was discussed at the Conference of Government Experts on the Reaffirmation and Development of International Humanitarian Law applicable in Armed Conflicts in 1971.

[14] See R. Brett. 'Non-Governmental Human Rights Organizations and International Humanitarian Law' (1998) 324 International Review of the Red Cross 531–6, 533 for an early illustration of this point. See also Andrew Clapham's discussion of this article: A. Clapham, *Human Rights Obligations of Non-State Actors* (OUP, Oxford 2006) 46–8.

[15] Protection of Victims of Non-International Armed Conflict, Report dated January 1971 submitted by the International Committee of the Red Cross to the Conference of Government Experts on the Reaffirmation and Development of International Humanitarian Law applicable in Armed Conflicts, Geneva, 24 May–12 June 1971, 36 (hereafter ICRC Report on Protection of Victims of Non-International Armed Conflict) <http://1.usa.gov/VEnVHc> accessed 20 January 2017.

[16] See *Prosecutor v Boškoski and Tarčulovski* (Trial Judgment) IT-04-82-T (10 July 2008) [185–91] (hereafter *Boškoski*). Here the Trial Chamber confirms that States' categorizations of certain 'acts' as 'terrorist' are of minimal relevance. However, see [238], [243], and [245–7] of the *Boškoski* judgment in which the chamber took note of the language that the State authority used to describe the violence as well as the legal framework that has been applied. See also *Prosecutor v Milutinović* et al. (Trial Judgment) IT-05-87-T (26 February 2009) Vol I, [800] (hereafter *Milutinović* Vol I).

[17] ICRC Report on Protection of Victims of Non-International Armed Conflict, 37 <http://1.usa.gov/VEnVHc> accessed 20 January 2017, which states: 'Article 3 leaves a broad power of appraisal to the Parties to the conflict, but nevertheless does not give them the power of sovereign decisions as to the application of its provisions.' See for example, L. Arimatsu and M. Choudbury, 'The Legal Classification of the Armed Conflicts in Syria, Yemen and Libya, Chatham House', March 2014 *International Law PP 2014/01*, 12 (hereafter Chatham House Report on the Legal Classification of Armed Conflicts).

2.2 No deciding body to decide application of international humanitarian law

In 1971, the ICRC prepared a report on the legal framework which applied in non-international armed conflict recommending that a new protocol be drafted to supplement common Article 3 of the Geneva Conventions. In the report, which was submitted to government experts, the ICRC considered at length the idea that a procedure or body should be established for the 'objective finding' of armed conflicts.[18] While recognizing that the establishment of such a body might be helpful, ultimately the report concluded that it would be 'too difficult' to create a procedure that 'would have the confidence of all in order to reach decisions considered as impartial by the States involved'.[19] The ICRC also made it clear that it would not want to assume this role itself as it felt that the 'delicate relations which exist between the ICRC and the government faced with non-international armed conflict on its territory would be dangerously jeopardised if the ICRC regularly and publicly expressed its conclusions on the nature of the confrontation'.[20] Instead, the ICRC noted that the application of international humanitarian law might be determined by statements by existing bodies, such as the United Nations Security Council or other regional organizations.[21]

Today, the determination of whether international humanitarian law applies to a certain situation is generally only decided authoritatively by criminal tribunals and commissions of inquiries, in many cases after the conflict has ended and in the majority of cases long after the threshold of international humanitarian law has passed. While a conflict is ongoing and before such a ruling has taken place, an observer seeking to know whether international humanitarian law applies to a particular situation, is forced to analyse the threshold test him or herself, assessing whether there is a steadily growing consensus that the situation should be designated as an armed conflict, from influential voices such as the Security Council, the General Assembly, the International Committee of the Red Cross, the High Commissioner for Human Rights, Human Rights Watch, and Amnesty International.[22] Clues as to these bodies' designation of situation may be found in references to 'international humanitarian law', 'war crimes', the existence of a 'non-international armed conflict'.[23] Yet while some of these views are authoritative, none are determinative. In recent times, there have been a few instances in which media sources have reported that the ICRC has 'ruled' that international humanitarian law applies to particular situations. While the ICRC made a public

[18] ICRC, Report on Protection of Victims of Non-International Armed Conflict (n 15) 37–41.

[19] Ibid, 41. [20] Ibid. [21] Ibid.

[22] For an indication of how such an appraisal is conducted by international lawyers see Chatham House Report on the Legal Classification of Armed Conflicts (n 17).

[23] See K. Fortin, 'Syria in Civil War, says ICRC' (*Armed Groups and International Law*, 15 July 2012) <http://armedgroups-internationallaw.org/2012/07/15/syria-in-state-of-civil-war-says-icrc/> accessed 20 January 2017. See also R. Bartels, 'Follow-up on the organizational requirement: ICRC statements and conflict qualification' (*Armed Groups and International Law*, 10 August 2012) <http://armedgroups-internationallaw.org/2012/08/10/follow-up-on-the-organisational-requirement-icrc-statements-and-conflict-qualification/> accessed 20 January 2017.

pronouncement on this in Syria, the circumstances in which it happened were somewhat exceptional[24] and in general it still appears that the ICRC is keen to refrain from making such explicit statements that can be interpreted as 'rulings'.

2.3 Definition of non-international armed conflict

It was also noted by the ICRC in its 1971 Report, that another effective way to protect the 'threshold test' of international humanitarian law was to provide a better definition of non-international armed conflict.[25] Despite this recommendation, little progress was made in defining a non-international armed conflict until the 1990s when the two ad hoc criminal tribunals for the former Yugoslavia and Rwanda[26] (ICTY and ICTR) dealt with the definition comprehensively in its case law in order to establish whether the alleged crimes could be considered 'war crimes'. In doing so, the Tribunals developed a legal test for determining the application of common Article 3. This was first set out by the ICTY Appeals Chamber in its so often cited Decision on the Defence Motion for Interlocutory Appeal on Jurisdiction *Tadic* and has been applied consistently since. The test was set out follows:

> An armed conflict exists whenever there is a resort to armed force between States or protracted armed violence between governmental authorities and organised armed groups or between such groups within a State.[27]

Later, the Trial Chamber in the *Tadic* Judgment distilled this test into two 'closely related' criteria: (i) the intensity of the conflict; and (ii) the organization of the parties.[28] In the context of a non-international armed conflict, the Appeals Chamber also required that the armed violence be 'protracted'.[29]

Since the Appeal Chamber's first pronouncement on the matter in its *Tadic* Jurisdiction Decision, the ICTY has built a significant body of case law determining when the threshold for a non-international armed conflict is reached under customary international law, which has broadly been followed by the International Criminal Court (ICC).[30] Today, the ICTY's jurisprudence on the 'organization

[24] See K. Fortin, 'Syria and the geographical scope of international humanitarian law: moving towards a localized approach?' (*Armed Groups and International Law*, 2 October 2012) <http://armedgroups-internationallaw.org/2012/10/02/syria-and-the-geographical-scope-of-international-humanitarian-law-moving-towards-a-localised-approach/> accessed 20 January 2017.

[25] ICRC Report on Protection of Victims of Non-International Armed Conflict (n 15) 37, 41.

[26] United Nations International Criminal Tribunal for the former Yugoslavia created by means of UN Security Council Resolution 827 (25 May 1993) UN Doc S/RES/827. United Nations International Criminal Tribunal for Rwanda created by means of UN Security Council Resolution 955 (8 November 1994) UN Doc S/RES/955.

[27] *Prosecutor v Tadić* (Jurisdiction Decision) IT-94-I-T (2 October 1995) [70] (hereafter *Tadić* Jurisdiction Decision).

[28] *Prosecutor v Tadić* (Trial Judgment) IT-94-I-T (7 May 1997) [562] (hereafter *Tadić*).

[29] *Tadić* Jurisdiction Decision (n 27) [70]: 'protracted armed violence between governmental authorities and organised armed groups or between such groups within a State'.

[30] *Tadić* (n 28) [561–2]; *Prosecutor v Delalić, Mucić, Delić and Landžo,* (Trial Judgment) IT-96-21-T (16 November 1998) [183–5] (hereafter *Celebici*); *Prosecutor v Krnojelac* (Trial Judgment) IT-97-25-T, (15 March 2002) [51]; *Prosecutor v Kunarac, Kovac and Vukovic* (Appeals Judgment)

requirement' and the 'intensity requirement' provides important information about when the 'threshold' of international humanitarian law has been reached. The existence of this case law protects the threshold of non-international armed conflict from manipulation by third parties. It also provides a framework of analysis against which decisions to invoke international humanitarian law and assert criminal jurisdiction over 'war crimes' can be more easily justified by all parties. The observation that the application of international humanitarian law is beyond the control of individual States is important when analysing how armed groups acquire international legal personality from a theoretical perspective because it is an indication that the legal framework does not reflect a 'recognition conception' of international legal personality. While a fuller reflection on the theoretical significance of the paragraphs above is conducted later in the chapter, the chapter continues by first examining the threshold test from a material perspective to see what it tells us about the international legal personality of armed groups.

3. Threshold of IHL: Material Perspective

We are told by the Trial Chamber in the *Tadic* Trial Judgment, in a statement which has been subsequently much repeated, that the two criteria of intensity and organization 'are used solely for the purpose, of distinguishing an armed conflict from banditry, unorganized and short-lived insurrections, or terrorist activities which are not subject to international humanitarian law'.[31] Yet this chapter argues that, on a fundamental level, the two criteria of 'organization' and 'intensity' which were identified in the *Tadic* case are closely connected to the issue of international legal personality of armed groups. Indeed, it is argued that one of the main functions of the organization test is to determine whether the armed group is a legal entity capable of adhering to the international obligations contained in common Article 3. Likewise, it is argued that one of the main functions of the intensity test is to determine whether the situation is severe enough to justify the imposition of international law obligations on the armed group. As a result, the threshold test is of great value when seeking to understand how armed groups are bound by international human rights law. A full explanation of these arguments is set out fully below, together with a detailed examination of both requirements.

IT-96-23&IT-96-23/1-A (12 June 2002) [56] (*Kunarac* Appeals Judgment); *Prosecutor v Kordić and Čerkez* (Appeal Judgment) IT-95-14/2-A (17 December 2004) [336] (hereafter *Kordić*); *Prosecutor v Limaj, Bala and Musliu* (Trial Judgment) IT-03-66-T (30 November 2005) [83–4] (hereafter *Limaj*); *Prosecutor v Naletilic and Martinovic* (Trial Judgment) IT-98-34-T (31 March 2003) [225]; *Boškoski* (n 16). For ICC jurisprudence see *Prosecutor v Thomas Lubanga Dyilo* (Trial Judgment) ICC-01/04-01/06 (14 March 2012) [533–8] (hereafter *Lubanga*); *Prosecutor v Germain Katanga* (Trial Judgment) ICC-01/04-01/07 (7 March 2014) [1186–7] (hereafter *Katanga*).

[31] *Tadić* (n 28) [562]; *Boškoski* (n 16) [175]; *Limaj* (n 30) [89]; *Prosecutor v Djordjević* (Trial Judgment) IT-05-87/1-T (23 February 2011) [1522] (hereafter *Djordjević*).

3.1 Organization test

3.1.1 Functions to determine whether armed group is a 'legal entity'

When one examines the case law on 'threshold' from the perspective of 'legal personality' of armed groups, it is seen that one of its main functions is to address the requirement that there should be a distinguishable 'legal entity' which can be bound by common Article 3, as a counterpart to the State.[32] The implicit need for such a test stems from the fact that common Article 3 can only be applied to a particular factual situation if the norms which it contains are applied by both parties to the conflict, i.e. the State and the armed group or both armed groups. It was observed at the start of this chapter that the entire philosophy of both common Article 3 and Additional Protocol II is based on the notion that their provisions are binding equally on both parties to the conflict. As a result, in order for common Article 3 to apply, the armed group in question needs to be an entity which is organized enough to be responsible, as a legal entity, for its implementation.[33] Indeed, the question of when an 'organization' crystallizes into a legal entity is particularly relevant when dealing with armed groups because, unlike other non-State actors, there is no formal moment of their incorporation or creation which is evidenced by constitutional documents. Instead, armed groups evolve into legal entities organically with the passing of time. As a result, there is a need for a formal examination of the armed group's cohesion in order to discern whether and when it can be treated as a legal entity as a matter of law.

3.1.2 ICJ Western Sahara case conducts similar appraisal of legal entity

Interestingly, a similar appraisal of whether it was possible to treat a non-legally constituted non-State actor as a legal entity was conducted by the ICJ in its Advisory Opinion on *Western Sahara*.[34] Here, the ICJ determined whether the 'Mauritanian entity'—now known as Mauritania—was a 'legal entity' at the time under analysis. In order to do so, the court heard submissions on how the people who lived in the Mauritanian entity had a common language, a common way

[32] See *Advisory Opinion on Western Sahara* [1975] 12 ICJ Reports, 16 October 1975, 63, [148] (hereafter *Western Sahara Advisory Opinion*) which states that, 'Some criterion has, however, to be employed to determine in any particular case whether what confronts the law is or is not legally an "entity" '.

[33] See Pictet, *Commentary to Geneva Convention I* (n 1) 49, which states: 'That the Party in revolt against the de jure Government possesses an organized military force, an authority responsible for its acts, acting within a determinate territory and having the means of respecting and ensuring respect for the Convention.'

[34] In its *Western Sahara Advisory Opinion* (n 32) the ICJ stated that the 'essential test' to determine whether 'a group' is 'a legal entity distinct from its members' is the test that the Court set out in its Advisory Opinion on *Reparations*. However, in fact the test set out in the *Reparations* Opinion is not as helpful as the *Western Sahara Advisory Opinion* when looking at the legal personality of armed groups, because (i) it related to whether an organization was organized enough to take a claim against its member governments; and (ii) it related to an 'incorporated' entity, rather than an unincorporated entity. See 63 [148].

of life, religion, and system of laws. It also heard how, in the eyes of the region's inhabitants, the Mauritanian entity was a 'distinct entity'. It took note of the fact that the Mauritanian entity had two types of political authority: emirates and tribal groups.[35] In considering whether the Mauritanian entity had reached the threshold of a 'legal entity', the ICJ found it relevant to determine whether there was any cohesion or central administration amongst its constituent parts. It made clear that it was not sufficient for there to be 'forms of common activity' between the various tribes and emirates. Instead, it said that it was necessary to determine that the Mauritanian entity had 'common institutions or organs'.[36] On finding an absence of such common institutions 'even of a quite minimal character' and determining that many of the emirates and tribes lived independently from one another, the Court concluded that the Mauritanian entity 'did not have the character of a personality or corporate entity distinct from the several emirates and tribes which composed it'.[37] Notably, the ICJ was considering whether the Mauritanian entity was a subject of international law per se rather than a subject of a particular body of international law, such as international humanitarian law.

3.1.3 Closer examination of the 'organization requirement'

It is argued that the ICTY's appraisal of the organization requirement in its threshold test has a similar function to the ICJ's appraisal of the Mauritanian entity in its Advisory Opinion on *Western Sahara*, although it is more detailed. As a result, the case law on the organization requirement clarifies how organized an armed group must be before it will be bound by common Article 3. It also identifies some of the factual indicators that are relevant to a determination of whether a particular group meets this requirement. As a first point, it clarifies that there is no requirement that an armed group should be as organized as a State[38] or even a 'modern, well-organised and supplied, trained and disciplined, efficient fighting force' for it to be bound by common Article 3.[39] Despite this, the case law confirms that 'some degree of organisation' is clearly required.[40] In two of its most recent cases on the matter, the ICTY Trial Chambers have noted five broad categories of indicators which have been taken into account when the group's organization is assessed: (i) factors signalling the presence of a command structure; (ii) factors indicating that an armed group can carry out operations in an organized manner;

[35] The ICJ considered this question in the context of examining the legal ties which existed between Western Sahara and the Mauritanian entity. The label 'Mauritanian entity' recognized the fact that at the time in question, there was no Mauritanian State in existence. The first point for the Court's consideration was the legal nature of that entity which Mauritania claimed had legal ties with Western Sahara at the time of colonization by Spain. Ibid, 57 [130], [132], [133].

[36] Ibid, 63 [149]. [37] Ibid, 63 [149].

[38] *Boškoski* (n 16) [197], citing *Prosecutor v Orić* (Trial Judgment) IT-03-68-T (30 June 2006) [254]. See also *Djordjević* (n 31) [1525].

[39] *Boškoski* (n 16) [289]. Here the Judgment found that the NLA met the organizational requirement despite the fact that at no time was it 'a modern, well-organised and supplied, trained and disciplined, efficient fighting force'.

[40] *Djordjević* (n 31) [1525]; *Limaj* (n 30) [89].

(iii) factors indicating a level of logistics; and (iv) factors relevant to determining whether an armed group possessed a level of discipline and the ability to implement the basic obligations of common Article 3; and (v) factors indicating that the armed group is able to speak with one voice.[41] It is notable that the ICC has had recourse to the same five factors in its case law determining whether an armed conflict is not of an international character.[42] The identification of these five categories is helpful as it facilitates a systematic analysis of what makes a group 'organized' although they are by no means an exhaustive list.[43]

3.1.3.1 Command structure

In considering whether a group is organized, the ICTY has shown an attentiveness to factors pertaining to the group's command structure. Factors which have been considered relevant to this question have included the question of whether or not the group has a centralized General Staff which takes decisions about important combat operations and coordinates the action of the various sub-divisions of the group.[44] In that respect, the ICTY has also taken note of the organization of the group from a strategic point of view. Relevant to this determination has been an assessment of whether the group has divided the territory under its control into operational zones of responsibility.[45] The question of whether the group has organized itself into brigades, battalions, companies, and platoons has also been deemed relevant.[46] Likewise attention has been given to whether a hierarchical command structure can be discerned within the group[47] and the question of whether the group has a headquarters or regional headquarters.[48] Trial Chambers have also taken note of the way in which the centralized structure exerts control over the subordinate individuals and groups.[49] For example, evidence has been given on the existence of protocols establishing the circumstances in which a zone commander must seek the approval of the General Staff before initiating a combat operation.[50] Similarly relevant might be the existence of a protocol setting out what a zone commander should do if he has given orders without having obtained approval first, i.e. must he seek retroactive approval?[51] Also relevant is the way in which coordination between units takes place. Are there regular centralized meetings between the General Staff and the zone commanders? If so, are minutes taken?[52]

41 *Boškoski* (n 16) [199]; *Djordjević* (n 31) [1526].

42 *Katanga* (n 30) [1186].

43 *Boškoski* (n 16) [198].

44 *Djordjević* (n 31) [1541–2]; *Milutinović* Vol I (n 16); *Limaj* (n 30) [99].

45 *Djordjević* (n 31) [1546]; *Milutinović* Vol I (n 16) [827]; *Limaj* (n 30) [95].

46 *Boškoski* (n 16) [271]; *Djordjević* (n 31) [1547]; *Milutinović* Vol 1 (n 16) [826].

47 *Djordjević* (n 31) [1541], [1546], [1548–55]; *Limaj* (n 30) [99], [111]; *Boškoski* (n 16) [271].

48 *Djordjević* (n 31) [1548]; *Boškoski* (n 16) [270]. It has been noted that the fact a group does not have a consistent location for its general headquarters may be explained by the fact that it functions as a secret organization, *Limaj* (n 30) [104].

49 *Djordjević* (n 31) [1542]; *Milutinović* Vol I (n 16) [829].

50 *Milutinović* Vol I (n 16) [829], *Djordjević* (n 31) [1543].

51 *Djordjević* (n 31) [1544].

52 *Djordjević* (n 31) [1542–3]; *Milutinović* Vol I (n 16) [829].

All these factors, taken together, have been deemed relevant to the assessment of the group's command structure.

3.1.3.2 Ability to carry out operations in an organized manner

The second issue relevant to whether a group is organized has been said to be its ability to carry out operations in an organized manner. While many of the factors relevant to a group's command structure might be relevant to this category, Trial Chambers have also shown interest in a group's general military capabilities. It has been noted that:

> indicative of the level or organization of an armed group is its ability to carry out military operations, including troop movements and logistics.[53]

Particularly relevant seems to be the question of whether the group has demonstrated an ability to coordinate its planning and operations. An example of such coordination might be a group's ability to launch an effective military response to developments as they unfold. This might be illustrated by an armed group's ability to link up various sub-groups of fighters by radio or its ability to move soldiers from one location to assist soldiers in another location.[54] The case law shows that a group's ability to carry out operations in an organized manner might also be evidenced by the level of compliance with orders that is achieved.[55] For example, in the *Boskoski* case, the Trial Chamber enquired into whether the group was able to achieve substantial compliance with ceasefire agreements that had been brokered at the highest level of the organization. Finding that 'substantial compliance' had followed the signing of the Ohrid Agreement, it also noted numerous contrary examples of instances where Albanian National Liberation Army (NLA) troops on the ground had failed to act in accordance with the position expressed by the General Staff.[56] It concluded that the NLA 'had developed some capacity to implement a ceasefire, although its results were far from uniform'.[57] Other factors indicating a group's 'ability to carry out operations in an organized manner' include its ability to blockade roads[58], establish checkpoints[59], control territory[60], issue ID cards[61], collect donations,[62] and take control of civilian installations.[63]

3.1.3.3 Logistics

The third category of factors which has been deemed relevant to a group's organization relates to its logistics, i.e. how it deals with the procurement, supply, and maintenance of equipment, with the movement, evacuation, and hospitalization of personnel, the provision of facilities and services, and related matters. Relevant to this category is the group's capacity to recruit new members and the arrangements

[53] *Boškoski* (n 16) [277]. [54] *Limaj* (n 30) [108]; *Boškoski* (n 16) [277].
[55] *Limaj* (n 30) [98]; *Boškoski* (n 16) [279]. [56] *Boškoski* (n 16) [279–80].
[57] Ibid, [280]. [58] *Djordjević* (n 31) [1557]. [59] Ibid. [60] Ibid.
[61] Ibid. [62] Ibid. [63] Ibid.

that it has made for training new and existing members.[64] For example, in the *Djordjević* case the Trial Chamber stated:

> The training of new recruits by personnel with particular experience is an indication of the KLA's effectiveness in developing itself into an organized military unit with trained fighters.[65]

Also relevant has been the establishment of training centres by the group.[66] Likewise indicative of the organization of the group is the group's use of uniforms. Did uniforms exist? How common were they? How where they supplied?[67] While Trial Chambers heard considerable evidence on these questions, the Trial chamber in the *Limaj* case found:

> While the existence of a uniform may be an indicator of the existence of a well-organised entity, in the view of the Chamber, this factor alone is not determinative in this case of the existence of an organized military structure, as it has little bearing on the functioning of the KLA.[68]

Of equal interest to Trial Chambers has been the manner in which the group procures weapons, the kind of weapons it has and the means that it has for the transportation of weapons.[69] Likewise, the sophistication of the communications equipment used by the group has clearly been deemed to be indicative of its organization.[70]

3.1.3.4 Discipline and ability to implement IHL provisions

The fourth set of factors relevant to a group's organization relates to whether an armed group possesses a level of discipline and the ability to implement the basic obligations of common Article 3. This fourth overarching requirement has not consistently been applied in the jurisprudence. Indeed, in the *Limaj* case, when the defence submitted that 'at the bare minimum' a party to a conflict 'must be able to implement international humanitarian law and … possess: a basic understanding of the principles laid down in common Article 3, a capacity to disseminate rules and a method of sanctioning breaches'[71], the Trial Chamber appeared to disagree, reminding the Defence that only 'some degree of organisation by the parties' was required and clarifying that this was a lower level of organization than that required for the responsibility of superiors.[72] However, in the *Boskoski* case the Trial Chamber explicitly included this requirement as one of the five key prerequisites for a group to be deemed 'organized' and further stated:

64 Ibid, [1560], *Limaj* (n 30) [118]; *Boškoski* (n 16) [283–4].

65 *Djordjević* (n 31) [1560]. See also *Milutinović* Vol I (n 16) [824]; *Limaj* (n 30) [120].

66 *Djordjević* (n 31) [1561].

67 *Djordjević* (n 31) [1562], *Milutinović* Vol I (n 16) [837–9]; *Limaj* (n 30) [123]; *Boškoski* (n 16) [276], [285].

68 *Limaj* (n 30) [123].

69 *Djordjević* (n 31) [1566], [1568]; *Milutinović* Vol I (n 16) [835]; *Limaj* (n 30) [121–2]; *Boškoski* (n 16) [276], [281].

70 *Djordjević* (n 31) [1569–70]; *Milutinović* Vol I (n 16) [828]; *Limaj* (n 30) [104], [124].

71 *Limaj* (n 30) [88].

72 Ibid [89]. See also *Prosecutor v Mrkšić, Radić, Šljivančanin* (Trial Judgment) IT-95-13/1-T (27 September 2007) [407] (hereafter *Mrkšić*).

The leadership of the group, must, as a minimum, have the ability to exercise some control over its members so that the basis of Common Article 3 may be implemented.[73]

It later stated:

so long as the armed group possesses the organisational ability to comply with the obligations of international humanitarian law, even a pattern of ... violations would not necessarily suggest that the party did not possess the level of organisation required to be a party to an armed conflict. The Chamber cannot merely infer a lack of organisation of the armed group by reason of the fact that international humanitarian law was frequently violated by its members.[74]

This provides clarity as to whether an armed group must actually comply with international humanitarian law to be deemed bound by it, or whether it must merely be deemed *capable of* complying with international humanitarian law to be bound by it.[75]

In determining whether a particular group has a level of discipline and the ability to implement the basic obligations of common Article 3, Trial Chambers from the ICTY have found it relevant to consider the structures that were in place for the dissemination of internal rules and international humanitarian law. For example, it has been noted that the armed group in question had a code of conduct that was distributed to zone commanders and subordinates.[76] In the Kosovo cases, the Trial Chamber also found it relevant that booklets containing the rules of warfare had been distributed. In *Djordjevic* the Trial Chamber noted:

the distribution of Rulebooks reflected the ongoing process of developing and enforcing coordination within the growing KLA.[77]

Equally noteworthy was the fact that training sessions had taken place on the laws of war and Geneva Conventions.[78] The Trial Chambers likewise noted a fairly well-developed system of enforcing military discipline[79] including the existence of a military police force[80] and a military court.[81] It was also remarked that the fact that there may be some disconnect between theory and practice in the enforcement of discipline would not necessarily mean that a group had not reached a required level of organization for common Article 3 to apply. In the *Limaj* case,

[73] *Boškoski* (n 16) [196]. See also *Djordjević* (n 31) [1525–6].

[74] *Boškoski* (n 16) [205].

[75] See F. Hampson, 'Human Rights and Humanitarian Law Internal Conflicts' in M. Meyer (ed), *Armed Conflict and the New Law* (British Institute for Comparative and International Law, 1990) 55–80, 67. Uncertainty in this regard may be traced to the tendency elsewhere in international humanitarian law of certain statuses only being granted to groups who manifest their ability to apply international humanitarian law. For example, the Hague Regulations state that belligerent status will only be granted to military forces (whether the army of militias and volunteer corps) 'provided that they conduct their operations in accordance with the laws and customs of war.' See also Article 4A(2) of Geneva Convention III.

[76] *Djordjević* (n 31) [1571]; *Milutinović* Vol 1 (n 16) [826], [830]; *Limaj* (n 30) [98], [110–12].

[77] *Djordjević* (n 31) [1571].

[78] Ibid, also *Milutinović* Vol 1 (n 16) [830].

[79] *Djordjević* (n 31) [1572], [1575]; *Milutinović* Vol 1 (n 16) [831].

[80] *Limaj* (n 30) [113].

[81] *Milutinović* Vol 1 (n 16) [831]; *Djordjević* (n 31) [1572–4].

the Court stated even if disciplinary rules are not consistently enforced, the step of setting up a structure that will be capable of securing compliance gave evidence of the 'growing formality and effectiveness of the organizational structure'.[82]

However, despite the fairly high level of disciplinary structures in existence within the Kosovo Liberation Army (KLA), it is clear that no such sophistication is necessary in order to fulfil the requirement specified. In the *Boskoski* case relating to the Macedonian conflict, where no such comparable structures were found to exist, the Trial Chamber concluded that nonetheless:

> there was ... a basic system of discipline within the NLA that allowed it to function with some effectiveness.[83]

It has also been noted that internal command structures within an armed group may be difficult for the outside world to discern because of the conditions of secrecy within which the group is forced to operate.[84]

3.1.3.5 Ability of the armed group to 'speak with one voice'

Finally, the last overarching criteria which is deemed to be a condition of organization is the ability of the armed group to 'speak with one voice'. The group's practice of issuing political statements and communiqués to the public about its policies and practice will be relevant to this.[85] Likewise, when looking at the KLA, the Trial Chamber noted that it had an official spokesperson whose role was to communicate with the domestic and foreign media.[86] Also relevant to the group's ability to speak with one voice is the way in which it is perceived by the international community, particularly with respect to peace negotiations.[87] For example, the *Limaj* Trial Chamber took note of relationships between the group and foreign diplomatic representatives.[88] In this regard, it will also be important to ascertain how 'key' the group is considered in any negotiations taking place to resolve the crisis. In the *Limaj* case, the Trial Chamber noted the acceptance of the KLA by international representatives as a key party in political negotiations to resolve the crisis in Kosovo. It stated that:

> this discloses and confirms that by that time the KLA had achieved a level of organizational stability and effectiveness. In particular this gave it the recognized ability to speak with one voice and with a level of persuasive authority on behalf of its members.[89]

Other factors which have been placed in the preceding four categories could also be seen to be relevant in this category. For example, the level of compliance achieved after ceasefire negotiations could be deemed to be indicative of the extent to which the individuals taking part in the negotiations on behalf of the KLA are expressing the will of, and sufficiently connected to, the views of their members. Also relevant in this respect are the factors placed under the heading 'command structure' as this

[82] *Limaj* (n 30) [117]. [83] *Boškoski* (n 16) [274]. [84] *Limaj* (n 30) [132].
[85] *Boškoski* (n 16) [269]. [86] *Limaj* (n 30) [102].
[87] *Djordjević* (n 31) [1576]; *Limaj* (n 30) [129]. [88] *Limaj* (n 30) [124].
[89] Ibid, [129].

enquiry seems based on a desire to ascertain whether what happens at operational level reflects the will of a centralized General Staff.

3.1.4 Analysis of the five indicators of 'organization'

An examination of these kinds of factors supports the theory that one of the main purposes of the organization requirement is to determine whether the armed group under scrutiny can be deemed to be a legal entity capable of being bound by international humanitarian law. When reviewing the jurisprudence of the ICTY, it is striking that many of the factors analysed are indicators of a group's unity as a cohesive whole. This is of course most obvious when looking at the fifth criterion; the ability of the group to speak with one voice. The purpose of this requirement is clearly directed at ascertaining the extent to which the group can be seen to be a unified whole, rather than a loose alliance of actors. It asks whether the group has a level of unity that allows the individuals at the 'top' to represent the whole armed group, either on the ground or at international level. Trial Chambers seem satisfied that this is the case in instances where there is proof that individuals who are nominally identified as a representatives of the group, in terms of strategy or international negotiations, prove themselves capable of influencing the members' behaviour. In doing so, it is demonstrated that the group has matured into being a coherent entity which is separate from its individual members and can act as a single entity. But a similar purpose can be read into the other four requirements too. In focusing on the group's command structure, ability to carry out its operations in an organized manner, logistics, and discipline, the court is also effectively evaluating whether the armed group is a 'group', rather than a loose collection of individuals. In fact, it is striking that almost all the factors which are examined within these five broad headings contribute to an appraisal of an armed group's unity.[90] This lends credence to the argument that one of the main functions of the organization requirement is to provide an analytical framework by which it can be determined whether a particular armed group can be said to be, in the words of the ICJ in the *Western Sahara* case, a 'personality or corporate entity distinct from' its individual members.

The case law makes clear that not all the various criteria listed above need to be satisfied for a group to meet the 'organizational' requirement. Indeed, it remains to be seen how the organization requirement would be applied in a situation where the armed group had a horizontal structure, rather than a pyramidal one.[91] Clearly, in a situation where an armed group is made up of discrete operational cells which

[90] This is true of the armed group's command structure, centrality of command, hierarchy, existence of a headquarters, existence of a uniform, ability to conduct coordinated operations, capacity to achieve compliance with orders on the ground, ability to conduct operations in an organized manner, use of centralized systems for procurement, supply and maintenance of equipment, training, recruitment, ownership and use of communications systems, existence and dissemination of a disciplinary code, and enforcement of discipline.

[91] S. Sivakumaran, *The Law of Non-International Armed Conflict* (OUP, Oxford, 2014) 172–4 (hereafter Sivakumaran, *Non-International Armed Conflict*).

do not have clear lines of contact between them, it will be harder to prove that an armed group is a 'single entity' than if the armed group has a classic structure with clear vertical command structures. Further challenges will be posed in conflicts where an armed group either fragments, or never initially coalesces into a single coordinated force. In these instances, the 'group' may consist of loosely coordinated groups with a similar cause but no clear leadership.[92] In such cases, it may be difficult to judge whether the armed group can be deemed a subject of international humanitarian law or even several different separate subjects of international humanitarian law. Yet clearly the fact that an armed group has a pyramidal structure will not alone be a reason for it per se not to meet the threshold of organization required by international humanitarian law. In such cases, it will likely be more important to prove lines of communication between horizontal units and leadership command centres.

Importantly, the case law from the ICTY shows that the question of whether an armed group can be deemed an entity for the purposes of international humanitarian law is looked at in conjunction with the normative content of common Article 3. This is implicit in the Court's evaluation of whether the armed group is capable of complying with the international humanitarian norms contained within common Article 3. A focus on the armed group's normative capacity was particularly seen in the *Boskoski* case, where the Trial Chamber paid attention to whether or not the leadership of the armed group exercised sufficient control over its members 'so that the basis of common Article 3' could be implemented. This shows that unlike in the *Western Sahara* case where the ICJ was concerned with whether the Western Sahara was capable of having international legal personality per se, the ICTY is concerned with whether an armed group is capable of having international legal personality under a particular normative framework, i.e. common Article 3. Moreover, in the *Boskoski* judgment, the Trial Chamber points out that the level of organization required to fulfil the obligations set out in common Article 3 is 'minimal' as the norms it contains are purely humanitarian in nature.[93]

3.1.5 'Organization requirement' in the Additional Protocol II threshold

The need to match an entity's normative capacity with a particular normative framework explains why a higher organizational threshold is required for an armed group to be considered bound by Additional Protocol II, than for common Article

[92] The challenges situations raise are illustrated in the Chatham House Report on the Legal Classification of Armed Conflicts (n 17). For example, in the Syrian armed conflict, there was considerable fragmentation and non-coordination among armed groups that were part of the 'opposition'. See 9–11. The Libya conflict posed another challenge because here many of the anti-Gaddafi groups were far from being organized under any kind of command. See 40–1.

[93] *Boškoski* (n 16) [197]. It is questionable whether this statement is really accurate as an armed group will rarely 'only' be bound to the humanitarian provisions in common Article 3 but will often very soon afterwards, or indeed contemporaneously, be bound to the basic rules on conduct of hostilities that probably require a greater level of organization. For further discussion of this point, see section 5.1.6 of Chapter 7.

3. Article 1 of the Additional Protocol II requires that an armed group has 'responsible command' and 'control over a part of its territory' in order to 'implement' the Protocol. By 'responsible command', the commentary states that the armed group must have a degree of organization 'capable, on the one hand, of planning and carrying out sustained and concerted military operations, and on the other, of imposing discipline in the name of the de facto authority'.[94] Explaining the term 'control over a part of its territory', the commentary states that the control 'must be sufficient to allow sustained concerted military operations to be carried out and for the Protocol to be applied, e.g. caring for the wounded and the sick, or detaining prisoners and treating them decently, as provided in Articles 4 and 5'.[95] The commentary continues by noting that there must be some stability of control over 'even a modest area of land' for the group to be 'capable of effectively applying the rules of the Protocol'.[96] Indeed, it finds the notion that an armed group should be able to 'implement the Protocol' before it is deemed to apply a 'fundamental criterion'.[97] Moreover, acknowledging that the threshold of Additional Protocol II is quite high, the commentary finds it to be nonetheless 'realistic' in the light of the 'rules' it contains.[98] It goes on to state that it is only in instances where an armed group meets this threshold that it will have the 'minimum infrastructure' required to apply the rules developed in the Protocol.

In recent years, there have been developments in international criminal law which suggest that the traditional divide between common Article 3 conflicts and Additional Protocol II conflicts has been partly eliminated.[99] Certainly, a reading of Article 8(2)(e) and (f) of the Rome Statute indicates that a number of the norms in Additional Protocol II also apply in non-international armed conflicts where there is 'protracted armed conflict between governmental authorities and organized armed groups or between such groups', but no control of territory.[100]

[94] ICRC, *Commentary to the Additional Protocols of 8 June 1977* (n 12) [4463].

[95] Ibid, [4464]. [96] Ibid, [4467]. [97] Ibid, [4470]. [98] Ibid.

[99] To be clear, Article 8(2)(c) of the Rome Statute refers to serious violations of Article 3 common to the four Geneva Conventions of 12 August 1949. Article 8(2)(d) of the Rome Statute states that paragraph (2)(c) applies to armed conflicts not of an international character and thus does not apply to situations of internal disturbances and tensions, such as riots, isolated and sporadic acts of violence or other acts of a similar nature. Article 8(2)(e) of the Rome Statute refers to 'other serious violations of the laws and customs applicable in armed conflicts not of an international character' and then lists acts (i)–(xii). At least seven of these provisions can be seen to have their origin in Additional Protocol II. Article 8(2)(f) states that paragraph (2)(e) applies to armed conflicts not of an international character and thus does not apply to situations of internal disturbances and tensions, such as riots, isolated and sporadic acts of violence, and other acts of a similar nature. It applies to armed conflicts that take place in the territory of a State when there is protracted armed conflict between governmental authorities and organized armed groups or between such groups. Notably, Article 8(2)(f) does not list a requirement that the armed groups should have control of territory, which is generally the classic differentiation between a common Article 3 conflict and an Additional Protocol II conflict.

[100] Article 8(2)(e)(i) of the Rome Statute can be seen to correspond with Article 13(2) of APII, Article 8(2)(e)(ii) with Articles 11 and 12 of APII, Article 8(2)(e)(iv) with Article 16 of APII, Article 8(2)(e)(v) with Article 4(2)(g) of APII, Article 8(2)(e)(vi) with Article 4(2)(e) and (f) of APII, Article 8(2)(e)(vii) with Article 4(3)(c) of APII, Article 8(2)(e)(viii) with Article 17(1) of APII, and Article 8(2)(e)(xi) with Article 4(2)(a) of APII. The absence of a requirement that the armed group has a 'control over a part of territory' in the wording Article 8(2)(f) implies that 'territory' is no longer required for the corresponding international humanitarian law norms to apply.

Indeed, the Trial Chamber in the *Lubanga* case confirmed that there was no need for the Prosecution to establish either that the armed group was under responsible command or that it had control over a portion of a territory for there to be a non-international armed conflict for the purposes of Article 8(2)(f).[101] Yet when considering the significance of Article 8(2)(f) for the framework of international humanitarian law, it is helpful to remember that all the norms which are contained in Article 8(2)(e) of the Rome Statute, which originate from Additional Protocol II, are those which can be violated by individuals. They include the crimes of intentionally directing attacks against the civilian population, intentionally attacking buildings or persons using the emblems of the Geneva Conventions, intentionally attacking religious buildings or those dedicated to art and science, intentionally attacking hospitals, pillaging a town, committing rape or other acts of sexual violence, and conscripting or enlisting children. In capacity terms, they all relate to obligations in the Additional Protocol II, which can be adhered to, or violated, just as much by individuals as by armed groups. As a result, their observance requires less organizational capacity than positive obligations.

Indeed, conspicuously absent from the crimes listed in Article 8(2)(e) of the Rome Statute are references to any of the obligations in Additional Protocol II that require an amount of 'infrastructure' or 'territory' to be implemented. These include the rules relating to detention, education, and penal prosecutions. The reason for their absence in Article 8(2)(e) can nominally be explained by the fact that violations of these provisions, although serious, do not amount to crimes under international criminal law. But it is also notable that many of the obligations in Additional Protocol II which are absent from Article 8(2)(e) are those obligations which cannot be fulfilled by individuals alone, and require an 'organization' which has control of territory for their implementation. Most significantly, their absence from Article 8(2)(e) precludes an argument that Article 8(2) (f) of the Additional Protocol has eliminated the threshold of Additional Protocol II. Rather, Article 8(2)(e) merely indicates that there is an emerging category of norms which apply in non-international armed conflicts which do not require control of territory. This category of norms relates largely to conduct of hostilities and is also thought to be binding in non-international armed conflicts as a matter of customary international law. It is generally thought that this category of norms will become binding at the lowest level of non-international armed conflict, alongside common Article 3.[102]

In summary, when examining the legal framework through the lens of legal personality it can be seen that it reflects an acceptance of the fact that armed groups operating in non-international armed conflict will have a spectrum of international legal personality under treaty law that is tied to their normative capacity.

[101] *Lubanga* (n 30) [538].

[102] This conclusion is supported by the ICRC's study on Customary International Humanitarian Law which concluded that the main rules relating to conduct of hostilities apply in non-international armed conflicts and international armed conflicts. J. Henckaerts and L. Doswald-Beck, *Customary International Humanitarian Law, Volume I: Rules* (CUP, Cambridge 2005) 3–76.

It identifies clearly two recognizable points along this spectrum which are matched with three discrete packages of norms: (i) those in common Article 3; (ii) the further norms in Article 8(2)(e) of the Rome Statute that apply at the same time; and (iii) the remaining norms in Additional Protocol II which are not reflected in Article 8(2)(e) and which require territory. The fact that international humanitarian law and international criminal law combined provide these two graduated thresholds of international legal personality matched with normative capacity is helpful because it allows an evaluation of an armed group's international legal personality against objective criteria that is tied to a realistic framework of normative accountability. It would not be realistic to hold every armed group responsible for all the provisions of Additional Protocol II. In other words, the normative framework and case law indicates that there is no value in designating an entity as the bearer of a set of international norms if it does not have the capacity to enforce them. Having identified the important function of the organization requirement, it is now time to provide a similar analysis of the intensity requirement.

3.2 'Intensity requirement'

3.2.1 Introduction

The paragraphs below demonstrate that the intensity requirement also has an important role in determining the legal personality of armed groups. Under the heading 'intensity', it is also important to examine the criteria of 'protractedness' which was mentioned in the first *Tadić* Jurisdiction Decision but has since been largely subsumed into the 'intensity' criterion.[103] As the *Haradinaj* Trial Chamber stated:

> The criterion of protracted armed violence has therefore been interpreted in practice, including by the Tadić Trial Chamber itself, as referring more to the intensity of the armed violence than to its duration.[104]

Yet, despite the fact that the requirement of 'protractedness' has been analysed by ICTY Trial and Appeals Chambers under the heading of 'intensity', it is clear that it brings a 'temporal element to the definition of armed conflict' which the intensity requirement on its own does not always capture.[105] The fact that separate attention must be given to whether a conflict is 'protracted' has also be confirmed by Article 8(2)(f) of the Rome Statute that requires there to be '*protracted* armed conflict between governmental authorities and organized armed groups or between

[103] *Boškoski* (n 16) [186]. The *Milutinović* Trial Judgment is an exception to this, as it analyses the existence of an armed conflict under the headings (a) protracted armed violence and (b) the KLA as an organized armed group. It concluded that the armed violence in Kosovo was of 'sufficient duration and intensity to amount to the 'protracted armed violence' envisaged by the first prong of the test for an internal armed conflict'.

[104] *Prosecutor v Haradinaj* et al. (Trial Judgment) IT-04-84 (3 April 2008) [49] (hereafter *Haradinaj*).

[105] *Boškoski* (n 16) [186].

such groups'.[106] As a result of its importance, the nature of the protractedness requirement is briefly described in the following paragraph.

3.2.2 Protractedness requirement

The purpose of the 'protractedness' requirement is to distinguish isolated incidents which occur in peacetime from acts which are part of a protracted campaign of violence which entails the engagement of both parties in hostilities.[107] Clarifying this, the *Boskoski* Trial Chamber cited the *Kordic* Appeals Chamber which stated:

> [t]he requirement of protracted fighting is significant in excluding mere cases of civil unrest or single acts of terrorism.[108]

However, because in practice the requirements of 'intensity' and 'protractedness' are analysed together, it is hard to say exactly what it entails. It is noted in the *Boskoski* case that there has been a 'significant pattern' of Trial Chambers examining incidents of violence that precede the temporal limits of the indictment to determine whether the violence is 'protracted', particularly when the indictment period is less than one year.[109] The purpose of Trial Chambers seems to have been to examine how a pattern of violence by both sides emerges over time, as the armed group becomes increasingly organized. The duration of the distinct episodes of hostilities that make up the greater picture of protracted armed violence has also been held to be relevant.[110] Usually at the point at which the existence of an armed conflict is affirmed there are daily instances of violence.[111] Yet the case law makes clear that daily clashes are not required for the protractedness requirement to be fulfilled.[112] In other words, violence does not need to be constant to be 'protracted'. However, it does suggest that a pattern of armed violence must be discerned which continues over a period of significant duration.

3.2.3 'Intensity requirement'

It is easier to discern the factors which have been deemed to be indicative of 'intensity' as in many cases these are listed at the beginning of the legal analysis. Many of these factors are also relevant to the protracted nature of the violence. They include the seriousness of the attacks and whether there has been an increase or spread of clashes over territory and over a period of time,[113] the

[106] *Lubanga* (n 30) [536], [538]; *Katanga* (n 30) [1185].

[107] *Boškoski* (n 16) [185].

[108] *Boškoski* (n 16) [185] citing *Kordić* (n 30) [341] (second emphasis added by the *Boškoski* Trial Chamber).

[109] *Boškoski* (n 16) fn 758.

[110] *Limaj* (n 30) [142], [149], [153], [155], [156], [168].

[111] *Boškoski* (n 16) [234]; *Milutinović Vol I* (n 16) [803]; *Haradinaj* (n 104) [96–9]; *Limaj* (n 30) [172].

[112] *Limaj* (n 30) [168].

[113] *Boškoski* (n 16) [177]; *Tadić* (n 28), [565–6]; *Celebici* (n 30) [186], [189]; *Prosecutor v Milosević* (Decision on Motion for Judgment of Acquittal) IT-02-54-T (16 June 2004) [28–9] (hereafter *Milosević* Rule 98 *bis* Decision); *Kordić* (n 30) [340–1]; *Prosecutor v Halilovic* (Trial Judgment)

number of government forces mobilized,[114] the mobilization of reservists,[115] the use of weapons by the parties to the conflict and in distinct engagements,[116] as well as whether the conflict has attracted the attention of the United Nations Security Council.[117] Also relevant in this respect will be whether statements have been made on the matter by either the United Nations Security Council or any other regional organizations, or whether any resolutions have been passed.[118] Trial Chambers have paid attention to the number of civilians which have been displaced from combat zones as a result of the fighting[119] and the number which have been evacuated.[120] They have taken into account the number of casualties caused by the hostilities[121] and the extent of destruction of houses and property,[122] the weapons used by other sides,[123] in particular the use of heavy weapons and equipment.[124] Also relevant to the intensity requirement has been the blockading, besieging, or shelling of towns,[125] the existence of front lines between the parties,[126] the number of persons kidnapped or detained by the parties,[127] and the occupation of territory, towns, and villages.[128] The ICRC's involvement in the release of detainees on both sides and role in passing messages to families of detainees has also been noted.[129] Additionally, attention has been given to the deployment of the army rather than the police to crisis areas,[130] the

IT-01-48-T (16 November 2005) [163–6] (hereafter *Halilovic*); *Haradinaj* (n 104) [91–9]; *Limaj* (n 30) [168], [169]; *Milutinović* Vol I (n 16) [803]; *Boškoski* (n 16) [243]; *Djordjević* (n 31) [1533].

114 *Limaj* (n 30) [164]; *Boškoski* (n 16) [213]; *Haradinaj* (n 104) [92], [99].

115 *Boškoski* (n 16) [213], [243].

116 *Milosević* Rule 98 *bis* Decision (n 113) [31]; *Limaj* (n 30) [166]; *Haradinaj* (n 104) [49]; *Boškoski* (n 16) [243] and often a detailed description of weapons used by both parties in each engagement.

117 *Djordjević* (n 31) [1535]; *Boškoski* (n 16) [214]; *Tadić* (n 28) [567]; *Haradinaj* (n 104) [49]; *Celebici* (n 30) [190].

118 *Boškoski* (n 16) [213], [215], [243]; *Djordjević* (n 31) [1535]; *Tadić* (n 28) [567].

119 *Boškoski* (n 16) [240], [248]; *Djordjević* (n 31) [1533–4]; *Limaj* (n 30) [161], [167]; *Haradinaj* (n 104) [49], [97].

120 *Boškoski* (n 16) [216]; *Kordić* (n 30) [340].

121 *Djordjević* (n 31) [1533]; *Milutinović* Vol I (n 16) [797]; *Boškoski* (n 16) [239]; *Tadić* (n 28) [565]; *Haradinaj* (n 104) [92], *Limaj* (n 30) [142]; *Kordić* (n 30) [339].

122 *Limaj* (n 30) [142], [152]; *Boškoski* (n 16) [241]; *Tadić* (n 28) [565]; *Haradinaj* (n 104) [92]; *Kordić* (n 30) [339].

123 *Limaj* (n 30) [158], [161]; *Milosević* Rule 98 *bis* Decision (n 113) [31]; *Boškoski* (n 16) [208–49] (the *Boškoski* Trial Judgment and the *Limaj* Trial Judgment are particularly attentive to the use of weapons used).

124 *Limaj* (n 30) [138], [149], [158], [161], [163], [165], [166], [171]; *Haradinaj* (n 104) [94]; *Tadić* (n 28) [143]; *Halilovic* (n 113) [166].

125 *Limaj* (n 30) [153]; *Boškoski* (n 16) [243]; *Tadić* (n 28) [143]; *Haradinaj* (n 104) [96]; *Halilovic* (n 113) [165–7], [168].

126 *Limaj* (n 30) [142]; *Halilovic* (n 113) [161], [169], [172].

127 *Limaj* (n 30) [162]; *Milutinović* Vol I (n 16) [819].

128 *Limaj* (n 30) [143], 146, 163; *Milutinović* Vol I (n 16) [799], [801]; *Djordjević* (n 31) [1533]; *Tadić* (n 28) [566]; *Halilovic* (n 113) [162], [163], [164]; *Boškoski* (n 16) [242].

129 *Boškoski* (n 16) [243].

130 *Limaj* (n 30) [159]; *Haradinaj* (n 104) [98]; *Milutinović* Vol I (n 16) [798]; *Boškoski* (n 16) [178].

estimated size of the armed group,[131] the closure of roads by both sides,[132] the setting up of checkpoints,[133] the appeals for intervention from the international community by both sides,[134] and the involvement of international organizations in the brokering and monitoring of ceasefire agreements.[135] The language that the State authority has used to describe the violence has been noted, as well as the legal framework that has been applied.[136] In particular, it has been seen to be relevant that the State has prosecuted persons for offences which are only applicable in times of armed conflict or that it has granted a broad amnesty to those who participated.[137]

One of the disadvantages of the ICTY jurisprudence is that it is not so helpful for fine-tuning the placement of the threshold of non-international armed conflict. The main reason for this is that the bulk of the case law from the ICTY relates to the conflict in Kosovo where the fighting reached a considerable level of protractedness and intensity, which easily met the thresholds required. As a result, the *Boskoski* case is the most helpful case for fine-tuning the positioning of the threshold of intensity. The reason for this is that it dealt with the conflict in Macedonia where the attacks against the State forces by the NLA were on a much smaller scale than those of the KLA in Kosovo. This is reflected in the relatively few casualties on both sides and the relatively small-scale material damage to property and housing. The highest estimates put the total number of civilians killed during 2001 as a result of the armed clashes at 168.[138] In its judgment, the Trial Chamber considered whether these low figures might be an indication that the police and army were working within a law enforcement paradigm, rather than a conduct of hostilities framework. Yet, it concluded that the figures reflected the fact that the NLA often employed guerrilla tactics in their fight against the Macedonian government which produced many fewer casualties than larger-scale military offensives.[139] This confirms that an armed conflict characterized by guerrilla tactics can still theoretically meet the threshold of violence required for the existence of a non-international armed conflict. Whether this is the case will depend on the frequency of the attacks, their geographical extent, the weapons employed, and the effect they have on the government and the civilian population. Having looked in detail at the substance of the intensity requirement, it remains to examine what it says about the legal personality of armed groups.

[131] *Milutinović* Vol I (n 16) [802]. This is a factor which is more commonly discussed in the context of the organization requirement. See *Milutinović* Vol I (n 16) [823]; *Djordjević* (n 31) [1540]; *Boškoski* (n 16) [267].

[132] *Limaj* (n 30) [144]; *Milutinović* Vol I (n 16) [797]. This factor is also sometimes seen as an indication of a group's organization, see *Haradinaj* (n 104) [75].

[133] *Limaj* (n 30) [145]. This factor is also sometimes seen as an indication of a group's organization, see *Haradinaj* (n 104) [75].

[134] *Boškoski* (n 16) [243]; *Djordjević* (n 31) [1535]; *Prosecutor v Hadzihasanovic and Kubura* (Trial Judgment) IT-01-47-T (15 March 2006) [23] (hereafter *Hadzihasanovic and Kubura*).

[135] *Milutinović* Vol I (n 16) [812]; *Djordjević* (n 31) [1535]; *Boškoski* (n 16) [233], [243].

[136] *Milutinović* Vol I (n 16) [800]; *Boškoski* (n 16) [238], [245–7].

[137] *Boškoski* (n 16) [238], [243].

[138] Ibid, [244].

[139] Ibid.

3.2.4 *The rationale behind the 'intensity requirement'*

When examining the intensity threshold from the perspective of legal personality, it is seen that it is reminiscent of the factors which were also at play in the application of the law of belligerency and insurgency, described in the previous chapter. In instances where a *de jure* government's capacities are compromised, there is greater justification for making armed groups the addressee of international norms. This was demonstrated in the belligerency and insurgency framework which both included in their definition the idea that third States were *compelled* to have some kind of relation with the insurgent group because of the absence or inabilities of the *de jure* government.[140] To a large extent, it is argued that the intensity requirement plays the same role in the international humanitarian law framework. Together with the 'protractedness' requirement it acts as a confirmation of the parent State's inability to confront the violence by ordinary law enforcement means. The significance of this inability is twofold; first it gives deference to the notion that the application of international humanitarian law will only be justified when law enforcement measures have been proved insufficient. The motivation for verifying a government's 'need' to apply the international humanitarian law framework stems from the observation that a government should not be able to exploit the legal framework by escalating its operations against an insurgent group in order to self-trigger the application of international humanitarian law.[141] But it also proves that the capacities of the parent State are significantly compromised. Likewise, a requirement that the State is partly absent before international norms can be applied is seen in the threshold test for Additional Protocol II which implicitly includes a requirement that the State has lost control of a portion of its territory in its Article 1. Inherent in the fulfilment of this requirement is an acknowledgement that the government is no longer single-handedly able to secure the safety of its citizens across its whole territory. It also confirms the situation as 'international' in character.

Another major function of the intensity requirement relates to the need to prove the international aspect of non-international armed conflict. When examining the law of belligerency and insurgency, it was seen how the application of international legal norms to armed groups was precipitated by, and justified by, the involvement of third States' in the conflict. It is likely as a result of similar motivations that the intensity requirement takes note of the involvement of third parties in the conflict. Yet it is notable in this respect that in the ICTY's assessment, more attention is given to the involvement of the United Nations and other international organizations than to the involvement of third States as such. For example, Trial Chambers have considered whether the conflict has reached the agenda of the United Nations Security Council and taken note of the involvement of the ICRC in the release

[140] See sections 2.1, 2.4, and 3.3.3.2 of Chapter 4 on the belligerency and insurgency frameworks.

[141] The relevance of such a determination seems to be hinted in the *Boškoski* case when the Trial Chamber found it relevant that the NLA had *'compelled'* the government to commit the full weight of its military resources to fighting the insurgency, *Boškoski* (n 16) [289].

of detainees and their communication with the outside world.[142] They have also considered the involvement of international organizations in the brokering and monitoring of ceasefire agreements. Perhaps this change of emphasis reflects the changed international landscape today. Because international organizations exist nowadays, it is more legitimate for third States to protect their interests vis-à-vis an armed group via international organizations, than bilaterally. Trial Chambers have also paid attention to a number of humanitarian issues such as refugee flows, IDP numbers, the number of casualties, and the extent of destruction of civilian infrastructure. In that sense, attention is seen to be given to whether the violence has reached 'international' proportions such that it poses a threat to international peace and security as a whole. Of course, it is also important to note that the intensity of the violence is also an indicator of the operational capability of the armed group. Recognizing this, it is seen that the two limbs of the threshold test overlap in their function. The factors examined as part of the intensity requirement also provide an added confirmation that the group is organized enough to orchestrate a certain scale of damage.

4. Threshold of IHL: Theoretical Perspective

4.1 Introduction

It will be shown in this section that the threshold test also assists in answering the more difficult question of what the threshold test tells us about the theoretical aspect of international legal personality of armed groups. The purpose of the analysis that follows is twofold. First, it aims to gain insights into the way in which armed groups are deemed, explicitly or implicitly, to acquire international legal personality under international law. In doing so, the analysis pays particular attention to the role of State consent in the legal framework and the manner in which the legal personality of armed groups is perceived. These conclusions are interesting in their own right but are particularly employed in Chapter 6 which examines how the conclusions from Chapters 4 and 5 can enhance our understanding of how armed groups may be bound by international human rights law. The second purpose of the analysis is to seek objective justification for a later recourse to a particular conception of international legal personality when looking at the legal personality of armed groups under international human rights law. This is particularly important from a methodological perspective because it helps address two crucial questions that are relevant later in the study: first, the question of whether the practice of armed groups should be taken into account in a determination of customary international law binding upon them and second, the question of the relevance of State consent to the acquisition of legal personality by armed groups.

[142] See *Prosecutor v Simic* et al. (Decision on the Prosecution Motion under Rule 73 for a Ruling concerning the Testimony of a Witness) IT-95-9-T (27 July 1999), fn 9, which confirmed a '*general acknowledgment*' that the ICRC has international legal personality.

4.2 Scope of international legal personality of armed groups under IHL

The first theoretical question to consider is what the international legal framework of international humanitarian law says about the scope of the international legal personality of armed groups. On a formal reading of the treaties, armed groups are bound principally to respect the international humanitarian norms vis-à-vis the other parties to the conflict. This is uncontested. In that sense, it can be said without doubt that the international humanitarian law legal framework constitutes recognition of the fact that armed groups have specific international legal personality vis-à-vis the parties against which they are fighting. That being said, there are also strong reasons to conclude that the international legal personality of armed groups under international humanitarian law is of a general nature, i.e. that their obligations are owed to third States too.[143] The first reason for this is that the obligations in common Article 3 have been said to be 'elementary considerations of humanity'.[144] This recognizes that the norms in common Article 3 have a status akin to *erga omnes* norms.[145] A similar conclusion can be drawn from common Article 1 of the Geneva Conventions which contains an obligation on all States parties to 'ensure respect for the present Convention'. On the face of it, this would seem to include an obligation on all States to secure the respect of common Article 3 by States and armed groups.[146] The notion that common Article 3 is *erga omnes* was also seemingly confirmed by the ICJ in the *Nicaragua case* where it concluded that the United States was 'under an obligation not to encourage persons or groups engaged in the conflict to act in violation of the provisions of Article 3 common to the 1949 Geneva Conventions'.[147]

The idea that the obligations owed under common Article 3 are owed to more entities than just the parties to the conflict is also supported by the case law of the ICTY which has stated on several occasions that most norms of international humanitarian law are either *jus cogens* or *erga omnes.*[148] Its assertions in this regard are not well substantiated but it has been shown above that they can be defended at

[143] See discussion of international legal personality being 'general' or 'specific' in section 3.2 of Chapter 4.

[144] *Case Concerning Military and Paramilitary Activities in and against Nicaragua (Nicaragua v United States of America)* [1986] ICJ Reports 14, 27 June 1986 [218] (hereafter *Nicaragua v USA*)

[145] The use of the term *erga omnes* in the following paragraphs refers specifically to the notion set out in *Barcelona Traction, Light and Power Company, Limited (Belgium v Spain)* [1970] ICJ Reports, 5 February 1970, 3 [33] (hereafter *Barcelona Traction*). Here, the ICJ referred to norms which are *'the concern of all States'*. It stated that 'in view of the importance of the rights involved, all States can be held to have a legal interest in their protection'.

[146] It is relevant to note at this juncture that the Geneva Conventions have been universally ratified.

[147] *Nicaragua v USA* (n 144) [220].

[148] It is noted that it is generally thought that the fact that a norm has *jus cogens* status will mean that it has *erga omnes* effect. See also E. de Wet, 'Jus Cogens and Obligations Erga Omnes' in D. Shelton (ed) *The Oxford Handbook of International Human Rights Law* (OUP, Oxford, 2013) 542–3 (hereafter de Wet, 'Obligations Erga Omnes'). On which see *Prosecutor v Furundzija* (Trial Judgment) IT-95-17/1-T (10 December 1998) [151–7]; *Prosecutor v Kupreskic* et al. (Trial Judgment) IT-95-16-T (14 January 2000) [520].

least in relation to common Article 3. Although universal jurisdiction for common Article 3 is not provided by the Geneva Conventions themselves, the right of third States to assert jurisdiction over these crimes has been asserted by the ICRC to be a rule of customary international law.[149] There have also been several prosecutions at national level on the basis of universal jurisdiction for violations of international humanitarian law committed in non-international armed conflicts.[150] It is also noteworthy that the Rome Statute defines 'war crimes' as the most serious crimes of concern 'to the international community as a whole'.[151] The notion that common Article 3 establishes legal obligations for armed groups *erga omnes* is also confirmed by the practice of the United Nations Security Council which routinely calls upon the parties to non-international armed conflicts to abide by their obligations under international humanitarian law.[152] Taken together, this practice suggests that the international legal personality of armed groups bound by common Article 3 is general in character. Such a conclusion cannot be drawn with as much certainty when it comes to all the norms in Additional Protocol II because the protocol is not universally ratified. Likewise, not all the norms in Additional Protocol II are considered to have the status of customary international humanitarian law and nor are all its provisions reflected in international criminal law.[153]

4.3 Treaties as ultimate source of international legal personality

A more important point to note is that the threshold test under international humanitarian law, although crucial, cannot properly be said to be the first step in armed groups acquiring international legal personality under modern international humanitarian law. Such a suggestion would overlook the fact that, unlike the law of belligerency and insurgency, the norms contained in the modern international humanitarian law which applies to non-international armed conflict are enshrined in treaty law. As a result, unlike the framework of belligerency or insurgency, international humanitarian law is explicitly the product of States' drafting and consent. The ability of States to bind non-State actors by means of treaty law is examined in

[149] The Geneva Conventions provide universal jurisdiction for 'grave breaches' of the Conventions. The breaches enumerated as 'grave' do not wholly correspond with breaches of common Article 3. See J. Henckaerts and L. Doswald-Beck, *Customary International Humanitarian Law, Volume I: Rules* (CUP, Cambridge 2005) 604–5.

[150] See the cases in Belgium, Switzerland and the Netherlands cited at footnote 196 of ibid. See also commentary by C. Ryngaert, 'Another Afghan Case in the Hague District Court: Universal Jurisdiction over common Article 3', *Hague Justice Portal* 2007 <http://www.haguejusticeportal.net/index.php?id=8213> accessed 20 January 2017.

[151] See Preamble to the Rome Statute. See also de Wet, 'Obligations Erga Omnes' (n 148) 554.

[152] See for example, UN Security Council Resolution 2175 (29 August 2014) (Protection of civilians in armed conflict) UN Doc S/RES/2175; UNSC Resolution 2173 (27 August 2014) (Sudan and South Sudan) UN Doc S/RES/2173; UNSC Resolution 2165(2014) (Syria); UNSC Resolution 2145 (17 March 2014) (Afghanistan) UN Doc S/RES/2145.

[153] Having said that, it has earlier been observed that many of the norms in Additional Protocol II which are not linked to a corresponding crime under international law, are those which relate to an armed groups' control of territory. This raises another reason to argue that they may be general in character, as this has been the case for analogous norms in the belligerency and insurgency framework.

Chapter 7 in depth, and will not be explored in detail here. For now, it is sufficient to observe that the treaty landscape of international humanitarian law that applies in non-international armed conflicts represents a consent by States that armed groups be held bound by certain pre-identified norms in certain circumstances of non-international armed conflict. In that sense, the existence of the treaty framework of common Article 3 and Additional Protocol II embodies a strong element of State consent, which is usually a characteristic of the recognition conception of international legal personality. It is a strong indication of the fact that at the time of the treaties' drafting, the States parties consented to the conferral of a specific measure of legal personality to armed groups.[154]

However, it is also important to observe that the bestowal of international legal personality on armed groups by common Article 3 and Additional Protocol II, if it can be called that, operates in the abstract. Neither common Article 3 nor Additional Protocol II gives, or seeks to give, specific armed groups legal personality. This means that specific armed groups only 'step up' and take their place in the legal framework at the moment at which the threshold of international humanitarian law is reached. As a result, it is argued that this is the second, and more interesting, temporal moment to analyse when seeking to draw conclusions about the legal personality of armed groups because this is the moment at which specific armed groups acquire legal personality in a concrete sense. In particular, the threshold test tells us how and when international legal personality is acquired and how that international legal personality is conceived. The paragraphs below draw theoretical conclusions on this issue. These conclusions emerge from the description above about *how* the threshold of international humanitarian law is reached. They also emerge from the organization and intensity requirements which pinpoint *when* the threshold of international humanitarian law is met.

In view of the different conceptions of international legal personality, it is almost inevitable that there will be disagreement about whether the threshold test should be seen to be the moment at which an armed groups gains international legal personality or the moment at which the legal personality of armed groups is confirmed, i.e. whether the threshold of common Article 3 and Additional Protocol II is a transformative moment or a confirmatory moment. The difference is slight but takes us to yet another version of the circular conundrum which has been so endlessly debated in writings about international legal personality.[155] Does international legal personality precede the application of an international norm? Or does the acquisition of international legal personality follow or coincide with the acquisition of international legal personality? A prolonged consideration of these questions exposes 'time' to be an inadequate continuum against which to judge matters relating to the international legal personality of non-State actors. This is

[154] The analysis of Sassòli is recalled in this regard. M. Sassòli and A. Bouvier, *How Does Law Protect In Law? Cases, Documents and Teaching Materials on Contemporary Practice in International Humanitarian Law* (2nd edn, ICRC, Geneva 2006) 266.

[155] See Chapter 3 on the differences between the recognition conception of international legal personality and the individualistic, formal, and actor conception of legal personality.

particularly the case when looking at non-State actors like armed groups which do not have an easily identifiable moment of incorporation. It is noted that the legal framework postulates that an armed group will begin as a group of individuals and end up as an organized entity capable of bearing obligations under international law. It is argued in this chapter that the threshold test functions as a tool to identify the moment at which this moment of transition takes place. But while the legal framework gives the impression that the threshold test is able to do this quite successfully, in fact we must admit that the moment remains hard to pin down in scientific terms. The reason for this is that the threshold of armed conflict is not measured by criteria that can be counted or computed mathematically. We do not say 'that any armed group with more than x members' is an 'organization'. We do not say that once more than x people have been killed, the threshold of intensity has been reached. If we did, the question of whether the threshold has been reached would be a relatively straightforward calculation.

Instead, the question of whether a particular situation of violence is 'intense enough' and the question of whether a particular armed group is 'organized enough' are determined with reference to factors which are not easily evaluated mathematically. Even when quantifiable figures are relevant (e.g. number of casualties), they are evaluated by reference to other non-quantifiable factors (e.g. the manner of death, the author of the casualty etc). This points to the fact that the threshold tests which are built into international humanitarian law, while indisputably important for legal certainty, are inherently unscientific and inevitably rather arbitrary in application. This is exacerbated by the fact that there is no single objective body to 'rule' that the threshold has been reached. As a result, there is no possibility to ensure that the criteria relevant for a non-international armed conflict have been applied uniformly. Stepping back, one can see that the threshold test, as it is accepted, requires us to 'buy into' the intellectual fiction that at a particular moment in time, during the course of a situation of unrest or non-international armed conflict, the various thresholds of international humanitarian law have been reached. This exposes the paradox that although we accept the threshold test at a conceptual level, we can also recognize that it is ultimately an artificial notion which can rarely be expressed accurately at the level of days or minutes. This is reflected in the fact that bodies asserting that international humanitarian law applies rarely argue that international humanitarian law begins to apply on a particular day. Instead, such statements generally confirm that international humanitarian law applies 'now' or confirm that it applied at a particular date in the past, without seeking to pinpoint when exactly international humanitarian law started to apply.[156]

[156] See for example the judgment in *Limaj* (n 30) [171] in which the Trial Chamber found that it was satisfied that 'before the end of May 1998 an armed conflict existed in Kosovo between the Serbian forces and the KLA'. See also the judgment in *Djordjević* (n 31) [1579] in which the Trial Chamber declared itself satisfied that 'as of the end of May 1998 an armed conflict existed in Kosovo between Serbian forces, in particular forces of the VJ and the MUP, and the KLA'. See also *Milutinović* Vol I (n 16) [841] which states that 'starting in 1998 and no later than summer of that year, VJ and MUP forces, and the KLA as an organized group, engaged in protracted armed violence throughout

The significance of the inherent artificiality of the threshold test confirms the legal framework of international humanitarian law, as all legal frameworks, to be an intellectual fiction created by States. It might be tempting to conclude from this fiction that threshold test is a *post posteriori* confirmation of an already existing legal situation, in a manner similar to some declarations of belligerency. But such a conclusion would ignore the fact that, however artificial, the threshold of international humanitarian law is largely respected in practical terms. This highlights the paradox highlighted above. Although, as scholars, we can recognize that the different thresholds for the application of international humanitarian law are artificial, in practice we respect them. The most likely reason for this is that the threshold test, and its integrity as a transformative moment, is important from a legal certainty perspective. The first reason for this is that it makes clear the protections that people are entitled to in times of armed conflicts. Secondly, and connectedly, it dictates the rules of international law which are binding on particular actors at a certain moment. Thirdly, and perhaps most importantly when justifying a rigorous attention to the temporal element of the test, the threshold test identifies a distinct moment at which individuals can be held criminally responsible for war crimes. As a consequence, it is seen that the legal framework of international humanitarian law, combined with an evaluation of how it is applied in practice, confirms a notion that the application of the international humanitarian law precedes, or coincides with, the application of international legal personality. It does not leave room for the possibility that an armed group may have international legal personality under international humanitarian law before the formal threshold of international humanitarian law is met.[157] The coincidence between the normative framework and the acquisition of legal personality has strong features of the formal conception of international legal personality, under which legal personality is a consequence of an entity being bound by international norms.

4.4 Relevance of State consent to application of IHL to particular armed groups

A further point to note is that because the legal framework that applies to non-international armed conflict is created by States, it might be tempting to conclude that it corresponds most closely with the recognition conception of international legal personality. The temptation to draw this conclusion would be based on the fact that the 'source' of the international legal personality of armed groups is, at a fundamental level, the consent of States reflected in treaty law. Yet there are several aspects of the legal framework which do not fit with traditional features of the recognition conception of international legal personality. The most important of

Kosovo'. See finally *Boškoski* (n 16) [292], in which the Trial Chamber stated: 'Having regard to the law applicable and the analysis of the evidence made above, the Chamber is persuaded that in August 2001, at the times material to the Indictment, there was a state of internal armed conflict in FYROM.'

[157] That is not to say that an armed group may not gain international legal personality under another body of law, for example human rights law, prior to that moment.

these is the observation that the application of international humanitarian law to a particular non-international armed conflict is beyond the consent of States. By that it is meant that a parent State is not able to block the application of international humanitarian law in circumstances where it does not want to acknowledge that international humanitarian law applies. Nor can a parent State legitimately declare international humanitarian law to apply to a situation of armed violence in circumstances where the threshold is not deemed to have been met. Likewise, the opinions of third States are only relevant to the extent that they are contribute to, and can be said to be evidenced by, resolutions from the United Nations Security Council and General Assembly. In that sense, while the opinions of States are relevant to ascertaining the legal threshold, they cannot unilaterally make a difference to the application or non-application of the international humanitarian law framework. It has been seen above that this was a deliberate strategy on the part of the drafters of common Article 3 to de-politicize the legal framework and prevent a parent State or third States from having the power to control the legal framework. In that sense, modern international humanitarian law as it applies to specific armed conflicts is crucially different from the core aspects of the belligerency framework where the parent State and third States were able to 'bestow' or 'withhold' aspects of an armed group's international legal personality at will. As a result, it does not bear the same hallmarks of the recognition conception of international legal personality.

Instead, the legal framework of international humanitarian law indicates that the acquisition of legal personality by an armed group is governed by the development of the armed group's organization, in combination with the context in which it is operating. In other words, the legal framework indicates that the acquisition of legal personality by armed groups is largely circumstance-driven, rather than State-driven. The case law demonstrates that the most important aspects which determine an armed group's journey to legal personality relate to its organization, its functional capacity, its participation on the international sphere, the severity of the hostilities, the humanitarian consequences of the conflict, and the reduced capacities of the parent State. These have much in common with the actor and individualistic conceptions of international legal personality which pay close attention to the functioning of the armed group on an international sphere. However, it has been seen that the legal framework makes a clear connection between the armed group's functional capacity and its *normative* capacity. This is seen in the different thresholds of international humanitarian law which exist, each of which links distinct packages of norms with distinct organizational requirements for armed groups. It is argued that attention to the armed group's functionality makes the legal framework lean more towards the individualistic conception of international legal personality than the actor conception of legal personality.

Chapter 3 demonstrated that the individualistic conception of legal personality places store on a group's 'legal interaction' with third States and the international community, rather than its interaction in general. Likewise, the legal framework of international humanitarian law is at odds with the notion central to the actor conception that all legal norms are constantly subject to change and flux according to the needs of the participants to whom they address. It is also at odds with the notion that, in formal terms, the opinion of an armed group is irrelevant in determining whether the threshold of international humanitarian law has been met and whether a particular armed group is bound to its provisions.[158] Instead, the legal framework of international humanitarian law contains a strongly prescriptive element which manifests itself in the role of State consent in the legal framework, the existence of *jus cogens* norms, and a rigorous deference to the threshold test determining when armed groups will be bound. The legal framework's strong focus on norms and strict insistence on the fact that the 'threshold' of international humanitarian law should be treated as a 'transformative moment' leads to the conclusion that the legal framework also contains features of the formal conception of international legal personality.

5. Conclusions

This chapter's review of the framework of international humanitarian law has demonstrated that the 'threshold' test for the application of international humanitarian law is a rich source of information when seeking to determine how, and when, armed groups acquire legal personality under international law. In particular, the chapter demonstrates that an armed group needs to be organized to the point at which it can be treated as an entity separate from its members. It also demonstrates that there needs to be an 'international' dimension of the situation which justifies an otherwise domestic actor being the subject of international obligations. In exploring these ideas, the chapter showed how the organization requirement serves to determine whether a group of individuals has evolved into a legal entity capable of adhering to the international legal obligations contained with common Article 3. In examining whether the group has a common structure, an ability to carry out operations in an organized manner, a level of logistics, a level of discipline, an ability to implement international humanitarian law norms, and an ability to speak with one voice, the purpose of the organization requirement seems to be to establish whether the group is a cohesive entity that it capable of complying with the rules contained in common Article 3, i.e. a party to the armed conflict and a duty-bearer under the legal framework. The chapter argues that the intensity requirement acts as a confirmation of the parent State's inability to confront the violence by ordinary law enforcement means. In doing so, it confirms that the capacities of the parent State are significantly compromised. It also confirms the situation as 'international' in character, in a manner that justifies the imposition of international legal personality upon the armed group. In examining the threshold test, the chapter argues that it serves another important function, which is to protect the legal framework from manipulation by political actors.

[158] This will be explored in more detail in Chapter 7.

From a theoretical perspective, the chapter has shown that the framework of international humanitarian law which applies to non-international armed conflict has features of the formal and individualistic approach to international legal personality. In particular, it has been seen that the legal framework in the abstract which is contained in common Article 3 and Additional Protocol II reflects the formal approach to international legal personality. But the legal framework also corresponds with some aspects of the individualistic approach to international legal personality. This is particularly seen in the second level of the analysis, when specific armed groups 'step up' into the legal framework of common Article 3 or Additional Protocol II. Here, the threshold test's two limbs of 'organization' and 'intensity' repeatedly emphasize an armed group's functionality, capacity, and participation on the international stage. Similarities with the individualistic conception are also seen in the legal framework's examination of the involvement of the international community. Another feature of the legal framework which is reminiscent of the individualistic conception of international personality is the focus on the armed group as an entity which has emerged out of an incorporation of individuals. Seeing individuals as the base unit of international law is a core concept that is explored by Hersch Lauterpacht in his writings.[159] A further similarity with the individualistic conception of international legal personality can be seen in the notion that the application of international humanitarian law, and the coincident acquisition of international legal personality by armed groups should be dictated by concerns of humanity. Although not stated explicitly in the threshold test, the application of international humanitarian law to a particular conflict is clearly motivated by humanitarian concerns.

During the course of this analysis, it has become increasingly clear that the international legal framework of international humanitarian law does not correspond easily with the features of the actor concept of international legal personality. It has been seen that are several main reasons for this. The first is that the treaty law framework of international humanitarian law which applies to armed groups does not take into account the consent of armed groups. As a result, the legal framework does not reflect the central premise of the actor school of international legal personality which asserts that those who are bound by the law will generally also be the makers of the law. The legal framework also demonstrates a focus on legal norms which is not per se a feature of the actor conception of international legal personality, which tends to focus equally on non-legal participation. Its focus on legal norms is particularly observed in the fact that the legal framework is deferential to the notion that the acquisition of legal personality by armed groups is coincident to the application of international humanitarian law, and does not precede it. This anomaly was described in detail above and is incompatible with the actor school's conception of international legal personality, which is largely descriptive. It has been seen in the fact that the legal framework contains a strong normative element which dictates that the international legal personality of armed groups is

[159] This will be explained in more detail in Chapter 7.

closely related to the normative framework to which they are bound. This sets it apart from the actor conception of international law which is rooted in a deference to the 'actual', over the 'normative'. An analysis of what these conclusions tell us about when and how armed groups may gain international legal personality under international human rights law is conducted in Chapter 6.

6

International Legal Personality of Armed Groups under Human Rights Law

1. Introduction

The previous two chapters have demonstrated how the legal frameworks of belligerency, insurgency, and international humanitarian law conceive the legal personality of armed groups. Providing a historical and contemporary perspective, Chapters 4 and 5 show that many of the problems associated with holding armed groups accountable under human rights law have been dealt with before in other frameworks. For example, the chapters show how the different frameworks have coped with the problem that armed groups come into being organically, rather than having a readily identifiable moment of legal incorporation. They also demonstrate how the three legal frameworks are vulnerable to political manipulation and identify some of the main tools that have been employed to combat that vulnerability. In doing so, they demonstrate the importance of identifying the 'moment' at which a particular body of law applies to armed groups. They show that the ability to identify this moment, with reference to clear objective criteria, protects the legal framework from politicization. In doing so, the chapters identify and corroborate the importance of achieving a better understanding of the international legal personality of armed groups under human rights law. In the light of this observation, the purpose of this chapter is to draw together the analysis of the two previous chapters in order to see what they can tell us about when and how it may be justifiable to find armed groups responsible under human rights law. The chapter concludes by applying these conclusions to the analysis contained in Chapter 2 in order to explore how different thresholds of human rights obligations for armed groups might be operationalized.

2. International Legal Personality Exists Along a Spectrum

The insurgency, belligerency, and international humanitarian law frameworks show a strong acceptance of the fact that international legal personality is a concept that exists along a spectrum. The historical legal framework of belligerency and insurgency shows a historical acceptance that recognizing that armed groups have obligations under international law does not mean that they are States. It also does not mean that the armed groups are approaching statehood per se. Indeed, all three legal frameworks show a strong acceptance that the international legal personality of armed groups has historically been understood as a *sui generis* product of the exceptional circumstances of armed conflict in which it arises. When turning to the human rights law framework, this observation reinforces the message that the fact that an armed group is held accountable under human rights law does not have any formal consequences from a legal perspective. It does not mean that the armed group is being recognized as a State. Nor does it give the armed group equal status in law to the incumbent government. It also does not mean that the armed group has attained the status of belligerency. Indeed, the three legal frameworks examined also show an acceptance of the fact that the legal personality of armed groups *inter se* is rarely uniform. In other words, the legal personality of one armed group, manifested by the normative scope of its obligations, will likely be different from that of another armed group. It has also shown that the variations between different armed groups' personality can manifest themselves either procedurally or substantively.

3. Legal Personality Can Be General or Specific

From a procedural perspective, it has been seen that armed groups may have international legal personality in the general, i.e. *erga omnes* or in the specific, against one or two States or international organizations. A clear example of armed groups manifesting general legal personality was shown to arise in instances where a parent State recognized an armed group as a belligerent. In this instance, it was seen that armed groups were considered bound to the law on belligerency in relation to their warlike operations vis-à-vis all third States. General legal personality was also seen to be possible in instances where an armed group had control of territory. In such instances, it was demonstrated that third States could hold an armed group responsible for the obligations of the parent State under customary international law or treaty law. The procedural scope of these obligations would, it is argued, be the same as the original obligation which was binding on the parent State. Specific legal personality was seen to arise in instances where an armed group brokered a specific agreement with a third State. It was also seen to arise in instances where a specific third State recognized an armed group as a belligerent. From a procedural perspective, it was shown that the normative scope of the obligations of armed groups under international humanitarian law is less clear. However, it was demonstrated that there are strong arguments that the legal personality of armed groups bound by common Article 3 is general in nature. It was also shown that aspects of the legal personality of armed groups bound by Additional Protocol II may be general in nature. The significance of this for human rights law is that it provides a strong argument that the legal personality of armed groups will be general in instances where it is deemed to have arisen out of the control of territory. In instances where an armed group's legal personality under international human rights law has arisen out of treaty law or specific agreements with other international entities it could be general or specific.

4. Legal Personality of Different Armed Groups

From a substantive perspective, an analysis of the three legal frameworks demonstrated that different armed groups have different levels of substantive legal personality. By that it is meant that different armed groups may have different levels of normative responsibility, even within the same normative framework. This conclusion stems from the observation that in every framework the normative responsibilities of armed groups was seen to be fundamentally linked to their capacities, their relations with third parties, and the circumstances in which they operate. In addition to the obligations associated with their warlike operations, belligerent armed groups were also held bound by further bundles of norms arising out of their control of territory or ad hoc legal interaction with third States. The scope of this second branch of normative responsibility was determined by the specific facts of the armed conflict and the issues on which the interests of third States were engaged. The legal framework of insurgency demonstrated that armed groups which had not been recognized as belligerents could be held bound by a similar package of norms arising out of their control of territory or legal interaction with third States. In both the frameworks of insurgency and belligerency it was demonstrated that these norms would not necessarily have any connection to the armed group's warlike operations per se. Instead, it was seen that they would relate more to the protection of assets and foreign nationals. A recognition that armed groups can have varying levels of international legal personality is also a feature of international humanitarian law. This was demonstrated by the fact that international humanitarian law has built-in thresholds of normative responsibility with concurrently matched organization requirements.

5. Legal Frameworks Can Accommodate High Degree of Heterogeneity Within Category 'Armed Groups'

There are several conclusions which can be drawn from the conclusions above which are relevant to the human rights law framework. Perhaps the most important of these is the observation that all three legal frameworks recognize that there is a high level of factual and legal heterogeneity within the category of armed groups. This stems from the differences in armed groups' capacity, territorial control, relations with third States, relations with the parent State, and operational practices. It is noteworthy that none of the three legal frameworks treat armed groups as a generic category of actors with common features. Nor do they advocate an 'on/off' approach to their normative responsibilities. Instead, all three legal frameworks recognize that the normative framework to which an armed group is held bound will match its capacity. It was stated above that in different ways, each legal framework supports the notion that armed groups will be held bound by a spectrum of norms. In the international humanitarian law framework, this spectrum is formalized by the creation of distinct categories of norms which match distinct thresholds of organization capacity. This observation provides support for an argument that it is sensible to hold armed groups accountable under a spectrum of human rights obligations that match their capacity and functionality. Whether this is possible as a matter of law is a different question and will be examined in more detail below. For now it can simply be commented that the legal frameworks of belligerency, insurgency, and international humanitarian law indicate the impracticability of holding *all* armed groups bound to the *whole range* of human rights obligations found in the International Covenant on Civil and Political Rights (ICCPR) and International Covenant on Economic, Social and Cultural Rights (ICESCR).

6. International Legal Personality of Armed Groups May Have Different Sources

A review of the law relating to belligerency and insurgency and a survey of the international humanitarian law framework has shown that the international legal personality of armed groups may have different sources. The three legal frameworks has shown that the international legal personality of armed groups may arise out of treaty law, customary international law, bilateral agreements, and control of territory or people. The law on belligerency and insurgency in particular has shown that a single armed group is capable of having obligations which come from different sources. This allows the conclusion that an armed group may concurrently have obligations under international humanitarian law and obligations under human rights law. It also supports the notion that an armed group's obligations under human rights law may arise from different sources. They may arise out of treaties which, like the Geneva Conventions, explicitly seek to bind armed groups. But they may also arise out of the armed group's control of territory. In this case, it has been argued that their source in the formal sense is likely the legal obligations of the State itself. The legal frameworks also support the notion that different armed groups can, and likely will, have a different set of obligations from each other. They support the idea that the obligations of armed groups under international law are inherently linked to their function and capacity. As a result, the normative scope of an armed group's legal personality will be directly linked to the specific circumstances of the situation in which they are operating.

7. Link between Legal Personality of Armed Groups and Control of Territory is Not New

A review of the law on insurgency and belligerency has shown that the notion that an armed group may accrue responsibilities under international law as a result of its control of territory is far from new. Instead, the legal frameworks of insurgency and belligerency have demonstrated that it has long been recognized that an armed group may be held to have taken on the responsibilities of the State in instances where it controls territory to the exclusion of the government. The situation of the American Civil War demonstrated that the obligations deemed binding on the Confederate States by Great Britain went far beyond obligations relating to the military operations of the two sides. Instead, they related to the due diligence obligations of a parent State under customary international law. Chapter 4 commented that these obligations were not dissimilar to modern-day human rights law conceptions of due diligence. Moreover, it was demonstrated that the instances in which armed groups were held bound by the obligations of the parent State were not restricted to situations of belligerency. The juxtaposition of the analysis of the legal framework of insurgency with the legal framework of belligerency demonstrated that the responsibilities that an armed group accrued by virtue of its control of territory were not dependent on a declaration of belligerency per se. Chapter 4 showed that during the Spanish Civil War, the Franco insurgents were regularly held bound by third States to provide compensation for damages that they suffered to persons or assets. This is relevant when considering how armed groups are bound by human rights law because it demonstrates that the practice of holding armed groups to be bound by international law in circumstances where they control territory has important historical precedent.

In the exploration of the above principle, instances were seen in which armed groups were held responsible by third States for the obligations of their parent States under customary international law and treaty law. It is argued that the instances in which armed groups were held bound to protect foreign assets or nations are essentially examples of armed groups being held bound to the customary international law obligations of the parent State. With regard to treaty law, the view was articulated in 1864 that an armed group would also be held bound by the treaty law obligations undertaken by a parent State. A similar view was taken by the Spanish government in 1936 where it informed the Portuguese government that, because of its control of territory, the Franco rebels should be held responsible under 'international treaties' in its place.[1] From these words, it can be assumed that the Spanish government viewed the Franco insurgents to be responsible for the State's obligations under treaty law in the area under its control. Taken together, these examples provide evidence, albeit a little scanty, of an acceptance that armed groups could be held bound to the obligations of the parent State in customary law and treaty law in instances where they had control over territory.

The significance of these conclusions for the accountability of armed groups under human rights law is that they provide an endorsement of the practice of calling armed groups accountable under international human rights law, in instances where they exercise control over a territory. They show that the practice of recognizing that armed groups may be held bound by the legal obligations of the State in circumstances where they control territory is not new. They also support the

[1] C. Rousseau, 'La Non-Intervention en Espagne' (1938) 3 Revue de Droit International et de Législation Comparée 217, 279.

idea that in such instances, the armed group is essentially being held bound by the obligations of the State. In that sense, the conclusions indicate that the source of an armed group's human rights obligations in instances where it controls territory is likely to be the State's own human rights obligations under either treaty law or customary international law. The idea that armed groups may be bound by the obligations of the parent State in instances where they control territory is examined in more detail in later chapters of this book which examine more thoroughly how armed groups are bound by humanitarian law and how armed groups might be bound by international human rights law. In particular, it is explored in Chapter 9, which analyses the theory that an armed group may be bound by the obligations of the parent State in instances where it has control of territory in default of the government.

8. Legal Threshold for Application of Human Rights Law to Armed Groups

8.1 Importance of determining when legal framework applies

The analysis of the international humanitarian law framework has highlighted the importance of clarifying the question of 'when' the legal framework of human rights can be applied to armed groups. It demonstrated that the absence of a clearly defined threshold makes the legal framework vulnerable to manipulation, which ultimately affects its legitimacy. It also demonstrated that the best way of protecting against such malleability is for there to be a widely recognized threshold of application which is recognized by all parties. For the purposes of human rights law, this suggests that there is much work to be done in defining the point at which international human rights law will apply to armed groups. It will be shown below that this will include defining an organizational criterion that serves not only to check whether an armed group can be treated as a legal entity but also whether it can be an entity under 'human rights law'. A better understanding will also need to be developed of what external factors need to be in existence before an armed group is recognized to be an entity of international law. It was seen in the international humanitarian law framework that the organization requirement needed to be evaluated in tandem with the context in which the armed group was operating, i.e. 'the intensity requirement'. Attention must be given to whether a different, but functionally equivalent, contextual framework may be required before human rights law is deemed to be binding upon armed groups.

8.1.1 Functional equivalent to the 'intensity requirement' for the human rights framework

Unlike international humanitarian law, international human rights law is accepted to apply at all times, in peacetime and in times of armed conflict. As a result, any threshold test for the application of international human rights law to armed groups will not need to refer to the existence of the armed conflict per se. There is no reason of law why there needs to be an armed conflict for armed groups to be bound by human rights law. As a result, any threshold test for the acquisition of international legal personality by armed groups under international human rights law is unlikely to contain an 'intensity' requirement as such. That being said, the analysis above has shown that the intensity test provides important information about the circumstances in which armed groups may acquire legal personality under human rights law. For example, it indicates that the situation will need to have an 'international' dimension which justifies, or possibly even necessitates, the legal personality of the armed group. In that regard, it is noteworthy that the theoretical conclusions of Chapters 4 and 5 indicated that armed groups acquire legal personality under international law not because of the consent of individual States and not as a result of their own consent to be bound to those norms. Instead, they found that armed groups acquire legal personality under international law as a result of their own functionality and as a result of the incapacity of the State. These requirements would be satisfied in instances where an armed group was exercising control over a territory to the exclusion of the *de jure* government.

Identifying the fact that there is a need for the situation to be 'international' raises the important question of whether an armed group can attain international legal personality outside of an armed conflict situation. To a great extent this question is outside the scope of this book which focuses exclusively on armed groups operating in the context of non-international armed conflicts. However, the conclusions of Chapters 4 and 5 indicate that it will only be possible for an armed group to acquire legal personality outside an armed conflict situation in circumstances where the armed group is organized and the capacities of the State are significantly diminished. The latter requirement may be demonstrated by significant State failure or absence in a particular area or in circumstances where the crimes that an armed group commits are so heinous that they constitute a State-default and engage the interest of the international community as a whole. It is argued in Chapter 10 that this may occur if, for example, an armed group commits crimes against humanity outside the threshold of non-international armed conflict.

8.1.2 'Organization requirement' for the human rights framework

A review of the contemporary framework of international humanitarian law also makes clear that there will need to be some kind of preliminary checking mechanism to verify whether an armed group can be spoken of as a legal entity before it is described as bearing responsibility under international human rights law. A preliminary test to check the armed group's 'cohesion' should include a similar assessment of the group's unity and cohesion that is conducted in the case law from the ICTY and by the ICJ in the *Western Sahara* case. Attention should be given whether the armed group can be said to be an entity separate from its individual members. When assessing this requirement, attention may be given to similar criteria which have been identified case law on the 'organization' criteria in the international humanitarian law framework above. For example, attention may be given to an armed group's ability to speak in one voice, its command structures, its capacity to hold a ceasefire, ability to represent itself at international level, its organizational structure, and its disciplinary codes. Attention may be given to any aspects of the group's organization which suggest that it has a strong or central leadership. This may be demonstrated by the way the armed group manages its logistics, how it obtains its weapons, how it acquires its funding, and whether it has a centralized command. On the basis that the same type of entity is being examined for 'organizational' coherence when considering whether an armed group is bound by international human rights law, it makes sense that the same external and internal features may be taken as indicators of the armed group's basic cohesion.

However, it has also been observed that the test of whether an armed group can be said to be a 'legal entity' has not been undertaken in isolation. Instead, it has been conducted with reference to the legal framework towards which legal personality is being assessed, e.g. international humanitarian law. This has been shown to be a consequence of the linkage between international legal personality and an armed group's normative capacity. In other words, it has been shown that the organization test, which is part of the threshold test for the application of international humanitarian law, also has the function of ascertaining whether the armed group has the capability of fulfilling the normative framework of international humanitarian law. The case law on 'organization' asks not only 'is this entity sufficiently organised to be a subject of international law?' but 'is this entity sufficiently organised to be a subject of international humanitarian law e.g. common Article 3 or common Article 3 *and* Additional Protocol?' This explains why the organization test for common Article 3 puts such store on the armed group's command structure, disciplinary systems, and its ability to secure adherence to common Article 3. The test's focus on these elements reflects the fact that a party to an armed conflict, whether State or non-State in character, can only properly secure its own adherence to international humanitarian law norms if it secures their implementation throughout all the levels of command, down to the individual soldier taking part in hostilities.

As a result, when considering whether an armed group is unified enough for it to be bound by human rights law, one must ask not only 'is this armed group organized enough to be a subject of international law?' but 'is this armed group organized enough to be able to be a subject of international human rights law'? In other words, 'is this armed group organized enough to be able to implement the human rights framework'? In doing so, it will be important to consider features of the group which are specifically relevant to the human rights framework. For example, it might be relevant to take notice of whether an armed group operates a basic law enforcement system or is providing healthcare or education in the area in which it controls. It may also be relevant to determine whether it has a system of registering births and deaths, officiating over marriages, or resolving family or land disputes. These are strong indicators that an armed group has 'common institutions or organs' which allow it to adhere to certain norms within the human rights framework. But the observation that an armed group's obligations under human rights law need to be linked to its capacity poses a problem. For while it has been seen that the modern framework of international humanitarian law has two built-in thresholds of normative responsibility for armed groups, there are currently no equivalent normative thresholds built into the international human rights framework.

8.2 Normative accountability must be graduated to correspond with capacity

The fact that there are no equivalent normative thresholds in human rights law is due to the structure of human rights law and the fact that it applies, at least in theory, at all times. Moreover, as a body of law traditionally binding on States, the common and classical view has been that human rights norms should be indivisible. In other words, if a State signs up to a human rights treaty, it is held responsible for *all* the rights therein unless it derogates from particular obligations, because of the exigencies of the situation. From this perspective, it could easily be argued that human rights law should be seen as an indivisible block of norms. Taking this position, it can be understood why it might be concluded that an armed group would need a very consolidated control of territory before it is bound by human rights law, if this means adhering to the full gamut of the human rights in the UDHR, ICCPR or ICESCR. However, there are a number of current developments in human rights law which challenge the idea that human rights law must apply in its entirety or not at all. The most important of these developments is the fact that it is increasingly recognized that a State may exercise jurisdiction extraterritorially in instances where it is only capable of adhering to some human rights norms and not others. The acknowledgement that this is possible has become particularly evident in instances where States are exercising control over territory or persons abroad.

8.2.1 Al-Skeini case

Indeed, there are a number of important cases from the European Court of Human Rights which have recognized that where a State exercises physical power and control over a person, its ability to respect human rights law will be restricted to those rights which are 'relevant' to the situation. It is this concept which forms the basis of the European Court of Human Right's statement in *Al-Skeini* et al that:

> [w]henever the State through its agents exercises control and authority over an individual, and thus jurisdiction, the State is under an obligation under Article 1 to secure to that individual the rights and freedoms under Section 1 of the Convention that are relevant to the situation of that individual. In this sense, therefore, the Convention rights can be 'divided and tailored'.[2]

The test of what rights will be 'relevant' in a given situation will likely be those rights which are within the capability of the State agent to respect, at the given

[2] *Al-Skeini and Others v United Kingdom*, Application No. 5572/07 (ECHR, July 2011)(Grand Chamber Judgment) [137] (hereafter *Al-Skeini*). It is noted that the Court's statement that Convention rights can be 'divided and tailored' is not the same as refuting the fact that human rights are indivisible.

moment that authority over the individual is exercised. In other words, where the State's authority is short-lived or fleeting, the case law from the European Court of Human Rights recognizes that it is not realistic to hold States to the entire range of substantive rights set out in the Convention.[3] Importantly, the Court's statement that 'Convention rights' *can* be 'divided and tailored' is misleading. Actually, this case can better be seen as an authority that Convention *obligations* can be 'divided and tailored' between duty-bearers. The fact that a State may be found not to be responsible for the full gamut of human rights does not mean that the individuals within its sphere of influence no longer possess the full spectrum of rights.

8.2.2 Ilascu v Moldova case

In the *Ilascu v Moldova* case, the European Court of Human Rights also recognized that a State's obligations can be tailored to its capacity. Here, the Court held that a State which has lost control over a portion of its territory will not be held responsible for the full range of rights under the convention in that portion of its territory.[4] Instead, the Court held that the fact the State did not have *de facto* control over a part of its territory served to reduce the scope of the State's jurisdiction in that area so that was only held bound to secure 'positive obligations' towards persons.[5] In the circumstances, this constituted an obligation for Moldova to take all diplomatic and legal efforts vis-à-vis third States and international organizations to try and guarantee the rights in the Convention for the people living outside its areas of factual authority. In other words, the Court held Moldova to be responsible only for the aspects of the human rights framework which were reasonable in the circumstances.[6] In effect then, the *Ilascu* case provides another example of an instance in which the European Court of Human Rights has demonstrated a willingness to take a flexible approach to what human rights obligations a State owes in circumstances where it has a reduced capacity.

8.2.3 Tailoring obligations to normative capacity

The appreciation that human rights can be amended according to the capacities of the obligation-bearer opens the door for a similar argument to be made in respect

It simply recognizes that while individuals have the full range of rights at all times, not all these rights may be enforceable or they may not all be enforceable against the same State.

[3] This is limited to situations in which a State has 'effective control over an area'. See *Al-Skeini v UK* (n 2) [138]. See also J. P. Cerone, 'Peace Operations and the Complementarity of Human Rights and International Humanitarian Law' in Human Rights and Peace Operations, International Institute of Humanitarian Law, '31st Round Table on Current Problems of International Humanitarian Law, Sanremo' (4–6 September 2008) 110–11, for the argument that in instances where a State is acting extraterritorially, the range of applicable rights may be limited by the scope of the State's authority or control.

[4] *Ilaşcu and Others v Moldova and Russia*, Application No. 48787/99 (ECHR, 8 July 2004) (hereafter *Ilaşcu).*

[5] *Al-Skeini* (n 2) [332–3]. [6] Ibid, [347].

of armed groups.[7] In other words, it opens the door to an argument that an armed group may be bound by different human rights standards depending on its capacity and control over the civilian population. It suggests that from a *lex ferenda* perspective, it might be possible for the adoption of an approach similar to that in the belligerency, insurgency, and international humanitarian law framework under which armed groups with less developed functional capacities are held bound to a lesser range of obligations. Seen from this perspective, any law governing the accountability of armed groups under human rights law, whether it develops by means of treaty law or custom, might benefit from recognizing a 'lower threshold' of human rights for armed groups with little control over a territory and a 'higher threshold' of human rights for armed groups with more, but not total, control over a territory. The lower threshold would likely contain norms which require little or no control of territory. The higher threshold would contain norms that require a greater degree of control and institutional capacity. While a fuller examination of this idea will have to be carried out with reference to discrete norms in future research, the chapter continues by drawing upon the analysis contained in Chapter 2 to examine how different thresholds of human rights obligations for different kinds of armed groups could be operationalized.[8]

8.2.3.1 Situations where an armed group has no territorial control

It is unrealistic to imagine that many armed groups which do not control territory will be able to devote significant resources to 'progressively realizing' the social and economic rights of the civilian population.[9] But it is certainly possible to imagine that such armed groups could adhere to the core set of obligations that relate to the right to an adequate standard of living, food, water, clothing, housing, and physical and mental health, i.e. the obligation to 'ensure the satisfaction of, at the very least, minimum essential levels of the rights'.[10] It is equally possible to see that armed groups without control of territory will be able to 'respect' many civil and political rights. For while some civil and political rights need a sophisticated level of organization to be implemented, others need little organization or territory to be respected. For example, the prohibition of torture only requires an individual to refrain from torturing for it to be adhered to. Likewise,

[7] It is asserted that the reference to rights being 'divided and tailored' confuses issues of possessing rights and having recourse to a claim against an entity for a violation of rights.

[8] See D. Murray, *Human Rights Obligations of Non-State Armed Groups* (Bloomsbury, London 2015) (hereafter Murray, *Human Rights Obligations*) for an examination of these issues with a specific focus on prosecution, detention, and the right to health.

[9] See Article 2 of the ICESCR for the obligation to 'undertake steps, individually and through international assistance and co-operation … to the maximum of its available resources, with a view to *achieving progressively the full realization* of the rights recognized in the Covenant by all appropriate measures' (emphasis added).

[10] The UN Committee on Economic, Social and Cultural Rights has stated that economic, social and cultural rights have a 'minimum core obligation' that will ensure the satisfaction of 'minimum essential levels' of each of the ICESCR rights. See UN Committee on Economic, Social and Cultural Rights, 'General Comment 3 (The Nature of States Parties' Obligations)' (14 December 1990) UN Doc E/1991/23, [10] (hereafter CESCR General Comment 3, Obligations).

in instances where an armed group does not have territorial control, it can still refrain from taking actions which interfere with people's freedom of movement, physical security, property, and liberty in these circumstances. It can also refrain from taking any measures which would prevent people from enjoying social and economic rights like the right to health and the right to education, by destroying schools or making medical clinics the subject of attack. Additionally, it can refrain from taking action that might interfere with people enjoying their right to health, food, and water, e.g. by refusing humanitarian organizations access to the territory.

The idea that an armed group's obligations could be less extensive where its control over a territory is less than complete corresponds with the fact that a State's human rights obligations in such a situation will still be in existence and enforceable. For example, it was established in arbitral case law from the nineteenth century that a State can be held responsible for its failure to protect individuals or assets from the harmful acts of an armed group, in circumstances where prevention or protection was a realistic possibility.[11] In such circumstances, a State will be held responsible not for the acts for the armed group per se but for its own failure to prevent the harm in question.[12] A similar principle is found in case law from human rights courts and monitoring bodies which have at times found States to be responsible for protecting civilians from the acts of armed groups.[13] States' positive obligations in respect to armed groups may include preventing armed attacks or taking efforts to secure the prosecution of persons conducting armed attacks.[14] Case law has also found States to be under the obligation to conduct their military operations against the armed group in such a manner that respects civilians' right to life.[15] States have also been found to be under more general obligations to protect civilians from violations by armed groups.[16] For example, they have been held

[11] See extensive review of this case law in ILC, Yearbook of the International Law Commission 1975 (5 May–25 July 1975) Vol II, UN Doc A/CN.4/SER.A/1975/Add.1, [179] 94–7 (hereafter ILC Yearbook 1975 Vol II). See also ILC, Yearbook of the International Law Commission 1972 (2 May–7 July 1972) Vol II, UN Doc A/CN.4/SER.A/1972/Add.1, [161–80] 133–9 (hereafter ILC Yearbook 1972 Vol II).

[12] ILC Yearbook 1972 Vol II (n 12) 139. See also ILC Yearbook 1975 Vol II (n 12) 97; L. Zegveld, *The Accountability of Armed Opposition Groups in International Law*, (CUP, Cambridge 2002) 52 (hereafter Zegveld, *Armed Opposition Groups*) 181.

[13] Zegveld, *Armed Opposition Groups* (n 12) 189–96. See also UN Human Rights Committee, 'General Comment 35 (Article 9 Liberty and Security of Person)' (28 October 2014) UN Doc CCPR/C/GC/35, [7] (hereafter HRC General Comment 35, Liberty and Security).

[14] See for example UN Human Rights Committee, 'Concluding Observations on Colombia' (4 August 2010) UN Doc CCPR/COL/CO/6, [18], [25] (hereafter HRC Colombia Observations 2010); UN Human Rights Committee, 'Concluding Observations on the Democratic Republic of Congo' (26 April 2006) UN Doc CCPR/C/COD/CO/3, [15–16] (hereafter HRC Congo Observations 2006); UN Human Rights Committee, 'Concluding Observations on Colombia' (26 May 2004) UN Doc CCPR/CO/80/COL, [8]; UN Committee on Economic, Social and Cultural Rights, 'Concluding Observations on Colombia' (7 June 2010) UN Doc E/C.12/COL/CO/5, [15] (hereafter CESCR Colombia Observations 2010).

[15] See for example *Ergi v Turkey*, Application No. 23818/94 (ECHR, 28 July 1998) [79–81]; See discussion of it in Zegveld, *Armed Opposition Groups* (n 12) 190.

[16] HRC Congo Observations 2006 (n 14) [13].

bound to take steps to prevent children being recruited by armed groups.[17] With regard to these kinds of obligations, a State is not under an obligation to succeed, but merely under an obligation to take appropriate measures to protect the persons within its territory.[18] In that sense, it is seen how the various layers of human rights obligations under the two Covenants could be divided and tailored between two duty-bearers according to their capabilities and immediate relevance.

8.2.3.2 Situations where an armed group has territorial control

Equally in situations where an armed group has territorial control, it makes sense for an armed group's obligations to be more extensive. Case law shows that when a State has lost control over a portion of its territory, its obligations in respect of that territory will often be adjusted so that it is only held bound by its positive obligations towards persons within that territory.[19] These positive obligations have been stated to include (i) an obligation to re-establish its control over territory; and (ii) take measures to ensure respect for the applicants' rights.[20] In respect of the first set of obligations, it is clear that a State does not have an obligation to use military means to re-take control of a territory.[21] Nor does a State have an obligation to extinguish an armed insurrection when it occurs.[22] In respect of the second set of obligations, a State has been held to be under the obligation to make efforts to secure the protection of persons in a territory outside its control.[23] That being said, the State is not required to protect individuals, in a physical sense, from harm by the armed group or other individuals as such efforts would be 'ineffectual'.[24] Indeed, it is a long-established principle of law that a State will not be held responsible for the damage caused by armed groups to third parties in territory outside of its control.[25]

[17] UN Human Rights Committee, 'Concluding Observations on Yemen' (23 April 2012) UN Doc CCPR/C/YEM/CO/5, [24]; HRC Colombia Observations 2010 (n 14) [24]; HRC Congo Observations 2006 (n 14) [18]; UN Committee on Economic, Social and Cultural Rights, 'Concluding Observations on Afghanistan' (7 June 2010) UN Doc E/C.12/AFG/CO/2-4, [30]; CESCR Colombia Observations 2010 (n 14) [16].

[18] Zegveld, *Armed Opposition Groups* (n 12) 191.

[19] This principle has been stated by the European Court of Human Rights but there is no reason to think that it would not hold true for the HRC interpreting the ICCPR. See *Ilaşcu* (n 4) para 339.

[20] Ibid.

[21] Ibid, paras 340–5. Here, the Court clearly considered that it was unrealistic to expect Moldova to have managed to re-establish its control over the Transdniestrian territory. As a result, the European Court of Human Rights seemed to take the view that Moldova's obligations to re-establish its control could have been fulfilled largely by its diplomatic efforts to assert sovereignty over the territory and its efforts to secure the release of the individuals from custody in its bilateral negotiations with the Russian Federation.

[22] See also ILC, Yearbook of the International Law Commission, 1975, Vol II, UN Doc. No. A/CN.4/SER.A/1975/Add.1, (ILC Yearbook 1975, Vol II), para 179.

[23] See *Ilaşcu* (n 4) para 347. The European Court of Human Rights recognized that it would have been 'ineffectual' for Moldova to try and investigate or prosecute members of the Transdniestrian regime who were living in Transdnietria or offences committed in Transniestria.

[24] See *Ilaşcu* (n 4) para 339.

[25] For a very detailed review of these cases and State practice in this regard see the ILC Yearbook 1975, Vol II (see note 22) p 94–7. See also ILC, Yearbook of the International Law Commission, 1972 Vol II, UN Doc. No. A/CN.4/SER.A/1972/Add.1, paras 161–80.

This principle can be found in copious jurisprudence from arbitral tribunals in the nineteenth century.[26]

The lack of capacity of the State combined with the heightened capacity of the armed group creates an argument that an armed group controlling territory should have more extensive human rights obligations, than an armed group without control over territory. Yet, the analysis conducted in Chapter 2 suggests that even in these situations, it may be sensible to tailor a group's obligations to match its capacity. For Chapter 2 demonstrated that even armed groups with a very consolidated control of territory do not often have the capacity to fulfil the full range of State functions. Moreover, it was commented above that there is already judicial authority for the idea of modifying the *range* of obligations that an entity is bound to, to match its capacity. Importantly, there is also authority for the idea that the normative content of particular obligation can also be tailored to match a duty-bearer's capacity. For example, the ICESCR recognizes that there will be differing degrees of capacity among duty-bearers, ranging from the very minimal to the quite developed.[27] As a result, while the ICESCR obliges ratifying States to adhere to a set of core obligations which are designed to 'ensure the satisfaction of, at the very least, minimum essential levels of each of the rights', it also provides for the progressive realization of these rights to the maximum of a States' available resources, it.[28] This latter obligation demonstrates that there is scope to mould the content of economic, social and cultural rights—beyond their essential core—to match the capacities of a duty bearer.

There is less established precedent for the idea of adjusting the content of civil and political rights. The legal framework does not contain pre-existing latitude for modifying the content of the norm to match the capacities of the duty-bearer. Nevertheless, there is scope for consideration whether certain civil and political rights might be applied differently when applied to armed groups. For example, notions such as 'legality', 'democracy', 'arbitrariness' could be interpreted in a different manner so that emphasis is placed instead on concepts like 'transparency' and 'civilian participation' instead.[29] This could be a means of determining whether the limits which have been placed on a particular rights by an armed group, are justifiable. Similarly, when human rights norms require that particular actions should be 'in accordance with the law', consideration could be given to whether a similar approach could be taken to that taken in Geneva Convention IV.[30] Article 64 of

[26] See *Ilaşcu* (n 4) para 339. [27] See CESCR General Comment 3, Obligations (n 10)

[28] See Article 2 of the ICESCR for the obligation to 'undertake steps, individually and through international assistance and co-operation … to the maximum of its available resources, with a view to *achieving progressively the full realization* of the rights recognized in the Covenant by all appropriate measures' (emphasis added).

[29] It is noted in this respect that authors like Weinstein find notions of civilian 'participation' to be a relevant dynamic in some situations of rebel governance. J. Weinstein, *Inside Rebellion: The Politics of Insurgent Violence* (CUP, Cambridge 2007) 187 (hereafter Weinstein, *Inside Rebellion*).

[30] A similar suggestion is made by D. Casalin, 'Taking Prisoners: Reviewing the International Humanitarian Law Grounds for Deprivation of Liberty by Armed Opposition Groups' (2011) 883 International Review of the Red Cross 743, 757.

Geneva Convention IV stipulates that the criminal law of the occupied territory must remain in force. It adds that an occupying power is only allowed to repeal or suspend the criminal law of the occupied territory if it constitutes a threat to the occupying power's security or prevents it from fulfilling its obligations under Geneva Convention IV.[31] In any instances where an occupying power enacts new penal legislation, the Convention states that it is under an obligation to publish it and bring it to the attention of the inhabitants in their own language. It also provides that an occupying power is prevented from making any provisions retroactive in character.

If similar rules were applied in situations where an armed group occupied territory over a long period of time, an armed group would be obliged to keep the criminal legislation of the State intact unless it was contrary to human rights law or international law more generally. In any instance where an armed group brought in new laws with the effect of creating new crimes or restricting people's freedoms, it would be under a duty to bring it to the attention of the local population. Such an approach might constitute an important step towards reducing the arbitrariness of detention by armed groups, which is often based on 'rough guidelines' or approximations.[32] A similar approach could also be applied to rules restricting freedom of movement, freedom of association, freedom of thought, conscience, and religion, or freedom of expression which also require any restrictions on these rights to be 'provided by law'.[33] Of course, armed groups would have duties of 'immediate realisation' under both the ICESCR and ICCPR to 'respect *and ensure*' the rights contained in the Covenants. In other words, an armed group controlling territory would be bound to do more than simply refrain from certain actions. Instead, in order to fulfil its obligations under human rights law it would also be bound to take positive action to ensure that the rights contained therein are protected and fulfilled.[34] With regard to economic and social rights, this may include taking an active role in food distribution if there is a situation of humanitarian disaster or food shortage. It may also include the active provision of healthcare and education, within the boundaries of the armed group's capability. With regard to civil and political rights, the armed group's positive obligations may include preventing third parties violating the rights of others, by means of exercising policing

[31] Article 64 of Geneva Convention IV. See S. Sivakumaran, 'Courts of Armed Opposition Groups, Fair Trials Or Summary Justice?' (2009) 7 Journal of International Criminal Justice 489, 507–8 (hereafter Sivakumaran, 'Fair Trials Or Summary Justice?') for a discussion of how Additional Protocol II treats the notion of armed groups enacting legislation.

[32] In 2007, at a time when the Forces Nouvelles had held the north of the country for approximately five years, Colonel Ouattara Seydou stated that there were 'rough guidelines' on periods of detention in relation to common crime. 'For small crimes, like petty theft, we keep people for a month and then free them.' He then corrected himself and said 'a month or two'. With respect to murderers and rapists, he said 'we have to keep the person a bit longer, for the time it takes residents to feel safe again'. D. Balint-Kurti, 'Cote D'Ivoire's Forces Nouvelles, Chatham House' (Africa Programme Armed Non-State Actors Series, September 2009) 29.

[33] See Articles 12(3), Article 18(3), Article 19(3) and Article 22(2) of the ICCPR.

[34] See Murray, *Human Rights Obligations* (n 8) 186–91 for a detailed analysis of the obligation to fulfil.

actions.[35] It is noteworthy that it does not take a sophisticated State apparatus to adhere to the core human rights principles relevant to the right to life, including proportionality, imminent danger, and strict necessity. In 2009, the UN mission in Ivory Coast trained the Forces Nouvelles police in 'human rights and law enforcement' when they did not have a functioning judiciary or a significant police force.[36] The obligation to protect would also require armed groups in control of a territory investigate and prosecute perpetrators of common crime.[37]

The notion that an armed group controlling territory will often address common crime through prosecutions raises the thorny issue of whether an armed group could ever conduct judicial proceedings or detain in a manner which would satisfy Article 14 or Article 9 of the ICCPR. In particular, it seems unlikely that an armed group could satisfy the human rights requirement that a court be 'established by law' in the manner the phrase is meant under human rights law.[38] However, in instances where an armed group is operating a court system in an area where the government is entirely absent, consideration may be given whether the courts are 'competent, independent and impartial'.[39] This is a requirement has been deemed by the Human Rights Committee to be an absolute right and requires consideration to be given to issues like the independence and qualification of the judges and the independence of the court, as an institution, from the executive and legislature.[40] While it has already been commented above that it may also pose a challenge for armed groups to satisfy the requirement of *nullum crimen sine lege*, the situation is

[35] Ibid, 195–6 on the obligation to protect.

[36] There are also reports that ONUCI conducted trainings for Forces Nouvelles officers on specific aspects of law enforcement giving particular attention to issues like arbitrary detention, preventative detention and physical violence in April 2009. Opération des Nations Unies en Côte d'Ivoire, 'Droits de l'Homme l'ONUCI des Forces Nouvelles' (2001) <https://onuci.unmissions.org/droits-de-l%E2%80%99homme-l%E2%80%99onuci-forme-des-officiers-des-forces-nouvelles> last accessed 20 January 2017.

[37] Evidence that this is realistic is seen for example in the Deed of Commitment under Geneva Call for the Prohibition of Sexual Violence in Situations of Armed Conflict and Towards the Elimination of Gender Discrimination which contains the commitment to 'take all feasible measures towards effectively preventing and responding to acts of sexual violence committed by any person, in areas where we exercise authority'. It also contains the commitment to 'endeavour to provide victims of sexual violence with the assistance and support they require in order to address the impact of such violence'. See paras 3 and 4 at http://www.genevacall.org/wp-content/uploads/dlm_uploads/2013/12/DoC-Prohibiting-sexual-violence-and-gender-discrimination.pdf. This Deed of Commitment has been signed by the Chin National Front/ Army and the Karen National Union/ Karen National Liberation Army in Burma/ Myanmar and several non-State armed groups in India.

[38] This is somewhat similar to the reference in common Article 3(1)(f) to 'regularly constituted court'. Sivakumaran (n 31) 489–500 on whether courts of armed opposition groups can be 'regularly constituted'? See also J. Somer, 'Jungle Justice: Passing Sentence on the Equality of Belligerents in Non-International Armed Conflict' (2007) 89 International Review of the Red Cross 655, 665–6 (hereafter Somer, 'Jungle Justice') on the meaning of 'established by law' with relation to armed groups and 671–76 on the term 'regularly constituted court'.

[39] See HRC General Comment 32, Article 14: Right to Equality before Courts and Tribunals and to a Fair Trial), UN Doc. No. CCPR/C/GC/32, 23 August 2007, paras 18–21. It is noted that this interpretation is broadly in line with the Elements of Crimes description of Article 8(2)(c)(iv) which defines not being 'regularly constituted' as being analogous with not affording the essential guarantees of independence and impartiality *or* not affording all the other judicial guarantees. Somer, 'Jungle Justice' (n 38) 674

[40] Somer, 'Jungle Justice' (n 38) 674.

more hopeful in terms of whether an armed group can ever satisfy the obligation to provide accused persons with 'minimal guarantees' of fairness. The international humanitarian law provisions on fair trial in common Article 3 and Article 5 of Additional Protocol II provide evidence of a view that the 'essence' of these rights may be respected by armed groups controlling territory. In particular, when the judicial guarantees in Article 14 are reviewed, it is seen that many of them can be adhered to without sophisticated structures or resources.[41]

8.2.4 Shared obligations

When considering how the obligations of armed groups may be operationalized, it is important to observe that the fact that an armed group controls territory does not mean that the State no longer has any obligations in that area. Indeed, it was commented above that a State will still be held bound by its positive obligations towards persons in a territory *even* when it is wholly controlled by an armed group.[42] Importantly, it was also shown in Chapter 2 that States may sometimes cooperate with armed groups on the provision of public services. A vivid example of where this happened was during the non-international armed conflict between Sri Lanka and the LTTE where the Sri Lankan government continued to provide a significant number of public services in the North and East of the country even after these areas had fallen under LTTE control. Between 1983 and 1987 the administration of justice and the police force remained in the hands of the incumbent government throughout the rebel-held area.[43] Later, when the LTTE become more organized, the provision of services in the LTTE-controlled territory became what has been described as a 'complex interface between state and rebel governmental efforts'.[44] While the security sector, which included the judiciary and police, was completely under the control of the LTTE, the health and education sectors were a joint concern.[45] The Sri Lankan government remained involved in the region primarily by continuing to pay the salaries of teachers, doctors, nurses, and other professionals in the health and education sectors.[46] It also continued to appoint government agents for the country districts which under rebel control.[47] While the arrangement in Sri Lanka may seem unusual, it provided an important measure by which the Sri Lankan government could keep its connection between the people in the North and East of the island and the government in Colombo alive.[48]

[41] For example, the right to a presumption of innocence, the right to be informed promptly in a language the defendant understands of nature and cause of charge, the right to be tried without undue delay, the right to be tried in one's presence and to defend oneself in person, the right to examine witnesses against you, the right not to be compelled to testify to one's own guilt.

[42] This principle has been stated by the European Court of Human Rights in *Ilaşcu* (n 4) [339].

[43] Z. C. Mampilly, *Rebel Rulers: Insurgent Governance and Civilian Life during War War* (Cornell University Press, Ithaca and London 2011) 109 (hereafter Mampilly, *Rebel Rulers*).

[44] Ibid, 112. [45] Ibid, 112. [46] Ibid, 115.

[47] Government agents were assigned to every district in Sri Lanka and were responsible for implementing centrally issued directives.

[48] Mampilly, *Rebel Rulers* (n 43) 94.

Indeed, it can be noted that continued government involvement in rebel-held areas is also common in the early stages of an armed conflict where the government continues to retain a foothold in rebel held areas. For example, a government may continue to pay government employees' salaries in times of non-international armed conflict despite the fact that the area in which they work has fallen outside the government's control. An example of this can be seen in Syria where in many towns, public officials, for a time at least, continued to be able exercise government functions by virtue of their government salary. Reporting from Qualaat Al-Mudiq in June 2012, two months after it fell to rebel control, journalist David Enders described this phenomenon as one of the 'ironies of war'. Interviewing a local resident, he reported:

> 'I am still drawing my government check as a teacher,' Mousab al-Hamadee, an anti-government activist, said, smiling. The Syrian government continues to provide services such as electricity and water without interruption.[49]

Likewise, the Iraqi central government long continued to pay the salaries of employees in Islamic State controlled areas.[50] The existence of these arrangements serves as a reminder that it should not be assumed that just because a State has lost physical control of a portion of territory, it has ceased to have any normative capacity in that region.

8.2.5 Advantages of this approach

From a policy perspective, it can be noted that there are important advantages to an approach which matches an armed group's obligations to its capacity. Perhaps most importantly it ensures that the legal framework remains realistic. Yet equally it reduces the aspirational aspect of human rights law. Normally if a State signs a human rights convention, it is bound to adhere to the full range of rights contained within it, even if their attainment is impossible at the moment of ratification. The fact that a State has difficulties in complying with the human rights legal framework at the time it ratifies a convention is not a reason for a State to refrain from signing the convention. There is no prior check to determine whether a State is capable of adhering to all the rights in the convention at the time of ratification because there is an assumption that States, as a matter of capacity, are able to fulfil the rights within human rights treaties. In that sense, human rights law sets 'end goals' for States to work with and use as an agenda for democratic and institutional reform. The aspirational aspect of human rights law, as opposed to international humanitarian law which is ultimately about damage limitation, is one of

[49] 'Rebels Carve out a Safe Haven in Northern and Central Syria' (*Seattle Times*, 7 June 2012) < http://www.seattletimes.com/nation-world/rebels-carve-out-a-safe-haven-in-northern-and-central-syria/> accessed 20 January 2017.

[50] al-Tamimi, Aymenn, 'The Evolution of the Islamic State Administration: The Documentary Evidence' (2015) 9 (4) Perspectives on Terrorism http://www.terrorismanalysts.com/pt/index.php/pot/article/view/447/html accessed 19 January 2017.

the reasons that makes States particularly reluctant to recognize human rights law as binding upon armed groups. They fear that such a recognition may suggests a desire on the part of the international community that armed groups engage in a process of institution-building, the result of which may lead to a further consolidation of their control of territory. However, an approach that asserts that armed groups are not bound by the full range of human rights law but bound to a threshold of norms that match their existing capacity may serve somewhat to allay these fears. It reduces the aspirational aspect of human rights law and makes it instead a framework which matches, responds to and seeks to regulate what armed groups are already doing.

The notion that armed groups' capacity will determine the legal framework of human rights to which they are bound highlights the need for any further discussion of the normative framework to take place against the backdrop of political science research. Chapter 2 illustrated that there is an extensive and growing body of research on what armed groups actually do, in terms of government functions and provision of public services. It also highlights the need for further research to be conducted on human rights norms themselves and the organizational capacity that is needed for them to be adhered to. There have been several studies on armed groups exercising judicial functions in the context of international humanitarian law, but more research is needed on human rights norms.[51] Most pertinently, Murray has conducted important research in relation to prosecution, detention, and the right to health. His in-depth research on these topics examines how these specific human rights can be applied to armed groups in practice.[52] Using a context-dependent approach, Murray has examined the different capacities that are necessary for armed groups to adhere to these key human rights norms. In order to solve these kinds of problems, further multidisciplinary or interdisplinary approach on additional discrete norms is necessary to clarify how the legal framework can be matched with what is happening on the ground.

9. Role of Armed Groups in Creation of Customary International Law

In addition to providing guidance on how the obligations of armed groups may be operationalized alongside those of the States, Chapters 4 and 5 allow important conclusions to be drawn about the manner in which the legal personality of armed groups is conceived, from a theoretical perspective. Indeed, the conclusion that the legal frameworks of belligerency, insurgency, and international humanitarian law support an individualistic or formal approach to legal personality of armed groups is of assistance in subsequent chapters which review the manner in which

[51] See Somer, 'Jungle Justice' (n 38) 655–90; also Sivakumaran, 'Fair Trials or Summary justice?' (n 31) 489–513.

[52] Murray, *Human Rights Obligations* (n 8) 205–271.

armed groups might be bound by international human rights law. In particular, the conclusion helps to address the divergence of practice and a lack of consensus in academic literature about the role that non-State actors should play in the creation of customary international law.[53] It is argued that the challenge of finding an objective answer to this question is assisted by the conclusion that the existing legal framework on armed groups reflected in international humanitarian law reflects a formal and individualistic conception of international legal personality. The consequences of this view provide justification for a conclusion that the practice of armed groups need not be taken into account when determining what customary international law is binding upon them. The reason for this is that the individualistic and formal conceptions of international legal personality do not support the proposition that subjects of international law should by definition have a role in law-creation. Indeed, it has been stated in Chapter 3 that the formal conception, in particular, is explicit that entities can be bound by customary international law without having taken part in its creation. It is argued that this view reflects the reality that customary international law is much less 'democratic' in character than it is often thought to be.

While views on this point are expanded in Chapter 11, it is important to note that Part II's conclusions on this issue do not preclude armed groups being encouraged to become involved in norm creation, at the invitation of States. This reflects the conclusion that a finding that the international legal framework of international humanitarian law as it exists in treaties is closer to the formal or individualistic conceptions of international humanitarian law, does not exclude the value of the actor conception of international legal personality as a parallel track of responsibility and norms. Indeed, it is recognized that there might be important advantages in armed groups participating in the creation and development of international human rights law.[54] Such involvement might include attendance at negotiation of new instruments of international human rights law, in the same manner as a number of armed groups attended the drafting conferences of the Additional Protocols with 'observer status without voting rights'.[55] It might also involve armed groups taking part in academic and civil society discussions relating to new legal instruments or the existing legal framework.[56] It is acknowledged

[53] See A. Roberts and S. Sivakumaran, 'Lawmaking by Non-State Actors: Engaging Armed Groups in the Creation of International Humanitarian Law' (2012) 37 Yale Journal of International Law 107, citing A. Clapham, *Human Rights Obligations of Non-State Actors* (OUP, Oxford 2006) 28–29, and R. McCorquodale, 'An Inclusive International Legal System' (2004) 17 Leiden Journal of International Law 477, 479–80.

[54] See S. Rondeau, 'Participation of Armed Groups in the Development of the Law Applicable to Armed Conflicts' (2011) 93 International Review of the Red Cross 649–72 (hereafter Rondeau, 'Participation of Armed Groups') for a thorough and convincing discussion of these advantages.

[55] Ibid, 658.

[56] Rondeau mentions a number of successful examples of members of armed groups taking part in projects run by academic institutions and non-governmental organizations. See in particular, Geneva Academy of International Humanitarian Law and Human Rights, 'Armed Non-State Actors and International Norms: Towards a Better Protection of Civilians in Armed Conflict' (March 2010). This initiative involved armed groups from Colombia, Congo, Darfur, Kosovo, Kurdistan,

that such participation might be helpful in encouraging an ownership of norms and ensuring that armed groups' view on the law is at least known and taken into account in the drafting. This may provide some safety net in ensuring that any normative frameworks which are developed for non-international armed conflicts are realistic and as a matter of policy, can be adhered to by both sides of the fighting.[57] The chapter's conclusions also do not detract from a view that it is fundamentally important to continue persuading armed groups to sign special agreements and declarations on the law in accordance with common Article 3 of the Geneva Conventions.[58] Likewise, armed groups should be encouraged to make unilateral declarations stating their commitment to human rights norms.

The advantages of armed groups signing up to such commitments are multifold. First the opportunity to sign such a commitment provides a valuable means for international actors to engage with armed groups on the subject of international norms and forces armed groups' leaders to reflect on their internal codes of conduct.[59] Secondly, they provide a means for an armed group to commit itself to a certain code of conduct which is in accordance with international norms. This is beneficial from the perspective of ownership as it enables the armed groups to see the norms as a code adopted from within, rather than as having been imposed from the outside.[60] Logic and psychology dictates that this may have a positive effect on compliance with the instrument and produce a more effective model of accountability.[61] But finally, the other advantage of engaging with armed groups in a structured manner is that even if armed groups do not take part in drafting conferences on the development of the law, a record will be kept of their views and concerns and these can be presented to the delegates.[62] Also, the more standardized the codes of conduct become, the less chance there will be that an armed group will sign a declaration or publish a code of conduct which is at odds with international humanitarian law or human rights law standards. An organization

Malaysia, Nepal, Nigeria, Northern Ireland, Palestine, Sierra Leone, and Sri Lanka. It also refers to the 'Viewpoints' project of the Centre of Humanitarian Dialogue which brought together a two-volume edited collection of viewpoints from researchers, policy, advisers, former members of armed groups, academics, NGO directors, mediators, and consultants (hereafter Geneva Academy, 'Towards a Better Protection of Civilians'). See Rondeau, 'Participation of Armed Groups' (n 54) 661–3.

[57] See M. Sassòli, 'Taking Armed Groups Seriously: Ways to Improve Their Compliance with International Humanitarian Law' (2010) 1 International Humanitarian Legal Studies 5, 21 (hereafter Sassòli, 'Taking Armed Groups Seriously').

[58] Common Article 3 has been argued to put a duty on the parties of a non-international armed conflict to broker special agreements to reflect their intention to abide by more extensive provisions of the Geneva Conventions than those contained in common Article 3. The article states 'The Parties to the conflict should further endeavour to bring into force, by means of special agreements, all or part of the other provisions of the present Convention.'

[59] Geneva Academy, 'Towards a Better Protection of Civilians' (n 56) 7, advises that engagement should take place at the highest level of an armed group.

[60] See discussion of 'ownership' in A. Bell and S. Casey-Maslen, 'Enhancing Compliance with International Law by Armed Non-State Actors' (2011) 3 Goettingen Journal of International Law 175.

[61] See the definition of accountability Chapter 1. See Sassòli, 'Taking Armed Groups Seriously' (n 57) 20–1.

[62] For similar ideas, see Rondeau, 'Participation of Armed Groups' (n 54) 662.

engaging with armed groups to sign codes of conduct may have more success convincing an armed group to sign the 'standard' code of conduct, if it can demonstrate that other armed groups were prepared to sign it too.

10. Conclusions

While the whole spirit of this chapter is to state conclusions, a few final overarching conclusions to Part II of the book are stated here. Part II has shown that the legal frameworks of belligerency, insurgency, and international humanitarian law hold valuable information about the legal personality of armed groups per se. First, they clarify the material factors which are needed for an armed group to acquire international legal personality under international law. In other words, they establish how organized an armed group must be before it can be held bound by international law and how that organization may be manifested. The three legal frameworks also provide authority for an argument that there is a further 'international element' which must be proved before an armed group can be treated as a subject of international law. The legal frameworks indicate that this international element may be satisfied by demonstrating a combination of the following factors: either that the armed group is operating in the context of a non-international armed conflict, that the parent State has reduced capacities, has lost control over a portion of territory, that the situation is such to merit the attention of the international community as a whole, or that the interests of third States are involved. The identification of these kinds of criteria holds great value in identifying the equivalent material conditions that will be required before an accountability mechanism can consider holding an armed group responsible under human rights law. They also provide legitimacy for an exploration of how armed groups may be held bound by human rights obligations, in a manner that matches their capacities.

Secondly, the conclusions identify important information about the manner in which the legal personality of armed groups is perceived from a theoretical perspective. In particular, they find that the legal frameworks reflect a conception of legal personality which has elements of the formal conception of legal personality and elements of the individualistic conception of legal personality. They clarify that while there is a strong deference to State consent in the legal frameworks, equal attention is given to the functionality of armed groups and their normative capacity. The conclusions also demonstrate that all three legal frameworks are imbued with a level of flexibility which understand the legal personality of armed groups to exist along a spectrum. They highlight that there is significant precedent for an approach under which armed groups are held accountable under international law, in a manner that reflects their normative capacity. This provides legitimacy for an argument that armed groups should be held accountable to different thresholds of human rights law, according to their functionality and normative capacity. The identification of answers on these questions have an important value in furthering the debate on when and how armed groups will gain legal personality under international human rights law.

PART III

HOW AND WHEN ARE ARMED GROUPS BOUND BY HUMAN RIGHTS LAW?

7

How are Armed Groups Bound by International Humanitarian Law?

1. Introduction

This chapter analyses how armed groups are bound by international law humanitarian law. On the basis that it is universally agreed that armed groups are bound by international humanitarian law, international humanitarian law presents a concrete and uncontroversial example of armed groups being bound by international law.[1] As such, it presents an opportunity to dissect the mechanics of '*how armed groups can be bound by international law*' without the distraction of parallel discussions about the desirability of them being bound in the first place. It is also helpful that a large number of theories already abound in this field as to how armed groups are bound by international humanitarian law. This body of literature constitutes a valuable resource when considering how armed groups might be bound by international human rights law. When using one field of law to elucidate another, it helps if the field of law which is being called upon for clarity is settled and free of controversy. Unfortunately this is not so when drawing upon international humanitarian law. For although it is generally accepted that armed groups *are* bound by international humanitarian law, the question of *how* armed groups are bound by international humanitarian law has puzzled and divided academics ever since common Article 3 of the Geneva Conventions was first discussed.[2] In the years since it was drafted common Article 3 has been described variously as

[1] L. Moir, *The Law of Internal Armed Conflict* (CUP, Cambridge 2002) 52 (hereafter Moir, *Internal Armed Conflict*); J. Kleffner. 'The Applicability of International Humanitarian Law to Organized Armed Groups' (2011) 882 International Review of the Red Cross 443–61, 443–4 (hereafter Kleffner, 'Organized Armed Groups').

[2] F. Siordet. 'Les Conventions de Genève et La Guerre Civile, Revue Internationale de la Croix Rouge' (1950) 81 Bulletin International des Sociétés de la Croix Rouge 105 (hereafter Siordet, 'La Guerre Civile'); Y. Dinstein. 'The International Law of Civil Wars and Human Rights' (1976) 6 Israel Yearbook on Human Rights 62–80, 68 (hereafter Dinstein, 'Civil Wars and Human Rights'); R. Baxter, 'Jus in Bello Interno: The Present and Future Law' in J. Moore (ed), *Law and Civil War in the Modern World* (Johns Hopkins, Baltimore 1974) 527 (hereafter Baxter, 'Jus in Bello Interno'); A. Cassese. 'The Status of Rebels under the 1977 Geneva Protocol on Non-International Armed Conflicts' (1981) 30 International and Comparative Law Quarterly 416 (hereafter Cassese, 'Status of Rebels'); T. Fleiner-Gerster and M. Meyer. 'New Developments in Humanitarian Law: A Challenge to the Concept of Sovereignty' (1985) 34 International and Comparative Law Quarterly 267, 272.

'revolutionary'[3], an 'audacious and paradoxical provision'[4], 'a legal heresy' and a 'legal aberration'.[5] Even now, over sixty years since the Geneva Conventions were drafted, the question of how armed groups are bound by common Article 3 and Additional Protocol II represents a complex legal problem on which consensus remains elusive.[6]

2. Existing Theories on How Armed Groups are Bound by IHL

Since the Geneva Conventions were drafted, a number of different theories have been put forward to explain how armed groups are bound by the laws of war. Although different authors have perceived, categorized, and explained these theories different ways, it is broadly possible to discern five main theories of how armed groups are bound: (i) by being third parties to the Geneva Conventions and Additional Protocol II; (ii) by domestic legislation; (iii) through their members being bound directly by international law; (iv) by having effective control over part of the territory; and (v) through customary international law. These theories are evaluated below to see whether how they provide an explanation for how armed groups are bound by international humanitarian law. When considering the legislative jurisdiction theory, the chapter finds that there has been little attention given to how the fact that an armed group's members are bound by international humanitarian law translates into a finding that the armed group itself is bound. In grappling with this problem, the chapter introduces a sixth theory, which it calls the 'extended legislative jurisdiction' theory. In examining these theories below, the chapter demonstrates that an armed group may be bound by international humanitarian law due to a combination of these theories working in parallel to each other. In a similar manner, the chapter shows that that some of these theories are not as separate as they may first appear.

In discussing the relative merits of the above theories, authors have often, particularly in recent literature, focused equally on both the legal merits of the particular theory and the prospect of it promoting compliance with international humanitarian law.[7] The driving force behind this dual focus has been an increased

[3] J. Gutteridge, 'The Geneva Conventions of 1949' (1949) 26 British Yearbook of International Law 294.

[4] J. Pictet, 'The Twentieth International Conference of the Red Cross' (1966) 8 ICJ Journal 1, 15, cited by A. H. Robertson, *Human Rights in the World* (Manchester University Press, Manchester 1982) 217.

[5] T. Meron, *Human Rights in Internal Strife, Their International Protection* (CUP, Cambridge 1987) 39. Meron states: 'Article 3 should no longer be regarded as a legal aberration'.

[6] M. Milanovic, 'Is the Rome Statute binding on individuals (and why we should care?)' [2011] Journal of International Criminal Justice 25, 40 (hereafter Milanovic, 'Is the Rome Statute binding on individuals?'): Kleffner, 'Organized Armed Groups' (n 1) 443. See also C. Tomuschat, 'The Applicability of Human Rights Law to Insurgent Movements' in H. Fischer et al. (ed), *Krisensicherung und Humanitarer Schutz—Crisis Management and Humanitarian Protection: Festschrif fur Dieter Fleck* (Berliner Wissenschafts-Verlag, Berlin 2004) 573–91, 587.

[7] It is noted that the practice of addressing the second question is not new, but it has certainly been the subject of increased focus in recent years. For literature particularly focusing on the latter

perception that compliance with international humanitarian law by armed groups is currently in a state of crisis.[8] One of the causes of this crisis is widely thought to be rooted in the notion that some armed groups feel no affinity with the norms contained in the Geneva Conventions and Additional Protocol II.[9] It is in order to address this psychological aspect of the legal framework that authors writing in the field have paid increased attention to whether the various theories lend themselves to compliance by the armed groups themselves.[10] In considering these issues there has been much attention given to issues such as legitimacy and ownership of norms.[11] For the purposes of this chapter, only minimal attention is given to whether a particular theory is persuasive to armed groups. Such considerations are considered technically peripheral to the question of whether armed groups are bound *in a legal sense*.[12] That being said, the chapter takes note in passing whether one theory is more prone to being accepted than another, as, although largely outside the scope of this study, many of the same legitimacy questions will apply when dealing with international human rights law.

3. Armed Groups Bound as Third Parties to the Geneva Conventions

One of the most influential and early articles on the question of how armed groups are bound by international humanitarian law was that by Cassese. Writing in 1981, Cassese suggested that armed groups are bound to the Geneva Conventions and Additional Protocol II as 'third parties'.[13] As armed groups are non-State actors, Cassese recognized that the rules in the Vienna Convention on the Law of Treaties 1966 on third parties will not apply *strictu sensu*. As a result, Cassese asserted

aspect see Baxter, 'Jus in Bello Interno' (n 2) 527–8; C. Ryngaert, 'Non-State Actors in International Humanitarian Law' in J. d'Aspremont (ed), *Participants in the International Legal System: Multiple Perspectives on Non-State Actors in International Law* (Routledge, Abingdon 2011) 284–94 (hereafter Ryngaert, 'Non-State Actors in IHL')

8 C. M. Bassiouni, 'The New Wars and the Crisis of Compliance with the Law of Armed Conflict by Non-State Actors' (2008) 3 Journal of Criminal Law and Criminology 711.

9 V. Bernard. 'Editorial: Understanding Armed Groups and the Law' (2011) 93 International Review of the Red Cross 261, 266.

10 Kleffner, 'Organized Armed Groups' (n 1); M. Sassòli, 'Possible Legal Mechanisms to Improve Compliance by Armed Groups with International Humanitarian Law and International Human Rights Law, Paper Submitted at the University of Quebec in Montreal, Canada at the Armed Groups Conference, Vancouver' (13–15 November 2003).

11 C. Ryngaert, 'Imposing International Duties on Non-State Actors and the Legitimacy of International Law' (2010) Working Paper No. 42 (hereafter Ryngaert, 'Imposing International Duties'); A. Bell and S. Casey-Maslen, 'Enhancing Compliance with International Law by Armed Non-State Actors' (2011) 3 Goettingen Journal of International Law 175.

12 This observation is supported by the finding in Chapters 5 and 6 that the legal framework of international humanitarian law does not reflect an actor conception of legal personality.

13 Cassese, 'Status of Rebels' (n 2) 416. See Moir, *Internal Armed Conflict* (n 1) 52–3; S. Sivakumaran, 'Binding Armed Opposition Groups' (2006) 5 International and Comparative Law Quarterly 369, 377–9 (hereafter Sivakumaran 'Binding Armed Opposition Groups'); Kleffner, 'Organized Armed Groups' (n 1) 457 for a discussion of this theory.

that the customary international law on third parties must be applied instead.[14] This, he argued, is broadly analogous to the rules in Articles 35–38 to the Vienna Convention determining the instances in which treaty law can bind third States.[15] Article 35 of the Vienna Convention is clearly the most relevant provision when it comes to explaining how armed groups are bound by international humanitarian law because it deals with treaties which, like international humanitarian law treaties, confer obligations upon third parties, i.e. armed groups.[16] Article 35 of the Vienna Convention provides that third States can be bound by obligations contained in a treaty in instances where it is clear that: (i) the contracting parties intended the treaty to confer such duties on those third parties; and (ii) the third party has accepted that obligation in writing. Applying this article by analogy to armed groups, it can be seen that armed groups are bound by treaty law in instances where the contracting parties intended the treaty to create such obligations for armed groups and when the armed group has accepted the obligation in writing.

3.1 The Intention of the Drafters of GC3 and APII

When examining the first of these requirements, Cassese concluded that the *travaux préparatoires* to the Geneva Conventions and Additional Protocol II and the text of the treaties themselves provided sufficient evidence that it was the intention of the contracting parties that they should bind armed groups. On the basis that several of the theories which are examined in this chapter rely on the 'intention of the parties', the section below reviews and adds to Cassese's analysis of this issue. Indeed, the *travaux préparatoires* to the Geneva Conventions show that the delegates found it hard to agree *how* armed groups could be bound by international humanitarian law. They show that the idea that an international treaty could bind an armed group which did not exist yet was radical. Frédéric Siordet, who was present at the drafting meetings, reported later that long discussions took place about whether or not it was legally possible.[17] Yet the drafters were finally united in the view that it was possible. The final text of common Article 3 very clearly imposes obligations on 'each Party to the [armed] conflict [not of an international character]' i.e. the

[14] Cassese, 'Status of Rebels' (n 2) 423.

[15] C. Chinkin, *Third Parties in International Law* (Clarendon Press, Oxford 1993) 39 seems to support Cassese's approach. She states that: '[the] law applicable to the claims by or against other entities [which are not States] must be articulated either by analogy to the Convention, or under general international law'.

[16] Article 35 and Article 36 of the Vienna Convention distinguish between treaties providing for obligations for third States and treaties providing for rights for third States. In instances where the treaty contains obligations for third States, Article 35 states the third State must accept the obligation in writing. In instances where the treaty provides the third State with rights, Article 36 states that a third party's assent shall be presumed, unless the contrary is indicated. The rationale behind this distinction is that a treaty conferring legal obligations is more burdensome for a third party State than a treaty conferring rights. Although individual members of an armed group gain rights under international humanitarian law, the armed group itself only assumes obligations.

[17] Siordet, 'La Guerre Civile' (n 2) 105.

State and the armed group. Indeed ever since common Article 3 was drafted, it has rarely been questioned that its drafters intended it to bind armed groups. As a result, the discussion that common Article 3 has provoked has rarely been about *whether* armed groups are bound by its provisions, but always about *how* armed groups are bound by its provisions.[18]

Interestingly, the idea that armed groups can be bound by treaty law was more controversial in the 1970s, than at the end of the 1940s when the Geneva Conventions were drafted. This is illustrated in the *travaux préparatoires* to Additional Protocol II. These show that the States that attended the Diplomatic Conference had highly divergent views on the issue. There were even a few States who thought that armed groups would not be bound by the Protocol's provisions at all.[19] For example, the Italian delegation stated:

> In ratifying this instrument, the High Contracting Parties will assume obligations, not towards rebel forces (which are neither subjects of international law nor Parties to Protocol II) but towards the other Contracting Parties, the international community and world opinion.[20]

According to the Italian delegation, the obligations contained in Additional Protocol II would only be assumed by States and owed to other States. The rebel group would presumably not be legally obliged to comply with the Protocol's provisions.[21]

It is clear that the Italian delegation was not alone in viewing the Protocol this way. The Colombian delegation expressed the view that:

> the Protocol would bind only the signatory states since there is no practical way of imposing obligations on dissident armed forces or organized armed groups.[22]

Likewise, the Nigerian delegation stated that the fact that the Additional Protocol addressed armed groups rendered the document as a whole non-binding. It stated that in order to have been a legally binding document the Protocol would have had to contain 'reciprocal obligations between States Parties'.[23] Instead, it was a

[18] See also ICRC, *Commentary to the Additional Protocols of 8 June 1977 to the Geneva Conventions of 12 December 1949* (Martinus Nijhoff, Geneva 1987) 1345 [4444] (hereafter ICRC, *Commentary to the Additional Protocols of 8 June 1977)*, which states: 'The question is often raised how the insurgent party can be bound by a treaty to which it is not a High Contracting Party. It may therefore be appropriate to recall here the explanation given in 1949. Although this argument has occasionally been questioned in legal literature, the validity of the obligation imposed upon insurgents has never been contested.'

[19] See Cassese, 'Status of Rebels' (n 2) 420–3 for an overview of further comments made by State delegations during the drafting process of Additional Protocol II which relate to: (i) the subjectivity of armed groups; and (ii) the way in which armed groups are bound by international humanitarian law.

[20] Geneva Conference, 'Official Records of the Diplomatic Conference on the Reaffirmation and Development of International Humanitarian Law Applicable in Armed Conflicts' (1974–1977) Vol VII, CDDH/SR.5.1/Annex, 122 1977 (hereafter Geneva Conference 1974–1977).

[21] See Cassese who confirms that this was the view held by the Italian delegation. Cassese, 'Status of Rebels' (n 2) 420, 421.

[22] Geneva Conference 1974–1977 (n 20) Vol VII, CDDH/SR.49, 79 [2].

[23] Ibid, 63 [22].

'statement of good intention . . not law'.[24] It is relevant to note that Nigeria and Colombia cannot be strictly considered to be contracting parties when assessing the intentions of the Protocol's drafters for the purpose of Article 35 of the Vienna Convention because they only signed Additional Protocol II many years after it came into force.[25] As a result, their opinions can be given less weight than those States who considered that armed groups were bound by Additional Protocol II and went on to ratify it.

Indeed the records of the Diplomatic Conference show that many, if not most, of the delegations in attendance accepted the fact that Additional Protocol II would be binding upon armed groups. The drafting papers make clear that States were well aware that the main aim of Additional Protocol II was to bind both the government and the rebel groups. For example, while commenting on the difficulties of striking the right balance between the scope and content of Additional Protocol II, the United Kingdom delegation stated:

> *The obligations imposed on States and dissidents* should not be so vague as to be nugatory or so high as to set an impossible standard. (emphasis added)[26]

This is a sign that the normative content of the Protocol was expressly formulated to take account of the fact that it was intended to bind both States and rebel groups. This is confirmed by the Commentary.[27] In a similar manner, when commenting on draft Article 22 on the denial of quarter, the Soviet delegate stated that if the article were accepted:

> it would impose an obligation not only on Governments but on those who, for various reasons, were engaged in movements against Governments.[28]

At the time the Protocols were being drafted, the Soviet view on such an issue would have been significant as it would have influenced and been representative of a considerable number of other countries in the Soviet bloc. Likewise, the Belgian delegation was very clear that Additional Protocol II was based on the same 'entire philosophy' of common Article 3, namely the 'basic sovereign principle that the obligations … are equally binding on both Parties to the conflict'.[29]

The ICRC was also very clear from the beginning of the drafting process that the Additional Protocol should be binding on both parties to a non-international armed conflict. As the Additional Protocols' main sponsor, its voice on these issues was undoubtedly an important authority during the drafting debates. As early as the 1971 Conference of Government Experts, the ICRC stated:

[24] Ibid, 63 [22].

[25] By the time Nigeria and Colombia acceded to the Additional Protocol in 1988 and 1995 respectively, it would likely have become clear to them that Additional Protocol II would be binding upon all parties to a non-international armed conflict. Certainly, neither State appended a reservation or declaration stating otherwise.

[26] Geneva Conference 1974–1977 (n 20) Vol VIII, CDDH/I/SR.24, 236 [37].

[27] ICRC, *Commentary to the Additional Protocols of 8 June 1977* (n 18) 1335.

[28] Geneva Conference 1974–1977 (n 20) Vol XIV, CDDH/III/SR.32, 314 [22].

[29] Geneva Conference 1974–1977 (n 20) Vol VII, CDDH/SR.49, 76.

In order to dispel any doubts or misgivings on the part of experts about the obligations which rebels should assume and the means of compelling them to do so, the ICRC representative wished to state that the ICRC had always held the view that Article 3 was binding not only on the governments of Contracting States but also on the population as a whole and, hence, on rebel forces. The obligation dated from 1949. This would not be changed if Article 3 were expanded by means of an additional protocol.[30]

Its view had clearly not changed by the time of the diplomatic conference on the reaffirmation and development of international humanitarian law applicable in armed conflicts held in Geneva in 1974–1977. In a drafting session in 1975 dealing with draft Article 5 which addressed the rights and duties of the parties to the Additional Protocol, the ICRC representative was equally adamant on this point, stating that:

the purpose of article 5 was to make it clear that draft Protocol II should be applied to all the Parties to a conflict, whether established Governments or rebels. The rights and duties laid down in it were valid for all.[31]

The fact that the ICRC view can be considered the majority view on the matter is confirmed by the final text of Additional Protocol II. This provides further evidence that its drafters intended its provisions to be binding upon State parties and rebels alike.

When reviewing the text of Additional Protocol II, it becomes immediately apparent that the term 'Parties to the conflict' is notably absent from Article 1. Indeed, every mention of the phrase 'parties to the conflict' was removed in the final round of the Protocol's drafting in response to a fear that the phrase might be interpreted as a recognition of the insurgent party.[32] Despite this deletion, it is clear that Additional Protocol II's provisions were intended to be applied by both States and armed groups.[33] For a start, Article 1 of the Additional Protocol states that it 'develops and supplements' common Article 3 of the Geneva Conventions. On this basis, it can be concluded that Additional Protocol II was intended to bind the same parties as common Article 3, i.e. States and armed groups.[34] Likewise, Article 1 of Additional Protocol II states that the protocol's provisions will apply to situations where armed opposition groups exercise such control over the territory to enable them to 'implement this Protocol'. This is a strong indication that its drafters considered armed groups to be bound by its provisions.[35] Moreover, the scope of the Additional Protocol is clearly stated to be 'all persons affected by

[30] Conference of Government Experts on the Reaffirmation and Development of International Humanitarian Law Applicable in Armed Conflicts, Geneva, 'Report on the Work of the Conference' (24 May–12 June 1971) 44 [223].

[31] Geneva Conference 1974–1977 (n 20) Vol VIII, CDDH/I/SR.24, 239. It is not clear how other delegations reacted to this statement as the drafting session for the day ended almost immediately after this statement was made.

[32] ICRC, *Commentary to the Additional Protocols of 8 June 1977* (n 18) 1339 [4415].

[33] M. Bothe, 'Conflits Armés Internes de Droit International Humanitaire' (1978) 1 Revue Générale de Droit International Public 82, 93.

[34] Cassese, 'Status of Rebels' (n 2) 416. [35] Ibid.

an armed conflict as defined in Article 1'.[36] It would be contrary to this stated field of application if its provisions were only binding on States because Article 1 of Additional Protocol II makes it clear that the Protocol will only apply in circumstances where an armed group holds a substantial swathe of territory. Taking the whole weight of these observations on the *travaux préparatoires* and text of Additional Protocol II into account, it seems that there is very little doubt that it was intended to bind both States parties and armed groups.

3.2 The relevance of an armed group's 'consent' to treaty provisions

It is clear from the section above that it is reasonably easy to satisfy the first of the requirements for third parties to be bound by treaty law. It is clear from the *travaux préparatories* that the drafting States intended common Article 3 of the Geneva Conventions and Additional Protocol II to establish duties on those third parties, i.e. armed groups. However, it is much harder to satisfy the second requirement of the third party theory, that an armed group must have explicitly consented to be bound by the treaty's provisions. While the provision of unilateral declarations by armed groups confirming their obligations under international law would presumably fulfil this criterion, they are often on discrete issues such as child soldiers.[37] It is rare that declarations by armed groups cover the whole range of obligations under common Article 3 and Additional Protocol II. Furthermore, the notion that an armed group must consent before it is bound by international humanitarian law does not correspond with the manner in which we understand international humanitarian law to operate, from a practical or theoretical perspective.[38] When a member of an armed group appears before the International Criminal Court in The Hague on war crimes charges, at no point does the judge ask whether he, or the armed group to which he belongs, consented to be bound by international humanitarian law. Indeed, ever since the International Military Tribunal at Nuremberg, it has been accepted that all members of society are bound by international humanitarian law, without any of us having been consulted as to whether we consent to it.[39]

[36] See Article 2(1) of Additional Protocol II.

[37] A. Roberts and S. Sivakumaran, 'Lawmaking by Non-State Actors: Engaging Armed Groups in the Creation of International Humanitarian Law' (2012) 37 Yale Journal of International Law 107, 141–2 (hereafter Roberts and Sivakumaran 'Engaging Armed Groups'). Roberts and Sivakumaran argue that unilateral declarations made by armed groups should be given the same weight as unilateral declarations by States. They cite the *Nuclear Tests* case in this regard, where the ICJ stated: 'declarations made by way of unilateral acts, concerning legal or factual situations, may have the effect of creating legal obligations' depending on the intention of the State making the declaration and how it may be reasonably understood by other actors. *Nuclear Tests (Australia v France)* [1974] ICJ Reports 253, 20 December 1974 [43–6].

[38] It also does not correspond with the conclusion in Chapters 5 and 6 which concludes that the legal framework of international humanitarian law does not reflect an 'actor' conception of legal personality.

[39] This idea is expounded more fully later in the chapter in the section on the 'legislative jurisdiction' theory.

A further point casting doubt on this requirement is that there is no indication in the drafting papers reviewed above that the bindingness of common Article 3 and Additional Protocol II was ever considered to be conditional upon an armed group's consent. Such a provision would allow members of armed groups which have not consented to international humanitarian law 'off the hook' in terms of their individual criminal responsibility.[40] While research show that the wholesale rejection of international humanitarian law and principles by armed groups is not common, there are clear examples where this has happened and continues to happen.[41] During the Vietnam war, the Vietnamese National Front (VNF) repeatedly stated that it did not consider itself to be legally bound by the provisions of the 1949 Geneva Conventions because it had not signed them.[42] Likewise, several Salafi groups have publically rejected the provisions of international humanitarian law, arguing that they are contrary to Islam.[43] Under the framework of international law relating to third parties which has been set out above, a group which rejects international humanitarian law in this way would not be considered bound to its provisions. Nor, importantly, would an armed group who has made no statement at all on the law. For according to the principles of Article 35 of the Vienna Convention, an armed group must expressly provide its consent in writing (i.e. take *positive action*) in order to be bound by international humanitarian law's provisions. It is this unrealistic result which has led to a general conclusion that, although from a technical perspective armed groups are indeed 'third parties' to international humanitarian treaty law, the law on third parties as it is generally strictly applied to States does not provide a convincing explanation for *how* armed groups in general are bound by it.[44]

4. Armed Groups Bound as a Result of the Domestic Implementation of Treaty Law

Another explanation for how armed groups are bound by international humanitarian law asserts that armed groups are bound as a result of implementing domestic legislation. The attraction of this theory, which was once the more widespread view, is that it presents the most straightforward *legal* explanation of how armed groups are bound by international humanitarian law.[45] Under this approach,

[40] Sivakumaran 'Binding Armed Opposition Groups' (n 13) 278.

[41] See O. Bangerter, 'Reasons Why Armed Groups Choose to Respect International Humanitarian Law or Not' (2011) 93 International Review of the Red Cross 353, 380–2 (hereafter Bangerter, 'Reasons') for research on the reasons why armed groups choose not to respect international humanitarian law.

[42] See D. Forsythe, *Humanitarian Politics: The International Committee of the Red Cross* (John Hopkins University Press, Baltimore and London 1977) 156. See also Roberts and Sivakumaran, 'Engaging Armed Groups' (n 37) 127.

[43] See Bangerter, 'Reasons' (n 41) 380–2.

[44] Sivakumaran 'Binding Armed Opposition Groups' (n 13) 379.

[45] For authors examining this view see Cassese, 'Status of Rebels' (n 2) 416; T. Fleiner-Gerster and M. Meyer, 'New Developments in Humanitarian Law: A Challenge to the Concept of Sovereignty'

armed groups derive their legal personality and their obligations entirely through the workings of domestic law. As a result, the theory avoids any need to acknowledge armed groups as subjects of international law. Furthermore, the theory that armed groups are only *indirectly* bound by international humanitarian law avoids the seeming paradox of a domestic entity being able to be directly bound by international law without its explicit consent. Yet this theory also makes the question of whether or not armed groups are bound in a particular situation dependent upon external factors which may or not be satisfied in a particular armed conflict situation. In particular, there has been a fear that it will depend on whether or not the State in question has taken the legislative or administrative steps necessary to make the Geneva Conventions and Additional Protocols binding by way of domestic law.[46] In many States around the world, much international treaty law is held to have no binding effect unless it has been explicitly incorporated into domestic law or unless it is recognized to be 'self-executing' (i.e. immediately incorporated into the domestic legal order without domestic legislation).[47] This is the case in *inter alia* the UK[48], the US[49] and the majority of the Commonwealth States.[50] If armed groups are only bound as a result of the domestic implementation of treaty law, then in situations where a State has failed to incorporate treaty law into its domestic law where it was necessary, the group is not bound.[51]

The idea that international humanitarian law is binding upon armed groups is a matter of domestic law does not fit with significant evidence that international humanitarian law becomes binding upon its addressees directly, irrespective of whether it has been implemented into domestic legislation, and irrespective of whether such a step would normally be constitutionally necessary. This is supported by the case law from the war crimes tribunals after the Second World War which found that individuals were obliged to adhere to the laws and customs of

(1985) 34 International and Comparative Law Quarterly 267–83, 272 (hereafter Fleiner-Gerser and Meyer, 'A Challenge to the Concept of Sovereignty'); G. Abi-Saab, *Non-International Armed Conflicts* (Henry Dunant Institute, Geneva 1988) 217–39.

[46] See Fleiner-Gerser and Meyer, 'A Challenge to the Concept of Sovereignty' (n 45) 272; M. Bothe, K. J. Partsch and W. Solf, *New Rules for Victims of Armed Conflicts: Commentary on the Two 1977 Protocols Additional to the Geneva Conventions of 1949* (1982); M. Bothe, 'Article 3 and Protocol II: Case Studies of Nigeria and El Salvador' (1981–1982) 31 American University Law Review 899, 700. While in many countries customary international law is deemed automatically to form part of the domestic law, treaty law often needs to be implemented into domestic law by means of enabling legislation. See for example I. Brownlie, *Principles of Public International Law* (7th edn, OUP, Oxford 2008) 41–9. It is noted that while Sierra Leone had ratified the Geneva Conventions and Additional Protocol II, it had not implemented it into law by means of domestic legislation. The Trial Chamber of the Special Tribunal for Sierra Leone found that this was not an issue that it needed to consider, because it had already found that the crimes under consideration constituted customary international law. See *Prosecutor v Issa Hassan Sesay, Morris Kallon and Augustine Gbao (Judgment)* SCSL-04-15-T (2 March 2009) [69].

[47] M. Shaw, *International Law* (6th edn, CUP, Cambridge 2008) 150, 166.

[48] See ibid, 152. [49] See ibid, 162–3. [50] See ibid, 172.

[51] See T. Meron, *Human Rights in Internal Strife, Their International Protection* (CUP, Cambridge 1987) 39; D. Forsythe, 'Legal Management of Internal War: The 1977 Protocol on Non-International Armed Conflicts' (1978) 72 American Journal of International Law 272, 292; Baxter, 'Jus in Bello Interno' (n 2) 527–8.

war, even in circumstances where the national law does not contain the same obligation. The International Military Tribunal (IMT) stated:

> The very essence of the Charter [of the IMT] is that individuals have individual duties which transcend the national obligations of obedience imposed by the individual State. He who violates the laws of war cannot obtain immunity while acting in pursuance of the authority of the State if the State in authorizing action moves outside its competence under international law.[52]

The Tribunal clearly understood international humanitarian law to be binding upon individuals, as a matter of international law. The advantage of such a finding is that it safeguards against the rejection of national laws by armed groups.[53] In many situations where an armed group takes control in a portion of the territory, it immediately declares the national law to be invalid and imposes its own law.[54] These declarations will be legally irrelevant if the armed group is bound directly by international humanitarian law as an independent legal entity from the State. The paragraphs below consider whether this is possible, by an evaluation of what has been termed the 'legislative jurisdiction' theory.[55]

5. Armed Groups Bound Directly through Constituent Members or as an Entity

5.1 'Legislative jurisdiction' theory

5.1.1 Introduction to the 'legislative jurisdiction' theory

The 'legislative jurisdiction' theory is based on the argument that armed groups are bound by international humanitarian law as a result of the Geneva Conventions and the Additional Protocols creating *direct* obligations upon individuals.[56] The theory is rooted in the view that international humanitarian law is an exception to the principle that an international treaty will only create direct international rights and obligations for individuals in instances where the State is *monist* or the treaty is self-executing. Instead, it is based on the proposition that

[52] 'International Military Tribunal (Judgement and Sentence)' (1947) 41 American Journal of International Law 172, 221. See A. Cassese, *International Law* (OUP, Oxford 2001) 79–80. See also Sivakumaran 'Binding Armed Opposition Groups' (n 13) 385.

[53] See below for more detail on this view which was held during the ICRC during the drafting of common Article 3. See also D. Petrasek, 'Ends & means: human rights approaches to armed groups' [2000] International Council on Human Rights Policy 60 (hereafter Petrasek, 'Ends and Means').

[54] See for example, L. Polgreen, 'Timbuktu Endured Terror under Harsh Sharia Law' (*New York Times*, 31 January 2013) <http://www.nytimes.com/2013/02/01/world/africa/timbuktu-endured-terror-under-harsh-shariah-law.html?_r=0> accessed 20 January 2017.

[55] Moir, *Internal Armed Conflict* (n 1) 53. See also Baxter, 'Jus in Bello Interno' (n 2) 527-8.

[56] This was a term first coined in Moir, *Internal Armed Conflict* (n 1) 53. It is sometimes called the 'prescriptive jurisdiction' theory. See Murray, 'How International Humanitarian Law Treaties Bind Non-state Armed Groups' (2014) 20(1) Journal of Conflict and Security Law 101 (hereafter Murray, *Humanitarian Law Treaties*),

international treaty law is capable of directly creating rights or duties for individuals in instances where this was the intention of the treaty's drafters. Support for this idea is found in the Permanent Court of International Justice's *Advisory Opinion on the Jurisdiction of the Courts of Danzig* in 1928.[57] In this case, the Permanent Court of International Justice was requested to rule on whether the courts of the Free City of Danzig were able to hear pecuniary claims from railway employees against the Polish Railway Administration based on an international agreement between the Free City of Danzig and Poland dated 22 October 1922 called the *Beamtenabkommen*. The question before the Court was whether the *Beamtenabkommen* created direct rights and obligations under international law for the employees of the Railway Administration which could be enforced in a national court in Danzig.

In its Advisory Opinion, the Permanent Court of Justice started out by admitting that usually international agreements do not create direct rights and obligations for individuals. However, it went on to say, that there may be exceptions to this rule where the very object of the international agreement is the creation of individual rights and duties for individuals which are to be enforceable in the national courts.[58] According to the Court, the question of whether such rights and duties have been created in a particular instance can be ascertained from the provisions of the agreement itself and the intention of the parties, as evidenced in the 'wording' and 'tenor' of the agreement.[59] The Permanent Court of Justice held that the *Beamtenabkommen* created direct rights and duties for individuals, even though its provisions had not been incorporated into domestic law.[60] It also found that individual holders of those rights were able to enforce them in the courts of Danzig against the Polish Railways Authority. In effect, the Permanent Court of Justice's *Advisory Opinion* confirms an exception to the rules on third parties set out above. It confirms the possibility of third parties, crucially non-States actors, acquiring direct rights and duties from a treaty in instances where they have not explicitly consented to be bound by the treaty's provisions. Effectively, the *Advisory Opinion* confirms that this is possible in instances where the treaty demonstrates a specific intention on the part of the contracting parties to create such direct rights and duties for individuals.

The idea that international law can create direct rights and duties for individuals has been used as an explanation for how armed groups are bound by international humanitarian law.[61] It has been called the 'legislative jurisdiction' theory because it contemplates the fact that in exceptional circumstances the signing of an

[57] *Advisory Opinion on the Jurisdiction of the Courts of Danzig* [1928] 5 PCIJ Reports 15, 3 March 1928. Support for this idea has also more recently been articulated by the Appeals Chamber of the Special Tribunal for Lebanon. See *Interlocutory Decision on the Applicable Law: Terrorism, Conspiracy, Homicide, Perpetration, Cumulative Charging* STL-11-01/I/AC/R176bis (16 February 2011) [74].

[58] *Courts of Danzig*, ibid, 17–18. [59] Ibid, 17–18. [60] Ibid, 20.

[61] Ibid, 17–18. Sivakumaran 'Binding Armed Opposition Groups' (n 13) 384. It is noted that Cassese who took a critical view of the possibility of international humanitarian law directly binding individuals in his early article on armed groups in Cassese, 'Status of Rebels' (n 2) 429, seems to have come around to the idea in A. Cassese, *International Law* (OUP, Oxford 2005) 144.

international treaty by the State can have the same effect as a State legislating for all individuals within its jurisdiction. The advantage of the so-called 'legislative jurisdiction' theory is that it explains how armed groups are bound by international humanitarian law irrespective of whether the State in which they are operating has correctly implemented the Geneva Conventions or Additional Protocol II into domestic law. It also provides a credible explanation for how armed groups can be held to have obligations under international humanitarian law irrespective of whether they have control over a territory or have provided their consent to its provisions.[62] In considering this theory, the first point to consider is whether international humanitarian law really does seek to create direct rights and obligations upon individuals.

5.1.2 Drafters of Geneva Conventions and Additional Protocols intended to bind individuals

There is considerable evidence that it was the intention of the drafters of the Geneva Conventions and Additional Protocols that the treaties would create direct obligations upon individuals. During the drafting of the Geneva Conventions, and even before 1949 in the preliminary drafting sessions, the ICRC made clear that the undertaking by each State party to respect the Conventions' provisions would not just bind the State itself, but should be understood to bind each one of the State's citizens. This concept was so important to the ICRC that it took efforts to make sure that it was clear in the text of the Conventions themselves. It was with this aim in mind that the ICRC included the phrase 'in the name of their people' in the 1948 Stockholm draft of the Convention. The draft Convention began:

> the High Contracting Parties undertake, *in the name of their people*, to respect and ensure the respect of the current Convention in all circumstances. (emphasis added)[63]

The phase 'in the name of their people' was deleted by the Stockholm Conference[64], but was discussed again during the Diplomatic Conference in 1949 when the Finnish delegation suggested that it should feature in the preamble of the Geneva Conventions. Although the ICRC welcomed the prospect of the reinsertion of the phrase[65], the preambles to the Conventions were eventually not included so the phrase was never reinserted. The fact that the phrase did not return to the

[62] In that sense, the notion that individuals can be directly bound by a treaty can be seen as an exception to the rules relating to third parties and international law considered above for there is no consent requirement in *Courts of Danzig* criteria. The reason for this must be that a consent requirement would be entirely unworkable when the third parties are individuals.

[63] Siordet, 'La Guerre Civile' (n 2) 120, author's translation.

[64] 'Final Record of the Diplomatic Conference of Geneva of 1949, Vol II (B), Seventh Meeting' (17 May 1949) 26.

[65] 'Final Record of the Diplomatic Conference of Geneva of 1949, Vol II (B), Twenty Fourth Meeting' (15 June 1949) 79. It is noted that the insertion of the words 'in the name of the peoples' was also suggested by the Finnish delegation and adopted by the Working Party as part of the proposed Preamble of Geneva Convention IV, 'Final Record of the Diplomatic Conference of Geneva of 1949', Vol III, 97–8.

Conventions may also have been influenced by a view expressed by the French delegation that the expression 'to ensure respect' which appears in common Article 1 of the Conventions ultimately played the same role as the phrase 'in the name of the peoples'.[66]

5.1.3 Idea that individuals are bound by international humanitarian law accepted in criminal jurisprudence

Moreover, at the time that the Geneva Conventions were drafted, the idea that international humanitarian law was binding on civilians was not new. The case law from the Second World War military tribunals had already found that the 'mere fact of being a civilian affords no protection whatever to a charge based on criminal law'.[67] There had been numerous cases before the Tokyo and Nuremberg Tribunals where the defendants were civilian administrators, political party officials, industrialists, judges, prosecutors, doctors, nurses, prison wardens, and concentration camp inmates.[68] Most notably, the cases against the German industrialists contain explicit judicial confirmation that ordinary civilians, as well as public officials, are bound by the laws of war.[69] Even more striking are those cases against ordinary individuals who were not associated with German industry. In the *Essen Lynching* case, five of the accused were members of a crowd of onlookers who spontaneously attacked and killed three prisoners of war in the streets of Essen.[70] In the trial of Alois and Anna Bommer and their daughters, the accused were German settlers in occupied France who were accused of dealing in stolen property belonging to French citizens. In finding the parents and two daughters guilty of war crimes, the Tribunal confirmed that:

[66] 'Final Record of the Diplomatic Conference of Geneva of 1949, Vol II (B), Ninth Meeting' (25 May 1949) 53. See also comment from the Monaco delegation at 87.

[67] UN War Crimes Commission, 'Digest of Laws and Cases, Law Reports Of Trials Of War Criminals, Selected and prepared by The United Nations War Crimes Commission' (London 1949) Vol 15, 59.

[68] Ibid.

[69] See *Trial of Frederick Flick and Five Others* (United States Military Tribunal, Nuremburg, 1949) Law Reports Of Trials Of War Criminals, Selected and prepared by The United Nations War Crimes Commission (20 April–22 December 1947) Vol IX, 18 (hereafter *Flick*). See also *Trial of Carl Krauch and Twenty-Two Others* (United States Military Tribunal, Nuremberg, 1949) Law Reports Of Trials Of War Criminals, Selected and prepared by The United Nations War Crimes Commission (14 August 1947–29 July 1948) Vol X, 47. See also *Trial of Alfried Felix Alwyn Krupp Von Bohlen Und Halbach and Eleven Others* (United States Military Tribunal, Nuremberg, 1949) Law Reports Of Trials Of War Criminals, Selected and prepared by The United Nations War Crimes Commission (17 November 1947–30 June 1948) Vol X (hereafter *Krupp*), and *Trial of Bruno Tesch and Two Others (Zyklon B* case*)* (British Military Court, Hamburg, 1949) Law Reports Of Trials Of War Criminals, Selected and prepared by The United Nations War Crimes Commission (1–8 March 1946) Vol I (hereafter *Zyklon B).*

[70] *Trial of Erich Heyer and Six Others* (British Military Court for the Trial of War Criminals, Essen, 1949) Law Reports Of Trials Of War Criminals, Selected and prepared by The United Nations War Crimes Commission, (18–19 and 21–22 December 1945) Vol I, 88–92. Two of the seven accused were members of the German Army but the other five accused were civilian inhabitants of Essen. Two of these five were acquitted.

laws and customs of war are applicable not only to military personnel, combatant or acting as members of occupying authorities, or, generally speaking, to organs of the State and other public authorities, but also to any civilian who violates these laws and customs.[71]

These cases constitute an important confirmation of the fact that even before the drafting of the Geneva Conventions, it was already understood that ordinary individuals are bound by international humanitarian law.[72]

5.1.4 Individuals considered to be directly bound by international humanitarian law

Post-Second World War case law makes clear that, in terms of mechanics, individuals were thought to be *directly* bound by the provisions of international humanitarian law, without the need for additional implementing domestic legislation. The United States Military Tribunal in the *Flick* trial stated:

> *International law, as such binds every citizen just as does ordinary municipal law.* Acts adjudged criminal when done by an officer of the Government are criminal also when done by a private individual ... The application of international law to individuals is no novelty. (emphasis added)[73]

The fact that individuals were considered directly bound by international law is also illustrated by the extract from the IMT Judgment cited in section 4 above confirming that national law offers no defence to a violation of international law. In stating that 'individuals have individual duties which transcend the national obligations of obedience imposed by the individual State', the Tribunal made clear that individuals were being prosecuted on the basis of their direct obligations under international law, rather than their obligations under domestic law. [74]

Interestingly, it appears that the war crimes tribunals relied upon a mixture of treaty law and customary international law in their deliberations. A passage in the judgment of the *Einsatzgruppen Trial* indicates a reliance on treaty law. The Tribunal stated:

> It is a fallacy of no small proportion that international obligations can apply only to the abstract legal entities called States. Nations can act only through human beings, and when Germany signed, ratified and promulgated the Hague and Geneva Conventions, she bound each one of her subjects to their observance.[75]

[71] *Trial of Alois and Anna Bommer and their Daughters* (Permanent Military Tribunal at Metz, 1949) Law Reports Of Trials Of War Criminals, Selected and prepared by The United Nations War Crimes Commission (19 February 1947) Vol IX, 62.

[72] The fact that common Article 3 applies to everyone without discrimination, irrespective of whether they have a special relationship to one of the parties of the conflict has been confirmed by the Appeals Chamber of the ICTR in *Prosecutor v Akayesu (Judgment)* ICTR-96-4-T (2 September 1998) [437–44].

[73] *Flick* (n 69) 18.

[74] See 'International Military Tribunal (Judgement and Sentence)' (n 52), 221.

[75] *Trial of Otto Ohlendorf and Twenty Four Others* (United States Military Tribunal II) Trials Of War Criminals before the Nuremberg Military Tribunals under Control Council 10 (8–9 April 1948) Vol IV/1, cited in *Krupp* (n 69) 173.

This statement is essentially an articulation of the *legislative jurisdiction* theory, whereby every individual in the country is directly bound by international humanitarian law by virtue of the State signing the treaty in question. Yet there are also instances where the military tribunals relied on customary international law as well. For example, the war crimes courts often treated the Hague Conventions and the general principles of the 1929 Geneva Convention on Prisoners of War as 'mere codifications' of existing customary international law.[76]

5.1.5 Armed groups bound through their members

The paragraphs above confirm that at the time the Geneva Conventions were drafted, it was already understood that individuals could be directly bound by at least some provisions of international humanitarian law, as a matter of treaty law or customary international law.[77] But it was the intention of the drafters of common Article 3 and Additional Protocol II to make the armed groups themselves, rather than just their members, responsible for their implementation. How did they seek to achieve this? In an article written in 1950, Frederic Siordet, an ICRC Member who had been involved in the drafting process of the Geneva Conventions and who assisted Jean Pictet in drafting their commentaries, explained that the ICRC was aware, prior to the Geneva Conventions' drafting, that the idea of binding a rebel group might seem to be a 'juridical heresy'.[78] Yet he explained it was partly in order to rationalize this heresy and clarify the legal mechanics of how the Geneva Conventions would bind armed groups, that the ICRC had been so keen to include the phrase 'in the name of their people' in the Geneva Conventions. He explained that the ICRC had included this phrase in the Stockhom draft in order to make it clear that armed groups would be bound by international humanitarian law, by virtue of their constituent members being bound *directly* by international humanitarian law.

A similar explanation was given by the ICRC at the 1971 Conference of Government Experts on the Reaffirmation and Development of International Humanitarian Law Applicable in Armed Conflicts. The representative stated that it wished to address any doubts or misgivings on the part of experts about the obligations that rebels should assume by clarifying that:

[76] With relation to the Hague Convention, the I.M.T's finding on this point was crucial to circumventing the potential effect of the 'general participation' clause in Article 2 of the convention. The Nuremberg and Tokyo Tribunals later followed the I.M.T's approach of relying on the provisions of the Hague Convention, as a matter of customary law rather than treaty. This was explicitly confirmed by the U.S. Military Tribunal in the *High Command* case and the *Krupp* case. For a discussion of these cases, see Digest of Laws and Cases, *Law Reports Of Trials Of War Criminals, Selected and prepared by The United Nations War Crimes Commission* (London 1949) Vol XV, 12.

[77] See also H. Lauterpacht, *International Law and Human Rights* (Stevens & Sons, London 1950) 10, 28, for a discussion of the laws of war being an instance of international law imposing duties upon individuals without recourse to State legislation.

[78] Siordet, 'La Guerre Civile' (n 2) 120.

the ICRC had always held the view that Article 3 was binding not only on the governments of Contracting States but also on the population as a whole and, hence, on rebel forces. (emphasis added)[79]

A similar sentiment was repeated by the ICRC representative during a drafting session of Additional Protocol II. Here the ICRC representative stated that common Article 3 was based on the principle that engagements entered into by the State were binding not only upon the established Government but also upon all private individuals on the territory of the High Contracting Party. This meant that the legal obligations undertaken by the State were also binding upon the insurgent party.[80]

It can be presumed that the ICRC's explanation that armed groups would be bound through their members was based on the notion that an armed group is bound by *identical obligations* to its members.[81] To some extent, this theory that armed groups would be bound through its members tallies with the finding in Chapter 4 that an armed group comes into existence as a legal entity—a bearer of rights and obligations under international law—at the moment when it reaches a level of 'organization', for it to be recognized as a separate legal entity from its members. This moment is partly defined by the idea that at a certain point an armed group becomes collectively capable of bearing the rights and obligations set out in international humanitarian law. Chapter 4 demonstrates that the 'organization' threshold is a fundamental part of the two-pronged threshold test for the application of common Article 3. As a matter of common sense, an armed group must be sufficiently organized before it, as a group, can be deemed bound by common Article 3.[82] It is noted that this legal theory has similarities with the concept of 'unincorporated associations' in domestic law. An unincorporated organization is one of the simplest forms of legal structure in many countries comprising of a group of people who have come together, with common goals. Indeed, it is noteworthy that there are

[79] Conference of Government Experts on the Reaffirmation and Development of International Humanitarian Law Applicable in Armed Conflicts, Geneva 24 May–12 June 1971, 44 [223].

[80] Geneva Conference 1974–1977 (n 22), Vol VIII, 239 [55]. See also the Commentary to Additional Protocol II which states: 'the question is often raised how the insurgent party can be bound by a treaty to which it is not a High Contracting Party. It may therefore be appropriate to recall here the explanation given in 1949: the commitment made by a State not only applies to the government but also to any established authorities and private individuals within the national territory of that State and certain obligations are therefore imposed upon them. The extent of rights and duties of private individuals is therefore the same as that of the rights and duties of the State. Although this argument has occasionally been questioned in legal literature, the validity of the obligation imposed upon insurgents has never been contested.' ICRC, *Commentary to the Additional Protocols of 8 June 1977* (n 18) 1345 [4444].

[81] See also Dinstein, 'Civil Wars and Human Rights' (n 2) 68, who accepts that individuals belonging to rebel forces have international human duties but questions whether it is yet possible to talk of collective duties imposed on the rebel groups.

[82] *Prosecutor v Boškoski and Tarčulovski (Trial Judgment)* IT-04-82-T (10 July 2008) [197] (hereafter *Boškoski*), importantly points out that as the obligations set out in common Article 3 are purely humanitarian, the level of organization required to fulfil them is only 'minimal'. This 'organization' requirement is explored at length in Chapter 5.

examples of armed groups having been sued in domestic law as 'unincorporated associations'.[83]

5.1.6 Limitations of the 'legislative jurisdiction' theory

However, the theory that armed groups are bound by international humanitarian law *through their members* is not without weaknesses. The main limitations of the theory stem from the fact that it draws a very tight correlation between the armed group and its members. For a start, it asserts that the legal obligations of the armed group are identical to its members. As a result, it relies upon the idea that all norms of international humanitarian law which apply in common Article 3 conflicts and Additional Protocol II conflicts are firstly binding upon individuals and armed groups alike and secondly, are able to be adhered to by individuals and armed groups alike. When it comes to the text of common Article 3, this may be maintained as a reality. First, there is legal precedent to confirm that individuals are bound by common Article 3.[84] Second, there is good argument that individuals *can* adhere to all the provisions of common Article 3, by refraining from committing the prohibited acts and offering the humane treatment to protected persons that the article requires. But with respect to norms of international humanitarian law beyond the text common Article 3, the theory becomes harder to sustain.

For example, it remains unclear whether ordinary individuals can be reasonably held bound by international humanitarian law norms relating to the conduct of hostilities that apply alongside common Article.[85] It remains questionable whether ordinary individuals can reasonably be expected to take precautions in attack or weigh up whether the losses to civilian life and infrastructure will be excessive to the military advantage gained by a particular attack. Moreover, although there are some provisions of Additional Protocol II which are clearly binding on individuals and armed groups equally, there are also several provisions which seem to be only directed at the *group* and not its members.[86] Examples of such provisions include

[83] See for example *Mark Christopher Breslin and Others v Seamus McKenna and Others* [2009] NIQB 50, where five defendants were sued for the planning, production, planting and detonation of the bomb which exploded in Omagh on 15 August 1998, two as representing the IRA. Under the law in Northern Ireland, such an entity did not have separate legal personality so could not be a defendant in its own right but could be sued through named individuals.

[84] The fact that common Article 3 applies to everyone without discrimination irrespective of whether they have a special relationship to one of the parties of the conflict has been confirmed by the Appeals Chamber of the ICTR in *Prosecutor v Akayesu (Judgment)* ICTR-96-4-T (2 September 1998) [437–44].

[85] See M. Sassòli and A. Bouvier, *How does Law Protect in War?, Cases, Documents and Teaching Materials on Contemporary Practice in International Humanitarian Law, Volume I* (2nd edn, ICRC, Geneva 2006) 267 (hereafter Sassòli and Bouvier, 'How does Law Protect in War?'), where the pertinent comment is made that '[i]f such individuals are not considered as addressees of IHL, most acts committed in anarchic conflicts would not be covered by IHL nor consequently punishable as violations of IHL'.

[86] These include the prohibition of declaring that no quarter shall be given in Article 4(1), the fundamental guarantees contained in Article 4(2), on passing penal sentences or penalties except pursuant to a conviction pronounced by a court offering essential guarantees of independence and impartiality in Article 6(2), prohibition against making the civilian population an object of attack in Article 13(2),

the obligation to provide children with the care and aid they require,[87] the obligations relating to persons whose liberty has been restricted in Article 5,[88] and the obligations relating to penal prosecutions and fair trial in Article 6.[89] It seems clear that these provisions are directed at the armed group as a collective entity and are not addressed to its members.[90] Likewise, there is a strong argument that the obligations in Article 6(5) regarding amnesty are addressed exclusively to the armed group. Like the provisions relating to conduct of hostilities, many of these provisions require responsible command and a degree of organization to be carried out effectively.[91] These provisions demonstrate that there it is problematic to argue that armed groups are bound *through their members* because in both common Article 3 situations and Additional Protocol II situations, the obligations of an armed group do not exactly correspond to the obligations of its constituent members.[92]

The theory also takes little account of the fact that the connection between an armed group group and its members inevitably reduces as an armed group becomes more established. With the adoption of disciplinary codes, establishment of bureaucratic structures, and implementation of complex command structures, an armed group inevitably takes on an impersonal 'organizational' character that is separate to its members.[93] The group also develops a functional capacity that is more extensive than its individual members. From a legal perspective, this indicates that the legal personality of an armed group is quickly bigger than its constituent members. As an armed group becomes more established its legal obligations increase and become greater than those of its members, who are not always bound by the same norms. This is an expression of the important truth that parties to an armed conflict are much more than simply the sum of their members.[94] An armed group's power to act is made greater by its organizational structure. Despite these difficulties in the legislative jurisdiction theory, the *travaux préparatoires* of Additional Protocol II suggests that the theory may have another limb to it, which has hitherto been either neglected or not explicitly articulated. For the purpose of the analysis below, this is referred to as the 'extended legislative jurisdiction' theory.

the prohibition against attacking buildings dedicated to culture or religion in Article 16 and the prohibition against forcibly displacing the civilian population in Article 17(1).

[87] Articles 4(3)(a)(b) and (e) of Additional Protocol II: an obligation that includes the provision of an education, the facilitation of family reunion and the removal of children from the area of hostilities.

[88] Articles 5(1)(b), 5(2)(a), and 5(2)(b) of Additional Protocol II: obligations which include the obligation to provide detained persons with food and drinking water in a hygienic and safe conditions and the right of the prisoners to be accommodated as a family and the right to send and receive letters and cards.

[89] Article 6 of Additional Protocol II.

[90] See Kleffner, 'Organized Armed Groups' (n 1) 451.

[91] ICRC, *Commentary to the Additional Protocols of 8 June 1977* (n 18) 1353 [4467].

[92] See L. Zegveld, *The Accountability of Armed Opposition Groups in International Law* (CUP, Cambridge 2002) 16, for a similar argument.

[93] See also J. Kleffner, 'The Collective Accountability of Organized Armed Groups for System Crimes' in A. Nollkaemper and H. van der Wilt (eds), *System Criminality in International Law* (CUP, Cambridge 2009) 238–69, 241–7 for further observations on this point.

[94] Kleffner, 'Organized Armed Groups' (n 1) 450.

5.2 'Extended legislative jurisdiction' theory

5.2.1 Drafters also intended to bind constituent/established authorities

During the drafting conferences of the Additional Protocols in the 1970s, the ICRC stated that the draft Additional Protocol II was based on the same principles as common Article 3. It continued that any engagement entered into by the State should be considered binding not only on the established government but also on 'the constituent authorities and all private individuals on the territory of the High Contracting Party concerned'. According to the ICRC, this principle meant that the engagement entered into by the State was binding upon the armed group.[95] Likewise, in its commentary to APII, the ICRC stated:

> The commitment made by a State not only applies to the government but also to any *established authorities* and private individuals within the national territory of that State and certain obligations are therefore imposed upon them. The extent of rights and duties of private individuals is therefore the same as that of the rights and duties of the State (emphasis added).[96]

In analysing these statements earlier in this chapter, the sections above have focused on the references to 'individuals' ('in the name of the people'). But it is argued below that that a better explanation for the obligations of armed groups lies in the words 'constituent authorities' and 'established authorities' in these paragraphs.

5.2.2 Definition of constituent/established authorities

In both passages above, the ICRC says that the commitment made by the State is binding on: (i) the State; (ii) private individuals; and (iii) constituent/ established authorities. It is noteworthy that there is no further discussion of the meaning of the phrases 'constituent authorities' or 'established authorities' in the drafting papers of Additional Protocol II or the commentary to Additional Protocol II. While the term could be said to refer only to 'government' authorities, it could also be interpreted broadly to mean any entity exercising authority over a population. Indeed, there is a strong case to be made that the ICRC used the phrases 'constituent authorities' and 'established authorities' in this broad manner. It is noted that the ICRC representative used the phrase 'authorities' and 'constituted authorities' in other places to refer to the sides of a non-international armed conflict falling under Additional Protocol II, i.e. the State forces and the armed group.[97] For example, when discussing the fundamental guarantees section of the draft protocol, the ICRC representative stated that it was:

> designed to protect all persons who took no direct part or who had ceased to take a part in hostilities against abuse of power and inhuman and cruel treatment by the *military or*

[95] Geneva Conference 1974–1977 (n 20) Vol VIII, 239 [55].
[96] ICRC, *Commentary to the Additional Protocols of 8 June 1977* (n 18) 1345 [4444].
[97] Geneva Conference 1974–1977 (n 20) Vol VIII, CDDH/I/SR.33, 346 [23].

civilian authorities of the Parties to the conflict in whose power they might be (emphasis added).[98]

In this context, the term 'authorities' clearly relates to the 'military or civilian authorities' of the State and the armed group.

Likewise, the ICRC representative at the Diplomatic Conference referred to the 'special nature' of the 'authorities of the insurgent party' who she said were 'not representatives appointed in conformity with national legislation but self-*established de facto* authorities' (emphasis added).[99] A wide interpretation of the term 'authorities' is also supported by Article 6(5) of Additional Protocol II which states that the 'authorities in power' at the end of a non-international armed conflict shall endeavour to grant the broadest possible amnesty. Likewise, the term 'competent authority' was used in draft Article 11(e), which eventually got amended, to refer to 'a competent authority of [either] party to the conflict'.[100] Further evidence that the ICRC was referring to both sides the conflict is found in Additional Protocol I. Significantly, throughout Additional Protocol I, the term 'authority' is used to apply to both sides of the conflict, whether the conflict is between two States or a State and a national liberation movement.[101] In the latter instance, the term 'authority' is clearly being used explicitly to refer to the legal non-State entity which assumes rights and duties under the Additional Protocol.

If the term 'constituent authorities' and 'established authorities' is understood to include the 'authority' of a rebel group, the 'gap' in the 'legislative jurisdiction' theory is filled. For it suggests that the ICRC intended armed groups to be bound by IHL not only by virtue of their individual members being bound but also directly as a group (i.e. 'authority').[102] From a legal perspective, this approach can be understood as an extension of the principle in *Advisory Opinion on the Jurisdiction of the Courts of Danzig* explained above. It is a recognition that a treaty between States may bind not only individuals, but also other non-State actors which are organized enough to have personality under international law. It is argued below that such an extension would be a natural development of the principle evidenced in the *Jurisdiction of the Courts of*

[98] Ibid, 323 [3]. [99] Geneva Conference 1974–1977 (n 20) Vol IX, 288 [29].

[100] In Article 11(e) of draft Additional Protocol II, 'means of medical transport' is defined as 'any means of transport assigned exclusively to medical transport, under the control of a competent authority of a party to the conflict'. See Geneva Conference 1974–1977 (n 20) Vol I, Part III, Draft Additional Protocol, 37.

[101] Article 1(4) of Additional Protocol I states that the protocol will apply to armed conflicts in which peoples are fighting against colonial domination and alien occupation and against racist regimes in the exercise of their right of self-determination, as enshrined in the Charter of the United Nations and the Declaration on Principles of International Law concerning Friendly Relations and Co-operation among States in accordance with the Charter of the United Nations. See also wording of Articles 83(2) and 96(3).

[102] See the ICRC's words 'the engagement entered into by the State was not only binding upon the established Government but also upon the constituent authorities and all private individuals on the territory of the High Contracting Party concerned'. See Kleffner, 'Organized Armed Groups' (n 1) 450.

Danzig case before the ICJ. Indeed, there is no reason of logic why the principle established in the *Jurisdiction of the Courts of Danzig* case should only extend to individuals and not to all non-State actors. With respect to States, there are good arguments why the notion of privity of contract should be applied rigorously. The most obvious of these is that States are able to sign treaties. But the nature of non-State actors makes it hard, and often impossible, to solicit their consent to be bound by treaty norms, whether a party or as a third Party.[103] This is particularly the case for individuals whose sheer number on the planet makes obtaining their individual consent impossible. It is also true of armed groups.[104]

Indeed, the nature of armed groups makes it less likely that they would sign international humanitarian law instruments, even if they could. Notably, States parties mainly ratify international humanitarian law provisions in times of peace.[105] After an armed conflict has broken out, it is generally more difficult to persuade a State to accept constraints on the way on which it conducts its hostilities.[106] Applying this argument by analogy to armed groups, one quickly sees the problem. Before the armed conflict breaks out, the armed group in question does not exist. Once the conflict has broken out, strategic and logistical influences create a strong risk that the armed group will not wish to sign such a treaty.[107] In the light of this problem, one can see that the endorsement of a 'legislative' approach to international law in this instance can not only be justified legally, but also conceptually. In a similar vein, it is significant to note that the driving force behind a finding that armed groups are 'bound' directly by international humanitarian law is humanitarian in character. Humanitarian concerns, according to Chinkin in her authoritative study on third parties in international law, are likely to provide justification for 'any discrepancy with the rigid treaty rule' on third parties contained in the Vienna Convention.[108]

[103] The ability of non-State actors to sign treaties is a matter which needs further consideration under international law. C. Chinkin, *Third Parties in International Law* (Clarendon Press, Oxford 1993) (hereafter Chinkin, *Third Parties in International Law*).

[104] See Murray, *Humanitarian Law Treaties* (n 56), 120–1 for the inapplicability of the *pacta tertiis* rule for armed groups

[105] It is noted that all the Geneva Conventions and the Additional Protocols make it impossible for States Parties to denounce them effectively in instances where the denouncing party is involved in an armed conflict. See Article 63 of GC1, Article 62 of GC2, Article 142 of GC3, Article 158 of GC4, Article 99 of API and Article 25 of APII.

[106] It has been noted in this respect that many of the States which have not signed Additional Protocol I or II of the Geneva Conventions are those which continue to be, or have recently been, involved in armed conflicts, e.g. India, Pakistan, Israel, United States of America, Syrian Arab Republic, Sri Lanka, Nepal, Iraq. There are of course important instances in which States involved in ongoing armed conflict have signed international humanitarian law treaties. Examples include Afghanistan which acceded to Additional Protocol I and II of the Geneva Convention in November 2009 and Colombia which acceded to Additional Protocol I in 1993 and Additional Protocol II in 1995.

[107] Exceptions to this rule are of course seen in the numerous Deeds of Commitments which have been signed by armed groups under the auspices of Geneva Call. Yet the armed groups that have signed these commitments still represent a fraction of the armed groups active in the world today.

[108] Chinkin, *Third Parties in International Law* (n 15) 133.

6. Armed Groups Bound as a Result of Controlling Territory

6.1 Legal reasoning behind this argument

The extended jurisdiction theory set out above has strong connections with the fourth theory of how armed groups are bound by international humanitarian law which asserts that they are bound by virtue of their control of territory. The legal reasoning behind such a proposition has been only modestly explored so far in legal literature and when it has, it has tended to be explained with reference to logic, rather than law. For example, it has been argued that armed groups are bound by common Article 3 by virtue of the fact, and to the extent to which, they claim to represent the State or part of it.[109] It is argued that if an armed group is successful in overthrowing an existing government, it will be bound by international humanitarian law in its role as the representative of the State. The argument runs broadly as follows: if an armed group is going to be held bound by these norms eventually, why should it not be held bound by these norms at the moment it becomes a serious threat to the State?.[110] Yet this argument is legally problematic. First, it overlooks the fact that after a conflict, a successful armed group will be bound by international humanitarian law in its new incarnation as the State, rather than in its old incarnation as an armed opposition group.[111] While the members of the armed group will undoubtedly form a fundamental part of the State's administrative structures, the legal subjectivity of the armed group will no longer exist as an independent legal entity.[112] The argument also does not explain why an armed group which fails to become the new government is also considered bound by international humanitarian law for the duration of the conflict.

The second explanation for the notion that armed groups are bound by international humanitarian law by virtue of their control of territory is based on the principle in Article 10 of the Articles on State Responsibility. Article 10 states that the 'conduct of an insurrectional movement which becomes the new government of a State shall be considered *an act of that State* under international law' (emphasis added).[113] The existence of this legal principle has been pointed to as

[109] J. Pictet, *Commentary to the Geneva Convention for the Amelioration of the Condition of the Wounded and Sick in Armed Forces in the Field of August 12, 1949* (International Committee of the Red Cross, Geneva 1952) 51. See also Moir, *Internal Armed Conflict* (n 1) 55, citing Baxter, 'Jus in Bello Interno' (n 2) 151

[110] Moir, *Internal Armed Conflict* (n 1) 55; Cassese, 'Status of Rebels' (n 2) 427.

[111] Sivakumaran, 'Binding Armed Opposition Groups' (n 13) 380.

[112] See ILC, Yearbook of the International Law Commission 1972 (2 May–7 July 1972) Vol II, UN Doc A/CN.4/SER.A/1972/Add.1, 145 [199] (hereafter ILC Yearbook 1972 Vol II) for a discussion of this.

[113] Moir does not reference Article 10 specifically (and indeed they may not have been adopted when his book went to press) but the principle in Article 10 is clearly what he is referring to. Moir, *Internal Armed Conflict* (n 1) 55. The text of these Articles and Commentaries are found in UN General Assembly, 'Report of the International Law Commission, Fifty-third session, Official Records, Fifty-Sixth Session, Supplement No. 10' (23 April–1 June 2001 and 2 July–10 August 2001) UN Doc A/56/10.

evidence that armed groups which are already exercising *de facto* authority over a portion of the country are held to the same international law norms as the State during the armed conflict.[114] Yet while such a conclusion may seem logical, there is little evidence that the rationale behind the principle is rooted in an armed group's prior control of territory.[115] In arbitral decisions where the principle has been put into practice, no relevance has been attached to whether the armed group in question was exercising effective control over part of the territory at the time at which the acts were committed.[116] Indeed, the International Law Commission has concluded that the principle in Article 10 can be better explained by the fact that the State apparatus which emerges at the end of an armed conflict is often, in practical terms, a continuation of both organizations which fought against each other during the armed conflict itself.[117] Taking this into account, it makes sense for the State to be held responsible for the acts not only of the pre-existing government but also of the armed group that now forms part of it. In terms of administration and structures, the post-conflict government is likely to contain core elements of both legal entities.[118]

6.2 Principle of effectiveness

The notion that armed groups are bound by international humanitarian law by virtue of their control of territory has also been explained with reference to the principle of effectiveness.[119] It has been argued that in situations of non-international armed conflict the principle of effectiveness requires not only the established government to adhere to treaty obligations, but also any other authority which claims to exercise, or actually exercises, powers which usually belong to the State.[120] The principle of effectiveness has been described as the principle of international law that states that a legal order must be efficacious to be valid.[121] According to this principle, the constitution of a State, its legitimate government, legal order and community are only valid as long as the legal order upon which they are founded remains efficacious.[122] A legal order may lose its efficacy in multiple scenarios when it no longer corresponds to reality. Principal among these scenarios is a State's loss

[114] Ibid, 55. [115] ILC Yearbook 1972 Vol II (n 112) 145 [198]. [116] Ibid.

[117] ILC Yearbook 1972 Vol II (n 112) 146 [199].

[118] In situations where a successful revolution causes the complete breakdown of the State organization against which the armed group was fighting, the pre-existing State may be deemed to no longer exist and a new State, endowed with an international personality different from that of the former one, emerges. If this is the case, the new State will only be responsible for the acts of the armed group that now makes up its ranks. It will not be responsible for the acts of the previous government. See ILC Yearbook 1972 Vol II (n 112) 146 [195].

[119] Kleffner, 'Organized Armed Groups' (n 1) 451.

[120] R. Pinto, 'Les Règles du Droit International Concernant La Guerre Civile' (1965) 114 Recueil des Courts 528, cited by Kleffner, 'Organized Armed Groups' (n 1) 451, fn 33.

[121] H. Kelsen, *General Theory of Law and State* (Harvard University Press, Cambridge 1949) 121.

[122] See ibid, 121: 'According to this principle of international law [the principle of effectiveness], an actually established authority is the legitimate government, the coercive order enacted by this government is the legal order, and the community constituted by this order is a State in the sense of international law, insofar as this order is, on the whole, efficacious.'

of control of territory[123] or a State's inability to exert effective control over all of its territory.[124] The most extreme example is seen when a part of a State's population creates a new State on part of the territory of an old State. Here, the coming into existence of the new State takes place in accordance with the principle of effectiveness: a new national legal order becomes efficacious in that territory and the old national legal order ceases to be effective.[125] In other less extreme instances where, for example, an armed group exerts only a degree of control over a portion of the territory, the pre-existing legal order may cease to be effective in that territory to varying degrees. Depending on the level of control exercised by the armed group, the State may not be able fully to enforce national law over that region or fully adhere to its obligations under international law. In such circumstances, the armed group may or may not have set up a competing national legal order. However, if it controls a portion of the territory, it is likely to be capable of adhering to, and thereby making efficacious, at least some of the pre-existing international legal obligations of the State. By usurping some of the key prerogatives of State, for example by asserting control over territory and people, the armed group has become in many situations the only actor capable of adhering to the international legal obligations of that State.

One of the benefits of an explanation based on the principle of effectiveness is that it is rooted dually in the control exercised by the armed group in a particular situation and the absence of the State in such a situation. In discussing the accountability of armed groups under international humanitarian law the second of these justifications is often overlooked. Instead, the focus of the legal argument is usually placed on the control and functions exerted by the armed group in question. Yet importantly Part II of the book showed that a lack of control by the *de jure* government, and its inability to be an effective duty-bearer under international law in situations where armed groups have taken control of an area of the country, seems to be an equally fundamental part of understanding how and why armed groups may bear obligations under international law in particular circumstances. It recognizes that the idea that armed groups may bear obligations under international law is partly a pragmatic response to the *de jure* government's loss of control over a part of its territory. In such instances, it is no longer efficacious for the State to be the sole duty-bearer of international law obligations and limited obligations may have to be borne by other actors.[126] While the parameters of this principle have been little explored, Chapter 4 showed that its underlying rationale is supported by examples from history which indicate that when a certain degree

[123] Ibid, 220.

[124] Ibid, 217. The example is given of the validity of a State's legal order only being able to extend to that part of the territory over which the State has effective control. The example that Kelsen uses is the air space that may lie within a state's sovereignty but which is outside their control. It seems that the same principle could be applied in instances where a State has 'lost' its effective control over a portion of a territory as a result of conflict.

[125] Ibid, 216.

[126] There may be multiple actors which step in in such a scenario (e.g. church organizations and humanitarian organizations), but only some of them will be deemed to have international legal personality.

of control of territory has been achieved by an armed group, third States may begin to address the armed group as the duty-bearer of international norms, rather than State, via the *de jure* government.

While the invocation of the principle of effectiveness may well be relevant when explaining how armed group might be bound by human rights law, and will be explored further in Chapter 9, it is observed that the underlying reasoning does not wholly fit as an explanation of how armed groups are bound by international humanitarian law.[127] Most importantly, the international humanitarian law of non-international armed conflict always entails two duty-bearers; a State actor and a non-State actor. As a result, unlike the examples from the Spanish Civil War and the American Civil War explored in Chapter 4, the application of international humanitarian law to armed groups does not represent an example of a non-State actor being held responsible in 'default' of the government in instances where the State's duty to fulfil its obligations throughout the whole territory has been interrupted or compromised as a result of the armed group usurping the government's position.[128] Instead, the international humanitarian law norms which apply in situations of non-international armed conflict can better be seen as legal framework which, from its very conception, codifies the effectiveness principle. This is particularly true for Geneva law which codifies a series of protection which covers issues which in times of peace would be the sole prerogative of the State.[129] The provisions in international humanitarian treaty law are designed to bind the State and the rebel group in anticipation of the fact that in times of non-international armed conflict, the State on its own will not be able to secure the protection to which international humanitarian law aspires.[130]

6.3 Explanation based on territory another manifestation of the extended jurisdiction theory

Indeed, it is asserted that a better explanation of why armed groups are bound by international humanitarian law in instances where they control territory is found in the 'extended jurisdiction' theory above. This asserts that as a result of signing the Geneva Conventions and the Additional Protocols, States have bound not only on the individual citizens of the State, but also other 'authorities' in the State territory. Under this theory, the armed group is not held bound by the obligation of the State per se (as under the theory of effectiveness) but instead, it is bound in its own right by an obligation created by the State, which is designed *ab initio* to be binding upon it. The difference between these theories is subtle and at times not wholly

[127] A similar comment is made by Ryngaert, 'Non-State Actors in IHL' (n 7) 287.

[128] In a way, international humanitarian treaty law can be seen to be a codification of the effectiveness principle whereby it was recognized by the drafters at the outset that in times of armed conflict the State would be unable to secure the protection of all the civilians within its territory.

[129] See also Ryngaert, 'Non-State Actors in IHL' (n 7) 287.

[130] The relevance of the effectiveness theory is arguably stronger for Geneva law (the law on protected persons) than Hague law (the law on hostilities).

recognized in the manner in which the theories are discussed. Yet ultimately, the difference between the theories reflects the fact that the principle of effectiveness is a much more far-reaching and radical theory than the extended jurisdiction theory. It holds that in times of non-international armed conflict, other subjects of international law may be held bound by the obligations of the State, even in the absence of any explicitly articulated intention by the State. The extended jurisdiction theory, on the other hand, is essentially an articulation of States' intention to bind armed groups. It holds that States can bind armed groups by means of international treaty law and that those obligations will become binding at the moment at which the armed groups have legal personality under international law.

From the perspective of the 'extended jurisdiction' theory, the fact that an armed group has control over territory is simply one indication of the fact that the armed group is an 'authority' capable of bearing direct obligations under international humanitarian law. From this perspective, the theory based on 'control of territory' is not in fact a theory in its own right. Instead, it can better be seen as part of the 'extended jurisdiction' theory. In a similar vein, it will be shown below that it is part of the equivalent theory based on customary international law. Seeing 'control of territory' to be one element of other theories in fact solves several of the 'problems' which arise if the question of how armed groups are bound by international humanitarian law is too exclusively linked to a control of territory. For a theory that says that an armed group is bound by international humanitarian law because it effectively controls a portion of the territory does not explain how armed groups are bound by international humanitarian law in situations where they either do not control a portion of the territory or do not claim to represent the State or a part of it. This will often be the case in non-international armed conflicts which do not reach the threshold of Additional Protocol II.[131] Moreover, Article 8(2)(f) of the Rome makes clear that no effective control of territory is required for some of the norms contained in Additional Protocol II to apply.[132] Such a theory also fails to take note of the fact that an armed group's control of a territory can be fluid and will vary as the conflict progresses from day to day and week to week.[133] These factors make it problematic to make territory or claims of sovereignty the sole factor on which to determine international personality for the purpose of international humanitarian law.[134]

7. Armed Groups Bound through Customary International Law

The final theory of how armed groups are bound by international humanitarian law finds its explanation in customary international law. This theory asserts that

[131] Kleffner, 'Organized Armed Groups' (n 1) 453.
[132] See Article 8(2)(e) and (f) of the Rome Statute and section 3.1.5 in Chapter 5.
[133] Milanovic, 'Is the Rome Statute binding on individuals?' (n 6) 41.
[134] See A. Cassese, *International Law* (OUP, Oxford 2001) 69.

armed groups are bound by international humanitarian law, as a matter of customary international law rather than treaty law per se. There are two approaches to a theory that armed groups are bound by customary international law. The first approach is that an armed group is bound as an entity by customary international law because its individual members are bound by customary international law. This theory is so similar to the jurisdictional legislation theory that it is not considered separately in this chapter. The second approach is that an armed group is bound by international humanitarian law because of its status as an independent subject of international law. It argues that armed groups are bound by international humanitarian law as a consequence 'of the international personality that they [the armed groups] possess'.[135] It has been commented above that this theory has similarities with the extended legislative jurisdiction theory above. The strength of this theory lies the fact that it deals with armed groups directly as groups, without relying on their constituent individual members. This takes appropriate account of the fact that armed groups are entities which possess power and functions that are greater than the sum of the power and functions of their constituent members.[136] The theory recognizes that the organizational structure of an armed group often heightens its potential to acquire arms, devise military strategy, coordinate military campaigns or indeed systematically terrorize the civilian population. Like the explanation rooted in the principle of effectiveness above, it also allows the legal personality of armed groups to be understood as being a feature of, and also a result of, the compromised capacities of the State during the armed conflict. Another argued advantage of this explanation is that it is imbued with a measure of realism for it demonstrates an explicit preparedness to recognize armed groups as subjects of international law, in their own right, albeit to less limited extent than States.

However, one of the problems of this theory is that it is often articulated in terms which fail to take due note of the specifics of the place of armed groups in the legal framework. For example, it is often implied that customary international law is a fixed body of international norms that is binding equally upon all new subjects of international law when they first come into existence, no matter whether they be States or non-State actors.[137] As a result, it is sometimes argued that armed groups are bound by customary international law because they become a subject of international law.[138] Such an approach fails to give due attention to the fact that not all subjects of international law are bound by the same norms of customary international law.[139] For, while both States and individuals are subjects

[135] Kleffner, 'Organized Armed Groups' (n 1) 454. [136] Ibid, 455, 450.

[137] See Sivakumaran 'Binding Armed Opposition Groups' (n 13) 373; F. Hampson, 'Other Areas of Customary International Law in Relation to the Study' in E. Wilmshurt and S. Breau (eds), *Perspectives on the ICRC Study on Customary International Humanitarian Law* (CUP, Cambridge 2007) 52.

[138] See Murray, *Humanitarian Law Treaties* (n 56) 108

[139] While the ICJ stated has stated that customary rules 'by their nature, must have equal force for all members of the international community', it is submitted that the ICJ was referring only to States as for the reason given above its comment does not hold true for all subjects of international law. See *North Sea Continental Shelf (Federal Republic of Germany v Netherlands)* [1969] ICJ Reports 3, 20 February 1969, [38].

of international law, it is important to be clear that as subjects of international law, they have extremely different obligations. For example, while States have obligations under the law of the sea and law relevant to the use of force, individuals do not. In other words, international legal personality under customary international law exists along a spectrum. Accordingly, the legal personality of armed groups under customary international law will be first, limited and secondly, a different nature to that of States. Moreover, it is only meaningful to say that armed groups are bound by customary international law, if due attention is given to the notion of what customary international law *is* when it comes to non-State actors and how it is constituted.[140] It is argued in Chapter 11 of the book that customary international law binding on armed groups is created through State action and *opinio juris,* although the State practice must demonstrate an intention on the part of States that armed groups are also bound, i.e. that the norm applies in the context of a non-international armed conflict.

Another problem with an explanation that armed groups are bound by customary international humanitarian law is its circularity.[141] To some extent this circularity is inherent in the most widely accepted definition of a subject of international law.[142] It is noted in this respect that established legal doctrine tends to define a subject of international law as an entity that is capable of holding rights and obligations under international law.[143] If this definition is applied to armed groups, the following circular argument is constructed: 'Armed groups bear rights and duties under international law because they are subjects of international law. Armed groups are subjects of international law because they bear rights and duties under international law'.[144] Unhelpful as this argument may be, it reflects the uneasy relationship between a declaratory and constitutive approach to international legal personality that was demonstrated in Chapters 3, 4, and 5. It reflects the fact that we understand armed groups as bearing obligations under international humanitarian law at the moment at which : the conflict has reached a certain degree of intensity; and (ii) they become sufficiently organized to be treated as a legal entity under international humanitarian law. At that moment, as has been shown in Chapter 5 of the book, armed groups 'step up' into the pre-existing framework of rights and obligations that make up international humanitarian law, and which have been made by States by virtue of treaty law and customary international law.

[140] This is discussed in Chapter 11 at length. See also T. Rodenhauser, 'Human Rights Obligations of Non-State Armed Groups in Other Situations of Violence: The Syria Example' (2012) 3 International Humanitarian Legal Studies 263, 274–9; Sivakumaran 'Binding Armed Opposition Groups' (n 13) 373.

[141] See Kleffner, 'Organized Armed Groups' (n 1) 454, where he cites the Darfur Commission of Inquiry which states: 'all insurgents that have reached a certain threshold of organization, stability and effective control of territory, possess international legal personality and are therefore bound by the relevant rules of customary international law on internal armed conflicts'.

[142] See ibid, 456, for the specific point and I. Brownlie, *Principles of Public International Law* (7th edn, OUP, Oxford 2008) 57 for the general.

[143] J. Crawford, *The Creation of States in International Law* (2nd edn, Clarendon Press, Oxford 2006) 28.

[144] Kleffner, 'Organized Armed Groups' (n 1) 456.

Perhaps entanglement in this circularity can be somewhat avoided if the international legal personality of the armed group is understood to be based not on a formal assessment of an entity's assumption of rights and duties under international law, but on its functionality. When this approach is taken, an armed group's legal personality can be conceived to be a construct which is linked not only to its formal possession of rights and duties, but also to its capacity. An armed group at the lower end of the scale of capability and organization will only be bound by common Article 3, which exists as a matter of treaty law and customary international law. An armed group possessing a higher level of organization and effective control over a territory will be bound to the norms in Additional Protocol II, which are deemed to be customary. This will include the fundamental guarantees, the fair trial guarantees, the broad humanitarian principles relating to detention, protection, and care of the wounded, sick and shipwrecked, and medical and religious personnel, use and respect of the ICRC emblem, and protection of the civilian population.[145] It may not include some of the more detailed provisions such as the obligation to ensure that children receive an education and the duty to provide detainees with medical examinations.

In a sense, it is seen that the argument that armed groups are bound by customary international law is, in many ways, a 'customary law' version of the extended jurisdiction theory above. It is the theory that armed groups are bound by international humanitarian law on the basis that States have created a customary international law framework which holds armed groups to be bound when certain contextual and capacity-related triggers are in place, i.e. the organization and intensity requirement. One of the important advantages of a theory based on customary international law is that it finds an individual armed group to be bound as a result of behaviour of the collectively of States, rather than the fact that the State, against whom the armed group is fighting, has signed a particular treaty.[146] From a psychological perspective, this may present a more acceptable explanation for an armed group which will likely wish to distance itself from its parent State. A key disadvantage to this theory is that it does not explain how armed groups are bound by international humanitarian treaty law, as it was drafted and finalized in 1949 and 1977. As a result, it is hard to accept it as the *only* theory of how armed groups are bound by international humanitarian law.

8. Conclusions

The conclusions of this chapter are divided into those that apply to treaty law and those that apply to customary international law. In terms of treaty law, the chapter has concluded that the 'legislative jurisdiction theory' and the 'extended legislative

[145] See Sivakumaran, 'Binding Armed Opposition Groups' (n 13) 372 and L. Zegveld, *The Accountability of Armed Opposition Groups in International Law* (CUP, Cambridge 2002) 20–1.

[146] Kleffner, 'Organized Armed Groups' (n 1) 454.

jurisdiction theory' provide most assistance when explaining how armed groups might be bound by treaty law. These two interconnected theories, which constitute an exception to the *pacta tertiis* rule, demonstrate that an armed group can be bound by international human rights treaty law in instances where the treaty shows on its face that it was intended to bind either: (i) the armed group's members; or (ii) the armed group as a whole. Building on the conclusions of Chapter 6, the chapter argues that it is important to be able to identify the moment at which the armed group becomes a subject of international law, separate to that of its members, because this is the moment at which these treaty obligations will become binding upon the group as a separate entity of international law. The legislative jurisdiction theory and the extended legislative jurisdiction theory carry the potential disadvantage that they reinforce an image of the State as the ultimate 'legislator'. As a result in practical terms, the theories may also not be the most attractive explanations to promote compliance with the norm by the armed group because their rationale is based on the authority of the State.

Two main theories have been put forward to explain how armed groups may be bound by customary international law. The first is the customary international law version of the 'legislative jurisdiction theory'. This is based on the notion that individuals are bound by international humanitarian law as a matter of customary international humanitarian law. As a result, when individuals form collectivities which constitute separate subjects of international law, these new subjects of international law will be bound by, at the very minimum, the same obligations as their members. As a hypothesis, this theory has not been given separate attention as it is essentially the 'customary law version' of the 'legislative jurisdiction' theory and has the same scope and is subject to similar disadvantages and advantages. The second theory which has been put forward to explain how armed groups are bound by customary international law is premised on armed groups' status as subjects of international law. In many ways, it has been interpreted as a 'customary law version' of the extended legislative jurisdiction theory. It is based on an understanding of international legal personality that exists along a spectrum and is inherently connected to an armed group's capability and functionality. It is constructed on the premise that as an armed group incrementally gains capability and interacts with other international actors, it will gain legal personality under international law and become bound to relevant legal obligations broadly commensurate with its activities.

The chapter has emphasized that the fact that an armed group becomes a subject of international law does not mean that it becomes bound by all rules of customary law. Instead, it becomes bound by the rules of international law which are confirmed by State practice and *opinio juris* to be binding upon the parties to a non-international armed conflict. It has shown that the theory that armed groups are bound by international humanitarian law *because they have control of a territory* should in fact be considered connected to the extended legislative jurisdiction theory and customary international law theory. It has been demonstrated that this much-offered explanation of how armed groups are bound by international humanitarian law is better understood as simply one indicator of an armed group's international legal personality under international humanitarian law. Understanding territory as a single indicator of legal personality, explains why armed groups may still be bound by international humanitarian law in instances where they do not control a portion of the territory. It also provides reassurance that armed group's obligations under international humanitarian law will remain largely static, in circumstances where their control over territory is more fluid.

The strength of the argument that armed groups are bound by international humanitarian law by virtue of their functionality and capability is that, like the extended jurisdiction theory above, it treats armed groups directly as groups. It does not make their subjectivity dependent upon their individual members, as does, for example, the legislative jurisdiction theory. Another advantage of the theory that armed groups are bound by customary international humanitarian law is that, unlike under the 'extended jurisdiction' theory, the fact that armed groups are bound by international norms is not explained by the fact that the parent State has signed a particular treaty. Instead, it is explained on the basis of the behaviour of the international community of States. In examining the theory which asserts that armed groups accrue responsibilities under international law by virtue of their control of territory, the chapter examined the 'effectiveness' theory. While this theory was largely rejected as an explanation for how armed groups are bound by international humanitarian law, the chapter found it likely to be of major assistance in understanding how armed groups are bound by human rights law. In the light of these conclusions, the effectiveness theory will be examined much more closely in Chapter 9.

8

Armed Groups and Treaty Law

1. Introduction

It was shown in the introduction to the book that over time, academics have disagreed as to whether and when armed groups might be bound by human rights treaty law. Matas, an early commentator on the subject, argued that several major human rights treaties (i.e. the Convention against Torture and the International Covenant on Civil and Political Rights) applied 'to groups and persons directly'.[1] Likewise, Tomuschat has asserted that the armed groups will be bound by the ICCPR and other human rights instruments in instances where they exercise government control.[2] Yet the majority of authors seem to reject the notion that armed groups can be held bound by human rights treaties, finding customary international law the most convincing source of law to explain how armed groups are bound by human rights law. In view of this disagreement, the purpose of this chapter is to analyse this issue more fully by utilizing *inter alia* the theories explored in Chapter 7. Indeed, it was shown in Chapter 7 that there are three main explanations to explain how armed groups can be bound by international treaty law: (i) the 'legislative jurisdiction theory'; (ii) the 'extended legislative jurisdiction theory'; and (iii) the idea that treaty obligations can become binding upon armed groups as a result of territorial control. As Chapter 7 demonstrated that the third theory relating to the relevance of 'control of territory' provides a potential explanation for how armed groups are bound by treaty law *and* customary international law, this theory is examined separately in Chapter 9. As a result of the separate treatment of this issue, a complete picture of how armed groups may be bound by treaty law is only gleaned by reading Chapters 8 and 9 together.

Chapter 7 demonstrated that both the legislative jurisdiction theory and the extended legislative jurisdiction theory are based on the intention of the parties to bind armed groups or their members. As a result, this chapter's primary purpose is to consider whether the *travaux préparatoires* to the main human rights treaties or their texts evidence an intention on the part of their drafters

[1] D. Matas, 'Armed Opposition Groups' (1997) 3 Manatoba Law Journal 621, 632 (hereafter Matas, 'Armed Opposition Groups').

[2] C. Tomuschat, 'The Applicability of Human Rights Law to Insurgent Movements' in H. Fischer et al. (eds), *Krisensicherung Und Humanitarer Schutz—Crisis Management and Humanitarian Protection: Festschrif Fur Dieter Fleck* (Berliner Wissencschafts-Verlag, Berlin 2004) 573, 588.

that armed groups or their constituent members (i.e. individuals) should be bound by their provisions. In doing so, the chapter's aim is to see whether it is possible to argue that armed groups are bound by human rights treaty law. In considering these questions, the chapter begins by evaluating three of the core international human rights treaties, namely the International Covenant on Civil and Political Rights (ICCPR), the International Covenant on Economic, Social and Cultural Rights (ICESCR) and the Convention against Torture and Other Cruel, Inhuman or Degrading Treatment or Punishment (CAT). In examining these treaties, the chapter evaluates whether it can be said that armed groups are bound by these treaties and also analyses how their three treaty bodies, the Human Rights Committee, the Committee on Economic, Social and Cultural Rights and the Committee against Torture address the acts of armed groups under their mandates. The chapter ends by examining the two human rights treaties which address armed groups directly: the Optional Protocol of the Convention on the Rights of the Child and the African Union Convention for the Protection and Assistance of Internally Displaced Persons in Africa (the Kampala Convention). While the chapter does not address other human rights treaties, such as the Convention on the Elimination of all Forms of Discrimination Against Women (CEDAW) which has explicitly mentioned the possibility of armed groups being bound by human rights law in its General Comment 30 on armed conflict, its analysis will nevertheless be able to be applied by analogy to these treaties.[3]

2. The ICCPR and ICESCR

2.1 Drafting papers and text of the ICCPR and ICESCR

2.1.1 Classic vertical paradigm between State and individual

There is no indication in the *travaux préparatoires* of the ICCPR (1966) and ICESCR (1966) that their drafters discussed the question of whether the treaties should bind armed groups in the 1940s and early 1950s. Both the ICCPR and the ICESCR are drafted in a manner which makes clear that the State is the ultimate duty-bearer of the rights they contain. Both Covenants begin with the words 'The States Parties to the present Covenant'. This opening phrase, which is common to most international treaties, is an immediate signal that the drafters of the ICCPR and ICESCR sought to bind States parties. Likewise, both Covenants have a clause containing State 'undertakings' in Article 2. In particular, Article 2 of the ICCPR forms the basis of the legal framework that the Covenant creates. It sets out the nature of the States' obligations to 'respect and ensure' the rights recognized in the Covenant. It guarantees the individual freedom of interference *from the State*

[3] CEDAW 'General Recommendation No. 30 on Women in Conflict Prevention, Conflict and Post-Conflict Situations' (18 October 2013) UN Doc CEDAW/C/GC/30 [16].

and ensures that the individual has access *to the State*.[4] In a similar fashion, Article 2 of the ICESCR sets out an undertaking by each State party that it will 'take steps ... to the maximum of its available resources, with a view to achieving progressively the full realization of the rights recognized in the present Covenant'. With this wording, Article 2 of the ICESCR explicitly identifies the State as the key actor responsible for achieving the realization of the economic, social, and cultural rights enshrined in the Covenant. In Article 3 of both Covenants, States parties 'undertake to ensure the equal right of men and women to the enjoyment of all ... rights set forth in the present Covenant'. This again confirms the State as the ultimate duty-bearer of the rights the Covenants contain. Accordingly, Articles 2 and 3 of both Covenants articulate a classical vertical framework of human rights obligations owed by States to individuals.

2.1.2 Support for notion that non-State actors may have obligations under human rights law

2.1.2.1 Core declaratory language of rights

Despite the State-orientated nature of Article 2 of the ICCPR, the core 'rights language' employed in the Covenant is broadly supportive of the idea that States may not be the only duty-bearers within the broader human rights framework.[5] It is noted that the substantive core rights set out in Part III of the ICCPR are not articulated with reference to a specific duty-bearer. Instead, the core rights in the ICCPR contain no details of the duty-bearer at all but are declaratory in nature, beginning with phrases such as, 'Everyone has' or 'No one shall'. For instance, Article 6 states that 'Every human being has the inherent right to life'. Article 7 holds that 'No one shall be subjected to torture or to cruel, inhumane or degrading treatment or punishment'. Indeed, it is noteworthy that the core rights in Part III of the ICCPR mirror the same broader declaratory concept of human rights contained in the Universal Declaration on Human Rights (UDHR) which focuses on rights for 'everyone' and 'all'. As a result, although making clear that the Covenant is only binding upon States, the text of Part III does not exclude the possibility that the rights referred to may have a broader scope outside the Covenant. Such a conclusion is less pronounced in the text of the ICESCR where the substantive rights in Part III are repeatedly linked to the State's obligations.[6] However, there are several other indications in the text of the ICESCR that suggest that its drafters nonetheless supported the idea that other non-State actors might be duty-bearers under human rights law.

[4] See M. Nowak, *U.N. Covenant on Civil and Political Rights, CCPR Commentary* (2nd revised edn, Engel Verlap, Kehl am Rhein 2005) (hereafter Nowak, *CCPR Commentary*), where he makes the distinction that 'civil rights—from an historical viewpoint—guarantee the liberal freedom of the individual "from the State" but political rights guarantee the democratic freedom of access "to the State"'.

[5] See Matas, 'Armed Opposition Groups' (n 1) 621–34.

[6] For an example, see Article 6, which states: 'The States Parties to the present Covenant recognize the right to work.'

2.1.2.2 Preambles of ICCPR and ICESCR

The first of these indications is found in the Preambles of the ICESCR and the ICCPR. The Preambles of both Covenants refer not only to the 'obligation of States … to promote universal respect for an observance of, human rights and freedoms', but also state that:

> the individual, having duties to other individuals and to the community to which he belongs, is under a responsibility to strive for the promotion and observance of the rights recognized in the present Covenant.

This statement, repeated in the Preambles to both Covenants, seems to articulate a view on the part of the Covenants' drafters, that individuals, as well as States, have responsibilities to 'promote and observe' the rights contained in the ICCPR and ICESCR. The fact that the drafters decided not to refer to these duties again in the binding part of the Covenant (except in Article 5(1) which is discussed below), does not detract from the force of these words. Instead, it simply indicates that the drafters wished the Covenant's binding force to be limited to States.[7]

2.1.2.3 Article 5(1) of ICCPR and ICESCR

A similar indication that the drafters of the ICCPR and ICESCR did not believe obligations under international human rights law to be limited to States is found in Article 5(1) which is common to the ICCPR and ICESCR. In words reminiscent of Article 30 of the UDHR, Article 5(1) of the ICCPR and ICESCR states:

> Nothing in the present Covenant may be interpreted as implying for any State, group or person any right to engage in any activity or perform any act aimed at the destruction of any of the rights and freedoms recognized herein or at their limitation to a greater extent than is provided for in the present Covenant. [8]

The *travaux préparatoires* to Article 5(1) of the ICCPR shows that Article 5(1) was motivated by the post-Second World War context in which it was drafted. It was particularly aimed at providing protection against individuals or groups wishing to exploit the human rights framework to abuse or destroy rights for others. It was intended to stop individuals asserting rights such as the right to freedom of expression or assembly to further ideologies (e.g. fascism or totalitarianism) which would destroy key cornerstones of the human rights framework such as democracy or the rule of law.[9] Like Article 30 of the UDHR, Article 5(1) recognizes that rights can be destroyed not only by States, but also by individuals or groups. In recognizing that individuals can 'destroy' the rights and freedoms of others, Article 5(1) may be seen as further evidence that the Covenant's drafters understood individuals to owe some kind of human rights obligations to each other.

[7] See Nowak, *CCPR Commentary* (n 4) 3–4.

[8] Article 30 of the UDHR states: 'Nothing in this Declaration may be interpreted as implying for any State, group or person any right to engage in any activity or to perform any act aimed at the destruction of any of the rights and freedoms set forth herein.'

[9] See Nowak, *CCPR Commentary* (n 4) 115.

2.1.2.4 Positive obligations evidence of horizontality of obligations

The view that individuals owe some kind of human rights obligations to each other is also seen in the fact that both the ICCPR and the ICESCR find States to be under an obligation to ensure that individuals are protected against human rights abuses by private persons.[10] In its General Comment No. 31 on the nature of the general legal obligation imposed on States parties to the Covenant, the Human Rights Committee stated that the ICCPR protects 'not just against violations of Covenant rights by its agents, but also against acts committed by private persons or entities that would impair the enjoyment of Covenant rights in so far as they are amenable to application between private persons or entities'.[11] The Human Rights Committee reminded States parties that a failure to 'ensure' Covenant rights by exercising due diligence to prevent, punish, investigate, or redress the harm caused by such acts by private entities or persons may lead to a violation on the part of the State party. In confirming that Convention rights may 'apply' between private persons and entities, the Human Rights Committee demonstrated an openness to the notion that non-State actors (e.g. individuals or groups) have horizontal obligations under human rights law, albeit not directly enforceable by the Committee.[12]

In a similar manner to the Human Rights Committee, the Committee on Economic, Social and Cultural Rights has also recognized that States have a duty to prevent non-State actors from infringing individuals' rights. In its General Comment on the Right to Water the Committee stated that 'steps should be taken by States Parties to prevent their own citizens and companies from violating the right to water of individuals and communities in other countries'.[13] Importantly, this constitutes an explicit recognition by the Committee that individuals and non-State actors can 'violate' the rights of individuals.[14] A similar statement was made by the Committee on Economic Social and Cultural Rights in its General Comment on the Right to Social Security.[15] Here the Committee also said that States parties should take steps to influence third parties (non-State actors) to *respect*

[10] See Nowak, *CCPR Commentary* (n 4) 37–41, on the duty to 'ensure' the rights in the Covenant (which includes the duty to 'protect' and 'fulfil') and how the obligation to 'protect' in particular may create 'horizontal effects'.

[11] UN Human Rights Committee, 'General Comment 31 (Nature of the General Legal Obligation Imposed on States Parties to the Covenant)' (26 May 2004) UN Doc CCPR/C/21/Rev.1/Add.13, [8] (hereafter HRC General Comment 31).

[12] A. Clapham, *Human Rights Obligations of Non-State Actors* (OUP, Oxford 2006) 329 (hereafter Clapham, *Non-State Actors*).

[13] See UN Committee on Economic, Social and Cultural Rights, 'General Comment 15 (The Right to Water)' (20 January 2003) UN Doc E/C.12/2002/11, [23–4]. See also UN Committee on Economic, Social and Cultural Rights, 'Statement on the obligations of States Parties regarding the corporate sector and economic, social and cultural rights' (20 May 2011) UN Doc E/C.12/2011/1.

[14] It has been noted in the introduction to this study that the term 'violate' (as opposed to 'abuse') is generally used to refer to the breach of a binding norm. As a result, this comment by the Committee on Economic, Social and Cultural Rights can be seen as evidence of a view by the committee that citizens and companies are bound to respect the right to water.

[15] UN Committee on Economic, Social and Cultural Rights, 'General Comment 19 (The Right to Social Security)' (4 February 2008) UN Doc E/C.12/GC/19, [54].

the right, through legal or political means.[16] Likewise, in its General Comment on the Right to Adequate Food, the Committee stated:

> While only States are parties to the Covenant and are thus ultimately accountable for compliance with it, all members of society individuals, families, local communities, nongovernmental organizations, civil society organizations, as well as the private business sector have responsibilities in the realization of the right to adequate food. The State should provide an environment that facilitates implementation of these responsibilities.[17]

The significance of these statements are considered further in the paragraphs below.

The statements by the Human Rights Committee and the Committee on Economic, Social and Cultural Rights recognize that at least some of the rights articulated in the Covenant may have horizontal effect and be binding upon individuals and other non-State actors, such as armed groups and companies. This is particularly seen in the statements by the ICESCR which refer to third parties 'respect[ing]' rights and 'violating' the rights in the Covenant.[18] In the case of the ICCPR, the Committee's General Comment refrains from using the word 'violations' to describe the acts of private individuals but acknowledges that when individuals or entities harm other individuals, they may 'impair' the rights of those individuals. In this sense, statements from both Committees reinforce the message in the two Covenants' preambular paragraphs by indicating that individuals have duties to other individuals and to the community and are under a responsibility to strive for the promotion and observance of the rights they contain. Yet it is noteworthy that at the same time, the two Committees make clear that their own main focus is not on the actions of the non-State actors as such, but on the States' response to these actions. They focus on whether a State has taken sufficient and appropriate steps to prevent, punish, investigate, prosecute, or provide redress for the harm suffered. In taking this approach, both Committees confirm that the responsibility of non-State actors for human rights violations, as a matter of international or domestic law, is largely outside their scope.

Further support for the conclusion that the ICCPR does not create binding obligations for non-State actors is found in the Human Rights Committee's General Comment 31 which states:

> The article 2, paragraph 1, obligations are binding on States [Parties] and do not, as such, have direct horizontal effect as a matter of international law.[19]

It is also noteworthy that when the Human Rights Committee was drafting its recent General Comment No. 35 on Article 9 in 2014, it chose to remain silent on

[16] Ibid.

[17] UN Committee on Economic, Social and Cultural Rights, 'General Comment 12 (The Right to Adequate Food)' (12 May 1999) UN Doc E/C.12/1999/5, [20].

[18] The term 'respect' is generally used to refer to the obligation to refrain from restricting the exercise of rights where such restriction is not allowed. See Nowak, *CCPR Commentary* (n 4) 37.

[19] HRC General Comment 31 (n 11) [8].

the question of whether Article 9 might directly bind armed groups despite having been directly urged by non-governmental organizations (NGOs) to include a passage clarifying Article 9's relevance to armed groups.[20] In the final draft of the General Comment, the Committee stated simply:

> States parties have the duty to take appropriate measures to protect the right to liberty of person against deprivations by third parties. States parties must protect individuals against abduction or detention by individual criminals or irregular groups including armed or terrorist groups, operating unlawfully within their territory.[21]

This seems to confirm that the Human Rights Committee considered the acts of armed groups to be relevant to its treaty-based mandate only in so far as they can be linked to States' obligations to protect individuals from their acts.

2.1.3 State-focused paradigm in the enforcement mandates

The analysis above has shown that there is little indication in the texts or drafting papers of the ICCPR or the ICESCR that their drafters intended them to create binding obligations for individuals or armed groups. Even if the texts of the two Covenants support a broader vision of human rights under which non-State actors can be duty-bearers, they create binding obligations only for States. This is inherent in the States' undertaking in Article 2 of the Covenants. It is also made clear in the systems that the Covenants and their Optional Protocols create for reporting inter-state complaints and individual complaints.[22] These complaints systems confirm that the primary focus of the Human Rights Committee and Committee on Economic, Social and Cultural Rights is to observe States' progress in respecting and realizing the rights contained in the Covenants and to monitor alleged violations of those rights by States. The Covenants do not provide individuals with the ability to complain that their rights have been violated by private actors, unless their complaint relates specifically to a State's failure to prevent, prosecute, investigate, or punish that harm. This is in line with the focus on the State's response to actions of individuals.

[20] K. Fortin, 'General Comment on Article 9 of ICCPR and detention by non-state actors' (*Armed Groups and International Law*, 31 October 2012) <http://armedgroups-internationallaw.org/2012/10/31/general-comment-on-article-9-of-iccpr-and-detention-by-non-state-actors/> accessed 20 January 2017.

[21] UN Human Rights Committee, 'Draft General Comment 35 (Article 9: Liberty and Security of Person)' (28 October 2014) UN Doc CCPR/C/GC/ 35, [7].

[22] The ICCPR created a system of reporting (see Article 40) and inter-State complaints (Article 41). The Optional Protocol to the ICCPR adopted and opened for signature ratification and accession by General Assembly Resolution 2200A(XXI) of 16 December 1966, creates a process for individuals who claim to be victims of a violation by any State party. The ICESCR also created a system of reporting (Article 16). The Optional Protocol to the ICESCR which was adopted by the Human Rights Council, by its Resolution 8/2 of 18 June 2008 creates an individual complaint procedure under which individuals or groups of individuals can complain that they are victims of a violation of any of the economic, social, and cultural rights set forth in the Covenant by a State party. The Optional Protocol of the ICESCR came into force on 5 May 2013.

2.2 Practice of the Human Rights Committee and Committee on Economic, Social and Cultural Rights with regard to armed groups

The fact that States are obliged to take positive action to protect civilians from the acts of armed groups has been confirmed in the Concluding Observations of the Human Rights Committee and the Committee on Economic, Social and Cultural Rights. These confirm that States' positive obligations under the Covenants may extend to ensuring civilians are not caught in the cross-fire between States and armed groups and taking efforts to secure the prosecution of members of armed groups.[23] States have also been found to be under more general obligations to protect civilians from violations by armed groups.[24] For example, States have been repeatedly instructed to take steps to prevent children being recruited by armed groups.[25] They have also been instructed to take adequate measures to protect camps for internally displaced persons.[26] The Human Rights Committee has also criticized States parties for arbitrarily refusing to grant access to life-saving humanitarian assistance to areas under the control of armed groups.[27] In emphasizing these positive obligations, both Committees have demonstrated that although they are not prepared to directly address the acts of armed groups, they are willing to focus on States' failure to prevent, prosecute, investigate, punish, or provide redress for their harm.

2.3 Concluding remarks on the ICCPR and ICESCR

The section above shows that there is little evidence that the drafters of the ICCPR and the ICESR intended the Covenants to directly bind either armed groups or individuals. As a result, there is little opportunity to employ the 'legislative

[23] See for example UN Human Rights Committee, 'Concluding Observations on Iraq' (3 December 2015) UN Doc CCPR/C/IRQ/CO/5, [20(a)]; UN Human Rights Committee, 'Concluding Observations on Colombia' (4 August 2010) UN Doc CCPR/COL/CO/6, [25], [18]; UN Human Rights Committee, 'Concluding Observations on the Democratic Republic of Congo' (26 April 2006) UN Doc CCPR/C/COD/CO/3, [15–16] (hereafter Congo HRC Observations 2006); UN Human Rights Committee, 'Concluding Observations on Colombia' (26 May 2004) UN Doc CCPR/CO/80/COL, [8] (hereafter Colombia HRC Observations 2004); UN Committee on Economic, Social and Cultural Rights, 'Concluding Observations on Iraq' (27 October 2015) UN Doc E/C.12/IRQ/4, [26(d)] (hereafter Iraq CESCR Observations 2015); UN Committee on Economic, Social and Cultural Rights, 'Concluding Observations on Colombia' (7 June 2010) UN Doc E/C.12/COL/CO/5, [15] (hereafter Colombia CESCR Observations 2010).

[24] Congo HRC Observations 2006 (n 23) [13] and Iraq CESCR Observations 2015 (n 23) [26(d)].

[25] UN Human Rights Committee, 'Concluding Observations on Yemen' (23 April 2012) UN Doc CCPR/C/YEM/CO/5, [24] (hereafter Yemen HRC Observations 2012); Colombia HRC Observations 2004 (n 23) [24]; Congo HRC Observations 2006 (n 23) [18]; UN Committee on Economic, Social and Cultural Rights, 'Concluding Observations on Afghanistan' (7 June 2010) UN Doc E/C.12/AFG/CO/2-4, [30]; Colombia CESCR Observations 2010 (n 23) [16].

[26] UN Human Rights Committee, 'Concluding Observations on Sudan' (19 August 2014) UN Doc CCPR/C/SDN/CO/4, [9] (hereafter Sudan HRC Observations 2014); Yemen HRC Observations 2012 (n 25) [22].

[27] Sudan HRC Observations 2014 (n 26) [8].

jurisdiction' theory or the 'extended legislative jurisdiction' theory identified in Chapter 7. Instead, the analysis above has shown that the Human Rights Committee and the International Committee on Economic, Social and Cultural Rights are only willing to consider the acts of armed groups in the context of their mandate when the State has failed in its duties to prevent, punish, investigate, or punish their acts. However, the section above has also shown that both Covenants contain indications that their drafters believed that human rights obligations may be borne by other actors, in addition to States. Evidence for this was found in the Preambles to both Covenants and their common Article 5(1). It is also implicit in the findings by two treaty bodies that States have a positive obligation to protect the rights of persons from harm caused by other individuals or private entities. In a sense then, it can be said the Covenants provide support for the idea that other actors can have human rights obligations under international law, although they also make clear that the Covenants themselves cannot be seen to be the source of that obligation.

3. The Convention against Torture and Other Cruel, Inhuman or Degrading Treatment or Punishment (CAT)

Having examined the ICCPR and the ICESCR, the chapter now turns its attention to the Convention against Torture and Other Cruel, Inhuman or Degrading Treatment or Punishment (CAT). In a departure from the definition of torture in the ICCPR, the CAT's definition of torture in Article 1 contains an explicit requirement that the prohibited act be 'inflicted by or at the instigation of or with the consent or acquiescence of a *public official or other person acting in an official capacity*'. As a consequence of this wording, the definition of torture in the CAT has been much criticized by feminist commentators who have argued that its 'State' focus leaves little room for taking into account pain and suffering experienced in the private sphere, most often by women.[28] Yet, it has also been argued that the term 'public official or other person acting in an official capacity' in Article 1 is *in fact* a positive addition because it is wide enough for the Convention to address the acts of members of armed groups in instances where they act in an 'official capacity'.[29] The following section evaluates the merits of such an argument and

[28] See H. Charlesworth, C. Chinkin, and S. Wright, 'Feminist Approaches to International Law' (1991) 85 American Journal of International Law 613, 627, who argued that the CAT demonstrates the 'grip' that the private/public dichotomy has on international law.

[29] See in particular the UK criminal law case of *R v Zardad*, Case No. T2203/7676 (UK Central Criminal Court, 7 April 2004) (hereafter *R v Zardad*) which found an Afghan warlord guilty of torture under section 134(1) of the Criminal Justice Act 1988 which enacted Article 1 of the CAT into English law. Here, the UK found that Mr Zardad was a 'person acting in a public capacity' for the purposes of section 134(1) relying upon case law from the Committee against Torture. See also S. Sivakumaran, 'Torture in International Human Rights and International Humanitarian Law' (2005) 18 Leiden Journal of International Law 541 (hereafter Sivakumaran, 'Torture'); R. McCorquodale and R. La Forgia, 'Taking Off the Blindfolds: Torture by Non-State Actors' (2001) 2 Human Rights

the ability of Article 1 of the CAT to address acts by members of armed groups. In doing so, the section first turns to the *travaux préparatoires* of the CAT to consider what its drafters intended by the term.

3.1 *Travaux préparatoires* on 'Public Official' requirement and final text of CAT

The *travaux préparatoires* of the CAT demonstrate that the States that drafted it had different visions about the new Convention's purpose and scope. During the discussions about the Convention's purpose, it was considered whether the Convention should cover acts by *de facto* public officials or whether it should be limited to acts by *de jure* public officials.[30] The Convention's predecessor, the 1975 Declaration on the Protection of All Persons from Being Subjected to Torture and Other Cruel, Inhuman or Degrading Treatment or Punishment, had been limited to acts committed by 'public officials'. This term was widely accepted to refer only to *de jure* public officials or agents of the State. In the light of this precedent, several States argued that the Convention should also only cover acts by *de jure* officials.[31] According to these States, the primary purpose of the Convention was to tackle the high likelihood that States perpetrating torture would not prosecute or investigate instances in which it was alleged to have happened.[32] With this aim in mind, the drafters found it predominantly necessary to create a Convention which placed an obligation upon States to prevent and prosecute acts of torture committed by or at the instigation of, consent or acquiescence of a State agent or persons wielding official authority.[33] For these States, it was sufficient that the Convention should contain a relatively narrow definition of 'torture' that focused exclusively on persons with official authority.

However, a few States clearly believed that the Convention's purpose was to address the crime of torture, irrespective of the status of perpetrator. France, Spain, and Panama, for example, advocated a wide definition of torture which focused on the nature of the act, and did not give as much attention to the identity or status of the perpetrator.[34] Likewise the Federal Republic of Germany, advocated that the Convention should have a broader reach than the Declaration and apply to persons 'regardless of their legal status' who:

Law Review 189 (hereafter McCorquodale and La Forgia, 'Taking Off the Blindfolds') for excellent discussions of these issues.

[30] See J. H. Burgers and H. Danelius, *The United Nations Convention Against Torture: A Handbook on the Convention Against Torture and Other Cruel, Inhuman or Degrading Treatment or Punishment* (Martinus Nijhoff Publishers, Dordrecht 1988) 45–6 (hereafter Burgers and Danelius, *Handbook on the Convention Against Torture*).

[31] The UK, an adherent of this position, suggested that the definition of torture in Article 1 should read, 'public official[s] or any other agent of the State'. Ibid, 45–6.

[32] Ibid, 120. [33] Ibid, 45–6.

[34] Burgers and Danelius, *Handbook on the Convention Against Torture* (n 30) 45–6; A. Boulesbaa, *The UN Convention on Torture and the Prospects for Enforcement* (Martinus Nijhoff, The Hague 1999) 24 (hereafter Boulesbaa, *Prospects for Enforcement*).

have been assigned public authority by State organs on a permanent basis or in an individual case, but also to person[s] who, in certain regions or under particular conditions, actually hold and exercise authority over others, and whose authority is comparable to government authority or – be it only temporarily has replaced government authority or whose authority has been derived from such persons [35]

While this proposal was not incorporated into the Convention by the Working Group, the final text of Article 1 seems to indicate that the Convention's drafters agreed that its scope should be greater than that of the Declaration.[36] In the final text of Article 1 of the CAT, the phrase 'public official' included in the Declaration is expanded to read 'public official *or other person acting in an official capacity*'. Unfortunately, despite the addition of the phrase, the *travaux préparatoires* of the Convention do not clarify what the drafters intended by the phrase 'other person acting in an official capacity'. In order to address this uncertainty, the following paragraphs examine how the term 'other person acting in an official capacity' has been interpreted by the Committee against Torture. In particular, they consider whether and when the Committee has utilized the phrase to facilitate the inclusion of rebel groups within the scope of Article 1 of the CAT.

3.2 Practice of the CAT with regard to armed groups

3.2.1 Elmi v Australia

A comprehensive review of the Committee against Torture's 'jurisprudence' shows that it has generally taken a restrictive approach to the phrase 'public official or other person acting in an official capacity'. The Committee has only been prepared to include an armed group within the scope of Article 1 of the CAT in one case, *Elmi v Australia*.[37] This case related to Somalia in 1999 at a time when the Somali State apparatus had entirely collapsed and various warring clans had taken on some of the functions of government. In this case, the author of the communication, Mr Elmi, claimed that he would face torture from the Hawiye clan if he was returned to Somalia. The Committee agreed, finding that the members of the Hawiye clan fell within the phrase 'public officials or other persons acting in an official capacity'. It stated:

The Committee notes that for a number of years Somalia has been without a central government, that the international community negotiates with the warring factions and that some of the factions operating in Mogadishu have set up quasi-governmental institutions and are negotiating the establishment of a common administration. It follows then that, de facto, those factions exercise certain prerogatives that are comparable to those normally

[35] Burgers and Danelius, *Handbook on the Convention Against Torture* (n 30) 45.

[36] See Boulesbaa, *Prospects for Enforcement* (n 34) 28.

[37] This case is also discussed in Chapter 9 on the link between an armed groups obligations and international law and its control of territory. For further discussions on this case, and its significance, see also Sivakumaran, 'Torture' (n 29) 541–56; McCorquodale and La Forgia, 'Taking Off the Blindfolds' (n 29) 189–218.

exercised by legitimate governments. Accordingly, the members of those factions can fall, for the purposes of the application of the Convention, within the phrase 'public officials or other persons acting in an official capacity' contained in Article 1.

While the Committee's finding in *Elmi v Australia* may appear quite ground-breaking,[38] later cases have shown that the Committee's finding in regard to Hawiye clan in this case was quite exceptional and was likely intrinsically linked to the fact that the group had been exercising quasi-governmental authority, at a time where the government was wholly lacking in capacity due to complete State failure.[39]

3.2.2 Case law subsequent to Elmi v Australia

The exceptional nature of the Committee against Torture's conclusion in *Elmi v Australia* is illustrated by comparing it with similar cases which have subsequently come before the Committee in situations where the central government still exists. In these cases, the Committee has consistently taken the position that the actions of the armed groups fall outside Article 1's scope, irrespective of whether the State has lost control over a portion of the country and irrespective of whether any control the State has, is durable or effective. This is illustrated most starkly in the case of *H.M.H.I. v Australia* which also related to the situation in Somalia. Crucially, the case related to facts in 2002, three years after the case of *Elmi v Australia* had been decided. At this point the Somali Transitional National Government had been established but controlled little more than the Somali capital, Mogadishu.[40] Despite the government's limited effectiveness, the Committee's finding in *H.M.H.I. v Australia* differed significantly from its finding in *Elmi v Australia*. The Committee stated:

> with three years having elapsed since the Elmi decision, Somalia currently possesses a State authority in the form of the Transitional National Government, which has relations with the international community in its capacity as central Government, *though some doubts may exist as to the reach of its territorial authority and its permanence*. Accordingly, the Committee does not consider this case to fall within the exceptional situation in Elmi, and takes the view that acts of such entities as are now in Somalia commonly fall outside the scope of article 3 of the Convention. (emphasis added)[41]

The Committee's position in this regard takes almost no account of the level of control exercised by the government and apparently shows no interest in the level

[38] See McCorquodale and La Forgia, 'Taking Off the Blindfolds' (n 29) 218.

[39] Compare *Elmi v Australia,* Communication No. 120/1998 (14 May 1999) UN Doc CAT/C/22/D/120/1998, 6.5–6.7, with *H.M.H.I. v Australia*, Communication No. 177/2001 (1 May 2002) UN Doc CAT/C/28/D/177/2001, 6.4 (hereafter *H.M.H.I. v Australia)*.

[40] This particular point was not reported as having been discussed by the Committee against Torture but it is assumed that it was known. It can be readily be found out by referring to contemporaneous reports of the situation in Somali, e.g. Crisis Group, 'Somalia: Countering Terrorism in a Failed State', International Crisis Group, Africa Report No. 45 (23 May 2003) <https://www.crisisgroup.org/africa/horn-africa/somalia/somalia-countering-terrorism-failed-state> accessed 20 January 2017.

[41] *H.M.H.I. v Australia* (n 39) 6.4.

of control exercised by the armed group in question. A similar approach was seen in a further two cases from 2000 and 2001.

The cases of *M.P.S. v Australia* and *S.V. v Canada* related to events in Sri Lanka and were decided in 2000 and 2001 at a time when the Liberation Tigers of Tamil Eelam (LTTE) had a very consolidated control over a significant part of the country and an administration which included a sophisticated structure courts and police stations.[42] Against this factual background, it is doubly noteworthy that the Committee paid almost no attention to the level of control exercised by the LTTE at the time. In *S.V. v Canada* the Committee stated simply:

> The Committee considers that the issue of whether the State party has an obligation to refrain from expelling a person who might risk pain or suffering inflicted by a non-governmental entity, without the consent or acquiescence of the Government falls outside the scope of article 3 of the Convention. Consequently, the issue, on which the authors base part of their claim that they would suffer torture by LTTE or other non-governmental entities on return to Sri Lanka, cannot be considered by the Committee.[43]

A comparison of these cases indicates strongly that the legal rationale for the Committee against Torture's approach lies in the fact that that in the *Elmi v Australia* case, the Somalian government had completely ceased to exist.[44] Whether such an approach by the Committee against Torture can be justified legally is considered in more detail in Chapter 9 which comprehensively analyses the relationship between territorial control and international obligations.[45] It is important to add that in 2003, the Committee indicated that it might take a wider view on the matter, extending its scope to armed groups exercising quasi-governmental authority over territory but until now, such an extension has not been seen.[46]

[42] According to the LTTE, by 2002 over 23,000 cases had been tried in the rebel court system. Z. C. Mampilly, *Rebel Rulers: Insurgent Governance and Civilian Life during War* (Cornell University Press, Ithaca and London 2011) 110.

[43] *S.V. v Canada,* Communication No. 49/1996 (15 May 2001) UN Doc CAT/C/26/D/49/1996, 9.5. See also *M.P.S. v Australia,* Communication No. 138/1999 (30 April 2002) UN Doc CAT/C/28/D/138/1999, 7.4. For the Committee's earlier jurisprudence on non-State actors, see *G.R.B. v Sweden*, Communication No. 83/1997 (15 May 1998) UN Doc CAT/C/20/D/83/1997, 6.5 (relating to the Shining Path).

[44] Indeed this was explicitly stated by the Committee in *H.M.H.I. v Australia* (n 39).

[45] See conclusions of Chapter 9. Here, the significance of this case is discussed in relation to Article 9 of the Articles on State Responsibility for Internationally Wrongful Acts.

[46] It should be noted that the Committee appears to take a somewhat more liberal view to the question of whether rebel groups might fall within the scope of Article 1 of the CAT in the case of *S.S. v The Netherlands*, Communication No. 191/2001 (5 May 2003) UN Doc CAT/C/30/D/191/2001. Here, the Committee states: 'The Committee observes that the issue whether the State party has an obligation to refrain from expelling a person who might risk pain or suffering inflicted by a non-governmental entity, without the consent or acquiescence of the Government, falls outside the scope of Article 3 of the Convention, unless the non-governmental entity occupies or exercises quasi-governmental authority over the territory to which the complainant would be returned.' However, in this case, it ruled that the applicant could be returned to territory other than that under the control of the LTTE, so this issue was not looked at any further.

3.3 The obligation to define 'torture' in domestic law: strict approach to 'public official' requirement

A similar approach is seen in Committee's attitude to States' incorporation of the definition of torture into their national law. While initially the Committee appeared unperturbed by States treating issues like 'ill-treatment and assault' and 'torture' synonymously, in more recent reports it has made clear that national definitions of torture must follow the definition in Article 1.[47] Such an attitude is also evidenced in the Committee against Torture's second General Comment. Here, the Committee instructs States parties to 'make the offence of torture punishable as an offence under its criminal law, in accordance, at a minimum, with the elements of torture as defined in article 1 of the Convention'. It also reminds States that it is important to define the offence of torture in a manner that distinguishes it from common assault or other crimes.[48]

3.4 Openness to broader definitions of torture in other areas of international law

Yet despite the Committee's State-focused approach, the Convention clearly recognizes that non-State actors are capable of perpetrating acts of 'torture' in other areas of law, outside the Convention against Torture. Article 1(2) of the Convention states:

> This article is without prejudice to any international instrument or national legislation which does or may contain provisions of wider application.

The existence of Article 1(2) makes clear that the Convention's drafters were prepared to recognize that wider definitions of torture can co-exist with the definition of torture advanced by Article 1 of the CAT. An example of such a wider definition of torture is that contained in international humanitarian law. It has been explicitly clarified by international criminal tribunals that the definition of 'torture' under international humanitarian law does not require the 'severe pain or suffering' to be perpetrated by a public official or other person acting in an official capacity. Instead, the offence applies to public officials, members of armed groups, and private person equally.[49]

[47] Ingelse, conducting a review of the Committee's attitude to the definition of torture in Article 1, notes that it has changed its attitude to the way in which States incorporate the definition of torture into their domestic law. C. Ingelse, *The UN Committee against Torture: An Assessment* (Kluwer International, The Hague 2001) 221–2. See for example UN Committee against Torture, 'Conclusions and Recommendations: Third Periodic Report' (3 April 2006) UN Doc CAT/C/FRA/CO/3, [5].

[48] It should be pointed out that, in a somewhat contradictory fashion, the Committee also states that it 'recognizes that broader domestic definitions also advance the object and purpose of this Convention as long as they contain and are applied in accordance with the standards of the Convention, at a minimum'. UN Committee against Torture, 'General Comment 2 (Implementation of Article 2 by States Parties)' (24 January 2008) UN Doc CAT/C/GC/2 [9] (hereafter CAT General Comment 2).

[49] Although early decisions from the ICTY saw the Tribunal turning to Article 1 of the Convention against Torture for guidance, it rapidly moved away from the State-responsibility orientated human rights definition of torture towards a definition based on the pain and suffering of the victim. This move

3.5 'Due diligence' developed under 'acquiescence'

It is also clear that the Committee against Torture is willing to find States responsible for their failure to prevent acts of torture by non-State actors, even though the wording of Article 1 of the CAT makes it difficult for the Committee against Torture to address acts by non-State actors in the same way as they are addressed under the ICCPR and ICESCR. In fact, the definition makes clear that acts by non-State actors will only constitute 'torture' in instances where the State has 'acquiesced' or consented to the acts in question. The implication of this requirement is that a State will have to have a higher level of involvement in the acts of a private actor for its responsibility to be engaged. Read literally, it would imply that the CAT only imposes duties on States to prosecute, investigate, or provide redress for acts of pain and suffering perpetrated by private individuals in instances where the acts were committed with the consent or acquiescence of the State. However, this is not the approach that the Committee has taken. Instead, the Committee has interpreted the terms 'consent' and 'acquiescence' widely so that in instances where a State fails to prevent, investigate, prosecute, or punish the acts of non-State officials, a State is held to be consenting or acquiescing to these acts for the purposes of Article 1.

The Committee's approach to the term 'acquiescence' is apparent from its second General Comment published in November 2007. Here, the Committee stated:

> where State authorities or others acting in official capacity or under color of law, know or have reasonable grounds to believe that acts of torture or ill-treatment are being committed by non-State officials or private actors and they fail to exercise due-diligence to prevent, investigate, prosecute and punish such non-State officials or private actors consistently with this Convention, the State bears responsibility and its officials should be considered as authors, complicit or otherwise responsible under the Convention for consenting to or acquiescing in such permissible acts.[50]

This confirms that the Committee is willing to use the term 'acquiescence' to hold States responsible for their failure to protect individuals from harm caused by private actors.[51] Indeed, this author has shown elsewhere that although the concept of 'acquiescence' has only rarely been addressed by the Committee in its

can be seen in *Prosecutor v Furundzija (Trial Judgment)* IT-95-17/1-T (10 December 1998) [162–3]; *Prosecutor v Delalić, Mucić, Delić and Landžo (Trial Judgment)* IT-96-21-I (16 November 1998) [473]; *Prosecutor v Kunarac, Kovač and Vuković (Trial Judgment)* IT-96-23, IT-96-23-A, IT-96-23/1, IT-96-23/1-A22 (12 June 2002) [470(i)]; *Prosecutor v Kvočka, Radić, Žigić and Pracać (Trial Judgment)* IT-98-30/1-A (28 February 2005). See Sivakumaran, 'Torture' (n 29) for a thorough review of this jurisprudence.

50 CAT General Comment 2 (n 48).

51 For a fuller analysis of the Committee's approach to the term 'acquiescence' see K. Fortin, 'Rape as Torture: An Evaluation of the Committee against Torture's Attitude to Sexual Violence' (2008) 4(3) Utrecht Law Review 145, 153–9.

'jurisprudence', it is a central part of the Committee's analysis when it considers a State's reports under Article 19.[52]

3.6 General practice of the Committee against Torture with regard to armed groups

A review of the Committee against Torture's Conclusions and Recommendations demonstrates that the Committee is willing to address the acts of armed groups through the notion of due diligence that it has created under the terms 'acquiescence' and 'consent' in Article 1.[53] Consistent with this approach, the Committee does not show concern for the acts of the armed groups themselves and does not refer to such groups as fitting within the definition of 'public official or other person acting in an official capacity'. Instead, its references to armed groups are always articulated with a focus on the State party's failure to prevent or punish the abuses by armed groups. For example, the Committee has criticized instances when armed groups enjoy impunity for their actions. On such occasions, its comments are followed by an appeal to the State party to investigate and prosecute the armed group's abuses.[54] In a similar vein, the Committee has criticized the giving of amnesties to members of armed groups. These, it argues, are contrary to a State's obligation to carry out prompt, impartial, and thorough investigations, bring the perpetrators to justice, and provide adequate compensation for the victims.[55] With regard to the situation in Iraq with relation to ISIL, the Committee has urged Iraqi authorities to keep thorough documentation on the types of violations in the territory under ISIL's control so that when control is re-established, the perpetrators can be punished.[56]

The Committee has also indicated that States may be obliged to take forcible measures against armed opposition groups to prevent them from attacking civilians. In the case of Uganda, the Committee recommended that the government:

> act without delay to protect the civilian population in areas of armed conflict in northern Uganda from violations by the Lord's Resistance Army and members of security forces. In

[52] Ibid, 161.

[53] UN Committee Against Torture, 'Conclusions and Recommendations: Initial Report of Burundi' (15 February 2007) UN Doc CAT/C/BD/CO/1, [11] (hereafter CAT Burundi Report 2007); UN Committee Against Torture, 'Conclusions and Recommendations: Third Periodic Report of Colombia' (4 February 2004) UN Doc CAT/C/CR/31/3, [9(c)], [10(a)] (hereafter CAT Colombia Report 2004); UN Committee Against Torture, 'Conclusions and Recommendations: Initial Report of Uganda' (21 June 2005) UN Doc CAT/C/CR/34/UGA, [10(n)] (hereafter CAT Uganda Report 2005); UN Committee Against Torture, 'Conclusions and Recommendations: Nepal' (13 April 2007) UN Doc CAT/C/NPL/CO/2l, [33] (hereafter CAT Nepal Report 2007); UN Committee Against Torture, 'Conclusions and Recommendations: Sri Lanka' (15 December 2005) UN Doc CAT/C/LKA/CO/2, [17] (hereafter CAT Sri Lanka Report 2005).

[54] CAT Burundi Report 2007 (n 53) [11]. See also the UN Committee Against Torture, 'Conclusions and Recommendations: Syria (29 June 2012) UN Doc CAT/C/SYR/CO/1/Add.2 [23(d)] where it urged the Syrian authorities to conduct investigations into summary executions, enforced disappearances, arbitrary arrests and detention, and torture or cruel, inhuman or degrading treatment or punishment by State agents or non-State actors.

[55] CAT Colombia Report 2004 (n 53) [9(c)], [10(a)].

[56] UN Committee Against Torture, 'Conclusions and Recommendations: Initial Report of Iraq' (7 September 2015) UN Doc CAT/C/IRQ/CO/1 [12(b)].

particularly, the State party should protect internally displaced persons confined in camps, which are constantly exposed to attacks by the Lord's Resistance Army.[57]

Further examples can be found in which the Committee against Torture has indicated that States are under an obligation to prevent violations by armed groups. The Committee has stated that the Nepali, Sri Lankan, and Ugandan authorities are required to 'take the necessary steps, in a comprehensive manner to prevent the abduction of children' by the CPN-Maoist in Nepal, the Liberation Tigers of Tamil Eelam in Sri Lanka, and the Lord's Resistance Army in Uganda and to take positive measures to 'facilitate the reintegration of former child soldiers into society'.[58] Likewise, it has stated that authorities in the Philippines are required, as much as possible, to prevent the abduction and military recruitment of children by armed groups.[59]

3.7 Concluding remarks on the CAT

The analysis above has shown that like the Human Rights Committee and the Committee on Economic, Social and Cultural, the Committee against Torture has resisted addressing the acts of armed groups directly. Its reluctance to do so may be explained by the fact that the Committee against Torture is a treaty body with a limited mandate to hear complaints against States. In that sense, it has interpreted the phrase 'public official or other person acting in an official capacity' restrictively in its jurisprudence so that it functions as a gateway through which it can make a finding of State responsibility. The Committee's caution in this regard may stem from the fact that under Article 22 of the CAT, the Committee only has the competence to receive and consider communications from individuals 'who claim to be victims of a violation by a State Party of the provisions of the Convention'.[60] That being said, it may be questioned whether there is not greater scope for the Committee to encourage a broader interpretation of torture when it comes to the prohibition of *non-refoulement* in Article 3 and domestic prosecutions of torture.[61] In such cases, it is significant that the definition of torture is not applied to make

[57] CAT Uganda Report 2005 (n 53) [10(n)].

[58] CAT Nepal Report 2007 (n 53) [33]; CAT Sri Lanka Report 2005 (n 53) [17]; CAT Uganda Report 2005 (n 53) [22].

[59] UN Committee Against Torture, 'Conclusions and Recommendations: Third Report of the Philippines' (2 June 2016) UN Doc CAT/C/PHL/3, [38(e)].

[60] It is noted that this does not explain its approach to non-State actors when it hears complaints under Article 3, because here it is not being asked to make a finding that the respondent State has committed torture but that the complainant risks torture at the hands of a third State. As a result, if the Committee made a finding that the complainant risked torture at the hands of an armed group, it would not exceed the mandate it has been given to hear individual complaints against a State party (as opposed to an armed group).

[61] This would bring the CAT's approach in line with the position of the European Court of Human Rights which has held that a State sending an individual back to a country where he or she may face torture at the hands of a non-State actor may still be considered to violate Article 3 (prohibition of torture) stating, 'Owing to the absolute character of the right guaranteed, the Court does not rule out the possibility that Article 3 of the Convention may also apply where the danger emanates from persons or groups or persons who are not public officials.' See *H.L.R. v France*, Application No. 24573/94 (ECHR, 29 April 1997)(Grand Chamber Judgment) [40], as discussed by McCorquodale and La Forgia, 'Taking Off the Blindfolds' (n 29) 201.

a finding of State responsibility per se.[62] Accordingly there is more potential to interpret the phrase 'public official or other person acting in an official capacity' broadly, to also take into account the acts of armed groups controlling territory.

This potential was illustrated in the case of *R v Zardad* from the UK Criminal Court, where the UK extended its universal jurisdiction under the Convention against Torture and found Mr Zardad guilty of torture under s134(1) of the Criminal Justice Act 1988 which enacts Article 1 of the Convention against Torture.[63] Mr Zardad had been a senior commander in the Hezb-I-Islam, a fighting faction that had held complete control over the south of Afghanistan from 1992 to 1996. The question of whether he could be found guilty of torture depended on whether the Court found him to fit within the term 'public official or other person acting in an official capacity'. In its judgment, the Court took a wide interpretation to the *Elmi v Australia* case and found that Mr Zardad was a 'person acting in a public capacity'. Its conclusion in this respect was based on the fact that Hezb-I-Islam had 'a sufficient degree of organisation, a sufficient degree of actual control of an area and ... exercised the type of functions which a government or governmental organisation would exercise'.[64] Its conclusion on this point seems sensible considering the text of Article 1 is wide enough to include the acts of armed groups in instances where they are exercising control over the territory and considering the court did not have to make a finding of State responsibility. However, it is pertinent to note that the UK's court wider definition to 'torture' does not on its face accord with the Committee against Torture's approach to the definition. Having reviewed the text of the CAT, the chapter now turns two human rights treaties which seem to address armed groups directly: the Optional Protocol of the Convention on the Rights of the Child and the African Union Convention for the Protection and Assistance of Internally Displaced Persons in Africa (the Kampala Convention).

4. The Optional Protocol to the Convention on the Rights of the Child on the Involvement of Children in Armed Conflict

4.1 A human rights treaty?

The Optional Protocol to the Convention on the Rights of the Child on the Involvement of Children in Armed Conflict (the 'Optional Protocol') is one of the only two human rights treaties which directly refers to armed groups and deals exclusively with situations of armed conflict.[65] Importantly, on the basis of

[62] A State is simply found guilty of a breach of Article 3 of the CAT which prohibits States from expelling, returning, or extraditing a person to another State where there are substantial grounds for believing that they would be in danger of being subjected to torture.

[63] *R v Zardad* (n 29). For a discussion of this case, see Clapham, *Non-State Actors* (n 12) 342–3.

[64] *R v Zardad* (n 29) [33].

[65] This was adopted and opened for signature, ratification, and accession by UN General Assembly, 'Optional protocols to the Convention on the Rights of the Child on the involvement of children in armed conflict and on the sale of children, child prostitution and child pornography' (25 May

its normative content, it may be legitimately questioned whether the Optional Protocol qualifies as a human rights treaty at all or whether considering its focus on an issue traditionally dealt with by international humanitarian law—the recruitment of child soldiers—it can be better qualified as an international humanitarian law treaty.[66] Clearly the Protocol is the product of an age in which it is generally accepted that the two bodies of law are complementary in scope. Yet despite the Protocol's hybrid nature, there are good reasons to see it to be first and foremost a human rights treaty. First, it is appended to the Convention on the Rights of the Child (the CRC). Equally, it departs from the standards in international humanitarian law. It does this by making the minimum age of recruitment of children 'eighteen', instead of 'fifteen' as set out by Article 77(2) of API and Article 3(c) of Additional Protocol II of the Geneva Conventions.[67] In departing from international humanitarian law standards, the Optional Protocol's purpose was to bring the CRC's approach to the recruitment of children in line with the definition of 'child' that is central to the CRC.[68] This reflects the fact that as a treaty, the Optional Protocol was intended to 'strengthen further the implementation of rights recognised' in the CRC.[69] Interestingly,the question of whether Article 4, which addresses armed groups directly, should better be characterized as a human rights norm or international humanitarian law norm was also discussed by the drafters of the Optional Protocol. After some discussion, along similar lines to those discussed here, the drafters also decided that Article 4 was a human rights provision.[70]

4.2 Is Article 4 of the Optional Protocol binding on armed groups?

4.2.1 Drafting papers and the text of the Optional Protocol

The Optional Protocol on the Involvement of Children in Armed Conflict constitutes a marked departure from all previous human rights treaties because it addresses armed groups directly.[71] Article 4 of the Optional Protocol states:

1. Armed groups that are distinct from the armed forces of a State should not, under any circumstances, recruit or use in hostilities persons under the age of 18 years.

2000) UN Doc A/RES/54/263, and came into force on 12 February 2002 (hereafter Optional Protocol on involvement of children in armed conflict).

[66] C. Droege, 'Elective Affinities? Human Rights and Humanitarian Law' (2008) 871 International Review of the Red Cross 501, 507.

[67] This standard was repeated in Article 38 of the Convention of the Rights of the Child (CRC) and referred to as the 'rules of international humanitarian law'.

[68] Article 1 of the CRC defines a child as 'every human being below the age of eighteen years'. Article 38(2) of the CRC required States parties to take all feasible measures to ensure that persons who have not attained the age of fifteen years do not take a direct part in hostilities.

[69] See preamble to the Optional Protocol on involvement of children in armed conflict (n 65) 222.

[70] OHCHR, 'Outcome of the Expert Consultation on the Issue of Protecting the Human Rights of Civilians in Armed Conflict' (4 June 2009) UN Doc A/HRC/11/31, 12 [27].

[71] It should be noted that the Optional Protocol *does* contain the traditional beginning 'The States Parties to the present Protocol have agreed as follows'.

2. States Parties shall take all feasible measures to prevent such recruitment and use, including the adoption of legal measures necessary to prohibit and criminalize such practices.
3. The application of the present article under this Protocol shall not affect the legal status of any party to an armed conflict.

Yet despite its wording, there remains an important disagreement amongst commentators as to whether Article 4(1) of the Optional Protocol was intended to bind armed groups. Legal scholars who say that it was not, point to the fact that Article 4(1) uses the term 'should' which is a soft exhortation compared to the 'shall' which is used elsewhere, when States parties are addressed, e.g. in Article 4(2).[72] Legal scholars who say it was intended to be binding upon armed groups, point out that the terms 'under any circumstances' can be interpreted as a 'clear indication that the drafters intended to create (or crystallize) a meaningful obligation that allows for no delay or derogation'.[73] The *travaux préparatoires* of the Optional Protocol demonstrate that the Optional Protocol's ambiguity on this point reflects the fact that there was disagreement among its drafters as to whether non-State actors could be bound by an inter-State treaty.[74] Indeed, it has been argued by some authors that this ambiguity was intended as a solution to deal with this disagreement.[75]

Interestingly, there are several other indicators that a considerable number of the Protocol's drafting States intended it to create binding obligations for armed groups. The first of these is found in the fact that Article 4 was retained in the body of the Protocol and not relegated to the preamble, as some States had suggested.[76] Another is found in Article 4(3) which confirms that nothing in Article 4 will affect the legal status of any party to an armed conflict. This article is a clear and obvious borrowing from common Article 3 of the Geneva Convention which was unambiguously intended to bind armed groups. The last line of common Article 3 states that the application of the article 'shall not affect the legal status of the Parties to the conflict'. The existence of this text in common Article 3 was designed to address States' concerns that the placing of obligations upon armed groups would be used by armed groups, or other actors, to argue that they had attained belligerent status.[77] The fact that drafting

[72] C. Ryngaert, 'Human Rights Obligations of Armed Groups' (2008) 2 Revue Belge de Droit International 355, 364.

[73] A. Clapham, 'The Rights and Responsibilities of Non-State Actors: The Legal Landscape & Issues Surrounding Engagement, Draft for Comment available on SSRN' (Geneva Academy of International Humanitarian Law and Human Rights, February 2010) 25.

[74] Human Rights Commission, 'Report of the working group on a draft optional protocol to the Convention on the Rights of the Child on involvement of children in armed conflicts on its sixth session' (27 March 2000) UN Doc E/CN.4/2000/74, [37–40] (hereafter HRC Report on draft optional CRC protocol on children in armed conflicts).

[75] See also J. A. Hessbruegge, 'Human Rights Violations Arising from Conduct of Non-State Actors' [2005] Buffalo Human Rights Law Review 21, 31.

[76] HRC Report on draft optional CRC protocol on children in armed conflicts (n 74) [38].

[77] A similar clause is found in Article 7 of the African Union Convention for the Protection and Assistance of Internally Displaced Persons in Africa (hereafter the Kampala Convention) which very

States felt the need for such a clause in the Optional Protocol of the Convention on the Rights of the Child suggested that at least some of its drafters understood Article 4(1) to place legal obligations upon armed groups. If Article 4(1) had been not intended to impose obligations upon armed groups, Article 4(3) would have been redundant.

4.2.2 State practice on interpretation of the Optional Protocol

In line with Article 31(3)(b) of the Vienna Convention on the Law of Treaties, there is a significant body of 'subsequent practice' that suggests agreement amongst the drafters of the Optional Protocol that Article 4(1) should be interpreted to directly bind armed groups and not just the signing States parties. On ratifying the Optional Protocol, Mexico appended an interpretive declaration that stated:

> In ratifying the Optional Protocol to the Convention on the Rights of the Child on the involvement of children in armed conflict, adopted by the General Assembly of the United Nations on 25 May 2000, the Government of the United Mexican States considers that any responsibility deriving therefrom for non-governmental armed groups for the recruitment of children under 18 years or their use in hostilities lies solely with such groups and shall not be applicable to the Mexican State as such. The latter shall have a duty to apply at all times the principles governing international humanitarian law.[78]

The reports of the Secretary-General of the United Nations and his Special Representatives for Children and Armed Conflict indicate a similar view. Although the words chosen by these individuals have not been uniform over the years, many of these reports confirm a view that the Optional Protocol 'prohibits insurgent groups "under any circumstances" from recruiting persons under 18 years or using them in hostilities'.[79]

The Secretary-General of the United Nations has also confirmed a view that armed groups in States that have ratified the Optional Protocol will be held accountable to a higher standard than that set out in the Convention on the Rights

explicitly sets out prohibitions addressed to the members of armed groups, stating: 'The provisions of this Article shall not, in any way whatsoever, be construed as affording legal status or legitimizing or recognizing armed groups.'

[78] UN, 'Interpretative Declaration made by Mexico upon ratification of the Protocol' (15 March 2002) <https://treaties.un.org/Pages/ViewDetails.aspx?src=IND&mtdsg_no=IV-11-b&chapter=4&clang=_en#11.> accessed 20 January 2017. Intriguingly, Mexico withdrew this interpretative declaration on 28 May 2013 but did not provide an explanation for its actions.

[79] See UN Security Council, 'Report of the Secretary-General on children and armed conflict' (26 November 2002) UN Doc S/2002/1299, [3] (hereafter 'SG Report 2002, children and armed conflict'); UN Human Rights Council, 'Annual Report of the Special Representative of the Secretary-General for children and armed conflict, Radhika Coomaraswamy' (3 September 2010) UN Doc A/HRC/15/58, [16], [64]; UN Economic and Social Council, 'Annual Report of the Special Representative of the Secretary-General for children and armed conflict, O. A. Otunno' (3 March 2003) UN Doc E/CN.4/2003/77, 6 [2].

of the Child,[80] Additional Protocols I and II to the Geneva Conventions[81] and the Rome Statute of the International Criminal Court.[82] By that he has indicated that such groups will be considered to be prohibited from recruiting or using children under the age of eighteen, rather than children under fifteen.[83] The Working Group on Children and Armed Conflict which, significantly for an assessment of subsequent practice, is made up of the fifteen Security Council members, has also been seen to state that armed groups using children in capabilities related to military operations are in 'contradiction' to the Optional Protocol to the Convention on the Rights of the Child on the involvement of children in armed conflict.[84] In such situations, the Working Group has directly called upon the leadership of such groups requesting that clear military orders 'strictly prohibiting the recruitment and use of children, consistent with both the national legislation of [the country in question] and the Optional Protocol to the Convention on the Rights of the Child on the involvement of children in armed conflict, are enforced'.[85]

Further support for a prevalent view that armed groups are directly bound by the Optional Protocol can also be found in action plans between an armed groups and the United Nations. For example, the action plan which was drawn up in 2009 between the Moro Islamic Liberation Front (MILF) and the United Nations in the Philippines states that the MILF accepts the 'obligations' under international humanitarian law and international human rights law 'specifically the Optional Protocol to the Convention on the Rights of the Child on the involvement of children in armed conflict'.[86] This is another indication of an understanding by both the United Nations and the armed group that the Optional Protocol's text

[80] Article 38(3) of the Convention on the Rights of the Child prohibits States parties from recruiting any person who has not attained fifteen years.

[81] Article 77(2) of API states that the parties to the conflict (NB: these may include armed groups with the status of national liberation movements) shall take all feasible measures to ensure that children who have not attained the age of fifteen years do not take a direct part in hostilities and shall refrain from recruiting them into their armed forces. Article 4(3)(c) of APII requires that children who have not attained the age of fifteen years shall neither be recruited in the armed forces or groups nor allowed to take part in hostilities.

[82] See Articles 8(2)(b)(xxvi) and 8(2)(e)(vii) of the Rome Statute that make it a war crime to conscript or enlist children under the age of fifteen years into the national armed forces armed groups or use them to participate actively in hostilities in international armed conflicts and non-international armed conflicts.

[83] See 'SG Report 2002, children and armed conflict' (n 79) [31].

[84] The Working Group on Children and Armed Conflict was established in July 2005 pursuant to UN Security Council, 'Children in armed conflict' (26 July 2005) UN Doc S/RES/1612.

[85] UN Security Council, 'Conclusions on children and armed conflict in the Philippines, Working Group on Children and Armed Conflict' (3 October 2008) UN Doc S/AC.51/2008/10, [5(b)], [5(d)(ii)], [5(2b)], [2(d)(ii)]. It is noted that this instance of the Working Group on Children and Armed Conflict referring directly to the Optional Protocol seems rather exceptional. Usually, the Working Group is not as explicit when citing the source of armed groups' obligations in this regard. See, for example, UN Security Council, 'Conclusions on children and armed conflict in Afghanistan, Working Group on Children and Armed Conflict' (13 July 2009) UN Doc S/AC.51/2009/1.

[86] Action Plan between the Moro Islamic Liberation Front and the United Nations in the Philippines at http://theirwords.org/media/transfer/doc/1_ph_milf_biaf_2009_13-d74703efad5c37df5ab9842bc87e67a2.pdf accessed 14 April 2017.

creates 'obligations' for armed groups and was intended to create obligations for armed groups by its drafters. Also noteworthy is the fact that the Commission of Inquiry for Syria has held that the Optional Protocol 'by its terms applies to non-State actors'.[87]

4.3 Concluding remarks on the Optional Protocol

When considering the theories set out in the previous chapter, it can be seen that the 'extended legislative jurisdiction' theory provides the best explanation for how the Optional Protocol achieves its goal to bind armed groups. In directly addressing armed groups, the treaty's drafters create direct duties for the armed groups under international treaty law. It has been seen in the previous chapter that this constitutes an exception to the *pacta tertiis* rule. However, it has also been shown in the previous chapter that such exceptions to the rules on third parties and treaties can be justified in strictly defined circumstances. The first requirement is that there is clear evidence that the drafters of the treaty intended it to have this effect and create direct obligations for third parties. When examining the Optional Protocol to the Convention on the Rights of the Child on the involvement of children in armed conflict, it has been noted that there are ambiguities in the text of Article 4 as to whether it was intended to bind armed groups. However, despite this textual ambiguity, it has also been shown that there is a significant body of evidence indicating that it was the drafters' intention to bind armed groups. There is also a considerable amount of subsequent practice demonstrating that this is how the Optional Protocol is interpreted in practice. It has also been shown in the previous chapter that a departure from the *pacta tertiis* principle is less controversial in instances where it is justified by a strict humanitarian imperative. On the basis that the Optional Protocol was intended to 'increase the protection of children from involvement in armed conflict', it seems clear that this requirement can be satisfied in this instance.

It has also been argued in the previous chapter that the direct application of obligations or rights to third parties by means of treaty law is usually in response to it being impossible or impracticable to seek the consent of the entity in question at the time the treaty is drafted. It was argued that this is very often the case with armed groups. Indeed, the fact that there is no procedure under the Optional Protocol on the involvement of children in armed conflict for armed groups to sign up to its provisions can be explained by the difficulties that would be inherent in a system that required armed groups to sign up to the Optional Protocol at the

[87] UN Human Rights Council, 'Report of the Independent International Commission of Inquiry on the Syrian Arab Republic' (5 February 2013) UN Doc A/HRC/22/59, 86, as highlighted by T. Rodenhauser, 'Human Rights Obligations of Non-State Armed Groups in Other Situations of Violence: The Syria Example' (2012) 3 International Humanitarian Legal Studies 263, 272.

moment that an armed conflict breaks out. It may also be explained by an understanding that armed groups can be bound by treaty law without their consent, i.e. through a legislative approach. As a final point, it is important to remember that the conclusions in Chapter 6 indicates that armed groups will only be bound by Article 4(1) of the Optional Protocol on the Involvement of Children in Armed Conflict in instances where they have reached an organizational threshold that allows them to adhere to the norms it contains, and ensure that they are enforced. On the basis that the Optional Protocol relates to 'armed conflict', it is submitted that this will likely be similar to the lower threshold of application of Common Article 3 of the Geneva Conventions.

5. The African Union Convention for the Protection and Assistance of Internally Displaced Persons in Africa (the Kampala Convention)

The most recent treaty which appears to contain human rights obligations addressed to armed groups is the Kampala Convention. The text of the Kampala Convention was adopted by the African Union Ministerial Conference in November 2008 and came into force on 6 December 2012. Article 7(5) of the Kampala Convention states as follows that:

Members of armed groups shall be prohibited from:

a) Carrying out arbitrary displacement;
b) Hampering the provision of protection and assistance to internally displaced persons under any circumstances;
c) Denying internally displaced persons the right to live in satisfactory conditions of dignity, security, sanitation, food, water, health and shelter; and separating members of the same family;
d) Restricting the freedom of movement of internally displaced persons within and outside their areas of residence;
e) Recruiting children or requiring or permitting them to take part in hostilities under any circumstances;
f) Forcibly recruiting persons, kidnapping, abduction or hostage taking, engaging in sexual slavery and trafficking in persons especially women and children;
g) Impeding humanitarian assistance and passage of all relief consignments, equipment and personnel to internally displaced persons;
h) Attacking or otherwise harming humanitarian personnel and resources or other materials deployed for the assistance or benefit of internally displaced persons and shall not destroy, confiscate or divert such materials; and
i) Violating the civilian and humanitarian character of the places where internally displaced persons are sheltered and shall not infiltrate such places.

Before looking in more detail at the obligations set out in Article 7(5) and the choice of words employed by its drafters, a few brief words are given on the content of these obligations.

5.1 A human rights treaty?

It has been noted that the list of prohibited acts in Article 7(5) broadly reproduces key international humanitarian law provisions relevant to the protection of civilians.[88] However, a closer look at Article 7(5) shows that the provisions addressing armed groups have their origins in both international humanitarian law and international human rights law. For example, it is clear that several of the prohibitions set out above in Article 7(5) have their origins in human rights law. This is true of Article 7(5)(d)'s prohibition on restricting the freedom of movement of internally displaced persons within and outside their areas of residence. The origins of this provision are in Article 12 of the ICCPR which recognizes that everyone has the right to freedom of movement and residence within the border of each State.[89] Likewise, the wording of Article 7(5)(c) seems to originate from both human rights law and international humanitarian law. This is apparent in the Article's comment that internally displaced persons (IDPs) have a 'right to live in satisfactory conditions of dignity, security, sanitation, food, water, health and shelter'. This rights-based wording makes clear that this provision is based not only on Article 17(1) and Article 4(3)(b) of Additional Protocol II[90] but also on the human right to life, dignity, security, an adequate standard of living, and right to health in human rights law.[91] Similarly, Article 7(5)(e) of the Kampala Convention's prohibition on the recruitment of children or use of children in hostilities relies dually on international humanitarian law and international human rights law.[92] It is noted

[88] S. Ojeda, 'The Kampala Convention on Internally Displaced Persons: Some International Humanitarian Law Aspects' (2010) 3 Refugee Survey Quarterly 58, 66, and fn 41 (hereafter Ojeda, 'Kampala Convention Humanitarian Law Aspects'). While many of these provisions have their origin in treaty law, they also reflect 'rules' from the ICRC's Customary International Humanitarian Law Study: Article 7(5)(a) can be seen to be based on ICRC customary international law Rule 129, Article 7(5)(b) can be seen to be based on ICRC customary international law Rules 55 and 56, Article 7(5)(c) can be seen to be based on ICRC customary international law Rule 131, Article 7(5)(e) can be seen to be based on ICRC customary international law Rules 136 and 137, Article 7(5)(f) can be seen to be based on ICRC customary international law Rules 93 and 94, Article 7(5)(g) can be seen to be based on ICRC customary international law Rules 55 and 56, Article 7(5)(h) can be seen to be based on ICRC customary international law Rules 31, 32, 35, 36, 37 and Article 7(5)(i) can be seen to be based on ICRC customary international law Rules 1, 7, and 10. See J. Henckaerts and L. Doswald-Beck, *Customary International Humanitarian Law, Volume I: Rules* (CUP, Cambridge 2005) (hereafter Henckaerts and Doswald-Beck, *Rules*).

[89] It is noted that this provision was also contained in UN Commission on Human Rights, 'Guiding Principles on Internal Displacement' (22 July 1998) UN Doc E/CN.4/1998/53/Add.2, Article 14(1), which states: 'Every internally displaced person has the right to liberty of movement and freedom to choose his or her residence.'

[90] These provisions together form Rule 131 of the ICRC's study on customary international humanitarian law, which states: 'In case of displacement, all possible measures must be taken in order that the civilians concerned are received under satisfactory conditions of shelter, hygiene, health, safety and nutrition and that numbers of the same family are not separated.' See n 88 above.

[91] See for example the preamble of the Universal Declaration of Human Rights (UDHR), which states: 'Whereas recognition of the inherent dignity and of the equal and inalienable rights of all members of the human family is the foundation of freedom, justice and peace in the world'. See also Article 6 of the ICCPR, which states that 'every human being has the inherent right to life'.

[92] It is noted that the Kampala Convention (n 77) adopts the same age limit as the Optional Protocol to the Convention on the Rights of the Child, i.e. eighteen. While Article 4 of the Optional Protocol prohibits the recruitment or use in hostilities of persons under 18 years, Article 4(3)(c) adopts the lower age limit of fifteen years.

in this respect that the Kampala Convention adopts the same age limit for its prohibition on the recruitment and use of children in hostilities as the Optional Protocol to the Convention on the Rights of the Child, i.e. eighteen.[93]

The mixture of human rights law and humanitarian law in Article 7(5) reflects a recognition that internally displaced persons require recourse to a 'web of international humanitarian and human rights law' for their protection.[94] This observation is stated explicitly in the Explanatory Note to the Kampala Convention which was published by the African Union after its text was agreed. The fact that the Kampala Convention contains a mixture of international human rights law and international humanitarian law is also stated in the Convention's preamble. This preamble states that the inherent rights of internally displaced persons are provided for and protected in international human rights and humanitarian law and recalls a comprehensive list of both human rights law and international humanitarian law treaties. It is also noted that the African Union's Press Release announcing the adoption of the Convention calls it a 'landmark legal instrument in international human rights and humanitarian law'.[95] Having demonstrated that the Kampala Convention articulates obligations to 'members of armed groups' that originate in human rights law and international humanitarian law, it remains to consider whether in practice it is used as a tool to binds armed groups as such, and/or their members, and if so, how this is achieved.

5.2 Drafting papers and text of Article 7(5) of the Kampala Convention

5.2.1 A troubled drafting history

It is noted in this regard that although the Kampala Convention is often referred to as containing obligations for 'armed groups', questions remain about whether the Convention actually binds armed groups or was intended to bind armed groups.[96] Moreover, according to those were present at the drafting process of the Convention, Article 7 'was among the most debated provisions'[97] of the entire Convention. Records of the drafting process indicate that earlier attempts to include obligations of armed groups in the Convention were met by criticism

[93] See Article 1(h) of the Kampala Convention (n 77) which defines 'child' as below the age of eighteen years.

[94] African Commission on Human and Peoples' Rights, 'Explanatory Note on the African Union Convention for the Protection and Assistance of Internally Displaced Persons' (undated but clearly drafted after the Convention was adopted) <http://www.internal-displacement.org/assets/publications/Tools-and-Frameworks/200910-training-KC-Explanatory-Note-Eng.pdf> accessed 20 January 2017 (hereafter Explanatory Note on Kampala Convention).

[95] Commissioner Bahame Tom Nyanduga, African Commission on Human and Peoples' Rights, 'Press Release for the African Union Special Summit on Internally Displaced Persons' (22 October 2009) <http://www.achpr.org/press/2009/10/d25/> accessed 20 January 2017 (hereafter Press Release).

[96] See Ojeda, 'Kampala Convention Humanitarian Law Aspects' (n 88) 64, 65.

[97] Ibid, 65.

by various members of the NGO community.[98] In particular, some NGOs expressed misgivings about a previous draft of the Convention in which the obligations of States and armed groups were listed together in the same article. In response to this draft, a number of NGOs requested that the responsibilities of armed groups and States be listed in separate articles because they were afraid that the proposed format would imply that the responsibilities of States and armed groups were identical.[99] A later draft of the Convention shows that the NGOs' suggestion was taken onboard as it included a separate paragraph (now Article 7) which was then entitled 'Obligations of Armed Groups Relating to Protection and Assistance'.[100]

During the drafting process that followed, it is clear that this new article was yet again subject to criticism. While it has not been possible to find an exact record of the debate, it seems probable that the notion of armed groups bearing obligations under the Convention remained contentious, especially when originating from international humanitarian law *and human rights law*.[101] By the time that the final draft of the Convention was adopted, all reference to armed groups had been removed from Article 7's heading. As a result, although the provisions of the final version of Article 7 continue to relate only to armed groups and their members, the article is now rather cryptically entitled 'Protection and Assistance to Internally Displaced Persons in Situations of Armed Conflict'. Somewhat strangely, the generic sounding title of the article does not provide any indication that its content relates exclusively to armed groups, and not States. Crucially the final version of Article 7(5) also refers to the obligations of the 'members' of armed groups, rather than the armed groups themselves. It is this final change which is relied upon most often by those who argue that the Convention does not actually bind armed groups. Yet despite the final wording of Article 7, the following section shows that indications can also be found in the final draft that at least some of its drafters continued to believe that the Convention was binding upon armed groups too.[102]

[98] Amnesty International, Fédération Internationale des Droits de l'Homme, IDP Action, Institute for Human Rights and Development in Africa, Laws for Human Rights (South Africa) and Refugees International, 'Internally Displaced Persons in Aprica need a strong Convention' (Letter to the African Union, 6 June 2008) <http://www.fidh.org/IMG/pdf/IDPconventionAUngoComments.pdf> accessed 20 January 2017 (hereafter Letter to African Union and NGO Commentary to Kampala Convention draft).

[99] NGO Commentary to Kampala Convention (n 98) [3].

[100] F. Z. Giustiniani, 'New Hopes and Challenges for the Protection of IDPs in Africa: The Kampala Convention for the Protection and Assistance of Internally Displaced Persons in Africa' (2010–2011) 2 Denver Journal of International Law and Policy 347, 359 (hereafter Giustiniani, 'Hopes and Challenges'). Some scholars have expressed disappointment that the obligations of States and armed groups are listed in separate articles. See Ojeda, 'Kampala Convention Humanitarian Law Aspects' (n 88) 65.

[101] See Giustiniani, 'Hopes and Challenges' (n 100) 359.

[102] It is noteworthy that a number of commentators continue to assert that the Convention places obligations upon armed groups without seemingly noticing that this may be controversial or disputed. See for example Ojeda, 'Kampala Convention Humanitarian Law Aspects' (n 88) 65; K. Ridderbos, 'The Kampala Convention and Obligations of Armed Groups' (2011) 37 Forced Migration

5.2.2 Indications that Article 7(5)(b) was intended to bind armed groups

The first and clearest indication that the Kampala Convention was considered by its drafters to be binding upon armed groups is found in Article 5(11) of the Kampala Convention which refers to the obligations of 'armed groups' in Article 7. Article 5(11) states: 'States Parties shall take measures aimed at ensuring that armed groups act in conformity with their obligations under Article 7.' This phrase indicates a continued view that Article 7 entails obligations for armed groups, as well as their members. In a similar manner, Article 2(e) of the Convention elaborates that one of the 'objectives' of the Kampala Convention was to 'provide for the respective *obligations responsibilities and roles of armed groups*, non-state actors and other relevant actors' (emphasis added). This is another indication that the final text of the Convention was intended to place obligations on armed groups, as well as their members. Furthermore, the Press Release issued by the Commissioner Bahame Tom Nayanduga after the Convention was drafted states that the Kampala Convention 'prohibits *armed groups* and their members from engaging in arbitrary displacement, or other such violations of the basic human rights of internally displaced persons' (emphasis added). Likewise, the Explanatory Note to the Kampala Convention, which was published by the African Union after the Convention's text was finalized, states that Article 7 'outline[e]s the obligations of *Armed Groups*' (my emphasis).[103] The note goes on to say that armed groups 'inter-alia, have the obligation to prevent forced displacement in the territories under their control, provide humanitarian organizations with access to the displaced and facilitate the delivery of relief'. In doing so, the Explanatory Note interprets Article 7(5) as conferring obligations upon armed groups. All these sources indicate that, despite the wording of the final draft of Article 7(5) being restricted to 'members of armed groups', its drafters intended it to contain obligations for armed groups as well.

Noting the differences between Article 7(5) (which refers only to the obligations of the members of armed groups) and Article 5 and Article 2 (which refers to the obligations of the armed groups as such), one commentator has said that these inconsistencies represent an oversight on the part of the drafters.[104] From this perspective, Articles 2 and 5's continued reference to the obligations of armed groups, simply reflects a 'mistake' on the part of the Convention's drafters.[105] Yet another explanation for these anomalies could be that the drafters of the Kampala Convention intended armed groups to be bound 'through their members'. This idea is far from unimaginable. For it was shown in the preceding chapter that this is how the ICRC explained the fact that armed groups are bound by common Article 3 of the Geneva Conventions. Indeed, while from a technical legal

Review; Norwegian Refugee Council and Internal Displacement Monitoring Centre, 'A review of the legal framework in Zimbabwe relating to the protection of IDPs' (December 2014) 2 [9].

[103] Explanatory Note on Convention (n 94) 4.

[104] M. T. Maru, 'The Kampala Convention and its Contribution in Filling the Protection Gap in International Law' (2011) 1 Journal of Internal Displacement 91, 121.

[105] Ibid.

perspective, the theory is quite complex, it has an attractive conceptual simplicity. It is premised on the notion that legal entities are, in their essence, made up of individuals. Moreover, recourse to this theory would explain why Articles 2 and 5 continue to refer to the obligations of armed groups, when Article 7 only refers to their members. It would also explain the African Union's Explanatory Note on the Convention which refers not only to the 'obligations of Armed Groups' in Article 7 but also refers to 'the obligations of the Members of Armed Groups'.[106] In referring to 'both' these types of obligations, carelessness becomes a less likely explanation for the anomalies in the Convention's drafting. Instead, this is an important indication that at least some of the Convention's drafters understood the Kampala Convention to be binding on both armed groups and their members. A similar conclusion can be drawn from the Press Release drafted by Commissioner Bahame Tom Nayanduga which states that the Convention contains prohibitions for 'armed groups and their members'.[107]

5.3 Nature of obligations set out in Article 7(5)

As a final point, it is interesting to note how the provisions included in Article 7 of the Kampala Convention compare to the obligations in Articles 3, 4 and 5 of the Convention that are introduced to States. One of the main differences is that the obligations addressed to States parties are mainly articulated in the form of positive obligations. For example, States undertake to 'respect and ensure respect and protection of the human rights of internally displaced persons, including humane treatment, non-discrimination and equal protection of law'.[108] States also undertake to 'respect and ensure respect for international humanitarian law regarding the protection of internally displaced persons'. In contrast, Article 7 is phrased in terms of 'prohibitions'. Members of armed groups are stated to be 'prohibited from' carrying out the specific acts set out in the article, some of which, restricting the freedom of movement of internally displaced persons, can be seen to have their origin in human rights law. As a consequence the members of armed groups are bound by a much narrower set of obligations to those imposed on States parties. While it is understood that it may not be desirable or realistic to seek to bind armed groups, or their members, to the same range of obligations as States, the final text of the Kampala Convention raises questions as to why either armed group members or the armed groups themselves could not be held to at least some of the other positive obligations which the Convention articulates for State parties. An obvious and somewhat mysterious omission in this respect is an obligation to respect international humanitarian law.[109]

[106] Explanatory Note on Kampala Convention (n 94) 2.

[107] See Press Release (n 95).

[108] See Article 3(1)(d).

[109] Article 3(1)(e) of the Kampala Convention requires States parties to respect and ensure respect for international humanitarian law regarding the protection of internally displaced persons. There is no equivalent provision in Article 7(5).

5.4 Concluding remarks on the Kampala Convention

The section above has shown that a comparison of different articles of the Kampala Convention leaves a scholar in a degree of some bewilderment as to the intentions of its drafters. Articles 2 and 5 of the Convention suggest that it was intended to bind armed groups. Article 7 of the Convention indicates that it was intended to bind armed groups' members. Despite this ambiguity, the Convention unequivocally indicates that its drafters understood individuals (i.e. the members of armed groups) to be bound by certain core human rights norms, including the obligation to respect freedom of movement, the obligation to respect the right to life, and the obligation to respect the right to 'live in satisfactory conditions of dignity, security, sanitation, food, water, health and shelter'.[110] This fact alone makes the Kampala Convention a very significant document as it has been shown in this chapter that most major human rights treaties generally bind only States, and not individuals. Moreover, recourse to the theories evaluated in Chapter 7 shows that, despite the internal contradictions in its drafting history and text, the fact that the treaty is binding upon individuals allows a good argument to be made that the Kampala Convention also binds armed groups. This requires recourse to the 'legislative jurisdiction' theory that was set out in detail in Chapter 7.

6. Conclusions

The chapter has found little evidence that the ICCPR, ICESCR, and CAT can be cited as a 'source' of human rights obligations for armed groups or individuals. Instead, it has shown that there are no indications in the *travaux préparatoires* of these treaties that they were intended to be binding upon armed groups. Rather, the texts of the treaties, and the procedural mechanisms that they establish, provide a powerful argument that they are binding only upon States. This textual interpretation is also supported by the practice of the treaty bodies. However, it has been shown that the human rights treaties analysed above demonstrate support for the notion that non-State actors may bear obligations under wider human rights law. Evidence for such support has been shown to exist in the text of the Conventions themselves, either explicitly or implicitly. The clearest example of where this is explicitly stated is the Preamble of the ICCPR and ICESCR. A similar idea is also found in Article 5(1) of the ICCPR and ICESC. Likewise, the chapter has shown that statements from the treaty bodies demonstrate a consistent openness to the notion that human rights obligations may apply horizontally between non-State actors.

A similar openness is also found in the treaty bodies' jurisprudence on positive obligations. Here, it has been repeatedly confirmed that the idea that States have positive obligations to protect private individuals is inherently linked to the notion

[110] See Article 7(5)(a)(c) and (d).

that individuals owe human rights obligations to each other *inter se*. Different treaty bodies have approached this concept in different ways and to different extents but they have all recognized that private actors are capable of infringing the rights of others. This constitutes an implicit recognition of the fact that individuals and other non-State actors are bound by human rights law to a certain degree. However, the treaty bodies' statements in this regard are generally brief and leave a lot to conjecture. Indeed, a review of the practice of treaty bodies in this respect has indicated that horizontal obligations are only commented upon by the treaty bodies if it triggers State responsibility. This brevity notwithstanding, it seems clear that the treaty bodies reviewed do not consider the source of these obligations for non-State actors to lie in human rights treaty law. There is little indication that the Human Rights Committee, the Committee on Economic, Social and Cultural Rights, and the Committee on Torture consider the treaty texts to create international obligations which are binding upon non-State actors. Instead, the repeated suggestion is that the human rights obligations of individuals and non-State actors exist outside the treaty framework, for example, in customary international law or national law.

The latter part of the chapter has shown that a good argument can be made that armed groups and their members are bound by the two human rights treaties which explicitly address armed groups, i.e. the Optional Protocol on the Involvement of Children in Armed Conflict and Kampala Convention. However, in doing so, the chapter has demonstrated that the question in each case remains controversial. Indeed, it shows that the drafting histories of both treaties were plagued by discussions of the question of whether armed groups can be bound by treaty law. They were also afflicted by disagreement about what it would mean if armed groups were bound by treaty law. During the drafting of the Kampala Convention there were also lengthy discussions about 'what kind of obligations' an armed group may have. The chapter has shown that the disagreement on these issues clearly manifests itself in the final text of both treaties. Both treaties contain ambiguities that may have been a deliberate attempt on the part of their drafters to achieve a compromise between proponents of different positions. While to an extent it is true that all treaties are 'disagreement[s] reduced to writing', ambiguities of this magnitude are damaging to the accountability framework that both treaties set up, as they have both led to an argument *after* the treaty's ratification about what their respective drafters intended.[111] Ultimately, these observations confirm the pressing need to deepen our understanding and scholarship on the legal personality of armed groups so that any future human rights documents that seek to bind armed groups can be free of such doubts. It is hoped that this book may contribute to this effort.

[111] P. Allott, 'The Concept of International Law' (1999) 10 European Journal of International Law 31, 43.

9

Control of Territory and Human Rights Obligations of Armed Groups

1. Introduction

The purpose of this chapter is to consider whether and how an armed group's control of territory may provide a legal explanation for how it is bound by international human rights law.[1] It was shown in the introduction to the book that many instances of armed groups being held responsible under human rights law are explained by the fact that they exercise 'some degree of control over a given territory and population'.[2] The idea that territorial control holds the key to understanding how and when armed groups are bound by human rights law has been raised by multiple commentators. For example, Matas, in his early writing on the subject stated: '[w]hen a government undertakes an obligation on behalf of the state, the obligation is taken on behalf of the whole state, governmental and non-governmental people alike, and not just on behalf of the government'.[3] Likewise,

[1] It is acknowledged in Chapter 4, 6 and 7 that there is precedent for armed groups acquiring legal obligations in instances where they control territory. This chapter takes a more theoretical approach to probe the legal principles from which such a norm may have emerged.

[2] The majority of reports limit their observations to instances in which the armed group in question has effective control. See for example, UN Human Rights Council, 'Report of the Independent International Fact-Finding Mission on the Gaza Conflict, Human Rights In Palestine And Other Occupied Arab Territories' (23 September 2009) UN Doc A/HRC/12/48, [304]; UN Human Rights Council, 'Report of the Independent International Commission of Inquiry to investigate all alleged violations of international human rights law in the Libyan Arab Jamahiriya' (1 June 2011) UN Doc A/HRC/17/44, [72]. For examples of reports where territorial control is not required see UN Human Rights Council, 'Report of the Independent International Commission of Inquiry on the Syrian Arab Republic' (22 February 2012) UN Doc A/HRC/19/69; UNMISS, 'Conflict in South Sudan: A Human Rights Report' (8 May 2014) <https://unmiss.unmissions.org/sites/default/files/unmiss_conflict_in_south_sudan_-_a_human_rights_report.pdf> accessed 20 January 2017. See also J. Henckaerts and C. Wiesner, 'Human Rights Obligations of Non-State Armed Groups: A Possible Contribution from Customary International Law?' in R. Kolb and G. Gaggioli (eds), *Research Handbook on Human Rights and Humanitarian Law* (Edward Elgar Publishing, Cheltenham 2013) 146–69, 154–60 (hereafter Henckaerts and Wiesner, 'A Possible Contribution from Customary International Law') for a further review of practice in that respect.

[3] D. Matas, 'Armed Opposition Groups' (1997) 3 Manatoba Law Journal 621, 632. See also A. Constantinides, 'Human Rights Obligations and Accountability of Armed Opposition Groups: The Practice of the UN Security Council' (2010) 4 Human Rights and International Legal Discourse

Tomuschat, writing in 2004, wrote that '[t]o the extent that elements of governmental authority have fallen into the hands of a rebel movement, that movement cannot escape its responsibilities under the CCPR—and other human rights instruments, including the elementary rules that have crystallized as customary law'.[4] Providing a significant contribution to the literature on the topic, Part II of the book has already demonstrated that the legal frameworks of belligerency and insurgency both provide strong historical precedents of armed groups being held bound by 'human rights-like' obligations in instances where they control territory.[5] While the substantive conclusions on this point are not rehearsed again here, the chapter now finds it important to consider these precedents from a technical perspective, in a bid to understand the source of obligations arising out of territorial control. It conducts this examination through the lens of the theory of effectiveness and its role as a tool to mend schisms between the normative and the actual. While this theory was largely rejected as providing an explanation for how armed groups are bound by international humanitarian law, it was identified in Chapter 7 as having significant potential to explain how armed groups are bound by international human rights law.

The chapter is structured as follows. It begins by reviewing the principle of effectiveness and its potential relevance for explaining how armed groups may be bound by international human rights law. It then examines how a number of different courts and claims commissions have dealt with situations in which armed groups have controlled territory to the exclusion of the incumbent government. In doing so, the chapter illustrates a number of instances in which international law has been prepared to treat the conduct of armed groups as acts of the State in certain exceptional situations. In particular, the chapter finds authority for this idea in the case law from the Franco-Italian Conciliation Commission from the 1950s, Article 9 of the Articles on State Responsibility, case law from the General Claims Commission of 1923 between the United States and Mexico, and case law of the US Supreme Court. Recognizing that such a principle constitutes a major exception to the law on State responsibility, the chapter seeks to clarify the ambiguities and parameters of this case law in some depth. Finally, it examines what legal significance the reviewed legal authorities on State responsibility have to an examination of the legal *obligations* of armed groups. It considers this question from a substantive and procedural perspective. The chapter concludes by taking a longer perspective on its findings and their significance for wider legal debates.

89, 101–3 which reviews Security Council Resolutions referring to the armed group's control of territory.

[4] C. Tomuschat, 'The Applicability of Human Rights Law to Insurgent Movements' in H. Fischer et al. (eds), *Krisensicherung Und Humanitarer Schutz—Crisis Management and Humanitarian Protection: Festschrif Fur Dieter Fleck* (Berliner Wissenschafts-Verlag, Berlin 2004) 573–91 (hereafter Tomuschat, 'Insurgent Movements').

[5] See Chapters 4 and 6.

2. Principle of Effectiveness

On the basis that the principle of effectiveness is a recurring theme in this chapter, it is helpful to describe it briefly at the start. The principle of effectiveness was already identified in Chapter 7 as being a means of understanding how armed groups are bound by the obligations of the State.[6] In international law more generally, it derives from the larger principle *ut res magis valeat quam pereat*, i.e. the principle that a legal order must be efficacious to be valid.[7] The principle of effectiveness operates at two levels in the international legal order: micro and macro. At a micro level it refers specifically to the interpretation of international legal norms.[8] In particular, it refers to the notion that legal norms must be interpreted in a manner that best takes into account their object and purposes.[9] Although the principle of effectiveness is not referred to explicitly in the Vienna Convention on the Law of Treaties, it is often thought to be incorporated into Article 31(1) of the Vienna Convention which states that a treaty should be interpreted in 'good faith in accordance with the ordinary meaning to be given to the terms of the treaty in their context and in the light of its object and purpose'.[10] Yet it is argued that the principle of effectiveness is of most interest to this chapter at a macro level. Here, the principle of effectiveness is a restorative force on a legal order that has lost its effectiveness or is at risk of losing its effectiveness. Generally, one of the principal scenarios in which a legal order loses its effectiveness is where a schism emerges between the normative order and the facts on the ground.

2.1 Principle of effectiveness in the modern legal system

The macro principle of effectiveness is sometimes described as the principle of *ex factis jus oritur*.[11] This principle has been said to 'permeate' the structure of international law and to 'influence' it completely by 'systematically connecting the

[6] See section 6.2 of Chapter 7. Also, R. Pinto. 'Les Règles du Droit International Concernant La Guerre Civile' (1965) 114 Recueil des Courts 528, cited by J. Kleffner, 'The Applicability of International Humanitarian Law to Organized Armed Groups' (2011) 882 International Review of the Red Cross 443, 451 fn 33 (hereafter Kleffner, 'The applicability of international humanitarian law'). Pinto states: 'Au cours de la période de guerre civile, l'exécution des obligations conventionnelles relève du governement légal et de toute autorité qui prétend exercer et exerce un pouvoir, à ce titre, le droit inernational général et conventionnel. C'est là une conséquence du principe d'effectivité.'

[7] H. Kelsen, *General Theory of Law and State* (Harvard University Press, Cambridge 1949) 121.

[8] H. Lauterpacht, 'Restrictive Interpretation and the Principle of Effectiveness in the Interpretation of Treaties' (1949) 26 British Yearbook of International Law 48.

[9] See *Fisheries Jurisdiction (Spain v Canada) (Jurisdiction of the Court)* [1998] ICJ Reports 432, 4 December 1998, 455, where the ICJ stated that the principle of effectiveness has 'an important role in the law of treaties'.

[10] J. Pauwelyn, *Conflict of Norms in Public International Law* (CUP, Cambridge 2008) 248.

[11] This Latin phrase translates as 'the law arises from the facts'. The discussion in this paragraph owes much to Salvatore Zappalà's reflection on the role of effectiveness in world society today and its relationship with universal values. S. Zappalà, 'Can Legality Trump Effectiveness in Today's International Law' in A. Cassese, *Realizing Utopia: The Future of International Law* (OUP, Oxford 2012) 105–17.

world of law to its ability to display effects in the world of fact and vice versa'.[12] This description of the principle leads to the observation that the principle of effectiveness is connected to the theories of international legal personality which are represented by the 'actor' and 'individualistic' school of international legal personality explored in Chapter 3. Like both these theories, the principle of effectiveness gives priority to the 'actual', as well as the 'normative'. It represents an inquiry into actual and effective power, rather than formalities of legal norms. In doing so, the principle provides a tool to mend schisms between the normative order and factual reality. It is the means by which a normative order that is at risk of becoming ineffective may be made effective again. In the modern system of international law, it has been commented that the role of the principle of effectiveness has declined.[13] Indeed, Salvatore Zappalà notes in a thoughtful article on the topic that in the present day legal framework, more priority is given to notions of 'legitimacy, lawfulness, and legality', than to any 'factual element'.[14] Moreover, Zappalà argues that the emergence of a set of 'universal values' (e.g. the prohibition of the use of force, the principle of self-determination, the role of fundamental human rights) has created resistance to attempts to give priority to arguments of expediency over legality.[15] However, Zappalà also observes that when the principle of effectiveness and universal values are not in conflict they can sometimes be seen to work together to enable the international community to fix instances of misalignment between fact and law.[16] The truth of this observation is reflected in much of the legal authority reviewed below.

2.2 Principle of effectiveness and the human rights framework

In the light of the description above, it is clear that the principle of effectiveness is likely to be relevant when explaining how armed groups may be bound by human rights obligations in instances where they control territory. In instances where an armed group controls a portion of the territory of a country it becomes hard, if not impossible, for the *de jure* government to 'respect' human rights in that area of the State's territory.[17] Chapters 4 and 5 of the book have already demonstrated the problems which arise when a government is unable to enforce laws throughout its territory in relation to the legal frameworks of belligerency and insurgency. Chapters 2, 6 and 7 observed the same problems in the specific context of human rights law. Chapter 7 in particular demonstrated that in instances where a State is suffering violence at the hands of armed groups, it remains bound under human rights law to take reasonable measures to protect individuals in their territory from the acts of private actors.[18] According to the due diligence principle, a State is under the obligation to protect individuals from harmful acts by private

[12] Ibid, 105. [13] Ibid, 106. [14] Ibid, 106. [15] Ibid, 109.
[16] Ibid, 117.
[17] C. Ryngaert, 'Human Rights Obligations of Armed Groups' (2008) 2 Revue Belge de Droit International 355, 368 (hereafter Ryngaert, 'Human Rights Obligations of Armed Groups').
[18] This jurisprudence is reviewed in detail in Chapter 7.

individuals and has an obligation to investigate, prosecute, and punish the perpetrators and provide compensation to the victims of such harm.[19] Yet, like the due diligence principle in general public international law from which human rights due diligence principle partly originates, a State's efforts under human rights law are measured by what can 'reasonably' be expected from the State in the circumstances, and by 'result'.[20] As a result, a State will rarely be held responsible for its failure to exercise due diligence in relation to the conduct of armed groups in a territory beyond its control.

In such situations, it will be almost impossible for the government to protect individuals from the acts of armed groups. This practical reality is vividly illustrated below in a report written by the Special Rapporteur for Extrajudicial Killings after his visit to Sri Lanka in 2006. Here, the Special Rapporteur recounted:

> When I asked police officers why a particular killing had not been resolved, I generally received the same answer: the suspect escaped into an LTTE-controlled area ... it is true that the police are unable to enter these areas ... In September 2005, government police entered an LTTE-controlled area in Mannar in pursuit of a suspected paedophile. The police officers were captured by the LTTE, and three were still being held in early January 2006. In the meantime, the suspect escaped and was detained only when he turned himself in to the police in Colombo.[21]

This is a powerful account of the physical limitations of a government's abilities in circumstances where an armed group has control of the territory. If a government does not have effective control over a particular portion of its territory, its ability to protect individuals from harm or prosecute wrong-doers is severely compromised because its law enforcement officers are not able to physically enter the territory to take any action at all.[22]

The limitations of the due diligence principle under human rights law are also apparent in cases case where an armed group does not have control of the territory but is operating in difficult terrain where State structures are almost absent. This is illustrated in the Special Rapporteur for Extrajudicial Killings' Report on his return from the Democratic Republic of the Congo (DRC) in 2010. Here, the Special Rapporteur recounted the logistical constraints that the DRC government and United Nations Organization Mission in the Democratic Republic of

[19] See Chapter 7.

[20] See later in the chapter for an explanation of how the due diligence principle manifested itself in relation to a State's duties towards private actors in public international law. See also J.A. Hessbruegge, 'Human Rights Violations Arising from Conduct of Non-State Actors' (2005) Buffalo Human Rights Law Review 21, 30 (hereafter Hessbruegge, 'Violations from Conduct of Non-State Actors').

[21] Special Rapporteur on extrajudicial, summary or arbitrary killings, 'Report on Mission to Sri Lanka' (27 March 2006) UN Doc E/CN.4/2006/53/Add.5, [34].

[22] See also *Ilaşcu and Others v Moldova and Russia*, Application No. 48787/99 (ECHR, 8 July 2004) [339]. In this case, it was explained how a State's positive obligations with regard to territory outside its control will be distilled down to the obligation to take actions at diplomatic levels to secure the safety of the individuals within that territory. For example, at [347] the European Court of Human Rights recognized that it would have been 'ineffectual' for Moldova to try and investigate or prosecute members of the Transdniestrian regime who were living in Transdniestria or offences committed in Transdniestria.

the Congo (MONUC) faced in protecting civilians from the acts of the Lord's Resistance Army (LRA). The Special Rapporteur stated:

> I spoke with many humanitarian actors, UN and Government officials, and military commanders in Province Orientale. There is no doubt that effectively protecting civilians from the LRA is a daunting task. Many villages are remote and sometimes inaccessible without days of travel or the use of helicopters, and state presence through the region is negligible. Communication systems are poor or non-existent, and villagers must sometimes run for days to deliver warnings of impending, or news of on-going, LRA attacks. The LRA often conduct well-planned and sudden attacks, and the Government and MONUC face resource constraints that limit their capacity to have troops on the ground where needed, or to respond rapidly to attacks.[23]

These reports provide anecdotal 'real-life' accounts of how, in many instances, the due diligence principle is very quickly rendered incapable of providing any meaningful assistance to those seeking protection from the actions of armed groups. In such circumstances, the classic human rights law framework where the State, represented by the *de jure* government, is the duty-bearer, is at grave risk of becoming completely ineffective.

When an armed group controls territory, the local population faces severe risk of harm from an entity that, in international law terms, is treated as a private actor because of its status as a 'non-State actor'. Yet the government is unable to implement the State's obligations to 'protect' the individuals from the acts of that 'private actor'. As a result, when applying the classic human rights framework where the State is the only duty-bearer, a schism arises between the actual and the normative. While the armed group, the entity with power, has no obligations under the human rights framework, the State, the entity with the obligations, has no power to implement them. It is argued that it is in order to address this schism and in an effort to realign the actual and the normative that the international community has come to address armed groups directly. In doing so, it is seen how the practice of holding armed groups to account under human rights law is an example of the international community's willingness to give priority to effectiveness over strict legality. In identifying this pattern, the rest of the chapter investigates whether there are any legal precedents or rules which allow us to better understand the practice of holding armed groups bound by human rights law, in situations where they control territory, as a matter of law. If such precedents can be identified, the practice of UN accountability mechanisms reviewed in the book's introduction can be understood as a manifestation of a wider principle in international law that, when armed groups control territory to the exclusion of the *de jure* government, they can be addressed directly. The first step in this investigation is the law on State responsibility as set out in the Draft Articles on State Responsibility.[24]

[23] Special Rapporteur on Extrajudicial Killings, 'Report on Mission to the Democratic Republic of the Congo' (1 June 2010) UN Doc A/HRC/14/24/Add.3, 15 [55].

[24] ILC, Draft Articles on Responsibility of States for Internationally Wrongful Acts (9 August 2001) UN Doc A/56/83 (hereafter ILC Articles on State Responsibility) and Commentary.

3. Law on State Responsibility Regarding Armed Groups

3.1 General rule

Under the law on State responsibility, States are not generally responsible for the acts of armed groups.[25] This reflects the fact that a State is generally only responsible for the actions of its organs of government or for individuals who have acted under the direction, instigation, or control of those organs, i.e. 'agents' of the State. In an earlier draft of the Articles on State Responsibility, the principle that States are not responsible for the acts of armed groups was deemed so important that it was contained in an article in its own right.[26] However, in the final version of the Articles, the principle is relegated to the Commentary to Article 10. This states:

> The general principle in respect of the conduct of such movements, committed during the continuing struggle with the constituted authority, is that it is not attributable to the State under international law.[27]

Copious and unequivocal support for this principle is found in the jurisprudence of arbitral tribunals from the nineteenth and early twentieth century.[28]

In the nineteenth and early twentieth century, many mixed claims commissions were asked to consider the question of whether a parent State could be held responsible for damage or injury to foreign nations and foreign assets in times of riots, insurrection, and armed conflict.[29] In their conclusions, the arbitral tribunals repeatedly held that a State will not be held responsible for actions which are outside of its control and will only incur responsibility in relation to an insurrection if it is guilty of a breach of good faith or of negligence in suppressing the insurrection. Even in those situations, the tribunals repeatedly emphasized that the responsibility incurred by a State was not responsibility for the acts of the armed groups as such, but for the State's omission to provide due protection and vigilance in the particular circumstances.[30] Commenting on this case law, Special Rapporteur Ago clarified that damage caused by insurgents should be seen as 'nothing more than the external event which serves as a catalyst for the wrongfulness of that conduct [by the State]'.[31] In the multiple reports that were produced during the drafting of

[25] See the Commentary to Article 10 of the ILC Articles on State Responsibility (n 24) 50 [2].

[26] In an earlier draft of the Articles, this principle was stated explicitly. See draft Article 14 in ILC, Yearbook of the International Law Commission 1975 (5 May–25 July 1975) Vol II, UN Doc A/CN.4/SER.A/1975/Add.1, 91 (hereafter ILC Yearbook 1975 Vol II), which states: 'The conduct of an organ of an insurrectional movement which is established in the territory of a State or in any other territory under its administration, shall not be considered as an act of that State under international law.' See also Fourth Report on State Responsibility by Roberto Ago, Special Rapporteur, ILC, Yearbook of the International Law Commission 1972 (2 May–7 July 1972) Vol II, UN Doc A/CN.4/264 and Add. 1, 143 [192] (hereafter ILC Yearbook 1972 Vol II).

[27] See the Commentary to Article 10 of the ILC Articles on State Responsibility (n 24) 50 [2].

[28] For a review of these cases and State practice in this regard see ILC Yearbook 1975 Vol II (n 26) 94–7.

[29] See also ILC Yearbook 1972 Vol II (n 26) [90–135], [153–92].

[30] Ibid, [179].

[31] Ibid, [179].

the Articles on State Responsibility it was repeatedly recognized that a State would only very rarely incur due diligence responsibility for the violent conduct of armed groups.[32] The reports noted in this respect that arbitral case law on the issue from the nineteenth century made consistently clear that a State would generally only be held responsible for its failure to take action in respect of armed groups if its organs had been in a position to take appropriate preventive and punitive action but omitted to do so.[33]

3.2 Exceptions to general rule for armed groups

However, the Articles on State Responsibility recognize that there are several key exceptions to the rule that States are not responsible for the acts of armed groups.[34] The principal and most obvious exceptions in this regard are set out in Article 10. This article makes clear that States will be responsible for the conduct of: (i) insurgent groups which have been successful in their attempt to either take over the government of the country; or (ii) insurgent groups which have established a new State in part of the old State's territory.[35] Neither of these exceptions relate to the type of armed groups under examination in this study which is limited to an examination of those armed groups which are still engaged in *ongoing* non-international armed conflicts, whether against the government or another armed group. However, the paragraphs below will show that a good case can be made that a further exception to the general principle for armed groups is found in Article 9 of the Articles. Most significantly, the Commentary to Article 10 states that 'unsuccessful' insurrectional movements may be attributed to the State in the special circumstances envisaged by Article 9 of the Articles on State Responsibility. It states:

> In other words, the acts of unsuccessful insurrectional movements are not attributed to the State *unless* under some other article of Chapter II, *for example in the special circumstances envisaged by article 9.* (emphasis added)[36]

The Commentary does not make clear how the term 'unsuccessful armed group' should be defined. Yet there is a suggestion in the Commentary that it was intended to counter the concept of a 'successful' armed group in Article 10. If so, the term 'unsuccessful armed group' in the Commentary to Article 10 can be read as including acts of armed groups which are still engaged in a continuing struggle with the *de jure* government and the acts of armed groups which have been defeated and no

[32] Ibid, [153]. [33] Ibid, 135 [167].

[34] The due diligence principle is not strictly seen as an 'exception' to this principle as the State is not found responsible for the conduct of the armed group per se but its failure to exercise due diligence with regard to that conduct.

[35] Article 10(1) states that the conduct of an armed group may be considered an act of State under international law in instances where the armed group becomes the new Government of that State. Article 10 (2) states that the conduct of a movement, insurrectional or other, which succeeds in establishing a new State in part of the territory of a pre-existing State or in a territory under its administration shall be considered an act of the new State under international law.

[36] See Commentary to Article 10 of the ILC Articles on State Responsibility (n 24) 50 [2].

longer exist.[37] Crucially, the statement that the acts of 'unsuccessful insurrectional movements' can fall under Article 9 constitutes a specific acknowledgement that the acts of armed groups that do not succeed in usurping the *de jure* government may sometimes also be considered an 'act of State' for the purposes of State responsibility. On the basis that this principle constitutes a major exception to the general rule that States will not be responsible for the acts of armed groups, it is explored in more detail below.[38]

3.3 Closer analysis of Article 9

In order to examine the significance of the statement in the Commentary to Article 10 it is first important to look more closely at the text and scope of Article 9 of the Articles on State Responsibility. Article 9 states:

> The conduct of a person or group of persons shall be considered an act of a State under international law if the person or group of persons is in fact exercising elements of the governmental authority in the absence or default of the official authorities and in circumstances such as to call for the exercise of those elements of authority.

The words of the article indicate that three conditions must be met for the conduct to fall within the scope of Article 9: (i) the person or group must be in fact exercising elements of governmental authority; (ii) in the absence of default of the official authorities; and (iii) in circumstances such as to call for the exercise of those elements of authority. While more attention to these three criteria will be given later in this section, it is helpful to first make some general comments about Article 9's scope. Research into the drafting of the article shows that Article 9 was intended to deal with a very 'exceptional' situation under international law.[39] It

[37] This can be gleaned from a comparison of the word 'unsuccessful' with the concept articulated in Article 10. The observation that the term 'unsuccessful' could refer to armed groups that are engaged in an 'continuing struggle' with the *de jure* government and those who have been defeated is derived from a study of the sentence in combination with the sentence that precedes it: 'The general principle in respect of the conduct of such movements, committed *during the continuing struggle with the constituted authority*, is that it is not attributable to the State under international law. In other words, the acts of unsuccessful insurrectional movements are not attributable to the State, unless under some other article of chapter II, for example in the special circumstances envisaged by article 9' (emphasis added). See ibid.

[38] The longest previous discussion of the application of Article 9 to armed groups is found in T. Ruys, 'Crossing the Thin Blue Line: An Inquiry into Israel's Recourse to Self-Defense against Hezbollah' (2007) 43 Stanford Journal of International Law 265, 285–90 (hereafter Ruys, 'Crossing the Thin Blue Line'). For further shorter mentions of the potential of Article 9 to address the acts of armed groups, see V. Bílková, 'Establishing Direct Responsibility of Armed Opposition Groups for Violations of International Humanitarian Law' in Ryngaert (ed), *Responsibilities of the Non-State Actor in Armed Conflict and the Market Place* (Brill, Leiden 2015) 269 (hereafter Bílková, 'Establishing Direct Responsibility'); Ryngaert, 'Human Rights Obligations of Armed Groups' (n 17) 361; S. Sivakumaran, 'Torture in International Human Rights and International Humanitarian Law' (2005) 18 Leiden Journal of International Law 541, 551; R. McCorquodale and R. La Forgia, 'Taking Off the Blindfolds: Torture by Non-State Actors' (2001) 2 Human Rights Law Review 189, 213–14 (hereafter McCorquodale and La Forgia, 'Taking Off the Blindfolds'); Hessbruegge, 'Violations from Conduct of Non-State Actors' (n 20) 62–3.

[39] Commentary to Article 9 of the ILC Articles on State Responsibility (n 24) 49 [1].

was included in the Articles on State Responsibility to deal with circumstances in which persons who are not State officials are required to perform State functions, as a result of the exigencies of the situation.[40] It is stated in the Article's Commentary that Article 9 owes something to the old idea of the '*levée en masse*' and is 'a form of agency of necessity'.[41] The Commentary to Article 9 also states that the situations in which Article 9 will be invoked will only occur rarely, for example 'during revolution, armed conflict or foreign occupation, where the regular authorities dissolve, are disintegrating, have been suppressed or are for the time being inoperative'.[42]

Indeed in order to convey an idea of the circumstances in which Article 9 might be invoked, it is helpful to restate some of the specific factual examples cited by the Special Rapporteur in previous discussions of the article[43] and cited in the Commentary to an earlier version of the article.[44] These include the instances early in the Second World War when local administrations fled before the invading German army. They also include instances later in the Second World War when occupying administrations fled before the liberating Allied Forces. In such situations, the drafters of Article 9 noted that private individuals or groups of individuals sometimes filled the administrative void that was created by the fleeing government by taking over government functions on their own initiative. The Commentary also cites instances where committees of private persons provisionally took charge of an area's administration in these circumstances, issuing ordnances, performing legal acts, administering property, or pronouncing judgments.[45] Furthermore, it notes that private persons are sometimes driven to assume military functions in default of the national army. Examples of this include local residents taking up arms to defend a town (*levée en masse*) or the decision of the Paris taxi-drivers in the First World War to assume the function of auxiliaries to the regular armed forces.[46] In his fourth report Special Rapporteur Ago also mentions that Article 9 might be relevant in the circumstances of a major natural disaster. In such a situation, the Special Rapporteur noted, the local people might have to take over the exercise of some of the prerogatives of public power, e.g. police or health services. This had occurred in parts of Italy after the Messina earthquake in 1908.[47] Having introduced the general context of the article, it is now necessary to see how Article 9 might apply to the acts of armed groups; a question that until now remains little explored in legal doctrine.[48]

[40] See ILC, Yearbook of the International Law Commission 1974 (6 May–26 July 1974) Vol I, UN Doc A/CN.4/SER.A/1974, 32 [3] (hereafter ILC Yearbook 1974 Vol I).

[41] Commentary to Article 9 of the ILC Articles on State Responsibility (n 24) 49 [2].

[42] Ibid, [1].

[43] See ILC Yearbook 1974 Vol I (n 40) 32–3.

[44] See ILC, Yearbook of the International Law Commission 1974 (6 May–26 July 1974) Vol II, UN Doc A/CN.4/SER.A/1974/Add.1 (Part One), 283–6 (hereafter ILC Yearbook 1974 Vol II).

[45] Ibid, 285 [9].

[46] ILC Yearbook 1974 Vol I (n 40) 32–3, 32 [5].

[47] Ibid, 32 [5]; ILC Yearbook 1974 Vol II (n 44) 285 [9].

[48] See (n 38) for commentators who have commented on the potential for Article 9 to apply to armed groups. Notably, Ruys, 'Crossing the Thin Blue Line' (n 38) 287 comments that 'much, unfortunately, remains unclear with regard to the principles governing this type of situation'.

3.3.1 The application of Article 9 to armed groups

Somewhat frustratingly despite the Commentary to Article 10 stating that Article 9 can apply to armed groups, the Commentary to Article 9 does not mention this possibility again. Yet, it can be noted that the idea that Article 9 might apply to armed groups was mentioned by International Law Commission member Mr Ramangasoavina during one of the Commission's many discussions of Article 9. Mr Ramangasoavina stated:

> If the insurrectional movement failed, but it was subsequently found that some of its acts had been carried out in the interests of the community, then those acts–if internationally wrongful–must engage the State's responsibility under Article 8 [now Article 9].[49]

The fact that there is no record of any members of the Commission disagreeing with Mr Ramangasoavina is an indication that his comment was not considered unreasonable.[50] However in earlier drafts of the Articles, Special Rapporteur Ago, who worked closest on the draft Articles relating to insurrectional groups, explicitly dismissed the possibility that a State could ever be responsible for the acts of armed groups.[51] His rationale in this respect was that whenever an armed group becomes an entity of international law in its own right, it will rather incur its own responsibility under international law.[52] Noting this contradiction as troubling, this chapter notes that at the time the Articles were finalized in 2001, the Commentary to Article 10 explicitly contemplates that the acts of 'unsuccessful armed groups' might fall under Article 9.[53] It also notes that Ago's comments were restricted to instances in which armed groups caused *harm* to assets and people. This type of damage is far from the sort of quasi governmental acts which are contemplated by Article 9.

[49] ILC Yearbook 1974 Vol I (n 40) 37 [8].

[50] Another indication that armed groups can fall under Article 9 is also found in the Commentary to Article 5 of the Articles which relates to parastatal entities, i.e. entities empowered by internal law to exercise governmental authority. The Commentary to Article 5 takes pains to distinguish situations covered by Article 5 from situations in which an 'entity or group seizes power in the absence of State organs but in situations where the exercise of governmental authority is called for'. In making this distinction, the Commentary to Article 5 affirms, that the latter situation will be covered by Article 9 of the Articles. The reference to an entity or group 'seizing power' in the Commentary to Article 5 seems to support the possible application of Article 9 to armed groups. See Commentary to Article 5 of the ILC Articles on State Responsibility (n 24) 43 [7].

[51] See ILC Yearbook 1975 Vol II (n 26) 98 [26]; ILC Yearbook 1972 Vol II (n 26) 142 [186].

[52] Special Rapporteur Ago's view on this is evidenced in draft Article 14 of the Articles which was later deleted. This stated: '(1) The conduct of an organ of an insurrectional movement, which is established in the territory of a State or in any other territory under its administration, shall not be considered as an act of that State under international law (2) Paragraph 1 is without prejudice to the attribution to a State of any other conduct which is related to that of the organ of the insurrectional movement and which is to be considered as an act of that State by virtue of articles 5 to 10 (3) Similarly, paragraph 1 is without prejudice to the attribution of the conduct of the organ of the insurrectional movement to that movement in any case in which such attribution may be made under international law.' See ILC Yearbook 1975 Vol II (n 26) 98, 91–106.

[53] The decision to introduce this phrase into the Commentary was made in May 2001. See ILC, 'Summary Record of the 2681st Meeting' (29 May 2001) UN Doc A/CN.4/SR.2681, 94 [32]. The phrase was inserted in response to a comment by The Netherlands that Article 10, when read with Article 9 (then Article 7) implied that all acts of unsuccessful insurrectional groups could be attributable to the State. The Drafting Committee confirmed that this would not be the case, unless the State was responsible under some other Article in chapter II, for example Article 9. Indeed, the question

3.3.1.1 Functions must be 'governmental' in nature

Taking this Commentary to Article 10 at face value, it would appear that the Commentary to Article 9 can then be taken as containing important guidance about when the conduct of armed groups may be treated as State acts. In doing so, the Commentary provides guidance on the location of the dividing line between the core principle that States are generally not responsible for private actors and the principle that in some exceptional circumstances States may incur responsibility for the acts of private actors. Indeed, it was noted already in section 3.3 of this chapter that the Commentary confirms that three conditions must be met for the conduct of a person or group of individuals exercising elements of the governmental authority to be considered an 'act of State under international law'. The Commentary states:

> First, the conduct must effectively relate to the exercise of the governmental authority, secondly, the conduct must have been carried out in the absence or default of the official authorities, and thirdly, the circumstances must have been such as to call for the exercise of those elements of authority.[54]

With relation to the first condition, the Commentary makes clear that the persons must be exercising some kind of function which is 'governmental' in nature. In its earlier discussions of the article, the International Law Commission provides examples of activities which might be included within this category. These include the assumption of military duties in support of the government, the exercise of policing roles, the issuance of judgments and ordnances, the performance of legal acts, the taking charge of administration, the provision of health services, or the administration of property.[55] It is important to note that such governmental actions are significantly different in character from the type of ravaging and wrecking actions by armed groups which lies at the heart of the copious case law establishing the general principle that States are generally not responsible for the *damage* to persons or objects caused by armed groups, in the course of their insurrection.[56]

3.3.1.2 Functions must be performed in the absence of or default of the government

Expounding on the second condition, the Commentary states that the phrase 'in the absence of or default of' in Article 9 was intended to cover the situations of a 'total collapse of State apparatus' as well as cases where 'the official authorities are not exercising their functions in some specific respect, for instance, in the case of a partial collapse of the State or its loss of control over a certain locality'.[57] The Commentary also contains the clarification that Article 9 does apply to entities

from the Netherlands was explicitly drafted in such a way to imply a view that Article 9 applied to unsuccessful insurrectional groups. See The Netherlands comments on Article 10, 'Comments and Observations Received from Governments' (3 April 2001) UN Doc A/CN.4/515 and Add.1-3, 50.

[54] Commentary to Article 9 of the ILC Articles on State Responsibility (n 24) 49 [3].

[55] See ILC Yearbook 1974 Vol I (n 40) 32 [5]; ILC Yearbook 1974 Vol II (n 44) 285 [9].

[56] See n 28.

[57] See the Commentary to Article 9 of the ILC Articles on State Responsibility (n 24) 49 [5].

which constitute 'general *de facto* government[s]'. The Commentary clarifies that such entities will be better treated as State organs under Article 4 of the Articles on State Responsibility.[58] It elaborates further:

> the cases envisaged by article 9 presuppose the existence of a Government in office and of State machinery whose place is taken by irregulars or whose action is supplemented in certain cases. This may happen on part of the territory of a State which is for the time being out of control, or in other specific circumstances. A general de facto Government, on the other hand, is itself an apparatus of the State, replacing that which existed previously.

It is not exactly clear what the Commission meant by 'general *de facto* governments' but earlier Commentary suggests that it was referring to a government that completely 'replaced' the previous government as a result of a *coup d'état*, military defeat, or total State failure.[59] The Commission was of the view that any 'general *de facto* Government' emerging out of the ashes of the previous government in these scenarios would be better covered by either Article 4 of the Articles or possibly Article 10.[60] In making this distinction, it can be concluded that Article 9 can apply to the acts of a *local de facto* government set up by an insurgent group, existing contemporaneously with the legal government, and controlling territory in the absence of that government.

3.3.1.3 Circumstances must have been such 'to call for the exercise of elements of the governmental authority by private person'

The third condition set out in the Commentary requires that the circumstances must have been such 'to call for the exercise of elements of the governmental authority by private persons'. The Commentary elaborates:

> The term 'call for' conveys the idea that some exercise of governmental functions was called for, though not necessarily the conduct in question. In other words, the circumstances surrounding the exercise of elements of the governmental authority by private persons must have justified the attempt to exercise police or other functions in the absence of any constituted authority.[61]

[58] Article 4(1) states: 'The conduct of any State organ shall be considered an act of that State under international law, whether the organ exercises legislative, executive, judicial or any other functions, whatever position it holds in the organization of the State, and whatever its character as an organ of the central Government or of a territorial unit of the State.' Article 4(2) states: 'An organ includes any person or entity which has that status in accordance with the internal law of the State.'

[59] It is noteworthy in this regard that the Commentary to an earlier version of this Article states: 'A de facto government, on the other hand, is itself a State apparatus which has replaced the State machinery that exited previously. The term "de facto government" or "general de facto" government is sometimes used to denote a government which, though not invested with power in accordance with the previously established constitutional forms, has fully and finally taken power, the previous government having disappeared.' See ILC Yearbook 1974 Vol II (n 44) 286 [12].

[60] See Commentary to Article 9 of the ILC Articles on State Responsibility (n 24) 49 [4]. The same result is reached by reliance on Article 10(1). It is observed that Article 10(1) is simply a reinforcement of the fact that Article 4 will apply to a new government of a State which is comprised of an entity which was previously an insurgency.

[61] See Commentary to Article 9 of the ILC Articles on State Responsibility (n 24) 49 [6].

Crucially, the Commentary then goes on to say:

There is thus a normative element in the form of agency entailed by article 9, and this distinguishes these situations from the normal principle that conduct of private parties, including insurrectionary forces, is not attributable to the State.[62]

While the Commentary indicates that this 'normative' element will be of principal assistance in identifying the dividing line between armed groups treated purely as 'private actors' and armed groups whose acts are capable of incurring State responsibility, its brevity leaves considerable uncertainty about what this 'normative element' may refer to.[63]

It has been suggested that this normative requirement can only be met by an armed opposition group seeking to re-establish public order when it has not been implicated in having caused the State 'default' in the first place, because such a group lacks a *bona fide* attitude.[64] Although frustratingly, the drafting records of Article 9 do not provide guidance on this point, they also do not provide support for the notion that a *bona fide* attitude was necessarily what was meant by the 'normative element' mentioned in the Commentary. Instead, it is argued that it seems more likely that the words 'call for' seem to simply require recourse to determining whether the exercise of governance was objectively necessary in the circumstances. Indeed, the application of a *bona fide* test would be hard to apply in reality to armed groups because it would be difficult to measure which party to a non-international armed conflict was to blame for the absence of the *de jure* government in a particular location, at any given moment. In a similar vein, it has been argued that Article 9 will only apply to armed groups which are tolerated by the government, rather than armed *opposition* groups as such, e.g. the Revolutionary Guards in the immediate aftermath of the revolution in Iran.[65] Yet it is argued that the necessity of such a condition is not borne out in the Commentary which explicitly uses the adjective 'insurrectional' to describe the movements that can sometimes fall within the scope of Article 9.[66] Further analysis of this position is given at section 9.3 below.

3.3.2 Article 9 applies to certain acts of certain armed groups and not armed groups per se

In the light of these conclusions, it is argued that the Commentary to Article 9 suggests that the factors which will be relevant to determining whether the acts of an armed group may be treated as an act of a State include: the nature of the act committed by the armed group; (ii) the position of the incumbent government in

[62] Ibid.
[63] Ruys, 'Crossing the Thin Blue Line' (n 38) 289, calls this the 'vaguest of the three criteria'.
[64] Bílková, 'Establishing Direct Responsibility' (n 38) 269.
[65] Eatwell, T, 'State Responsibility and the Conduct of Armed Group Governors', paper on file with author
[66] See Commentary to Article 10 of the Articles on State Responsibility (n 24).

the factual context; and (ii) whether the situation required some exercise of government function, although not necessarily the conduct in question. Crucially, the Commentary suggests that Article 9 of the Articles should be understood to apply to 'distinct acts' rather than 'distinct entities'.[67] In other words, the Commentary indicates that Article 9 should not be understood as applying to specific armed groups per se but rather should be understood as applying to certain acts of certain armed groups. Such an approach is supported by the wording of the heading to Article 9 which states that the Article applies to '*conduct* carried out in the absence or default of the official authorities' (emphasis added). It is also supported by Commentary which states that when considering whether a person or group is performing governmental functions 'the nature of the activity performed [should be] given more weight than the existence of a formal link between the actors and the organisation of the State'.[68] According to this line of thinking, only some of the acts of a particular armed group can be attributed to the State. Having demonstrated in the paragraphs above that Article 9 provides support for the idea that the acts of armed groups may, in some circumstances, be considered acts of State, the following section of the chapter continues by reviewing a further series of cases that can be read to support and clarify this idea.

4. Case Law from the General Claims Commission of 1923 between the United States and Mexico

When considering the idea that some acts by an armed group may be considered to be acts of State, it is noteworthy that a similar argument was made by Silvanie and other legal scholars in the 1930s. Silvanie argued that international law requires acts of insurgents to be treated differently depending on whether they are acts of 'government routine' or acts of a revolutionary government in its personal character.[69] In his book *Responsibility of States for Acts of Unsuccessful Insurgent Governments*, Silvanie relied upon a line of case law from the General Claims Commission of 1923 between the United States and Mexico and also cases from the Supreme Court of the United States after the American Civil War.[70] The first line of case law arose out of instances in which the United States requested the government of Mexico to abide by contracts signed by the revolutionary Huerta government, which had taken control of large swathes of Mexico for a period of months in 1913

[67] This seems contrary to the approach taken by Ruys, 'Crossing the Thin Blue Line' (n 38) 289

[68] See Commentary to Article 9 of the ILC Articles on State Responsibility (n 24) 49 [4].

[69] See fairly strong criticism of these authorities in the Fourth Report on State Responsibility by Roberto Ago, Special Rapporteur, ILC Yearbook 1972 Vol II (n 26) 142. Ago states that similar ideas are found in writings by Reuter, Schwarzenberger, and O'Connell. Yet in dismissing Silvanie's argument Special Rapporteur Ago states that Silvanie does not cite a 'single case' in support of this argument. This is not the case as is shown below.

[70] H. Silvanie, *Responsibility of States for Acts of Unsuccessful Insurgent Governments* (Colombia University Press, London 1939) (hereafter Silvanie, *Insurgent Governments*).

and 1914.[71] In response to these claims, the General Claims Commission adopted a position which is broadly in line with the legal principles reflected in Article 9 of the Articles on State Responsibility. The General Claims Commission stated that the acts of the Huerta insurgents could bind the Mexican State, but only in instances where it had been exercising functions related to the administration of impersonal government. In other words, it argued that a distinction needed to be made between acts of a revolutionary administration in its personal character and acts of purely government routine.[72]

4.1 Differentiation necessary between personal and impersonal conduct

The General Claims Commission continued to explain that if the Huerta administration had had control over more or less the whole of the country at the time under consideration, the State would have been bound by all its acts, irrespective of whether they were personal or impersonal. Its statement in this regard can be compared to the Commentary to Article 9's conclusion regarding 'general *de facto* governments' above. It reflects the observation that in instances where an armed group is the sole entity exercising governmental functions in a territory, and has instituted an entirely new government structure, its conduct will be better treated under either Article 4 or 10(1) of the Articles on State Responsibility. The General Claims Commission continued that at the times when the Huerta administration had a less than complete control over the country, its acts of a personal nature would not ordinarily bind the nation.[73] In other words, in instances where an armed group only had partial control over the State's territory, the General Claims Commission found it necessary to distinguish between its 'personal' and 'impersonal' conduct. Again, this is similar to the approach evidenced in Article 9 when applied to armed groups. It holds that the conduct of an armed group will only be considered an act of State, in instances where it is: (i) governmental in nature; and

[71] On 18 February 1913, General José Victoriana Huerta Márquez declared himself to be the provisional president of Mexico and shortly afterwards compelled the President and Vice President to tender their resignations. Huerta forced the provisional acting president to appoint him to the position of ranking minister in office and then forced him too to resign. During the second half of February, March, and April 1913, Huerta had control over nearly the whole of the country. Between January to July 1914, Huerta's power diminished rapidly. The postal money orders which formed the subject of the *Hopkins* case were purchased by the claimant between April 1914 and June 1913. At this time, control of the country was split between Carranza, as First Chief of the Constitutional Army and Huerta. See facts set out in *George W. Hopkins (U.S.A.) v United Mexican States* (Reports of International Arbitral Awards, 31 March 1926) 42–51, 42, 45–6.

[72] Ibid, 43.

[73] The General Claims Commission stated in this regard (Ibid, 45): 'The binding force of such acts of the Huerta administration as partook of the personal character as contradistinguished from the Government itself will depend upon its real control and paramountcy at the time of the act over a major portion of the territory and a majority of the people of Mexico ... Even while still in possession of the capital and therefore dominating the foreign office, the treasure, and Mexico's representatives abroad, its acts of a personal nature could not ordinarily bind the nation from the moment it apparently was no longer the real master of the nation.'

(ii) called for by the absence of the *de jure* government combined with the people's need for governance.

4.1.1 Impersonal government function

In explaining its view, the General Claims Commission touched on several similar elements to those raised in the Commentary of Article 9. In order to shed light on its approach, it is helpful to cite from the *George W. Hopkins (U.S.A) v United Mexican States* (the *Hopkins* case) in full. Here the Commission found:

> The greater part of governmental machinery in every modern country is not affected by changes in the higher administrative offices. The sale of postage stamps, the registration of letters, the acceptance of money orders and telegrams (where post and telegraph are government services), the sale of railroad tickets (where railroads are operated by the government), the registration of births, deaths, and marriages, even many rulings by the police and the collection of several types of taxes, go on, *and must go on*, without being affected by new elections, government crises, dissolutions of parliament, and even state strokes. A resident in Mexico who cleans the government bureaus or pays his school fee to the administration does not and cannot take into consideration the regularity or even legality of the present administration and the present congress; his business is not with personal rules, not one with a specific administration, but one with the government itself in its unpersonal aspect.
>
> The difficulty of distinguishing between the government itself and the administration of that government arises at the point where the voluntary dealings and relations between the individual and the government agencies assume a personal character in support of the particular agencies administering the government for the time being. To this class belong *voluntary undertakings to provide a revolutionary administration with money or arms or munitions and the like*. But the ordinary agencies, departments and bureaus of the government must continue to function notwithstanding its principal administrative offices may be in the hands of usurper, and in such a case the sale and delivery to these necessary and legitimate agencies of supplies, merchandise, and the like, to enable the government itself in its unpersonal aspect to function is a very different transaction from *one having for its object the support of an individual or group of individuals seeking to maintain themselves in office*. The character of each transaction must be judged and determined by the facts of the particular case (emphasis added).[74]

It is can be seen in this regard that the General Claims Commission took the view that some of the acts of the Huerta administration could be treated as acts of State and some could not. In coming to this conclusion, the Commission was persuaded by the notion that some elements of administration of government are purely functional and necessary for life to go on in a particular area of the country.

The General Claims Commission's comments point to the fact that the force of human life is, in many ways, much stronger than the authorities that control it. This was commented on at length in Chapter 2 and was referred to as the 'life-goes-on-driver'.[75] In addition, the General Claims Commission identifies the fungibility of

[74] Ibid, [44–5], cited by Silvanie, *Insurgent Governments* (n 70) 84–5.

[75] See section 3.2.3.2(a) of Chapter 2.

some aspects of government administration in times of non-international armed conflict. The Commission expressed the view that it may be more important to the people on the ground that certain public services continues to exist, than that they are provided by specific entities. The General Claims Commission also indicates that the fungible nature of the service-provider and the continuity of the service itself are important aspects in determining whether particular conduct is personal or impersonal. In circumstances, where an insurgent group utilizes mechanisms or structures which are already in existence, the Claims Commission suggests that its conduct in will be more likely to be seen to be 'impersonal' in nature. The Claims Commission also touches on the same notion of 'necessity' which is reflected in the 'normative' aspect of the Commentary to Article 9. The Claims Commission refers to the fact that the provision of certain services, *inter alia*, the sale of postage stamps, the registration of births, deaths, and marriages, many rulings by the police, and the collection of several types of taxes '*must* go on' in times of non-international armed conflict. Moreover, the Commission found the fact that certain services are necessary or inevitable to be a useful indicator in a determination of whether the conduct under examination is 'personal' or 'impersonal'.

4.1.2 Personal government function

The General Claims Commission countered these characteristics of fungiblity, continuity, and necessity with the idea that some other acts conducted by an insurgent group are entirely directed at maintaining its power dominance over the territory. These relate to the armed group's military struggle against the incumbent government. In other words, rather than relating to 'the government itself in its unpersonal aspect', the armed group's 'personal' acts have for their 'object the support of an individual or group or individuals seeking to maintain themselves in office'.[76] In conducting a review of the Claims Commission's jurisprudence, Silvanie observed that the Commission did not find any of the acts that it examined to be the 'so-called acts of an unsuccessful revolutionary administration in its *personal character*'.[77] The Commission did, however state, that examples of such 'personal' acts might include the borrowing of money and purchase of arms and munitions in furtherance of the rebellion.[78] In identifying these acts, it was clear that the General Claims Commission sought to distinguish acts of impersonal governance by an armed group from those acts which were intricately linked to the Huerta regime's military identity and campaign against the Mexican government.

4.1.3 Doubtful zone between personal and impersonal

In developing a bifurcated approach to the conduct of the Huerta insurgency, the General Claims Commission recognized that there was a 'large doubtful zone' of actions which did not fall easily into either of the two categories set out above. The

[76] Ibid. [77] Silvanie, *Insurgent Governments* (n 70) 87. [78] Ibid.

difficulty of categorizing acts which fell into the 'doubtful zone' was demonstrated when the Commission had to consider whether the purchase of two ambulances by the Chief of the Military Section of the Huerta government at the order of the Department of War and Navy constituted the purchase of 'war material' or the act of the government 'as an abstract entity in its unpersonal aspect'.[79] Here, both parties relied on the principles of law set out in the *Hopkins* case cited above but disagreed as to whether the purchase of the ambulances had been 'personal' or 'impersonal' in character. The Mexican government argued that the ambulances constituted 'war material' purchased by the Huerta regime. The US government argued that the purchase of ambulances had been an impersonal act which should be binding upon the Mexican State. It is clear from the judgment that the question posed the Commissioners considerable difficulty. Indeed the Presiding Commissioner stated that, in his view, the purchase of ambulances by the Huerta regime fell into the 'doubtful zone'.[80] Despite this, the Commissioners concluded that the purchase of ambulances had been an act of impersonal government. Ultimately, the Commissioners were persuaded by the fact that it was harder to categorize the purchase of ambulances as an act designed to support the Heurta regime, than an act of impersonal government. [81] When seeking to determine where this 'dividing line' should be placed, the paragraphs below show that it is also instructive to turn to the case law from the American Civil War which articulates similar ideas and is similarly helpful in achieving a better understanding of the principles contained in Article 9 of the Articles on State Responsibility.

5. Case Law from the American Civil War

The second line of case law which Silvanie draws attention to also supports the principle that certain acts of unsuccessful governments can bind the State. This line of case law is of a national, rather than international, in character. It is the case law from the Supreme Court of the United States which arose after the conclusion of the Civil War. Here, the US Supreme Court was asked to decide what effect should be given to the various acts of the Confederate Government and the separate governments of the revolting States, during the Civil War. In reviewing this case law, Silvanie noted that as a result of the formal division of power between the Confederate Government and the individual revolting States, the Confederate Government's activities were almost exclusively military and related almost solely to its rebellion against the United States. As a result, the Confederate Government had almost no involvement in acts of 'government routine'.[82] According to the US Supreme Court, the Confederate Government was 'simply the military

[79] *The Peerless Motor Car Company (U.S.A.) v United Mexican States* (Reports of International Arbitral Awards, 13 May 1927) 203–5, 204.

[80] Ibid. [81] Ibid. [82] Silvanie, *Insurgent Governments* (n 70) 99.

representative of the insurrection against the authority of the United States'.[83] In Silvanie's view, it was this finding that caused the US Supreme Court to conclude that none of the Confederate Government's actions could be held to have created binding obligations on the State in international law terms.

When examining the conduct of the individual revolting States, as opposed to the Confederate Government, the US Supreme Court's conclusions were very different. Here, the US Supreme Court remarked that in many of the revolting States, 'the same constitutions, the same laws for the protection of property and personal rights remained, and were administered by the same officers'.[84] As a result, in order to determine whether the acts of the separate States were binding upon the nation, the US Supreme Court found that it was necessary to make a distinction between: (i) 'acts necessary to peace and good order among citizens, such, for example, as acts sanctioning and protecting marriage and the domestic relations, governing the course of descents, regulating the conveyance and transfer of property, real and personal, and providing remedies for injuries to person and estate, and other similar acts, which would be valid if emanating from a lawful government'; and (ii) 'acts in furtherance or support of rebellion against the United States, or intended to defeat the just rights of citizens, and other acts of like nature'.[85] While the Supreme Court found the former type of actions would be binding on the State as such, it found that the latter type would not.[86]

The US Supreme Court elaborated its approach most clearly in the case of *Horn v Lockhart* where it stated:

> We admit that the acts of the several States in their individual capacities, and of their different departments of government, executive, judicial, and legislative, during the war, so far as they did not impair or tend to impair the supremacy of the national authority, or the just rights of citizens under the Constitution, are in general, to be treated as valid and binding. The existence of a state of insurrection and war did not loosen the bonds of society, or do away with civil government, or the regular administration of the laws. Order was to be preserved, police regulations maintained, crime prosecuted, property protected, contracts enforced, marriages celebrated, estates settled, and the transfer and descent of property regulated precisely as in time of peace. No one that we are aware of seriously questions the validity of judicial or legislative acts in the insurrectionary States touching these and kindred subjects, where *they were not hostile in their purpose or mode of enforcement to the authority of the National Government, and did not impair the rights of citizens under the Constitution* (emphasis added).[87]

[83] *Thorington v Smith*, 75 US [8 Wallace] (1868) 1, 9, cited by Silvanie, *Insurgent Governments* (n 70) 98.

[84] Ibid.

[85] *Texas v White*, 74 US [7 Wallace] (1969) 700, cited by Silvanie, *Insurgent Governments* (n 70) 100.

[86] It is noteworthy that the US Supreme Court's finding that acts intended to defeat the rights of citizens could not be considered binding on the US government is contrary to the argument made below that there is no need to consider whether an armed group's act is qualitatively appropriate or in the interests of the citizens in question.

[87] *Horn v Lockhart*, 84 US [17 Wallace] (1873) 570, cited by Silvanie, *Insurgent Governments* (n 70) 100.

In doing so, the US Supreme Court also advocated an approach whereby the acts of an armed group are divided into those which 'aid the rebellion' and those which are 'done in the ordinary course of governmental routine'.[88] The US Supreme Court found that acts falling into the second category *could* be held to be acts of the nation State whereas those which fell into the first category *could not*. In clarifying the scope of the first category of acts, the US Supreme Court said that 'all the enactments of the *de facto* legislatures in the insurrectionary States during the war, which were not hostile to the Union, or the authority of the general government, and which were not in conflict with the Constitution of the United States, or of the States, have the same validity as if they had been enactments of legitimate legislatures'.[89] The approach of the US Supreme Court reveals an application of similar principles of law to those found in the case law from the General Claims Commission of 1923 and Article 9 of the Articles on State Responsibility discussed above.

6. ICJ Namibia Principle and European Court of Human Rights Jurisprudence

6.1 ICJ found conventions of a humanitarian character to be an exception to non-recognition rule

One of the core ideas which emerges from the sources reviewed above is that when one subject of international law unlawfully exercises impersonal powers of government within the territory of another State in default of that State's *de jure* government, its acts may be considered an act of the territorial State. Moreover the case law above demonstrates that a court's willingness to give effect to the actions of an unlawful entity is particularly apparent where the resulting realignment of the actual and the normative furthers universal values. In the cases before the General Claims Commission and the US Supreme Court, the recognition of the insurgent acts gave 'effect' to acts related to civil administration and the protection of individual rights. Interestingly, support for the wider principle on which this case law is based can also be found in the ICJ's 1971 Advisory Opinion on the continued illegal presence of South Africa in Namibia.[90] The question before the ICJ was the effect of Security Council Resolution 276(1970) which stated that because the continued presence of the South African authorities in Namibia was illegal, all acts taken by the Government of South Africa on behalf of or concerning Namibia should be treated by third States as being illegal and invalid.[91] In its Advisory

[88] Silvanie, *Insurgent Governments* (n 70) 101.
[89] *United States v Insurance Companies*, 89 US [22 Wallace] (1874) 99.
[90] *Advisory Opinion on Legal Consequences for State of the Continued Presence of South Africa in Namibia (South West Africa) notwithstanding Security Council Resolution 275/1970* [1971] ICJ Reports 16, 21 June 1971 (hereafter *Namibia Advisory Opinion)*.
[91] UN Security Council, 'Admission of new Members to the UN: Algeria' (30 January 1970) UN Doc S/RES/176, [2].

Opinion, the ICJ clarified that the Security Council Resolution 276(1970) had the effect of placing third States under an obligation to abstain from entering into treaty relations with South Africa, in all instances where South Africa was purporting to act on behalf of Namibia. The ICJ also confirmed that third States were under an obligation not to invoke or apply any existing treaties which had been entered into by South Africa on behalf of Namibia.[92] According to the ICJ, the resolution also required States to abstain from including Namibia in the jurisdiction of any diplomatic or special missions which they sent to South Africa and imposed an obligation upon UN Member States not to enter into economic relationships with South Africa in instances in which South Africa purported to represent Namibia.[93]

But importantly, the ICJ also found that the non-recognition of South Africa's administration of Namibia by third States should have limits. In particular, the ICJ stated the non-recognition principle 'should not result in depriving the people of Namibia of any advantages derived from international co-operation'.[94] The ICJ clarified that third States should not treat the government of South Africa's acts as nullities, in instances where to do so would be to the 'detriment of the inhabitants of the Territory'.[95] As examples of acts which might fall into this category, the ICJ cited 'the registration of births, deaths and marriages'. It also stated that the obligation on third States to abstain from invoking treaties signed by South Africa on behalf of Namibia did not extend to 'general conventions such as those of a humanitarian character, the non-performance of which may adversely affect the people of Namibia'.[96] In his separate opinion, Judge de Castro provided further examples to illustrate these points. In doing so, he stated that transactions by the *de facto* authorities which related to 'public property' must be distinguished from acts which related to the 'acts and rights of private persons [which] should be regarded as valid (validity of entries in the civil registers and in the Land Registry, validity of marriages, validity of judgments of the civil courts etc)'.[97]

6.2 European Court of Human Rights Judgment in the *Cyprus v Turkey* Case

The ICJ's comments in this case, although clearly not directed to armed groups, give credence to the notion that when one subject of international law exercises *impersonal powers of government* within the territory of another State in default of that State's *de jure* government, those acts may be given validity under international law and considered as binding on the territorial State. In articulating this idea, the ICJ's Advisory Opinion seems to give further support to the idea that there are some functions of State that are so intimately connected with the administration of

92 *Nambia Advisory Opinion* (n 90) [121]. 93 Ibid, [123]. 94 Ibid, [125].
95 Ibid, [125]. 96 Ibid, [122].
97 *Nambia Advisory Opinion* (n 90) Individual Opinion of Judge de Castro, [206–7].

government in its impersonal sense that they may be performed by fungible actors. Support for this second principle is also seen in the case law of the European Court of Human Rights relating to the Turkish Republic of Northern Cyprus (TRNC). Here, applicants have repeatedly argued that the remedies and law enforcement systems which have been established by the TRNC should be seen to be unlawful per se because they are an integral part of the unlawful occupation of Northern Cyprus by Turkey. In response, the European Court of Human Rights has cited the ICJ's Advisory Opinion on Namibia in support of a contrary view. Using words which strikingly reflect the diverse authorities above, the European Court of Human Rights expounded:

> The obligation to disregard acts of de facto entities is far from absolute. Life goes on in the territory concerned for its inhabitants. That life must be made tolerable and be protected by the de facto authorities, including their courts; and, in the very interest of the inhabitants, the acts of these authorities related thereto cannot simply be ignored by third State or by international institutions, especially courts, including this one. To hold otherwise would amount to stripping the inhabitants of the territory of all their rights whenever they are discussed in an international context, which would amount to depriving them even of the minimum standard of rights to which they are entitled.[98]

In doing so, the European Court gave further support for the principle that the acts of a subject of international law, usurping the *de jure* government, may be given limited recognition if they are the impersonal acts of a State and ensure that life can continue when the government is unable to exercise its usual functions.

The case *Cyprus v Turkey* case can be distinguished from the *Namibia* case and the case law from the General Claims Commission and US Supreme Court because it involved three, rather than two, subjects of international law. Also, unlike the case law from the General Claims Commission and the US Supreme Court, it pertained to a situation where the usurping entity was still exercising power in the area in question, as opposed to a situation where the usurping entity had subsequently ceased to exist. As a result, the European Court of Human Rights found the occupying power (i.e. Turkey) not the territorial State (i.e. Cyprus) responsible for the violations of human rights in the TRNC. Its driving rationale was clearly that Turkey is a subject of international law in its own right, still in existence, and capable of being held responsible for its own wrongful acts. At a procedural and a substantive level, it would have been inappropriate in this case, and moreover contrary to the principle of effectiveness, to hold Cyprus responsible for human rights violations perpetrated by its occupier, Turkey. In a sense then, the case gives support for the idea that in instances where the usurping entity is a subject of international law in its own right, it makes more sense to hold it responsible for its own acts. This idea will be returned to later in the chapter.

[98] *Cyprus v Turkey*, Application No. 25781/94 (ECHR, 10 May 2001) [96].

6.2.1 Tensions between universal values and the principle of effectiveness

In many ways, the cases from the ICJ and European Court of Human Rights illustrate the different set of issues that must be considered in situations of ongoing illegality as opposed to unlawful situations which have already come to an end. They also powerfully illustrate the difficulties that are faced when two or more universal values are in conflict. In both these cases, there was clearly a tension between the Court's desire to safeguard the principle of non-recognition on the one hand and its desire to protect the fundamental rights of the persons who live in the territory on the other. Standing back, the decisions of these courts may be explained by the fact that the principle of non-recognition exerted a force on the legal framework that pushed in a different direction to the principle of effectiveness. In contrast, the concern to safeguard rights exerted a force on the legal framework which worked in the same direction as the principle of effectiveness.[99] Ultimately, the two forces together can be seen to have justified carving out an exception to the non-recognition principle. As a result, in both these cases, the Courts demonstrated a willingness to place the rights of the persons living in the territory above the wider illegality of the situation in which the people lived. While some deny that any acts can be lawful in an unlawful situation, both Courts justified their position along similar lines as the legal precedent so far reviewed.[100] Both courts articulated the view that because some aspects of administrative government are: (i) 'impersonal'; and (ii) designed to further universal values, the legality of the service provider in the wider framework with respect to those services can be somewhat overlooked.

It is important to state here that there will be less likelihood of a tension between two universal values when the entity usurping the territorial States' power is an armed group rather than another State. It is noteworthy that Hersch Lauterpacht made the same distinction, when he said:

> A rule of law which compels third States to regard as invalid, for a prolonged period of time, the law and administration of a de facto authority and to regard as valid within the territory of that authority the laws and administration of the de jure government, is not one which commends itself to sound principle (*unless, perhaps, in a particular case, the de facto authority is established* in violation not only of the constitutional law of the State concerned but *also of international law*). (emphasis added)[101]

[99] It is noted that the European Court of Human Rights stated: 'recognizing the effectiveness of those bodies [the TRNC Courts] for the limited purpose of protecting the rights of the territory's inhabitants does not, in the Court's view and following the Advisory Opinion of the International Court of Justice, legitimize the TRNC in any way'. See ibid, [92].

[100] The finding of the European Court of Human Rights in particular was controversial as it led to a further finding by the Court that the applicants were under an obligation to use the Courts of the TRNC in order to be deemed to have exhausted their domestic remedies. See L. G. Loucaides, 'The Judgement of the European Court of Human Rights in the Case of *Cyprus v Turkey*' in Loucaides, L. G., *The European Convention in Human Rights* (Martinus Nijhoff, Leiden 2007) 107–20.

[101] H. Lauterpacht, 'Recognition of Insurgents as a *de facto* Government' (1939) 1 Modern Law Review 1, 9.

He went on to emphasize that revolutions and rebellions are not contrary to international law. As a result, international law permits such 'measures of recognition as is necessary for the acknowledgement of the validity of the acts of the *de facto* authority within its territory'.[102] This observation identifies the fact that the application of the principle of effectiveness is much less controversial when it comes to armed groups than when it comes to an occupying State. Similar authority for this principle is found in the case law from the *Franco-Italian Conciliation Commission* below.

7. Cases from the Franco-Italian Conciliation Commission

Ideas similar to those articulated by Lauterpacht above are also articulated in a series of cases from the Franco-Italian Conciliation Commission established under Article 83 of the 1947 Treaty of Peace.[103] The cases from the Franco-Italian Conciliation Commission emanated out of acts perpetrated by the Italian Social Republic during the Second World War. The Italian Social Republic, otherwise known as the Salo Republic, was established by Nazi Germany on 28 September 1943. The Salo Republic had its own local Government and exercised powers through its own administrative and judicial organs. The rules it decreed were obligatory to the people who were subjected to that legal order and liable to penalties.[104] The cases before the Franco-Italian Conciliation Commission related to the confiscation, destruction, or damage of assets by officials belonging to the Salo regime. The broad question that the Conciliation Commission had to decide was whether post-war, the laws passed by the Salo Republic could be treated as the laws of Italy.[105] If the Commission found in the affirmative, the people who had been deprived of their property by the Salo Republic, who were mainly Jewish, would

[102] Ibid.

[103] *Fubini Case, Decision No. 201* (Reports of International Arbitral Awards, 12 December 1959) Volume XIV, 420–34 (hereafter *Fubini*); *Baer Case, Decision No. 199* (Reports of International Arbitral Awards, 12 December 1959) Volume XIV, 402–7 (hereafter *Baer*); *Falco Case, Decision No. 200* (Reports of International Arbitral Awards, 12 December 1959) Volume XIV, 408–19 (hereafter *Falco*); *Différend Dame Mossé, Decision Nos. 144–157* (Reports of International Arbitral Awards, 17 January 1953 and 6 October 1953) Volume XIII, 486–500 (hereafter *Différend Dame Mossé*).

[104] *Fubini* (n 103) 429–30.

[105] Article 78(6) of the Treaty of Peace stated: 'United Nations nationals and their property shall be exempted from any exceptional taxes, levies or imports imposed on their capital assets in Italy by the Italian Government or any Italian authority between September 3, 1943, and the coming into force of the present Treaty for the specific purpose of meeting charges arising out of the war or of meeting the costs of occupying forces or of reparation payable to any of the United Nations. Any sums which have been so paid shall be refunded.' Article 78(9)(a) of the Treaty of Peace stated that: '"United Nations nationals" means individuals who are nationals of any of the United Nations, or corporations or associations organized under the laws of any of the United Nations, at the coming into force of the present Treaty, provided that the said individuals, corporations or associations also had this status on September 3, 1943, the date of the Armistice with Italy. The term "United Nations nationals" also includes all individuals, corporations or associations which, *under the laws in force in Italy during the war*, have been treated as enemy' (emphasis added).

be entitled to compensation or tax exemption.[106] In examining the factual circumstances of the situation in Italy at the time, the Commission rejected the Italy's argument that the Salo Republic was an agent of the German Reich whose forces occupied a part of Italian territory.[107] Instead, it found that the Salo Republic should be treated in a manner akin to an insurrectional group operating alongside the incumbent government. Explicitly basing its reasoning on the principle of effectiveness, the Conciliation Commission found that the 'legal order' of the insurgents should be treated as part of the legal order of the State as a whole. As a result of its approach, the Commission found that the laws that had been passed by the Salo Republic during the Second World War certainly fell within the definition of 'laws in force' in Italy.

Considering the Commission's reasoning, this line of cases provides an interesting elaboration of how the principle of 'effectiveness' can be invoked, at both an international law and a domestic law level, in situations where a portion of the territory has fallen out of the central government's control. In the *Fubini* case, the Conciliation Commission set out the principle which the existence of the Salo Republic had presented, as follows:

> The condition that thus materialized in Italy is not unknown in international law; it is one of co-existence of a legal government and an insurrectional government fighting one another for the possession of power in a State. It is by an application of the general principles of international law that this condition must be judged and that its effects on the provisions of the Treaty of Peace must be determined.
>
> The rules of the law of nations are determined in this field are controlled by the principle of effectiveness which plays a fundamental part in establishing the legal order of the insurgents. In view of the fact that there did exist, during a period of nineteen months, two Governments of Italy, each of which denied the power to the other, the question arises whether the laws enacted by the insurrectional Government must be considered as part of the laws in force in Italy during the war ...

The Commission answered this question in the affirmative, saying it had been persuaded by the fact that the laws in question had emanated from an entity which 'in fact, exercised the political power over that part of the Italian territory' where the confiscated property had been located.[108] In other words, the Commission took note of the fact that: (i) the Salo Republic had actual power in that area; and (ii) the Italian government had had no power in that area.

The Commission then went on to affirm the role played by the 'principle of effectiveness' in its confirmation of the status of the insurrectional Government's

[106] The result of the Conciliation Commission's decision in this respect was different in each case. In the *Fubini* case (n 103), it resulted in the applicants being exempted from payment of the tax on their property. In the *Baer, Falco* and *Différend Dame Mossé* cases (n 103), it resulted in the claimant receiving compensation from the Italian government for losses suffered during the war as a result of damage to a building owned by the claimant.

[107] *Fubini* (n 103) 429. Although the Commission's conclusions were the same in each case, it articulated its reasoning slightly differently in each case and relied on slightly different legal authorities in each.

[108] Ibid, 429.

legal order. In support of this finding, the Commission cited Professor Guggenheim who wrote:

The seizure of power by belligerents and insurgents in a part of the territory of the State conflicts with State positive law, entails the creation of a new provisional legal order. It is what one often describes as a 'local de facto Government'. The latter may establish international law intercourse with the Central Government, as well as with third States, on the condition that its legal order be an effective one (Traité de droit international public, I, p. 203).[109]

The Commission then continued by citing the Italian jurist Professor Balladore Pallieri. His opinion from his *Diritto internationazle pubblico* is cited in full below because it is rare to find such a full articulation of the principle of effectiveness applied to armed groups. He stated:

The international organisation to which the international system refers is that which, de facto, really exists within the State. International law does not consider as a system, in this respect, that system which should exist according to domestic rules, but those which effectively and positively do exist. An international revolutionary movement can, in a violent manner and without legal continuity, substitute new systems for those which formerly existed, but as far as the international order is concerned it is not important that these agencies have no basis in the former regime and that they assert themselves to be Government agencies only de facto, by the success of the revolution that has brought them to power. It is this fact which is important, and without any limitation whatever with regard to both international law and the international order ... The imputation concerns whoever is in possession of real public authority in the interior of the State and, consequently, ... Those who, whatever the reason, come to be in a similar position, become agencies of the State.[110]

Demonstrating a preparedness to give more priority to the 'actual' exercise of power than the 'formal' exercise of power, the Commission found that the rules of the Salo Republic should be treated as the 'laws in force in Italy during the war'. In doing so, it demonstrated a willingness to treat an insurrectional movement as an informal and unsanctioned 'agency of the State' because of its exercise of actual power.

In a similar manner, in the *Falco* case, the Commission stated that it would be contrary to the 'principle of effectiveness' to accept Italy's argument that the Salo Republic's laws should not be included in the phrase 'laws in force in Italy during the war'. It elaborated that, by virtue of the principle of effectiveness:

when a local government and an insurrectional government share power in a State, the laws enacted by each one in the parts of the territory which they respectively occupy are considered as laws in force, which obtain validity, under the Law of Nations, from the effective power which each of the two Governments exercises over the territory wherein it is in a position to assure the execution of its determinations.[111]

109 Ibid. 430. 110 Ibid.

111 Ibid, 417. A similar statement is found in *Baer* (n 103) 406.

The Commission also found it relevant that this interpretation of the phrase 'laws in force in Italy during the war' fitted with a teleological reading of the Treaty which had the aim of benefiting persons whose property, rights, or interests had sustained damages under the laws in force in Italy during the war.[112] The force of this detail should not be overlooked because it highlights the important fact that the application of the principle of effectiveness in this case was also in accordance with the protection of universal values. The effect of the Commission finding that the Salo Republic's laws were to be treated as the 'laws of Italy' was that the people who had suffered from those laws should be compensated for their loss.[113]

8. Comparison of Emerging Conclusions with Political Science Analysis of Armed Conflict

Although emerging from different factual contexts, these disparate sources give credence to the idea that the effectiveness principle can work in tandem with universal values to give limited recognition to the acts of a usurping entity. Before seeking to synthesize these ideas into some concluding remarks and show how they are relevant to human rights law, the following paragraphs will first consider briefly how the ideas expressed in the preceding paragraphs are reflected in 'real life' in non-international armed conflicts. In doing so, recourse is briefly had to some of the observations in Chapter 2 about life under rebel control. In particular, it is interesting to note that the conclusions of Chapter 2 largely support the comments made by the General Claims Commission and the US Supreme Court above that there are some aspects of people's lives in conflict which are not related to the conflict itself. The social and political science literature reviewed for Chapter 2 showed that for the people that live in warzones, war is not an 'event' but the 'normal—in the sense of "expected"—context for the unfolding of social life'.[114] It showed, that to a large extent, life goes on in areas under rebel control. As a result, land and domestic disputes continue to occur, crime proliferates, and the population continues to require governance relating to the protection of their rights and everyday life. The idea that everyday life continues in rebel held areas has similarities with the view that certain aspects of governance have the impersonal qualities identified by the General Claims Commission. Indeed, it was shown in Chapter 2, that what is referred to as the 'life-goes-on-driver' often compels the armed group to provide some kind of governance structures or services in that area.

[112] *Falco* (n 103) 417.

[113] Reading the cases, one has the feeling that the Commission would have been much less willing to interpret the Salo Republic's laws as the 'laws of Italy' if the effect of such a finding had been to validate the effect of those laws, i.e. confirm the confiscation of property.

[114] S. C. Lubkemann, *Culture in Chaos: A Social Anthropology of the Social Condition of War* (University of Chicago Press, Chicago 2010) 1; see also Chapter 2 for a full discussion of this observation.

Chapter 2 confirms that there is often a strong 'need' for a continuance of public administration or government in some form during non-international armed conflicts. Accordingly, it provides support for the idea that government services may be 'called for', 'impersonal', and fulfilled by fungible entities. Perhaps most relevant of all, it shows that the division of governance tasks between government and rebel group is not always as clear-cut as is often assumed. Indeed, Chapter 2 showed that there are many instances where a State may continue to provide resources to provide some public services in the area under a rebel group's control. For example, it showed that in Sri Lanka, the provision of services in the LTTE-held areas was a 'complex interface between state and rebel governmental efforts'.[115] It also commented that in some situations of armed conflict, public services are also fulfilled by civilian committees. Moreover, it fits with the idea that an evaluation of whether a particular act should be considered an 'act of State' should be conducted on the basis of the conduct itself, rather than the identity of the actor. In broad terms, the findings in Chapter 2 seem to support the idea that in the exceptional circumstances of non-international armed conflict where the *de jure* government's powers no longer match the geographical contours of the State, the legal entity of a State under international law may be understood as being greater than its representative government. Having reviewed this diverse case law above, it now remains to consider whether it can be distilled down into a summary. In particular, it is helpful to try to identify the parameters of the principle that the acts of an armed group may be considered to be an act of State.

9. Conclusions on Circumstances in which Acts of an Armed Group Can Be Considered an Act of State

9.1 Functions must be 'governmental' in nature

The case law reviewed above suggests the 'impersonal' acts of governance by an armed group may be considered an act of State. It might be tempting to adopt a subjective approach to the definition of 'impersonal'. This would enquire into the group's professed motivation in providing the service in question. Yet, it is argued that a subjective approach in this instance would be imprudent. The reason for this is that a single motive is rarely found for any action by a political entity. It was shown in Chapter 2 that the provision of public services by an armed group may often serve a dual purpose. While on the one hand an armed group may claim to be performing government functions in response to the needs of the civilian population, it may also be serving its own political agenda by doing so.[116]

[115] Z. C. Mampilly, *Rebel Rulers: Insurgent Governance and Civilian Life during War* (Cornell University Press, Ithaca and London 2011) 112 (hereafter Mampilly, *Rebel Rulers*).

[116] Here, it is important to note that State inflicted terror is often 'justified' to the people and society at large on the basis that it is necessary to protect public order and in the best interest of society. Bassiouni states in this regard: 'Every tyrannical regime since the turn of this century has claimed to be acting for the greater good of the people and has justified its excesses as necessary to preserve

Under an objective approach, the acts of a rebel administration must be impartially examined and consideration must be given to whether they are wholly connected to the exercise of government in its impersonal aspect. The case law from the General Claims Commission, the US Supreme Court, the ICJ, and the European Court of Human Rights is of assistance in the identification of considerations which will be relevant in determining whether an act is 'impersonal' in nature. Attention must be given to whether the acts relate to the continuance of daily life in armed conflict. Consideration must also be given to whether the acts can be performed by fungible actors. These would include acts relating to the resolution of domestic disputes, the registration of births, deaths, and marriages, the administration of basic policing and judicial functions, the provision of healthcare and education, and the provision of telecommunication services in the territory.

In contrast, functions performed by an armed group which are intimately related to its military struggle with the government or their military or political agenda will not constitute acts of State. Examples of such activities would include actions relating to military campaigns, recruitment and training of troops, the conduct of hostilities, and the purchase and supply of weapons. However, ordinary policing activities could also fall into this category if it is found, on objective analysis, that they are intimately connected to an armed group's military strategy.[117] For example, in some extreme instances, the exercise of governance activities may be employed as a weapon of war; a means by which an armed group may achieve complete military dominance over a civilian population, thereby dissuading it from rising up against it.[118]

9.2 Functions must be performed in the absence of or default of the government

The Commentary to Article 9 makes clear that the conduct must be performed in the absence of or default of the government, in some part of the territory. It also makes clear that it does apply to circumstances where a *de facto* government has emerged out of complete State failure. Instead, the Commentary makes clear that the conduct of such an entity will be better treated under Article 4(1) of the Articles on State Responsibility which relate to State organs. In making this distinction, the Commentary to Article 9 confirms the point which was also made by the General Claims Commission with respect to the Huerta regime. Importantly, the second condition's requirement that the functions must be performed 'in the absence of or default of the official authorities' indicates that the principle will largely

and restore public order.' C. M. Bassiouni, *Crimes Against Humanity in International Criminal Law* (Kluwer Law International, The Hague 1999) 250.

117 See (n 116). See also K. Fortin, 'The Application of Human Rights Law to Everyday Civilian Life Under Rebel Control' [2016] NILR, 161 (hereafter Fortin 'Everyday Civilian Life'), 179.

118 This is currently seen in the tactics exerted in Raqqa in Syria by the Islamic State. See OHCHR, Independent International Commission of Inquiry on the Syrian Arab Republic, 'Rule of Terror: Living under ISIS in Syria' (14 November 2014) UN Doc HRC/CRP/ISIS, [73].

not apply to the acts of an armed group exercising governmental functions *in parallel to* the government in the same territory, unless they are fulfilling different functions.[119] Such a phenomenon may occur, as for example they did in the armed conflicts Afghanistan and Nepal, when a government and an armed group are locked in a struggle for legitimacy in a particular area of the country and neither entity has exclusive control of the territory.[120] In such instances, unless the government in that area is failing to a considerable degree, an armed group will not be exercising government functions 'in the absence of or default of the official authorities' but instead will be exercising parallel government functions which are deliberately in competition with those of the government. As a result, the authorities reviewed above imply that the principles underlying Article 9 will generally not apply in areas where both the armed group and the government are present and exercising governmental functions.

9.3 Circumstances must have been such 'to call for the exercise of elements of the governmental authority by private persons'

It has already been shown that it makes little sense to inquire into an armed group's stated motivations when seeking to determine whether an armed group's actions are 'impersonal'. For similar reasons, it is argued that when determining whether an armed group's actions were 'called for' it is not advisable to formulate a test that considers whether the armed group professed to have the populations' best interests at heart or whether the group was acting in *bona fide* manner.[121] While this argued position is contrary to the position taken by the US Supreme Court which did not consider acts which impaired the rights of citizens to be impersonal, it is justified by the fact that there will rarely be a consensus on whether a particular armed group is acting 'in the interest of the community' or following its own political agenda. Moreover, it is noted that in finding that the Salo Republic's laws were the 'laws in force in Italy', the *Franco Italian Claims Commission* gave little attention to the fact that the Salo Republic's laws were discriminatory against Jews. Instead, it focused only on the fact that the Salo Republic had established a 'new provisional legal order' in an area where the Italian *de jure* government was absent. It is also noted that an approach focusing on an armed group's conduct was 'called for' would not be in line with the general approach of the Articles on State Responsibility which is generally resistant to any enquiry into an individual or State's motivation or a qualitative assessment of a person or State's acts.

In the light of these arguments, it is argued that an assessment of whether the acts in question are 'called for' should not take heed of the quality of the armed

[119] See Ruys, 'Crossing the Thin Blue Line' (n 38) 288.

[120] See for example OHCHR, 'Nepal Conflict Report' (2012) 43 and 90–1 and E. L. Walker, 'Culturally Attuned Governance and Justice in Helmand Province, Afghanistan', (2010) ISAF/International Media Ventues 50, 867. See also D. Kilcullen, *Counterinsurgency* (Hurst & Co Publishers Ltd, London 2010) 157–8.

[121] See Bílková, 'Establishing Direct Responsibility' (n 38) 269.

group's response or the circumstances in which the armed group is exercising governance. Instead, it is argued that it should be considered whether the functions of government were 'necessary' in the circumstances ruling at the time; a condition which could easily be fulfilled by the absence of the *de jure* government in the territory in question. This approach to the 'normative' requirement is supported by the Commentary to Article 9. This states that, 'circumstances must have been such to call for the exercise of elements of the governmental authority by private persons' and continues significantly:

> the term 'call for' conveys the idea that some exercise of governmental functions was called for, *though not necessarily the conduct in question.* (emphasis added) [122]

This confirms a view that there is no need to embark on a qualitative evaluation of the service provided. The logic of such a position is confirmed by the fact that the Articles on State Responsibility deal wholly with 'wrongful acts'. This makes it clear that the principle underlying Article 9 is not limited to blameless acts that are designed to protect rights, but extends also to acts which impair rights.

10. Conclusions for International Humanitarian Law

Having set out the parameters of the circumstances in which the acts of armed groups may be considered to be acts of State, it is now time to consider what relevance these authorities have to the legal framework that applies in non-international armed conflict. In particular, attention will be given to how these conclusions are relevant to the question of whether and how an armed group's control of territory may provide a legal explanation for how armed groups may be bound by human rights law. The identification of the conditions above support the conclusion that an armed group's violations of international humanitarian law relating to the conduct of hostilities will not constitute acts of State because such violations are clearly related to conduct which is intimately linked to an armed group's military campaign. Such a conclusion is not so obvious for violations of international humanitarian law relating to protected persons. On first evaluation, such violations would appear to fall into the 'doubtful zone' identified above. For while a party's fulfilment or violation of international humanitarian law may constitute an exercise of government functions, it will also relate exclusively to the armed conflict. When forced to decide which side of the 'line' such acts fall, it is argued that this latter point is likely to be determinative, leading to a conclusion that violations of international humanitarian law do not fall within the principles of effectiveness underlying Article 9, no matter whether they relate to the conduct of hostilities or protected persons. Such a conclusion is justified by the observation that international humanitarian law obligations do not relate to fungible aspects of the administration of government per se that continue in peace and war. Instead,

[122] See Commentary to Article 9 of the ILC Articles on State Responsibility (n 24) 49 [6].

they are intrinsically related to, and emerge out of, the hostilities. It is also justified by the observation made in Chapter 7, that the legal framework of international humanitarian law is designed, in its very conception, to be binding upon two international actors.[123] As a result, from a conceptual perspective, the application of international humanitarian law obligations to armed groups does not reflect the idea at the core of the case law above, i.e. that the legal entity of a State under international law is greater than its representative government. Similarly, as it was commented in Chapter 7, nor does the international humanitarian law framework involve a non-State actor being held responsible 'in default of' the government, in instances where the State's duty to fulfil its obligations throughout the whole territory has been interrupted or compromised as a result of the armed group usurping the government's position in a part of the country.[124]

11. Conclusions for International Human Rights Law

However, when applying the same criteria to international human rights law, a different conclusion is reached. It was shown in Chapter 2 that the major role of human rights law in non-international armed conflict is the regulation of aspects of 'everyday' life, which are unconnected to the armed conflict. Indeed, it was demonstrated that human rights norms have an especially important role to play in relation to issues which exist equally in peacetime as well as during armed conflict. Moreover, it was also shown that human rights norms are particularly relevant to individuals' ability to maintain their daily life, e.g. their ability to travel to work, move around freely, access healthcare, express an opinion freely, gather in public places, and be protected from common crime. Human rights law contains a right to freedom of movement, a right to freedom of expression, and a right to freedom of assembly.[125] It contains provisions articulating the right to work, the right to just and favourable conditions of work, the right to an adequate standard of living, including adequate food, clothing, and housing.[126] It contains a right to health, in the sense of a positive right which extends to healthy people as well as those who are already sick and contains important provisions relating to family life.[127] It also contains provisions relevant to people's right to marry freely, children's rights to be registered after birth, and the resolution of domestic disputes. It is argued that many of these issues correspond with the aspects of 'government in its impersonal aspect' which were identified in the cases above and which fulfil the first criteria of Article 9. It is also relatively easy to fulfil the second criteria of Article 9 when looking at human rights law obligations. Because, unlike international humanitarian law, the application of human rights law obligations to armed groups clearly represents an example of a non-State actor being held responsible 'in default of' the

[123] See section 6.2 of Chapter 7. [124] Ibid.
[125] See Articles 12, 19, 22 of the ICCPR. [126] See Articles 6, 7, 11 of the ICESCR.
[127] See Article 12 of the ICESCR.

government, in instances where the State's duty to fulfil its obligations throughout the whole territory has been interrupted or compromised. It is also easier to fulfil the third criteria as it was demonstrated in Chapter 2 that armed groups often exercise governance functions in response to a 'need' to fulfil the gap left by the government. Taking these factors into consideration, it is seen that conduct relating to the fulfilment or violation of human rights norms fits more squarely into the conceptual framework presented by Article 9. On the basis of this observation, it is argued that the case law evaluated above provides an important contribution to understanding how armed groups which are controlling territory may be bound by international human rights law. This is explained further below.

12. Implications for How Armed Groups are Bound by Human Rights Law

The chapter so far has brought to light an little known line of case law that suggests that in certain exceptional circumstances armed groups can violate the international legal obligations of the State. Clearly the fact that armed groups can commit acts of State does not automatically lead to a conclusion that that armed groups are bound by the State's obligations. Instead, it leads to the thorny question of whether entities capable of violating a State's obligations are bound by those obligations, as a matter of international law.[128] This is a debate that is too lengthy to address comprehensively here but it is summarized briefly as follows. According to the majority theory, international law can bind the State but cannot make claims about how it is complied with internally within the State. Accordingly, under this theory which is sometimes called the 'black-box' theory, agents or organs of the State can violate the State's obligations under international law but are not necessarily bound by them directly. However, under a minority view, a State's organs are directly bound by international law largely because they are the means through which it must be enforced. Scholars reflecting on this debate have commented that there is growing support for this minority view in international and national authority, reflecting a 'changing approach to international law'.[129] Indeed, such an approach may be considered especially appropriate and indeed even compelling in the relatively unusual circumstances where the actor perpetrating the wrong is entirely outside the control of the entity representing the State, i.e. the *de jure*

[128] See W. Ferdinandusse, 'Out of the Black-box?: The International Legal Obligations of State Organs' (2003–2004) 29 Brooklyn Journal of International Law 45 (hereafter Ferdinandusse, 'Out of the Black-box?').

[129] See for example *LaGrand (Germany v United States of America) (Order, Request for Indication of Provisional Measures)* [1999] ICJ Reports 9, 3 March 1999, [28]. See also Ferdinandusse, 'Out of the Black-box?' (n 128) 68–9. See also E. Lauterpacht (ed), *International Law: Being the Collected Works of Hersch Lauterpacht: Vol I—the General Works* (CUP, Cambridge 1970) 280: 'To say that the State—and the State only—is the subject of international duties is to say . . . that international duties bind no one; it is to interpose a screen of irresponsibility between the rule of international law and the agency expected to give effect to it.' Cited by Ferdinandusse (n 128) 54.

government. Indeed, the argument is also supported by the principle of effectiveness that has been articulated above. Unless the subject of international law is held bound by the obligations of the State, the State's obligations become meaningless in that area of its territory. When this argument is accepted, the reasoning of the chapter so far comes together to provide a theoretical explanation for how armed groups are bound by international human rights law. It consists of three constitutive points: (i) armed groups exercising governmental functions in default of the *de jure* government are performing acts of State; (ii) with respect to those acts international law is prepared to treat the armed groups as unofficial and unsanctioned agents of the State whose actions can incur State responsibility; and (iii) the principle of effectiveness, and some recent judicial authority, supports the fact that in respect to those functions, the armed groups are bound by the international obligations of the State, i.e. human rights law.

13. A Bottom-Up Approach: Rights Devolving with Territory and Population

Before turning to the procedural implications of this conclusion, one final point is made on substance. It is commented that although so far the discussion has viewed the legal framework from the top-down perspective with a focus on the duty-bearers, there are also valid comments to be made from a bottom-up perspective, in relation to the rights holders.[130] Moreover, when looking at the legal framework from a bottom-up perspective, it is seen that there is also legal authority to argue that armed groups controlling territory should be bound by the legal obligations of the State. The main point is that human rights treaties are an exception to the widely accepted principle that independent States inherit a *tabula rasa* when it comes to treaty law (the 'clean slate' principle).[131] This has been explained on the basis that human rights treaties 'devolve with territory' and cannot be renounced.[132] The Human Rights Committee has stated in this regard that:

> The rights enshrined in the Covenant belong to the people living in the territory of the State party ... [Moreover] once the people are accorded the protection of the rights under the Covenant, such protection devolves with territory and continues to belong to them, notwithstanding change in government of the State party, including dismemberment in more

[130] Tomuschat, 'Insurgent Movements' (n 4) 588; Hessbruegge, 'Violations from Conduct of Non-State Actors' (n 20) 40.

[131] It is noted that this principle, although most deferential to State consent, is not uniformally accepted. Writing in 2003, Rasulov argues that there is also much scholarly support for the 'continuity' mechanism, under which a successor state inherits all the treaty obligations of its predecessor. A. Rasulov, 'Revisiting State Succession to Humanitarian Treaties: Is there a Case for Automaticity?' (2003) 14 European Journal of International Law 141 (hereafter Rasulov, 'Case for Automaticity').

[132] UN, 'Report of the Human Rights Committee Vol 1, General Assembly, Official Records, Fifty-first Session, Supplement No. 40' (13 April 1997) UN Doc A/51/40, 16 [72] (hereafter Human Rights Committee Report 13 April 1997).

than one State or State succession or any subsequent action of the State party designed to divest them of the rights guaranteed by the Covenant.[133]

Moreover, the issue was also brought to the attention of the ICJ when it was asked to consider whether the Genocide Convention was automatically applicable to Bosnia and Herzegovina after its succession from the former Socialist Republic of Yugoslavia.[134]

Although the ICJ found it unnecessary to address the question in order to decide the case, the question of whether there is automatic succession to a human rights Convention such as the Genocide Convention was addressed in separate opinions by Judge Weeramantry and Judge Shahabuddeen. Both judges agreed that the Genocide Convention should constitute a deviation from the clean slate principle and continue to apply to the populations to which it has applied in the past. In particular, Judge Weeramantry cited a number of relevant legal arguments to justify this position.[135] He pointed out *inter alia* that human rights treaties do not represent an 'exchange of interests and benefits between contracting States in the conventional sense'.[136] Instead, they represent a commitment of the participating States 'to certain norms and values recognized by the international community'.[137] He also found value in the argument that human rights treaties do not impose a burden on States per se, but are simple a 'formal recognition' of the human rights that their subjects have irrespective of any treaties.[138] He also found it persuasive that the principles contained in the Genocide Convention are also principles of customary international law.[139] Moreover, he found that the argument that human rights treaties were subject to automatic succession was an important means of avoiding a 'legal vacuum' for the people living in that territory 'precisely at the time they need it most—when there is instability in their State'.[140]

The notion that human rights treaties automatically devolve with territory and are owned by the populations in that territory is not universally accepted.[141] However, the underlying arguments on which the principle has been based

[133] See UN Human Rights Committee, 'General Comment No. 26, (Continuity of Obligations)' (12 August 1997) UN Doc CCPR/C/21/Rev.1/Add.8/Rev.1, [4]. For similar statements see also Human Rights Committee Report 13 April 1997 (n 134) [72], 17; UN Human Rights Committee, 'Concluding Observations on Portugal (Macao)' (4 November 1999) UN Doc CCPR/C/79/Add.115, [3]; UN Human Rights Committee, 'Summary Record of the 1178th Meeting' (5 November 1992) UN Doc CCPR/C/SR.1178/Add.1, [4], [12], [31].

[134] *Application of the Convention on the Prevention and Punishment of the Crime of Genocide (Bosnia and Herzegovina v Serbia and Montenegro)* [2007] ICJ Reports 43, 26 February 2007 (hereafter *Bosnia and Herzegovina v Serbia and Montenegro).* See F. Pocar, 'Some Remarks on the Continuity of Human Rights and International Humanitarian Law Treaties' in E. Cannizzaro, *The Law of Treaties Beyond the Vienna Convention* (OUP, Oxford 2011) for a review of the main sources on this issue.

[135] *Bosnia and Herzegovina v Serbia and Montenegro* (n 134) Separate Opinion of Judge Weeramantry, 641–53.

[136] Ibid, 645. [137] Ibid, 645. [138] Ibid, 647. [139] Ibid, 648.

[140] Ibid, 649–50.

[141] See Rasulov, 'Case for Automaticity' (n 131), for a view that is 'pessimistic' about the ability to justify such a rule with regard to State practice and *opinio juris.* See M. Kamminga, 'State Succession in Respect of Human Rights Treaties' (1996) 7 European Journal of International Law 469, who finds 'wide support' for the continuity of obligations under human rights treaties.

contribute convincing arguments for the idea that armed groups should be bound by the treaty obligations of the parent State. Indeed, the idea that areas under the territorial control of armed groups will become outside the reach of human rights law is contrary to the reality that individuals in those areas continue to have 'rights' in these areas. It was shown at the beginning of the chapter that when armed groups control territory, a vacuum of human rights may arise, in that populations under their control are left without human rights protection at the moment that they need it most. From this perspective, it is seen how the effectiveness principle may be employed from a both a top-down and bottom-up perspective. The emphasis of the chapter has been on how it creates an imperative to ensure that the framework of a State's legal *obligations* are effective throughout a State's territory. But it is argued here that there is an equal imperative to ensure that the framework of legal *rights* is effective throughout a State's territory. Moreover emphasis on the latter consideration is particularly relevant considering the nature of human rights conventions. Indeed, although not explicitly articulated, a study of the bottom-up approach highlights the fact that the principles articulated by the General Claims Commission, US Supreme Court, ICJ, and European Court of Human Rights were equally motivated by a concern to protect the 'rights' of the individuals in those territories. In particular, the European Court of Human Rights stated that if it disregarded the acts of *de facto* entities, it would amount to 'stripping the inhabitants of the territory of all their rights'.[142] In that sense, the rights at the bottom of the framework may be seen to represent the universal values which operate, together with the principle of effectiveness, to restore the effectiveness of the legal framework so that armed groups can be addressed directly, in regard to their State functions.

14. Allocation of Responsibility for Internationally Wrongful Acts Committed by Armed Groups

14.1 Parent State responsible for acts of State falling under Article 9

In the light of these legal findings, some closing comments must be made about the procedural consequences of the conclusions above. A strict reading of the cases above seems to lead to a finding that the parent State can be held responsible for acts of an armed group, when it conducts governance activities. In procedural terms, it can be seen such a finding may have merit once the conflict is over. Indeed, it has been seen in the case law from the Franco-Italian Conciliation Commission, the US Supreme Court, and the General Claims Commission between the United States and Mexico, that sometimes it makes sense to address a State for the wrongs of an armed group, in instances where the armed group no longer exists and the

[142] See n 98.

armed conflict is over. However, in instances where the armed conflict is ongoing, it makes much less sense because the armed group is a subject of international law in its own right. From a political perspective, it would also be unacceptable as it would hold a State responsible for the acts of the entity against which it was fighting. It would be akin to holding Iraq responsible for the human rights violations committed by Islamic State on its territory. It would also let the armed group completely off the hook. From a legal perspective, it would have the effect of reinstating into the legal framework another troubling disconnect between the normative order and reality. Indeed, considering that armed groups are subjects of international law in their own right, there are strong reasons to argue that in practical terms, they should bear their own responsibility under international law for their wrongs.[143] Considering the principle set out in Article 9, it is suggested that the entity's own responsibility will be concurrent to the international responsibility of the State, albeit that the State's responsibility is mainly not invoked.[144]

14.2 Responsibility of non-State actors outside remit of drafters of Articles

In instances where an armed group still exists, it seems sensible to argue that it will be responsible for its own acts. In particular, there is evidence that during the drafting of the Articles there was considerable discomfort at the suggestion that States should ever be responsible for the acts of an armed group, in instances where the armed group had its own legal personality under international law.[145] Indeed, it was often commented during the drafting of the articles that armed groups should bear their own responsibility for their conduct. In a Commentary to an earlier version of the Articles in 1975, the Commentary stated that the responsibility of a State for acts of insurgent groups should follow the same lines as the approach adopted for 'private individuals' during a riot or mass demonstration. By this the Commentary was essentially reiterating the general principle set out at the beginning of the chapter that States will not be responsible for the acts of armed groups per se, but may be responsible for their failure to exert sufficient due diligence to protect civilians from their actions. However, the Commentary then remarked that the situation may be different in circumstances where an armed group has assumed power over a portion of a State's territory. It was observed in this respect that there is not only a quantitative difference between cases of riot and mass demonstration and scenarios where the insurrectional group has assumed power over a portion

[143] Indeed this was Special Rapporteur Ago's main argument against the State being held responsible for the acts of an armed group that had its own legal personality under international law. See Bílková, 'Establishing Direct Responsibility' (n 38) and S. Verhoeven, 'International Responsibility of Armed Opposition Groups' in C. Ryngaert (ed), *Responsibilities of the Non-State Actor in Armed Conflict and the Market Place* (Brill 2015) for two recent explorations of how such a regime could be developed.

[144] See Ryngaert, 'Human Rights Obligations of Armed Groups' (n 17) 361, for the idea that the State and the armed group could be concurrently responsible for the same violation.

[145] ILC Yearbook 1974 Vol II (n 44) 98.

of the State's territory—i.e. the disruption is more intense—but also a qualitative difference.

In explaining this latter observation, the Commentary stated that at the point an insurrectional movement has 'its own machinery and … organs [which] … they may engage in conduct liable to bring an international responsibility upon the insurrectional movement itself if that conduct should constitute a breach of an international obligation recognized as incumbent on the insurrectional movement'.[146] In such instances, the Commentary stated, recourse would generally be had to the insurrectional group and not the State in question. It elaborated:

> It will rarely be possible to accuse a State of failing in its own obligations of vigilance and protection in relation to the conduct of organs of an insurrectional movement because, most of the time, the acts in question are entirely beyond its control. Even more rarely will such accusations be leveled against the State in cases where, after the insurrectional movement has succeeded in entrenching its authority over a sufficient portion of the State's territory, third States come to hold the movement itself responsible for internationally wrongful acts of its own organs.[147]

While these remarks were not made within the specific context of Article 9, they do confirm a view that in circumstances where an armed group has attained legal personality under international law, it will make more sense for the armed group itself to be held responsible for its own actions, while it still exists.[148]

14.3 Law on belligerency and insurgency supports practice of addressing armed groups directly

Moreover, further support for such an approach is found in the law of belligerency and insurgency. It is relevant to note that the conclusions of Part II of the book are broadly supportive of the conclusions reached in this chapter. They show that the idea that armed groups take on the international law obligations of the parent State when they control territory has significant historical precedent. In particular, Chapter 4 demonstrated that in instances where a third State or a parent State declared a belligerency, a parent State was thenceforth absolved of its international law obligations vis-à-vis foreign nationals and assets in that part of its territory. Instead from that point on, third States (if the parent State declared the belligerency) or the declaring third State (if a third State had declared the belligerency), would be forced to address the armed group itself for any claims relating to the protection of their assets and nationals in the portion of territory over which it had control. Indeed, it was shown in Chapter 4 that this shift of legal obligations and responsibility from the parent State to the armed group was often advantageous for both third States and the parent State, because, in essence, it facilitated a realignment of the situation on the ground with the legal framework. It allowed third States to engage directly on responsibility matters with the entity with control

[146] Ibid, 91–2 [3]. [147] Ibid, 92 [4]. [148] See n 137.

on the ground. This allowed third States to better secure the protection of their assets and gave them a better chance of receiving compensation for their losses. Moreover, the transfer of legal obligations from a parent State to an armed group also allowed parent States to relinquish their responsibility for territory outside their control. This would often be a welcome development in instances where an armed group controlled significant swathes of territories, as in those instances, the capabilities of the parent State would be limited to the point of being nugatory.

Similarly, Chapter 4 showed that third States would often address an armed group directly in situations that fell below a belligerency. It showed that in the Spanish Civil War, Britain, Norway, and Portugal pursued claims against the Franco insurgents despite the fact neither they, nor the Spanish Republic, had recognized the Franco administration as a belligerent. Indeed, Chapter 4 showed how Spain even encouraged Portugal to pursue Franco's administration for claims under 'international conventions', on the basis that in factual terms, the Franco administration was the entity responsible for the claims. Likewise, records from that time indicate that Britain, Norway, and Portugal addressed the Franco administration directly because that it made no sense to pursue Spain for matters outside its control, particularly in instances where the Franco administration was: (i) capable of protecting individuals and assets within territory under its control; (ii) factually responsible for the wrongs complained of ; (iii) procedurally willing to address them; and (iv) capable of providing reparation for them, in the form of compensation and guarantees of non-repetition. Ultimately, these examples are further manifestations of the broader principle of 'effectiveness' that has been reflected on throughout this chapter. They reflect the potential of the principle of effectiveness to work at both at a substantive level and a procedural level in the legal framework.

14.4 Support for the idea that one legal entity should be held responsible for another legal entity's obligations

The idea that one legal entity can be held responsible for the violation of another legal entity's obligations is not a notion that is foreign to the law on State responsibility. Article 17 of the Articles on the Responsibility of States for Internationally Wrongful Acts addresses the scenario where one State directs and controls the acts of another State. The Article confirms that a third State that is directing and controlling the international wrong of another State should be held responsible for that international wrong, even though the legal obligation which has been breached formally belongs to the other State.[149] For example, when one State is occupying another State and controls the police force of the occupied State, the occupying State will be responsible for any international wrong committed by that police force.[150] It is argued that although these situations are not analogous, a similar framework of attribution should be applied in instance where an armed

[149] See Commentary to Article 17 of the ILC Articles on State Responsibility (n 24) 68 [6].
[150] Ibid, [5].

group is exercising governmental functions in default of the government. Here, the armed group will be responsible for conduct amounting to an international wrong alongside the parent State, even though the legal obligation that has been breached in formal terms belongs to the parent State. A further analogous example was noted by Special Rapporteur Ago during the drafting of the Articles on State Responsibility when he referred to the 'situation which may arise when in the territory of a given State another subject or subjects of international law are acting in its place'. He stated:

> For reasons which vary from case to case, a State may be placed in a situation where another subject, or even other subjects, of international law are acting in its territory [here the footnote adds significantly: 'To avoid complicating the analysis of such situations still further, we shall refer here only to the case in which the other subject or subjects involved are also State. But they may be subjects of a different nature, such as an insurrectionary movement or even, to take an extreme case, an international organization'].
>
> If a situation of this kind occurs, the other subject or subjects may, for purposes of their own or else because of the need to fill gaps in the organization of the territorial State, entrust certain activities pertaining to the legal order of that State to elements of their own organization. The organs of the territorial State, those thorough which it normally discharges its international obligations, are then set aside as regards functions which may vary in scope …
>
> A particular example if that of a military occupation, whether in time of war or in time of peace, whether partial or total, temporary or permanent, in brief, regardless of the title, reason and character of the occupation; nor is there any need, for the purposes with which we are concerned here, to draw any distinction based on whether the occupation is regarded as legitimate or illegitimate by international law …
>
> If therefore, in exercising the activities entrusted to them within the framework of the legal order of the occupied State, these organs of the occupying State are guilty of acts or omissions in breach of an international law obligation of the occupied State, those acts or omissions must be imputed to the occupant and involve its responsibility. This is clearly a direct responsibility, a responsibility for its own act.
>
> It is scarcely necessary to add that since in these cases the organs of the occupying State are acting in place of those of the occupied State and within the framework of the latter's legal order, they are bound to act in compliance with the international obligations incumbent upon the organs of the occupied State which they are replacing.[151]

The broad principle articulated by the Special Rapporteur confirms the approach set out above. This asserts that in instances where an armed groups exercises governmental functions in default of the government, it will be bound by the legal obligations of the parent State. Moreover although in formal terms the parent State is responsible, the armed group will, by virtue of its own international legal

[151] Ibid.

personality, also be responsible for their breach itself.[152] After the conflict has ended, it may make more sense for a third party to pursue the State for the acts of the armed groups which it perpetrated while exercising governmental functions in default of the government.[153] At that point, the armed group will no longer have legal personality under international law and may not be an effective recipient of any claim for responsibility.

15. Conclusions

In this chapter it has been shown that there is significant legal precedent for the idea that armed groups may be bound by the legal obligations of the State, in certain circumstances. The root of this theory stems from the idea that some aspects of an armed group's conduct may be treated as the act of a State, in instances where it is controlling territory and exercising governmental functions. Support for this idea has been found in the case law from the *Franco-Italian Conciliation Commission*, the General Claims Commission between the United States and Mexico, and the United States Supreme Court. Support for this notion has also been found in Article 9 of the Articles on State Responsibility and its Commentaries. Indeed, an examination of this case law has shown how there is a precedent of treating the conduct of armed groups as acts of State in instances where the conduct is impersonal, governmental, and responds to a need of the community. The idea that this conduct can be treated as State conduct stems from an acknowledgement that in the exceptional circumstances of non-international armed conflict, where a *de jure* government has lost control of certain parts of its territory, the State, in legal terms, is more expansive than its *de jure* government. It also constitutes recognition that impersonal acts of government may be performed by fungible actors, especially in situations of armed conflict or humanitarian disaster. It has been shown that the merit of such a conceptual approach is supported by political science literature which often observes that the 'State' is much more than its government, and should also be perceived from a bottom-up perspective.[154]

[152] It is noted that this is the manner in which some accountability mechanisms seem to have explained the responsibility of armed groups under international human rights law. See for example, the statement by the UN Truth Commission on El Salvador which stated: 'However, it must be recognized that when insurgents assume government powers in territories under their control, they too can be required to observe certain human rights obligations that are binding on the State under international law. This would make them responsible for breaches of those obligations.' UN Security Council, 'Report of the UN Commission on Truth in El Salvador' (1 April 1993) UN Doc S/25500, Annex, 20, cited by Henckaerts and Wiesner, 'A Possible Contribution from Customary International Law' (n 2) 154.

[153] If the armed group is successful, the State will be the natural addressee of any request for compensation because Article 10 of the ILC Articles on State Responsibility (n 24) will apply.

[154] Mampilly, *Rebel Rulers* (n 115) 239, for example, calls for a 'perspective that recognizes multiple systems producing order within a single territory as an important contemporary reality, worthy of its own analysis'.

Likewise, this chapter has repeatedly argued that the principle of effectiveness is of crucial relevance in understanding how armed groups are bound by human rights law in instances where they control territory.[155] Moreover, it has asserted that there are strong reasons to hold that the armed group is bound by the obligations of the State directly on the basis that the traditional representative of the State—the *de jure* government—has no power to ensure an armed group's compliance with the State's legal obligations under international law throughout its territory.[156] The chapter has also asserted that while the armed conflict remains ongoing, an armed group will generally bear responsibility for the breach of those obligations itself. This is a consequence of the armed group's independent legal personality under international law and its ability to bear obligations as an independent entity from its members and from the State. Support for this notion has been found in the law on belligerency and insurgency. It was shown in Part II of the book that the law on belligerency and insurgency provides another strong precedent for the view that armed groups will take on 'human-rights-like' legal obligations in instances where they control territory, and bear responsibility for their breach themselves. A review of these diverse authorities leads to the observation that in instances where a State loses control over a portion of a territory, its obligations under international law acquire a multidimensional nature whereby different entities acquire different layers of obligation and incur different levels of responsibility for their breach.

It can be noted that the principles explored in this chapter, and their articulation through the effectiveness principle, have strong similarities with the 'actor' approach to international legal personality set out in Chapter 3, which prioritizes the 'actual' over the 'normative'. They also have similarities with the individualistic approach to international legal personality which shows a preparedness to take into account the actual, so far as it is legal in character. It was shown in Chapter 3 that both theories put store on the idea that legal personality is linked to an entity's participation on the international sphere. Indeed, in that sense, the legal principles explored in this chapter give less attention to the issue of State consent, than the international humanitarian law framework explored in Chapter 5. Instead, they articulate a view that obligations may emerge for armed groups as a result of the factual context in which they operate and the functions of government which they adopt. Indeed, the only consent that has been shown to be relevant in this framework is the State's own consent to be bound by the original human rights obligations over its whole territory. As a result, the legal framework gives little attention to whether the State 'consents' to the armed group being bound as a matter of

[155] It is noted that the principle of effectiveness was also held to be the driving force behind Article 9 of the ILC Articles on State Responsibility (n 24). See ILC, Yearbook of the International Law Commission 1980 (5 May–25 July 1980) Vol II Part I, UN Doc A/CN.4/SER.4/1980/Add.1 (Part I), 96 [12].

[156] It is noted that international obligations generally apply to the whole territory of a State. This is found in Article 29 of the Vienna Convention on the Law of Treaties (1969). See L. Zegveld, *The Accountability of Armed Opposition Groups in International Law* (CUP, Cambridge 2002) 209.

international law. From a technical perspective the armed group is treated as a manifestation of the State, in respect to its provision of public services. Moreover, the evidence points to an argument that the armed group is bound as a result of the State's own obligations. In that sense, the conclusions in this chapter confirm and build on the conclusions made in Part II which analysed the law of belligerency and insurgency.

This chapter also demonstrates a key additional element which is relevant to an armed group's acquisition of legal personality under international law; that is, the absence of the incumbent government. In this sense, this chapter has shown that an armed group may acquire obligations under international human rights law, not only through its own functionality but also through the absence of the *de jure* government. This is similar to the findings in Chapters 4, 5, and 6 which found that the incapacities of the *de jure* government was a key force which justified the acquisition by an armed group of legal personality. Of course, the problem with this theory is that it links the armed group's legal obligations to the legal obligations of the State. This makes the theory an unattractive explanation for armed groups, especially for treaty law whose bindingness is explicitly rooted in the individual consent of the parent State. It will be less unattractive when it is used to explain how armed groups are bound by customary international law which is based on the consent and practice of the community of States.[157] However, it can be seen that a more attractive perspective on the theory is found in the bottom-up perspective articulated at the end of the chapter. Armed groups may find it less confrontational to understand that their legal obligations arise out of the rights framework which have devolved with the territory and now belong to the population. From this perspective, the armed group is not taking responsibility for the duties of the State per se but for the rights of the people.

Before concluding, it must be commented that it can be seen that it was unlikely to be on the basis of the principles explored in this chapter that the Committee against Torture was willing to find that the acts of the Hawiye claim could incur State responsibility in the *Elmi v Australia* case that was discussed in Chapter 8.[158] This case has sometimes been cited as an example of the Committee against Torture showing a willingness to 'pierce' the State veil.[159] In many ways this observation is true, as the case demonstrates the Committee's willingness to treat the acts of an entity holding *de facto* powers of government in a situation of State failure, as 'State acts' which incur State responsibility. However, on the basis that the Somalian government had completely ceased to exist in the *Elmi* case, it is suggested that the Committee's decision in the *Elmi* case can be better seen to be an application of Article 4(1) of the Articles on State responsibility, which this chapter has shown can apply in instances where an armed group establishes a new government when there is a situation of complete State failure. That being so, the analysis of

[157] Kleffner, 'The applicability of international humanitarian law' (n 6) 454.

[158] *Elmi v Australia*, Communication No. 120/1998 (14 May 1999) UN Doc CAT/C/22/D/120/1998, discussed at sections 3.2.1 and 3.2.2 of Chapter 8.

[159] McCorquodale and La Forgia, 'Taking Off the Blindfolds' (n 38) 218.

this chapter shows that the Committee against Torture could theoretically take a broader approach in its case law to the 'public official' requirement in its Article 1 by relying instead on Article 9. This would enable the Committee to make a finding that a returning State had violated its obligations under Article 3, not only in instances of complete State failure but also in instances where armed groups exercised governmental functions in territory where the government was absent.[160]

Finally, it is noteworthy that the ideas explored in the chapter are relevant to questions beyond that of 'when and how do armed groups become bound by human rights law?' In particular, the invocation of the effectiveness principle at a domestic and international level by the Franco-Italian Conciliation Commission may provide a thought-provoking contribution to the current debate in international humanitarian law on whether armed groups can establish tribunals or pass laws that are considered legitimate under domestic or international law and allow them to prosecute or detain.[161] In its analysis of these issues, the Conciliation Commission found that the principle of effectiveness allowed it to treat the legislation of armed groups as the law of the State. It may also provide a contribution to the discussion of similar questions when looking at whether and when an armed group may be able to abide by the fair trial guarantees enshrined in Article 14 of the ICCPR.[162] Moreover, it is noted that the ideas explored in this chapter may also be relevant to discussions on self-defence and the question of whether attacks by armed non-State actors may be attributed to the State in which they are operating.[163]

[160] See for example *H.M.H.I v Australia*, Communication No. 177/2001 (1 May 2002) UN Doc CAT/C/28/D/177/2001.

[161] See section 8.2.3.2 in Chapter 6.

[162] See for example S. Sivakumaran, 'Courts of Armed Opposition Groups, Fair Trials Or Summary Justice?' (2009) 7 Journal of International Criminal Justice 489; J. Somer, 'Jungle Justice: Passing Sentence on the Equality of Belligerents in Non-International Armed Conflict' (2007) 89 International Review of the Red Cross 655. See also D. Murray, *Human Rights Obligations of Non-State Armed Groups* (Bloomsbury, London 2016) 205–56 for a review of armed group practice in this regard and an analysis of how the legal framework could be applied to this practice.

[163] Ruys, 'Crossing the Thin Blue Line' (n 38) 265–94.

10

Armed Groups and Crimes against Humanity

1. Introduction

This chapter analyses what the law on crimes against humanity tells us about how and when armed groups are bound by human rights law. Literature seeking to explain how armed groups are bound by human rights law has identified the significance of the relationship between human rights law and crimes against humanity, yet the subject remains only minimally explored.[1] For example, it has been noted that international criminal law imposes human rights obligations on individuals belonging to armed groups.[2] Likewise, it has been warned that an expansive interpretation of Article 7 of the Rome Statute may be used as a 'back door' for a 'progressive development of international human rights law'.[3] Similarly, several fact-finding missions have cited Article 7 of the Rome Statute on crimes against humanity as the legal justification for their findings that armed groups have committed human rights violations.[4] This suggests that the authors of the

[1] A. Clapham, 'Focusing on Armed Non-State Actors' in A. Clapham and P. Gaeta (eds), *The Oxford Handbook of International Law in Armed Conflict* (OUP, Oxford 2014) 766–810, 805–7; C. Ryngaert, 'Human Rights Obligations of Armed Groups' (2008) 2 Revue Belge de Droit International 355, 365 (hereafter Ryngaert, 'Human Rights Obligations of Armed Groups'); J. Henckaerts and C. Wiesener, 'Human Rights Obligations of Non-State Armed Groups: A Possible Contribution from Customary International Law?' in R. Kolb and G. Gaggioli (eds), *Research Handbook on Human Rights and Humanitarian Law* (Research Handbooks in Human Rights 2013) 146–69, by implication at 159–60.

[2] See Ryngaert, 'Human Rights Obligations of Armed Groups' (n 1) 365. N. Rodley, 'Non-State Actors and Human Rights' in S. Sheeran and N. Rodley (eds), *Routledge Handbook of International Human Rights Law* (Routledge, Abingdon 2013) 533 (hereafter Rodley, 'Non-State Actors and Human Rights')

[3] C. Kress, 'On the Outer Limits of Crimes Against Humanity: The Concept of Organisation within the Policy Requirement: Some Reflections on the March 2010 *Kenya* Decision' (2010) 23 Leiden Journal of International Law 855, 860–1 (hereafter Kress, 'Reflections on the March 2010 *Kenya* Decision').

[4] See for example, OHCHR, 'Special Report: Summary of fact finding missions on alleged human rights violations committed by the Lord's Resistance Army (LRA) in the districts of Haut-Uélé and Bas-Uélé in Orientale province of the Democratic Republic of Congo, United Nations Joint Human Rights Office in the DRC (United Nations Organization Mission in the Democratic Republic of the Congo and Office of the High Commissioner for Human Rights)' (December 2009) [6] (hereafter LRA Report, December 2009). See also UN Human Rights Council, 'Report of the Independent International Commission of Inquiry on the Syrian Arab Republic' (22 February 2012) UN Doc A/HRC/19/69, [106]; UNMISS, 'Conflict in South Sudan: A Human Rights Report' (8 May 2014) <https://unmiss.unmissions.org/sites/default/files/unmiss_conflict_in_south_sudan_-_a_human_

reports consider Article 7 of the Rome Statute to be evidence that armed groups have obligations under human rights law. While the view that international criminal law is the source of human rights obligations may be ambitious, it seems likely that the law on crimes against humanity can provide information about armed groups' obligations under human rights law. The chapter's aim is to evaluate how the law relating to crimes against humanity can be of assistance in explaining how and when armed groups are bound by human rights law. The chapter is divided into three parts. The first part considers whether armed groups, as opposed to their members, can commit crimes against humanity. Finding strong evidence to suggest that armed groups can commit crimes against humanity albeit in a non-criminal sense, the second part of the chapter considers what the law on crimes against humanity can tell us about *when* armed groups can commit crimes against humanity. The final part of the chapter evaluates what the law on crimes against humanity is able to reveal about the content of armed groups' responsibilities under human rights law.

2. Armed Groups and Crimes against Humanity

2.1 Armed groups and the jurisdiction of international courts and tribunals

The chapter begins with an evaluation of whether armed groups, as opposed to their members, can commit crimes against humanity. Interestingly, the draft Statute of the International Criminal Court (ICC) which was prepared for the Diplomatic Conference in Rome in 1998 contained a suggestion that the court should have jurisdiction over 'legal persons',[5] a phrase that could potentially have included armed groups.[6] The draft Statute also contained a suggestion that the International Criminal Court should be able to impose far-reaching sanctions over legal persons that included fines, dissolution, and the forfeiture of premises and assets.[7] However, this provision was controversial and it was rejected when, after weeks of discussion, no consensus had been reached on its contents. Accordingly, for now, Article 25(3) of the Rome Statute is entitled 'Individual Criminal Responsibility'

rights_report.pdf> [18] accessed 20 January 2017, which refers to armed groups being bound by *peremptory norms*. The wording of these reports is discussed further in Chapter 11.

[5] Article 23 [5], [6] of the draft Rome Statute.

[6] Although there is no indication that the provision was intended to extend to 'armed groups', it is likely that the term 'legal person' could have been interpreted to include armed groups. For a detailed discussion of this draft article see A. Clapham, 'The Question of Jurisdiction Under International Criminal Law Over Legal Persons' in M. T. Kamminga and S. Zia-Zarifi (eds), *Liability of Multinational Corporations Under International Law* (Kluwer Law International, The Hague 2000) 139–78, 143–58 (hereafter Clapham, 'Question of Jurisdiction'); O. Triffterer (ed), *Commentary on the Rome Statute of the International Criminal Court, Observers' Notes, Article by Article* (Nomos Verlagsgesellschaft, Baden Baden 1999) 477–8 (hereafter Triffterer, *Commentary*); L. Zegveld, *The Accountability of Armed Opposition Groups in International Law* (CUP, Cambridge 2002) 56–7.

[7] See n 5.

and only extends to individuals.[8] It reads: 'The Court shall have jurisdiction over *natural persons* pursuant to this Statute' (emphasis added). In excluding 'legal persons' from the Court's jurisdiction, the drafters of the Rome Statute chose not to follow in the footsteps of the International Military Tribunal (IMT) at Nuremberg which had the power to declare groups or organizations to be 'criminal'.[9] Instead, the drafters followed the example of the ad hoc Tribunals of the International Criminal Tribunal for the former Yugoslavia (ICTY) and International Criminal Tribunal for Rwanda (ICTR) which have also had jurisdiction only over natural persons.[10] Interestingly, the Appeals Chamber of the Special Tribunal for Lebanon has recently held that the Tribunal has jurisdiction to hear cases of contempt against legal persons.[11]

2.2 International criminal law holds information about the responsibility of armed groups under general international law and human rights law

The fact that the majority of existing international criminal law courts and tribunals only provide jurisdiction over individuals does not preclude the possibility that international criminal law holds important information about the responsibility of armed groups under general international law and under human rights law. International criminal law's ability to provide information on such issues emerges from the fact that in many instances where an individual commits an international crime, another legal entity may also incur responsibility for the act. This observation stems from the fact that many international crimes are peremptory norms (e.g. prohibitions of aggression, genocide, slavery, racial discrimination, crimes against humanity and torture, and the right to self-determination) and exist at the intersection of several different disciplines of international law:[12] international

[8] Article 123 of the Rome Statute states that the Secretary-General of the United Nations may convene a Review Conference to consider any amendments to the Rome Statute at the request of a State party if that request has the approval of the majority of States parties.

[9] Article 9 of the Charter of the International Military Tribunal—Annex to the Agreement for the prosecution and punishment of the major war criminals of the European Axis (London Agreement) (1945) gave the International Military Tribunal (IMT) the power to declare groups or organizations to be 'criminal organizations' during the trial of any individual member of that group or organization. For a discussion of this provision, see Clapham, 'Question of Jurisdiction' (n 6) 160–70. It is noted that the purpose of the provision in the London Charter was to make the prosecution of the crime of 'membership' more expedited. See L. van den Herik, 'Corporations as Future Subjects of the International Criminal Court: An Exploration of the Counterarguments and Consequences' in C. Stahn and L. van den Herik (eds), *Future Perspectives on International Criminal Justice* (CUP, Cambridge 2010) 350, 351.

[10] Article 6 of the Statute of the International Criminal Tribunal for the Former Yugoslavia (1993); Article 5 of the Statute of the International Criminal Tribunal Rwanda (1994).

[11] See *Decision on Interlocutory Appeal Concerning Personal Jurisdiction in Contempt Proceedings in the case against New T.V. S.A.L. Kharma Mohamed Tahsin Al Khayat (Appeals Panel)* STL-14-05/PT/AP/AR126.1 (2 October 2014).

[12] See A. Cassese, *International Criminal Law* (OUP, Oxford 2008) 7–8 (hereafter Cassese, *International Criminal Law*).

human rights law, international criminal law, general public international law, and international humanitarian law. As a result of this positioning, they have the potential to constitute more than one of the following: a crime perpetrated by an individual, a wrongful act of a State or non-State actor, a violation of international humanitarian law, and/or a violation of international human rights law.[13] The possibility of there being so many different jurisdictional manifestations of a single act was illustrated by the avalanche of case law which followed the conflict in the former Yugoslavia. The crimes committed during the armed conflict in the former Yugoslavia triggered a diverse range of procedures and litigation suits throughout the world and in a variety of fora: cases before the ICJ, prosecutions in front of the ICTY, consideration by the UN Human Rights Committee, and a civil claim in the US for the tort of torture.[14]

One of the clearest passages explaining this phenomenon in relation to the State paradigm is found in the judgment by the International Court of Justice (ICJ) in the case *Bosnia and Herzegovina v Serbia and Montenegro Case concerning the Application of the Convention on the Prevention and Punishment of the Crime of Genocide (Bosnia and Herzegovina v Serbia and Montenegro)*.[15] After examining the evidence, the ICJ's conclusions in this case are well-known. The Court concluded that the acts of the individuals who had committed the genocide at Srebrenica could not be attributed to Serbia and Montenegro under the rules of State responsibility.[16] Despite this, the ICJ found that Serbia and Montenegro had violated its 'obligation to prevent' and its 'obligation to punish' the genocide in Srebrenica so that its responsibility was engaged.[17] In coming to these conclusions, the ICJ observed that genocide is a 'crime' which entails a 'duality of responsibilities':[18] individual responsibility and State responsibility. It noted that this 'duality of responsibility' is a 'constant feature of international law' that is reflected in provisions of the Rome Statute[19] and the Articles on State

[13] Ibid.

[14] See for example, *Application of the Convention on the Prevention and Punishment of the Crime of Genocide (Bosnia and Herzegovina v Serbia and Montenegro) (Judgment)* [2007] ICJ Reports 43, 26 February 2007 (hereafter *Bosnia and Herzegovina v Serbia and Montenegro)*; UN, 'Procedural Decisions of the Human Rights Committee, Bosnia and Herzegovina, Croatia, Yugoslavia' (1993) UN Doc A/ 48/40, Annex VII; *Kadic v Karadzic (Opinion of 2nd Circuit re Subject Matter Jurisdiction)* Docket Nos. 94-9035, 94-9069 (United States Court of Appeals for the Second Circuit, 13 October 1995); UNSG, 'Report of the Secretary-General Pursuant to paragraph 2 of Security Council Resolution 808' (3 May 1993) UN Doc S/25704, establishing the International Criminal Tribunal for the former Yugoslavia.

[15] *Bosnia and Herzegovina v Serbia and Montenegro* (n 14) 43, 238.

[16] The ICJ found that the massacres were perpetrated by persons and groups of persons (the Army of the Republika Srpska in particular) who did not have the character of organs of the Respondent, and did not act on the instructions or under the effective control of the Respondent. The Court also did not find that the Respondent State's responsibility was engaged for acts of complicity in genocide as per Article III, paragraph (e), of the Convention. See *Bosnia and Herzegovina v Serbia and Montenegro* (n 14) 202–19, 237.

[17] *Bosnia and Herzegovina v Serbia and Montenegro* (n 14) 226, 229.

[18] Ibid, 112–3 [163].

[19] Article 25(4) of the Rome Statute states: 'No provision in this Statute relating to individual criminal responsibility shall affect the responsibility of States under international law', cited ibid. 116 [173].

Responsibility.[20] In citing these provisions, the ICJ made clear that the responsibility incurred by States and individuals for the underlying acts is different in character.[21] A State's responsibility is akin to a tortious or civil responsibility for an international wrong. An individual's responsibility is an individual criminal responsibility for a crime. Both types of responsibility can be triggered simultaneously by the same act but exist without prejudice to each other.[22] The fact that an individual has been prosecuted for a particular act does not exonerate the State from its own responsibility.[23] Nor is it necessary, as a matter of law, for there to have been a finding of individual criminal responsibility for it to be found that a State is responsible for that act.[24] The ICJ also made some important comments about how such an act can be attributed to States.

1.1. Attribution of responsibility for crimes against humanity to States

From the ICJ's comments in the *Bosnia and Herzegovina v Serbia and Montenegro* case, it can be seen that both individuals and States may incur responsibility for crimes against humanity. Moreover, the judgment demonstrates that a State's responsibility under international law can be assessed against a reasonably clear legal framework. International law accepts that States have international legal personality and can bear responsibility for internationally wrongful acts. Furthermore, the International Law Commission's Articles on State Responsibility for Internationally Wrongful Acts provide a clear framework of analysis against which to assess State responsibility.[25] The Articles demonstrate that in instances where State officials commit international crimes, the State itself will often also be responsible for the crimes under general international law.[26] If the State is not responsible for the crimes themselves, it may, as was found in the *Bosnia and Herzegovina v. Serbia and Montenegro* case, be responsible for its failure to prevent

[20] ILC, 'Draft Articles on Responsibility of States for Internationally Wrongful Acts' (9 August 2001) UN Doc A/56/83 (hereafter ILC Articles on State Responsibility). Article 58 states: 'These articles are without prejudice to any question of the individual responsibility under international law of any person acting on behalf of a State.' Cited at *Bosnia and Herzegovina v Serbia and Montenegro* (n 14) 116 [173].

[21] The ICJ cited the Commentary to Article 58 of the ILC Articles on State Responsibility (n 20) and stated: 'the question of individual responsibility is in principle distinct from the principle of State responsibility'. In *Bosnia and Herzegovina v Serbia and Montenegro* (n 14) 116 [173].

[22] *Bosnia and Herzegovina v Serbia and Montenegro* (n 14), [173].

[23] Ibid.

[24] *Bosnia and Herzegovina v Serbia and Montenegro* (n 14) 120 [182]. Cassese notes in this regard that the notion of individual criminal responsibility is a concept which followed the notion of State responsibility in terms of how the law developed. He notes that violations of international humanitarian law, for example, originally only generated State responsibility. See Cassese, *International Criminal Law* (n 12) 6. This was the legal *status quo* that the International Military Tribunal was seeking to change in its famous statement that: '[c]rimes against international law are committed by men, not by abstract entities'. See (n 9).

[25] See (n 20).

[26] This is explicitly stated in the Commentary to Article 58 of the ILC Articles on State Responsibility (n 20) and cited in *Bosnia and Herzegovina v Serbia and Montenegro* (n 14) 116 [173].

or punish the crimes.[27] In instances where crimes are committed by persons who are not State officials, the ICJ confirmed that the question of whether a State is responsible will be assessed on the basis of whether the State had 'effective control' over those individuals' actions.[28] The process of attributing State responsibility to crimes against humanity is also assisted by the fact that crimes against humanity, by definition, have a two-tiered authority.

2.3 Crimes against humanity usually have a two-tiered authorship

2.3.1 Widespread and systematic requirement

The ICJ's observation that international crimes often incur a duality of responsibility is supported, when it comes to crimes against humanity, by the fact that crimes against humanity almost always have a two-tiered authorship. While this observation is rarely noted, its truth is has been repeatedly confirmed in case law on the crime. For example, it was recognized already in the case law from the Military Tribunals operating under Control Council No. 10 that isolated acts cannot constitute crimes against humanity.[29] Summarizing the main findings of the Military Tribunals' jurisprudence in 1948, the United Nations War Crimes Commission stated that the trials had established that:

> Isolated offences did not fall within the notion of crimes against humanity. As a rule systematic mass action, particularly if it was authoritative, was necessary to transform a common crime, punishable only under municipal law, into a crime against humanity, which thus became also the concern of international law. Only crimes which either by their magnitude and savagery or by their large number or by the fact that a similar pattern was applied at different times and places, endangered the international community or shocked the conscience of mankind, warranted intervention by States other than that on whose territory the crimes had been committed, or whose subjects had become their victims.[30]

Clearly already in the1940s, it was recognized that acts needed to reach a certain magnitude or systematicity before they could be prosecuted as crimes against humanity.

[27] See *Bosnia and Herzegovina v Serbia and Montenegro* (n 14) 226, 229.

[28] *Case Concerning Military and Paramilitary Activities in and against Nicaragua (Nicaragua v United States of America)* [1986] ICJ Reports 14, 27 June 1986, 65 [116]. This was confirmed by the ICJ in *Bosnia and Herzegovina v Serbia and Montenegro* (n 14) 208 [400], where the court stated: 'it must however be shown that this "effective control" was exercised, or that the State's instructions were given, in respect of each operation in which the alleged violations occurred, not generally in respect of the overall actions taken by the persons or groups of persons having committed the violations'. This is a more rigorous test than the overall test set out by the ICTY in *Prosecutor v Tadić (Appeals Chamber Judgment)* IT-94-1-A (15 July 1999) [122] (hereafter *Tadić* Appeals Judgment). Here it was held that if a group of individuals could be held to be under the 'overall control' of a particular State, the activities of the group will engage the responsibility of the State, irrespective of whether each of them was specifically imposed, directed or requested by the State.

[29] *Trial Josef Altstötter and Others* (United States Military Tribunal, Nuremberg 1948) Law Reports Of Trials Of War Criminals Selected and Prepared by the United Nations War Crimes Commission (17 February–4 December 1947) Vol VI, 79.

[30] *History of the United Nations War Crimes Commission and the Development of the Laws of War* (His Majesty's Stationery Office, London 1948) 179.

There was also an appreciation that a pattern of crimes amounting to crimes against humanity would rarely ever be able to be committed by a single individual.[31]

Writing in 1996, the International Law Commission suggested that it was the fact that crimes against humanity had a dual authorship that elevated them to the status of 'international crimes' under international law. The Draft Code of Crimes against the Peace and Security of Mankind (ILC Draft Code of Crimes) stated that for acts to constitute a 'crime against humanity', they must be 'instigated or directed by a Government or by any organization or group'.[32] The Commentary elaborated as follows:

> The instigation or direction of a Government or any organization or group, which may or may not be affiliated with a Government *gives the act its great dimension* and *makes it a crime against humanity* imputable to private persons or agents of the State. (emphasis added)[33]

The fact that it is not possible to commit an isolated crime against humanity is also reflected in the law on crimes against humanity that has been developed by the ad hoc tribunals and the International Criminal Court.[34] Indeed, crimes against humanity have recently been described as a 'collective crime' because crimes against humanity comprise of an attack on a 'collectivity'[35] and are carried out 'collectively'.[36]

[31] Arguably the *Streicher* case before the IMT constitutes an example of an individual committing crimes against humanity. Julius Streicher the publisher of Der Sturmer, an anti-Semitic weekly newspaper in the Second World War was prosecuted for crimes against humanity. The systematicity in this case was achieved on the basis that over a period of years, Streicher was responsible for the newspaper's circulation which had a circulation of 600,000. As a result, single-handedly Streicher was able to achieve the systematic, mass action required for crimes against humanity. *International Military Tribunal (Judgment and Sentence)* (n 9) 294. It is doubtful whether such crimes committed by Streicher would be committed as crimes against humanity today. See *Prosecutor v Nikolić (Review of Indictment pursuant to Rule 61 of the Rules of Evidence and Procedure)* IT-94-2-R61 (20 October 1995) [26] (hereafter *Nikolić)*, where the Trial Chamber states: 'Although [crimes against humanity] need not be related to a policy established at State level in the conventional sense of the term, they cannot be the work of an isolated individual alone.' See also *Prosecutor v Germain Katanga and Mathieu Ngudjolo Chui (Trial Judgment)* ICC-01/04-01/07 (7 March 2014) [1123–24] (hereafter *Katanga* Trial Judgment). See also G. Simpson, 'Men and Abstract Entities: Individual Responsibility and Collective Guilt in International Criminal Law' in A. Nollkaemper and H. van der Wilt (eds), *System Criminality in International Law* (CUP, Cambridge 2009) 69–100, 90 (hereafter Simpson, 'Abstract Entities').

[32] See ILC, 'Draft Code of Crimes against the Peace and Security of Mankind with commentaries', Yearbook of the International Law Commission 1996 (6 May–26 July 1996) Vol II, Part 2, UN Doc A/CN.4/SER.A/1996/Add.1 (Part 2) (hereafter ILC Draft Code of Crimes and Commentary), Article 18 (Crimes against Humanity) 47.

[33] See Commentary to Article 18 in ILC Draft Code of Crimes and Commentary (n 32) 47. As cited in *Prosecutor v Tadić (Trial Judgment)* IT-94-I-T (7 May 1997) [655] (hereafter *Tadić* Trial Judgment).

[34] See (n 31).

[35] *Tadić* Trial Judgment (n 33) [644]. See also G. Sluiter, '"Chapeau Elements" of Crimes against Humanity' in L. Sadat (ed), *Forging a Convention for Crimes against Humanity* (CUP, Cambridge 2011) 102–41, 117 (hereafter Sluiter, '"Chapeau Elements"').

[36] See also *Prosecutor v Akayesu (Trial Judgment)* ICTR-96-4-T (2 September 1998) [580]; *Decision Pursuant to Article 15 of the Rome Statute on the Authorization of an Investigation into the Situation in the Republic of Kenya (Pre-Trial Chamber II)* ICC-01/09 (31 March 2010) [95] (hereafter Article 15 Decision); *Katanga* Trial Judgment (n 31) [1123].

Nowadays, an individual can only be found guilty of crimes against humanity today if his or her acts were committed as part of a wider campaign of crimes.[37] This is implicit in the requirement articulated in Article 7 of the Rome Statute and the case law from the ad hoc tribunals that the underlying acts which constitute crimes against humanity must be 'widespread or systematic'.[38] It is also inherent in the requirement that crimes against humanity must constitute an 'attack' upon a civilian population.[39] The term 'attack' in the chapeau of Article 7 has been held to refer to 'a course of conduct involving the multiple commission of acts'[40] or 'a campaign or operation' carried out against the civilian population.[41] This interpretation of these terms confirms that crimes against humanity will almost always be coordinated at a higher level. This is also reflected in the *mens rea* of the offence which requires that an accused knows that there is an attack on the civilian population and knows that his acts comprise part of that attack.[42] Accordingly, while an individual may in theory be prosecuted for a single crime against humanity, the prosecution will only be successful if the single act (e.g murder) forms part of a wider pattern of crimes.[43] This reflects the fact that the case law on crimes against humanity addresses collective criminal conduct: it addresses situations where at the bottom level there are individuals committing criminal acts which make up a widespread or systematic pattern of conduct and at the top-level there is higher organization or State organizing, directing, or facilitating the wider operation of criminal conduct.

2.3.2 Requirement that crimes against humanity be committed pursuant to a policy

In future case law in front of the ICC, the emphasis on the existence of higher 'entity' directing, facilitating, or ordering crimes against humanity is only likely to become more pronounced. This is because of Article 7(2)(a) of the Rome Statute requires that crimes against humanity must be perpetrated in furtherance to a

[37] See (n 31). [38] *Tadić* Trial Judgment (n 33) [644].

[39] See the chapeau of Article 7 of the Rome Statute which states that '"A crime against humanity" means any of the following acts when committed as part of a widespread or systematic attack directed against any civilian population, with knowledge of the attack.' G. Mettraux, 'Crimes against Humanity and the Question of the "Policy" Element' in L. Sadat (ed), *Forging a Convention for Crimes against Humanity* (CUP, Cambridge 2011) 142–76, 154 (hereafter Mettraux, 'The "Policy" Element').

[40] See Article 7(2)(a) which states that '"Attack directed against any civilian population" means a course of conduct involving the multiple commission of acts referred to in paragraph 1 against any civilian population.' See also *Prosecutor v Jean-Pierre Bemba Gombo (Decision Pursuant to Article 61(7)(a) and (b) of the Rome Statute on the Charges of the Prosecutor Against Jean-Pierre Bemba Gombo)(Pre-Trial Chamber II)* ICC-01/05-01/08 (15 June 2009) [75] (hereafter *Bemba Gombo*); Article 15 Decision (n 36) [80].

[41] *Bemba Gombo* (n 40) [75]; *Katanga* Trial Judgment (n 31) [1123].

[42] *Tadić* Appeals Judgment (n 28) [248]; *Prosecutor v Kunarac* et al. *(Appeals Judgment)* IT-96-23, 23-A, 23/1, 23/1-A, (12 June 2002) [99], [102] (hereafter *Kunarac* Appeals Judgment); *Prosecutor v Blaškić (Appeals Judgment)* IT-95-14-A (29 July 2004) [16] (hereafter *Blaškić* Appeals Judgment); *Katanga* Trial Judgment (n 31) [1125].

[43] See *Blaškić* Appeals Judgment (n 42) [101], which states: 'Only the attack, not the individual acts of the accused need only be a part of this attack, and all other conditions being met, a single or limited number of acts on his or her part would qualify as a crime against humanity, unless those acts may be said to be isolated or random.' Also *Katanga* Trial Judgment (n 31) [1124].

policy 'of a State or organization'. Effectively, this constitutes a requirement that the acts in question be the design of larger entity, be it a State or organization. We are told by delegates who attended the Rome Conference that the policy requirement was included in Article 7(2)(a) to assist in distinguishing crimes against humanity from ordinary crimes.[44] However, it constituted a controversial departure from the jurisprudence from the ad hoc tribunals, which rejected a 'policy requirement'.[45] Indeed, the discrepancy between the Rome Statute and the ad hoc tribunals on this point has prompted an animated academic debate about whether the 'policy requirement' in Article 7 is reflective of customary international law.[46] Those in favour of the requirement have criticized the meagre judicial authorities on which the ICTY Trial Chamber relied when it ruled that there was no policy requirement under customary international law.[47] They have also argued that a policy requirement is essential to distinguish crimes against humanity from municipal crimes or ordinary human rights violations.[48] Those who were against the inclusion of Article 7(2)(a) in the Rome Statute have asserted that there is little evidence that a policy requirement *is* part of customary international law. They argue that there was no policy requirement in the definition of crimes against humanity as they were prosecuted either before the IMT or the military tribunals set up under Control Council Law No. 10.[49] They also point out that there was no policy requirement in the Statutes for the ICTY, ICTR, or Special Court for

[44] D. Robinson, 'The Context of Crimes against Humanity' in R. S. Lee (ed), *The International Criminal Court: Elements of Crimes and Rules of Procedure and Evidence* (Transnational Publishers Inc, New York 2001) 62.

[45] See *Kunarac* Appeals Judgment (n 42) 28 fn 114. Unlike the ICC which applies its own Statute, the ICTY is bound to apply customary international criminal law. In his initial report in 1993, the Secretary-General of the United Nations made clear in his report that the ICTY should 'apply rules of international humanitarian law which are beyond any doubt part of customary law so that the problem of adherence of some but not all States to specific conventions does not arise'. UN Secretary General, 'Report of the Secretary-General Pursuant to paragraph 2 of Security Council Resolution 808' (3 May 1993) UN Doc S/25704, [34].

[46] See Mettraux, 'The "Policy" Element' (n 39) for an overview of the debate. At 145, Mettraux explains how 'the debate over the definition of that crime [crimes against humanity] is also a debate over its soul, over what it *should* be, as much as over what it is'.

[47] See *Kunarac* Appeals Judgment (n 42) 28 fn 114. Shabas refers to this as the 'famous footnote' in W. A. Schabas, 'Prosecuting Dr. Strangelove, Goldfinger, and the Joker at the ICC' (2010) 23 Leiden Journal of International Law 847, 849 (hereafter Schabas, 'Prosecuting Dr. Strangelove, Goldfinger, and the Joker'). See further criticism of this footnote see W. A. Shabas, 'Crimes against Humanity: The State Plan of Policy Element' in L. Sadat and M. Scharf (eds) *The Theory and Practice of International Criminal Law: Essays in Honor of M. Cherif Bassiouni* (Martinus Nijhoff, Leiden 2008) 347–64 (hereafter Shabas, 'Crimes against Humanity'). See also Kress, 'Reflections on the March 2010 *Kenya* Decision' (n 3) 870.

[48] See Mettraux, 'The "Policy" Element' (n 39) 148, for a summary of these arguments. Kress, 'Reflections on the March 2010 *Kenya* Decision' (n 3) 871, also conducts a thorough and thought-provoking review of Judge Kaul's dissenting opinion with which he largely agrees. He argues further that contrary to a number of bold jurisprudential assertions since the *Kunarac* Appeals Judgment (n 42), the customary definition of crimes against humanity includes the requirement of a policy by a State or a State-like organization.

[49] Notably the requirement was not included in the London Agreement, the Charter of the International Military Tribunal for the Far East (1946) or Article II(1)(c) of the Control Council Law No. 10, *Punishment of Persons Guilty of War Crimes, Crimes against Peace and against Humanity* (1945).

Sierra Leone. Nor does a policy requirement appear in other international conventions referring to crimes against humanity, for example the 1968 Convention on the Non-Applicability of Statutory Limitations to War Crimes and Crimes against Humanity, the Genocide Convention, or the Apartheid Convention.[50] They also assert that the policy requirement's apparent purpose, to provide an 'adhesive' to acts which might otherwise seem random or isolated, is already achieved by the requirement that the acts must be part of a 'widespread or systematic attack directed against any civilian population'.[51]

For the purposes of this chapter, it is important to note that even those authorities that contest the existence of a policy requirement often acknowledge that another entity in addition to the individual perpetrator, either State or non-State, will play a key role in the commission of crimes against humanity.[52] For example, in the *Limaj* et al case, which rejects the policy requirement, the Trial Chamber stated:

> Although [evidence of a policy or plan is] not a legal element of Article 5, ... it is an important indication that the acts in question are not merely the workings of individuals acting pursuant to haphazard or individual design, but instead have *a level of organisational coherence and support* of a magnitude sufficient to elevate them into the realm of crimes against humanity. (emphasis added)[53]

Likewise, the case law from the ICTY has repeatedly emphasized that crimes against humanity cannot be the work of 'isolated individuals alone'.[54] It seems clear that both sides of the debate agree that the actions of an individual accused of crimes against humanity will take place within the context of a wider course of conduct designed or facilitated by a larger organized entity. Ultimately, as it has been argued above, this inference can be principally gleaned as the requirement that the individual acts must be widespread or systematic, and form part of a larger attack against a civilian population.

[50] See Mettraux, 'The "Policy" Element' (n 39) 157–69, for a thorough review of these sources and a detailed historical analysis of the case law on crimes against humanity on this point.

[51] See ibid, 154. See also R. Dixon (revised by C. K. Hall), 'Crimes against Humanity—part 1 chapeau' in Triffterer, *Commentary* (n 6) 180, who remarks that the policy requirement 'introduced as part of a political compromise in Rome, is not part of customary international law and is essentially superfluous as the "widespread or systematic" nature of an attack on a civilian population itself demonstrates the existence of a plan or policy. It has been justified as a basis for ensuring that random or isolated acts are excluded from the scope of crimes against humanity, but that purpose is fully served by the requirement that the attack be widespread or systematic.'

[52] Moreover, the polarization between the two camps seems to have been reduced by the latest Trial Chamber judgment from the Court which suggests that the existence of a policy may be deduced from the 'widespread' or 'systematic' nature of the crimes. *Katanga* Trial Judgment (n 31) [1106–13].

[53] *Prosecutor v Limaj, Bala and Musliu (Trial Judgment)* IT-03-66-T (30 November 2005) [212] (hereafter *Limaj* Trial Judgment).

[54] See *Nikolić* (n 31) [26]. *Prosecutor v Tadić, (Jurisdiction Decision)* IT-94-I-T (2 October 1995) (hereafter *Tadić* Jurisdiction Decision) [251].

2.4 Conclusions on attribution of responsibility for crimes against humanity to States

The paragraphs above demonstrate that crimes against humanity not only have a dual authorship but can also trigger a duality of responsibility. Moreover, they demonstrate that when it comes to States, the contextual elements of crimes against humanity are helpful in determining a State's responsibility. The analysis has shown that in instances where the individuals committing the crimes are State officials and the entity behind the course of conduct is a State, a good case will be able to be made that the State should incur responsibility for the full pattern of crimes as a matter of international law.[55] Bassiouni has stated in this regard that:

> a 'state action or policy' aimed at committing 'crimes against humanity' creates state responsibility for its violation of a jus cogens norm.[56]

The drafters of the proposed International Convention on the Prevention and Punishment of Crimes against Humanity clearly came to a similar conclusion. The draft Conclusion states in its Preamble that 'crimes against humanity constitute crimes under international law which may give rise to the responsibility of States for internationally wrongful acts'.[57] Likewise, the draft Convention states at Article 1 that 'States may be held responsible for crimes against humanity pursuant to principles of State responsibility for internationally wrongful acts.'[58]

Identifying the role of the organization or State behind the individual crimes highlights the fact that the criminal prosecutions of individuals for crimes against humanity will rarely address the magnitude of the course of conduct which has been committed. Clearly individual criminal prosecutions only address certain acts that have been perpetrated during the wider course of that conduct.[59] This observation highlights the limitations of the oft-quoted words of the judgment of the International Military Tribunal at Nuremberg: '[c]rimes against international law are committed by men, not by abstract entities, and only by punishing individuals

[55] See (n 21).

[56] C. M. Bassiouni, *Crimes Against Humanity in International Criminal Law* (Kluwer Law International, The Hague 1999) 212 (hereafter Bassiouni, *Crimes Against Humanity*).

[57] Whitney R. Harris World Law Institute, 'Proposed International Convention on the Prevention and Prosecution of Crimes against Humanity' (Crimes against Humanity Initiative, Washington University School of Law, August 2010) <http://law.wustl.edu/harris/cah/docs/EnglishTreatyFinal.pdf> accessed 20 January 2017.

[58] The Commentary to the draft Convention clarifies that the word 'may' was intended to capture the fact that State responsibility will only be incurred if the act in question can be properly 'attributed' to a State. See point 3 of the Explanatory Note under Article 1. The consequences of a State committing an internationally wrongful act usually include the obligation of cessation, non-repetition, and the obligation to make full reparation for the injury. The consequences of a State committing a serious breach of a peremptory norm involve the imposition of obligations upon States which are not directly affected by the wrongful act to: (i) cooperate to bring an end to the serious breach; and (ii) not recognize as lawful the situation created out of the serious breach. See *inter alia* Articles 30, 31, 40 and 41 of the Articles on State Responsibility (n 20).

[59] A. Nollkaemper, 'Introduction' in A. Nollkaemper and H. van der Wilt (eds), *System Criminality in International Law* (CUP, Cambridge 2009) 1, 4 (hereafter Nollkaemper, 'Introduction').

who commit such crimes can the provisions of international law be enforced'.[60] It demonstrates that a sole focus on the culpability of the individual fails to address the greater responsibility of the entity which has masterminded the 'course of conduct' as a whole. Indeed, from a quantitative and qualitative perspective the entity behind the individuals will likely be far more at fault, than the individuals that make it up. The entity behind the crime, the State or organization, is in control of the whole pattern of the underlying conduct. The entity behind the crime may also be the vehicle by which the widespread or systematic nature of the crimes is achieved. Having demonstrated that States can be responsible for crimes against humanity, the purpose of the following section is to show that as a matter of law, there is a good argument that armed groups should also be able to incur responsibility for crimes against humanity.

2.5 Attribution of responsibility for crimes against humanity to armed groups

2.5.1 A changing legal landscape

It was once thought that crimes against humanity were only able to be committed by States. This was largely due to the fact that the law on crimes against humanity was developed out of the prosecutions which followed the Second World War which involved the imposing State apparatus of Nazi Germany. This case law prompted an understanding that crimes against humanity could be exclusively perpetrated by States, or individuals supported by States, because their commission would require recourse to State institutions, personnel, and resources.[61] Since the Second World War, non-State actors have repeatedly shown themselves able to perpetrate atrocities in a widespread or systematic manner. Moreover, already in 1991, the drafters of the 1991 ILC Draft Code of Crimes demonstrated an appreciation that States do not have a monopoly on the abilty to perpetrate widespread and systematic violence. The Commentary stated:

> [i]t is important to point out that the draft article does not confine possible perpetrators of the crimes to public officials or representatives alone... *the article does not rule out the possibility that private individuals with de facto power or organized in criminal gangs or groups might also commit the kind of systematic or mass violations of human rights covered by the article.* (emphasis added)[62]

[60] These words must be seen in their context. They were stated in a world where it was normally *only* possible to have recourse to abstract entities and never before possible to have recourse to the individuals behind the entity. Ironically, in today's world, the opposite is often true with individuals taking responsibility for international crimes, more often than States. See Nollkaemper, 'Introduction' (n 59) 8, where he also notes that when takes into account the manner in which 'systems' can contribute to the commission of international crimes, the words of the Nuremberg Tribunal are 'doubtful'.

[61] See C. M. Bassiouni, *International Criminal Law, Vol I, Sources, Subjects and Contents* (Martinus Nijhoff, Leiden 2008) 248–9 (hereafter Bassiouni, *Sources*).

[62] ILC Draft Code of Crimes and Commentary (n 32), 103.

This quote, which is returned to later in the chapter, was cited by the *Tadic* Trial Chamber when it found in 1997 that the policy behind crimes against humanity 'need not be the policy of a State'.[63]

Today, there is no question that members of armed groups can commit crimes against humanity. In 2009, Revolutionary United Front leaders, Issa Hassan Sesay, Morris Kallon, and Augustine Gbao were convicted of crimes against humanity by the Special Court for Sierra Leone.[64] Likewise in 2009, the Liberian Truth and Reconciliation Commission found that all sides of the non-international armed conflict had committed crimes against humanity.[65] There have also been numerous instances in which fact-finding missions or Commissions of Inquiry have found evidence to suggest that members of armed groups have committed crimes against humanity.[66] Also noteworthy is the fact that out of the thirty four individuals against whom the ICC has issued arrest warrants, ten have been members of armed groups which are facing charges of crimes against humanity.[67] In June 2014, the ICC confirmed charges of war crimes and crimes against humanity against Bosco Ntaganda who was associated with two paramilitary groups, the Union des Patriotes Congolais (UPC) and the Forces Patriotiques pour la Libération du Congo (FPLC) in the Democratic Republic of the Congo (DRC).[68] On 7 March 2014, the ICC found Germain Katanga, member of an armed group called the *Force de Résistance Patriotique en Ituri*, to be individually criminally responsible for the crime against humanity of murder committed during the attack on the village of Bogoro, in the Ituri district of the DRC.[69] On 21 March 2016, the ICC found Jean-Pierre Bemba Gombo, member of *Mouvement de Libération du Congo*, an armed group supporting President Patassé, guilty of the crime against humanity of rape and murder in the Central African Republic.[70]

[63] *Tadic* Trial Judgment (n 33) [655].

[64] All three were convicted of the crimes against humanity of extermination, murder, rape, sexual slavery, other inhumane acts (namely, forced marriage and physical violence), and enslavement. See *Prosecutor v Issa Hassan Sesay, Morris Kallon, Augustine Gbao (Trial Judgment)* SCSL-04-15-T (2 March 2009). These convictions were upheld on appeal.

[65] Republic of Liberia Truth and Reconciliation Commission, 'Volume II: Consolidated Final Report' (30 June 2009) 19.

[66] See for example LRA Report, December 2009 (n 4); UN Security Council, 'Mid-Term Report of the United Nations Joint Human Rights Office on Human Rights Violations committed by the M23 in North Kivu Province (April 2012–November 2013)' (19 July 2013) UN Doc S/2013/433; UN Human Rights Council, 'Report of the Independent International Commission of Inquiry on the Syrian Arab Republic' (5 February 2015) UN Doc A/HRC/28/69.

[67] These include Germain Katanga, Bosco Ntaganda, Callixte Mbarashimana, Mattieu Ngudjolo Chui, Jean-Pierre Bemba Gombo, Joseph Kony, Dominic Ongwen, Vincent Otti, Okot Odhiambo, Ali Kushayb.

[68] *Prosecutor v Bosco Ntaganda (Decision on the Confirmation of Charges)* ICC-01/04-02/06 (9 June 2014) (hereafter *Ntaganda* Confirmation of Charges Decision).

[69] *Katanga* Trial Judgment (n 31).

[70] *Prosecutor v Jean-Pierre Bemba Gombo (Trial Judgment)* ICC-01/05-01/08 (21 March 2016) (hereafter *Bemba* Trial Judgment).

2.5.2 Some challenges to attributing crimes against humanity to armed groups

The fact that individual members of armed groups can commit crimes against humanity produces a strong argument that, theoretically at least, armed groups should also be able to be held responsible for crimes against humanity as a matter of international law. This arises from an application of the same reasoning set out above in relation to States, to armed groups as well. When crimes against humanity are committed by individuals belonging to armed groups, the crimes equally have a two-tiered authorship and incur a 'duality of responsibility'. No matter whether the individual perpetrator belongs to a State or an armed group, it was shown above that the existence of a crime against humanity is rationalized by the idea that the individual crimes form part of a wider course of conduct directed and controlled by a 'higher' entity controlling and supporting a wider course of criminal conduct. The truth of this conclusion is seen most clearly in Article 7(2)(a) of the Rome Statute which explicitly recognizes that crimes against humanity must be perpetrated in furtherance to a policy 'of a State *or organization*' (emphasis added). This constitutes a clear indication that the drafters of the Rome Statute recognized that both States and non-State actors could be the facilitative engines behind the commission of crimes against humanity. Despite this factual reality, the process of attributing the wrongful act of an 'individual' to an 'armed group' will inevitably be harder than with States. There are several main reasons for this.

The first reason is that the international legal personality of an armed group is much less well understood under international law than that of a State. As a matter of fact, the internal organization and territorial control of armed groups varies greatly from group to group. Moreover, the organization of an armed group and its capability for bearing rights and obligations under international law may be subject to flux during the course of the armed conflict. Perhaps more challenging still, there is little guidance on when the conduct of an individual may be attributed to an armed group, as opposed to a State. It goes without saying that the Articles on State Responsibility do not cover the responsibility of non-State actors. Moreover, a serious attempt to find generalized clarity in this area would be fraught with difficulty. First, problems would arise out of the fact that the affiliation of individuals to armed groups is often much less formal than within a State, where contracts of employment and formal titles are often a reliable means of proving that an individual is a 'State official'.[71] Secondly, although reference is often made to an armed group's 'members', there is no consensus under international law about which individuals, if any, that designation should include for the purposes of attributing responsibility to the group.[72] The identification of what would count as an armed

[71] See ICRC, 'Interpretative Guidance on the Notion of Direct Participation in Hostilities Under International Humanitarian Law' (May 2009) 32–3.

[72] There are good arguments that any notion of membership developed for the purposes of attribution should be broader than the narrow notion of 'membership' which is often applied in the context of the Additional Protocol II of the Geneva Conventions. Under IHL, the notion of membership has been deliberately defined narrowly to restrict individuals' targetability and is defined according to whether a person has a 'continuous combat function'. See ibid, 33. While a definition of membership

group's organs is also unclear.[73] Most importantly, there is also currently no procedural forum for such a claim against an armed group to be heard.

Although the attribution of responsibility to armed groups would be hard, there is no reason why it should be impossible. Clearly, if a group has a clear vertical hierarchy of command, it will be easier to identify officials and organs. Indeed, it would seem that there is a solid argument to be made that the responsibility of an armed group will be triggered by the acts and omissions of its key fighters, its leaders, and any members of its law enforcement apparatus, such as its police and judiciary, if they exist. However, in each case, the affiliation of the individuals to the group would probably have to be proved, and could never be presumed, as with States. For example, it would likely have to be proved that that the individuals were fundamentally important to the group's existence and operation or that the individuals were acting under the armed group's close direction and control.[74] In the absence of rules on attribution relating to armed groups, an argument in a civil forum that an armed group was responsible for the acts of an individual would also be made easier if the prosecution of the individual(s) had already been conducted under the Article 25(3)(d)(i) and (ii) of the Rome Statute. Interestingly, when addressing the acts of individuals, Article 25(3)(d)(i) of the Rome Statute seems implicitly to recognize the possibility that a 'group' may commit crimes under international law.

Article 25(3)(d)(i) reads as follows:

In accordance with this Statute, a person shall be criminally responsible and liable for punishment for a crime within the jurisdiction of the Court if that person:

(d) In any other way contributes to the commission or attempted commission of such a crime *by a group of persons* acting with a common purpose. Such contribution shall be intentional and shall either:-
   (i) Be made with the aim of furthering *the criminal activity or criminal purpose of the group*, where such activity or purpose involves the commission of a crime within the jurisdiction of the Court; or
   (ii) Be made in the knowledge of *the intention of the group to commit the crime.* (emphasis added)

for the purposes of attribution should also be defined narrowly, it should include individuals in governance functions. Under the rules relating to State responsibility, State organs may include the executive and administration of government, the armed forces, the judicature, federal units, and the legislature. But conceptions of membership should clearly not be so broad as to include individuals only loosely connected to the group or living in the territory under the armed group's control.

[73] For a rare exploration of the legal dilemmas of direct responsibility for armed groups see V. Bílková, 'Establishing Direct Responsibility of Armed Opposition Groups for Violations of International Humanitarian Law' in Ryngaert (ed), *Responsibilities of the Non-State Actor in Armed Conflict and the Market Place* (Brill, Leiden 2015) 278–83 (hereafter Bílková, 'Establishing Direct Responsibility') and S. Verhoeven, 'International Responsibility of Armed Opposition Groups' in Ryngaert (ed), *Responsibilities of the Non-State Actor in Armed Conflict and the Market Place* (Brill, Leiden 2015) 299–303.

[74] See also L. Zegveld, *The Accountability of Armed Opposition Groups in International Law* (CUP, Cambridge 2002) 155

While for practical purposes, the effect of this provision is only to criminalize the defendant's participation in the crime, the wording of the Article goes some way towards anticipating or acknowledging the dual criminality of the group itself.[75] This is particularly illustrated by the italicized text above which suggests that both the group and the individual are committing the criminal conduct.[76]

The process of attributing responsibility to an armed group would be similarly assisted if the member of the armed group has been prosecuted either together with other members of the armed group by means of a common plan or joint criminal enterprise.[77] It will also be assisted in circumstances where the accused is prosecuted for having had control over the crime.[78] In circumstances where either of these arguments are made to establish individual criminal liability, evidence will have had to have been brought of the connection between the individual and the group. In addition, just as with States, if the contextual elements of crimes against humanity have been established, this will provide a strong indication that there is a connection between the individual perpetrator and the group. Having set out some of the challenges that would be involved in a finding that an armed group is responsible for crimes against humanity, the section below considers whether there is any support for this idea in legal doctrine.

2.5.3 Limited recognition of responsibility of armed groups for crimes against humanity

While there are currently no instances in which armed groups have been found responsible as groups for crimes against humanity by a judicial body, there are several instances in which the responsibility of armed groups for crimes against

[75] See Clapham, 'Question of Jurisdiction' (n 6) 145.

[76] See Bassiouni, *Sources* (n 61) 45, in this regard, who states: 'An individual may engage in concert of action with others with the requisite mental state to commit, collectively as opposed to individually, the violation of an existing norm. In such instances, when the collective individual conduct (whether by omission or commission) is performed for or on behalf of or under color of authority of a legal entity, that conduct may be ascribable to that legal entity, as well as to each individual person who has been a part of the decision-making process or the execution of the decision, which constitutes a violation of a particular legal norm.'

[77] The mode of liability known as 'Joint Criminal Enterprise' has been developed in the jurisprudence of the ICTY to prosecute crimes committed by multiple individuals with a common plan, design or purpose. It was first set out by the Appeals Chamber in the *Tadić* Appeals Judgment (n 28) [227–8].

[78] This refers to the manner in which *Thomas Lubanga Dyilo* was found guilty of committing war crimes 'jointly with another' pursuant to Article 25(3)(a) of the Rome Statute before the International Criminal Court. The ICC's interpretation of the term 'jointly with another', which relies heavily on what has become known as the 'control of the crime' theory, been criticized by *inter alia* Judge Fulford in his separate opinion in the *Lubanga* case and by Judge Van den Wyngaert in her Minority Opinion of in the *Katanga* case and her Concurring Opinion in *Ngudjolo Chui* case. For a longer critique of these modes of liability. See J. D. Ohlin, E. van Sliedregt & T. Weigend, 'Assessing the Control-Theory' (Cornell Law Faculty Publications, Paper 1242, September 2013) <http://scholarship.law.cornell.edu/facpub/1242> accessed 20 January 2017. The indirect perpetration theory seems particularly inappropriate for application to members of armed groups, as it was developed in prosecutions relating to *inter alia* the imposing State apparatus of Nazi Germany.

humanity has been implicitly recognized. Indeed, it is noteworthy that the Darfur Commission of Inquiry agreed in principle with the view that armed groups may be held responsible for both war crimes and crimes against humanity. It stated in this regard that 'serious violations of human rights law and international humanitarian law' would not only incur individual criminal responsibility but:

> may also involve the international responsibility of the State or of the international non-state entity to which those authors belong as officials (or for which they acted as de facto organs), with the consequence that the State or the non-state-entity may have to pay compensation to the victims of those violations.[79]

A similar view was also expressed during the drawing up of the Basic Principles and Guidelines on the Right to a Remedy and Reparation for Victims of Violations of International Human Rights and Humanitarian Law. Looking back on the drafting process, Theo van Boven reflected:

> While the Principles and Guidelines are drawn up on the basis of State responsibility, the issue of responsibility of non-State actors was also raised in the discussions and negotiations, notably insofar as movements or groups exercise effective control over a certain territory and people in that territory, but also with regard to business enterprises exercising economic power. It was generally felt that non-State actors are to be held responsible for their policies and practices, allowing victims to seek redress and reparation on the basis of legal liability and human solidarity, and not on the basis of State responsibility.[80]

[79] UN, 'Report of the Independent International Commission of Inquiry on Darfur to the United Nations Secretary-General pursuant to Security Council Resolution 1564 of 18 September 2004' (25 January 2005) <http://www.un.org/news/dh/sudan/com_inq_darfur.pdf> accessed 20 January 2017, [175]. It is noted that the International Commission of Inquiry on Darfur did not find evidence that suggested that the rebel groups had committed crimes against humanity. See [639].

[80] T. van Boven, 'An Introductory Note to the Basic Principles And Guidelines On The Right To A Remedy And Reparation For Victims Of Violations Of International Human Rights And Humanitarian Law' (*Reparation Law Blog*, 13 August 2012) <http://www.reparationlaw.com/resources/treaties-international-law-scholars-experts/> accessed 20 January 2017. He goes on to state: 'The Principles and Guidelines provide for equal and effective access to justice, "irrespective of who may ultimately be the bearer of responsibility for the violation" (principle 3 (c))'. In this connection reference is also made to the following provision: 'In cases where a person, a legal person, or other entity is found liable for reparation to a victim, such party should provide reparation to the victim or compensate the State if the State has already provided reparation to the victim (principle 15, last sentence). It is a victim-oriented perspective that was kept in mind in extending, albeit in a modest and cautious way, the scope of the Principles and Guidelines to include the responsibility and liability of non-State actors'. See also UN Economic and Social Council, 'Commentary to the draft Basic Principles And Guidelines On The Right To A Remedy And Reparation For Victims Of Violations Of International Human Rights And Humanitarian Law' (24 October 2003) UN Doc E/CN.4,/2004/57, which states: 'Another category of non-State actor consists of groups that assume effective control over certain territory and exercise over that territory and the people on that territory the equivalent control exercised by States. In some instances, these types of non-State actors receive limited international legal recognition. There is no legal reason why such non-State actors would be excluded either from responsibility for their actions or for the consequences of their policies and practices with respect to victims of these policies and practices. The intention here is not to make States responsible for the policies and practices of non-State actors, but to make these non-State actors responsible for their policies and practices, while at the same time allowing victims to seek redress on the basis of social and human solidarity and not on the basis of State responsibility.'

This illustrates a view that armed groups should be able to bear responsibility for violations of human rights law and international humanitarian law. It is noteworthy that in August 2014, the FARC declared itself willing to pay compensation to victims of the conflict in Colombia and stated its willingness to take responsibility for its acts under international humanitarian law.[81] This is evidence that the idea that an armed group may be held responsible, or even accept responsibility for, violations of internationally law is not practically unrealistic.[82]

The notion that the responsibility of armed groups is implicated when agents of the group commit crimes against humanity is also implicitly recognized in statements from international criminal tribunals. When addressing the actions of members of armed groups, there are many instances in which international criminal courts and tribunals have implicitly acknowledged the dual responsibility of the armed group itself. It is noteworthy in this respect that the case law often seems to tacitly acknowledge that it is often the armed group which commits, encourages, and facilitates the 'course of conduct' as a whole. For example, in the Pre-Trial Chamber's decision authorizing an investigation of crimes against humanity in the *Kenya* situation, the majority stated that the defining characteristic of whether a group may qualify as an 'organization' for the purposes of Article 7(2) of the Rome Statute is whether the 'group has the capability to perform acts which infringe on basic human values'.[83] In this statement, it is noteworthy that the Pre-Trial Chamber identifies the 'group' as the entity 'performing' the criminal acts. The understanding that an armed group can commit crimes against humanity, concurrently with an individual, is likewise seen in the ICC Pre-Trial Chamber's statement in the same case that 'organizations not linked to a State may, for the purposes of the Statute, elaborate and *carry out a policy* to commit an attack against a civilian population' (emphasis added).[84] Here again, it is noteworthy that Pre-Trial Chamber identified the armed group as the entity 'carrying out' the policy to commit crimes against humanity. The RUF case from the Special Court of Sierra Leone evidences a similar approach. Here, when analysing the contextual elements of 'crimes against humanity', the Trial Chamber repeatedly identifies the RUF in its judgment as being the author of the 'attack

[81] In August 2014, the FARC issued a statement expressing its willingness to assume responsibilities to the victims of the conflict, including its responsibility under international humanitarian law: 'Las FARC dicen que asumirán responsabilidades con las víctimas' (*BBC*, 13 August 2014) <http://www.bbc.co.uk/mundo/ultimas_noticias/2014/08/140813_ultnot_colombia_farc_responsabilidades_jgc.shtml.> accessed 20 January 2017: 'Así como demandaremos el reconocimiento de responsabilidades por parte de los múltiples actores responsables (del inicio y prolongación del conflicto), con todas las medidas y acciones que de ellas se deriven, manifestamos la voluntad de asumir las nuestras.' The FARC insisted that those responsibilities should take account of 'el carácter político-militar de nuestra organización, nuestros propósitos y definiciones programáticas, nuestros planes militares para la toma del poder, nuestras normas internas y de relacionamiento con la población civil y, desde luego, las leyes de la guerra y las normas del Derecho Internacional Humanitario.'

[82] See also A. Bellal, 'Establishing the Direct Responsibility of Non-State Armed Groups for Violations of International Norms: Issues of Attribution' in Ryngaert (ed), *Responsibilities of the Non-State Actor in Armed Conflict and the Market Place* (Brill, Leiden 2015) 313.

[83] Article 15 Decision (n 36) [90].

[84] Ibid, [92].

against the civilian population'.[85] It is also seen in the *Limaj* case in front of the ICTY. Here, the Trial Chamber observed that it is dealing with allegations that the 'attack against a civilian population *[was] perpetrated* by a non-state actor with extremely limited resources, personnel and organization' (emphasis added), i.e. the KLA. Here, again, we see the Trial Chamber identify the armed group as being the 'perpetrator' of the attack.

In the light of these developments, it seems a missed opportunity that there was no mention of the responsibility of armed groups in the draft Convention on Crimes against Humanity, which concentrated exclusively on the responsibility of States. Indeed, the drafters' decision not to address the responsibility of armed groups operating in non-international armed conflicts during the drafting process is particularly puzzling in light of the fact that during the drafting process, they *did* examine whether 'terrorist groups' could commit crimes against humanity.[86] To many scholars, recognition of the potential responsibility of armed groups operating in the context of non-international armed conflicts would be a less controversial proposition than the potential responsibility of terrorist groups, because armed groups are generally accepted to have limited legal personality under international law. Likewise, it is increasingly accepted that armed groups are not only bound by international humanitarian law but also capable of being held responsible for its violation.[87] Moreover, already in 1996, a version of Draft Articles on State Responsibility recognized the possibility of an armed group bearing responsibility for its own conduct under international law.[88] It is reassuring to see that there are signs that more attention may be given to this point, now that the International Law Commission has added the drafting of a treaty on crimes against humanity to its active agenda.[89]

3. What Kinds of Armed Groups Can Commit Crimes against Humanity?

The fact that armed groups exist along a spectrum of organization, functionality, and territorial control makes it necessary to consider *which* armed groups can commit crimes against humanity. A consideration of this question is particularly necessary in order to clarify what the law on crimes against humanity tells us about *when* and *how* armed groups can be bound by international human rights law. The first

[85] *Prosecutor v Issa Hassan Sesay, Morris Kallon, Augustine Gbao (Trial Judgment)* SCSL-040-15-T (2 March 2009) [944], [945], [947], [953], [955], [956].

[86] See M. P. Sharf and M. A. Newton, 'Terrorism and Crimes against Humanity' in L. Sadat (ed), *Forging a Convention for Crimes against Humanity* (CUP, Cambridge 2011) 269–78.

[87] See Bílková, 'Establishing Direct Responsibility' (n 73).

[88] See J. Henckaerts and L. Doswald-Beck, *Customary International Humanitarian Law, Volume I: Rules* (CUP, Cambridge 2005) 536 (hereafter Henckaerts and Doswald-Beck, *Rules*), citing the 1996 version of the ILC Articles on State Responsibility (n 20), Article 14(3).

[89] ILC, 'First Report on Crimes against Humanity, International Law Commission, Sixty-seventh session' (4 May–5 June and 6 July–7 August 2015) UN Doc A/CN.4/680 [70–3].

point to make is that the case law from the ad hoc tribunals and the ICC indicates a consensus that armed groups with control over a territory are generally capable of committing crimes against humanity. In 1997, when the *Tadic* Trial Chamber found that the policy behind crimes against humanity 'need not be the policy of a State' [90] it stated that the law in relation to crimes against humanity had now developed to take into account:

forces which, although not those of the legitimate government, have de facto control over ... defined territory.[91]

Nearly ten years later, the Trial Chamber in the *Limaj* et al. case agreed that armed groups with 'a level of *de facto* control over territory' would likely be capable of formulating a policy or plan to commit crimes against humanity.[92] In such situations, it said that an armed group would be likely to have the 'resources, personnel and organisation' needed to 'organise and deliver' such an attack.[93] In recent years, there have also been several decisions by ICC Pre-Trial Chambers confirming that armed group controlling territory will generally be able to fulfil the 'organization' requirement in Article 7(2)(a) of the Rome Statute.[94] Yet, there is much less consensus about whether armed groups can commit crimes against humanity when they do not control territory.

Section 2.5.1 of this chapter has shown that there was early support for the idea that many different sorts of private entities can commit crimes against humanity. In 1996, the Commentary to the ILC Draft Code of Crimes stated that 'private individuals with *de facto* power or organized in criminal gangs or groups' might also be able to commit crimes against humanity.[95] In 1997, the *Tadic* Trial Chamber stated that, in its view, armed groups which are 'able to move freely within [,] defined territory' are also able to commit crimes against humanity.[96] However, recently, the Pre-Trial Chamber's Majority decision in the ICC's *Kenya* case and the dissenting decision by Judge Kaul illustrated that these views are far from universally held.[97] In fact, the two decisions in the *Kenya* case prompted an important debate about some major questions related to the crime's definition and object and purpose. They raised the question whether an armed group needs to be 'State-like' to commit crimes against humanity;[98] whether an armed group needs to be 'military' to commit crimes against humanity, and whether armed groups can commit crimes against humanity outside of the armed conflict paradigm. Most pertinently for this chapter, the main focus of the debate was on the meaning of

[90] *Tadić* Trial Judgment (n 33) [655]. [91] Ibid.

[92] *Limaj* Trial Judgment (n 53) [213]. [93] Ibid, [191].

[94] *Bemba Gombo* (n 40) [81]; *Katanga* Trial Judgment (n 31) [396].

[95] See ILC Draft Code of Crimes and Commentary (n 32).

[96] *Tadić* Trial Judgment (n 33) [654]. [97] Article 15 Decision (n 36).

[98] See for example Kress, 'Reflections on the March 2010 *Kenya* Decision' (n 3); G. Werle and B. Burghardt, 'Do Crimes against Humanity Require the Participation of a State or a 'State-like' Organization?' (2012) Journal of International Criminal Justice 1; Shabas, 'Crimes against Humanity' (n 47); M. Halling, 'Push the Envelope—Watch it Bend: Removing the Policy Requirement and Extending Crimes against Humanity' (2010) 23 Leiden Journal of International Law 827.

the term 'organization' in Article 7(2)(a)'s requirement that crimes against humanity be committed 'pursuant to or in furtherance of a State *or organizational policy* to commit such an attack'.

Both the Majority and Judge Kaul agreed that the Rome Statute's drafters had intended to include non-State actors, as well as State actors, within Article 7's scope.[99] The point on which the judges disagreed was the question of *which non-State actors* could fulfil the organization requirement and what characteristics they should have. The Majority of the Pre-Trial Chamber found it unnecessary that an armed group's 'formal nature' or 'level of its organization' should be 'the defining criterion' in such an assessment.[100] Instead, the Majority found that the defining criterion in a determination of whether an armed group was 'organized' enough for Article 7(2) was the group's 'capability to perform acts which infringe on basic human values'.[101] From this perspective, it was important to assess the group's capacity to do harm on the scale and of the gravity necessary for the acts to be considered 'crimes against humanity'. The Majority went on to list some criteria relevant to determining this, which included whether the group: (i) is under responsible command, or has an established hierarchy; (ii) possesses the means to carry out a widespread or systematic attack against a civilian population; (iii) exercises control over a part of the territory; (iv) has criminal activities against the population as a primary purpose; (v) articulates an intention to attack a civilian population; and (vi) is part of a larger group which fulfils some or all of the above-mentioned criteria.[102] In contrast, Judge Kaul argued that only 'State-like' armed groups could fall within the definition of 'organization' in Article 7(2). The rationale for his position was that armed groups below this threshold of organization would better be treated under ordinary criminal law, rather than international criminal law. [103] Interestingly, Judge Kaul's dissent received considerable praise from several key scholars in the field of international criminal justice, despite having been criticized by others.[104]

[99] The majority of the Pre-Chamber determined that the term was wide enough to include 'organizations not linked to a State' [92]. Judge Kaul was likewise persuaded that the word 'organization' in the Statute would not have been included unless the drafters of the Rome Statute had intended to give it a meaning different from 'State'. As a result, Judge Kaul concluded in his dissenting opinion: 'it is permissive to conclude that an "organization" may be a private entity (a non-State actor) which is not an organ of a State or acting on behalf of a State'. Article 15 Decision (n 36) (Dissenting Opinion by Judge Hans-Peter Kaul) [45].

[100] Article 15 Decision (n 36) [90].

[101] Ibid.

[102] See Article 15 Decision (n 36) [93].

[103] Judge Kaul's dissenting opinion states that: 'It is imperative to enquire the content of the contextual element in article 7(2)(a) of the Statute in light of the fundamental rationale underlying crimes against humanity ... What is the object and purpose of crimes against humanity? What is in fact the underlying rationale or raison d'etre of crimes against humanity? What makes it different from other common crimes which fall solely under the jurisdiction of States?' See Article 15 Decision (n 36) [Dissenting Opinion by Judge Hans-Peter Kaul) [56].

[104] Schabas, 'Prosecuting Dr. Strangelove, Goldfinger, and the Joker' (n 47) 852, calls Judge Kaul's dissenting opinion 'compelling' and his review of the historical context of the adoption of crimes against humanity 'rare and refreshing' and 'very eloquent'. Kress, 'Reflections on the March 2010 *Kenya* Decision' (n 3) 862, states that he finds Judge Kaul's dissent to be 'more carefully reasoned and supported by references to relevant instances of international practice and to pertinent scholarly

Since the Kenya decisions, the Trial Chambers in the *Katanga* and *Bemba* cases have taken a similar position to the Majority decision in the *Kenya* case. In the *Katanga* Trial Judgment in March 2014, the Trial Chamber confirmed that Article 7 of the Rome Statute does not require a group to have an 'well-developed structure that could be described as State-like'.[105] Instead, the Trial Chamber said that it is only necessary to prove that the group, through its membership, means, and resources, is able to carry out an attack of the scale required by Article 7.[106] In taking a 'capability-based' approach to the 'organization' requirement in Article 7(2)(a), the *Katanga* judgment indicates a willingness to downscale the potential rigours of: (i) the policy requirement; and (ii) the 'organization' requirement in Article 7(2)(a) to an approach somewhat akin to that of the ICTY.[107] According to this approach, an armed group will be an organization for the purposes of Article 7(2)(a) if it can carry out the widespread or systematic commission of acts envisaged by Article 7(2)(a). In other words, it is not necessary for such a group to control territory, be a quasi-State, or to operate in the context of a non-international armed conflict for it to fall within the framework of Article 7(2)(a). In March 2016, Trial Chamber in the *Bemba* case affirmed the capability-based approach and also confirmed that the existence of a policy by a State or organization need not be made explicit.[108]

It is interestingly to note that the case law on crimes against humanity deals with the organization requirement much less systematically than the case law on war crimes which is reviewed in Chapter 5. This is probably because an evaluation of whether international humanitarian law applies to a particular factual situation necessarily starts with the identification of the parties, i.e. the State and the armed group. Moreover, the organizational entities behind the individual perpetrators are the primary means by which international humanitarian law is enforced. The concept of there being an 'organization' in the international humanitarian law framework is considered not only crucial to establishing the application of the legal framework but also crucial to its enforcement. The idea of an 'organization' is also necessary in order to understand the fighting between the two parties as 'hostilities' between two opposing military parties, meriting deference to the principle of military necessity. In contrast, the role that the State or armed groups play in the crimes against humanity legal framework is much less prominent. Generally, the law on crimes against humanity is approached from a bottom-up perspective whereby the overriding focus is on the harm suffered by the victims (i.e. the violation of rights), rather than on the obligation that has been breached and its duty-bearer. Likewise, the relationship between the law on crimes against humanity and its underlying legal sources is

writings [than the majority decision]'. At 863, Kress also states that he finds the Dissenting Opinion's third and final argument—on which its argument rests—'a truly fascinating piece of international judicial reasoning'. See also R. Bartels and K. Fortin, 'Law, Justice and a Potential Security Gap: The 'Organization' Requirement in International Humanitarian Law and International Criminal Law' (2015) 21 (1) Journal of Conflict and Security Law 29–48, 43–7

105 *Katanga* Trial Judgment (n 31) [1119]. 106 Ibid, [1120].

107 Ibid. [1109–11]. 108 *Bemba* Trial Judgment (n 70) [158–60].

much more oblique than the relationship between war crimes and international humanitarian law.

The comparative lack of attention given to the organization requirement in case law dealing with crimes against humanity is explicable in a criminal trial. Here, the priority of the forum is to make findings of individual guilt. However, if the purpose of the accountability mechanism is to reach a conclusion on an armed group's responsibility for crimes against humanity it will likely be necessary for more concentrated attention to be given to the organization requirement. For in a civil forum, it will be necessary to give more explicit consideration to the preliminary question of whether the group is sufficiently organized to be able to be treated as an entity of international law, such as is able to bear obligations under international law, because the goal of such a forum will be to find that legal entity—rather than the individuals that make it up—responsible for violations of those obligations. Indeed, it is argued that the need to spend time analysing this point will be particularly stringent in situations falling outside the threshold of armed conflict. In situations in which the threshold of international humanitarian law has already been reached, the legal personality of the armed group and its ability to bear basic legal obligations will have generally already been examined and proved, in order to satisfy the threshold test of international humanitarian law. [109] The only instance where significant further analysis of this point may be needed within armed conflict is when the armed group in question has fragmented significantly since the moment the threshold test for international humanitarian law has passed, in a manner that threatens its continued ability to be perceived to be a legal entity separate to its members.

4. Normative Significance of a Finding that Armed Groups Can Commit Crimes against Humanity

Having established that there is a legal argument to say that armed groups, as well as their members, can commit crimes against humanity, the final section of this chapter considers what these conclusions mean for an armed group's obligations under human rights law. More particularly, the final section builds upon the conclusions above to discover what information, if any, the law on crimes against humanity holds about the primary norms to which armed groups are bound. The ability of criminal law to provide information on this question is based on the fact that many of the substantive provisions of international criminal law have arisen out of a hybrid blend of international humanitarian law, international human rights law, and national criminal law.[110] As a result, the provisions of international

[109] See 3.2.2.2 of Chapter 11 for a fuller elaboration of this argument.

[110] See Cassese, *International Criminal Law* (n 12) 7: 'ICL is an essentially *hybrid branch of law*: it is public international law impregnated with notions, principles, and legal constructs derived from national criminal law, IHL as well as human rights law.' (emphasis added) See also Bassiouni, *Sources* (n 61) 37: 'ICL is a complex legal discipline consisting in the juxtaposition of several components originating in separate legal disciplines which are distinguishable as to their methods, techniques,

criminal law often overlap with, and articulate, primary norms from other bodies of law. For example, the fact that 'war crimes' are 'violations of international humanitarian law' means that the case law on 'war crimes' has been an important source of clarification for lawyers seeking to define the underlying norms of international humanitarian law that have been violated.[111] Evidence of this phenomenon is seen in the fact that the study on customary international humanitarian law conducted by the ICRC repeatedly relies on case law from the international criminal tribunals to assist in the identification and definition of primary norms of customary international humanitarian law.[112]

In the light of this example, it becomes apparent why international criminal law may hold information about the primary norms of human rights law too. It is often noted in this regard that international human rights law is one of the 'sources' of international criminal law.[113] Indeed, it was noted in the introduction to this book that it is often recognized that there is a strong connection between crimes against humanity and human rights law. Indeed, crimes against humanity are commonly referred to as 'serious human rights violations'.[114] When taken literally, this description indicates that human rights norms are the primary

contents, subjects, enforcement, modalities, institutions, structures, values, and policies ... The fact that the different components of ICL are either intertwined or interconnected does not, however, eliminate their separate legal characteristics. The umbilical cord between these components and their original disciplines remains unsevered.'

[111] See *Tadić* Appeals Judgment (n 28) [52], where the Appeals Chamber states that in order for Article 3 of the ICTY Statute to apply, 'the violation must constitute an infringement of a rule of international humanitarian law'. The Appeals Chamber clarifies that the further conditions that the violation must be 'serious' and the violation of the rule must entail individual criminal responsibility. See also R. Bartels, 'Discrepancies between International Humanitarian Law on the Battlefield and in the Courtroom: The Challenges of Applying International Humanitarian Law During International Criminal Trials' in M. Matthee et al. (eds), *Armed Conflict and International Law: In Search of the Human Face* (T.M.C. Asser Press, The Hague 2013) 339–78 on some of the tensions in this relationship.

[112] The ICRC Study states in this regard: 'Although decisions of international courts are subsidiary sources of international law, they do not constitute State practice. This is because, unlike national courts, international courts are not State organs. Their decisions have nevertheless been included because a finding by an international court that a rule of customary international law exists constitutes persuasive evidence to that effect. In addition, because of the precedential value of their decisions international courts can also contribute to the emergence of a rule of customary international law by influencing the subsequent practice of States and international organisations.' See Henckaerts and Doswald-Beck, *Rules* (n 88) 34.

[113] See Bassiouni, *Sources* (n 61) 37; Cassese, *International Criminal Law* (n 12) 6.

[114] See for example the fact that 'crimes against humanity' were labelled 'systematic or mass *violations* of human rights' (emphasis added) in the ILC Draft Code of Crimes and Commentary (n 32). See UN Human Rights Committee, 'General Comment 29 (States of Emergency: Article 4)' (31 August 2001) UN Doc CCPR/C/21/Rev.1/Add.11, [12], fn 7 (hereafter HRC General Comment 29), which states that many of the specific forms of conduct listed in article 7 of the Rome Statute are 'directly linked' to violations against human rights that are listed in the ICCPR. For example, it states that Article 7 of the Rome Statute covers practices that are related to Articles 6, 7, 8, 9, 12, 26, and 27 of the ICCPR. See also UN Human Rights Committee, 'General Comment 31 (Nature of the General Legal Obligation Imposed on States Parties to the Covenant)' (26 May 2004) UN Doc CCPR/C/21/Rev.1/Add.13, [18], which states: '[w]hen committed as part of a widespread or systematic attack on a civilian population, these violations of the Covenant are crimes against humanity (see Rome Statute of the International Criminal Court, Article 7)'.

norms which are being breached when a crime against humanity is committed. If this is the case, it is seen how the law on crimes against humanity may provide a strong confirmation of the fact that armed groups are bound by human rights law, albeit not necessarily the full spectrum of its provisions. For if armed groups *as such* are able to commit crimes against humanity, and those crimes against humanity are understood to constitute serious human rights violations, then international criminal law can be seen to provide an implicit confirmation that armed groups are bound by human right law. The legitimacy of such a conclusion depends mainly on whether crimes against humanity can be seen to be violations of human rights law in the 'literal' legal sense. The need to evaluate the legal accuracy of this description stems from the fact that although colloquially crimes against humanity are understood to be linked to human rights law, academic literature describing their origin often emphasizes that they originate in the law of war.[115] This observation raises a question whether the frequent use of the term 'serious human rights violations' when referring to crimes against humanity' is a kind of shorthand for particularly egregious harms, rather than a formal characterization of the crime.

4.1 The relationship between human rights law and crimes against humanity

In the earliest years in which they were prosecuted, crimes against humanity were often understood to have a close relationship with the laws of war. In his authoritative text on the subject, Bassiouni asserts that crimes against humanity originated as an 'extension of war crimes'.[116] However, although crimes against humanity have always had a close connection with international humanitarian law, it is clear they have always been understood as covering a broader scope of crimes than war crimes.[117] Indeed, from their first conception, they were understood to originate from the idea of the 'laws of humanity' referred to in the Martens clause in the Preambles of the 1899 and 1907 Hague Conventions.[118] Moreover, the Preambles to the Hague Conventions make clear that the 'law of humanity' was a legal framework that was supplementary to, and different to, the laws of war.[119] Likewise,

[115] C. M. Bassiouni, *International Criminal Law, Vol I, Crimes* (Transnational Publishers, New York 1999) 522, 536 (hereafter Bassiouni, *Crimes*).

[116] Convention with Respect to the Laws and Customs of War on Land (Hague II), 29 July 1899; Convention (IV) respecting the Laws and Customs of War on Land, and its annex, Regulations concerning the Laws and Customs of War on Land, The Hague, 18 October 1907.

[117] For a historical record of the conceptual beginnings of crimes against humanity see E. Schwelb, 'Crimes against Humanity' (1946) 23 British Yearbook of International Law 176 (hereafter Schwelb, 'Crimes against Humanity').

[118] See Bassiouni, *Crimes* (n 115) 522, 536.

[119] Both Preambles state that until a more complete code of the laws of war has been issued, the inhabitants and the belligerents will remain: 'under the protection and the rules of the principles of the law of nations, as they result from the usages established among civilized peoples, from the *laws of humanity*, and the dictates of the public conscience' (emphasis added).

when it was suggested after the First World War that individuals should be prosecuted for 'war crimes' and violations of the 'elementary laws of humanity', there was strong opposition to the latter suggestion on the basis that there was no precedent for the prosecution of violations of the 'law of humanity'.[120] Again, the fact that there was opposition to one category of crime but not the other is evidence that the two categories of crime have always been deemed to be partly separate in their origins and conception.

In a similar vein, historical records show that 'crimes against humanity' were included in the London Charter in order to ensure the International Military Tribunal could address conduct which fell outside the scope of the established laws and customs of war set out in the Hague Regulations.[121] The inclusion of Article 6(c) in the London Charter was reportedly due to the Allied States' wish to punish acts which would otherwise fall outside the legal category of war crimes, namely crimes which had been committed by Germany against German nationals in German territory.[122] In particular, there was a desire to prosecute the atrocities which were committed against German Jews and political opponents of the Nazi regime. These atrocities did not fall within the definition of 'war crimes' because they were not crimes that were committed against nationals of third States and they did not take place outside German territory. Again, this point evidences the fact that crimes against humanity had, from very early date, a different scope to war crimes. However, crimes against humanity were often talked about as if they were an 'extension' to the law on war crimes.[123] Literature shows that this description may have been a means to justify their existence as a 'new crime' under international law.

[120] Schwelb, 'Crimes against Humanity' (n 117) 180–2 also draws attention to the Report of the Commission of Fifteen Members created for the purpose of inquiring into the responsibilities relating to the First World War. The Commission concluded that the First World War was 'carried out on by the Central Empires together with their allies, Turkey and Bulgaria, by barbarous or illegitimate methods in violation of the established laws and customs of war *and* the elementary laws of humanity'. See also the dissent by the two US members of the Commission who objected to the Report's use of the term 'laws of humanity' on the basis that, unlike the law of war, the term was not a concept which was legally developed enough to form the basis of the administration of criminal law.

[121] Ibid, 183–8.

[122] Crimes committed during the war by Germany in relation to belligerents or belligerent nationals were war crimes no matter whether they were committed in Germany or in occupied territory. Crimes committed by Germany in relation to its own nationals were also war crimes, in instances where they were committed in occupied territory. Crimes committed by Germany to its own nations in German territory were not war crimes. See H. Lauterpacht, 'Draft Nuremberg Speeches' [2012] Cambridge Journal of International and Comparative Law 45, 95 (hereafter Lauterpacht, 'Draft Nuremberg Speeches'). See also Sluiter, '"Chapeau Elements"' (n 35) 117.

[123] Article 6 (c) states: 'Crimes against humanity: namely, murder, extermination, enslavement, deportation, and other inhumane acts committed against any civilian population, before or during the war; or persecutions on political, racial, or religious grounds *in execution of or in connection with any crime within the jurisdiction of the Tribunal, whether or not in violation of the domestic law of the country where perpetrated*' (emphasis added). For evidence of this, see P. Akhavan, 'Reconciling Crimes against Humanity with the Laws of War: Human Rights, Armed Conflict and the Limits of Progressive Jurisprudence' (2008) 6 Journal of International Criminal Justice 21, 24 (hereafter Akhavan, 'Limits of Progressive Jurisprudence').

4.1.1 Post-Second World War jurisprudence

Moreover, although human rights law was only in its infancy in the years after the Second World War, it took very little time for a connection between the two bodies of law to be identified. In Chief Prosecutor Hartley Shawcross's closing speech before the International Military Tribunal at Nuremberg in July 1946 he used the language of 'rights' to justify and explain the existence of crimes against humanity in international law. He stated:

> International Law has in the past made some claim that there is a limit to the omnipotence of the State and that the individual human being, the ultimate unit of all law, is not disentitled to the protection of mankind when the State tramples upon his rights in a manner which outrages the conscience of mankind.[124]

In doing so, Shawcross expressed the view that crimes against humanity found their legal justification in the egregiousness of the violations of 'human rights' by States against individuals. Although the Universal Declaration of Human Rights had not yet been drafted in 1946, the idea of 'human rights' had already taken a firm hold in these years. The 1945 Charter of the United Nations states in its first Article that the protection of human rights was to be one of the central concerns of the new international organization.[125] In June 1946, just a month before Hartley Shawcross made his speech, the United Nations Commission on Human Rights had been assigned the task of drafting 'an international bill of rights'.[126]

In a similar vein, the case law that emerged from the courts and tribunals established under Control Council No. 10 repeatedly calls upon the language and concept of 'human rights' to explain and define the concept of crimes against humanity. For example, in the *Einsatzgruppen Trial* judgment, the judges took note of a definition of 'crimes against humanity' that referred to the 'essential and inalienable rights of man'.[127] Evidently persuaded by this definition, the Military Tribunal went on to define 'crimes against humanity' itself in similar terms:

[124] Closing Speech, Sir Hartley Shawcross, 26 July 1946. See also (n 140).

[125] See Article 1(3) of the United Nations Charter which states that one of the purposes of the United Nations is to 'achieve international co-operation in solving international problems of an economic, social, cultural, or humanitarian character, and in promoting and encouraging respect for human rights and for fundamental freedoms for all without distinction as to race, sex, language, or religion'.

[126] See ESOSOC, 'Resolution 9(II)' (21 June 1946) UN Doc E/56/Rev.2, which assigned the task of making provision 'for the implementation of human rights and of an international bill of rights' to the new Commission on Human Rights.

[127] *Trial of Otto Ohlendorf and Twenty Four Others* (the *Einsatzgruppen* case) (United States Military Tribunal II, 8–9 April 1948) Trials of War Criminals before the Nuremberg Military Tribunals under Control Council 10, Vol IV/1,497 (hereafter the *Einsatzgruppen* case). This definition was put forward by the Counsellor of the Vatican at the VIIIth Conference for the Unification of Penal Law on 11 July 1947, and stated: 'The essential and inalienable rights of man cannot vary in time and space. They cannot be interpreted and limited by the social conscience of a people or a particular epoch for they are essentially immutable and eternal. Any injury ... done with the intention of extermination, mutilation or enslavement against the life, freedom of opinion ... the moral or physical integrity of the family ... or the dignity of the human being, by reason of his opinion, his race, caste, family or profession, is a crime against humanity.'

But now it has been seen that humanity need not supplicate for a tribunal in which to proclaim its rights ... It has been demonstrated here that the inalienable and fundamental rights of common man need not lack for a court to proclaim them and for a marshal to execute the court's judgments.[128]

The Military Tribunal's statement is further evidence that lawyers quickly connected crimes against humanity and human rights law in the years after the Second World War.

A similar connection can be seen in the judgments of the *Flick* trial[129] and *I.G.Farben* trial.[130] In these cases, the US Military Tribunal was asked to consider whether the confiscation of industrial property could be deemed to constitute crimes against humanity. The Military Tribunal concluded that it could not, explaining that it saw crimes against humanity to be crimes which are committed solely against the human person.[131] Reviewing these cases in 1949, the authors of the Digest of Laws and Cases of the Trials of War Criminals concluded that the judges' view on this point stemmed from a belief that crimes against humanity must be intrinsically linked to human rights violations.[132] The Digest stated:

it does not seem possible that war crimes in which there is no violation of human rights could possibly be regarded as crimes against humanity.[133]

More tellingly still, its conclusion was accompanied by a footnote which adds: the 'remark [cited above] assumes crimes against humanity to be restricted against human rights'.[134] Again, this shows that already in 1949, there was an understanding that crimes against humanity were essentially human rights violations. It also shows that while there is a connection between international humanitarian law and crimes against humanity, crimes against humanity require a special focus on the 'human person' that is not always present in 'war crimes' prosecutions.

[128] Ibid, 497.

[129] *Trial of Friedrich Flick and Five Others* (United States Military Tribunal, Nuremberg, 1949) Law Reports Of Trials Of War Criminals, Selected and prepared by the United Nations War Crimes Commission (20 April–22 December 1947) Vol IX, 48–50 (hereafter the *Flick* trial).

[130] *Trial of Carl Krauch and Twenty-Two Others* (*I.G. Farben* Judgment) (United States Military Tribunal, Nuremberg, 1949) Law Reports Of Trials Of War Criminals, Selected and prepared by The United Nations War Crimes Commission (14 August 1947–29 July 1948) Vol X, 41–2.

[131] In the *Flick* trial (n 129) 50, the Military Tribunal is reported to have left open the question of whether offences against personal property might constitute crimes against humanity. Its rationale in this regard was that such attacks (such as the burning of his house or depriving him of his food supply or his paid employment)—and their consequences—might amount to an assault upon the health and life of a human being.

[132] This is the final volume of volume of a fourteen volume series of law reports which was compiled from the prosecutions after the Second World War and published by the United Nations War Crimes Commission. The purpose of the Digest was to 'state briefly and succinctly the basic and most general rules' which had been established in the case law of the Military Tribunals. Digest of Laws and Cases, Law Reports Of Trials Of War Criminals, Selected and prepared by the United Nations War Crimes Commission (1949) Vol XV.

[133] Ibid, 135.

[134] Ibid, 135. See also fn 7, which states that the Commentary to which it refers 'assumes crimes against humanity to be restricted to offences against human rights'.

A similar view is found in the official historical record of the United Nations War Crimes Commission, published in 1948, which stated that the wording of Article 6(c) of the London Charter on 'crimes against humanity' presupposes the fact that:

> attacks on the fundamental liberties and constitutional rights of people and individual persons, that is inhuman acts, constitute international crimes not only in time of war, but also, in certain circumstances, in time of peace.[135]

The text goes on to state that 'a violation of a certain right, coming with the scope of Article 6(c), may also constitute a violation of the laws and customs of wars, as enumerated in Article 6(b)'.[136] This recognizes the important point that a given act may simultaneously constitute a war crime and a crime against humanity. It may also simultaneously constitute a violation of humanitarian law and a violation of human rights law.

4.1.2 Early academic writings

Another indication that crimes against humanity were very early understood to amount to human violations can be found in the writings of Sir Hersch Lauterpacht. In 1950, Lauterpacht wrote:

> To lay down that crimes against humanity are punishable is, therefore, to assert the existence of rights of man grounded in a law superior to the law of the State. Thus, upon analysis, the enactment of crimes against humanity in an international instrument signifies the acknowledgment of fundamental rights of the individual recognized by international law.[137]

He continued:

> In terms of law, with the conception of crimes against humanity there must correspond the notion of fundamental human rights recognised by international law and, as a further result, of an international status of the individual whose rights have thus been recognised.[138]

Hersch Lauterpacht's view on the relationship between crimes against humanity and human rights law is cited in full here because he was a jurist of considerable influence in a relatively small circle of lawyers writing and thinking about human rights law in post-War Europe. Significantly, Lauterpacht also played an influential role in the way in which the definition of crimes against humanity was developed before the military tribunals. It is said that Justice Robert H. Jackson inserted the term 'crimes against humanity' into the draft London Charter after a discussion he had with Sir Hersch Lauterpacht in London between 26 June and

[135] United Nations War Crimes Commission, *Complete History of the United Nations War Crimes Commission and the Development of the Laws of War* (His Majesty's Stationary Office, London 1948) 192–3.
[136] Ibid, 193.
[137] H. Lauterpacht, *International Law and Human Rights* (Stevens & Sons, London 1950) 36.
[138] Ibid, 37.

8 August 8 1945.[139] It also clear that Lauterpacht provided significant written input to the writing of Sir Hartley Shawcross's closing speech which has been cited above.[140]

In many ways, it is easy to see how the link between crimes against humanity and human rights law must have been obvious to lawyers in these years. Both legal concepts gave central focus to the human person above any other concern. Moreover, both concepts understood serious offences against the human person as offences against the individual victim and against humanity as a whole. This is evidenced by the term 'crimes against humanity'. It is also evidenced by the decision to make the promotion of 'human rights and fundamental freedoms' one of the key purposes and principles of the Charter of the United Nations.[141] Both nascent bodies of law allowed the scrutiny of acts which had traditionally been viewed as exclusively domestic matters. Moreover, unlike war crimes, the justification of crimes against humanity and human rights law did not find its validation in the involvement of a third State.[142] Instead, both bodies of law found their legal justification in the grave egregiousness of the acts to which they referred and the failure of the State to take action against those acts.[143] In the words of Mr Justice Jackson in his opening speech before the International Military Tribunal at Nuremberg,

[139] See Bassiouni, *Crimes* (n 115) 548.

[140] P. Sands, 'Twin Peaks: The Hersch Lauterpacht Draft Nuremberg Speeches' [2012] Cambridge Journal of International and Comparative Law 37, 38. This interpretation is also validated by the fact that the words cited by Sir Hartley Shawcross (at n 124) were taken almost exactly from the draft speech by Sir Hersch Lauterpacht. His draft speech reads: 'The Charter affirms the principle that with regard to the fundamental rights of man there exists a higher forum than the positive law of any single State. As a rule international law recognizes that it is for the State to decide how it shall treat its nationals this, in the current phrase, is a matter which is exclusively within the domestic jurisdiction of the State. The Covenant of the League of Nations and the Charter of the United Nations recognize that right. But at the same time international law claims that there is a limit to the omnipotence of the State, and the individual human being, the ultimate unit of all law, is entitled to the protection of the society of nations when the State tramples upon his rights in a manner which shocks and outrages the conscience of mankind.' Lauterpacht, 'Draft Nuremberg Speeches' (n 122) 96.

[141] See (n 126).

[142] While war crimes perpetrated in the context of an international armed conflict generally covered crimes committed by a perpetrator of one nationality against a victim of another nationality or acts which took place in occupied territory, the definition of crimes against humanity contained in the London Charter and later Article II(c) of Control Council Law No. 10 and Article 5(c) of the Charter of the International Military Tribunal for the Far East was wide enough to cover acts committed within the borders of one country, by a perpetrator of one nationality against an individual of the same nationality. In Article II(c) of the Control Council No. 10 particularly, the 'international' aspect of crimes against humanity was largely justified by the seriousness of the acts themselves, rather than by the international aspect of the crime. The same cannot be said so emphatically for Article 6(c) of the London Charter and Article 5(c) of the International Military Tribunal for the Far East because these both contained a requirement that the specific crimes should have a connection with 'crimes against peace' or 'war crimes'.

[143] See in this respect the *Einsatzgruppen* Case (n 127) 497, where the Court stated: 'Crimes against humanity are acts committed in the course of wholesale and systematic violation of life and liberty. It is to be observed that insofar as international jurisdiction is concerned, the concept of crimes against humanity does not apply to offenses for which the criminal code of any well-ordered state makes adequate provision. They can only come within the purview of this basic code of humanity because the state involved, owing to indifference, impotency or complicity, has been unable or has refused to halt the crimes and punish the criminals.'

the question of how a government treats its own people becomes the concern of other governments and the international community when it passes 'in magnitude or savagery any limits of what is tolerable by modern civilizations'.[144]

4.1.3 Legal developments in the 1990s

In the decades after the Nuremberg and Tokyo trials, the connection between crimes against humanity and human rights law has only become more pronounced. When the International Law Commission published its Draft Code of Crimes in 1991, it contained a clear reference to the connection between crimes against humanity and human rights law. Most significantly, in 1991, Article 21 of the Code, which eventually became the article entitled 'Crimes against Humanity', was entitled: 'Systematic or mass violations of human rights'.[145] The ensuing text of Article 21 then defined the crime as follows:

> An individual who commits or orders the commission of any of the following violations of human right.[146]

The Article then lists 'murder, torture, establishing or maintaining over persons a status of slavery, servitude or forced labour, persecution on social, political, racial, religious or cultural grounds'. The Commentary to this article states that 'the common factor in all the acts constituting crimes under this draft article was a serious violation of certain fundamental rights'.[147]

The International Law Commission's use of the term 'serious human rights violations' is even more significant when it is noted that in 1991 the Commission also saw Article 21 to extend to armed groups. It has been pointed out already in this chapter that the Commentary to Article 21 stated that the article did not rule out the possibility that 'individuals with *de facto* power or organised in criminal gangs or groups' might be able to commit crimes against humanity.[148] Likewise, in its Commentary to the suggested crime of 'persecution', the International Law Commission commented that the crime:

> related to human rights violations other than those covered by the previous paragraphs, committed in a systematic manner or on a mass scale by government officials or by groups that exercise de facto power over a particular territory and seek to subject individuals or groups of individuals to a life in which enjoyment of some of their basic rights is repeatedly or constantly denied.[149]

This Commentary makes it explicitly clear that the International Law Commission considered it possible that armed groups were able to commit crimes against humanity. It also makes it clear that the Commission believed that armed groups

[144] 'Opening Speech by Justice Robert H. Jackson before the International Military Tribunal at Nuremberg' (21 November 1945) <https://www.roberthjackson.org/speech-and-writing/opening-statement-before-the-international-military-tribunal/> accessed 20 January 2017.

[145] See ILC Draft Code of Crimes and Commentary (n 32) 103–4. [146] Ibid, 103.

[147] Ibid. [148] Ibid, 103 [5]. [149] Ibid, 104 [9].

committing human rights violations were essentially committing violations of human rights law.

4.1.4 Contemporary case law

Today the relationship between international human rights law and crimes against humanity is often taken for granted. Cassese writes:

> To a large extent, many concepts underlying this category of crimes derive from, or overlap with, those of human rights law....laid down in standard provisions of international human rights instruments (e.g. the Universal Declaration of Human Rights, the UN Covenant on Civil and Political Rights). Indeed, while ICL concerning war crimes largely derives from, or is closely linked to, IHL, ICL concerning crimes against humanity is to a great extent predicated upon international human rights law.[150]

Indeed by the time Article 7 of the ICC was drafted there was little remaining evidence in its text that crimes against humanity used to be linked to the laws of war.[151] It has been commented in this regard that Article 7 'definitively divorced crimes against humanity from armed conflict, enshrining [their] autonomy as a concept rooted in human rights law'.[152]

The fact that there is a strong connection between human rights law and crimes against humanity can be seen through a simple comparison between the acts which are enumerated as crimes against humanity in Article 7 of the Rome Statute and the Universal Declaration of Human Rights (UDHR).[153] Such a comparison reveals that the physical acts which constitute crimes against humanity can easily be connected to the rights enumerated in the UDHR. For example, the enumerated acts listed under the heading 'Crimes against Humanity' in (a)–(k) of Article 7 of the Rome Statute can be easily linked with articles of the UDHR: murder and extermination correspond to the right to life;[154]enslavement corresponds to the right not to be held in slavery or servitude;[155] deportation or forcible transfer of population relates to a number of rights including, the right to freedom of movement and residence,[156] the right not to be arbitrarily deprived of property,[157] and the right to family life;[158] imprisonment or other severe deprivation of physical liberty corresponds to the right not be subjected to arbitrary arrest or detention;[159] torture and rape, sexual slavery, enforced prostitution, forced pregnancy, enforced sterilization, or any forms of sexual violence

150 A. Cassese and P. Gaeta, *International Criminal Law* (OUP, Oxford 2013) 92.

151 There was no longer any requirement that crimes against humanity be connected to any other crime in the Rome Statute. It is notable in this respect that Article 5 of the ICTY Statute still required crimes against humanity to have a nexus with armed conflict. The *Tadić* Appeals Judgment (n 28) [25], found that this requirement was not necessary under customary international law. See Akhavan, 'Limits of Progressive Jurisprudence' (n 123) 25–6, for a discussion of this provision.

152 See Akhavan, 'Limits of Progressive Jurisprudence' (n 123) 26.

153 UN General Assembly, *Universal Declaration of Human Rights* (10 December 1948) UN Doc GA/RES/217A(III) (UDHR); Rodley, 'Non-State Actors and Human Rights' (n 2) 533.

154 UDHR, Article 3.

155 Ibid, Article 4.

156 Ibid, Article 13.

157 Ibid, Article 17(2).

158 Ibid, Article 12.

159 Ibid, Article 9.

of comparable violence relates to the right not to be subjected to torture or cruel, inhuman, or degrading punishment[160] and the right not to be held in slavery or servitude;[161]persecution relates to the right to be entitled to all rights and freedoms without distinction of any kind;[162] the crime of apartheid relates to the same right to equality before the law, notably in the enjoyment of human rights;[163] and 'other inhumane acts' of a similar character intentionally causing great suffering, or serious injury to body or to mental or physical health has a connection with the right not to be subjected to cruel, inhuman, or degrading treatment.[164]

Moreover, an understanding of crimes against humanity 'equalling' human rights violations is seen in contemporary case law from the international courts and tribunals on crimes against humanity which contains repeated confirmations that crimes against humanity constitute 'human rights violations'.[165] Indeed, there is no doubt that the crime of 'persecution' is where the link between crimes against humanity and human rights law is most unequivocal.[166] For the crime of 'persecutions' is explicitly defined with reference to human rights law. According to Article 7(2)(g) of the Rome Statute, it is defined as:

> the intentional and severe deprivation of *fundamental rights* contrary to international law by reason of the identity of the group or collectivity. (emphasis added)[167]

[160] Ibid, Article 5. [161] Ibid, Article 4. [162] Ibid, Article 2.

[163] Ibid, Article 2; Article 5, UN Convention on the Elimination of Racial Discrimination (1969).

[164] Article 5, UN Convention on the Elimination of Racial Discrimination (1969).

[165] The case law on 'persecutions' also implicitly replicates the view of the ILC above that *all* the other enumerated acts in Article 5 and Article 7 of the ICTY Statute and Rome Statute amount to human rights violations or violations of 'fundamental rights'. In *Prosecutor v Kupreskic* et al. *(Trial Judgment)* IT-95-16-T (14 January 2000) [629] (hereafter *Kupreskic* Trial Judgment), the ICTY Trial Chamber held that the 'deliberate and systematic killing of Bosnian Muslim civilians' as well as their 'organized detention and expulsion' should be automatically seen to constitute persecution (i.e. amount to blatant or gross violations of 'fundamental rights') because the crimes of 'murder', 'imprisonment', and 'deportation' were explicitly listed as crimes against humanity in the Statute under Article 5. This approach confirms that the Trial Chamber considered that the acts listed in Article 7 (a), (b), (c), (d), (e), (f), and (g) of the ICTY Statute automatically to constitute 'blatant or gross violations of fundamental rights'. As a result, when confronted with these crimes, it did not need to go through its usual process of assessing whether the particular rights infringed were 'fundamental'. The ICC Pre-Trial Chamber took a similar approach in its Confirmation of Charges Decision in *Prosecutor v William Samoei Ruto, Henry Kirpongo Kosgey and Joshua Arap Sang (Decision on the Confirmation of Charges Pursuant to Article 61(7)(a) and (b) of the Rome Statute)(Pre-Trial Chamber II)* ICC-01/09-01/11 (23 January 2012) [271]. Here, the ICC Pre-Trial Chamber made clear that it did not consider it necessary to determine whether the definition of persecution had been met because the Prosecutor was alleging that the crime of persecution had been committed through other enumerated acts in Article 7, i.e. acts of 'murder and deportation or forcible transfer of population which have been already assessed as separate charges of crimes against humanity'.

[166] Another reason for this is that unlike some of the other acts which are listed as constituting crimes against humanity (e.g. murder, rape, imprisonment), the crime of 'persecution' refers to a generic category of abuse rather than a specific act. The crime of persecutions has been described as an 'umbrella' crime (see *Kupreskic* Trial Judgment, ibid.). As a result, there is a significant body of case law on the crime's substantive scope that is helpful when seeking to elucidate the relationship between human rights law and crimes against humanity.

[167] See Article 7(2)(g).

Likewise, under the ICTY jurisprudence, the crime of persecutions has been defined as:

> an act or omission, which (i) discriminates in fact and which *denies or infringes upon a fundamental right laid down in international customary or treaty law*; and (ii) was carried out deliberately with the intention to discriminate on political, racial or religious grounds. (emphasis added)[168]

Both definitions make clear that an individual or entity deemed to have committed 'persecutions' will be deemed to have committed violations of 'fundamental rights'.[169] The case law on persecutions also repeatedly states that *all* the other enumerated acts constituting crimes against humanity should be considered to amount to human rights violations.[170]

4.2 Consequence of finding that crimes against humanity constitute violations of human rights law

The consequence of being able to equate crimes against humanity with human rights violations in a formal sense is important when seeking to understand the accountability of armed groups under human rights law. It confirms the legitimacy of treating the case law on crimes against humanity as evidence that both individuals and armed groups are bound by certain human rights obligations. Perhaps most importantly, it also allows some conclusions to be drawn about the scope of norms to which armed groups are bound. For example, the case law on crimes against humanity indicates that an individual or entity committing the crime against humanity of murder is violating the right to life. This allows a conclusion that the same individual or entity is bound to respect the right to life. In a similar vein, the analysis above has illustrated that an individual or entity committing an act of enslavement is essentially violating the right of every individual not to be held in slavery. This allows a conclusion that the same individual or entity is bound by the obligation not to hold people in slavery. Indeed, it was shown above that all the acts which are listed in Articles 7(a), (b),

[168] *Prosecutor v Krnojelac (Appeals Judgment)* IT-97-25-A (17 September 2003) [185].

[169] In surveying these definitions, it is sensible to briefly consider whether the employment of the terms 'deprivation', 'infringement', or 'denial' should be considered to refer to something other than a 'violation' in a legal sense. It is argued that such an argument would be hard to sustain. This is readily apparent from the repeated use of the term 'violation' in the case law on persecutions from the ICTY and the *travaux préparatoires* of the Rome Statute. See the words in the Digest of Laws and Cases of the Trials of War Criminals (n 133) which stated: 'it does not seem possible that war crimes in which there is no violation of human rights could possibly be regarded as crimes against humanity'. See also the words of the Trial Chamber in the *Tadić* Trial Judgment (n 33) [697]: '[The crime of 'persecution'] is the violation of the right to equality in some serious fashion that infringes on the enjoyment of a basic or fundamental right that constitutes persecution'. See also the fact that 'crimes against humanity' were labelled 'systematic or mass violations of human rights' in the ILC Draft Code of Crimes and Commentary (n 32). Furthermore the words of the Commentary to Article 21 of the ILC Draft Code at 103 noted that persecution 'relates to human rights violations other than those covered by the previous paragraphs'.

[170] See (n 166).

(c), (d), (e), (f), (g), (i), (j), and (k) of the Rome Statute correspond with human rights norms enumerated in the UDHR. Importantly, the case law on 'crimes against humanity' also indicates that *further* human rights violations, in addition to those which correspond with the enumerated acts in Article 7, may amount to crimes against humanity. This is clear from the case law on persecutions which shows that 'fundamental human rights violations' can constitute crimes against humanity in instances where they are sufficiently grave and are accompanied by a discriminatory intent.[171]

However, the case law on persecutions is ultimately not that helpful when seeking to determine what further human rights norms might amount to crimes against humanity. The case law repeatedly makes clear that Trial Chambers are unwilling to define the idea of 'fundamental rights' in any detail, for fear that they will end up accidentally excluding some rights from the term's scope.[172] As a result of this uncertainty, the only conclusion that can be drawn is that the law on crimes against humanity seems to confirm that individuals, States, and armed groups are bound *at the very least* by the human rights obligations which correspond to the violations explicitly referred to in Article 7, at the moment at which the crimes are committed. It is significant in this regard that all of these enumerated norms are accepted, albeit to varying degrees, as having *jus cogens* status.[173] This reflects the fact that the crimes enumerated in Article 7 of the Rome Statute are norms which protect exceptionally important rights and values within the international community. When reflecting on the significance of these conclusions for armed groups, it is also significant to note that all the crimes in Article 7 correspond to violations of obligations to 'refrain' from a particular action, e.g. unlawfully taking someone's life, subjecting someone to slavery, preventing someone from exercising their freedom of movement, subjecting someone to arbitrary detention, subjecting someone to torture or inhuman or degrading treatment, or subjecting them to discrimination. Significantly, Article 7 does not articulate

[171] *Kupreskić* Trial Judgment (n 165) [617].

[172] In the *Kupreskic* and *Brdjanin* cases, the Trial Chambers explained their reluctance by voicing a concern that an overly explicit identification of 'fundamental rights' may be interpreted as an implicit exclusion of other rights from that definition. See *Kupreskić* Trial Judgment (n 166) [623], where the Trial Chamber states that it 'does not see fit to identify which rights constitute fundamental rights for the purposes of persecution'. See also *Prosecutor v Brdjanin (Trial Judgment)* IT-99-36-T (1 September 2004) [1031], where the Trial Judgment 'reiterates its view that there is no list of established fundamental rights and that such decisions are best taken on a case by case basis'. Their reluctance in this regard may also stem from the fact that the notion that there may be a hierarchy of rights, with some being more fundamental than others, challenges the notion that human rights are indivisible and 'form ... a single package'. T. van Boven, 'Distinguishing Criteria of Human Rights' in K. Vasak and P. Alston (eds), *The International Dimensions of Human Rights* (Greenwood Press, Westport 1982) 43. Interestingly, van Boven goes on to state that 'there still remain weighty arguments which militate in favour of distinguishing fundamental human rights from other human rights'.

[173] See HRC General Comment 29 (n 114) [13(c)]. The qualification 'core' refers to the fact that the Human Rights Committee has stated that even rights which are derogable (e.g. the right to liberty of movement and freedom to choose his residence) can never been derogated from in a manner which would justify the commission of the crime against humanity of deportation or forcible transfer for population.

crimes which obviously correspond to the violation of positive obligations under human rights law. This limitation seems to correlate with the conclusion in section 2 of this chapter that armed groups can commit crimes against humanity without necessarily holding established territorial control over a portion of a territory. While territorial control is generally not considered necessary to 'refrain' from certain prohibited actions, it may be necessary in order to fulfil positive obligations under international human rights law.

However, when using international criminal law on crimes against humanity to elucidate the scope of human rights obligations on armed groups or any other subject of international law, it is important to acknowledge that any list of obligations which emerges from the case law will be far from exhaustive. To argue that it is would be tantamount to suggesting that the international law on war crimes could be used to map the full scope of international humanitarian law. Such an argument is clearly ill-conceived and does not do sufficient justice to the different thresholds, purposes, and origins of the related bodies of law. It also ignores the fact that the international criminal law on both war crimes and crimes against humanity has a 'gravity' threshold which is naturally not present in the underlying framework of positive norms upon which the criminal prohibitions are based.[174] As a result, there are many norms in both underlying bodies of law, humanitarian law, and human rights law which are not reflected in international criminal law at all. The breach of these norms is not serious enough to trigger individual criminal responsibility under international law. This leads to the important observation that the fact that certain human rights obligations, including the positive aspects of the ones enumerated, are not evidenced in international criminal law does not discount the possibility that armed groups *may have* these positive obligations under human rights law.[175] The reason for their absence could be explained by the fact that breaches of such positive obligations under international law are generally less likely to attract criminal sanction.[176] It is clear, therefore, that the case law on crimes against humanity cannot be used to map the outer limits of the obligations of armed groups under human rights law.

[174] See *Tadić* Jurisdiction Decision (n 54) [94], which states that for an offence to be subject to prosecution before the International Tribunal under Article 3, it must: (i) constitute an infringement of international humanitarian law; (ii) be customary in nature; (iii) be serious; and (iv) entail individual criminal responsibility. See also the statements confirming that an act will only constitute the crime of 'persecutions' if it is of equal gravity to the other enumerated acts in Article 5 of the ICTY Statute. See for example, *Prosecutor v Brdjanin (Appeals Judgment)* IT-99-36-A (3 April 2007) [296].

[175] For example, the right to life may be respected by refraining from killing but usually the right to life is much more multidimensional than this and will include an obligation to protect others from dangers emanating from third parties.

[176] The truth of this is seen in the fact that the positive obligations in APII that broadly reflect human rights obligations are not reflected in Article 8 of the Rome Statute. See for example, Article 4(3)(a) of APII which places on obligation on the parties to the conflict to ensure that children are provided with an education. See also Article 5(1)(d) of APII which requires the parties to allow persons in detention to practice their religion. These are not reflected in Article 8(2)(c), and (e) of the Rome Statute.

5. Conclusions

In a debate heavily characterized by a lack of law, this chapter has shown that the law on 'crimes against humanity' provides a valuable legal affirmation of the fact that individuals, and armed groups committing crimes against humanity are violating human rights. The chapter's findings on this point are based on the observation that crimes against humanity only exist as international crimes because they are committed at two different levels, by two different entities. As a result, in instances where individuals commit crimes against humanity, another higher entity will generally be responsible for the pattern of conduct as a whole. While there is currently no forum where such a legal finding of responsibility can be made, there is no reason why such a forum should not come into existence in the future. Indeed, the chapter has demonstrated that prosecuting individuals for crimes against humanity is generally an insufficient response to the underlying action because it fails to address the greater responsibility of the entity behind the crime. By comparing the legal framework as applied to States, with the legal framework applied to armed groups, the chapter finds there to be a good legal argument that armed groups can be responsible for crimes against humanity. However, the chapter nevertheless points out that the ability to attribute responsibility to an armed group for the acts of individuals will be harder than it will be for States. It argues that this process may be made easier by the requirement that crimes against humanity are committed in a 'widespread or systematic' manner. It will be also assisted by the Rome Statute's requirement that crimes against humanity be committed 'pursuant to or in furtherance of a State or organizational policy'. An attempt to attribute the acts of an individual to an armed group may also assisted by the manner in which individuals have been prosecuted, if prosecutions have taken place. For example, if members of armed groups have been prosecuted for their contribution to a wider criminal enterprise, the evidence brought at trial may serve to prove the connection between the individual and the group.

Evaluating the modern law on crimes against humanity, the chapter sheds light on what kinds of armed groups can commit crimes against humanity. It has clarified that there is no requirement for armed groups to be State-like or to be operating in the context of an armed conflict to commit crimes against humanity. Instead, armed groups only need to demonstrate a capacity to 'to perform acts which infringe on basic human values' on a widespread or systematic scale. The chapter has noted that this requirement will inevitably be easier to satisfy in the context of a non-international armed conflict, but it has argued that that there is no reason of law why it should not also be able to be met outside armed conflict, if the armed group is committing widescale atrocities. However, it is important to note that the law on crimes against humanity does not help with the fine-tuning of *when* armed groups acquire international legal personality, it only confirms that they possess it at a certain moment in time *when* the crimes are committed. Indeed, the idea that armed groups have international legal personality at the time that they commit crimes against humanity seems to correspond with the conclusions in Chapter 6 which finds that armed groups will only acquire international legal personality if there is an international dimension to their personality i.e. if their actions affect the international community or take place against the backdrop of a serious loss of control by the *de jure* government. Finally, presenting research on the conceptual origins of crimes against humanity, the chapter argued that there is a strong connection between crimes against humanity and human rights law. This connection allows the law on crimes against humanity to be seen as evidence that entities committing crimes against humanity also have obligations under human rights law. It also allows some conclusions to be drawn about the type of human rights norms to which armed groups are bound. Certainly it provides an indication that these primary norms will include the *jus cogens* norms which correspond with the human rights violations which are referred to in Article 7 of the Rome Statute.

By way of conclusion, it can be seen while the case law on crimes against humanity does not provide much information on how or when armed groups *acquire* obligations under human rights law, it does provide information about the circumstances in which such obligations exist. It provides an argument that armed groups are bound by human rights law matching *jus cogens* norms set out in Article 7 first, in instances where they do not control territory and secondly, outside the parameters of international humanitarian law. It would be sensible to validate these conclusions further through a study of State practice and *opinio juris* in relation to armed groups and human rights norms.[177] Indeed, it is judicious to note that the conclusions set out above rely upon legal arguments that have been little explored in practice, as there have been no instances in which armed groups have been held responsible for crimes against humanity in a civil forum. That being said, the chapter has found that there is no reason of law to prevent such a development in the coming years. There is a strong and growing acceptance that armed groups are capable of bearing obligations under international law and no reason why they should not also be held responsible for their breach. Now that the International Law Commission has voted to add the drafting of a treaty on crimes against humanity to its active agenda, it is hoped there may be room for more discussion of this point.[178] Finally, when revisiting the goals and introduction of this chapter, it is helpful to state that the chapter did not find that the law on crimes against humanity 'creates' human rights obligations for armed groups. The significance of these conclusions in terms of what they mean for *how* armed groups may be bound by international human rights law will be developed further in the chapter on customary international law.

[177] For a discussion of the constituent elements of customary international law binding upon armed groups see section 2.6 of Chapter 11.

[178] ILC, 'Report of the International Law Commission, Sixty-sixth session' (5 May–6 June and 7 July–8 August 2014) UN Doc A/69/10, 5 [23].

11

Armed Groups and Customary International Human Rights Law

1. Introduction

This chapter considers the different ways in which customary international law may hold answers to understanding when and how armed groups may be bound by international human rights law. The need for such an inquiry arises out of the mounting evidence in earlier chapters that customary international law provides the strongest theoretical basis to explain how armed groups are bound by human rights law. In particular, when read together, Chapters 8 and 9 demonstrate that there is little evidence to suggest that armed groups are bound by the main human rights treaties, except when they are controlling a portion of the State's territory and exercising governmental functions. The conclusion that human rights treaties are not generally binding upon armed groups places the onus on customary international law to explain how armed groups are bound by human rights law in any other circumstances. Likewise, Chapter 10 argues that the customary international law on crimes against humanity constitutes strong evidence that armed groups are bound by customary international human rights law. Similarly, Chapter 9 on territorial control and Chapter 4 on the law of belligerency find that there is significant precedent for the idea that armed groups will be bound by the customary international law obligations of the State in instances where they exercise control over territory. Also, Chapter 7 identified customary international law as providing a major explanation for how armed groups can be bound by international law in general.

Additionally, it can be seen that UN accountability mechanisms have repeatedly identified customary international law, as opposed to treaty law, as the source of armed groups' obligations under human rights norms.[1] Significantly, they have

[1] UN Special Rapporteur on extrajudicial, summary, or arbitrary executions, 'Mission to Sri Lanka' (27 March 2006) UN Doc E/CN.4/2006/53/Add.5, [25] (hereafter Sri Lanka Report 27 March 2006), which states: 'The Government [of Sri Lanka] has assumed the binding legal obligation to respect and ensure the rights recognized in the International Covenant on Civil and Political Rights (ICCPR). As a non-State actor, the LTTE does not have legal obligations under ICCPR, but it remains subject to the demand of the international community, first expressed in the Universal Declaration of Human Rights, that every organ of society respect and promote human rights.' This report has been cited by numerous other accountability mechanisms, see (n 64).

done so in different ways. Some accountability mechanisms have relied on the Universal Declaration of Human Rights (UDHR) to justify holding armed groups responsible under human rights law. Some have relied upon the idea that the armed groups are controlling territory and exercising governmental functions to justify holding armed groups responsible. Others have relied upon various different theories relating to *jus cogens* norms or argued that armed groups are bound by customary international law as a result of being legal persons.[2] This chapter's purpose is to evaluate whether the arguments that the reports employ to explain how armed groups are bound by customary international law can be justified. It also seeks to evaluate whether the manner in which the accountability mechanisms have utilized and applied these theories is effective. When evaluating these issues, the chapter draws significantly upon conclusions reached in Part II, Chapter 9 on control of territory and Chapter 10 on crimes against humanity. It also draws on the theories explored in Chapter 7 on how armed groups can be bound by international law more generally. The fact that it draws so heavily on the book's previous conclusions explains its position as the last substantive chapter in the book before its conclusions.

2. Can Armed Groups Contribute to the Formation of Custom?

2.1 Divergent practice on the question of whether armed groups can contribute to making of custom

The chapter begins by addressing the role of armed groups in the formation of customary international law.[3] The need to address this question at the start of the chapter arises from a perceived imperative to be clear about what customary international law is when we talk about customary norms binding upon armed groups. Crucially, there is not only a divergence of practice on this issue but also a lack of consensus in academic literature.[4] The divergence of practice is demonstrated by the different methodologies employed by the International

[2] D. Murray, *Human Rights Obligations of Non-State Armed Groups* (Bloomsbury, London 2016) 88 (hereafter Murray, *Human Rights Obligations of Non-State Armed Groups*).

[3] A. Roberts and S. Sivakumaran, 'Lawmaking by Nonstate Actors: Engaging Armed Groups in the Creation of International Humanitarian Law' (2012) 37 Yale Journal of International Law 107 (hereafter Roberts and Sivakumaran, 'Lawmaking by Nonstate Actors').

[4] See ibid, 118, citing A. Clapham, *Human Rights Obligations of Non-State Actors* (OUP, Oxford 2006) 28–9 (hereafter Clapham, *Human Rights Obligations of Non-State Actors*); R. McCorquodale, 'An Inclusive International Legal System' (2004) 17 Leiden Journal of International Law 477, 479–80 (hereafter McCorquodale, 'An Inclusive International Legal System'). It is noteworthy that the question of whether international organizations can contribute to the creation of customary international law has been discussed at the latest sessions of the International Law Commission in relation to its study on the 'Identification of Customary International Law' with no consensus on the issue. See UN General Assembly, 'Report of the International Law Commission, Sixty-sixth session' (5 May–6 June and 7 July–8 August 2014) UN Doc A/69/10, 244 [159]; J. d'Aspremont, 'Conclusion: Inclusive Law Making and Law-Enforcement Processes for an Exclusive International System' in J. d'Aspremont (ed), *Participants in the International Legal System: Multiple Perspectives on Non-State Actors in International Law* (Routledge, Abington 2011) 425, 429 (hereafter in d'Aspremont (ed), *Multiple Perspectives on*

Committee of the Red Cross (ICRC) Study on Customary International Law and the *Tadić* Appeal Chamber in its Decision on the Defence Motion for Interlocutory Appeal on Jurisdiction.[5] The ICRC's study on Customary International Law drew significant conclusions about *inter alia* the customary international humanitarian law norms which are considered binding upon armed groups. In setting out its methodology for the study, the ICRC notably restricted its analysis to State practice and *opinio juris*. As a result, the study excluded the practice of armed opposition groups, such as codes of conduct, unilateral declarations, and deeds of commitment. Although the ICRC acknowledged that such practice may contain evidence of 'the acceptance of certain rules in non-international armed conflicts', it justified its exclusion on the basis that it did not 'constitute State practice as such'.[6] The ICRC's position was at odds with the approach of the Appeals chamber in the *Tadić* case.[7] In its 1995 decision on jurisdiction, the Appeals Chamber had no qualms about referring to both State practice and the practice of armed groups when determining which rules applied to non-international armed conflict. It stated '[i]n addition to the behavior of belligerent States, Governments and insurgents, other factors have been instrumental in bringing about the formation of the customary rules at issue'.[8] In doing so, the ICTY Appeals Chamber confirmed that it considered the behaviour of 'insurgents' to be a valid source of customary international law. Saying this, it proceeded to take note of *inter alia* instructions issued by Mao Tse-Tung in 1949 and an undertaking issued by the Farabundo Marti National Liberation Front (FMLN) in El Salvador.[9]

2.2 Divergent academic opinion on the question of whether armed groups can contribute to the making of custom

The different methodologies adopted by the ICRC and ICTY Appeals Chamber highlight a dilemma that is also reflected in academic writings. Roberts and Sivakumaran writing on this topic identify the writings of Andrew Clapham and Robert McCorquodale as typifying opposing poles of thought on the question.[10] At one end of the spectrum, Clapham argues for the increased recognition of the legal personality of armed groups but does not argue that they should have an increased role in law creation.[11] At the other end of the spectrum, McCorquodale

Non-State Actors), who after surveying literature covering all different kinds of non-State actors calls this a 'classical controversy in the literature'. See also M. Noortman and C. Ryngaert (eds), *Non-State Actor Dynamics in International Law: From Law-takers to Law-makers* (Ashgate, Farnham 2010).

[5] See *Prosecutor v Tadić (Appeals Chamber Decision on the Defence Motion for Interlocutory Appeal on Jurisdiction)* IT-94-1-AR872 (2 October 1995) [102–8] (hereafter *Tadić* Jurisdiction Decision).

[6] J. Henckaerts and L. Doswald-Beck, *Customary International Humanitarian Law, Volume I: Rules* (CUP, Cambridge 2005) 36 (hereafter Henckaerts and Doswald-Beck, *Rules*).

[7] See *Tadić* Jurisdiction Decision (n 5) [102–8].

[8] See ibid, [108].

[9] See ibid, [102], [103], [107].

[10] Roberts and Sivakumaran, 'Lawmaking by Nonstate Actors' (n 3) 118.

[11] Clapham, *Human Rights Obligations of Non-State Actors* (n 4) 28–9.

finds that law-making is an essential element of international legal personality.[12] The fact that there is academic divergence on the topic confirms importance of this question from a legal perspective. But the literature on the topic also demonstrates that a resolution of the question may also be important from a societal and compliance perspective. In particular, it has been argued that the inclusion of armed groups practice in the formation of customary international law is important to ensure that customary international remains realistic and effective.[13] Moreover, it has been frequently asserted that a failure to take into account the practice of armed groups threatens the validity of customary rules because it deprives armed groups, who are an important category of subjects of the law, of any ownership of the norms binding upon them.[14] In other words, it has been said that the exclusion of armed groups' practice and views threatens customary international law's effectiveness which is often said to be founded on consent.[15] Expanding upon these kinds of arguments, there is a considerable body of commentary espousing the notion of 'ownership' of norms with the compliance of armed groups with international humanitarian law.[16] A number of authors make the point that it is important for armed groups to be involved in the development and reaffirmation of the law to increase this sense of ownership.[17]

On the opposite side of the coin, academics have expressed their concern that if the practice of armed groups is to be taken into account when determining the existence of customary rules it may 'disrupt' the formation of custom.[18] Perhaps of more concern still, it has been argued that the inclusion of the practice of non-State actors in the formation of customary law may lead to a 'regression' of the normative framework.[19] In other words, it has been highlighted that although the participation of armed groups may lead to better compliance with the law, it will not necessarily lead to 'better law', in the sense of the law offering better protection to victims of non-international armed conflict.[20] Such a concern arises out of

[12] McCorquodale, 'An Inclusive International Legal System' (n 4); R. McCorquodale, 'The Individual and the International Legal System' in M. Evans (ed), *International Law* (OUP, Oxford 2006) 307.

[13] M. Sassòli. 'Taking Armed Groups Seriously: Ways to Improve Their Compliance with International Humanitarian Law' (2010) 1 International Humanitarian Legal Studies 5, 20–1 (hereafter Sassòli, 'Taking Armed Groups Seriously').

[14] See S. Rondeau, 'Participation of Armed Groups in the Development of the Law Applicable to Armed Conflicts' (2011) 92 International Review of the Red Cross 1, 6 (hereafter Rondeau, 'Participation of Armed Groups'); J. Kleffner, 'The Applicability of International Humanitarian Law to Organized Armed Groups' (2011) 882 International Review of the Red Cross 443, 454.

[15] See M. N. Shaw, *International Law* (6th edn, CUP, Cambridge 2008) 74, for the notion that customary international law is 'democratic'.

[16] Rondeau, 'Participation of Armed Groups' (n 14) 6.

[17] See Sassòli, 'Taking Armed Groups Seriously' (n 13) 20–1.

[18] I. Scobbie, 'The approach to customary international law in the Study' in E. Wilmshurst and S. Breau (eds), *Perspectives on the ICRC Study on Customary International Humanitarian Law* (CUP, Cambridge 2007) 47 (hereafter Wilmshurst and Breau, *Perspectives on the ICRC Study*).

[19] C. Ryngaert, 'Non-State Actors in International Humanitarian Law' in d'Aspremont (ed), *Multiple Perspectives on Non-State Actors* (n 4) 284–94, 289 (hereafter Ryngaert, 'Non-State Actors').

[20] H. Charlesworth, 'The Unbearable Lightness of Customary International Law' (1998) *92 American Society International Law Proceedings* 44.

the fact inherent to the nature of customary international law that 'violations of law can lead to the formation of new law'.[21] Yet it is argued that such a concern is largely overstated because contrary practice alone does not erode the sanctity of a norm.[22] Moreover, even if the practice of armed groups is taken into account in the formation of customary law, it will no doubt be taken into account alongside that of States.[23] Although States are also prone to violate human rights norms, they are less likely to claim that their violation was lawful. This is partly because it would be politically unacceptable but also because many norms in customary international human rights law are also reflected in human rights treaty law, making it harder for States to disown. As a result, it is unlikely that contrary practice by armed groups would very often justify the emergence of a new norm.[24]

Perhaps a more pressing theoretical concern is that while it is possible to identify a generic set of legal characteristics marking the moment at which an armed group becomes an 'organization' for the purposes of international humanitarian law, armed groups are extremely diverse in real terms.[25] They differ from each other in almost every aspect, e.g. size, motivation, organization, ideology, relationship with the civilian population. According to the conclusions of Chapter 6, they also exist along a spectrum of legal personality. While a baseline of organization may be able to be identified for both international humanitarian law and international human rights law, the legal personality of some armed groups may significantly exceed this. The fact that armed groups are both legally and factually heterogeneous makes it difficult to talk about the practice of armed groups in the same way as one can with States. In particular, it makes it difficult to identify practice which is representative of armed groups as a class. This problem does not arise to the same extent with States, which although equally diverse in their outward characteristics, have largely the same extent of legal personality. States all exercise control over territory, have a fixed population, government, and capacity to enter into treaty relations with other States.[26] Moreover, another potential problem arises from the fact that unlike States, armed groups are inherently transitory. While it was noted in the introduction to this study that non-international armed conflicts are becoming more protracted, the lifespan of armed groups still cannot be compared to that

[21] R. Higgins, *Problems and Process, International Law and How We Use It* (Clarendon Press, Oxford 1994) 19 (hereafter Higgins, *Problems and Process*).

[22] *Case Concerning Military and Paramilitary Activities in and against Nicaragua (Nicaragua v USA)* [1986] ICJ Reports 14, 27 June 1986, [186] (hereafter *Nicaragua v USA*).

[23] The reason for this is the fact that international humanitarian norms must bind both States and armed groups. As a result, it cannot be right that there could ever be 'customary law created by armed groups themselves and only applicable to those groups'. To suggest otherwise undermines one of the key principles of international humanitarian law, equality of belligerents. See R. van Steenberghe, 'Non-state actors from the perspective of the International Committee of the Red Cross' in d'Aspremont (ed), *Multiple Perspectives on Non-State Actors* (n 4) 204–32, 222.

[24] See Higgins, *Problems and Process* (n 21) 20, for a discussion of contrary practice and customary international law.

[25] See Part II of this book for an analysis of the organizational requirement and its relevance to the international legal personality of armed groups.

[26] See Article 1 of the Montevideo Convention on Rights and Duties of States 1933.

of States. As a result, accepting that armed groups today can contribute to the formation of customary international law does not necessarily fix the problem of ownership of norms. There remains a risk that even if the armed groups of today contribute to the formation of international law, the armed groups of tomorrow will still not feel any ownership of these norms and will use that as an excuse not to comply with them.[27]

2.3 International legal personality and law-making

The need to establish the role that armed groups play in the formation of customary international law arises from the fact that different subjects of international law are bound by different norms of customary international law.[28] While individual entities within a particular category of legal persons (e.g. States or individuals) may be bound by the same customary norms as each other, each category is bound by a different set of norms.[29] States are not bound by the same customary duties as individuals and vice versa. Likewise, States do not enjoy the same rights under customary international law as individuals and vice versa. As a result, it is necessary to determine which norms of customary international law armed groups are bound by, through a separate empirical process. From a legal perspective, different opinions about the role that non- State actors play in law-making are generally bound-up with different perceptions of international legal personality. In Part II, it was commented that conceptions of legal personality are almost inevitably subjective and generally emerge out of a scholar's broader understanding of the whole system of international law. It is for this reason that many scholars disagree on the question of whether law-making is a 'necessary attribute' of a subject of international law.[30] In an effort to cut through that subjectivity, Part II sought answers about the legal personality of armed groups in the legal frameworks which have been applied to them. It argued that these legal frameworks represent the closest we can get to a dominant conceptual attitude to armed groups, the acceptance of which is evidenced by the practical application of the framework. In order to better be aware of, and in order to somewhat combat, the author of this study's own subjective

[27] The danger of this is illustrated by the fact that despite the fact that eleven armed groups including the Palestinian Liberation Organization (PLO) and the Southwest African Peoples Organization (SWAPO) attended the drafting conference of the Additional Protocols, several other armed groups have subsequently declared that they did not accept the international humanitarian law provisions applying to the conflicts because they were not involved in their negotiation. See Rondeau, 'Participation of Armed Groups' (n 14) 658. See also Roberts and Sivakumaran, 'Lawmaking by Nonstate Actors' (n 3) 127, who refer to the fact that the National Liberation Front of Vietnam wrote to the ICRC indicating that it did not consider itself bound by the Geneva Conventions because it did not participate in their creation.

[28] For a different view on this see Murray, *Human Rights Obligations of Non-State Armed Groups* (n 2) 84–5 and 87–8.

[29] See *North Sea Continental Shelf (Federal Republic of Germany v Netherlands)* [1969] ICJ Reports 3, 20 February 1969, [63].

[30] R. Portmann, *Legal Personality in International Law* (CUP, Cambridge 2010) 8 (hereafter Portmann, *Legal Personality*).

tendencies, Chapters 4 and 5 sought a heightened degree of transparency in this evaluation by analysing the legal frameworks of insurgency, belligerency, and international humanitarian law against five main conceptions of international legal personality put forward by Portmann in his monograph on the topic: States-only, recognition, formal, individualistic, and actor. Significantly, Part II concluded that the legal frameworks cited above support an individualistic and formal approach to legal personality.[31]

2.4 Role of consent in customary international law more generally

Part II's findings on these issues are relevant to the question whether the practice of armed groups should be taken into account in the making of customary international law binding upon them. In particular, Part II demonstrated that the individualistic and formal conceptions of international legal personality do not support the fact that subjects of international law should by definition have a role in law-creation. Indeed, the formal conception, in particular, is clear that entities can be bound by customary international law without having taken part in its creation. However, it is argued that further support for the conclusion that the practice of armed groups need not be taken into an account in the formation of international law is also found in the general character of customary law, as it is understood vis-à-vis States. This is particularly the case when it is observed that the role of consent in customary international law is much less central than it is sometimes thought. Indeed, views on customary international law's supposedly 'democratic nature' are difficult to justify when the role of 'consent' is examined.[32] For example, customary international law requires 'extensive' and not universal practice before it will be binding on all States.[33] Moreover, in measuring the extensiveness of a particular practice, attention is given to how 'representative' different States' practice is in relation to the particular issue.[34] As a result, special attention

[31] It is noteworthy in this regard that Portmann, ibid, who conducts a much more wide-ranging evaluation of these five conceptions of international legal personality against case law and legal practice, but who notably does not look at armed groups in this evaluation, also finds these two conceptions of legal personality to be the most legally relevant in today's legal world.

[32] It is also noted in this regard that it is not necessary for a majority of States to have engaged in State practice which becomes binding upon all States. It is only necessary that the participation is reasonably representative and that there is no significant dissent. The ICJ in *North Sea Continental Shelf* (n 29) [74] confirmed that the practice must 'include[e] that of States whose interests are specially affected'. See International Law Association, Committee on Formation of Customary (General) International Law, 'Statement of Principles Applicable to the Formation of General Customary International Law' (London Conference 2000) 26 (hereafter ILA Final Report on Formation of Customary International Law), where it states: 'The fact that the test [of what constitutes extensive practice] is not purely quantitative may appear undemocratic. But leaving aside the question of what is meant by "democratic" in this context, it should be noted that customary systems are rarely completely democratic: the more important participants play a particularly significant role in the process.'

[33] In *North Sea Continental Shelf* (n 29) [74].

[34] H. Kelsen, *Pure Theory of Law* (University of California Press, Berkeley 1967) 176 (hereafter Kelsen, *Pure Theory of Law*), states: '[t]he physical or juristic person who "has" obligations and rights as their holder, is these obligations and rights—a complex of legal obligations and rights whose totality is expressed figuratively in the concept of "person" '.

is given to the practice of those States which are 'specially affected' by a particular issue.[35] As a result, certain lesser affected States may find themselves bound by a customary norm which does take into account or reflect their own practice or views.[36]

Moreover, when considering armed groups, it is especially relevant to note that consent has very little relevance to how customary international law applies to new or emerging actors of international law. Before becoming a State, an emerging State is not able to contribute to the amendment of existing norms of customary international law or adopt a persistent objector approach to emerging norms.[37] Instead, a new State is automatically bound by the existing body of customary international law binding on all other existing States.[38] Significantly, a new State is not able to reject norms of customary international law that already exist at the time of its creation, on the basis that it did not participate in their formation.[39] It is only able to affect the formation of customary law after its emergence as a subject of international law. At this point, it can contribute to State practice and *opinio juris*[40] or adopt a persistent objector status towards emerging customary norms.[41] Yet a new State can never persistently object to norms which already have *peremptory* status.[42] These examples serve to illustrate that customary international law cannot easily be seen as a system which is solely based on the consent of addressees. Moreover, once it is acknowledged that contemporary practice does not support customary international law being 'tacit agreement' between its creators, the need for a strict link between its creators and subjects is greatly lessened.[43]

[35] See quotation from *North Sea Continental Shelf* (n 29) at (n 32).

[36] See ILA Final Report on Formation of Customary International Law (n 32) 24–6.

[37] G.I. Tunkin, 'Remarks on the Juridical Nature of Customary Norms of International Law' (1961) 49(3) California Law Review 419, 426.

[38] See *Application of the Convention on the Prevention and Punishment of the Crime of Genocide (Bosnia and Herzegovina v Serbia and Montenegro)* [1996] ICJ Reports 595, 11 February 1996, (Separate Opinion of Judge Weeramantry) [648], for an articulation of this principle where he states: 'The principles [of customary international law] continue to be applicable to both sovereign and subjects, irrespective of changes in sovereignty, for the new sovereign, equally with the old, is subject to customary international law. The customary rights which the subjects of that State enjoy continue to be enjoyed by them, whoever may be their sovereign. The correlative duties attach to the sovereign, whoever he may be.' This is significantly different to the 'consent-based' approach that is inherent in treaty law which manifests itself in the fact that a new State starts with a *tabula rasa* in terms of the treaty law to which it is considered bound and it is only bound to the treaties which it decides to ratify. That being said, this general rule is subject to an emerging exception that says that new States are bound by treaties which contain provisions which are 'owned' by the population. See I. Brownlie, *Principles of Public International Law* (7th edn, OUP, Oxford 2008) 661 (hereafter Brownlie, *Principles*).

[39] Ibid.

[40] ILA Final Report on Formation of Customary International Law (n 32) 25.

[41] Ibid, 27.

[42] See D. Kritsiotis, 'On the Possibilities of and for Persistent Objection' (2010) 21 Duke Journal of Comparative and International Law 121, 131–4 for a discussion of this. See also F. Hampson, 'Other Areas of Customary International Law in Relation to the Study' in Wilmshurst and Breau, *Perspectives on the ICRC Study* (n 18) 69.

[43] Portmann, *Legal Personality* (n 30) 257–9.

2.5 Role of armed group's consent generally in international law

When customary international law is uncoupled from individual State consent, it is better understood as 'rules originating in a general—but, crucially, not universal—practice to which specific states neither have to contribute nor subsequently to consent in order to be bound'.[44] It allows the observation that armed groups are not the only actors which are bound by customary international law norms without their consent. It is also relevant to observe that the conclusion that armed groups do not have a role in the creation of customary international law is broadly in line with the conclusion in Chapter 7 which found that we already have broad acceptance of the fact that armed groups can be bound by international treaty law without their consent. From this perspective, it also seems reasonable to conclude that armed groups may be also bound by human rights law on the basis of State practice and *opinio juris*. However, it is cautioned that State practice and *opinio juris* can only be determinative of customary international law binding upon armed groups if it demonstrates an intention on the part of States for armed groups to be bound. The fact that such intention exists is implicit in a review of State practice and *opinio juris* in respect to the international humanitarian law that applies in non-international armed conflicts. If a State asserts that a particular rule of international humanitarian will apply to that framework, it can be assumed in most instances that the State intends it to apply to both States and non-State actors.[45] Yet the same cannot be assumed for human rights law and a finding that a particular rule of human rights law is binding upon States as a matter of customary international law does not automatically mean that it is also binding upon armed groups. It is argued that this factor is not given due consideration in the ICRC study on customary international humanitarian law which approaches its evaluation of international humanitarian law and international human rights law in the same way. Ultimately, this argument reflects the observation that was made in Chapter 7 that customary international law cannot be treated as a fixed bundle of norms that is binding upon all actors of international law. Having put forward the view that there is no need to consider the acts of armed groups in an appraisal of custom, this chapter now continues by considering what kinds of State practice and *opinio juris* will be relevant.

2.6 Formation of customary international law binding upon armed groups

2.6.1 State practice

It was long ago noted by the *Tadić* Appeals Chamber in its Jurisdiction Decision that when attempting to ascertain State practice in the context of armed conflict,

[44] Ibid, 258.

[45] This is a consequence of the principle of equality within the international humanitarian law framework. An exception to the idea that rules that apply in non-international armed conflicts will apply to both parties is found in Article 1 of the Geneva Conventions which is binding upon only High Contracting Parties, i.e. States. See ICRC, 'Commentary of 2016 to Common Article 1' (2016) C.1, [125].

emphasis will be generally given to verbal acts rather than physical practice as such.[46] This need not necessarily be the case when it comes to an assessment of what State practice indicates about the obligations of armed groups, but is likely considering that physical practice may be interpreted as threatening to a parent State. Examples of such verbal acts have been identified by the International Law Association as including diplomatic statements, policy statements, press releases, official manuals, instructions to the armed forces, comments by governments on draft treaties, legislation, decisions of national courts and executive authorities, pleadings before international tribunals, statements in international organizations, and the resolutions these bodies adopt.[47] Of particular relevance in terms of assessing whether armed groups are bound by international human rights law will be the legal framework contained in government human rights reports, statements by representatives of governments, and statements and approaches taken within international organizations. Resolutions of the General Assembly and the Security Council will also constitute evidence of the opinions of governments on the law.[48] Decisions of international courts and treaty bodies are generally thought not to constitute State practice. However, their pronouncements on the issue of armed groups and human rights law will have precedential value in terms of the law.[49] A question is raised as to the pronouncements by thematic special rapporteurs. Although these cannot be seen to be representative of States, it has been recognized that the articulation of standards by Special Rapporteurs has contributed to the interpretation and development of State practice and as a result cannot be 'lightly ignored'.[50] Evidence of physical practice may include actions such as sending human rights monitoring missions to particular rebel-controlled areas and the provision of training for rebel forces in human rights law.[51] An example of the latter practice can be seen by the United Nations Operation in Côte d'Ivoire (UNOCI) mission in Ivory Coast which provided training to fifty members of the Forces Nouvelles on human rights in April 2009.[52]

[46] *Tadić* Jurisdiction Decision (n 5) [99]. The Appeals Chamber's reasoning was that it is difficult, if not impossible, to ascertain the actual behaviour of the troops in the field for the purpose of establishing whether they in fact comply with, or disregard, certain standards of behaviour.

[47] ILA Final Report on Formation of Customary International Law (n 32) 14 [4(a)].

[48] Brownlie, *Principles* (n 38) 15.

[49] ILA Final Report on Formation of Customary International Law (n 32) 18–19. See also Henckaerts and Doswald-Beck, *Rules* (n 6) 34.

[50] N. Melzer, *Targeted Killing in International Law* (OUP, Oxford 2009) 203–4 (hereafter Melzer, *Targeted Killing*).

[51] Indeed this can be seen to be a feature of the fact that State practice is being relied upon as an indication of a third party being bound. It is hard to imagine what physical acts of States could be relevant in this regard: perhaps the 'sending' of human rights monitors to a particular region or the setting up of human rights monitoring missions.

[52] ONUCI, 'Droits de L'Homme: L'Onuci Forme des Officiers des Forces Nouvelles' (Press Release, 2 April 2009) <http://www.onuci.org/spip.php?article2001> accessed 20 January 2017.

2.6.2 *Opinio juris*

In addition to State practice, attention must be given to *opinio juris* or evidence that a particular provision is 'accepted as law'.[53] It is also noted that any study of armed groups and customary international law will no doubt come up against the same issue as the study conducted by the ICRC on customary international humanitarian law. Having relied heavily upon verbal acts for State practice, the ICRC found it difficult to differentiate them from *opinio juris*. It observed: '[m]ore often than not, one and the same act reflects practice and legal conviction'.[54] However, the observation that a statement by a State may be both State practice and *opinio juris* is not necessarily problematic. The ILA has recognized that some verbal State practice may equally be held to constitute *opinio juris*.[55] It can also be noted that contrary to tradition, it has been observed that in the area of human rights law, there is often a tendency to emphasize *opinio juris* over State practice.[56] This tendency was seen in the ICJ decision in the *Nicaragua* case where the Court found that it 'must satisfy itself that the existence of the rule in the *opinio juris* of States is confirmed by practice'.[57] A similar approach has been put forward by the ICTY in the *Tadić* case which advocated that it was sensible to focus on *opinio juris* rather than State practice because military operations are notoriously secretive. The ICTY has advocated a similar approach in the *Kupreskic* case, where the Trial Chamber advocated that *opinio juris* could be the 'decisive element heralding

[53] The phrase *opinio juris*, which comes from the expression *opinio juris sive necessitas* ('opinion of law or necessity'), is interpreted by some to mean the 'consent' or 'will' that something be law. For others, it is interpreted to refer to a 'belief' that a particular practice is a rule. See ILA Final Report on Formation of Customary International Law (n 32) 30. In the International Law Commission's current work on customary international law, it has been proposed that the 'subjective element' be referred as the requirement that a particular practice is 'accepted as law'. In doing so, the Special Rapporteur advocates using the same language as is found in Article 38|(1)(b) of the Statute of the International Court of Justice which refers to 'international custom, as evidence of a general practice accepted as law'. ILC, 'Second report on identification of customary international law by Special Rapporteur Wood' (22 May 2014) UN Doc A/CN.4/672, 7–14.

[54] Henckaerts and Doswald-Beck, *Rules* (n 6) 15. See also ILA Final Report on Formation of Customary International Law (n 32) 7 [10(c)]. The ICRC was criticized for this by the US government which stated that a more 'rigorous approach' to establishing *opinio juris* was required. See J. B. Bellinger III and W. J. Haynes II, 'A US Government Response to the International Committee of the Red Cross study on Customary International Humanitarian Law' (2007) 89 International Review of the Red Cross 443, 447.

[55] See ILA Final Report on Formation of Customary International Law (n 32) 7 [10(c)].

[56] It is noteworthy that Wouters and Ryngaert find some support for an emphasis on *opinio juris* in the ICJ's comments in *Nicaragua v USA* (n 22) [184], that '[t]he Court must satisfy itself that the existence of the rule in the opinio juris of States is confirmed by practice'. See J. Wouters and C. Ryngaert, 'The Impact of Human Rights and International Humanitarian Law on the Process of the Formation of Customary International Law' in M. Kamminga and M. Sheinen (eds), *The Impact of Human Rights Law on General International Law* (OUP, Oxford 2008) 111–12 (hereafter Wouters and Ryngaert, 'Impact of Human Rights Law'). For further discussion of this phenomenon see B. Simma and P. Alston, 'The Source of Human Rights Law: Custom, Jus Cogens and General Principles' (1988–1989) 12 *Australian Yearbook of International Law* 82, 88–90 (hereafter Simma and Alston, 'Source of Human Rights Law'); ILA Final Report on Formation of Customary International Law (n 32) 41–2.

[57] *Nicaragua v USA* (n 22) [184].

the emergence of a general rule or principle of humanitarian law', even if State practice was inconsistent or absent.[58] The Chamber explained its reasoning by the humanitarian nature of the norm in question. A similar approach was also taken by the ICRC in its study of customary international humanitarian law where it used *opinio juris* to clarify the existence of a rule when State practice was ambiguous.[59] While not all these reasons would be relevant when evaluating customary international human rights law applying to armed groups (i.e. military secrecy), a similar approach could be justified on the basis of the humanitarian nature of the norms. It might also be justified by the fact that States are often not able to be present in areas where armed groups operate.

3. Evaluation of Practice Holding Armed Groups Bound by Customary International Human Rights Law

Having confirmed how customary international law is formed when it comes to armed groups, the chapter now proceeds by examining the three main theories that have been relied upon by the various accountability mechanisms to justify holding armed groups responsible under customary international human rights law. The chapter's purpose in inspecting these statements is not to determine whether they constitute evidence whether armed groups are bound by customary international law per se.[60] In part, conclusions on this question have been drawn in Chapters 9 and 10. Equally, in part, conclusions on this question will rely on further study of State practice and *opinio juris* along lines set out above, particularly for armed groups without control of territory. Instead, in line with the objectives of this study, the chapter's aim is to see whether the theories that the statements draw upon provide a good explanation for *how* and *when* armed groups may be bound by customary international human rights law. In analysing these questions, the chapter's has significant recourse to the main theories which explain how armed groups are bound by international humanitarian law which were set out in Chapter 7. It also has recourse to the conclusions which have been drawn on the international legal personality of armed groups in Part II and the conclusions from Chapters 9 and 10. As a result, the remainder of the chapter is structured into three sections which match the three different theories that are most often employed to explain how armed groups are bound by customary international human rights law. The first section considers the statements that rely on the fact that the armed group has control of territory

[58] *Prosecutor v Kupreskic (Trial Judgment)* IT-95-16-T (14 January 2000) [527].

[59] Henckaerts and Doswald-Beck, *Rules* (n 6) 46. This observation was made in Wouters and Ryngaert, 'Impact of Human Rights Law' (n 56).

[60] For an appraisal of this question see J. M. Henckaerts and C. Wiesener, 'Human Rights Obligations of Non-State Armed Groups: a Possible Contribution from Customary International Law?' in R. Kolb and G. Gaggioli (eds), *Research Handbook on Human Rights and Humanitarian Law* (Edward Elgar, Cheltenham 2013) 146–69 (hereafter Henckaerts and Wiesener, 'Possible Contribution from Customary International Law').

and population. The second section examines the statements that rely on *jus cogens* norms and the final section considers the statements that rely on the Universal Declaration of Human Rights. Each section of analysis is divided into three sub-sections. The first sub-section examines practice in which the theory under examination has been involved. The second sub-section considers whether this practice can be justified legally and the third sub-section draws conclusions.

3.1 Effective control and governance functions as source of binding legal obligations

3.1.1 Practice citing effective control and governance functions as a source of binding legal obligations

3.1.1.1 UN Special Rapporteurs

In an influential report written in 2006, Special Rapporteur Philip Alston justified his decision to hold the Liberation Tigers of Tamil Eelam (LTTE) accountable under human rights law on the grounds that 'it is especially appropriate and feasible to call for an armed group to respect human rights norms when it exercises significant control over territory and population and has an identifiable political structure'.[61] In doing so, the Special Rapporteur implied that the LTTE's armed group's control of territory and governmental function held the key to how and why the LTTE was bound by human rights law. A review of statements holding armed groups to account under human rights law shows that they are most often justified by the fact that the armed group in question controls territory.[62] The Special Rapporteur's approach towards the LTTE in Sri Lanka was followed soon afterwards by four other special procedure holders after a joint mission to Lebanon and Israel in September 2006. This joint report similarly concluded that it was appropriate and feasible to call for an armed group to respect human rights norms in instances where it 'exercises significant control over territory and population and has a identifiable political structure'.[63] A similar approach was also taken by nine special procedure holders after a joint mission to Palestine and the other Occupied Arab Territories.[64] It is shown below that a similar approach has also been repeatedly taken by the Office of the High Commissioner for Human Rights, fact-finding missions and commissions of inquiry set up under the auspices of the Human Rights Council and Security Council, and in Security Council and Human Rights Council resolutions.

[61] Sri Lanka Report 27 March 2006 (n 1).

[62] See (n 82 of Introduction).

[63] Ibid.

[64] UN Human Rights Council, 'Report on Human Rights Situation in Palestine and other Occupied Arab Territories, Combined report of the Special Rapporteur on the right of everyone to the enjoyment of the highest attainable standard of physical and mental health, the Special Representative of the Secretary-General for Children and Armed Conflict, the Special Rapporteur on violence against women, its causes and consequences, the Representative of the Secretary-General on the human rights of internally displaced persons, the Special Rapporteur on adequate housing as a component of the right to an adequate standard of living, and on the right to non-discrimination in this context, the

3.1.1.2 Office of the High Commissioner for Human Rights

In recent times, the Office of the High Commissioner of Human Rights has been likewise outspoken about armed groups 'violating' human rights, alongside State forces, in situations where they control territory. In her statement on Mali in 2012, Ms Navi Pillay, the High Commissioner for Human Rights, stated: 'According to credible reports that my office has received, the various armed groups currently occupying northern Mali have been committing serious human rights violations and possibly war crimes.'[65] She elaborated as follows:

> These include cruel punishments, such as amputations, the stoning to death of an unmarried couple, summary executions, recruitment of child soldiers, as well as violations of women's rights, children's rights, freedom of expression, the rights to food, health, education, to freedom of religion and belief and cultural rights.[66]

Moreover there are numerous examples of spokespeople from the Office of the High Commissioner of Human Rights referring to 'human rights violations' by armed groups.[67] This serves to prove that the Mali statement above is not an isolated incident and there are strong indications that the Office of the High Commissioner of Human Rights holds armed groups controlling territory to be bound by international human rights law as a matter of policy.

Indeed, the official approach of the Office of the High Commissioner of Human Rights towards armed groups and human rights law was clarified in its 2011 publication, 'International Legal Protection of Human Rights in Armed Conflict'.[68] In section C entitled 'Duty Bearers in International Human Rights Law and International Humanitarian Law', the report notes international human rights law and international humanitarian law have different rules regarding the type of actors that bear responsibilities and can be bound by the law. It goes on to say that '[d]espite their differences, both bodies of law are

Special Rapporteur on the right to food, the Special Rapporteur on extrajudicial, summary or arbitrary executions, the Special Rapporteur on the right to education and the independent expert on the question of human rights and extreme poverty' (20 March 2009) UN Doc A/HRC/10/22, [22] (hereafter HRC Palestine Report March 2009).

[65] 'Top UN official condemns amputations, human rights violations in northern Mali' (*UN News Centre*, 17 September 2012) <http://www.un.org/apps/news/story.asp?NewsID=42907&Cr=+Mali+&Cr1=> accessed 20 January 2017; OHCHR, 'Human Rights Council holds debate on Human Rights situations requiring the Council's attention' (17 September 2012) <http://www.unmultimedia.org/radio/english/2012/09/possible-war-crimes-committed-in-northern-mali/> accessed 20 January 2017, where Navi Pillay repeated that the area of Northern Mali had seen 'several serious human rights violations and possibly war crimes'.

[66] UN Human Rights Council, 'Oral report of the United Nations High Commissioner for Human Rights on the human rights situation in Mali, 21st session of the Human Rights Council' (13 September 2012) UN Doc A/HRC/21/64.

[67] See for example Statement by United Nations Assistant Secretary-General for Human Rights, Ivan Šimonović, 'Islamic Extremists Violate Human Rights in Northern Mali' (*UN Radio*, 10 October 2012) <http://www.unmultimedia.org/radio/english/2012/10/islamic-extremists-violate-human-rights-in-northern-mali/> accessed 20 January 2017.

[68] International Protection of Human Rights in Armed Conflict, United Nations Human Rights Office of the High Commissioner, New York/Geneva, 2011.

increasingly understood as imposing obligations on both State and non-State actors, albeit in different conditions and to differing degrees'.[69] In the subsequent separate section on non-State actors, the report reviews the evolving practice of the Security Council and the reports of the Special Rapporteur on extrajudicial, summary, or arbitrary executions and makes the following finding:

It is clear that the application of human rights standards to non-State actors is particularly relevant in situations where they exercise some degree of control over a given territory or population ... non-State armed groups are increasingly called upon to observe human rights protections, albeit in a manner that is in accordance with the particular situation on the ground.[70]

In the light of the Office's formal policy in this regard, it can be understood why the High Commissioner of Human Rights does not refrain from using the language of human rights to describe the acts of armed groups, in instances like Mali when they have control over a territory.

3.1.1.3 Fact-finding missions and commissions of inquiry

The above practice by the Office of the High Commissioner of Human Rights is evidence of a wider view that armed groups bear responsibility under human rights law when they have control over territory and exercise functions of government. In September 2009, the Report of the United Nations Fact-finding Mission on the Gaza Conflict addressed this question as follows, stating:

The relationship between IHL and IHRL is rapidly evolving, in particular in relation to non-State actors' obligations, with the ultimate goal of enhancing the protection of people and to enable them to enjoy their human rights in all circumstances. In the context of the matter within the Mission's mandate, it is clear that non-State actors that exercise government-like functions over a territory have a duty to respect human rights.[71]

In doing so, Mission Report cited the already-mentioned report on the human rights situation in Palestine and the other Occupied Arab Territories which was drafted by nine special procedures of the Human Rights Council.[72]

Similarly, in March 2011, the Report of the Secretary-General's Panel of Experts on Accountability in Sri Lanka made clear that it considered the LTTE to be bound to respect 'the most basic human rights of persons within its power, including the rights to life and physical security and integrity of the person, and freedom from

[69] Ibid, 21.

[70] Ibid, 25.

[71] UN Human Rights Council, Report of the Independent International Fact-Finding Mission on the Gaza Conflict, 'Human Rights In Palestine And Other Occupied Arab Territories' (23 September 2009) UN Doc A/HRC/12/48, 80 [305–7] (hereafter Gaza Fact-Finding Mission Report). The Fact-Finding Mission was established under the auspices of the Human Rights Council and had as its members: Richard Goldstone, Christine Chinkin, Hina Jilani, and Desmond Travers.

[72] HRC Palestine Report March 2009 (n 64) [22].

torture and cruel, inhuman or degrading treatment or punishment'.[73] The Panel explained its decision by stating:

> With respect to the LTTE, although non-state actors cannot formally become party to a human rights treaty, it is now increasingly accepted that non-state groups exercising de facto control over a part of a State's territory must respect fundamental human rights of persons in that territory. Various organs of the United Nations, including the Security Council, have repeatedly demanded that such actors respect human rights law.[74]

The Panel of Experts' conclusions in this regard, despite being rather lacking in sources, have more recently been cited by other United Nations fact-finding bodies to justify their own subsequent decision to hold non-State actors accountable under human rights law.

The Report of the Independent International Commission of Inquiry on the Syrian Arab Republic in August 2012 cited the Sri Lanka report, saying although '[n]on-state actors cannot formally become parties to international human rights treaties[,] ... [t]hey must nevertheless respect the fundamental human rights of persons forming customary international law, in areas where such actors exercise *de facto* control'.[75] The Sri Lanka report was also cited by the International Commission of Inquiry on Libya. Reporting in June 2012, the International Commission of Inquiry explained that, although armed groups are not bound by the international human rights treaties, they are increasingly recognized to be under an obligation to respect fundamental human rights of persons in that territory in instances where they are exercising *de facto* control over territory. On the basis that the Libyan National Transitional Council (NTC) had been 'exercising de facto control over territory akin to that of a Government authority', the Commission concluded that the allegations of human rights violations by the NTC fell within its mandate. It also found it relevant that the NTC had made a public undertaking in which it committed to 'build a constitutional democratic civil state based on the rule of law, respect for human rights and the guarantee of equal rights and opportunities for all its citizens including full political participations by all citizens and equal opportunities between men and women and the promotion of women empowerment'.[76]

[73] UN, 'Report of the Secretary General's Panel of Experts on Accountability in Sri Lanka' (31 March 2011) <http://www.un.org/News/dh/infocus/Sri_Lanka/POE_Report_Full.pdf> accessed 20 January 2017 (hereafter UNSG Sri Lanka Report March 2011). The experts on the panel were Marzuki Darusman, Steven Ratner, and Yasmin Sooka. The panel was set up after a joint commitment by the President of Sri Lanka and the UN Secretary General which 'underlined the importance of an accountability process'.

[74] Ibid.

[75] See UN Human Rights Council, 'Report of the Independent International Commission of Inquiry on the Syrian Arab Republic' (15 August 2012) UN Doc A/HRC/21/50, 47, Annex II, [10] (Applicable Law). See also 22 [34]: 'Non-State actors may also bear responsibility for gross abuses of human rights, in particular those that amount to international crimes.' The Independent International Commission of Inquiry was established under the auspices of the Human Rights Council and had as its members: Paulo Sergio Pinheiro, Yakin Ertürk, and Karen Koning AbuZayd.

[76] UN Human Rights Council, 'Report of the Independent International Commission of Inquiry to investigate all alleged violations of international human rights law in the Libyan Arab Jamahariya'

A similar approach was taken by the International Commission of Inquiry on the Central African Republic set up under in accordance with Security Council Resolution 2127(2013) which was constituted by Fatimata M'Baye, Professor Philip Alston, and Bernard A Muna. Here, the Commission held that it adopted 'the widely accepted understanding that non-state groups that exercise de facto control over territory must respect human rights in their activities'.[77] It then continued at some length:

Non-state actors are not able to become parties to international human rights treaties and thus those operating in the CAR, such as the Séléka and the anti-balaka, cannot formally undertake to be bound by the specific obligations contained in those treaties. Debates that took place in the late part of the twentieth century as to whether such non-state actors are nevertheless bound by the standards of international human rights law, have today been replaced by a general understanding that non-state groups that exercise de facto control over territory must respect human rights in their activities. The Security Council acted consistently with this approach in relation to the CAR when it strongly condemned 'the continued violations of international humanitarian law and the widespread human rights violations and abuses, perpetrated by armed groups'. The ICRC has consistently adopted a very cautious approach to this issue, but it now accepts the view that '[a] group which by virtue of exercising stable control over territory is able to act like a state authority may be recognized de facto as having human rights responsibilities.' [78]

Similar, but not such expansive reasoning is found in reports issued by United Nations human rights field offices, such as UNAMA in Afghanistan and MONUSCO in the DRC.[79] These also mention territory as the factor justifying holding the Taliban and the M23 accountable under human rights law.

(1 June 2011) UN Doc A/HRC/17/44, 32–3. This Commission of Inquiry was established under the auspices of the Human Rights Council and had as its members: Cherif Bassiouni, Asma Khader, Philippe Kirsch.

[77] UN Security Council, 'Final Report of the Independent International Commission of Inquiry on the Central African Republic' (22 December 2014) UN Doc S/2014/928, [41] (hereafter CAR Report 22 December 2014). This Commission of Inquiry was established under auspices of the United Nations Security Council and had as its members: Jorge Castaneda (later replaced by Philip Alston), Fatimata M'Baye, Bernard Acho Muna.

[78] Ibid, [107]. It is relevant to note in this respect that the Commission's reference to the ICRC's position is supported by a footnote referring to A. Breitegger, 'The Legal Framework Applicable to Insecurity and Violence Affecting the Delivery of Health Care in Armed Conflicts and Other Emergencies' (2013) 95 International Review of the Red Cross 83, 103–4.

[79] See UNAMA, 'Annual Report on the Protection of Civilians in Armed Conflict in Afghanistan' (2016) <https://unama.unmissions.org/sites/default/files/protection_of_civilians_in_armed_conflict_annual_report_2016_final280317.pdf> accessed 19 April 2017, p. 103. Prepared by the Human Rights Unit of the United Nations Assistance Mission in Afghanistan, this states: 'While they cannot become parties to international human rights treaties, non-State actors, including armed groups, are not precluded from being subject to human rights obligations under customary international law. Non-state actors are increasingly deemed to be bound by certain human rights obligations, particularly those exercising *de facto* control over some areas, such as Taliban.' The same or equivalent wording has appeared in each one of UNAMA's biannual Reports on the Protection of Civilians in Armed Conflict since 2011. See also UN Security Council, 'Report of the United Nations Joint Human

3.1.1.4 United Nations Security Council resolutions and resolutions from the Human Rights Council

It can be noted that the United Nations Security Council has shown a marked tendency to call upon all the parties of non-international armed conflicts to abide by norms of international humanitarian law and international human rights law.[80] An example of what has now almost become standard practice in this regard is seen in the United Nations Resolution 1894(2009) on the protection of civilians in armed conflict which:

> Demands that parties to armed conflicts comply strictly with the obligations applicable to them under international humanitarian law, human rights law and refugee law, as well as to implement all relevant decisions of the Security Council.

There are also numerous instances in which the Security Council has condemned 'violations' of human rights law by armed groups, in instances where they control territory or constitute a *de facto* authority.[81] Yet a review of Security Council Resolutions from 2014 indicates that the Security Council is more willing to demand that armed groups 'comply' with their 'obligations' under human rights law, than to condemn their 'violation'. Indeed, it is notable that in recent times, the Security Council uses the term 'human rights violations' for States and 'human rights abuses' for armed groups, despite often reiterating that both parties to the non-international armed conflict have 'obligations' under human rights law.[82] It is hard to see how this contradiction can be legally justified, but it may be motivated by a desire to differentiate linguistically between the obligations of a State and an armed group under international law.

While it might be tempting to think that the Security Council's language in this regard is incidental, it has been pointed out that it would be naïve to imagine

Rights Office on Human Rights Violations committed by the M23 in North Kivu Province' (April 2012–November 2013) UN Doc S/2013/433, [11].

[80] For a detailed review of this practice see C. Tomuschat, 'The Applicability of Human Rights Law to Insurgent Movements' in H. Fischer et al., *Crisis Management and Humanitarian Protection* (Berliner Wissenschafts-Verlag, Berlin 2004) 573–91 (hereafter Tomuschat, 'Insurgent Movements'); A. Constantinides, 'Human Rights Obligations and Accountability of Armed Opposition Groups: The Practice of the UN Security Council' (2010) 4 Human Rights and International Legal Discourse 89 (hereafter Constantinides, 'Obligations and Accountability').

[81] Constantinides, 'Obligations and Accountability' (n 80) 101–3.

[82] A review of the Security Council Resolutions from 2014 to 2016 reveal a more consistent use of the term 'violations' for State and 'abuses' for armed groups than prior to 2014. It may be assumed but it is not always explicitly clear that the term 'abuses' is used to refer to acts by armed groups. See for example UN Security Council Resolutions: 'Reports of the Secretary-General on the Sudan and South Sudan' (12 August 2016) UN Doc S/RES/2304 (2016); 'The Situation in the Central African Republic' (26 July 2016) UN Doc S/RES/2301 (2016); 'The situation concerning Iraq' (25 July 2016) UN Doc S/RES/2299 (2016); 'Situation in Mali' (29 June 2016) UN Doc S/RES/2295 (2016); 'The situation concerning the Democratic Republic of Congo' (29 June 2016) UN Doc S/RES/2293 (2016); 'The situation in Afghanistan' (15 March 2016) UN Doc S/RES/2274; 'Reports of the Secretary-General on the Sudan and South Sudan (15 December 2015) UN Doc S/RES/2252; 'Iraq' (29 July 2015) UN Doc S/RES/2233; 'Children and armed conflict' (18 June 2015) UN Doc S/RES/2225.

that Security Council documents are not scrutinized by lawyers.[83] Furthermore, in his 2004 Report on the Protection of Civilians in Armed Conflicts, the Secretary-General recognized that the language employed by Security Council resolutions is important. He stated in this regard:

> By using its resolutions to stress to all parties to armed conflicts, including non-State armed groups, that human rights violations and a denial of humanitarian access are unacceptable, the Security Council reinforces a message that humanitarian and other actors on the ground can use.[84]

This statement constitutes further confirmation that the Security Council and its member States are aware that the language it uses is important, both legally and in the field. It can also noted that while the Human Rights Council often makes the same distinction between its use of the word 'abuses' for armed groups and 'violations' for States, it has shown itself notably more willing to use the word violation when it comes to armed groups controlling territory to the exclusion of the *de jure* government.[85]

3.1.2 Assessment of justifiability of practice from a theoretical perspective

Finally, it should also be mentioned that in 2013 the Committee on the Elimination of Discrimination against Woman noted that that under certain circumstances, in particular where an armed group with an identifiable political structure exercises significant control over territory and population, it is obliged to respect international human rights.[86] The theory that armed groups may acquire obligations through their control of territory has been examined in detail in Chapter 9 which was devoted to explaining how and why armed groups exercising governmental

[83] Tomuschat, 'Insurgent Movements' (n 80) 585.

[84] UN Security Council, 'Report of the Secretary-General to the Security Council on the Protection of Civilians in Armed Conflict' (28 May 2004) UN Doc S/2004/431, [8].

[85] See UN Human Rights Council, 'Resolution on the Human Rights Situation in Mali' (17 July 2012) UN Doc A/HRC/RES/20/17, which '[condemned] the human rights violations and acts of violence committed in northern Mali, in particular by the rebels, terrorist groups and other organized transnational crime networks, including the violence perpetrated against women and children, the killings, hostage-takings, pillaging, theft and destruction of religious and cultural sites, as well as the recruitment of child soldiers, and call[ed] for the perpetrators of these acts to be brought to justice'. See also A. Clapham, 'Focusing on Armed Non-State Actors' in A. Clapham and P. Gaeta (eds), *The Oxford Handbook of International Law in Armed Conflict* (OUP, Oxford 2014) 766–810, 796, fn 115, for a discussion of this resolution and its later version in October which spoke of 'abuses' rather than violations. See also Human Rights Council, 'Resolution on the Human Rights Situation in Iraq in the light of abuses committed by the so-called Islamic State in Iraq and the Levant and associated groups' (3 September 2014) UN Doc A/HRC/RES/S-22/1. For examples of where the Human Rights Council makes a distinction see UN Human Rights Council, 'Report on the continuing grave deterioration in the human rights and humanitarian situation in the Syrian Arab Republic' (25 June 2014) UN Doc A/HRC/26/L.4/Rev.1; UN Human Rights Council, 'Report on technical assistance and capacity-building in the field of human rights in the Central African Republic' (26 September 2014) UN Doc A/HRC/27/L.31.

[86] CEDAW, 'General Recommendation No. 30 on Women in Conflict Prevention, Conflict and Post-Conflict Situations' (18 October 2013) UN Doc CEDAW/C/GC/30, [16].

functions in default of the government can be held bound by human rights norms. Conceptually, the chapter explained this phenomenon as representing an acknowledgement that the geographical contours of the State and the *de jure* government may become incongruent. The practice seems to manifest a readiness on the part of the international community to understand that in exceptional circumstances, different actors may perform acts of 'State' and be bound by the obligations of the State. The chapter argues that the instances in which armed groups are held to account under human rights law, like the situation of the LTTE in Sri Lanka, are essentially manifestations of the principle of effectiveness. It shows that deference to this principle facilitates the restoration of legal systems which have been made ineffective through the acts of a third party, albeit only in respect to fundamental rights. While noting that the principle of effectiveness has been generally usurped in the modern legal system by issues such as legality and legitimacy, the chapter observes that the practice of armed groups being held accountable under human rights law is a demonstration that it is still in operation in instances where it has the effect of protecting universal values.[87]

In exploring these arguments, Chapter 9 highlighted a diverse set of legal authorities which provides support for the idea that certain aspects of State function are fungible and can be performed by a variety of actors. Drawing these authorities together, the chapter concluded that there are respectable legal arguments that armed groups controlling territory and exercising government functions can be held bound by the legal obligations of the State in respect to those functions. Concentrating first on the top-down analysis set out above, the chapter concluded by observing that very similar dynamics can be seen to be at play with relation to rights-bearers. The chapter illustrated this by commenting that the phenomenon of armed groups being held bound by human rights law can also be justified by the argument that rights devolve with territory. This can be seen to be a bottom-up manifestation of the principle of effectiveness which works to ensure that a population's rights remain effective. The chapter concluded by making the important clarification that although the obligations of the State can be seen to be the source of the armed group's obligations under human rights law, the armed group itself will be responsible for their violation.

Support for the notion that armed groups can be bound by human rights law when they control territory was also found in Chapter 7 which explored the idea that armed groups can be bound by customary international law, in their own right, as a subject of international law. Under this theory, the source of the obligation binding upon the armed group is not the legal obligation of the State per se but an independent legal obligation that emerges solely out of State practice and *opinio juris*. In other words, the theory that armed groups can be bound by customary international law is not strictly a manifestation of the principle of effectiveness as much as a recognition that there are diverse actors in the international

[87] S. Zappalà, 'Can Legality Trump Effectiveness in Today's International Law' in A. Cassese, *Realizing Utopia: The Future of International Law* (OUP, Oxford 2012) 105–17.

system that are capable of bearing obligations as a result of the will of States, and partly also as a result of their own functionality. In exploring this argument, Chapter 7 argued that an armed group's control of territory was just one indicator of an armed group's 'legal personality' under international law. It was argued that other indicators of an armed group's legal personality in those instances would be the absence of the *de jure* government, the group's functionality on the international sphere, and its organization.

3.1.3 Conclusions on practice

In the light of the findings in Chapter 9, it can be concluded that there is reasonable legal precedent for the now widespread practice of holding armed groups to be bound by human rights law, in instances where they control territory. Likewise, in the light of the findings contained in Chapter 7 it can be seen that obligations binding upon armed groups may be also found to exist in customary international law, after a review of State practice and *opinio juris*. However, while as a collection, the statements reviewed above may seem to represent an convincing body of authority on the matter, the individual legal justification upon which they rely is less worked out and leaves much to be desired. Indeed, it is noted that again and again, the reports reviewed above cite each other as legal precedent and leave the hard questions like 'how' and 'when' unsolved and under-analysed. In relation to the question 'when' armed groups are bound by customary international law, it has been shown above that the conclusions in Chapters 7 and 9 provide significant insight which also feeds into answering the 'how' question. In relation to both these questions, much knowledge has been gleaned in Part II of this book which provides answers about when armed groups may acquire obligations under international law. This demonstrates the importance of proving that armed groups have legal personality under international law before holding them accountable under international law. In other words, it is necessary to appraise whether the armed group had 'the character of a personality or corporate entity distinct from [its members]'.[88] It also requires an evaluation of whether that personality is 'international'.

However, when examining these reports, one has the impression that the various versions of the phrase 'it is now increasingly accepted that non-state groups exercising de facto control over a part of a State's territory must respect fundamental human rights of persons in that territory' is repeated as a formula phrase that then gives the Commission or Inquiry a licence to apply human rights law to the armed group in question. Significantly, there is almost never any explicit analysis of whether the armed group in question fulfils the criteria mentioned in the formula phrase. First, there is rarely any explicit analysis of whether the armed group is organized enough to be treated as a separate legal entity under international human rights law. Secondly, there is also hardly any attention given to demonstrating that

[88] *Advisory Opinion on Western Sahara* [1975] ICJ Reports 12 (16 October 1975) 63 [149]. See discussion of this case in relation to legal personality at section 3.1.2 of Chapter 5.

the armed group in question indeed controls territory, let alone any attention given to the extent of that control, in temporal and geographical terms.[89] Attention is also seldom given to the requirement that the armed group in question is exercising government functions in the area in question.[90] While the groups' activities are not always mentioned as a relevant criteria by the reports, Chapter 6 has demonstrated that it is relevant to a determination of the armed group's normative capacity, i.e. the spectrum of human rights norms to which it might be held bound.[91] There are several explanations for this lack of attention. It might be considered that a particular armed group's control of territory (e.g. Hezbollah or LTTE) is so well-known by the wider international community that it need not be commented upon.[92] Alternatively, it might felt that the analysis of whether an armed group fulfils the organizational requirement for international humanitarian law automatically means that the same group will be organized enough to be a legal entity separate from its members for the purposes of international human rights law too.[93]

Yet from a legal perspective, these reasons do not excuse the oversight of addressing the issue. Indeed, it is argued that the lack of analysis above risks doing a serious injustice to the legal framework's development. Moreover, in some instances, for example in the Central African Republic in 2014, the territorial control exercised by the anti-balaka groups and their organization was certainly not something that could be assumed.[94] Without a more systematic analysis of these issues, it is feared that the legal personality of armed groups under international human rights law will remain something of an enigma and may lose, rather than gain, validity. Indeed, it is seen that while these reports constitute support for the notion that armed groups are bound by customary international human rights law when they control territory and exercise governmental functions, they currently contribute

[89] Minimal attention to this is given in the Sri Lanka Report 27 March 2006 (n 1) [14].

[90] Minimal attention to this is given in UN Security Council, 'Mid-Term Report of the United Nations Joint Human Rights Office on Human Rights Violations Committed by the M23 in North Kivu Province (April 2012–November 2013)' (19 July 2013) UN Doc S/2013/433. Minimal attention to this is also given in Sri Lanka Report 27 March 2006 (n 1) [23].

[91] The need to exercise governmental functions is not mentioned in CAR Report 22 December 2014 (n 77), [107]; UN Human Rights Council, 'Report of the Independent International Commission of Inquiry on the Syrian Arab Republic' (15 August 2012) UN Doc A/HRC/21/50, [10] of Annex II; UNSG Sri Lanka Report March 2011 (n 73) 54.

[92] UN Human Rights Council, 'Combined Report of the Special Rapporteur on extrajudicial, summary or arbitrary executions, Philip Alston; the Special Rapporteur on the right of everyone to the enjoyment of the highest attainable standard of physical and mental health, Paul Hunt; the Representative of the Secretary-General on human rights of internally displaced persons, Walter Kälin; and the Special Rapporteur on adequate housing as a component of the right to an adequate standard of living, Miloon Kothari—Mission to Lebanon and Israel' (2 October 2006) UN Doc A/HRC/2/7, where there is no analysis of Hezbollah's control or exercise of government functions.

[93] While the report from the CAR gave minimal attention to whether the Seleka and anti-balaka fulfilled the organization requirement for IHL at various points in the conflict, it gave no attention to whether they were organized enough to adhere to human rights norms. It also provided no factual analysis of the normative capacity of armed groups or analysis of the extent of their de facto control. CAR Report 22 December 2014 (n 77–9) 86–101.

[94] Ibid.

little to a greater understanding, or development, of this principle. Their lack of analysis of these points also means that they do not add to an understanding of what armed groups do on the ground in terms of providing governance activities and how the legal framework can respond. They also give very little attention to the scope of legal obligations which an armed group controlling territory will be bound. As a result, unlike the ICTY and ICC jurisprudence (which clarifies the legal justification of the application of international humanitarian law to armed groups) these documents and reports do not assist in clarifying the legal justification of the application of human rights law to armed groups, and contribute only a modest amount towards clarifying its parameters. Having examined the practice relating to armed groups controlling territory, the chapter now turns to examine the theory that armed groups are bound through *jus cogens* norms.

3.2 Jus cogens

3.2.1 Practice citing jus cogens *norms as source of obligations for armed groups under human rights law*

In instances where an armed group does not have control over territory, the fact that armed groups are bound by human rights law has been justified with reference to the fact that they are peremptory norms.[95] For example, this is the argument which was employed in the early reports from the Syria Commission on Inquiry which have held that:

> Human rights obligations constituting peremptory international law (ius cogens) bind States, individuals and non-State collective entities. Acts violating jus cogens—for instance, torture or enforced disappearances—can never be justified.[96]

Critically, the Syria Commission made this finding in relation to a time when international humanitarian law did not yet apply.[97] Similar language was also used

[95] Article 53 of the Vienna Convention on the Law of Treaties defines peremptory norms as: 'a norm accepted and recognized by the international community of States as a whole as a norm from which no derogation is permitted and which can be modified only by a subsequent norm of general international law having the same character'. In her study on *jus cogens* norms Dinah Shelton notes that neither the International Law Commission nor the Vienna Conference on the Law of Treaties developed an accepted list of peremptory norms, but made reference to 'genocide, slave trading and use of force other than in self defense' in commentaries and discussion. D. Shelton, 'Normative Hierarchy in International Law' (2006) 100(2) American Journal of International Law 292, 302 (hereafter Shelton, 'Normative Hierarchy'). The Human Rights Committee has identified a longer list of norms with *jus cogens* status in UN Human Rights Committee, 'General Comment 29 (States of Emergency: Article 4)' (31 August 2001) UN Doc CCPR/C/21/Rev.1/Add.11, [11–15] (hereafter HRC General Comment 29).

[96] UN Human Rights Council, 'Report of the Independent International Commission of Inquiry on the Syrian Arab Republic' (22 February 2012) UN Doc A/HRC/19/69, [122] (hereafter Syria Report 22 February 2012). For an extended discussion of this report see T. Rodenhauser, 'Human Rights Obligations of Non-State Armed Groups in Other Situations of Violence: The Syria Example' (2012) 3 International Humanitarian Legal Studies 263.

[97] Syria Report 22 February 2012 (n 96) 13.

in the Human Rights Report of the United Nations Mission in the Republic of South Sudan, where it was stated that:

> The most basic human rights obligations, in particular those emanating from peremptory international law (ius cogens) bind both the State and armed opposition groups in times of peace and during armed conflict. In particular, international human rights law requires States, armed groups and others to respect the prohibitions of extrajudicial killing, maiming, torture, cruel inhuman or degrading treatment or punishment, enforced disappearance, rape, other conflict related sexual violence, sexual and other forms of slavery, the recruitment and use of children in hostilities, arbitrary detention as well as of any violations that amount to war crimes, crimes against humanity, or genocide.[98]

Yet it is argued in the paragraphs below that the reliance upon *jus cogens* norms in this manner is problematic.

3.2.2 Assessment of justification of practice

3.2.2.1 *Jus cogens* norms not necessarily binding on armed groups

The first problem of employing *jus cogens* arguments stems from the fact that there is 'no definitive list of human rights that constitute peremptory norms of international law'.[99] But perhaps more problematic still is the fact that the statements from the Syria Commission and United Nations Mission in the Republic of South Sudan can be criticized for implying that because a norm is *jus cogens* it is binding upon every entity of international law. While this was one of the findings of the European Court of Justice in the *Kadi* case before the European Court of Justice, it does not stand up to legal scrutiny.[100] For while many norms which have been identified as *jus cogens* in character *are* arguably binding upon States and non-State actors equally (e.g. genocide, crimes against humanity, torture),[101] there are clearly some *jus cogens* norms which are binding upon States, but not on individuals or armed groups. A prominent example of such a norm is the prohibition on the use of force which is binding only on States.[102] Likewise, there are some *jus cogens*

[98] UNMISS, 'Conflict in South Sudan: A Human Rights Report, United Nations Mission in the Republic of South Sudan' (8 May 2014) <https://unmiss.unmissions.org/sites/default/files/unmiss_conflict_in_south_sudan_-_a_human_rights_report.pdf> accessed 20 January 2017, [17].

[99] Henckaerts and Wiesener, 'Possible Contribution from Customary International Law' (n 60) 159.

[100] See for example, *Kadi v Council and Commission*, CFEU, T-315/01 (21 September 2005) [226]. The Court of First Instance of the European Union held that *jus cogens* norms were understood to be 'a body of higher rules of public international law binding on all subjects of international law, and including the bodies of the United Nations, and from which no derogation is possible'. This aspect of the judgment has been subject to criticism. See for example Shelton, 'Normative Hierarchy' (n 95) 312, who calls it an 'astonishing conclusion'.

[101] See ILC, 'Draft Articles on Responsibility of States for Internationally Wrongful Acts with Commentary' (9 August 2001) UN Doc A/56/83, 85, which identifies the 'prohibitions of aggression, genocide, slavery, racial discrimination, crimes against humanity and torture, and the right to self-determination' as peremptory norms.

[102] For the *jus cogens* status of this norm see the ICJ in *Nicaragua v USA* (n 22): 'A further confirmation of the validity as customary law of the principle of the prohibition of force expressed in Article 2, paragraph 4 of the Charter of the United Nations may be found in the fact that it is frequently referred

crimes which can be committed only by non-State actors and not by States (e.g. piracy, which is by its nature a non-State activity).[103] This is clear evidence of the fact that just as the fact that a norm is customary in character does not allow for a conclusion that it is binding upon every subject of international law, nor does the fact that a norm is *jus cogens* allow for a conclusion that it is binding upon every subject of international law.[104] It is noted that these identified problems are largely solved by a linking the statements on *jus cogens* above with the law on crimes against humanity.[105] For there is strong agreement that crimes against humanity are based on *jus cogens* human rights obligations.[106] Moreover, Chapter 10 has shown that a reasonable argument can be made that the *jus cogens* norms prohibiting crimes against humanity are binding upon States, armed groups, and individuals. However, a more wide-reaching future study of State practice and *opinio juris* in relation to armed groups and human rights norms would be a valuable addition to the debate on this topic.

3.2.2.2 Crimes against humanity

Seen from this perspective, Chapter 10 has argued that there is a reasonable argument to be made that the *jus cogens* human rights obligations underlying Article 7 of the Rome Statute can be held binding upon armed groups, in instances where the armed group is sufficiently organized to fulfil those norms. Either the group can be held bound *through its members* or it can be held bound as an entity in its own right.[107] Indeed, support for the notion that armed groups are bound by human rights law through their members may be found in fact-finding reports which focus almost entirely on the criminal responsibility

to by State representatives as being not only a principle of customary international law but also a fundamental or cardinal principle of such law. The International Law Commission, in the course of its work on the codification of the law of treaties, expressed the view that "the law of the Charter concerning the prohibition of the law of force in itself constitutes a conspicuous example of a rule of international law, having the character of jus cogens"'.

[103] See ILC, Yearbook of the International Law Commission 1966 (4 May–19 July 1966) Vol II, UN Doc A/CN.4/SER.A/1966/Add.1, 248 [3].

[104] On the contrary, it seems that the question of who a norm is binding upon may rather be seen as *one* factor relevant to a determination of whether a particular norm is *jus cogens* status.

[105] In other words, it would be more legally justifiable if the report from South Sudan was worded as follows: 'The most basic human rights obligations, in particular those *corresponding with* the peremptory international law (ius cogens) *on crimes against humanity* bind both the State and armed opposition groups in times of peace and during armed conflict. In particular, international human rights law requires States, armed groups and others to respect the prohibitions of extrajudicial killing, maiming, torture, cruel inhuman or degrading treatment or punishment, enforced disappearance, rape, other conflict related sexual violence, sexual and other forms of slavery, the recruitment and use of children in hostilities, arbitrary detention as well as of any violations that amount to war crimes, crimes against humanity, or genocide.' (emphasis added)

[106] See HRC General Comment 29 (n 95) [11–15].

[107] See Chapter 7 for a full explanation for these theories and their advantages and disadvantages. It is noteworthy that Y. Dinstein, 'The International Law of Civil Wars and Human Rights' (1976) 6 Israel Yearbook of Human Rights 62, 68, seems to employ a similar argument to the legislative jurisdiction theory to explain how armed groups may be bound by human rights law.

of the armed group's members under international criminal law.[108] Such a theory may also be behind the Syria Commission's statement that human rights obligations constituting peremptory norms bind 'States, individuals and *non State collective entities*' (emphasis added).[109] Moreover, when the law on crimes against humanity is taken as evidence that armed groups are responsible under human rights law, there is no need to prove that the armed group in question is operating in the context of an armed conflict. There is also no strict need to demonstrate that the armed group had effective control of territory or was exercising functions of government, although these will be strong indicators of a group's personality.

However, in such situations, it is argued that there is a particularly pressing need to demonstrate that the armed group is 'an organization'; in the sense of a legal entity, separate to its members, capable of adhering to the basic human rights norms reflected in Article 7 of the Rome Statute. The need to give this factor more attention in situations falling below the threshold of armed conflict stems from the fact that the appraisal of whether the group has met the 'organizational requirement' of international humanitarian law has not been conducted anywhere else. If the armed group in question has already been proven to be organized enough to bear obligations under international humanitarian law, there will be a stronger argument to make that it is also organized enough to bear obligations under international human rights law. However, in line with the conclusions in Part II of this book, there will also be a need to address why the situation has reached the concern of international law. Part II has argued that this may be proved by reference to the level of the group's atrocities, the absence or incapacities of the *de jure* government, or involvement of the international community. Before developing these statements further, attention will be given to the reports in which these arguments have been employed.

3.2.2.3 Instances in which *jus cogens* has been replied upon correspond with lack of territorial control

The fact that Chapter 10 has found that an armed group can commit crimes against humanity without territorial control and outside the international humanitarian law framework, makes it reasonable that *jus cogens* norms have been employed as justification for armed groups being bound by human rights law, in instances where the armed group in question has not had a high degree of territorial control and has not been exercising governmental functions. It also likely explains why *jus cogens* norms were referred to by the Syrian Commission before the threshold

[108] OHCHR, 'Special Report: Summary of fact finding missions on alleged human rights violations committed by the Lord's Resistance Army (LRA) in the districts of Haut-Uélé and Bas-Uélé in Orientale province of the Democratic Republic of Congo, United Nations Joint Human Rights Office in the DRC (United Nations Organization Mission in the Democratic Republic of the Congo and Office of the High Commissioner for Human Rights)' (December 2009) (hereafter LRA Report, December 2009). It is noteworthy that while this report finds that the LRA has committed human rights violations, it seems to rely solely on the law on crimes against humanity to justify this.

[109] See Syria Report 22 February 2012 (n 96).

of international humanitarian law had been reached.[110] It may also be the reason why the law on crimes against humanity has been employed to address the acts of the Lords Resistance Army, a group famed for its nomadic nature and lack of control of territory.[111] However, when examining these reports, it is seen that there is a significant lack of analysis of the organization of the armed groups in question. There is also little attention given to their activities, their discipline, or capacity to adhere to the human rights norms identified. For example, in 2012 the Syrian Commission of Inquiry explicitly stated that the links between the FSA (Free Syrian Army) leadership abroad and the groups on the ground was unclear.[112] It also stated that it was unable to verify the existence of a functional chain of command or superior/subordinate relationship between the FSA leadership and local units.[113] On the basis of this observation, it proceeded to address violations by 'FSA groups' but it did not consider whether they formed one legal entity. Nor did it conduct any discernible analysis of the organization of these individual groups.

More significantly still, when considering whether the threshold of international humanitarian law was met, the Commission stated that although it was satisfied that the violence in some areas had met the required level of intensity: 'it was unable to verify that the (FSA), local groups identifying themselves as such or other anti-Government armed groups had reached the necessary level of organization' for international humanitarian law to apply.[114] On that basis, the Commission found that the threshold of international humanitarian law had not been met. Yet, despite this, it significantly went on to make a finding that the same groups 'committed gross human rights abuses'. In theoretical terms, there is no reason why an armed group cannot have legal personality under international human rights law outside the parameters of international humanitarian law. Indeed, it is also theoretically possible that the 'organization requirement' may be less demanding under human rights law than under international human rights law. However, it is argued that the Commission's approach could only be justified in early 2012 from the perspective of legal personality, if had been accompanied with an explanation why despite its view that the armed group did not have legal personality under international humanitarian law, it was nevertheless organized enough to have legal personality under international human rights law. It was found in Part II of the book that it is also necessary to point to the international component of the legal personality in question. Here it may be sufficient to point to the scale of the group's atrocities, the involvement of the international community, or the incapacities of the *de jure* government.

3.2.3 Conclusions on practice

This section has found that accountability mechanisms should be cautious about holding armed groups bound to *jus cogens* norms per se. However, on the

[110] Ibid. [111] See LRA Report, December 2009 (n 108).
[112] Syria Report 22 February 2012 (n 96) [18], [108]. [113] Ibid, [109].
[114] Ibid, [13].

basis of the arguments in Chapter 10, the chapter asserts that there is a good argument to be made that armed groups can be held responsible for breaches of the *jus cogens* norms in Article 7 of the Rome Statute. As a result, it is argued that that accountability mechanisms should be more specific in their reports and refer explicitly to the *jus cogens* norms reflected in the Rome Statute, rather drawing upon *jus cogens* norms more generally. In employing this argument outside of the international humanitarian law framework, the paragraphs above have argued that there will be an added imperative to prove that the armed group in question has international legal personality. This will require a systematic assessment of whether the armed group in question is organized enough to respect the *jus cogens* human rights norms underpinning Article 7 of the Rome Statute. It will also require attention to whether the armed group's personality is 'international' in character. It has been argued that this second requirement can be fulfilled by pointing to *inter alia* the extent of the armed group's brutality, the engagement of the international community, and the loss of function of the *de jure* government.

3.3 Universal Declaration of Human Rights as a source of customary international law

3.3.1 Practice citing the Universal Declaration of Human Rights

On the basis that the UDHR is the 'parent document, the primary inspiration, for most rights instruments in the world today',[115] it is no surprise that the UDHR has often been cited as a means to justify holding armed groups responsible under international human rights law. Most notably, after a visit to Sri Lanka in March 2006, Mr Philip Alston, the Special Rapporteur on extrajudicial, summary or arbitrary executions stated:

> Human right norms operate on three levels—as the rights of individuals, as obligations assumed by States, and as legitimate expectations of the international community. The Government has assumed the binding legal obligation to respect and ensure the rights recognized in the International Covenant on Civil and Political Rights (ICCPR). As a non-State actor, the LTTE does not have legal obligations under ICCPR, but it remains subject to the demand of the international community, first expressed in the Universal Declaration of Human Rights, that every organ of society respect and promote human rights.
>
> It is increasingly understood, however, that the human rights expectations of the international community operate to protect people, while not thereby affecting the legitimacy of the actors to whom they are addressed. The Security Council has long called upon various groups that Member States do not recognize as having the capacity to formally assume international obligations to respect human rights. The LTTE and other armed groups must accept that insofar as they aspire to represent a people before the world, the international

[115] M. Glendon, *A World Made New: Eleanor Roosevelt and the Universal Declaration of Human Rights* (Random House, New York 2002) 16.

community will evaluate their conduct according to the Universal Declaration's 'common standard of achievement'.[116]

Likewise, when four special mandate holders (one of whom was the Special Rapporteur on extrajudicial, summary and arbitrary executions, Mr Philip Alston) visited Lebanon in the aftermath of the 2006 war, they justified their scrutiny of Hezbollah's actions with a similar reference to the UDHR.[117] Since then, the Special Rapporteur's reference to the UDHR and use of the term 'organ of society' to justify armed groups being bound by human rights law has subsequently been repeated by[118] or cited[119] in an approving manner by numerous Special Mandate holders and fact-finding bodies.

3.3.2 Assessment of justification of practice

3.3.2.1 Universal Declaration addresses 'every organ of society'

By referring to the Universal Declaration of Human Rights, the reports seem to assert that armed groups are bound by the customary international law embodied in the Universal Declaration of Human Rights, either through their members or in their own right.[120] Conceptually, there is merit to this approach, for the Preamble to the UDHR famously states that it is a 'common standard of achievement' for 'every individual' and 'every organ of society'. It describes the Declaration as:

> a common standard of achievement for all peoples and all nations, to the end that *every individual and every organ of society*, keeping this Declaration constantly in mind, *shall strive* by teaching and education *to promote respect* for these rights and freedoms and by progressive measures, national and international, *to secure* their universal and effective recognition and observance,

[116] Sri Lanka Report 27 March 2006 (n 1) [25–7].

[117] UN Human Rights Council, 'Combined Report of the Special Rapporteur on extrajudicial, summary or arbitrary executions, Philip Alston; the Special Rapporteur on the right of everyone to the enjoyment of the highest attainable standard of physical and mental health, Paul Hunt; the Representative of the Secretary-General on human rights of internally displaced persons, Walter Kälin; and the Special Rapporteur on adequate housing as a component of the right to an adequate standard of living, Miloon Kothari, Mission to Lebanon and Israel' (2 October 2006) UN Doc A/HRC/2/7, [19].

[118] UN Human Rights Council, 'Report of the Representative of the Secretary-General on the Human Rights of Internally Displaced Persons, Walter Kälin, Mission to Sri Lanka' (21 May 2008) UN Doc A/HRC/8/6/Add.4, [10]; UN Human Rights Council, 'Report of the Special Rapporteur on extrajudicial, summary or arbitrary executions, Mission To The Philippines' (16 April 2008) UN Doc A/HRC/8/3/Add.2, [5].

[119] UN Human Rights Council, 'Report on Human Rights Situation in Palestine and other Occupied Arab Territories, Human rights violations emanating from Israeli military attacks and incursions in the Occupied Palestinian Territory, particularly the recent ones in the occupied Gaza Strip, Report of the High Commissioner for Human Rights on the implementation of Human Rights Council resolution 7/1' (6 June 2008) UN Doc A/HRC/8/17, [9] fn 12; HRC Palestine Report March 2009 (n 64) [22] fn 12. See also Gaza Fact-Finding Mission Report (n 70), [307] fn 186, [1369] fn 700.

[120] This is a reference to the conclusions in Article 7 which explains that armed groups may be bound by international law through their members or in their own right.

both among the peoples of Member States themselves and among the peoples of territories under the jurisdiction. (emphasis added)

The Preamble of the UDHR is remarkable for its choice to identify 'every individual and every organ of society', rather than Member States, as being the entities responsible for 'promot[ing]' the rights and freedoms therein and 'secur[ing]' their universal and effective recognition, and observance.

Indeed it is hard to read the preambular passage of the UDHR and come to any other conclusion except that its drafters believed that human rights should be 'secured' not just by States (which are notably not mentioned) but by a wider spectrum of duty-holders that would include a breakdown of all society's constituent units, from the most basic (i.e. individuals), to the more complex (i.e. organs of society), to the most sophisticated (i.e. States). It has been argued that the terms 'individual' and 'organ of society' should be interpreted widely. Louis Henkin has commented:

> Every individual includes juridical persons. Every individual and every organ of society excludes no one, no company, no market, no cyberspace. The Universal Declaration applies to them all.[121]

While Henkin does not mention armed groups in this passage, they clearly fit within the spirit of his definition of 'individual' and 'organ of society' which excludes no one. From Henkin's perspective, no entity is too small or too large to be excluded from the Declaration's reach.[122] Moreover, there seems merit in this view for the phrase 'every individual and every unit of society' gives the impression that the UDHR's drafters deliberately wished to adopt an inclusive approach which included most legal entities under international law, including individuals, organizations, entities, and corporations.

3.3.2.2 Agreement that some of the provisions of the UDHR are customary international law

At the time the UDHR was drafted there was broad agreement that it was a non-binding document.[123] However, in the years since its drafting, there have been a number of assertions that it has gained a binding character. Indeed there have been several studies assessing the UDHR's legal relevance that have noted that the Declaration has been repeatedly cited by UN Resolutions, reaffirmed by States at World Human Rights Conferences such those held in Vienna and Tehran,

[121] See L. Henkin, 'The Universal Declaration at 50' (1999) 25 Brooklyn Journal of International Law 17, 25.

[122] In fact Henkin seems to go further than this because it is hard to imagine how cyberspace can be deemed to be a legal entity under international law. Ibid.

[123] Eleanor Roosevelt stated in this regard when the UDHR was adopted: 'In giving our approval to the declaration today, it is of primary importance that we keep clearly in mind the basis character of the document. It is not a treaty; it is not an international agreement. It is not and does not purport to be a statement of law or of legal obligation. It is a declaration of basic principles of human rights and freedoms, to be stamped with approval by the General Assembly by formal vote of its members, and to serve as a common standard of achievement for all peoples of all nations.' Cited by H. Hannum, 'The Status of the Universal Declaration of Human Rights in National and International

referred to by national courts, and cited in domestic constitutions.[124] In the light of this kind of State practice, some scholars have taken the view that the UDHR has acquired customary international law status in its entirety.[125] However, this is a minority view. The majority of scholars who have written on the topic have suggested that only some of the UDHR's provisions have a binding character.[126] Adopting a slightly different approach, the ICJ has stated that the UDHR contains 'fundamental principles' of human rights.[127] Yet despite these widespread views, there remains no authoritative study on customary international human rights today. As a result, many legal scholars are unwilling to assert a strong view about: (i) which rights in the UDHR are customary; and (ii) which entities are bound to the corresponding obligations.[128] As a result, although there is no doubt that the UDHR is a document of 'central importance' in the 'human rights firmament' and although there is an emerging consensus that some of its norms have customary international status, its ability to be cited *in toto* as a source of customary international law in its own right remains controversial.[129]

3.3.3 Conclusions on practice

The lack of certainty surrounding this topic may explain why the so-often cited statement from the Special Rapporteur on Extrajudicial Killings uses such soft language. When the words of the Special Rapporteur are studied closely, it seems that he deliberately refrained from referring to the UDHR as a binding source of legal obligations for armed groups. Instead, he refers to the LTTE as being subject to the '*demand* of the international community' (emphasis added) and refers to the 'human rights *expectations* of the international community' (emphasis added). However, his use of this soft language does not necessarily mean that the Special

Law' (1995–1996) 25 Georgia Journal of International and Comparative Law 287, 318 (hereafter Hannum, 'Status of the Universal Declaration').

[124] Ibid. Also W. A. Schabas, 'Introductory Essay' in W. A. Schabas (ed), *The Universal Declaration of Travaux Préparatoires* (CUP, Cambridge 2013) (hereafter Schabas, 'Introductory Essay').

[125] See review of these authors in Simma and Alston, 'Source of Human Rights Law' (n 56) 90–9; Hannum, 'Status of the Universal Declaration' (n 123) 323.

[126] They point out that the view that the UDHR is binding in its entirety is difficult to justify when one looks at the UDHR's right to leisure, periodic holidays with pay and protection against unemployment, a majority of scholars. Simma and Alston, 'Source of Human Rights Law' (n 56) 92; Hannum, 'Status of the Universal Declaration' (n 123) 342.

[127] See *United States Diplomatic and Consular Staff in Tehran (United States of America v Iran)* [1980] ICJ Reports 3, 24 May 1980, [91].

[128] See Schabas, 'Introductory Essay' (n 124) 119, where he says that he is unwilling to cross the 'heretical Rubicon' by '[a]sserting that there is no distinction in terms of legal effect between the Universal Declaration of Human Rights and treaties'. He notes in this essay that the Universal Declaration of Human Rights forms the legal basis for the Universal Periodic Review system under the Human Rights Council, which every Member of the United States complied with between 2008 and 2011.

[129] Ibid, 113, comparing the view of John Humphrey and Egon Schwelb after the UDHR was drafted with scholars such as Hersch Lauterpacht. None of these scholars claimed that it was 'binding' per se, but differed in their view of its legal import. For the quote see Hannum, 'Status of the Universal Declaration' (n 123) 353.

Rapporteur did not consider the norms referred to as binding, as is sometimes assumed.[130] It is interesting to note that in earlier writings by Philip Alston, he referred to the same phrase 'legitimate expectations' as being 'characteristic of customary international law'.[131] In the light of this observation, it is hypothesized that that the Special Rapporteur used the phrase 'legitimate expectations' to distinguish the customary law obligations he found in the UDHR, from treaty law obligations.[132] Indeed, this reading tallies with the fact that the Special Rapporteur requests the LTTE to refrain from 'violating' human rights obligations.[133] The use of the word 'violations' indicates that, despite the Special Rapporteur's references to 'expectations' and 'demands', he nevertheless considered the LTTE to be bound by human rights norms, albeit with the source in custom and not treaty law.

It seems likely therefore that the Special Rapporteur considered the UDHR to be the source of binding legal obligations upon armed groups. This conclusion is particularly reasonable, considering that the mandate of the Special Rapporteur on Extrajudicial Killings is based on the right to life, which is a strong contender for customary international law status.[134] Moreover, it was shown in Chapter 10 that the case law on crimes against humanity provides a strong argument that armed groups have obligations relative to the 'right to life'.[135] In the light of these remarks, it is commented that it is justifiable for UN accountability entities to rely on the Universal Declaration of Human Rights, but only in regard to specifically articulated rights. That being said, it is also argued that there is also a pressing need for a further assessment of whether the armed group in question, in this case, the LTTE is organized sufficiently to be a subject of international human rights law. The manner in which such an assessment should be carried out has been

[130] Ryngaert, 'Non-State Actors' (n 19) 371–81.

[131] It is notable that Simma and Alston cited this phrase in their article on whether or not the UDHR had customary status written in 1988. Simma and Alston, 'Source of Human Rights Law' (n 56) 91, 98. The phrase 'these expectations characteristic of customary international law' is cited from L. Chen, 'Restatement: Protection of Persons' (1989) 14 Yale Journal of International Law 542, 546–7. In using the words, 'legitimate expectations', the article by Simma and Alston also refers to the work by M. McDougal, H. Lasswell and L. Chen, *Human Rights and World Public Order* (Yale University Press, New Haven and London 1980) 273–4, 325–7, which very clearly uses these terms to express the view that the UDHR is customary law, stating: 'The Universal Declaration of Human Rights had acquired, as we have already described, the attributes of authority in two different ways. First, it is commonly accepted as an authoritative specification of the content of the human rights provisions of the United Nations Charter. Secondly, its frequent invocation and application by officials, at all levels of government, have *conferred upon its content those crystallized expectations of future invocation and application characteristic of customary law*' (emphasis added and footnotes omitted).

[132] Henckaerts and Wiesener, 'Possible Contribution from Customary International Law' (n 60) 158, appear to agree with this analysis, stating: 'The question of whether such a legitimate expectation is closely related to the existence of a rule of customary international law. It may be argued that the existence of a legitimate expectation that armed groups respect human rights law supports or forms the basis of a customary law rule to the effect that human rights law binds armed groups' (footnote omitted).

[133] Sri Lanka Report 27 March 2006 (n 1) [85].

[134] Melzer, *Targeted Killing* (n 50) 184–9. See also African Commission on Human and People's Rights, 'General Comment No. 3 on the African Charter on Human and People's Rights: The Right to Life (Article 4)' (adopted during the session 4–18 November 2015) [5].

[135] See sections 4.1.4 and 4.2 of Chapter 10.

discussed in detail in Chapter 6 as well as in the two sections above. Likewise, further analysis is needed of whether the armed group in question controls territory and whether it exercises government functions, as these will be strong indications of its legal personality under international law. Further comment relating to this recommendation has been made already on this topic in the previous two sections and this applies equally here.

4. Conclusions

The main point that emerges from this chapter is that no matter what theory is employed to explain how armed groups are bound by customary international human rights law, it is important to identify the moment at which armed groups become a subject of customary international human rights law that is separate to its members. With regard to international humanitarian law, it was argued in Chapter 7 that there are two different levels of international legal personality built into the legal framework. The first level is symbolized by the threshold of common Article 3. This requires the armed group to be organized to the extent that it can be seen to be a legal entity separate to its members. It also requires proof that the armed group's legal personality is 'international in character'. Chapters 4, 5, 6, and 10 of this book have indicated that this 'international' element may be proved by an examination of whether the armed group is operating in an armed conflict context (the 'intensity requirement'), whether the *de jure* government is incapacitated, whether the level of atrocities by the armed group are such to have garnered the attention or intervention of the international community. Chapter 7 argued that the second level of legal personality was represented by Additional Protocol II. This required the armed group to have territorial control and a higher level of normative capacity. Inherent in this territorial threshold, was a demonstration that the *de jure* government was incapacitated and that the situation had reached 'international' proportions.

Applying this analysis to the practice surveyed above, it is significant that the practice from UN accountability bodies seems to indicate the similar emergence of two different thresholds at which customary international human rights law will apply to armed groups. The lower threshold seems to be based on the armed group being bound by *jus cogens* customary norms of the sort represented in Article 7 of the Rome Statute. The second higher threshold seems to be based on the idea that the armed group controls territory. However, the chapter has highlighted that there is currently insufficient attention given to whether these emerging thresholds have been met. With regard to the lower threshold, it is argued that there will be a greater imperative to show that the armed group is organized in a manner sufficient to confirm that it has legal personality separate from its members. Moreover, it has also been argued that there will need to be more attention given to establishing the 'international' element of an armed group's character. While this international dimension will automatically be confirmed when the armed group is operating in the context of an armed conflict or controlling territory, it cannot be taken for granted in situations where international humanitarian law does not apply. In those situations, it was argued that there is a need to confirm that the situation, and the role that the armed group plays in it, is one which is of interest to the international community as a whole which justifies the recourse to international law. This may be proved by the scale of the atrocities that the armed group has committed or by proving that the capacities of the *de jure* government have been severely compromised.

The higher threshold seems to require the armed group to have control of persons or territory, in default of the government. In instances where this is the case, Chapter 9 has shown that there is a strong case that the armed group is held bound to international law obligations of the State. Chapter 7 has shown that an armed group can also be held to be bound to its own legal obligations under customary international law, when State practice and *opinio juris* confirm these obligations. No matter which theory is relied upon, it has been suggested that more attention needs to be given to whether the armed group in question *actually does* control territory. The chapter has shown that this is all too often taken for granted in reports holding armed groups to account under human rights law. It is also argued that more attention should be given to the armed group's functionality and normative capacity, as the fact that an armed group controls territory does not mean that it will be able to adhere to anywhere near the full spectrum of human rights norms.[136] While this chapter has given some important insights into the question of when and how armed groups are bound by customary international humanitarian law, it is argued that a fuller understanding of these questions will be achieved when the suggestions made in this chapter start being addressed in practice. Only at this point will a body of 'jurisprudence' on the responsibility of armed groups under international human rights law start to emerge.

[136] See conclusions to Part II.

PART IV

CONCLUSIONS

12
Conclusions

This book took as its starting point the academic debate about whether armed groups can be deemed bound by human rights law, and in what circumstances. It showed that there are differing views about *whether* armed groups are bound by human rights law and also differing views about *when* they are bound by human rights law. Some academics argue that armed groups are not bound by human rights law at all. Others argue that armed groups are only bound by human rights law when they control territory and exercise functions of government. Yet others argue that armed groups can be bound by human rights law in a broader set of circumstances, including those where the threshold of armed conflict has not been reached. The introduction of the book showed that the academic debate on this topic has existed for almost two decades. Despite this, many angles of the debate have been only moderately explored and a plethora of questions relevant to the debate remain unanswered. For example, there is a significant lack of understanding of the relevance of territory to an armed group's acquisition of legal obligations under international law. There is also a considerable lack of clarity about the relevance of the law on crimes against humanity to understanding how and when armed groups may be bound by human rights law. Additionally, there is a general lack of understanding and scholarship on the question of how and when armed groups acquire international legal personality under human rights law. Yet despite the fact that these issues remain under-theorized, the introduction noted that the practice of armed groups being held accountable under human rights law only seems to gather pace.

1. Accountability in Peril

It is this disconnect between the accountability of armed groups under human rights law and our understanding of the obligations of armed groups under human rights law which was the primary motivation for this study. The introduction noted that doubt on these questions clearly manifests itself in the accountability framework. It observes that the manner in which accountability mechanisms justify holding armed groups to be bound by human rights law is distressingly inconsistent. Some accountability mechanisms use the word 'violations', while others seem to shy away from the word 'violations', preferring the word 'abuses'. The word 'violation' is generally thought to refer to the breach of a hard legal norm while the word 'abuse' is generally thought to refer to the breach of a 'soft law' norm'. Heightening the confusion even more, the Security Council seems to have recently adopted a policy of 'sitting on the fence' as to its terminology it uses: it urges armed groups to abide by their 'obligations' under international human rights law while condemning their 'abuses' of it. A further inconsistency relates to when armed groups are held bound by human rights law. While many accountability mechanisms seem to require armed groups to control territory to be held bound by human rights norms, other accountability mechanisms have held armed groups bound to human rights norms in instances where they do not control territory. A further uncertainty relates to whether or not armed groups are bound by human rights law outside of the armed conflict framework. The footnotes that accompany this varied practice do not give comfort that it is backed up by clear legal reasoning or theory. Indeed, it is clear that the inconsistency of practice broadly reflects the wide spectrum of different academic views about when armed groups can be bound.

It has been argued that the lack of understanding in this area manifests itself not only in inconsistent practice in terms of the factual situations concerning when armed groups are held bound by human rights law and how it is referenced (i.e. violations/ abuses), but also in the manner in which the varied practice is justified from a legal perspective. In many instances, reports holding armed groups accountable make little attempt to justify the practice legally at all. In instances where they do, their legal justification is flimsy. In many instances, reports simply reference a previous report which has held armed groups accountable under human rights law in a vaguely similar situation. Sometimes the practice is explained with reference to the fact that armed groups are bound by the 'demands of the international community', sometimes with reference to their control of territory or exercise of government functions, and sometimes with reference to *jus cogens* norms. Yet existing academic literature on the topic indicates that all these explanations are currently far from satisfactory as a matter of law. The introduction argues that the legal uncertainty about how and when armed groups are bound by human rights law risks inflicting damage on the accountability framework. It discusses this view by explaining that 'accountability' is only achieved if *inter alia* there is an external body which has the authority to scrutinize an entity's conduct against 'established rules and principles'.[1]

Finding that a process of 'accountability' must be based on 'established rules and principles', the introduction argues that any normative value that may be attained by holding armed groups 'to account' under human rights law is currently compromised by the lack of clarity about the 'rules and principles' upon which that accountability is based. It argues that as long as doubt remains as to whether, when, and how armed groups are bound by human rights law, uncertainty will remain as to whether the practice is legitimate. Moreover, the fact that the legal backdrop to this fast developing practice is so little understood

[1] D. Curtin and A. Nollkaemper, 'Conceptualizing Accountability in International and European Law' (2005) 36 *Netherlands Yearbook of International Law* 3, 8.

means that the practice itself risks losing validity. Many of the reports, from fact-finding commissions and commissions of inquiry, which have held armed groups accountable under human rights law, justify their practice with the inclusion of the stock phrase 'non-State groups exercising *de facto* control over a part of a States' territory must respect fundamental human rights of persons in the territory'. The book notes that this phrase is seldom accompanied by any analysis of whether these conditions have been fulfilled. One has the feeling that the drafters of the reports know that this is a thorny issue but hope that the repetition of this now often-cited formula phrase will give them a licence to apply human rights law to the armed group in question, without having to engage in further explanation or analysis.

2. Overriding Purpose of the Book

The overriding purpose of this study is to bring greater clarity and understanding in this area. The book aims to clarify the circumstances of how and when it may be justifiable for UN accountability mechanisms to say that armed groups have obligations under human rights law. In the light of this aim, the study has addressed four major questions. Part I addressed the first question and sought to evaluate whether there is any added value in the practice of holding armed groups accountable under human rights law at all, from a normative perspective. The purpose of Part II was to address the second and third research questions, thereby bringing overall clarity to the moment at which armed groups gain legal personality under international human rights law. The second question sought to gain insight into the manner in which the legal community is, and has been, willing to understand the legal personality of armed groups per se today and in the past. It investigated questions like the role of State consent and the role of control of territory in the acquisition of legal rights and obligations by armed groups. The third question considered what these conclusions tell us about when and how armed groups may gain international legal personality under human rights law. The fourth research question, which overlaps a little with the second and third, was addressed in Part III. It sought to gain a better understanding of *how* and *when* armed groups can be held bound by human rights law in a more technical sense. Drawing on the research in Parts I and II, it concentrated on the sources of those legal obligations and the circumstances when those sources may become binding upon armed groups.

3. Conclusions on 'Added Value' of International Human Rights Law

3.1 Greatest value in law enforcement paradigm

Part I confirms that international humanitarian law and international human rights are complementary to each other. It also confirms that international humanitarian law constitutes the most important element of the legal framework which applies in times of non-international armed conflict. Unlike human rights law, international humanitarian law was designed with the exclusive purpose of addressing the particular problems which arise in armed conflict. That being said, Chapter 2 demonstrates that in certain circumstances the practice of holding armed groups accountable under human rights law has the potential of bringing significant value to the legal framework, if it can be legally justified. In particular, it shows that human rights law brings most value to the law enforcement paradigm. The book defines the law enforcement paradigm as activities connected to the exercise of authority over persons or territory, the maintenance of public order, and the suppression of criminal or subversive activity outside the conduct of hostilities. Drawing upon literature from political science and anthropology, Chapter 2 demonstrates that the law enforcement paradigm is more important than it is often thought in territory controlled by armed groups. First, armed groups exercise 'governance' activities more regularly than it is often appreciated. Literature from the social sciences shows that it is a mistake to see territory under the control of rebel groups as a Hobbesian chaos. Instead, research shows that, on taking control of a particular area, armed groups will often feel compelled to quickly impose a form of order on the local population. This may involve basic policing, efforts to control people's movements, a clampdown on common crime, and controls on expressions of dissent. Armed groups may stop the broadcast of radio and television stations, prevent public gatherings, and round up and punish people for alleged collaboration with the enemy. In other words, an armed group does not need to be in control of a huge swathe of territory for a protracted period in order to exercise governance activities.

Secondly, the study observes that everyday life continues much more than is often thought in areas under rebel control. Research from the social sciences, especially that adopting a micropolitical approach, increasingly illustrates that not every aspect of an individual's life is defined by the fighting that takes place in times of armed conflict. Literature from political science and anthropology shows that in times of armed conflict, civilians continue to prioritize agendas which are not immediately connected to the armed conflict. Individuals get married, have children, get divorced, and have all kinds of legal disputes with those around them. Likewise, people get ill, need medical treatment, continue to work, and continue to suffer from, and perpetrate, common crime. Calling this the 'life goes on driver', Chapter 2 of the study identifies this force as a particularly important dynamic in the types of protracted armed conflicts that are so commonly seen today. In such situations, territory may be frozen under the control of one of the parties and the armed group will have the time and resources to focus on governance activities. On the basis that governance activities by armed groups are often instigated in response to the life goes on driver, and a population's ability to continue everyday life is likewise facilitated by governance structures, the study argues that the two forces can be seen as interdependent and mutually enforcing phenomena. Both are directly relevant to the identification of the value of human rights law on the legal landscape.

The book argues that these factual observations are crucial to identifying the value of human rights law in the law enforcement paradigm. The main reason for this is that the protections offered by international humanitarian law only cover aspects of life which are directly connected to the armed conflict. International humanitarian law does not govern the manner in which individuals are detained and prosecuted for offences relating to common crime. Nor does it cover the manner in which such individuals are treated whilst in detention. The drafters of the Additional Protocols were keen to restrict the scope of international humanitarian law, partly because they were acutely cognisant of the fact that not every aspect of an individual's life is connected to the armed conflict. After considering whether to limit the scope of international humanitarian law by geography, the drafters decided instead to limit it by 'persons'. In accordance with this approach, international humanitarian law would apply everywhere in the country but only to *some* people. In drawing the conceptual net of international humanitarian law relatively narrowly, its drafters also sought to give due deference to national law and human rights law. The study shows that these natural parameters of international humanitarian law are helpful in identifying the correspondent limits of international human rights law.

Correspondingly, Chapter 2 demonstrates that human rights law often brings value on issues unrelated to the armed conflict, i.e. issues that exist equally in peacetime as in armed conflict. Indeed, many issues relating to daily life, family life, and daily subsistence are regulated *only* by human rights law. Unlike international humanitarian law, international human rights law contains a right to freedom of movement, a right to freedom of expression, a right to freedom of assembly. It also contains provisions articulating the right to work, the right to just and favourable conditions at work, the right to an adequate standard of living, including adequate food, clothing, and housing. Only human rights law contains a provision on the right to health, in the sense of a positive right which extends to healthy people, as well as those who are already sick or wounded. This is particularly important for people seeking vaccinations or medical services related to nutrition, hygiene, or contraception. Likewise, only human rights law contains provisions relating to people's right to marry freely and the right of children to have their birth registered. Human rights law also contains detailed provisions on the rights of women, including their right not to be discriminated against in society. These are an important complement to the equivalent provisions in international humanitarian law which is generally designed to address a 'state of emergency' perspective.

Likewise, international human rights law contains key protections for persons subjected to the criminal justice system as a result of being suspected of having committed common crimes. Indeed, human rights norms such as the right to life, the right not to be detained arbitrarily, and the right to fair trial provide individuals with human rights protection at every stage of the criminal justice system. Such norms govern how the police arrest people who are suspected of crime or who pose a danger to the general public. They govern the manner in which people are detained and provide individuals with important safeguards in detention. They also provide protection for people prosecuted on criminal charges. Human rights law also contains a unique series of positive provisions designed to protect people from harm by others. In the area of combating sexual violence against women for example, a State is generally considered to be under a duty to legislate to ensure that sexual violence crimes can be adequately prosecuted. It is also considered to be under a duty to investigate, prosecute, and provide redress for the harm committed by private individuals. In that sense, human rights law contains important protections for the establishment and maintenance of public order and law enforcement in the literal sense of the term. While positive obligations exist in international humanitarian law too, they do not extend to the prevention of crime unless it has a clear nexus to the armed conflict.

The conceptual parameters of international human rights law are particularly helpful for addressing the 'life goes on driver' identified above and regulating the phenomenon of armed groups conducting governance activities. By connecting the literature from social sciences and the legal framework, the chapter demonstrates that human rights law has a particularly valuable role in ensuring that the legal framework addresses the full needs of people in times of armed conflict. For while international humanitarian law provides crucial emergency protection in times of armed conflict, the study argues that it also reproduces a reductionist narrative of armed conflict where individuals are addressed as being either 'fighters' or 'civilians'. It takes a top-down approach to the conflict that starts with the identification of its parties. While this is essential for the legal framework and people's protection in times of armed conflict, a review of the literature from social sciences shows that it does not address the full human experience of armed conflict. Human rights law is able to complement it by responding to the multidimensional human experiences of armed conflict that is rooted in people's roles as individuals: mothers, fathers, daughters, sons, and neighbours. The fact that human rights law does not rely upon allocating individuals particular statuses, and instead treats everyone equally as individuals, means that it is better able to provide protection to the individual as a participant in the social fabric of life with a full measure of agency. It also is able to respond to the extent of the 'life goes on driver' and the truth that in times of non-international armed conflict, the majority of individuals are interacting in a non-violent manner.

3.2 Humanitarian assistance

The book shows that humanitarian assistance is another major issue on which human rights law provides important complementarity to international humanitarian law. The ability of human rights law to play an important role in this area stems from the fact that the positive obligations under human rights law in respect to the provision of key life-saving assistance such as food, water, housing, and medicine, are more far-reaching than the equivalent positive obligations under international humanitarian law. Human rights law also adds value on the issue of whether parties to an armed conflict are required to consent to granting access to humanitarian organizations. The ICRC has held that under customary international humanitarian law, a State cannot withhold its consent in situations where: (i) people are starving; or (ii) its refusal is arbitrary. However, in the light of the fact that neither common Article 3 or Article 18 of APII contains any explicit provisions to this effect, recourse is often additionally had to human rights law. Within the human rights framework, the rights to life, freedom from inhuman and degrading treatment, an adequate standard of living, including adequate food, clothing and housing, and the right to the enjoyment of the highest attainable standard of health are a particularly important means of finding an obligation upon States parties to consent to humanitarian access. In particular, the Committee on Economic, Social and Cultural Rights has consistently drawn attention to the obligation of States to cooperate with international partners when taking steps to realize the rights contained in the Covenant.

3.3 Different perspectives of IHRL and IHL brings net gain

Generally, Part I shows that human rights law's value vis-à-vis international humanitarian law emerges from the fact that it brings a different perspective into the legal framework. Although the two bodies of law often cover similar issues, they have different philosophies, different ways of perceiving individuals, and different concerns. Naturally these differences filter down into the normative content of the two bodies of law. It is argued that these differences are at the heart of why the two bodies of law complement each other so effectively in responding to: (i) issues related to the armed conflict; and (ii) matters related to everyday life. In relation to individual norms and issues, the two bodies of law often cover the same issue, but provide a different, complementary normative perspective on it. For example, while international humanitarian law provides important protections for people who are sick and wounded, international human rights law provides protection for people who are healthy but nevertheless need medical assistance. Likewise, while humanitarian law prohibits people from being moved against their will, international human rights law protects people from being confined to a single location against their will in an arbitrary manner. The study shows that the two bodies of law repeatedly approach the same problems from a slightly different perspective with the result that together they create a net-normative gain. Likewise, these conceptual differences manifest themselves in the manner in which a particular provision is drafted. Human rights law is based in the language of 'rights' whereas international humanitarian law is generally based in the language of instruction or prohibition.

The study argues that these small drafting differences are often helpful for those working on the ground as they provide different routes to engagement. Human rights law allows a 'rights-based approach' where the starting question is what rights do people have? International humanitarian law facilitates a more cautionary approach where the starting point for engagement is the existence of a 'prohibition'. In general, the analysis of Part I on whether human rights law is able to bring any added value to the legal framework is conducted without consideration of the question of how or when armed groups may be bound by human rights norms or any consideration of how these norms might be applied differently by armed groups, than they are applied by States. This reflects the fact that the question of 'how and when' armed groups might be bound by human rights law is left until Part II and III. However, Part I concludes by making some observations about the relationship between the amount of territory that an armed group controls and the added value that is brought by human rights law. In doing so, it concludes that human rights law will be able to bring the most added value in situations where either: (i) an armed group controls territory; or (ii) the threshold of an armed conflict has not yet been met. In instances where the threshold of an armed conflict has been met, but an armed group does not control territory, the chapter concludes that the added value of human rights law vis-à-vis international humanitarian law will be less.

4. Conclusions on Legal Personality of Armed Groups under Human Rights Law

4.1 Framework of analysis

The purpose of Part II was to seek clarity on when and how armed groups can acquire legal personality under human rights law. The need for such an inquiry was motivated by the observation that most major questions plaguing the debate about whether armed groups are bound by human rights law relate to 'legal personality'. Debates as to when and how armed groups have obligations under human rights law run along the same fault lines that characterize debates about legal personality in international law more generally. Scholars from a positivist persuasion tend to reject the idea that armed groups can ever be bound by human rights law, unless they are State-like in character. Scholars who tend towards a more policy-orientated jurisprudential stance are generally more willing to embrace the idea that armed groups can be bound by human rights law in broader circumstances than this. The book argues that the polarization of views that is seen in the debate on armed groups and human rights law ultimately represents the different ways in which individual scholars conceive the whole system of international law. The manner in which a scholar views non-State actors within that system and the circumstances in which he or she argues that they may acquire international legal personality is largely defined by *inter alia* his or her views on the role of State consent in the international system, the manner in which legal personality can be acquired by non-State actors, and the way in which it manifests itself.

The study finds it necessary to employ several tools to guard against this subjectivity. In the first place, it aims to escape from the controversies of the debate about whether armed groups are bound by human rights law by looking at other areas of law, namely belligerency, insurgency, and international humanitarian law for answers. It treats these three frameworks of law as a valuable resource in seeking clarity on the legal personality of armed groups under international law per se. The particular value of these frameworks lies in the fact that unlike human rights law, there is broad agreement that these bodies of law, particularly international humanitarian law and the law on belligerency, bind armed groups. As a result, these legal frameworks provide important information about the manner in which armed groups can acquire legal personality under international law. As legal frameworks, they represent a consensus about how the international community is, or has been, willing to treat armed groups under international law. Although questions and controversies exist in these areas too, the fact that the application of these legal frameworks to armed groups is more established than human rights law, means they can provide more objective information about the source of legal obligations for armed groups, the circumstances in which armed groups may be held bound by international law, and the role that State consent plays in the acquisition of their legal personality.

The second tool that the study employs to combat this subjective element is an evaluative framework against which the legal personality of armed groups in these legal frameworks can be analysed. This evaluative framework, extracted from Portmann's monograph on the topic, distils legal scholarship on legal personality into five major schools of thought: States-only, recognition, formal, individualistic, and actor.[2] The study's decision to adopt and set out this evaluative framework was largely motivated by an acknowledgement that the subjectivity identified above is intrinsic and inescapable. As a result, it would be fallacious to argue that the author's analysis of these legal frameworks above is not influenced by that subjectivity. Recognizing that legal commentary is always informed by individual views, the study found it appropriate to analyse the question of armed group's legal personality with a heightened degree of openness and transparency. This allows the legal frameworks to be investigated against an identifiable benchmark of analysis. It also has the effect of forcing a more painstaking examination and helps the author of this study escape somewhat from, or at least be more aware of, her own inevitable scholarly biases.[3] Perhaps most importantly, the adoption of such a framework means that the conclusions of the study on these issues are immediately transparent and able to be challenged. This has the effect of facilitating a continuing debate on the topic and gives the study's conclusions more legitimacy. As a result, Part II does not seek to determine how and when an armed group may gain international legal personality per se as if there is an objective truth on the topic. Instead, it seeks to determine what the legal frameworks tell us about the dominant manner in which the legal personality of armed groups is conceived.

4.2 Legal personality of armed groups exists along a spectrum

Part II's analysis of the belligerency, insurgency, and international humanitarian law frameworks show a strong acceptance of the fact that the legal personality of

[2] R. Portmann, *Legal Personality in International Law* (CUP, Cambridge 2010) (hereafter Portmann, *Legal Personality*).

[3] R. Higgins, *Problems and Process, International Law and How We Use It* (Clarendon Press, Oxford 1994) 5.

armed groups can exist along a spectrum. The historical legal framework of belligerency and insurgency shows a long historical acceptance of the fact that armed groups may have obligations under international law without being treated as if they are States or approaching Statehood per se. Indeed, all three legal frameworks demonstrate a strong understanding of the fact that the legal personality of armed groups is a *sui generis* product of the exceptional circumstances that arise in armed conflict. In the field of human rights law, this confirms that the fact that an armed group has obligations under human rights law does not have any formal consequences as a matter of law. Instead, it can be seen as simply a modern manifestation of a long tradition of recognizing that armed groups may have legal personality under international law in the exceptional circumstances of non-international armed conflict. The analysis of the legal frameworks also provides strong support for the notion that the legal personality of one armed group will be different from the legal personality of another, in terms of its substantive and procedural scope. This is closely connected to another observation which is that the legal frameworks confirm that armed groups can acquire legal personality from different sources: treaty law, bilateral agreements with third States, customary international law, or control of territory.

4.3 Different procedural scope of different aspects of personality

The fact that an armed group can acquire legal personality from different sources means that different aspects of its legal personality will cover different issues and have a different procedural scope. The analysis of the legal frameworks of belligerency and insurgency demonstrate that while the obligations that an armed group accrues vis-à-vis a third State by means of a bilateral agreement are usually 'specific' in character, the obligations an armed group accrues as a result of controlling territory will usually be 'general' in character, i.e. able to be invoked by a multiplicity of third States and/or the international community in general. The significance of this for human rights law is that it provides a strong argument that any legal personality that an armed group acquires by virtue of controlling territory will be general in character. Another consequence of the observation that an armed group can acquire different levels of legal personality from different sources is the conclusion that armed groups can have different types of normative responsibility. Under the belligerency and insurgency frameworks, it was shown that an armed group's obligations can generally be divided into three distinct categories: those relating to the conduct of its warlike operations, those relating to its control of territory, and those emerging out of its bilateral obligations with third States.

4.4 Normative responsibilities of armed groups linked to their capabilities

Interestingly, all three legal frameworks support the notion that the normative responsibilities of armed groups will be linked to their capabilities. While more will be said on this at the end of this concluding chapter, some initial conclusions are stated here. Within the belligerency and insurgency framework, it was observed that an armed group's legal personality is inevitably tied to its functionality on the international sphere. As an armed group acquires a more consolidated territorial control, third States are often forced to interact with it in order to protect their own assets or citizens. In the earliest stages of an armed conflict, this interaction has been sometimes seen to result in the exchange of agents between the two parties and the brokering of individual agreements on discrete issues. At the moment at which a belligerency was declared, the armed group was seen to take over the State's due diligence obligations with respect to foreign assets and citizens. Significantly, these obligations were sometimes very similar to the modern day due diligence obligations that are a key part of human rights law. Also significant is the fact that a comparison of the framework of belligerency with the law on insurgency, showed that these territory-based obligations could sometimes also be triggered in situations falling below a formal belligerency. In particular, the example of the Spanish Civil War showed that armed groups exercising control over a territory, in default of the *de jure* government, could equally be held responsible for the harms that were committed on their territory and by their agents. As a result, the legal frameworks demonstrated that an armed group's obligations under international law would generally increase in a manner commensurate with its functionality.

4.5 Threshold test of international humanitarian law holds wealth of information about legal personality of armed groups

Further support for the notion that the normative responsibilities of armed groups will generally be linked to their capabilities was found in the international humanitarian law framework. The study argued that the threshold tests in international humanitarian law hold a wealth of information about the legal personality of armed groups under international humanitarian law. It argues that one of the key functions of the threshold test is to ascertain whether an armed group is organized enough to bear obligations under international humanitarian law. It argues that the lower threshold of common Article 3 is most interesting in this regard as it identifies clearly what is needed for a loose band of individuals to evolve into an entity with legal personality under international law. In contrast, the threshold test of Additional Protocol II identifies what is required for an entity to change from having 'some' international legal personality to having a 'more extensive' legal personality. While this transition is also of value, it is not as informative as the test which determines how international legal personality is acquired in the first place. The study shows that the need for such a threshold test stems from the fact that international humanitarian law only applies in circumstances of armed conflict. It also only applies if the norms that it contains can be applied by both parties to the non-international armed conflict, i.e. the State and the armed group or both armed groups. It also stems from the fact that armed groups are entities which come into existence organically. Unlike other non-State actors, such as companies or international organizations, armed groups do not have a formal moment of legal incorporation. Instead, they evolve into a corporate entity incrementally.

The book shows that a key benefit of having a clear threshold test which identifies when armed groups are bound by international humanitarian law is that it prevents the legal framework from being subjected to manipulation by political actors. Chapter 4 demonstrated that this was a major problem in the belligerency framework that ended up reducing its legitimacy so significantly that it proved unable to provide an effective or reliable legal framework in non-international armed conflicts. The study also showed that international humanitarian law is subject to the same pressures. We see different parties seeking to argue that it does or does not apply in particular circumstances, to meet their own ends. Yet in contrast to the law on belligerency, the application of international humanitarian law is not dependent on the views of the parent State or third States. Instead, it is based on an objective threshold test as to whether international humanitarian law has been met. While problems continue to be posed by the fact that there is no objective organization tasked with ruling whether the threshold of international humanitarian law has been met in a particular instances, the study shows that the establishment of a well-known and widely-respected threshold test for international humanitarian law has reduced the extent to which the application of international humanitarian law is vulnerable to manipulation or arbitrary application.

4.5.1 'Organization requirement'

In examining the threshold of common Article 3, Chapter 5 observes that it essentially has two different components: (i) the organization requirement; and (ii) the intensity requirement. It argues that both are equally valuable components in a determination of what is necessary for an armed group to acquire legal personality under international law per se. Turning to the organization requirement first, the study comments that it functions as an appraisal of whether an armed group can be seen to be an entity under international law. In that regard, it is somewhat analogous to the appraisal that the International Court of Justice (ICJ) conducted when it considered whether the Mauritanian entity was a 'legal entity' in its Advisory Opinion on *Western Sahara*. In that case, the ICJ considered whether the Mauritanian entity had the 'character of a personality or corporate entity distinct from the several emirates and tribes which composed it'. It is argued that the 'organization requirement' that has been developed by international criminal tribunals and courts has a similar purpose. Essentially its function is to check whether the armed group in question has a legal personality and is a corporate entity distinct from its members because only at that point can international humanitarian law apply. In doing so, case law has taken account of five broad categories of indicators: (i) factors signalling the presence of a command structure; (ii) factors indicting that an armed group can carry out operations in an organized manner;

(iii) factors indicating a level of logistics; (iv) factors relevant to determining whether an armed group possessed a level of discipline and the ability to implement the basis obligations of common Article 3; and (v) factors indicating that the armed group is able to speak with one voice. It will be shown below that the identification of these five factors is helpful in determining whether an armed group is 'organized' enough to have legal personality under human rights law.

4.5.2 'Intensity requirement'

The study finds the intensity criteria to have an equally important role to play in determining the legal personality of armed groups. In considering the 'intensity requirement', Chapter 5 found that the ICTY case law has paid attention to factors such as how protracted the violence has been, the seriousness of the attacks, the increase and spread of attacks over territory and over a period of time, the number of government forces mobilized, the kind of weapons used, and whether the conflict has attracted the attention of the United Nations Security Council. Trial Chambers have also paid attention to the number of civilians that have been killed, the number that have been displaced from conflict zones, and the number that have been evacuated. Case law has also taken into account the number of casualties, the number of houses destroyed, the use of heavy weapons, the blockading and shelling of towns, the existence of front lines, and the number of people detained. Attention has also been given to the ICRC's involvement in the release of detainees on both sides and its role in passing messages to families of detainees. Consideration has also been given to the manner in which the parent State has responded to the violence. For example, consideration has been given to whether it has deployed the army or the police to crisis areas and whether it has passed any emergency legislation or legislation that refers to 'war crimes'. The case law has also noted the extent to which the international community has been involved in trying to find a solution to the conflict.

In broad terms, the study has argued that the rationale behind the intensity requirement is similar to some of the factors which were seen relevant in the legal frameworks of insurgency and belligerency. The definition of both frameworks included the requirement: (i) that the situation was so serious to materially affect outside States; and (ii) that because of the absence of control by the States, outside States were forced to have some kind of relations with the insurgents. To a large extent, it is argued in this study that the intensity requirement plays the same role in the international humanitarian law framework. It acts as a confirmation of the parent State's inability to confront the violence by ordinary law enforcement means. The significance of this inability is twofold. First it confirms the necessity of the adoption of the international humanitarian law framework whose permissive aspect should not be able to be 'self-triggered' by States. Secondly, it confirms that the abilities of the *de jure* government are compromised in a manner that justifies the application of international law. It was seen in the insurgency and belligerency framework that the fact that a government had lost control of a portion of the State's territory was a major justification for the imposition of legal obligations upon armed groups. Connectedly, the third function of the intensity requirement is that it proves the international aspect of the situation in terms of seriousness meriting the attention of the international community. This plays an important role in confirming that the legal personality of the armed group has an international dimension to it. Part II of this book demonstrates that the relevance of this analysis for human rights law is considerable. The main points are briefly summarized below.

4.6 Importance of a threshold test in human rights law

4.6.1 'Organization requirement'

The analysis of the threshold test of the international humanitarian law framework demonstrates the importance of ascertaining when human rights law applies to armed groups. The advantage of having a clearly stated threshold test is that it will prevent the legal framework from being vulnerable to manipulation, which ultimately affects its legitimacy. It shows that any threshold test in human rights law will likewise have to evaluate the 'organization' of the armed group in question, to check that it is an entity capable of adhering to the norms in question. When assessing this requirement, attention will have to be given to whether the armed group can be seen to be a coherent corporate entity, separate from its members. Attention may be given to similar criteria to those identified in the case law from the ICTY on 'organization'. For example, attention may be given to an armed group's ability to speak in one voice, its command structures, its capacity to hold a ceasefire, its ability to represent itself at international level, its organizational structure, and its disciplinary codes. Attention may also be given to any features of the group's structure that suggest that it has a strong central leadership. Indications of this may be found in the manner in which an armed group manages its logistics, how it obtains its weapons, how it acquires its funding, and whether it has a centralized command. On the basis that the same kind of entity is being examined for 'organizational' coherence under human rights law as under international humanitarian law, the fact that an armed group has satisfied the organization requirement for international humanitarian law will be a strong indication that it can also be deemed an entity for the purposes of international human rights law. Likewise, the fact that an armed group controls territory will be a strong indication that it has satisfied the organization requirement but will not be determinative. Most attention to the organization requirement will be needed in any factual situation that falls outside the parameters of international humanitarian law, especially if the armed group in question has a horizontal structure or is fragmented.

However, Chapters 5 and 6 demonstrated that the question of whether an entity is organized must be evaluated specifically in relation to the normative framework in question. In other words, the purpose of the organization test is not only to demonstrate that an armed group has international legal personality per se but that it has legal personality under human rights law specifically. This requires attention to be given to whether the armed group is organized enough to comply with the obligations of international human rights law. The analysis also introduces the idea that there may be more than one threshold at which international human rights law applies to armed groups. It introduces the idea that different organization requirements may be matched with different bundles of human rights norms. At the higher end of the threshold, it may be relevant to note *inter alia* whether an armed group has promulgated legislation, administers prisons, has a system of basic civilian participation, provides public services, or exercises basic policing activities. At the lowest end of that threshold, it may be relevant to note *inter alia* that an armed group has a command structure that takes into account issues pertaining to basic law enforcement, i.e. the manner in which it exercises authority over persons or territory. Support for the idea that an armed group's normative responsibility should be tailored according to its capacity is found in the *Al-Skeini* case before the European Court of Human Rights which found that a State's normative responsibility can be adjusted according to its capacity.[4]

4.6.2 'International' requirement

Unlike international humanitarian law, international human rights law contains no natural threshold as it applies at all times, in peacetime and in armed conflict. As a result, any threshold test for the application of international human rights law to armed groups will not have to refer to the existence of an armed conflict per se. There is no reason of law that a test determining whether an armed group has legal personality under international human rights law should refer to the same 'intensity' requirement found in international humanitarian law. In fact, it would be inappropriate for it to do so because unlike international humanitarian law, human rights law applies at all times. That being said, Part II of the book found that some sort of equivalent contextual requirement will be needed in order to establish the 'international' aspect of the armed group's personality. This test will need to confirm the situation as one with international dimensions that justifies the armed group being bound by international law. The study indicates that proving the situation has reached one of international proportions may either be achieved by pointing to the scale or systematicity of the atrocities or by pointing to a significant default on the part of the *de jure* government, either because of its incapacities or loss of control over a portion of its territory or by demonstrating the involvement of the international community. Yet, the conclusions demonstrate that such a threshold test can only be developed alongside a more technical and legal understanding of *when* and *how* it is appropriate to hold groups accountable under human rights law.

[4] *Al-Skeini and Others v UK*, Application No. 55721/07, Grand Chamber Judgment, 7 July 2011, [137]. Chapter 2 argues that it is the 'obligations', not the 'rights', which are properly being divided and tailored in this instance.

4.7 Conclusions on when and how it is justifiable to hold armed groups bound by human rights law

Part III of the book was dedicated to achieving a better understanding of *when* and *how* armed groups can be held responsible under human rights law. It was commented above that the 'when' question overlaps somewhat with the inquiry into legal personality, but approaches the topic from a more technical perspective. It asks not 'at what point in time can an armed group be bound by human rights law?' but 'how' do those obligations arise. In examining this question, Part III began by considering the theories of how armed groups can be bound by international law per se as its starting point. It also notes the conclusions from Part II which suggest that armed groups can be bound to international humanitarian obligations as a result of controlling territory, treaty law, and ad hoc agreements. Ordering its analysis in accordance with the main theories that have been put forward for why armed groups are bound by human rights law, Part III proceeds by considering how these conclusions help explain how armed groups are bound by human rights law. As a result Part III comprised four separate chapters dealing with: (i) treaty law; (ii) control of territory; (iii) crimes against humanity; and (iv) customary international law. Each chapter considered how these various factors are relevant to building our understanding of how and when armed groups are bound by human rights law.

4.7.1 Treaty law

In a sense, the chapter on treaty law was the least ground-breaking in the study as it confirms that armed groups are generally not bound by the main human rights treaties, i.e. the ICCPR and the ICESCR. It also confirms that armed groups are not bound by the Convention against Torture. Chapter 8 comes to this conclusion by reviewing first the *travaux préparatoires* of the treaties, secondly their text, and thirdly the manner in which their scope has been interpreted by their treaty bodies. In each case, the chapter finds that there is little evidence that the drafters intended the treaties to bind armed groups. That being said, the chapter does not find this conclusion to be a rejection of the notion that armed groups may be bound by human rights law per se. On the contrary, the chapter identifies a number of signs in the treaty law framework which support a view that non-State actors may have human rights obligations under human rights law more generally, although the source of those obligations fall outside the treaty body framework. Nor does the chapter find this conclusion to be an indication that the members of the human rights treaty bodies consider armed groups to be outside their mandate per se. Indeed, the chapter shows that there are many indications that the treaty bodies are willing to press States parties to adhere to their positive obligations in providing populations with protection from armed groups.

These positive obligations include the obligation to ensure that civilians are not caught in the cross-fire between States and armed groups and the obligation to make efforts to secure the prosecution of members of armed groups. States have also been found to be under more general obligations to protect civilians from violations by armed groups. For example, States have repeatedly been instructed to take steps to prevent children being recruited by armed groups. They have also been instructed to take adequate measures to protect camps for internally displaced persons. The Human Rights Committee has also criticized States parties for arbitrarily refusing to grant access to life-saving humanitarian assistance to areas under the control of armed groups. In emphasizing these positive obligations, the treaty bodies which Chapter 8 analyses have demonstrated that, although they are not prepared to directly address the acts of armed groups, they are willing to focus on States' failures to prevent, prosecute, investigate, or punish their acts. However, the chapter also shows that it is possible to bind armed groups to human rights obligations by means of treaty law, in the same way as it is possible to bind armed groups to international humanitarian law norms by treaty law. It holds up the Optional Protocol to the Convention on the Rights of the Child on the Involvement of Children in Armed Conflict as an example of a treaty where that has arguably been achieved. It also identifies the African Union Convention for the Protection and Assistance of Internally Displaced Persons in Africa as another example of a convention that directly addresses armed groups and their members on human rights norms.

4.7.2 Relevance of control of territory

Chapter 8's finding that treaty bodies focus only on States' positive obligations to protect populations from the acts of armed groups, reinforces the need for Chapter 9's examination of the relevance of territory to the acquisition of legal obligations by armed groups. For a State's due diligence obligations under human rights treaty law are rendered quickly incapable of providing any meaningful assistance to those seeking protection from armed groups in instances where an armed group controls territory. In many ways, this is the practical problem which prompted armed groups to be addressed under human rights law in the first place. Such a situation represents a troubling schism between the actual and the normative. While the armed group, the entity with power in that territory, has no obligations in that territory, the entity with the obligations (i.e. the State) has no power to enforce them. Ultimately, it has been in order to address this rift, and in an effort to realign the normative and the actual, that the international community has come to address armed groups directly. The study argues that the practice of holding armed groups accountable under human rights law is a rare example of the principle of effectiveness overriding concerns of strict legality. It also gives support to the argument made by Salvatore Zappalà that the employment of the principle of effectiveness can only be justified in the modern world in instances where it is used to protect universal values, i.e. human rights protection.[5] Here, it is employed to prevent the persons in the territory under rebel control from existing in a human rights vacuum.

[5] S. Zappalà, 'Can Legality Trump Effectiveness in Today's International Law' in A. Cassese, *Realizing Utopia: The Future of International Law* (OUP, Oxford 2012).

In reviewing the relevance of territory to armed groups becoming bound by human rights norms it is useful to recall the conclusions from Part I of the book. The review of the law on insurgency and belligerency provided strong support for the notion that armed groups controlling territory were often held bound by international norms. It also suggested that armed groups controlling territory are ultimately being held bound by the obligations of the State. Support for this conclusion was found in the fact that the due diligence obligations to which the Confederacy was held to be bound are traditionally obligations binding upon States in international law. Likewise, there was a view articulated by British Law Officers advising the British government that it could consider the San Domingo belligerents bound to the terms of a treaty which had been signed by the parent State, Spain, before the conflict began. It was also seen in the fact that the Spanish government advised the Portuguese government that it should address any claims under 'international conventions' to the Franco insurgents because they were exercising control over the territory in which the wrong occurred. Further support for the idea that an armed group controlling territory can be held bound by the obligations of the parent State was also found in Part III. Chapter 9 brought to light multiple historical sources in which the acts of an armed group controlling territory to the exclusion of the *de jure* government have been treated as State acts. In reviewing these authorities from the Franco-Italian Claims Commission, the US Supreme Court, and the General Claims Commission between the United States and Mexico, the chapter found them to constitute authority for the notion that in certain exceptional circumstances, where the synchrony between the State and the *de jure* government has been lost, the international legal system is willing to hold other actors bound by the obligations of the State.

Reviewing the case law above in combination with case law from the ICJ and the European Court of Human Rights and the Commentary to Article 9 of the Articles on State Responsibility, Chapter 9 found the cases to lend support to the idea that when one subject of international law exercises impersonal powers of government within the territory of another State in default of that State's *de jure* government, those acts may be given validity under international law and considered as binding on the territorial State. The study found that this diverse case law provides further support for the idea that the usurping entity will be bound by the State's own international obligations under international law. Acknowledging that the practice is controversial, the chapter noted that there are increasing instances in which State organs have been held to be directly bound by a State's obligations under international law. With this in mind, the study argues that there is a particularly strong argument that armed groups controlling territory are bound by the obligations of the State, because in these situations the *de jure* government's ability to secure compliance with its obligations under international law throughout its territory is so severely compromised. In effect, the practice constitutes an understanding that in instances where the State and the *de jure* government are no longer geographically and functionally in synch, the State's obligations in respect to that territory may attach to other subjects of international law controlling that territory.

Crucially the study did not find that these cases demonstrated a preparedness to treat particular armed groups as unofficial and unsanctioned agents of the State per se, but only a willingness to treat some of their acts as State acts. In other words armed groups are treated as unofficial and unsanctioned agents of the State in respect of some of their acts but not others. The distinction is important and it is an expression of the idea that certain State functions are able to be performed by a multiplicity of actors in the exceptional circumstances of civil war or natural disaster, when the power of the *de jure* government no longer matches the full geographical contours of the State. Significantly, the study pointed out that echoes of this idea are repeatedly found in the political science literature referred to above. This repeatedly illustrates that some kind of informal 'governance' is required in instances where the *de jure* government is absent. It illustrates that it is often more important to the people on the ground that a particular service *is provided*, than who provides it. Likewise, the social science literature also highlighted that sometimes armed groups and governments will provide public services together in areas under rebel control. In the conflict in Sri Lanka the provision of services in the LTTE area of the country was said to be a 'complex interaction between state and rebel governmental efforts'.[6] Again, this observation, which is rarely commented upon in legal literature, supports the notion that in times of crisis, State functions may be performed by a multiplicity of actors.

Ultimately, the notion that an armed group may be bound by the obligations of the State when it is the only entity fulfilling core State functions in a particular area of the country was found to be key to understanding why the principle of effectiveness provides an explanation of why armed groups are bound by international human rights law but does not explain why they are bound by international humanitarian law. Unlike human rights law, international humanitarian law is entirely connected to the armed conflict. It is triggered at the moment at which the armed conflict commences and, in its very conception, is deemed binding upon two different actors. As a result, the application of international humanitarian law to armed groups is a feature of the legal framework's design. It is not caused by the inability of the *de jure* government to fulfil the State's obligations. It does not relate to a State's impersonal government function, but instead is more intimately connected with an armed group's struggle against the incumbent government. Human rights law on the other hand, is a body of law designed for one duty-bearer throughout a particular territory. It pertains to the governance relationship between the State and the individuals. As a result, it is inevitable that the effectiveness of human rights law is severely compromised in instances where the government loses control of a part of the State's territory. Moreover, while recognizing that in some exceptional circumstances some armed groups integrate governance functions into military strategies, the book takes the view that governance activities generally (e.g. detention, prosecution, provision of education, healthcare,

[6] Z. C. Mampilly, *Rebel Rulers: Insurgent Governance and Civilian Life during War* (Cornell University Press, Ithaca and London 2011) 112.

and the maintenance of public order) usually represent and relate to core State activities which are impersonal in character.

Further support for the notion that the State's obligations under international law are the ultimate source of the obligations binding upon armed groups was found in a bottom-up approach to the principle of effectiveness set out above. A bottom-up approach considers how individuals' rights, as opposed to a State's obligations, can remain effective throughout a State's territory, especially in instances where the government has lost control of a portion of it. Chapter 9 highlights legal authority for the notion that the rights at the bottom of the legal framework can act as an independent force that justifies and demands the identification of a new duty-bearer, in instances where the formal duty-bearer has lost its ability to respect, protect, and fulfil rights. Support for this view is found, for example, in the idea that human rights conventions are an exception to the 'clean state' principle. Building on this principle, the Human Rights Committee has held that the rights enshrined in the ICCPR 'belong to the people living in the territory of the State party' and as a result, cannot be revoked. Instead, it has held that the rights devolve with the territory. The chapter observes that the case law from the General Claims Commission, US Supreme Court, Italian-Franco Claims Commission, ICJ, and European Court of Human Rights was equally motivated by a desire to make effective the rights of the individuals at the bottom of the framework. In that sense, the study argues that the rights at the bottom of the framework can be seen as the source of the universal values which together with the principle of effectiveness, justifies giving legal effect to the actions of entities which have usurped the *de jure* government. In short, the study found that a respectable argument of law can be made that armed groups controlling territory are bound by the obligations of the State if they relate to impersonal governance and the protection of human rights.

4.7.3 Crimes against humanity

Chapter 10 continued by evaluating the relevance of the law on crimes against humanity to the question of when and how armed groups might be bound by human rights law. It observed that the connection between human rights law and the law on crimes against humanity has been often noted in the context of the debate on armed groups and human rights law, but has been only moderately explored. The chapter pointed out that the primary significance of the law on crimes against humanity to the debate stems from the fact that crimes against humanity are crimes which often trigger a duality of responsibility under international law; the responsibility of an individual under international criminal law and the responsibility of the entity 'behind' the crimes for the wider pattern of conduct which constitute international wrongs. The chapter explained that while this duality of responsibility is a common characteristic of international crimes, it is particularly relevant for 'crimes against humanity' which naturally have a two-tiered authorship. Individual acts are committed by individual perpetrators on the ground which form part of a widespread or systematic pattern of conduct committed by a higher entity. This higher entity, whether it be a State or armed group, masterminds the wider pattern of conduct and encourages, facilitates, or directs its perpetration. On the basis of the crime's structure, in instances that State officials commit international crimes, the State itself will also be responsible for those as international wrongs.

The chapter continues by arguing that there is also no reason of law why the same logic should not be applied to armed groups. This is particularly the case for armed groups operating within the context of a non-international armed conflict, who have already been proved to have international legal personality under international humanitarian law. Indeed, the chapter points out that there is now a wider acceptance of the fact that armed groups are capable of being found responsible for violations of international humanitarian law. The only elements missing are a forum for this responsibility to be realized and a generally accepted set of rules on attribution. It argues that there are equally strong legal arguments that armed groups should be able to be held responsible for crimes against humanity in a civil forum. To support this argument, the study identified general support for the idea that armed groups can commit crimes against humanity. It found specific support for the idea that armed groups can be responsible for crimes against humanity in a statement from the Darfur Commission of Inquiry and the Basic Principles and Guidelines on the Right to a Remedy and Reparation for Victims of Violations of International Human Rights Law and Humanitarian Law. The Commentary to these Guidelines stated 'non-State actors [such as groups or movements exercising effective control over a certain territory] should be held responsible for their policies and practices, allowing victims to seek redress and reparation on the basis of legal liability and human solidarity, and not on the basis of State responsibility'. The chapter recognized however that a process of attributing individual crimes to an armed group would be more complicated than attributing individual crimes to a State, although not impossible.

A finding that armed groups can commit and be held responsible for crimes against humanity is the first step in understanding why the law on crimes against humanity holds important information about how and when armed groups may be bound to international human rights law. The second step involves a fuller understanding of the relationship between international human rights law and the law on crimes against humanity. In academic literature, crimes against humanity are generally seen to have emerged from the law of war. Yet in popular parlance, crimes against humanity are recognized to have a strong connection with human rights law. Investigating this relationship more closely, the chapter found legitimacy for a formal link between crimes against humanity and human rights law. It found that the relationship between crimes against humanity and human rights law was in fact recognized from the earliest prosecutions of the crime after the Second World War. Prosecutors and judges in these early criminal tribunals repeatedly described crimes against humanity in human rights law terms, recognizing that crimes against humanity involved the systematic and widespread violation of individual 'rights'. As time went by, the study notes that the connection between the two bodies of law has become still more obvious. Today, it may be observed that the law on crimes against humanity and international human rights law have a more straightforward relationship than the relationship between crimes against humanity and its other parent, international humanitarian law.

A confirmation that crimes against humanity constitute literal violations of human rights law confirms why the law on crimes against humanity has been said to hold information about how and when armed groups are bound by human rights law. First, the case law is able to tell us something about the circumstances in which armed groups are bound by human rights law. Second, it is able to tell us something about the kinds of norms that armed groups may be bound by. On the first question, the study shows that the case law from international criminal tribunals and courts brings some important information to the table. In particular, it confirms that there is a wide appreciation that there is no need for an armed group to be State-like to be able to commit crimes against humanity. The case law also explicitly recognizes that armed groups with such a capability will likely control territory, be military in character, and have responsible command. That being said, the case law makes clear that no territory is formally required for an armed group to commit crimes against humanity. Nor is it necessary for the armed group to be operating in the context of a non-international armed conflict. Instead, all that is required is that the armed group is capable, as a group, of committing widespread and systematic crimes against humanity. The case law seems to suggest that atrocities by armed groups will amount to international crimes in instances where they are so widespread or so systematic that they have reached 'international' proportions. At this stage, they are no longer the concern of one State but are the concern of the international community as a whole. Moreover, the fact that they have occurred on the territory of a State arguably constitutes a failure on the part of the *territorial* State because it has failed in its duty to protect its population from the acts of private actors. It is noteworthy that this contains similar ideas to those found in the threshold test of international humanitarian law which likewise includes the concept of an 'organization' and a default of some kind by the *de jure* government.

The case law from the ICC which addresses the question of how organized an armed group needs to be to commit crimes against humanity addresses the issue much less directly, and much less systematically, than the case law appraising whether an armed group is 'organized enough' to be a subject of international humanitarian law. The reason for this is likely that the role of an organization in the perpetration of crimes against humanity is much less explicitly recognized than in international humanitarian law. Indeed, an armed group as an entity plays an important role in the landscape of international humanitarian law that is not at all mirrored in the law on crimes against humanity. The application of international humanitarian law to a particular factual situation starts with the identification of the parties, i.e. the State and the armed group. International humanitarian law explicitly recognizes that the parties to the conflict are of crucial importance to the enforcement of international humanitarian law by the group and by its members. The concept of there being an 'organization' is crucial to establishing the concept of 'responsible command' which is critical to international humanitarian law's enforcement. It is also necessary in order to understand the fighting between the two parties as 'hostilities' between two opposing military parties, meriting deference to the principle of military necessity.

The role played by the organizations behind the crime in the crimes against humanity case law is much less prominent. There are several reasons for the reduced prominence of the organization requirement in this case law. First, in the case law on crimes against humanity, a bottom-up perspective is often taken whereby the presiding focus is on the harm suffered by the victims (i.e. the violation of rights), rather than on the obligation that has been breached. Likewise, the relationship between the law on crimes against humanity and its underlying legal sources is much more oblique than the relationship between war crimes and international human rights law. These observations raise the question of whether the organizational requirement in the law on crimes against humanity should perhaps play a bigger role in prosecutions of crimes against humanity. It prompts a consideration of whether criminal tribunals should not engage in a more protracted assessment of whether armed groups are 'organized' rather than simply considering whether they are capable of committing widespread or systematic atrocities. Ultimately, the tests of 'capability' and 'organization' are linked because the fact that an armed group can commit widespread or systematic atrocities is an indication that it is organized. This observation is similar to the conclusion above that the intensity test also feeds into the question of whether an armed group fulfils the organization requirement under international law. While Chapter 10 concludes that it is not necessary for ICC judges to focus more explicitly on whether an armed group is organized enough to be a legal entity under international law, it argues that a more focused enquiry on this issue would be appropriate for accountability mechanisms that are focusing on both individual and organizational responsibility.

The law on crimes against humanity is also instructive when considering what human rights norms an armed group is bound by. The study showed that all the acts which are listed in Article 7(a)–(k) of the Rome Statute correspond with human rights norms enumerated in the UDHR *inter alia*: the right to life, the right not to be held in slavery or servitude, the right to freedom of movement and residence, the right not to be subjected to arbitrary arrest or detention, the right not to be subjected to torture or cruel, inhuman, or degrading punishment, and the right to be entitled to all rights and freedom without distinction of any kind. As a result, the law on crimes against humanity implicitly provides a strong indication that the entities capable of committing these crimes (e.g. individuals, States, and armed groups) are bound by the corresponding human rights norms, e.g. the obligation to respect the enumerated rights above. The case law also indicates that this list might not be exhaustive as the case law on the crimes against humanity on 'persecutions' states that 'fundamental human rights violations' can constitute the crime of persecution if it is accompanied by a discriminatory intent. Another reason to conclude that this list might not be exhaustive emerges from the observation that criminal law cannot be used to map exclusively the full extent of the primary norms from which it emerges. Such an argument would clearly be ill-conceived and would not do sufficient justice to the different thresholds, purposes, and origins of the related bodies of law. It also ignores the fact that the international criminal law on both war crimes and crimes against humanity has a gravity threshold which is naturally not present in the underlying frameworks of international humanitarian law and international human rights law. Further conclusions on the normative responsibility of armed groups are addressed later in these conclusions.

4.7.4 Customary international law

Finally the study considers whether customary international law can explain how and when armed groups may be bound by human rights law. As a preliminary question, it finds it necessary to consider how customary international law is made when it comes to evaluating the norms binding upon armed groups. The study considers it necessary to address this question because it is a subject of some debate in the literature on armed groups and fundamental to any discussion of how customary international law may be binding upon armed groups. Some scholars have taken the view that the legal framework will only remain valid if the practice of armed groups is taken into account in the formation of customary international law binding upon them. Others have argued that only an evaluation of State practice and *opinio juris* is necessary when seeking to discern the norms that are binding upon armed groups. In order to take a view on this question, the study draws upon the conclusions reached in Part II of the study which relate to how armed groups are treated under international law generally. It finds the idea that armed groups should contribute to the formation of customary international law a characteristic of the 'actor' school of legal thinking which considers less whether a particular normative framework is 'law' and more whether its subjects consider themselves to be bound by it. In appraising the legal frameworks of insurgency, belligerency, and international humanitarian law, Part II of the study found little evidence of such an approach reflected in the legal framework.

On the contrary, it was observed in Part II that the legal frameworks deemed binding upon armed groups generally give little attention to the question of whether the armed groups have agreed to be bound by the norm or rejected the norm in question. Likewise, the legal frameworks dismiss the notion, central to the actor conception, that all legal norms are constantly subject to change and flux according to the needs of the participants whom they address. Instead, the legal framework of international humanitarian law contains a strongly prescriptive element which manifests itself in the strong role of State consent in the legal framework, the existence of *jus cogens* norms, and a rigorous deference to the threshold test determining when armed groups will be bound. On the basis of these conclusions, Part I found that the legal frameworks addressing armed groups represent a mixture of the individualistic conception of international legal personality and the formal conception of international legal personality. Under the individualistic conception, attention is given to an entity's participation in the legal framework and its functionality. The legal framework of international law also betrays a disaggregated approach to legal subjectivity that is typical of the individualistic approach. This manifests itself in a willingness to see subjects of international law not only as impersonal corporate entities but also as aggregates of human beings. Under the formal approach to international legal personality, a strong deference is given to State consent and the notion that an entity gains legal personality as a consequence of being addressed by international norms.

Significantly, both these conceptions of legal personality do not find law-making to be an essential component of legal personality. This provides support for a view that the practice of armed groups need not be taken into account in the formation of customary international law. The study finds further support for a conclusion that the practice of armed groups need not be included in the formation of custom in the general character of customary international law which although sometimes described as being 'democratic' in nature, in fact can be better understood as 'rules originating in a general—but, crucially, not universal—practice to which specific states neither have to contribute nor subsequently consent in order to be bound'.[7] This observation is supported by the fact that new States are automatically bound by the existing body of customary law binding upon States. Significantly, new States are not able to reject norms of customary international law that already existed at the time of their creation. Likewise the formation of a rule of customary international law requires 'extensive' but not 'universal' practice before it will be binding upon all States. The study also takes a pragmatic approach to the argument that armed groups need to be involved in the creation of customary international law in order to comply with it or feel any ownership with it. It points out that there remains a risk that even if the armed groups of 'today' contribute to the formation of international law, the armed groups of 'tomorrow' will still not feel any ownership of these norms and may use that as an excuse not to comply with them.

On the basis of these findings, the chapter asserts that customary international human rights law binding upon armed groups will be formed through a combination of State practice and *opinio juris*. However, it finds that State practice and *opinio juris* will only be determinative of whether an armed group is bound by human rights law if both elements demonstrate an intention that armed groups are bound. This means that an appraisal of whether a norm is a customary international *human rights* law binding upon armed groups will need to be conducted differently to an appraisal of whether a particular norm of international *humanitarian* law is binding upon armed groups. If a State asserts that a particular rule of international humanitarian law applies in non-international armed conflict, the principle of equality in international humanitarian law generally allows for the assumption that the State intends the norm to be applied to State actors and armed groups. Importantly, the same cannot be said of human rights law. As a result, the chapter argues that any State practice cited to support the notion that armed groups are bound by customary international human rights law must involve an explicit mention of armed groups. For example, an example of State practice might involve an instance where a State trains or sensitizes armed groups on human rights norms. An example of *opinio juris* might be a statement from a

[7] Portmann, *Legal Personality* (n 2).

State pronouncing its belief that armed groups are bound by human rights law. Having set out these arguments, the study continued by evaluating the various theories that have been employed to justify holding armed groups bound by customary international law.

The study finds control of territory to be the strongest justification for the argument that armed groups are bound by customary international human rights law. Its strength derives from the fact that it can be articulated in two different ways, both of which are convincing. From one perspective, the armed group is bound by customary international human rights law as a result of it controlling territory in default of the *de jure* government. This explanation, which has already been examined above in section 4.7.2, has been seen to be grounded in judicial precedent and legal principles, making it the strongest theory reviewed. Under this theory, the armed group is essentially held bound by the customary or treaty obligations of the State, to the extent of its capacity. From the other perspective, the armed group is bound by customary international law when it controls territory by virtue of its functionality and State practice and *opinio juris* confirming that armed groups with that level of functionality are bound by human rights norms. From this angle, the fact that an armed group controls territory is not definitive. Instead, it is merely one indication that the armed group has gained sufficient functionality to have legal personality under international law. Fundamentally, the study emphasizes that the fact that an armed group gains legal personality under international law does not mean that it becomes bound by all rules of customary law. Instead, it means only that armed groups are bound by the rules of customary international law that, first, match their capacity, and when the second theory is relied upon, can be confirmed as binding upon armed groups. As a result, it can be seen how both theories *can* come together to justify how armed groups controlling territory may be bound by customary international human rights law. The first theory places more store on an armed groups exclusive control of territory. The second theory places store only on the armed group's existence as an legal entity separate from its members and its ability to adhere to human rights norms.

In situations where an armed group does not control territory, the study finds the legal justification for holding it bound by customary human rights law to have less historical precedent. The theory relies mainly upon the second theory above (i.e. the idea that the armed group has attained sufficient legal personality to be bound by customary international human rights law). Support for the idea is so far found mainly in international criminal law analysed above. The study argues that in instances where an armed group does not control territory, it will be important to prove that: (i) the armed group is an organization separate from its members; and (ii) the situation within which it is operating has reached international proportions. Indeed, in reviewing these theories, the chapter noted that there are a number of instances where armed groups have been held to be bound by human rights law on the basis that the norms in question are *jus cogens* norms. The study refutes the argument that because a norm is *jus cogens* it will per se be binding upon armed groups. It points out that such an approach fails to take into account the point already made above, that when talking about customary international law and non-State actors, it is important not to see customary international law as a fixed bundle of law. For just as not all customary international law norms are binding on all subjects of international law, so not all *jus cogens* norms are binding upon the same subjects of international law. However, the chapter finds it relevant that there is strong agreement that crimes against humanity and also genocide are *jus cogens* norms. Likewise, it points out that there is a good argument that these norms are binding upon individuals, States, and armed groups.

The study observed that there is a growing consensus that certain articles of the UDHR have now attained a status of customary international law. For example, there have been numerous declarations at international conferences since its adoption which affirm States' commitment to the UDHR's content. It has also been noted that references to the UDHR appear in numerous constitutions throughout the world. The UDHR also forms the legal basis of the Universal Periodic Review process which takes place under the auspices of the Human Rights Council. Furthermore, it forms the legal basis of the mandates of the charter-based Special Rapporteurs that operate under the Human Rights Council, addressing issues such as extrajudicial executions, arbitrary detention, the right to health, the right to adequate housing, the right to food, and the right to education. Yet, the chapter notes that there remains no authoritative study on the subject of customary international human rights law. As a result, scholars are generally reluctant to state definitively *which* norms contained in the Universal Declaration of Rights are binding and even less willing to state that which norms are binding upon non-State actors. However, in relation to some norms, for example the right to life, it seems as if a good case can be made that they are binding upon States and armed groups as a matter of customary law.

4.7.5 Evaluation of conclusions

Ultimately, the study shows that there may be more than one way to explain how armed groups are bound by human rights law in a technical sense. Clearly, the strongest situation in which the practice can be justified is in a situation where an armed group controls territory. The reason for this is that in this situation two of the theories come together to provide a justification for the practice. First, the armed group can be conceived to be bound due to the obligations of the State, under either treaty law or customary international law or both. In these situations, due to the exceptional circumstances of a schism having arisen between the State and the *de jure* government, the armed groups are bound by the obligations of the State. Significant precedent and support was found for such a principle of law in history and contemporary practice. Ultimately, the practice of holding armed groups bound by human rights law in these circumstances was seen to be a manifestation of the principle of effectiveness working in combination with universal values. Secondly, the fact that armed groups are bound by human rights law in these instances can be understood to be a consequence of their own legal personality, one of the strong features of which is control of territory.

In instances where an armed group does not control territory, the arguments that it is bound by human rights law are less consolidated in history and practice. Certainly the imposition of 'general' as opposed to 'specific' obligations upon an armed group in these circumstances does not have the same level of legal precedent behind them that as found in the law of belligerency, insurgency, and the diverse legal sources reviewed in chapter 9. However, the study finds evidence to suggest that armed groups may nevertheless be bound to customary international human rights law in these instances. The strongest evidence is found in the law relating to crimes against humanity which provides respectable evidence that armed groups can violate human rights norms in circumstances where they do not necessarily control territory. However, the study's conclusions make it hard to envisage that armed groups (e.g. the mafia), in existence outside of the context of a non-international armed conflict, which are not controlling territory and not committing widespread or systematic atrocities are bound by international human rights law unless some part of their operations can be linked to a significant default on the part of a State or has another international aspect meriting the attention of the international community. In these circumstances, a group may be organized enough to have legal personality but there is no international dimension to its personality to justify imbuing it with international legal personality and ongoing human rights obligations.

When studying the application of these various theories in practice, Chapter 11 has commented that there is a pressing need for accountability mechanisms to analyse the various requirements of the two emerging thresholds at which armed groups are being held responsible under human rights law. For example, in instances where the armed group's legal personality is based on their control of territory and exercise of government functions, there is a need for accountability mechanisms to comment on how much territory the armed group controls, whether the *de jure* government is absent or present, and evaluate the armed group's functionality, i.e. its normative capability. This will be evidenced by the kind of governance capabilities the armed group has and it may include a consideration of whether the armed group has a police force, court system, or legal code. It will also be relevant to note what public services the armed group provides in terms of healthcare, education, and public administration. In such situations, there will be less of an imperative to comment in detail on the armed group's 'organization' but a brief assessment of its organizational structure would be helpful. In instances where the armed group does not have control of territory, Chapter 11 argued that there will be a need for its legal personality to be analysed in a more detailed manner. This will require attention to whether the armed group is a legal entity separate from its members. In considering this question, it will be relevant to note whether the threshold of international humanitarian law been reached, whether the armed group has a command structure, whether it carries out operations in an organized manner, and whether it has a level of discipline and the ability to adhere to 'minimum core' human rights obligations.

Chapter 11 found that the greatest imperative to analyse the armed group's organization will be in circumstances where the threshold of a non-international armed conflict has not been reached or has receded. In these instances, the armed group has not already been proved to be a legal entity separate to its members by fulfilling the organization requirement under international humanitarian law. In such situations, there will also be a need to give attention to whether there are any outside factors which merit the armed group's personality being 'international' in character. This could be justified by the level of atrocities committed by the armed group (e.g. are they widespread or systematic?), the incapacities of the parent State or the involvement of the international community. It argued that it is only when these various factors are analysed more consistently that a body of 'jurisprudence' on the obligations of armed groups under international human rights law will start to emerge. This would be a valuable development to the legal framework as it would help protect human rights law from manipulation by outside parties and protect its validity. It would also increase the validity and effectiveness of accountability mechanisms holding armed groups accountable under human rights law and allow more consideration to be given to whether they are able to achieve the accountability of armed groups in the manner that corresponds with the definition of 'accountability' in the introduction of the study. This would involve consideration of whether armed groups could provide an account of their behaviour to the mechanisms, in response to allegations against them.

5. Operational Perspective

Finally, conclusions must be drawn on the operational side of the question to whether holding armed groups to be bound by human rights law has 'added value'. This issue has been left to the end of these conclusions because the preliminary conclusions drawn in Chapters 2 and 6 can be supplemented with the more technical comments and conclusions made in subsequent chapters. Chapters 2 and 6 made the observation that the obligations of armed groups under human rights law need to be looked at in the context of the obligations of the State. The rationale for such an approach is twofold. The first and most important reason is that one of the major justifications for the recognition that armed groups have legal personality under international law has been found to be the inability of a *de jure* government to adhere to the full range of its obligations under international law throughout the full territory of the State. As a result, in instances where the abilities of the *de jure* government are fully intact, there is very little rationale for a finding that an armed group has legal personality under international law. In that sense, the legal obligations of the two legal entities can be seen to have a kind of synchrony that is reflected in the principle of effectiveness. The study's findings indicate that in instances where the *de jure* government is most incapacitated, there is the greatest justification for an armed group to have international legal personality.

This conclusion leads to the connected observation that a State's ability to fulfil its obligations under human rights law are most compromised in instances where an armed group is controlling territory. In these situations a State's obligations under human rights law are generally distilled down to its positive obligations to re-establish its control over territory and take measures to ensure the respect for the applicants' rights. Indeed, it has been recognized that a State's obligations will be minimal and may simply involve negotiating with the armed group in question or taking action through diplomatic channels. A State will not be under an 'obligation' to re-take the territory through military means. Nor will it be under an obligation to protect individuals from harm in instances where they are outside its reach or control. It is a long-established principle of international law that a State's due diligence obligations under human rights law are obligations of 'means' rather than 'result'. Against this background, it is seen that in these circumstances there is the most need for armed groups to bear obligations under human rights law, from a protection perspective. Literature from social sciences has suggested that there will often be just as much of a 'need' for human rights protection in territory controlled by armed groups as in territory controlled by a State.

Indeed, in situations where an armed group is exclusively controlling territory, even temporarily, the study has shown that there is a high likelihood that everyday life will continue for the people under the armed group's control. It also showed that there is a high likelihood that armed groups will exercise governance functions. It has sometimes been argued that in instances where armed groups control territory, they should be held to the full range of human rights obligations to which States are bound. This study argues that it would be a mistake to take this view. The first reason for this is conceptual. So long as we carry on talking about armed groups as if they are aspiring States, or nearly States or State-like, we not only misconceive the majority of armed groups but also politicize the legal framework surrounding them. Research shows that many armed groups do not wish to usurp the incumbent government. It also seems clear that even armed groups with a very consolidated control of territory will not be State-like. It is partly in recognition of the fact that armed groups cannot be compared to States that the law of non-international armed conflict is less far-reaching than the law of international armed conflict. The international humanitarian law framework, created by States, takes care repeatedly to ensure that armed groups are only bound to obligations to which they can adhere, even when they control territory. It repeatedly indicates that the notion that the normative responsibility of armed groups must be tied to their capacity. This prompts the related observation that an armed group controlling territory will rarely be able to adhere to the full range of human rights norms. It also prompts the observation that armed groups may control territory in different ways and to different extents.

Indeed, the study points out that sometimes armed groups take control of a town very quickly after a short or even prolonged military confrontation with the State. In the early days after an armed group takes control of a town and the surrounding area, it may immediately instigate basic policing activities and institute a system of security in residential areas. Overnight, the armed group will become the prime entity able to affect these people's lives and also be responsible for the town's prison population. Such an armed group will have very different capabilities than an armed group that has been in control of a territory for several months or even years. It will not have the capability to provide sophisticated law enforcement activities but it will be able to interfere considerably with people's rights. Chapter 2 showed that it may institute curfews, stop children going to school, forbid public gatherings, close down radio and television broadcasting, and stop people travelling to their work. This leads to the observation that it will certainly be able to 'respect' many of the rights in ICCPR and ICESCR in these circumstances and may even be able to 'protect' others. For example, it would certainly be able to intervene if it found civilians raping or attacking another civilian or burning their houses or property.

In contrast, armed groups with a prolonged and consolidated control of territory may be able to adhere to a much fuller range of obligations. Yet, even then, armed groups will be unlikely to adhere to human rights obligations in the same way as States. It is noted in this respect that armed groups with even very prolonged and protracted control of territory, like the LTTE in Sri Lanka and the Forces Nouvelles in Ivory Coast, have been structurally unable to implement certain human rights norms. For example, the Sri Lankan government remained responsible for education and health in LTTE areas throughout the armed conflict. Likewise, the Forces Nouvelles in Ivory Coast did not have any working judicial system at all because all the judges had fled from the north of the country. Does it make sense then to address such groups on issues relating to the right to health and the right to a fair trial? An argument that armed groups should only be held bound to *some* human rights obligations may meet the criticism that human rights are indivisible and should not be divided and tailored. Yet Chapter 2 noted that the Grand Chamber of the European Court of Human Rights recently confirmed that rights can be divided and tailored when a State does not have full control of territory. In doing so, it confirmed the notion that the obligations that an entity bears must be tailored to match its normative capacity. Importantly, the study argues that it would have been more correct for the Court to have observed that the *obligations* that flow from human rights law can be divided and tailored, not the rights themselves. The individuals continue having the full range of human rights, but more than one entity may be responsible for implementing them.

In the light of these comments, the study has noted that many armed groups will be able to adhere to many human rights to a certain extent. For example, all the rights in the ICCPR have been noted to have an irreducible 'essence' that must be adhered to in every circumstance. In a similar manner the Committee on Economic, Social and Cultural Rights has stated that economic, social, and cultural rights have 'a minimum core obligation' that will ensure the satisfaction of 'minimal essential levels' of each of the ICESCR rights. The idea that rights may have a minimum core obligation may be useful in determining how they can be adhered to by entities other than States. Indeed, a right's minimum core will often be able to be adhered to by 'respecting' a right (i.e. failing to interfere with a right). For example, an armed group could easily respect the right to food and water by consenting to the provision of humanitarian relief by a humanitarian organization. An armed group could also respect the minimum core of economic, social, and cultural rights, by not taking any steps to deprive people of food, healthcare, or water. It would also be possible for members of an armed group to adhere to the basic principles of the right to life in law enforcement situations. It does not take a sophisticated State apparatus to adhere to the core human rights principles relevant to the right to life, including proportionality, imminent danger, and strict necessity. However, as an armed group becomes more consolidated and its control of territory is more protracted, it would be reasonable to expect more than this.

With regard to civil and political rights, the study has suggested that consideration needs to be given to the question of whether human rights norms can be applied differently when applied to armed groups. It suggests that notions such as legality, democracy, arbitrariness could be interpreted in a different manner so that emphasis is placed on concepts like transparency and civilian participation. It also suggests that guidance may be taken from the international humanitarian law on occupation about how to approach the requirement that certain measures are taken 'in accordance' with the law. Furthermore, it indicates that further consideration may be given to whether the approach of the Franco-Italian Conciliation Commission might be followed in determining whether courts established by armed groups are 'established by law'. It also suggests that consideration could be given to whether the courts were competent, independent, and impartial. In general, the study found that further research on particular norms must be the subject of a future study, so these comments must be taken as preliminary remarks rather than conclusions as such. The study argues that any research conducted on individual norms should be closely linked to literature from the social sciences or field research, so that it takes sufficient account of armed groups' varied functionalities and normative capacities.

In instances where armed groups do not control territory, the State's capability will of course be much stronger. In these instances, a State can much more easily fulfil its positive obligations under human rights law that it owes towards the populations affected by the armed conflict. The study also notes that in instances where an armed group does not control territory, it will generally either be on the attack or in retreat. As a result, the factual situation on the ground will be more akin to the conduct of hostilities paradigm than the law enforcement paradigm. Accordingly, human rights law will have a much less important role to play vis-à-vis international humanitarian law. This conclusion also arises from the observation that even if the law enforcement paradigm is relevant and people fall into the armed group's authority or control, it is much more likely that the situation will have a 'nexus' to the armed conflict. In other words, the individuals will more likely fall within the scope of international humanitarian law rules on law enforcement rather than within the scope of human rights law rules. Moreover, generally, the State will continue to have capacity in terms of service provision and will remain the entity from whom such services are expected. This conclusion is bolstered by research which indicates that armed groups will generally only focus on governance projects when they control territory. If they do not control territory, their focus will generally be on their military operations and their survival as an organization. On the basis of these observations, the study concludes that human rights law will have less relevance in these circumstances.

That being said, the study notes that an armed group will remain in a position to interfere considerably with people's freedom of movement, physical security, property, and liberty when it does not control territory. It will also be able to prevent people enjoying their right to education and their right to health, by destroying schools or making medical clinics the subject of attack. As a result, in instances where an armed group's control of territory is fluid or nugatory, it is suggested that an armed group may be held responsible to 'respect' the human rights that are relevant to the civilians in the territory in question, while the State may be held responsible to 'respect', 'protect', and 'fulfil' those rights. The State's positive obligations may include an obligation on the State to protect civilians in the course of its military operations against the armed group. In that sense, human rights obligations would once again be seen to have been divided and tailored between two duty-bearers according to their capabilities and immediate relevance. However, the study observes that in instances where an armed group does not control territory, the 'added' value brought by international human rights law applying to the armed group will be less, because the obligations to 'respect' under human rights law are quite similar to the basic provisions of international humanitarian law. However in some instances human rights norms may apply to a more far-reaching group of beneficiaries than international humanitarian law. For example the right to health will secure healthcare for people who are not sick or wounded, but trying to access advice regarding nutrition or family planning.

Accordingly, the study finds that in addition to situations where armed groups control territory to the default of the State, the main instances in which human rights law brings particular value is if the threshold of international humanitarian law has not yet been met, or has recently passed. It finds that it may also bring value in instances where an armed group exercises control over its own combatants and their families in a situation of otherwise high level hostilities, i.e. where it does not exert control over the civilian population per se. In these situations, the study notes that the ability to hold armed groups bound by international human rights law may bring significant value because it can regulate everyday family life under the armed group's command. Finally, the study has cast light on the possibility of States and armed groups sharing responsibility under human rights law. This possibility may arise in instances where an armed group has control over territory but the State and the armed group have come to some arrangement about the sharing of governance activities in that area. It also may potentially arise in instances where an armed group exercises governance activities alongside those of the State.

6. Value of Parallel Accountability Processes

The purpose of this book has been to find clarity on the question of when and how *all* armed groups may be bound by international human rights law. As a result, it has not focused in detail on the accountability processes which have been set up under the auspices of Geneva Call and the United Nations-led Monitoring and Reporting Mechanism on Children and Armed Conflict. However, it was commented in Chapter 6 that these mechanisms provide an important parallel track of accountability for armed groups that should be utilized to the full. The driving idea behind the Codes of Commitment instigated by Geneva Call and the action plans signed between the United Nations and armed groups pursuant to Security Council Resolution 1539(2004) is that armed groups are more likely to adhere to norms which they have signed themselves, than to norms which have been imposed upon them by the State against whom they are fighting. As a result, these mechanisms adhere to the philosophy at the heart of the pluralist concept of international legal personality which places greater store on the force of a norm, than an assessment of whether it is binding or not. Interestingly, these accountability processes which have been established by Geneva Call and the Security Council on these issues offer procedural mechanisms under which the voices of the armed groups are valid and can be heard. They also offer a means by which declarations by armed groups on particular discrete issues are monitored on the ground.

Indeed, it can be noted that a comparison of Geneva Call's monitoring processes and engagement programme with the definition of accountability explored and adopted in the introduction to this study, illustrates that Geneva Call is providing an effective model of procedural accountability. It is partly for this reason that such parallel tracks of accountability provide such a high value contribution to the accountability framework. However, the findings of this study highlight the fact that these parallel accountability mechanisms should not be seen as alternative tracks of accountability. From a legal perspective, the study has concluded that an armed group's consent to a particular norm is immaterial to the question of whether it is bound by it. As a result, if an armed group refused to sign such a commitment or renounced an existing commitment to humanitarian norms, it would still be considered bound by those norms under international humanitarian law or human rights law. Likewise, many of these accountability mechanisms are voluntary in nature. As a result, they only address the behaviour of armed groups which are willing to engage on humanitarian norms. This highlights the independent value of, and need for, accountability processes which are not based on consent, as these are more easily able to address the kind of armed groups that are unwilling to engage on the subject of international norms.

7. Concluding Remarks

As a final concluding remark, it is hoped that the research contained in this book will play an important role in alleviating the uncertainty at the core of the debate on whether and when armed groups can be held bound by human rights obligations. First, it identifies the added normative value that human rights law can bring to the legal framework, when applied to armed groups. It also brings clarity to the circumstances in which armed groups can have international legal personality under human rights law. In doing so, it sheds shed light on the material and theoretical circumstances which are required for armed groups to acquire legal personality under human rights law. It is hoped that this will be of value for organizations utilizing the human rights framework in times of armed conflict. The study also clarifies *when* the application of the human framework to armed groups can be legally justified. It also clarifies the legal foundations of the legal framework by providing an explanation to the question *how* armed groups are bound by international human rights law. In doing so, the book injects additional clarity into the heart of the accountability framework and provides firmer ground for it to develop and mature in the coming years.

Select Bibliography

ACADEMIC LITERATURE

Abi-Saab, G., *Non-International Armed Conflicts* (Henry Dunant Institute, Geneva 1988).

al-Tamimi, A. 'The Evolution of the Islamic State Administration: The Documentary Evidence', 2015 *Perspectives on Terrorism*, 9(4), <http://www.terrorismanalysts.com/pt/index.php/pot/article/view/447/html>

Akhavan, P. 'Reconciling Crimes against Humanity with the Laws of War: Human Rights, Armed Conflict and the Limits of Progressive Jurisprudence', 2008 *Journal of International Criminal Justice*, no. 6, 21–37.

Allott, P. 'The Concept of International Law', 1999 *European Journal of International Law*, no. 10, 31, 43.

Arimatsu, L. and Choudhury, M., 'The Legal Classification of the Armed Conflicts in Syria, Yemen and Libya, Chatham House', March 2014 *International Law PP 2014/01*.

Balint-Kurti, D., 'Cote d'Ivoire's Forces Nouvelles, Chatham House', September 2007 *Africa Programme Armed Non-State Actors Series*, 26.

Bangerter, O., 'Reasons Why Armed Groups Choose to Respect International Humanitarian Law or Not', 2011 *International Review of the Red Cross*, no. 93, 353.

Barber, R., 'Facilitating Humanitarian Assistance in International Humanitarian Law and Human Rights Law', 2009 *International Review of the Red Cross*, no. 874, 371–97.

Bartels, R., 'Discrepancies between International Humanitarian Law on the Battlefield and in the Courtroom: The Challenges of Applying International Humanitarian Law During International Criminal Trials' in Matthee, M. et al. (eds), *Armed Conflict and International Law: In Search of the Human Face* (T.M.C. Asser Press, The Hague 2013) 339–78.

Bartels, R., 'Follow-up on the organizational requirement: ICRC statements and conflict qualification', *Armed Groups and International Law blog*, 10 August 2012, <http://armedgroups-internationallaw.org/2012/08/10/follow-up-on-the-organisational-requirement-icrc-statements-and-conflict-qualification/>

Bartels, R. and Fortin, K., 'Law, Justice and a Potential Security Gap: The "Organization" Requirement in International Humanitarian Law and International Criminal Law', 2015 *Journal of Conflict and Security Law*, 21(1), 29–48.

Bassiouni, C. M., *Crimes against Humanity in International Criminal Law* (Kluwer Law International, The Hague 1999).

Bassiouni, C. M., *International Criminal Law, Vol I, Crimes* (Transnational Publishers, New York 1999).

Bassiouni, C. M., *International Criminal Law, Vol I, Sources, Subjects and Contents* (Martinus Nijhoff Publishers, Leiden 2008).

Bassiouni, C., M, 'The New Wars and the Crisis of Compliance with the Law of Armed Conflict by Non-State Actors', 2008 *The Journal of Criminal Law and Criminology*, no. 3, 711.

Baxter, R., 'Jus in Bello Interno: The Present and Future Law', in Moore, J. (ed), *Law and Civil War in the Modern World* (Johns Hopkins, Baltimore 1974) 527.

Baxter, R., *Some Existing Problems of Humanitarian Law in the Concept of International Armed Conflict: Further Outlook 1* (Proceedings of the International Symposium on Humanitarian Law, Brussels 1974).

Bell, C., 'Peace Agreements: Their Nature and Legal Status', 2006 *American Journal of International Law*, no. 100, 373–412.

Bellal, A., 'Establishing the Direct Responsibility of Non-State Armed Groups for Violations of International Norms: Issues of Attribution', in Ryngaert, C. et al. (eds), *Responsibilities of the Non-State Actor in Armed Conflict and the Market Place* (Brill, Leiden 2015) 304–22.

Bellal, A. and Casey-Maslen, S., 'Enhancing Compliance with International Law by Armed Non-State Actors', 2011 *Goettingen Journal of International Law*, no. 3, 175–97.

Bellinger, J. B. III and Haynes, W. J. II, 'A US Government Response to the International Committee of the Red Cross Study Customary International Humanitarian Law', 2007 *International Review of the Red Cross*, Vol. 89, no. 866, 443–71.

Berman, P. S., 'A Pluralist Approach to International Law', 2007 *Yale Journal of International Law*, no. 32, 301–29.

Bernard, V., 'Editorial: Understanding Armed Groups and the Law' 2011 *International Review of the Red Cross*, no.93, 261–7.

Bílková, V., 'Establishing Direct Responsibility of Armed Opposition Groups for Violations of International Humanitarian Law' in Ryngaert, C. et al. (eds), *Responsibilities of the Non-State Actor in Armed Conflict and the Market Place* (Brill, Leiden 2015) 263–84.

Bongard, P. and Somer, J., 'Monitoring Armed Non-State Actor Compliance with Humanitarian Norms: A Look at International Mechanisms and the Geneva Call Deed of Commitment', 2011 *International Review of the Red Cross*, Vol. 93, no. 883, 673–706.

Bothe, M., 'Conflits Armés Internes de Droit International Humanitaire', 1978 *Revue Générale de Droit International Public*, no. 1, 82–102.

Bothe, M., 'Article 3 and Protocol II: Case Studies of Nigeria and El Salvador', 1981–1982, *The American University Law Review*, no. 31, 899–909.

Bothe, M., Partsch, K. J., and Solf, W., *New Rules for Victims of Armed Conflicts: Commentary on the Two 1977 Protocols Additional to the Geneva Conventions of 1949* (Martinus Nijhoff Publishers, The Hague 1982).

Boulesbaa, A., *The UN Convention on Torture and the Prospects for Enforcement* (Martinus Nijhoff Publishers, Leiden 1999).

Bovens, M. 'Analysing and Assessing Accountability: A Conceptual Framework', 2007 *European Law Journal*, Vol. 13, no. 4, 447–68.

Bovens, M., 'Two Concepts of Accountability: Accountability as a Virtue and as a Mechanism', September 2010 *West European Politics*, no. 33(5), 946–67.

Breitegger, A., 'The Legal Framework Applicable to Insecurity and Violence Affecting the Delivery of Health Care in Armed Conflicts and Other Emergencies', 2013 *International Review of the Red Cross*, no. 95, 83.

Brett, R., 'Non-Governmental Human Rights Organizations and International Humanitarian Law', 1998 *International Review of the Red Cross*, no. 324, 531–6.

Brody, R., Parker, P., and Weissbrodt, D., 'Major Developments in 1990 at the UN Commission on Human Rights', 1990 *Human Rights Quarterly*, no. 12, 560–88.

Brownlie, I., *Principles of Public International Law* (7th edn Oxford University Press, Oxford 2008).

Brunée, J., 'International Legal Accountability through the Lens of State Responsibility', 2005 *Netherlands Yearbook of International Law*, Vol XXXVI, 21–56.

Burgers, J. H. and Danelius, H., *The United Nations Convention Against Torture: A Handbook on the Convention Against Torture and Other Cruel, Inhuman Or Degrading Treatment Or Punishment* (Martinus Nijhoff Publishers, Dordrecht 1988).

Casalin, D., 'Taking Prisoners: Reviewing the International Humanitarian Law Grounds for Deprivation of Liberty by Armed Opposition Groups', 2011 *International Review of the Red Cross*, no. 883, 743–82.

Cassese, A., 'The Status of Rebels under the 1977 Geneva Protocol on Non-International Armed Conflicts', 1981 *International and Comparative Law Quarterly*, no. 30, 416.

Cassese, A., *International Law* (Oxford University Press, Oxford 2001).

Cassese, A., 'The Special Court and International Law: The Decision concerning the Lomé Agreement Amnesty', 2004 *Journal of International Criminal Justice*, no. 2, 1130–40.

Cassese, A., *International Law* (Oxford University Press, Oxford 2005).

Cassese, A., *International Criminal Law* (Oxford University Press, Oxford 2008).

Cassese, A. and Gaeta, P., *International Criminal Law*, (Oxford University Press, Oxford 2013).

Cerone, J. P., 'Peace Operations and the Complementarity of Human Rights and International Humanitarian Law' in *Human Rights and Peace Operations, International Institute of Humanitarian Law, 31st Round Table on Current Problems of International Humanitarian Law, Sanremo, 4–6 September 2008* (2008).

Charlesworth, H., 'The Unbearable Lightness of Customary International Law', 1998 *American Society International Law Proceedings*, no. 92, 44–7.

Charlesworth, H., Chinkin, C., and Wright, S., 'Feminist Approaches to International Law', 1991 *American Journal of International Law*, no. 85, 613–45.

Chen, L., 'Restatement: Protection of Persons', 1989 *Yale Journal of International Law*, no. 14, 542.

Chinkin, C., *Third Parties in International Law* (Clarendon Press, Oxford 1993).

Clapham, A., 'The Question of Jurisdiction under International Criminal Law over Legal Persons' in Kamminga, M. T. and Zia-Zarifi, S. (eds), *Liability of Multinational Corporations under International Law* (Kluwer Law International, The Hague 2000) 139–78.

Clapham, A., *Human Rights Obligations of Non-State Actors* (Oxford University Press, Oxford 2006).

Clapham, A., 'Human Rights Obligations of Non-State Actors in Conflict Situations', September 2006 *International Review of the Red Cross*, Vol 88, no. 863, 491–523.

Clapham, A., 'The Rights and Responsibilities of Armed Non-State Actors: The Legal Landscape and Issues Surrounding Engagement, Ownership of Norms Project, Draft for Comment available on SSRN', February 2010 *Geneva Academy of International Humanitarian Law and Human Rights*.

Clapham, A., 'Human Rights Obligations of Organised Armed Groups' in Odello, M., and Beruto, G. L. (eds), *Non-State Actors and International Humanitarian Law: Organized Armed Groups: a Challenge for the 21st Century, 32nd Round Table on Current Issues of International Humanitarian Law, San Remo, 11–13 September 2009* (International Institute of Humanitarian Law, San Remo 2010).

Clapham, A., 'Focusing on Armed Non-State Actors' in Clapham, A. and Gaeta, P. (eds), *The Oxford Handbook of International Law in Armed Conflict* (Oxford University Press, Oxford 2014) 766–810.

Constantinides, A., 'Human Rights Obligations and Accountability of Armed Opposition Groups: The Practice of the UN Security Council', 2010 *Human Rights and International Legal Discourse*, no. 4, 89–110.

Cover, R. M., 'The Folktales of Justice: Tales of Jurisdiction', 1985 *Capital University Law Review*, no. 14, 179–203.

Crawford, J., *The Creation of States in International Law* (2nd edn Clarendon Press, Oxford 2006).

Curtin D. and Nollkaemper, A., 'Conceptualizing Accountability in International and European Law', 2005 *Netherlands Yearbook of International Law*, Vol XXXVI, 3–30.

d'Aspremont, J., 'Conclusion: Inclusive Law Making and Law-Enforcement Processes for an Exclusive International System' in d'Aspremont, J. (ed), *Participants in the International Legal System: Multiple Perspectives on Non-State Actors in International Law* (Routledge, Abingdon 2011).

de Wet, E., 'Jus Cogens and Obligations Erga Omnes', in Shelton, D. (ed), *Oxford Handbook on Human Rights* (Oxford University Press, Oxford 2013).

Dinstein, Y., 'The International Law of Civil Wars and Human Rights', 1976 *Israel Yearbook on Human Rights*, no. 6, 62–80.

Dinstein, Y., 'The Laws of Neutrality', 1984 *Israel Yearbook on Human Rights*, no. 14, 80–110.

Dixon, M., *Textbook on International Law* (Oxford University Press, Oxford 2007).

Draper, G. I. A. D., 'Humanitarian Law and Human Rights, Paper given at the First Conference on Human Rights in South Africa, Cape Town, 22–26 January 1979' in Meyer, M., and McCoubrey, H. (eds), *Reflections on Law and Armed Conflicts: The Selected Works on the Laws of War by the late Professor Colonel G.I.A.D. Draper, OBE* (Kluwer Law International, The Hague/Boston/London 1998).

Droege, C., 'The Interplay between International Humanitarian Law and International Human Rights Law in Situations of Armed Conflict', 2007 *Israel Law Review*, no. 2, 310–55.

Droege, C., 'Elective Affinities? Human Rights and Humanitarian Law', 2008 *International Review of the Red Cross*, no. 871, 501–48.

Dubnick, M. J., 'Seeking Salvation for Accountability', Paper presented at the 2002 Annual Meeting of the American Political Science Association, Boston.

Eissen, M., 'The European Convention on Human Rights and the Duties of the Individual', 1962 *Nordisk Tidsskrift International Ret*, 230–53.

Ellsberg, D., *Secrets: A Memoir of Vietnam and the Pentagon Papers* (Penguin, New York 2003).

Ferdinandusse, W., 'Out of the Black-box?: the international legal obligations of State organs', 2003–2004 *Brooklyn Journal of International Law*, Vol 29, 45–129.

Fleck, D., 'Humanitarian Protection against Non State Actors' in *Verhandeln fur den Frieden—Negotiating for Peace: Liber Amicorum Tono Eitel* (Springer, Berlin 2003).

Fleiner-Gerster, T. and Meyer M., 'New Developments in Humanitarian Law: A Challenge to the Concept of Sovereignty', 1985 *International and Comparative Law Quarterly*, no. 34, 267–83.

Forsythe, D., *Humanitarian Politics: The International Committee of the Red Cross* (The John Hopkins University Press, Baltimore and London 1977).

Forsythe, D., 'Legal Management of Internal War: The 1977 Protocol on Non-International Armed Conflicts', 1978 *American Journal of International Law*, no. 72, 272–95.

Fortin, K., 'Rape as Torture: An Evaluation of the Committee against Torture's Attitude to Sexual Violence', 2008 *Utrecht Law Review*, Vol 4, no. 3, 145–62.

Fortin, K., 'Complementarity between the ICRC and United Nations and International Humanitarian Law and International Human Rights Law 1948–1968', 2012 *International Review of the Red Cross*, no. 888, 1433–54.

Fortin, K., 'Syria in Civil War, says ICRC', *Armed Groups and International Law blog*, 15 July 2012, http://armedgroups-internationallaw.org/2012/07/15/syria-in-state-of-civil-war-says-icrc/

Fortin, K., 'Syria and the geographical scope of international humanitarian law: moving towards a localized approach?', *Armed Groups and International Law blog*, 2 October 2012, http://armedgroups-internationallaw.org/2012/10/02/syria-and-the-geographical-scope-of-international-humanitarian-law-moving-towards-a-localised-approach/

Fortin, K. 'The Application of Human Rights Law to Everyday Civilian Life Under Rebel Control' 2016 *Netherlands Yearbook of International Law*, 161.

Fox, R., 'On the Age of the Postmodern War, Beyond Clausewitz: the long and ragged conflicts of the coming millennium' *The Times Literary Supplement* (15 May 1998).

Garner, J. W., 'Questions of International Law in the Spanish Civil War' (1937) 31(1) *American Journal of International Law*, 66–73.

Gill, T., 'Some Thoughts on the Relationship between International Humanitarian Law and International Human Rights Law: a Plea for Mutual Respect and a Common Sense Approach' in Haeck, Y. et al. (eds), *The Realisation of Human Rights When Theory Meets Practice* (Intersentia, Cambridge 2013).

Giustiniani, F.Z., 'New Hopes and Challenges for the Protection of IDPs in Africa: The Kampala Convention for the Protection and Assistance of Internally Displaced Persons in Africa', 2010–2011 *Denver Journal of International Law and Policy*, no. 2, 347–70.

Glaser, M. P., 'Humanitarian engagement with non-state actors, The parameters of negotiated access', June 2005 *Network Paper, Humanitarian Practice Network*, no. 50.

Glendon, M. A., *World Made New: Eleanor Roosevelt and the Universal Declaration of Human Rights* (Random House, New York 2002).

Gowlland-Debbas, V., 'The Relevance of Paragraph 25 of the ICJ's Advisory Opinion on Nuclear Weapons', 2004 *American Society of International Law Proceedings*, no. 98, 358–63.

Grafton Wilson, G., 'Insurgency and International Maritime Law', 1907 *American Journal of International Law*, no. 1, 46–60.

Greenwood, C., 'Scope of Application of Humanitarian Law' in Fleck, D. (ed), *The Handbook of International Humanitarian Law* (Oxford University Press, Oxford 2009).

Griffiths, J., 'What is Legal Pluralism?', 1986 *Journal of Legal Pluralism*, no. 24, 1–55.

Gutteridge, J., 'The Geneva Conventions of 1949', 1949 *British Year Book of International Law*, no. 26, 294–326.

Hall, W. E., *International Law* (Clarendon Press, Oxford 1880).

Halling, M., 'Push the Envelope—Watch it Bend: Removing the Policy Requirement and Extending Crimes against Humanity', 2010 *Leiden Journal of International Law*, no. 23, 827–45.

Hampson, F., 'Human Rights and Humanitarian Law Internal Conflicts' in Meyer, M. (ed), *Armed Conflict and the New Law* (British Institute for Comparative and International Law, London 1990) 55–80.

Hampson, F., 'Other Areas of Customary International Law in Relation to the Study' in Wilmshurt, E., and Breau, S. (eds), *Perspectives on the ICRC Study on Customary International Humanitarian Law* (Cambridge University Press, Cambridge 2007).

Hannum, H., 'The Status of the Universal Declaration of Human Rights in National and International Law', 1995–1996 *Georgia Journal of International and Comparative Law*, no. 25, 287–397.

Henckaerts, J. and Doswald-Beck, L., *Customary International Humanitarian Law, Volume I: Rules* (Cambridge University Press, Cambridge 2005).

Henckaerts, J. and Wiesner, C., 'Human Rights Obligations of Non-State Armed Groups: A Possible Contribution from Customary International Law?' in Kolb, R. and Gaggioli, G. (eds), *Research Handbook on Human Rights and Humanitarian Law* (Edward Elgar Publishing, Cheltenham, 2013) 146–69.

Henkin, L., 'The Universal Declaration at 50', 1999 *Brooklyn Journal of International Law*, no. 25, 17–25.

Hessbruegge, J. A., 'Human Rights Violations Arising from Conduct of Non-State Actors', 2005 *Buffalo Human Rights Law Review*, 21–88.

Higgins, R., *Problems and Process, International Law and How We Use It* (Clarendon Press, Oxford 1994).

'International Military Tribunal (Judgement and Sentence)', 1947 *American Journal of International Law*, no. 41, 172–333.

Ingelse, C., *The UN Committee against Torture: An Assessment* (Kluwer International, The Hague 2001).

Jenks, C. W., 'The Conflict of Law-Making Treaties', 1953 *British Year Book of International Law*, 401–53.

Kahn, P. W., *The Cultural Study of Law* (University of Chicago Press, Chicago 1999).

Kalshoven, F., 'Applicability of Customary International Law in Non-International Armed Conflicts' in Cassese, A. (ed), *Current Problems of International Law* (University of Milan, Milan 1975).

Kalyvas, S., *The Logic of Violence in Civil War* (Cambridge University Press, Cambridge 2009).

Kamminga, M., 'State Succession in Respect of Human Rights Treaties', 1996 *European Journal of International Law*, Vol. 7, 469–84.

Kamminga, M. T., *Inter-State Accountability for Violations of Human Rights* (University of Pennsylvania Press, Philadelphia 1992).

Kelsen, H., *General Theory of Law and State* (Harvard University Press, Cambridge 1949).

Kelsen, H., *Pure Theory of Law* (University of California Press, Berkeley 1967).

Kilcullen, D., *Counterinsurgency* (Hurst & Co Publishers Ltd, London 2010).

Kleffner, J., 'The Collective Accountability of Organized Armed Groups for System Crimes' in Nolkaemper, A. and van der Wilt, H. (eds), *System Criminality in International Law* (Cambridge University Press, Cambridge 2009) 238–69.

Kleffner, J., 'Human Rights and International Humanitarian Law' in Gill, T. and Fleck, D. (eds), *The Handbook of International Law of Military Operations* (Oxford University Press, Oxford 2010).

Kleffner, J., 'The Applicability of International Humanitarian Law to Organized Armed Groups', 2011 *International Review of the Red Cross*, no. 882, 443–61.

Kolomba Beck, T., *The Normality of Civil War: Armed Groups and Everyday Life in Angola* (Campus, Frankfurt 2012).

Kooijmans, P. H., 'In the Shadowland Between Civil War and Civil Strife: Some Reflections on the Standard-Setting Process' in Delissen, A. and Tanja, G. (eds), *Humanitarian Law of Armed Conflict Challenges Ahead* (T.M.C. Asser Institute, The Hague 1991).

Kress, C., 'On the Outer Limits of Crimes against Humanity: The Concept of Organisation within the Policy Requirement: Some Reflections on the March 2010 *Kenya* Decision', 2010 *Leiden Journal of International Law*, no. 23, 855–73.

Kretzmer, D., 'Rethinking the Application of IHL in Non-International Armed Conflicts', 2009 *Israel Law Review*, no. 42, 8–45.

Krieger, H., 'A Conflict of Norms: The Relationship between Humanitarian Law and Human Rights Law in the ICRC Customary Law Study', 2006 *Journal of Conflict and Security Law*, no. 11(2), 265–91.

Kritsiotis, D., 'On the Possibilities of and for Persistent Objection', 2010 *Duke Journal of Comparative and International Law*, no. 21, 121–41.

Lauterpacht, H., 'Recognition of Insurgents as a *de facto* Government', 1939 *Modern Law Review*, no. 1, 1–20.

Lauterpacht, H., 'Restrictive Interpretation and the Principle of Effectiveness in the Interpretation of Treaties', 1949 *British Yearbook of International Law*, no. 26, 48–85.

Lauterpacht, H., *International Law and Human Rights* (Stevens & Sons, London 1950).

Lauterpacht, H., 'Draft Nuremberg Speeches', 2012 *Cambridge Journal of International and Comparative Law*, no. 1, 45–111.

Lindroos, A., 'Addressing Norm Conflicts in a Fragmented Legal System: The Doctrine of *Lex Specialis*', 2005 *Nordic Journal of International Law*, no. 74, 27–66.

Lootsteen, Y. M., 'The Concept of Belligerency in International Law', 2000 *Military Law Review*, no. 166, 109–41.

Loucaides, L. G., 'The Judgement of the European Court of Human Rights in the case of *Cyprus v Turkey*' in Loucaides, L. G., *The European Convention on Human Rights* (Martinus Nijhoff Publishers, Leiden 2007) 107–20.

Lubkemann, S. C., *Culture in Chaos: A Social Anthropology of the Social Condition of War* (University of Chicago Press, Chicago 2010).

Mampilly, Z. C., *Rebel Rulers: Insurgent Governance and Civilian Life During War* (Cornell University Press, Ithaca and London 2011).

Maru, M.T., 'The Kampala Convention and its Contribution in Filling the Protection Gap in International Law', 2011 *Journal of Internal Displacement*, no. 1, 91–130.

Matas, D., 'Armed Opposition Groups', 1997 *Manatoba Law Journal*, no. 3, 621–34.

May, L., *Crimes against Humanity: A Normative Account* (Cambridge University Press, Cambridge 2005).

McCorquodale, R., La Forgia, R., 'Taking Off the Blindfolds: Torture by Non-State Actors', 2001 *Human Rights Law Review*, no. 2, 189–218.

McCorquodale. R., 'An Inclusive International Legal System' 2004 *Leiden Journal of International Law*, no. 17, 477–504.

McCorquodale, R., 'The Individual and the International Legal System' in Evans D. M. (ed), *International Law* (Oxford University Press, Oxford 2006).

McDougal, M. S., Lasswell, H. D., and Reisman, W. M., 'The World Constitutive Process of Authoritative Decision' in Falk, R. A. and Black, C. E. (eds), *The Future of the International Legal Order, Volume I, Trends and Patterns* (Princeton University Press, Princeton 1969) 73–154.

McNair, A. D., *The Law of Treaties* (Clarendon Press, Oxford, 1961).

Melzer, N., *Targeted Killing in International Law* (Oxford University Press, Oxford 2009).

Melzer, N., 'Law Enforcement and the Conduct of Hostilities' in Gill, T. and Fleck, D. (eds), *The Handbook of the International Law of Military Operations* (Oxford University Press, Oxford 2010).

Meron, T., 'On the Inadequate Reach of Humanitarian and Human Rights Law and the Need for a New Instrument', 1983 *American Journal of International Law*, no. 77(3), 589–606.

Meron, T., *Human Rights in Internal Strife, Their International Protection* (Cambridge University Press, Cambridge 1987).

Mettraux, G., 'Crimes against Humanity and the Question of the "Policy" Element' in Sadat, L. (ed), *Forging a Convention for Crimes against Humanity* (Cambridge University Press, Cambridge 2011) 142–76.

Meyrowitz, H., 'Le Droit de La Guerre et Les Droits de L'Homme', 1972 *Revue du Droit Public et de la Science Politique en France et a` l'Etranger*, no. 88, 1059–105.

Milanovic, M., 'A Norm Conflict Perspective on the Relationship between International Humanitarian Law and Human Rights Law', 2010 *Journal of Conflict and Security Law*, no. 3, 459–83.

Milanovic, M., 'Is the Rome Statute Binding on Individuals (and Why We Should Care?)', 2011 *Journal of International Criminal Justice*, no. 9(1), 25–52.

Moir, L., *The Law of Internal Armed Conflict* (Cambridge University Press, Cambridge 2002).

Mongelard, E., 'Corporate Civil Liability for Violations of International Humanitarian Law', 2006 *International Review of the Red Cross*, no. 88, 665.

Mowbray, A., *The Development of Positive Obligations Under the European Convention on Human Rights by the European Court of Human Rights* (Hart Publishing, Oxford 2004).

Mulgan, R., "Accountability': An Ever-Expanding Concept', 2000 *Public Administration* no. 78(3), 555–73.

Műller, A., 'Limitations to and Derogations from Economic, Social and Cultural Rights' 2009 *Human Rights Law Review*, no. 4, 557–601.

Murray, D., 'How International Humanitarian Law Treaties Bind Non-state Armed Groups' 2014 *Journal of Conflict and Security Law*, 20(1) 101–31.

Murray, D., *Human Rights Obligations of Non-State Armed Groups* (Bloomsbury, London 2016).

Nijman, J., 'Non-State Actors and the International Rule of Law: Revisiting the 'Realist Theory' of International Legal Personality' in Noortmann, M. and Ryngaert, C. (eds), *Non-State Actor Dynamics in International Law: from Law-Takers to Law-Makers* (Ashgate, Farnham 2010).

Nollkaemper, A., 'Introduction' in Nollkaemper, A. and van der Wilt, H. (eds), *System Criminality in International Law* (Cambridge University Press, Cambridge 2009).

Noortmann, M. and Ryngaert, C. (eds), *Non-State Actor Dynamics in International Law: from Law-Takers to Law-Makers* (Ashgate, Farnham 2010).

Nowak, M., *U.N. Covenant on Civil and Political Rights, CCPR Commentary* (2nd revised edition) (Engel Verlap, Kehl am Rhein, 2005).

O'Connell, D. P., *International Law* (Stevens & Sons Limited, London 1965).

Ohlin, J. D., van Sliedregt, E and Weigend, T., 'Assessing the Control-Theory' (2013) *Cornell Law Faculty Publications*, Paper 1242, <http://scholarship.law.cornell.edu/facpub/1242>

Ojeda, S., 'The Kampala Convention on Internally Displaced Persons: Some International Humanitarian Law Aspects', 2010 *Refugee Survey Quarterly*, no. 3, 58–66.

Okowa, P., 'Interpreting Constitutive Instruments of International Criminal Tribunals: Reflections on the Special Court for Sierra Leone' in Fitzmaurice, M., Olufemi, I. A., and Merkouris, P. (eds), *Treaty Interpretation and the Vienna Convention on the Law of Treaties: 30 Years On* (Brill, Leiden 2010).

Oppenheim, L., *International Law, A Treatise* (Longmans, Harlow 1948).

Padelford, N. J., 'The International Non-Intervention Agreement and the Spanish Civil War', 1937 *American Journal of International Law*, no. 4, 578–603.

Pauwelyn, J., *Conflict of Norms in Public International Law* (Cambridge University Press, Cambridge 2008).

Peijic, J., 'Conflict Classification and the Law Applicable to Detention and the Use of Force', Wilmshurt, E. (ed), *International Law and the Classification of Conflicts* (Oxford University Press, Oxford 2002).

Petrasek, D., 'Ends & means: human rights approaches to armed groups', 2000 *International Council on Human Rights Policy*, 60.

Pictet, J., *Commentary to the Geneva Convention for the Amelioration of the Condition of the Wounded and Sick in Armed Forces in the Field of August 12, 1949* (International Committee of the Red Cross, Geneva 1952).

Pictet, J., *Commentary to the Geneva Convention for the Amelioration of the Condition of Wounded, Sick and Shipwrecked Members of Armed Forces at Sea of August 12, 1949* (International Committee of the Red Cross, Geneva 1952).

Pictet, J., 'The Twentieth International Conference of the Red Cross', 1966 *ICJ Journal*, Vol. VII, no. 1, 3–19.

Pinto, R., 'Les Règles du Droit International Concernant La Guerre Civile', 1965 *Recueil des Courts*, no. 114, 451–554.

Pocar, F., 'Some Remarks on the Continuity of Human Rights and International Humanitarian Law Treaties' in Cannizzaro, E., *The Law of Treaties Beyond the Vienna Convention* (Oxford University Press, Oxford 2011).

Portmann, R., *Legal Personality in International Law* (Cambridge University Press, Cambridge 2010).

Prud'homme, N., '*Lex Specialis*: Oversimplifying a More Complex and Multifaceted Relationship?', 2007 *Israel Law Review*, no. 40, 356–95.

Rasulov, A., 'Revisiting State Succession to Humanitarian Treaties: Is there a Case for Automaticity?', 2003 *European Journal of International Law*, Vol 14, no. 1, 141–70.

Ratner, S. and R., Slaughter A., 'Symposium in Method in International Law: Appraising the Methods of International Law: A Prospectus for Readers', 1999 *American Journal of International Law*, no. 93, 291–423.

Ridderbos, K., 'The Kampala Convention and Obligations of Armed Groups', March 2011 *Forced Migration Review*, no. 37 and December 2014 *Norwegian Refugee Council and Internal Displacement Monitoring Centre Briefing Paper*.

Roberts, A. and Sivakumaran, S., 'Lawmaking by Non-State Actors: Engaging Armed Groups in the Creation of International Humanitarian Law', 2012 *Yale Journal of International Law*, no. 37, 107–52.

Robertson, A. H., *Human Rights in the World* (Manchester University Press, Manchester 1982).

Robinson, D., 'The Context of Crimes against Humanity' in Lee, R. S. (ed), *The International Criminal Court: Elements of Crimes and Rules of Procedure and Evidence* (Transnational Publishers Inc, New York 2001) 62.

Rodenhauser, T., 'Human Rights Obligations of Non-State Armed Groups in Other Situations of Violence: The Syria Example', 2012 *International Humanitarian Legal Studies*, no. 3, 263–90.

Rodley, N. S., 'Can Armed Opposition Groups Violate Human Rights?' in Mahoney, K. E. and Mahoney, P. (eds), *Human Rights in the Twenty-first Century* (Kluwer Academic Publishers, The Netherlands 1993).

Rodley, N., 'Non-State Actors and Human Rights' in S. Sheeran and N. Rodley (eds), Routledge Handbook of International Human Rights Law (Routledge, Abingdon 2013).

Rondeau, S., 'Participation of Armed Groups in the Development of the Law Applicable to Armed Conflicts', 2011 *International Review of the Red Cross*, no. 92, 1–24.

Rosenau, J., 'Governance, Order and Change in World Politics' in Rosenau, J. and Czempiel, E. (eds), *Governance without Government: Order and Change in World Politics* (Cambridge University Press, Cambridge 1992).

Rousseau, C., 'La Non-Intervention en Espagne', 1938 *Revue de Droit International et de Législation Comparée*, no. 3, 217–80.

Rousseau, C., 'La Non-Intervention en Espagne—Section II', 1938 *Revue de Droit International et de Législation Comparée*, no. 3, 473–549.

Ruys, T., 'Crossing the Thin Blue Line: An Inquiry into Israel's Recourse to Self-Defense against Hezbollah', 2007 *Stanford Journal of International Law*, no. 43, 265–94.

Ryngaert, C., 'Another Afghan Case in the Hague District Court: Universal Jurisdiction over Common Article 3', *Hague Justice Portal* 2007, <http://www.haguejusticeportal.net/index.php?id=8213>.

Ryngaert, C., 'Human Rights Obligations of Armed Groups', 2008 *Revue Belge de Droit International*, no. 2, 355–81.

Ryngaert, C., 'Non-State Actors and International Humanitarian Law', 2008 Working Paper.

Ryngaert, C., 'Imposing International Duties on Non-State Actors and the Legitimacy of International Law', 2010 Working Paper no. 42.

Ryngaert, C., 'Non-State Actors in International Humanitarian Law' in d'Aspremont, J. (ed), *Participants in the International Legal System: Multiple Perspectives on Non-State Actors in International Law* (Routledge, Abingdon 2011), 284–94.

Sands, P., 'Twin Peaks: The Hersch Lauterpacht Draft Nuremberg Speeches', 2012 *Cambridge Journal of International and Comparative Law*, no. 1, 37–44.

Sassòli, M., 'Possible Legal Mechanisms to Improve Compliance by Armed Groups with International Humanitarian Law and International Human Rights Law', Paper Submitted at the University of Quebec in Montreal, Canada at the Armed Groups Conference, Vancouver' (13–15 November 2003).

Sassòli, M., 'The Status of Persons held in Guantánamo under International Humanitarian Law', 2004 *Journal of International Criminal Justice*, no. 2, 96–106.

Sassòli, M. 'Taking Armed Groups Seriously: Ways to Improve Their Compliance with International Humanitarian Law', 2010 *International Humanitarian Legal Studies*, no. 1, 5–51.

Sassòli, M. and Bouvier, A., *How Does Law Protect In War? Cases, Documents and Teaching Materials on Contemporary Practice in International Humanitarian Law* (2nd edn ICRC, Geneva 2006) Vol I.

Sassòli, M. and Olson, M. L., 'The Relationship between International Humanitarian and Human Rights Law Where it Matters: Admissible Killing and Internment of Fights in Non-International Armed Conflicts', 2008 *International Review of the Red Cross*, no. 90 (871), 599–627.

Shabas, W. A., 'Crimes against Humanity: The State Plan of Policy Element', in Sadat, L. and Scharf, M. (eds), *The Theory and Practice of International Criminal Law: Essays in Honor of M. Cherif Bassiouni* (Martinus Nijhoff Publishers, Leiden 2008) 347–64.

Schabas, W. A., '*Lex Specialis?* Belt and Suspenders? The Parallel Operation of Human Rights Law and the Law of Armed Conflict, and the Conundrum of *Jus ad Bellum*', 2007 *Israel Law Review*, no. 40, 592–613.

Schabas, W.A., 'Prosecuting Dr. Strangelove, Goldfinger, and the Joker at the ICC', 2010 *Leiden Journal of International Law*, no. 23, 847–53.

Schabas, W.A. 'Introductory Essay' in Schabas, W. A. (ed), *The Universal Declaration of Travaux Préparatoires* (Cambridge University Press, Cambridge 2013).

Sharf, M. P. and Newton, M. A., 'Terrorism and Crimes against Humanity' in Sadat, L. (ed), *Forging a Convention for Crimes against Humanity* (Cambridge University Press, Cambridge 2011) 269–78.

Schultz, T., *Transnational Legality: Stateless Law and International Arbitration* (Oxford University Press, Oxford 2014).

Schwelb, E., 'Crimes against Humanity', 1946 *British Year Book of International Law*, no. 23, 176–226.

Schwendimann, F., 'The Legal Framework of Humanitarian Access in Armed Conflict', 2011 *International Review of the Red Cross*, no. 844, 993–1008.

Scobbie, I., 'The approach to customary international law in the Study' in Wilmshurst, E. and Breau, S. (eds), *Perspectives on the ICRC Study on Customary International Humanitarian Law* (Cambridge University Press, Cambridge 2007).

Shaw, M. N., *International Law* (6th edn Cambridge University Press, Cambridge 2008).

Shelton, D., 'Normative Hierarchy in International Law', 2006 *American Journal of International Law*, Vol 100, no. 2, 292–323.

Silvanie, H., *Responsibility of States for Acts of Unsuccessful Insurgent Governments* (Columbia University Press, London 1939).

Simma, B. and Alston, P., 'The Source of Human Rights Law: Custom, Jus Cogens and General Principles', 1988–1989 *Australian Yearbook of International Law*, Vol 12, 82–108.

Simpson, G., 'Men and Abstract Entities: Individual Responsibility and Collective Guilt in International Criminal Law' in Nollkaemper, A. and van der Wilt, H. (eds), *System Criminality in International Law* (Cambridge University Press, Cambridge 2009).

Siordet, F., 'Les Conventions de Genève et La Guerre Civile, Revue Internationale de la Croix Rouge', 1950 *Bulletin International des Sociétés de la Croix Rouge*, no. 81, 104–23, 187–212.

Sivakumaran, S., 'Torture in International Human Rights and International Humanitarian Law', 2005 *Leiden Journal of International Law*, no. 18, 541–56.

Sivakumaran, S., 'Binding Armed Opposition Groups', 2006 *International and Comparative Law Quarterly*, no. 55, 369–94.

Sivakumaran, S., 'Courts of Armed Opposition Groups, Fair Trials or Summary justice?' 2009 *Journal of International Criminal Justice*, no. 7, 489–513.

Sivakumaran, S., *The Law of Non-International Armed Conflicts* (Oxford University Press, Oxford 2012).

Sivakumaran, S., 'International Humanitarian Law' in Moeckli, D., Sangeeta S., and Sivakumaran, S. (eds), *International Human Rights Law* (Oxford University Press, Oxford 2014).

Sluiter, G., '"Chapeau Elements" of Crimes against Humanity' in L. Sadat (ed), *Forging a Convention for Crimes against Humanity* (Cambridge University Press, Cambridge 2011) 102–41.

Snow, F., *Cases and Opinions on International Law with Notes and a Syllabus* (Boston Book Company, Boston 1893).

Somer, J., 'Jungle Justice: Passing Sentence on the Equality of Belligerents in Non-International Armed Conflict', 2007 *International Review of the Red Cross*, no. 89, 655–90.

Spieker, H., 'The Right to Give and Receive Humanitarian Assistance' in Heintze, H. and Zwitter, A. (eds), *Humanitarian Assistance: A Cross-cut Through Legal Issues Pertaining to Humanitarianism* (Springer, Heidelberg 2011).

Stoffels, R. A., 'Legal Regulation of Humanitarian Assistance in Armed Conflict: Achievements and Gaps', September 2004, *IRRC*, no. 855, 515.

Suter, K. D., 'An Enquiry into the Meaning of the Phrase "Human Rights in Armed Conflicts"', 1976 *Revue de Droit Penal Militaire et de Droit de la Guerre*, no. 3–4, 394–428.

Tilly, C., *The Politics of Collective Violence* (Cambridge University Press, Cambridge 2003).

Tomuschat, C., 'The Applicability of Human Rights Law to Insurgent Movements' in Fischer, H., Froissart, U., von Heinegg, H. and Raap, C. (eds), *Krisensicherung und Humanitarer Schutz—Crisis Management and Humanitarian Protection: Festschrif fur Dieter Fleck* (Berliner Wissenschafts-Verlag, Berlin 2004) 573–91.

Triffterer, O. (ed), *Commentary on the Rome Statute of the International Criminal Court, Observers' Notes, Article by Article* (Nomos Verlagsgesellschaft, Baden Baden 1999).

Tse-tung, M., 'Guerilla Warfare' in *Guerilla Warfare by Mao Tse-Tung and by Che Guevara with a forward by Captain B. H. Liddell Hart* (Cassell, London 1969).

Tuck, D., 'Detention by Armed Groups: Overcoming Challenges to Humanitarian Action', 2011 *International Review of the Red Cross*, no. 883, 759–82.

Tunkin, G. I., 'Remarks on the Juridical Nature of Customary Norms of International Law', 1961 *California Law Review*, 49(3), 419–30.

United Nations War Crimes Commission, *Complete History of the United Nations War Crimes Commission and the Development of the Laws of War* (His Majesty's Stationery Office, London 1948).

Valentino, B. A., 'Why we kill: the Political Science of Political Violence against Civilians', 2014 *Annual Review of Political Science*, no. 17, 89–103.

van Amstel, N., 'In Search of Legal Grounds to Detain for Armed Groups', 2012 *International Humanitarian Legal Studies*, 3, 160–91.

van den Herik, L., 'Corporations as Future Subjects of the International Criminal Court: an Exploration of the Counterarguments and Consequences' in Stahn, C. and van den Herik, L. (eds), *Future Perspectives on International Criminal Justice* (Cambridge University Press, Cambridge 2010).

van der Wilt, H., 'Crimes against Humanity: A Category Hors Concours in International Criminal Law?', *Amsterdam Law School Legal Studies Research Paper*, 2012, no. 2012–24.

van der Wilt, H., 'War Crimes and the Requirement of a Nexus with an Armed Conflict', 2012 *Journal of International Criminal Justice*, no. 10, 1–16.

van Steenberghe, R., 'Self-Defence in Response to Attacks by Non-State Actors in the Light of Recent State Practice: A Step Forward?', 2010 *Leiden Journal of International Law*, no. 23, 183.

van Steenberghe, R., 'Non-State Actors from the Perspective of the International Committee of the Red Cross' in d'Aspremont, J. (ed), *Participants in the International Legal System: Multiple Perspectives on Non-State Actors in International Law* (Routledge, Abingdon 2011) 204–32.

Vattel, E., *The Law of Nations*, 1797, Book III: Of War.

Verhoeven, H., 'The Self-fulfilling Prophecy of Failed States: Somalia, State Collapse and the Global War on Terror', 2009 *Journal of Eastern African Studies*, 3(3), 405–25.

Verhoeven, S., 'International Responsibility of Armed Opposition Groups' in Ryngaert, C. et al. (eds), *Responsibilities of the Non-State Actor in Armed Conflict and the Market Place* (Brill, Leiden 2015) 285–303.

Weinstein, J., *Inside Rebellion: The Politics of Insurgent Violence* (Cambridge University Press, Cambridge 2007).

Werle, G. and Burghardt, B., 'Do Crimes against Humanity Require the Participation of a State or a 'State-like' Organization?', 2012 *Journal of International Criminal Justice*, 10(5), 1–20.

Wheaton, H., *Elements of International Law* (Stevens & Sons, London 1904).

Wouters, J. and Ryngaert, C., 'The Impact of Human Rights and International Humanitarian Law on the Process of the Formation of Customary International Law' in Kamminga, M. and Sheinen, M. (eds), *The Impact of Human Rights Law on General International Law* (Oxford University Press, Oxford 2008) 111–31.

Xenos, D., *The Positive Obligations of the State Under the European Convention of Human Rights* (Routledge, Abingdon 2012).

Zappalà, S., 'Can Legality Trump Effectiveness in Today's International Law' in Cassese, A. (ed.), *Realizing Utopia: The Future of International Law* (Oxford University Press, Oxford 2012).

Zegveld, L., *The Accountability of Armed Opposition Groups in International Law* (Cambridge University Press, Cambridge 2002).

International Committee of the Red Cross

ICRC, *Commentary on the Additional Protocols of 8 June 1977 to the Geneva Conventions of 12 December 1949* (Martinus Nijhoff, Geneva 1987).

Final Record of the Diplomatic Conference of Geneva of 1949, Vol II (B), Seventh Meeting, Tuesday 17 May 1949.

Final Record of the Diplomatic Conference of Geneva of 1949, Vol II (B), Ninth Meeting, Wednesday 25 May 1949.

Final Record of the Diplomatic Conference of Geneva of 1949, Vol II (B), Twenty Fourth Meeting, Wednesday 15 June 1949.

Official Records of the Diplomatic Conference on the Reaffirmation and Development on International Humanitarian Law Applicable in Armed Conflicts, Geneva, 1974–1977, Vol I, Part III, Draft Additional Protocol II.

Official Records of the Diplomatic Conference on the Reaffirmation and Development of International Humanitarian Law Applicable in Armed Conflicts, Geneva, 1974–1977, Vol VII, CDDH/SR.5.1/annex.

Official Records of the Diplomatic Conference on the Reaffirmation and Development of International Humanitarian Law Applicable in Armed Conflicts, Geneva, 1974–1977, Vol IX.

Conference of Government Experts on the Reaffirmation and Development of International Humanitarian Law Applicable in Armed Conflicts, Geneva 24 May–12 June 1971, Report on the Work of the Conference.

ICRC, Annual Report of the International Committee of the Red Cross 2009, Geneva, May 2010.

Information sheet on the role of the ICRC during the Spanish Civil War which provides the dates and details of M. Junod's visits, <http://www.icrc.org/eng/resources/documents/misc/5gkdsb.htm>

ICRC in collaboration with the Secretariat of the League of Red Cross Societies, *The Red Cross and Human Rights*, October 1983, 27.
ICRC, Resolution II: Protection of the Civilian Population in Period of Armed Conflict, 7 December 1995.
ICRC, International Humanitarian Law and the Challenges of Contemporary Armed Conflicts, 28th International Conference of the Red Cross and Red Crescent, Geneva, 2 to 6 December 2003.
ICRC, Interpretative Guidance on the Notion of Direct Participation in Hostilities Under International Humanitarian Law, May 2009.
ICRC, International Humanitarian Law and the Challenges of Contemporary Armed Conflicts', 31st International Conference of the Red Cross and Red Crescent, October 2011.
ICRC, The Use of Force in Armed Conflicts: Interplay between the Conduct of Hostilities and Law Enforcement Paradigms, 2013.
ICRC, Internment in Armed Conflict: Basic Rules and Challenges, International Committee of the Red Cross, Opinion Paper, November 2014.
ICRC, Protection of Victims of Non-International Armed Conflict, Report dated January 1971 submitted by the International Committee of the Red Cross to the Conference of Government Experts on the Reaffirmation and Development of International Humanitarian Law applicable in Armed Conflicts, Geneva, 24 May–12 June, <http://1.usa.gov/VEnVHc>
ICRC, Q&A and Lexicon on Humanitarian Access, June 2014, <https://www.icrc.org/eng/assets/files/2014/icrc-q-and-a-lexison-on-humanitarian-access-06-2014.pdf>
ICRC, 'What is International Humanitarian Law?', <http://www.icrc.org/Web/eng/siteeng0.nsf/htmlall/humanitarian-law-factsheet/$File/What_is_IHL.pdf>

ICC Documents

ICC, Office of the Prosecutor, Situation in Nigeria, Article 5 Report, 5 August 2013.
ICC, Office of the Prosecutor, Report on Preliminary Examination Activities, November 2012.

International Law Association

Final Report on the Meaning of Armed Conflict in International Law, International Law Association, The Hague Conference 2010.
Statement of Principles Applicable to the Formation of General Customary International Law, ILA Final Report of the Committee on Formation of Customary (General) International Law, London Conference 2000.

International Law Commission

Comments and Observations Received from Governments, UN Doc. No. A/CN.4/515 and Add.1-3, 3 April 2001.
Conclusions of the work of the Study Group on the Fragmentation of International Law: Difficulties arising from the Diversification and Expansion of International Law, Yearbook of the International Law Commission, 2006, Vol II, Part Two.

Draft Articles on the Law of Treaties with Commentaries, Yearbook of the International Law Commission, 1966, Vol II, UN Doc. No. A/CN.4/SER. A/1966/Add. 1.
Draft Articles on Responsibility of States for Internationally Wrongful Acts, UN Doc. No. A/56/83, 9 August 2001.
Draft Code of Crimes against the Peace and Security of Mankind with commentaries, Yearbook of the International Law Commission 1996, Vol II, Part 2, A/CN.4/SER.A/ 1996/Add.1 (Part 2).
Fourth Report on State Responsibility by Roberto Ago, Special Rapporteur, Yearbook of the International Law Commission 1972, Vol II, UN Doc. No. A/CN.4/264 and Add. 1.
Report of the Commission to the General Assembly on the Law of Treaties, Vol II, UN Doc. No. A/6309/Rev.1.
Report of the International Law Commission, Fifty-third session, UN General Assembly Official Records, Fifty-sixth Session, Supplement No. 10, UN Doc. No. A/56/10, 23 April–1 June 2001 and 2 July–10 August 2001.
Report of the International Law Commission, Sixty-sixth session, UN Doc. No. A/69/ 10, 2014.
Second Report on State Responsibility by Special Rapporteur Ago, Yearbook of the International Law Commission, 1970, Vol II, UN Doc. No. A/CN.4/233.
Second Report on Identification of Customary International Law by Special Rapporteur Wood, UN Doc. No. A/CN.4/672, 22 May 2014.
Study on the Function and Scope of the Lex Specialis Rule and the Question of Self-Contained Regimes, ILC, 4 May 2004, UN Doc. No. ILC(LVI)/SG/FIL/CRD.1 Add.1.
Summary Record of the 2681st Meeting, UN Doc. No. A/CN.4/SR.2681.
Yearbook of the International Law Commission, 1958, Vol II, UN Doc. No. A/CN.4/ SER.A/1958/Add.1.
Yearbook of the International Law Commission, 1966, Vol II, UN Doc. No. A/CN.4/ SER.A/1966/Add.1.
Yearbook of the International Law Commission, 1967, Vol I, UN Doc. No. A/CN.4/ SER.A/1967.
Yearbook of the International Law Commission, 1969, Vol II, UN Doc. No. A/CN.4/SER. A/1969/Add. 1.
Yearbook of the International Law Commission, 1972, Vol II, UN Doc. No. A/CN.4/ SER.A/1972/Add.1.
Yearbook of the International Law Commission, 1974, Vol I, UN Doc. No. A/CN.4/ SER.A/1974.
Yearbook of the International Law Commission, 1974, Vol II, UN Doc. No. A/CN.4/ SER.A/1974/Add.1.
Yearbook of the International Law Commission, 1975, Vol II, UN Doc. No. A/CN.4/ SER.A/1975/Add.1.
Yearbook of the International Law Commission, 1980, Vol II, Part I, UN Doc. No. A/ CN.4/SER.4/1980/Add.1(Part I).

Kampala Convention Documents

Explanatory Note on Kampala Convention, <http://www.internal-displacement.org/assets/publications/Tools-and-Frameworks/200910-training-KC-Explanatory-Note-Eng.pdf>
Letter to the African Union dated 6 June 2008 from Amnesty International, Fédération Internationale des Droits de l'Homme, IDP Action, Institute for Human Rights

and Development in Africa, Laws for Human Rights (South Africa) and Refugees International, attaching NGO Commentary to the Kampala Convention, <http://www.fidh.org/IMG/pdf/IDPconventionAUngoComments.pdf>

Press Release, African Union, drafted by Commissioner Bahame Tom Nyanduga, 22 October 2009, <http://www.achpr.org/press/2009/10/d25/>

United Nations Documents

Children and armed conflict

Annual Report of the Special Representative of the Secretary-General for children and armed conflict, Olara A. Otunno, UN Doc. No. E/CN.4/2003/77, 3 March 2003.

Annual Report of the Special Representative of the Secretary-General for children and armed conflict, Radhika Coomaraswamy, UN Doc. No. A/HRC/15/58, 3 September 2010.

Annual Report on the Protection of Civilians in Armed Conflict in Afghanistan' (2016), <https://unama.unmissions.org/sites/default/files/protection_of_civilians_in_armed_conflict_annual_report_2016_final280317.pdf>

Conclusions on children and armed conflict in Afghanistan, Working Group on Children and Armed Conflict, UN Doc. No. S/AC.51/2009/1, 13 July 2009.

Conclusions on children and armed conflict in the Philippines, Working Group on Children and Armed Conflict, UN Doc. No. S/AC.51/2008/10, 3 October 2008.

Report of the Secretary-General on children and armed conflict, UN Doc. No. S/2002/1299, 26 November 2002.

Report of the working group on a draft optional protocol to the Convention on the Rights of the Child on involvement of children in armed conflicts on its sixth session, Commission on Human Rights, UN Doc. No. E/CN.4/2000/74, 27 March 2000.

Committee on the Elimination of Discrimination against Women

CEDAW 'General Recommendation No. 30 on Women in Conflict Prevention, Conflict and Post-Conflict Situations', UN Doc. No. CEDAW/C/GC/30, 18 October 2013.

Committee on Economic, Social and Cultural Rights

Concluding Observations of the CESCR on Afghanistan, UN Doc. No. E/C.12/AFG/CO/2-4, 7 June 2010.

Concluding Observations of the CESCR on Colombia, UN Doc. No. E/C.12/COL/CO/5, 7 June 2010.

Concluding Observations of the CESCR on Iraq, UN Doc. No. E/C.12/IRQ/4, 27 October 2015.

General Comment 3, The Nature of States Parties' Obligations, UN Doc. No. E/1991/23, 14 December 1990.

General Comment 12, The Right to Adequate Food, UN Doc. No. E/C.12/1999/5, 12 May 1999.

General Comment 14, The Right to the Highest Attainable Standard of Health, UN Doc. No. E/C.12/2000/4, 11 August 2000.

General Comment 15, The Right to Water (Article 11 and 12 of the Covenant), UN Doc. No. E/C.12/2002/11, 20 January 2003.

General Comment 19, The Right to Social Security, UN Doc. No. E/C.12/GC/19, 4 February 2008.

Statement on the obligations of States Parties regarding the corporate sector and economic, social and cultural rights, UN Doc. No. E/C.12/2011/1, 20 May 2011.

Committee against Torture

G.R.B. v Sweden, Communication No. 83/1997, UN Doc. No. CAT/C/20/D/83/1997, 15 May 1998.

Elmi v Australia, Communication No. 120/1998, UN Doc. No. CAT/C/22/D/120/199, 14 May 1999.

S.V. v Canada, Communication No. 49/1996, UN Doc. CAT/C/26/D/49/1996, 15 May 2001.

M.P.S. v Australia, Communication No. 138/1999, UN Doc. No. CAT/C/28/D/138/1999, 30 April 2002.

H.M. H.I. v Australia, Communication No. 177/2001, UN Doc. No. CAT/C/28/D/177/2001, 1 May 2002.

S.S. v The Netherlands, Communication No. 191/2001, UN Doc. No. CAT/C/30/D/191/2001, 5 May 2003.

Conclusions and Recommendations of the Committee against Torture, Third Periodic Report of Colombia, UN Doc. No. CAT/C/CR/31/3, 4 February 2004.

Conclusions and Recommendations of the Committee against Torture, Initial Report of Uganda, UN Doc. No. CAT/C/CR/34/UGA, 21 June 2005.

Conclusions and Recommendations of the Committee against Torture, Sri Lanka, UN Doc. No. CAT/C/LKA/CO/2, 15 December 2005.

Conclusions and Recommendations of the Committee against Torture, Third periodic Report of France, UN Doc. No. CAT/C/FRA/CO/3, 3 April 2006.

Conclusions and Recommendations of the Committee against Torture, Initial Report of Burundi, UN Doc. No. CAT/C/BD/CO/1, 15 February 2007.

Conclusions and Recommendations of the Committee against Torture, Nepal, UN Doc. No. CAT/C/NPL/CO/2l, 13 April 2007.

Conclusions and Recommendations of the Committee Against Torture, Syria UN Doc. No. CAT/C/SYR/CO/1/Add.2, 29 June 2012.

Conclusions and Recommendations of the Committee against Torture, Third periodic Report of the Philippines, UN Doc. No. CAT/C/PHL/3, 2 June 2016.

Conclusions and Recommendations of the Committee against Torture, Initial Report of Iraq, UN Doc. No. CAT/C/IRQ/CO/1, 2 June 2016.

CAT General Comment 2, Implementation of Article 2 by States Parties, UN Doc. No. CAT/C/GC/2, 24 January 2008.

Human Rights Committee

UN Human Rights Committee, *Pedro Pablo Camargo v Colombia*, Communication No. 45/1970, UN Doc. No. CCPR/C/OP/1.

UN Human Rights Committee, *John Khemraadi Baboeram et al v. Suriname*, Communication No. 146/1983 and 148 to 154/1983, UN Doc. No. 40 (A/40/40), 4 April 1985.

Concluding Observations of the HRC on Iraq, UN Doc. No. CCPR/C/IRQ/CO/5, 3 December 2015.

Concluding Observations of the HRC on Colombia, UN Doc. No. CCPR/CO/80/COL, 26 May 2004.

Concluding Observations of the HRC on Colombia, UN Doc. No. CCPR/COL/CO/6, 4 August 2010.

Concluding Observations of the HRC on the Democratic Republic of Congo, UN Doc. No. CCPR/C/COD/CO/3, 26 April 2006.
Concluding Observations of the HRC on the Initial Report of Haiti, UN Doc. No. CPPR/C/HTI/CO/1, 21 November 2014.
Concluding Observations of the HRC on the Initial Report of Malta, UN Doc. No. CPPR/C/MNE/CO/1, 21 November 2014.
Concluding Observations of the HRC on Israel's Initial Periodic Report to the HRC, UN Doc. No. CCPR/C/79/Add.93, 18 August 1998.
Concluding Observations of the HRC on Israel's Second Periodic Report, UN Doc. No. CCPR/CO/78/ISR, 21 August 2003.
Concluding Observations of the HRC on Israel's Third Periodic Report to the HRC, UN Doc. No. CCPR/C/ISR/CO/3, 3 September 2010.
Concluding Observations of the HRC on Israel's Fourth Periodic Report to the HRC, UN Doc. No. CCPR/C/ISR/CO/4, 21 November 2014.
Concluding Observations of the HRC on Portugal (Macao), UN Doc. No. CCPR/C/79/Add.115, 4 November 1999.
Concluding Observations of the HRC on the Second Periodic Report of Burundi, UN Doc. No. CCPR/C/BDI/CO/2, 21 November 2014.
Concluding Observations of the HRC on Sudan, UN Doc. No. CCPR/C/SDN/CO/4, 19 August 2014.
Concluding Observations of the HRC on Yemen, UN Doc. No. CCPR/C/YEM/CO/5, 23 April 2012.
General Comment 29, States of Emergency (article 4), UN Doc. No. CCPR/C/21/Rev.1/Add.11, 31 August 2001.
General Comment 31, Nature of the General Legal Obligation Imposed on States Parties to the Covenant, UN Doc. No. CCPR/C/21/Rev.1/Add.13, 26 May 2004.
General Comment 32, Article 14: Right to Equality before Courts and Tribunals and to a Fair Trial), UN Doc. No. CCPR/C/GC/32, 23 August 2007.
Draft General Comment 35, Article 9 Liberty and Security of Person, UN Doc. No. CCPR/C/GC/ 35, 28 October 2014.
General Comment 35, Article 9 Liberty and Security of Person, UN Doc. No. CCPR/C/GC/35, 28 October 2014.
Procedural Decisions of the Human Rights Committee, Bosnia and Herzegovina, Croatia, Yugoslavia, UN Doc. No. A/48/40, Annex VII, 1993.
Report of the Human Rights Committee, Vol I, General Assembly, Official Records, Fifty-first Session, Supplement No. 40, UN Doc. No A/51/40, 13 April 1997.
US Fourth Periodic Report to the HRC, 30 December 2011.

Economic and Social Council

UN Commission on Human Rights.
Resolution 9(II) of ECOSOC, UN Doc. No. E/56/Rev.2, 21 June 1946.

Field Office Reports

Afghanistan Mid-Year Report on the Protection of Civilians in Armed Conflict, United Nations Assistance Mission in Afghanistan, July 2013, Midterm Report of the Group of Experts on the Democratic Republic of Congo, UN Doc. No. S/2013/ 433, 19 July 2013.

'Conflict in South Sudan, A Human Rights Report, United Nations Mission in the Republic of South Sudan, 8 May 2014'.

Report of the United Nations Joint Human Rights Office on Human Rights Violations committed by the M23 in North Kivu Province, UN Doc. No. S/2013/433, April 2012–November 2013.

Report on the Protection of Civilians in Armed Conflict in Afghanistan prepared by the Human Rights Unit of the United Nations Assistance Mission in Afghanistan, 2014.

Summary of fact finding missions on alleged human rights violations committed by the Lord's Resistance Army (LRA) in the districts of Haut-Uele and Bas-Uele in Orientale province of the DRC, December 2009.

Human Rights Council and (Former) Commission on Human Rights

Combined Report of the Special Rapporteur on extrajudicial, summary or arbitrary executions, Philip Alston; the Special Rapporteur on the right of everyone to the enjoyment of the highest attainable standard of physical and mental health, Paul Hunt; the Representative of the Secretary-General on human rights of internally displaced persons, Walter Kälin; and the Special Rapporteur on adequate housing as a component of the right to an adequate standard of living, Miloon Kothari, Mission to Lebanon and Israel, UN Doc. No. A/HRC/2/7, 2 October 2006.

Combined Report of the Special Rapporteur on the right of everyone to the enjoyment of the highest attainable standard of physical and mental health, the Special Representative of the Secretary-General for Children and Armed Conflict, the Special Rapporteur on violence against women, its causes and consequences, the Representative of the Secretary-General on the human rights of internally displaced persons, the Special Rapporteur on adequate housing as a component of the right to an adequate standard of living, and on the right to non-discrimination in this context, the Special Rapporteur on the right to food, the Special Rapporteur on extrajudicial, summary or arbitrary executions, the Special Rapporteur on the right to education and the independent expert on the question of human rights and extreme poverty, UN Doc. No. A/HRC/10/22, 20 March 2009.

Commentary to the draft Basic Principles And Guidelines On The Right To A Remedy And Reparation For Victims Of Violations Of International Human Rights And Humanitarian Law, UN Doc. No. E/CN.4/2004/57, 24 October 2003, <http://www.un.org/ga/search/view_doc.asp?symbol=E/CN.4/2004/57>

Human Rights Council holds debate on Human Rights situations requiring the Council's attention, 17 September 2012, <http://www.ohchr.org/EN/NewsEvents/Pages/DisplayNews.aspx?NewsID=12534&LangID=E>

Report of the Independent International Fact-Finding Mission on the Gaza Conflict, UN Doc. No. A/64/490, 29 October 2009.

Report of the Independent International Commission of Inquiry on Libya, UN Doc. No. A/HRC/19/68, 2 March 2012.

Report of the Independent International Commission of Inquiry on the Syrian Arab Republic, UN Doc. No. A/HRC/19/69, 22 February 2012.

Report of the Independent International Commission of Inquiry on the Syrian Arab Republic, UN Doc. No. A/HRC/21/50, 15 August 2012.

Report of the Independent International Commission of Inquiry on the Syrian Arab Republic, UN. Doc. No. A/HRC/22/59, 5 February 2013.

Report of the Independent International Commission of Inquiry on the Syrian Arab Republic, 'Rule of Terror, Living under ISIS in Syria', 14 November 2014.

Report of the Independent International Commission of Inquiry on the Syrian Arab Republic, UN Doc. No. A/HRC/28/69, 5 February 2015.

Report of the Independent International Commission of Inquiry to investigate all alleged violations of international human rights law in the Libyan Arab Jamahiriya, UN Doc. No. A/HRC/17/44, 1 June 2011.

Report of the Special Rapporteur on extrajudicial, summary or arbitrary executions, Mission to Sri Lanka, UN Doc. No. E/CN.4/2006/53/Add.5, 27 March 2006.

Report of the Special Rapporteur on extrajudicial, summary or arbitrary executions, Philip Alston, Study on targeted killings, UN Doc. No. A/HRC/14/24/Add.6, 28 May 2010.

Report of the Special Rapporteur on extrajudicial, summary or arbitrary executions, Mission To Philippines, UN Doc. No. A/HRC/8/3/Add.2, 16 April 2008.

Report on the continuing grave deterioration in the human rights and humanitarian situation in the Syrian Arab Republic, UN Doc. No. A/HRC/26/L.4/Rev.1, 25 June 2014.

Report on Mission to Sri Lanka, UN Doc. No. E/CN.4/2006/53/Add.5, 27 March 2006.

Report on the Situation of Human Rights in Afghanistan Prepared by the Special Rapporteur Mr Felix Ermacora, in accordance with Commission on Human Rights Resolution 1988/67, UN ESCOR, Commission on Human Rights, 45th Session, Agenda Item, 12, para 68, UN Doc. No. E/CN.4/1989/24, 16 February 1989.

HRC 'Report of the Special Rapporteur on freedom of religion or belief, Heiner Bielefeldt' (29 December 2014) UN Doc. A/HRC/28/66.

Report on technical assistance and capacity-building in the field of human rights in the Central African Republic, UN Doc. No. A/HRC/27/L.31, 26 September 2014.

Resolution on the Human Rights Situation in Iraq in the light of abuses committed by the so-called Islamic State in Iraq and the Levant and associated groups, UN Doc. No. A/HRC/RES/S-22/1, 3 September 2014.

Resolution on the Human Rights Situation in Mali, UN Doc. No. A/HRC/RES/20/17, 17 July 2012.

The role of development cooperation and food aid in realizing the right to adequate food: moving from charity to obligation, UN Doc. No. A/HRC/10/5, 11 February 2009, <http://daccess-dds-ny.un.org/doc/UNDOC/GEN/G09/107/64/PDF/G0910764.pdf?OpenElement>

UN Commission on Human Rights, *Consequences of acts of violence committed by irregular armed groups and drug traffickers for the enjoyment of human rights.*, UN Doc. No. E/CN.4/RES/1990/75, 7 March 1990.

UN Commission on Human Rights, *Consequences on the enjoyment of human rights of acts of violence committed by armed groups that spread terror among the population and by drug traffickers*, UN Doc. No. E/CN.4/RES/1991/29, 5 March 1991.

UN Commission on Human Rights, *Consequences for the enjoyment of human rights of acts of violence committed by armed groups that spread terror among the population and by drug traffickers*, UN Doc. No. E/CN.4/RES/1993/48, 9 March 1993.

UN Commission on Human Rights, *Guiding Principles on Internal Displacement*, UN Doc. No. E/CN.4/1998/53/Add.2, 22 July 1998.

UN Commission on Human Rights, *Consequences on the enjoyment of human rights of acts of violence committed by armed groups that spread terror among the population and by drug trafficers*, UN Doc. No. E/CN.4/RES/1992/42, 28 February 1992.

Office of the High Commissioner of Human Rights

International Protection of Human Rights in Armed Conflict, United Nations Office of the High Commissioner, New York/ Geneva, 2011, p 25.

Outcome of the Expert Consultation on the Issue of Protecting the Human Rights of Civilians in Armed Conflict, Report of the Office of the High Commissioner for Human Rights, UN Doc. No. A/HRC/11/31, 4 June 2009.

Report for the United Nations High Commissioner for Human Rights on the situation of human rights in Mali, UN Doc. No. A/HRC/22/33, 7 January 2012.

Report of the High Commissioner for Human Rights on the implementation of Human Rights Council resolution 7/1, UN Doc. A/HRC/8/17, 6 June 2008.

'Report of the United Nations High Commissioner of Human Rights, Situation of Human Rights in the Central African Republic, UN Doc. No. A/HRC/24/59, 12 September 2013'.

Top UN official condemns amputations, human rights violations in northern Mali, 17 September 2012, <http://www.un.org/apps/news/story.asp?NewsID=42907&Cr=+Mali+&Cr1=#.VP7hgWSG-_Q>

'Twelfth periodic report of the United Nations High Commissioner for Human Rights on the situation of human rights in Sudan, Attacks on civilians in Western and Central Equatorial States, Southern Sudan between 15 December 2008 and 10 March 2009 by the Lord's Resistance Army (LRA)', UN Doc. No. A/HRC/18/2.

Reports of the Representatives of the Secretary-General

Report of the Representative of the Secretary-General on the Human Rights of Internally Displaced Persons, Walter Kälin, Mission to Sri Lanka, UN Doc. A/HRC/8/6/Add.4, 21 May 2008.

Reports of Commissions of Inquiry of the Secretary-General

Report of the Independent International Commission of Inquiry on Darfur to the United Nations Secretary-General pursuant to Security Council Resolution 1564 of 18 September 2004, 25 January 2005.

Final Report of the Independent International Commission of Inquiry on the Central African Republic, UN Doc. No. S/2014/928, 22 December 2014.

'Preliminary Report of the International Commission of Inquiry on the Central African Republic, UN Doc. No. S/2014/373, 26 June 2014'.

Secretary-General

Eighteenth Progress Report of the Secretary-General on the United Nations Operation in Côte d'Ivoire, UN Doc. No. S/2008/645.

'Report of the Secretary-General on the protection of civilians in armed conflict, UN Doc. No. S/2004/431, 28 May 2004'.

Report of the Secretary-General's Panel of Experts on Accountability in Sri Lanka, 31 March 2011, <http://www.un.org/News/dh/infocus/Sri_Lanka/POE_Report_Full.pdf>

Report of the Secretary-General Pursuant to paragraph 2 of Security Council Resolution 808/1993, UN Doc. No. S/25704, 3 May 1993.

Twenty-fourth report of the Secretary-General on the United Nations Operation in Côte d'Ivoire, UN Doc. No. S/2010/245.

Security Council

UN Commission on Truth in El Salvador, Report, UN Doc. No. S/25500, 1 April 1993, Annex.

UN Security Council Resolution 276(1970), UN Doc. No. S/RES/176 (1970).

UN Security Council Resolution 827(1993), UN Doc. No. S/RES/827 (1993).

UN Security Council Resolution 955 (1994), UN Doc. No. S/RES/955 (1994).

UN Security Council Resolution 1612(2005) (On children in armed conflict), UN Doc. No. S/RES/1612 (2005).

UN Security Council Resolution 2085(2012) (On authorization of the deployment of an African-led International Support Mission in Mali (AFISMA) for an initial period of one year), UN Doc. No. S/RES/2085 (2012).

UN Security Council Resolution 2098(2013) (On extension of the mandate of the UN Organization Stabilization Mission in the Democratic Republic of the Congo (MONUSCO).

UN Security Council Resolution 2145(2014) (On extension of the mandate of the UN Assistance Mission in Afghanistan (UNAMA)), UN Doc. No. S/RES/2145 (2014).

UN Security Council Resolution 2173(2014) (On extension of the mandate of the AU/UN Hybrid Operation in Darfur (UNAMID) until 30 June 2015), UN Doc. No. S/RES/2173 (2014).

UN Security Council Resolution 2175(2014) (On the protection of humanitarian personnel and UN and associated personnel in armed conflict), UN Doc. No. S/RES/2175 (2014).

UN Security Council Resolution 2304(2016) (Reports of the Secretary-General on the Sudan and South Sudan), UN Doc. No. S/RES/2304 (2016).

UN Security Council Resolution 2301(2016) (The situation in the Central African Republic), UN Doc. No. S/RES/2301 (2016).

UN Security Council Resolution 2299(2016) (The situation concerning Iraq), UN Doc. No. S/RES/2299 (2016).

UN Security Council Resolution 2295(2016) (Situation in Mali), UN Doc. No. S/RES/2295 (2016).

UN Security Council Resolution 2293(2016) (The situation concerning the Democratic Republic of Congo), UN Doc. No. S/RES/2293 (2016).

UN Security Council Resolution 2274(2016) (The situation in Afghanistan), UN Doc. No. UN Doc. S/RES/2274 (2016).

UN Security Council Resolution 2252(2016) (Reports of the Secretary-General on the Sudan and South Sudan), UN Doc. No. S/RES/2252.

UN Security Council Resolution 2233(2016) (Iraq), UN Doc. No. S/RES/2233.

UN Security Council Resolution 2225(2016) (Children and armed conflict), UN Doc. No. S/RES/2225.

Miscellaneous

Hampson, F. and Salama, I., 'Working paper on the relationship between human rights law and international law, Economic and Social Council', UN Doc. No. E/CN.4/Sub/2/3005/14.

OCHA, Oxford Institute for Ethics, Law and Armed Conflict and University of Oxford, Oxford Guidance on the Law Relating to Humanitarian Relief Operations in Situations of Armed Conflict (October 2016).

African Commission on Human and People's Rights

African Commission on Human and People's Rights 'General Comment No. 3 on the African Charter on Human and People's Rights: The Right to Life (Article 4) (adopted during the session 4–18 November 2015) [5].

Statements

Statement by the British Prime Minister, Hansard, House of Commons Debate, Vol 337, cc919-1045, 21 June 1938.
Statement by Lord Eden, Hansard, House of Commons Debate, Vol 328 cc1381-9, 8 November 1937.
Statement by the President of the Security Council, UN Doc. No. S/PRST/2002/27, 18 October 2002.

Newspaper Articles

A Battle for Syria One Court at a Time, The New York Times, 13 March 2013, <http://www.nytimes.com/2013/03/14/world/middleeast/a-battle-for-syria-one-court-at-a-time.html?ref=world&_r=2&>
An Audience with Ukraine Rebel Chief Igor Bezler, the Demon of Donetsk, The Guardian, 29 July 2014, <http://www.theguardian.com/world/2014/jul/29/-sp-ukraine-rebel-igor-bezler-interview-demon>
Bombardments Can't Stop the Disco Beat in Aleppo, Malay Mail Online, 23 November 2014, <http://m.themalaymailonline.com/features/article/bombardments-cant-stop-the-disco-beat-in-aleppo>
Congo Rebel Army Vows to Take Control of All DR Congo, The Telegraph, 21 November 2012, <http://www.telegraph.co.uk/news/worldnews/africaandindianocean/democraticrepublicofcongo/9693043/Congos-rebel-army-vows-to-take-control-of-all-DR-Congo.html>
Daily Life in Aleppo: The Struggle for Normality amid the Ruins of War, Spiegel Online, 26 February 2013, <http://www.spiegel.de/international/world/the-struggle-to-maintain-order-in-rebel-controlled-aleppo-in-syria-a-885396.html>
DR Congo Rebels Impose Unacceptable Curfew, UN', i24 News, 4 September 2013, <http://www.i24news.tv/en/news/international/africa/130905-dr-congo-rebels-impose-unacceptable-curfew-un>
Fighting Shortages, Syrian Civilians Take Reins in Rebel Areas, Associated Press, 28 February 2013, <http://www.nytimes.com/2013/03/01/world/middleeast/syrian-civilians-take-reins-in-test-of-self-government.html?ref=world&_r=0>
Goma Falls to Congo's M23 Rebels without Expected Bloodbath, The Telegraph, 20 November 2012, <http://www.telegraph.co.uk/news/worldnews/africaandindianocean/democraticrepublicofcongo/9691489/Goma-falls-to-Congos-M23-rebels-without-expected-bloodbath.html>

In Rebel-held Syria, Revolutionary Courts Decide Matters of Life, Death, Miami Herald, 18 June 2012, <http://www.miamiherald.com/2012/06/18/2855841/in-rebel-held-syria-revolutionary.html>

Las FARC dicen que asumirán responsabilidades con las víctimas, BBC, 13 August 2014, <http://www.bbc.co.uk/mundo/ultimas_noticias/2014/08/140813_ultnot_colombia_farc_responsabilidades_jgc.shtml>

Mali Rebel Groups Clash in Kidal, BBC, 8 June 2012, <http://www.bbc.co.uk/news/world-africa-18377168>

Mali: Rebels to Impose Islamic Law, Associated Press, 4 April 2012, <http://www.nytimes.com/2012/04/05/world/africa/mali-rebels-to-impose-islamic-law.html>

M23 Rebels Rape, Kill Civilians, Human Rights Watch, 22 July 2013, <http://www.hrw.org/news/2013/07/22/dr-congo-m23-rebels-kill-rape-civilians>

Rebel Court Fills Void amid Syrian Civil War, CNN, 26 January 2012, <http://edition.cnn.com/2013/01/25/world/meast/syria-rebel-court/>

Rebel-held Syrian Town Struggles to Keep the Peace, Associated Press, 25 June 2012, <http://www.guardian.co.uk/world/feedarticle/10306415>

Rebels Carve out a Safe Haven in Northern and Central Syria, The Seattle Times, 7 June 2012, <http://seattletimes.com/html/nationworld/2018381996_syriasafehaven08.html>

Timbuktu Endured Terror under Harsh Sharia Law, New York Times, 31 January 2013, <http://www.nytimes.com/2013/02/01/world/africa/timbuktu-endured-terror-under-harsh-shariah-law.html?_r=0>

TV Stations Silenced by M23 Resume Retransmitting in Goma, Reporters without Borders, 4 December 2012, <http://en.rsf.org/drc-concern-about-m23-s-news-control-21-11-2012,43706.html>

Miscellaneous Reports and Documents

Advisory Report on Humanitarian Assistance, Advisory Committee on Issues of Public International Law, The Hague, August 2014, <http://cms.webbeat.net/ContentSuite/upload/cav/doc/Report_nr._25_-_Humanitarian_assistance(1).pdf>

Closing Speech, Sir Hartley Shawcross, 26 July 1946.

Consolidated Report of the Republic of Liberia Truth and Reconciliation Commission, Vol II, 30 June 2009.

Deed of Commitment under Geneva Call for the Prohibition of Sexual Violence in Situations of Armed Conflict and Towards the Elimination of Gender Discrimination, <http://www.genevacall.org/wp-content/uploads/dlm_uploads/2013/12/DoC-Prohibiting-sexual-violence-and-gender-discrimination.pdf>

Digest of Laws and Cases, Law Reports Of Trials Of War Criminals, Selected and prepared by The United Nations War Crimes Commission, Vol XV, London, 1949.

Droits de l'Homme l'ONUCI des Forces Nouvelles, <http://www.onuci.org/IMG/article_PDF/article_2001.pdf>

Hottinger, J. T., The Engagement to Respect Humanitarian Law and Human Rights: A Prerequisite for Peace Negotiations, or a "Future" Component within Peace Negotiations, Exploring Criteria & Conditions for Engaging Armed Non-State Actors to Respect Humanitarian Law & Human Rights Law, Conference Report, 4–5 June 2007.

History of the United Nations War Crimes Commission and the Development of the Laws of War, His Majesty's Stationery Office, London 1948.

Interpretative Declaration made by Mexico upon ratification of the Protocol on 15 March 2002, see http://treaties.un.org/Pages/ViewDetails.aspx?src=TREATY&mtdsg_no=IV-11-b&chapter=4&lang=en

Introductory Note to the Basic Principles And Guidelines On The Right To A Remedy And Reparation For Victims Of Violations Of International Human Rights And Humanitarian Law by Prof. Dr. Theo van Boven.

Opening Speech by Justice Robert H. Jackson before the International Military Tribunal at Nuremberg, 21 November 1945, <http://www.roberthjackson.org/the-man/speeches-articles/speeches/speeches-by-robert-h-jackson/opening-statement-before-the-international-military-tribunal/>

Pretoria Agreement on the Peace Process in the Côte d'Ivoire (2005).

Principles of International Law Recognised in the Charter of the Nuremberg Tribunal and in the Judgment of the Tribunal, 1950, <http://legal.un.org/ilc/texts/instruments/english/draft_articles/7_1_1950.pdf>

Progress Report of the Chairperson of the Working Group on Economic, Social and Cultural Rights, 44th Session, Abuja, Nigeria.

Proposed International Convention on the Prevention and Prosecution of Crimes against Humanity, August 2010, Crimes against Humanity Initiative, Washington University School of Law, Whitney R. Harris World Law Institute, <http://law.wustl.edu/harris/cah/docs/EnglishTreatyFinal.pdf>

Report from Expert Meeting at Chatham House on Procedural Safeguards for Security Detention in Non-International Armed Conflicts, Chatham House and ICRC, London, 22–23 September 2008.

Resolution on Humanitarian Assistance, Sixteenth Commission, Institute of International Law, Bruges Session, 2nd September 2003.

The Rights-Based Approach to Emergencies, Action Aid, <http://www.actionaid.org.uk/doc_lib/110_1_rights_based_approach_guide.pdf>

Somalia, Countering Terrorism in a Failed State, International Crisis Group Africa Report No. 45, 23 May 2002, p i, <https://www.crisisgroup.org/africa/horn-africa/somalia/somalia-countering-terrorism-failed-state>

UN General Assembly Resolution, *Optional protocols to the Convention on the Rights of the Child on the involvement of children in armed conflict*, UN Doc. No. A/RES/54/263, 25 May 2000.

Walker, E. L., 'Culturally-Attuned Governance and Justice in Helmand Province, Afghanistan', ISAF/International Media Ventures, April 2010.

Index

The manufacturer's authorised representative in the EU for product safety is Oxford University Press España S.A. of El Parque Empresarial San Fernando de Henares, Avenida de Castilla, 2 - 28830 Madrid (www.oup.es/en or product.safety@oup.com). OUP España S.A. also acts as importer into Spain of products made by the manufacturer.

Printed and bound by CPI Group (UK) Ltd, Croydon, CR0 4YY

14/09/2026

02216288-0009